DATA ABSTRACTION AND STRUCTURES USING C++

DATA ABSTRACTION AND STRUCTURES USING C++

Mark R. Headington
University of Wisconsin–La Crosse

David D. Riley
University of Wisconsin–La Crosse

Jones and Bartlett Publishers

Sudbury, Massachusetts

Boston   London   Singapore

Editorial, Sales, and Customer Services Offices

Jones and Bartlett Publishers
40 Tall Pine Drive
Sudbury, MA 01776
(978) 443-5000
(800) 832-0034
info@jbpub.com
http://www.jbpub.com

Jones and Bartlett Publishers International
Barb House, Barb Mews
London W6 7PA
UK

Trademark Acknowledgments: Turbo C + + and Borland C + + are registered trademarks of Borland International, Inc.

Cover: James Crable "Empire State Plaza, Albany, NY." Reproduced courtesy of J.J. Brookings Gallery, San Jose, California.

Library of Congress Catalog Number: 92-75664

ISBN 0-7637-0295-1

Printed in the United States of America

00 99 98   10 9 8

To Anne, Brady, and Kari, who haven't seen much of me in the
last three years.

M. R. H.

To my wife, Sandi, and children, Derek and Kasandra.

D. D. R.

Data Abstraction and Structures Using C++ Program Disk

Jones and Bartlett Publishers offers free to students and instructors a program disk with all the complete programs found in *Data Abstraction and Structures Using C++*. The program disk is available through the Jones and Bartlett World Wide Web site on the Internet.*

Download Instructions

1. Connect to the Jones and Bartlett student diskette home page **(http://www.jbpub.com/disks/)**.

2. Choose *Data Abstraction and Structures Using C++*.

3. Follow the instructions for downloading and saving the *Data Abstraction and Structures Using C++* data disk.

4. If you need assistance downloading a Jones and Bartlett student diskette, please send e-mail to help@jbpub.com.

*Downloading the *Data Abstraction and Structures Using C++* program disk via the Jones and Bartlett home page requires access to the Internet and a World Wide Web browser such as Netscape Navigator or Microsoft Internet Explorer. Instructors at schools without Internet access may call 1-800-832-0034 and request a copy of the program disk. Jones and Bartlett grants adopters of *Data Abstraction and Structures Using C++* the right to duplicate copies of the program disk or to store the files on any stand-alone computer or network.

PREFACE

Software design has evolved dramatically in the past decade. In the 1970s, structured programming changed the way that programmers viewed control structures. More recently, the concepts of data abstraction and object-oriented software development have affected the way that programmers view data structures. Introductory computer science courses must embrace these techniques if they are to provide an adequate foundation in contemporary software development.

About This Book

Data Abstraction and Structures Using C++ is designed for a second course in computer science fundamentals, consistent with the ACM guidelines for the CS2 course (August 1985). The book is also compatible with a C102 course in ACM/IEEE's Computing Curricula 1991, covering elements from the following knowledge units: AL1 through AL4, AL6, SE1 through SE5, and PL3 through PL6.

The text's emphasis is on abstraction and its role in software development. The first chapter reviews (and extends) the principles of control abstraction that students learn in the first computer science course. Chapter 2 serves as a bridge between control abstraction and data abstraction, introducing separate compilation and the use of header files to separate specification from implementation. From Chapter 3 forward, the focus is on data abstraction— the separation of a data type's abstract properties from the details of its implementation.

Although this text is intended primarily for the second computer science course, it also can be used in a sophomore/junior-level data structures course (CS7) when supplemented with more advanced material on data structures.

Prerequisite Knowledge

This text assumes that the student has completed a first course in computer science that examined the tools and techniques of structured programming in a modern language—Pascal, Modula-2, Ada, C, C++, or Scheme, for example. Prior knowledge of C++ is not required. We have provided three appendices to aid in the transition from another language to C++, and it is in these appendices that many readers will want to begin. Appendix A (Introductory

Comparison of Pascal and C++) is a starting point for students with no background in C or C++. Appendix B (Introductory Comparison of C and C++) serves as a brief introduction to C++ for those already familiar with C. Appendix C (C++ Stream I/O) completes the introduction to C++ and should be read after either Appendix A or Appendix B.

The Use of C++

This book originated in response to the rapid adoption of C and C++ in the commercial arena and in academic curricula. A number of educators have expressed concern about the use of these languages, faulting them for being too unconstrained and for encouraging a tricky, unreadable style of programming. But it is well known that one can write bad code in any language. This text's approach is to present the language and program examples in a very disciplined manner so that potentially confusing coding practices (such as abundant use of side effects) do not obscure the primary subject: data abstraction and data structures.

The choice of C++ over C was a very clear one. C++ extends the C language to provide linguistic support for information hiding and abstract data types as well as for object-oriented programming (OOP). Regarding the latter, we have placed the material on object-oriented design and OOP in Chapters 10 and 11. We believe that these techniques are better appreciated, even natural, after a thorough grounding in the design and implementation of abstract data types. However, instructors wanting an earlier introduction to these topics will find flexibility in the chapter organization.

Distinguishing Features

Separation of Data Structure Definitions from Their Implementations

Students often confuse the abstract properties of a data structure with its implementation. Most textbooks interweave implementation issues with discussion of a data structure's characteristics and applications. A common result is that upper-division students almost invariably associate linked lists with dynamic data and machine-level pointers. They are surprised to learn (or remember) that alternative data representations exist and that an array of records using subscripts as "pointers" is in fact the preferred alternative for time-critical applications such as operating system software.

In this text, Part I (Abstraction) includes a chapter introducing well-known data structures as abstract data types. Their characteristics and applications are discussed without reference to possible implementations so students will be less apt to confuse abstract properties with implementation. Part II (Tools for Implementation) develops techniques and algorithms that culminate in alternative implementations of the major data structures.

Software Design Features

To highlight the importance of good program design techniques, we have sprinkled many separate *Designing with Wisdom, Using the Language*, and *Pursuing Correctness* sections throughout the text. Additionally, nearly every chapter has a special section entitled *A Study in Design*, an in-depth exposition of the development of a particular program, module, or abstract data type.

Development of Tools and Techniques

Every programmer needs a toolbox. This book includes numerous tools for the developing software engineer. Among these tools are modules, abstract data types, module and class interface diagrams, assertions, recursion, table-driven code, primitive models for data, Backus-Naur Form, performance analysis, and many widely used data structures with associated algorithms.

Assertions

We use assertions in the form of program comments throughout the text. Functions are documented with preconditions and postconditions to define precisely the contract between the caller and the called routine. Loop invariants document the semantics of loops. In addition, class invariants are introduced as a method of defining the expected behavior of class objects. Appendix D summarizes the assertion notation used in the book.

Problem Specification Form

We use a six-part problem specification form to emphasize the importance of precise and complete specifications. This form consists of the title, problem description, input specifications, output specifications, error handling, and a sample program execution. We frequently present larger programming examples and programming project assignments in this form.

Terminology

The computer scientist needs an extensive vocabulary. To build and reinforce this essential vocabulary, we accent important terms in boldface in the text and list them in a Key Terms section at the end of every chapter.

Extensive Selection of Examples

Most students learn by example. The text therefore includes many carefully selected examples illustrating program design and C++ code. We have compiled and executed each program and module on IBM PC-class machines using Borland's Turbo C++ (Second Edition), Borland C++ Version 3.0, and Microsoft C++ Version 7.0. In addition, in an early version of the manuscript, we developed and tested the programs in a UNIX environment with Apollo Domain C++ Version 1.2.1.

Programmers often model their software on examples drawn from texts. We have made a concerted effort to choose examples that not only support the material but also serve as good models for reference use.

Exercises and Programming Projects

Each chapter contains numerous student exercises and programming projects to reinforce and extend concepts presented in the chapter. Answers to selected exercises appear in the back of the book, for student review. The solutions to all unanswered exercises appear in the *Instructor's Guide*, available on request from Jones and Bartlett.

Class Testing

Instructors at several universities have successfully class-tested preliminary versions of this text over a period of six semesters. Students' suggestions have led to important improvements in pedagogy and accuracy.

Chapter Organization and Contents

Introduction The introduction establishes the importance of abstraction as a tool for managing complexity and develops the notions of functional (procedural) abstraction and data abstraction.

Part I: Abstraction

Chapter 1 (Control Abstraction) Chapter 1 builds on material learned in the CS1 course, focusing on control issues: control structures as abstractions for machine-level instructions, specification versus implementation of functions, functional decomposition and top-down design, and top-down versus bottom-up testing. The chapter also describes the use of program assertions, loop invariants, and function pre- and postconditions as documentation aids and contracts.

Chapter 2 (Modules and Information Hiding) Chapter 2 explores the use of modules to create off-the-shelf software packages. This material provides a transition from control abstraction to data abstraction. C++'s provision for separate compilation of program files is exploited by defining a module to be a pair of files: the specification (.h) file and the implementation (.cpp) file. In the design of modules, we stress the central issues of locality and information hiding. Students are taught to use specification files to design precise, abstract specifications for a module and then to translate this abstract view into concrete data and algorithms within the implementation file. Also included in this chapter are interfaces for many of the C++ standard library routines.

Chapter 3 (Data Abstraction Through Classes) This chapter introduces the concept of abstract data types (ADTs) and the C++ class mechanism. Because a class is a data type, many instances of one class can be declared. Information hiding is achieved by designating certain components of a class to be public and others to be private. Other issues addressed in this chapter include layered software and extending the language through operator overloading. Chapter 3 contains many examples of modules that employ classes. The early presentation of modules and classes permits their use throughout the remainder of the text.

Chapter 4 (Introduction to Data Structures) This chapter gives an overview of selected data structures, including arrays, records, linear lists, stacks, queues, and sets. We provide a taxonomy to differentiate among these data structures. Chapter 4 introduces a form for defining structured types that consists of the domain of permissible values, the structural relationships among components, and the set of operations for the type. In this chapter, we make no attempt to implement these data structures. Rather, we focus on their distinguishing properties and on applications that demonstrate their use.

Part II: Tools for Implementation

Chapter 5 (C++ Records (structs) and Unions) Chapter 5 examines records (structs in C++) and variant records (using unions in C++) in detail. Several examples illustrate the use of arrays and structs in building more complex structures.

Chapter 6 (Recursion) Recursion is another vital tool supporting data abstraction. Recursive (inductive) definitions frequently are needed to define data and associated operations, and recursive functions offer a powerful implementation facility. We use the technique of defining concepts recursively to introduce recursion as a control structure for designing algorithms and include Backus-Naur Form (BNF) as an illustration of using recursion in definitions. Finally, recursion, repetition, and table-driven code are compared as control structure alternatives.

Chapter 7 (Pointers and Dynamic Data) This chapter probes the use of pointer variables and C++ reference variables. The major application of pointers in Chapter 7 is to support allocation and deallocation of dynamic data through the new and delete operators. Related issues include inaccessible objects, memory leaks, dangling pointers, and shallow versus deep copying of class instances that point to dynamic data.

Chapter 8 (Linked Lists) Chapter 8 completes the presentation of fundamental implementation strategies by examining linked lists (single, double, and circular). Algorithms for list traversal, insertion, and deletion are discussed. Most of the techniques use dynamic data representations of linked lists, but array representations are also examined.

Chapter 9 (Design and Implementation of Abstract Data Types) Chapter 9 integrates the material from Chapters 1 through 8 to investigate ADTs at length. The issues involved in selecting the domain and operations for ADTs include categories of operations, completeness of the ADT, and testable preconditions. We examine set, stack, and queue implementations extensively and discuss alternative implementations for each of the examples. Additional significant topics include bounded versus unbounded ADTs, primitive models of abstraction, sequences, and N-tuples.

Part III: Additional Topics

Chapter 10 (Object-Oriented Design) The application of data abstraction to program design often takes the form of object-oriented design (OOD). In Chapter 10 students learn techniques for practicing OOD. A straightforward approach uses object tables to list the objects and their associated characteristics and operations. Two detailed design problems illustrate object-oriented design, incorporating ADTs from earlier chapters.

Chapter 11 (Object-Oriented Programming) Object-oriented programming (OOP) carries object-oriented design to the programming language level. OOP languages such as C++ are characterized by special linguistic features: classes, inheritance, and run-time binding of operations to objects. Chapter 11 demonstrates the benefits of these features in the context of software reuse and extensibility.

Chapter 12 (Algorithm Efficiency, Searching, and Sorting) This chapter introduces performance analysis (through big-O notation) and measurement (through benchmarking) in conjunction with searching and sorting algorithms. Linear searches, binary searches, hash tables, N^2 sorts, and $N \log N$ sorts are presented and analyzed.

Chapter 13 (Trees) Chapter 13 explores the tree as both an abstract concept and an implementation technique. We use an ADT for binary trees to describe many of the structures and algorithms and show both dynamic and array implementations of trees. Additional topics in this chapter include tree traversal algorithms, binary trees, binary search trees, expression trees, and tree-based sorting techniques.

Flexibility in Chapter Coverage

Although Chapters 1 through 9 are best covered in sequential order, the text's chapter organization allows considerable flexibility.

An Earlier Introduction to Object-Oriented Design and Programming

Some faculty will want to introduce OOD and OOP early in the course. Chapter 10 (OOD), which references stacks and queues but does not rely on pointers, can be covered immediately after Chapter 4. Chapter 11 (OOP), which does use pointers, can be introduced after Chapter 7. However, Chapter 11 requires a fair degree of sophistication on the part of the student, so the instructor may wish to assign only the earlier parts of the chapter at this time, returning to later material after students have completed Chapter 9.

An Earlier Introduction to Performance Analysis

Portions of Chapter 12 (Algorithm Efficiency, Searching, and Sorting) can be covered early in the course. Some instructors find it useful to discuss big-O measures of space and time efficiency throughout the course. The only topics in Chapter 12 that depend on earlier chapters are hash tables, which refer to linked lists (Chapter 8), and quicksort, which depends on recursion (Chapter 6).

Deemphasis of Certain Topics

Depending on curricular goals and students' backgrounds, instructors can quicken the pace by deemphasizing or eliminating certain topics in Chapters 1 through 9. Some instructors may assign Chapter 1 as outside reading if it overlaps substantially with material from the first computer science course. Chapter 5 on structs and unions may be eliminated if students are already familiar with structs and if unions are deemed to have minor importance in the course. Chapter 6 may also be eliminated if recursion was covered in the first course. Additional suggestions are given in the *Instructor's Guide*.

Supplements

Transparency Masters

A collection of 400 figures and program code in the text.

Instructor's Guide with Test Item File

The *Instructor's Guide*, prepared by the authors, contains chapter-by-chapter teaching suggestions, answers to all unanswered exercises, an extensive collection of transparency masters drawn from figures and program code in the text, and a compilation of exam questions. The *Instructor's Guide* is available on request from Jones and Bartlett.

Computerized Testing Disk

Also available on request from the publisher is an electronic version of the exam questions in the *Instructor's Guide*, distributed in IBM PC format (3.5-inch or 5.25-inch) or Macintosh format.

Acknowledgments

We wish to thank the many people at D. C. Heath who have seen this text through production, especially Karen Myer, Heather Monahan, Jennifer Raymond, and Randall Adams. Our gratitude is also due to our colleagues at the University of Wisconsin–La Crosse for their support in making our efforts possible.

We are grateful to the following reviewers for their many insightful comments and suggestions:

J. Eugene Ball, University of Delaware

Tim Budd, Oregon State University

A. L. Deal, Virginia Military Institute

Thomas F. Hain, University of South Alabama

Thomas W. Judson, University of Portland

David Littman, George Mason University

Paul Luker, California State University, Chico

Richard J. Reid, Michigan State University

David B. Teague, Western Carolina University

Charles N. Winton, University of North Florida

Edward B. Wright, Western Oregon State College

A special thanks to David Teague, who evidently spent nearly as much time critiquing the text as we did writing it.

Appreciation is also due to all of the people involved with IBM's University Level Computer Science Program courses. Participation in the PCS3 and PCS4 courses has shaped many of our beliefs regarding an introduction to this discipline. We thank the people who developed and maintain this educational material: Albert Baker, Debra Baker, Tony Baxter, John Bentley, Elaine Rich, and Mary Shaw.

We also wish to acknowledge David Moffat, whose article (D. Moffat, "Teaching a modern data structures course," *ACM SIGCSE Bulletin 18* (4), Dec. 1986, pp. 57–64.) sharpened our conviction that the definitions and applications of widely used data structures should be separated, both descriptively and through chapter organization, from the implementations of those structures.

Finally, we extend a very personal expression of gratitude to our families—Anne, Brady, and Kari; Sandra, Kasandra, and Derek—for their patience and encouragement throughout the development of this book.

M. R. H.

D. D. R.

BRIEF CONTENTS

CONTENTS

DATA ABSTRACTION AND STRUCTURES USING C++

INTRODUCTION

Few would disagree that the world is far more complex today than it was a thousand years ago. In much of the world, simple nomadic and agrarian life-styles have given way to fast-paced, highly interdependent social and commercial activities. Local tribes and cultural units have been swallowed up by national governments with complicated infrastructures. Shade-tree crafting of tools and clothing has evolved into technology-driven industrialization. The list goes on.

In simpler times, a person had at least some chance of thoroughly understanding how something worked, be it a tool, the structure of a tribal organization, or a simple machine. Today, most governmental and business operations, legal regulations, and highly technical products are too complicated for such understanding. Beyond some undefinable limit, the human mind is unable to cope with such complexity and engages in **abstraction,** the act of separating the essential qualities of an idea or object from the details of how it works or is composed.

With abstraction we tend to focus on the "what," not the "how." For example, our understanding of mail delivery is generally confined to *what* the postal service does (it delivers letters from senders to recipients), not *how* it does it (it transports the letters to a local post office, sorts them by zip code either manually or by machine, routes and transports them to regional facilities, sorts them into local carrier routes or redirects them to other facilities, and so forth).

Our understanding of automobiles is largely based on abstraction. Most of us know *what* the engine does (it propels the car), but fewer of us know—or want to know—precisely *how* the engine works (the pistons compress a mixture of fuel and air inducted from the intake manifold; the spark plugs ignite this mixture; the explosion forces the pistons down in their cylinders; this linear motion translates into rotational motion at the crankshaft, and so on).

Two different perceptions of an automobile

ABSTRACT VIEW　　　　　*DETAILED VIEW*

Abstraction is powerful because it allows us to discuss, think about, and use automobiles and mail delivery without having to know everything about how they work. It is through abstraction that we are able to cope with the myriad facts, details, and stimuli that constantly bombard us.

In the world of software design it is now recognized that abstraction is an absolute necessity for managing immense, complex software projects. In introductory computer science courses, programs are usually small (perhaps 50 to 200 lines of code) and understandable in their entirety by one person. Even in this book, space limitations require program examples to be both short and readily comprehensible. However, large commercial software products and system programs, such as computer operating systems and language compilers, stretch the limits of comprehension. Programs of hundreds of thousands, even millions, of lines of code cannot be designed, understood, or proven correct without using abstraction in various forms.

You have certainly practiced abstraction in programming, even if it was not labeled as such. A simple form of abstraction is **naming**—the use of descriptive identifiers to denote variables, constants, and complicated data types. A well-chosen variable name hides the details of where or how the data value is stored and emphasizes the more important issue of *what* is being stored. For example, the identifier

```
milesPerGallon
```

is a good abstraction because it emphasizes the variable's use. The identifiers

```
              m
dataStoredAtLocation1012
      someNumber
```

also could be used but are less effective abstractions.

Abstraction is also a central theme in **top-down design**—the design of an algorithm by decomposing a problem into subproblems, then successively decomposing each subproblem into further subproblems. This technique generates **levels** (or **layers**) **of abstraction.** The topmost level, an overall description of the problem solution, is the most abstract. The next level includes more detail, but not too much. With each succeeding level of the design, the programmer specifies the general actions but postpones to lower levels the details of how to perform them. From top to bottom, we proceed from the more general to the more specific, from the more abstract to the more detailed. Chapter 1 reviews this design strategy at length.

Another form of abstraction in programming is **functional** (or **procedural**) **abstraction.** By invoking a built-in function, as in the expression

```
3.5 * sqrt(alpha)
```

the programmer depends only on the function's **specification,** a written description of what it does. Use of the function does not require knowing its **implementation,** the mechanisms for accomplishing the result. The sqrt function may be implemented by a software algorithm for approximating

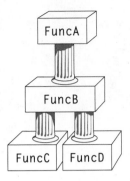

Layering of functions

square roots, or it may even be implemented directly by a machine's hardware. The power of functional abstraction arises from this separation of the function's behavior from its implementation. The program that invokes the `sqrt` routine is less complex because all the details involved in computing square roots are absent.

Functional abstractions are often layered on top of other functional abstractions. The code that implements a function `FuncA` may invoke function `FuncB`, which in turn invokes other functions. This layering is usually the result of top-down design.

The goal at each level is to abstract out the essential actions and tuck away further implementation details into lower level functions. Functional abstraction, discussed more fully in Chapters 1 and 2, is a basic tool we use throughout the remainder of this text.

Abstraction techniques also apply to data. Every data type is a set of values along with a collection of allowable operations on those values. For example, a program might need a data type `Stopwatch`, whose values are nonnegative floating point numbers and whose operations are `Start`, `Stop`, `Tick`, and `Display`. **Data abstraction** involves separating the properties of a data type (its values and operations) from the implementation of that data type. The implementation requires:

1. choosing a concrete **data representation** for the abstract values, and
2. implementing each allowable operation in terms of program instructions

For the `Stopwatch` type, a suitable data representation might be the standard `real` or `float` type in a programming language. Implementing the operations `Start`, `Stop`, `Tick`, and `Display` requires writing program code that manipulates the floating point representation of the stopwatch.

Data representations themselves can be viewed as layers of abstraction, each more abstract than the one below it, as shown for the `Stopwatch` type on the next page. Where this layering stops depends on a person's point of view (and what physicists can tell us about decomposition of atoms into more elementary particles).

What is significant is that the user of a data abstraction such as `Stopwatch` only needs to understand its properties, not its implementation. Suppression

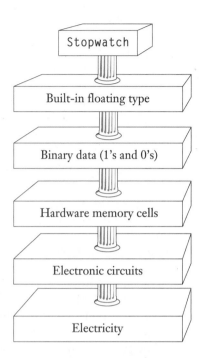

Layering of data representations

of the implementation details thus reduces complexity and also shields the user from subsequent changes in the implementation. The growing recognition of the importance of data abstraction is causing fundamental changes in approaches to software design.

This text explores the use of abstraction during the many stages of program design, coding, testing, and modification. Chapters 1 and 2 concentrate on flow of control and program structure, after which the primary emphasis is on data: data abstraction and data structures. Throughout, the goal is to stress the advantages of using abstraction to separate behavior from implementation.

Because the program examples and projects in this book are relatively small compared to major software systems, you may not see the benefits of abstraction immediately. However, it is important to maintain the following perspective throughout: The use of abstraction techniques can dramatically simplify the leap from small problems to huge projects. The tools we introduce in this text are intended to provide a firm foundation for appreciation of this perspective.

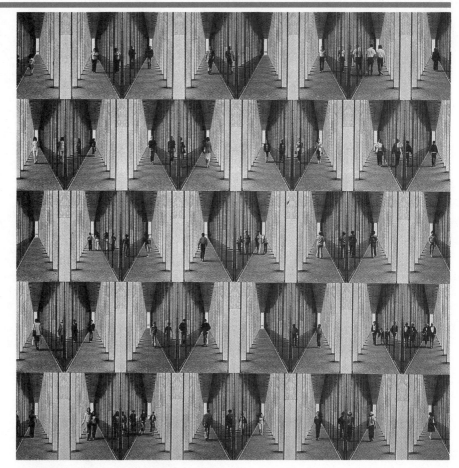

PART I

Abstraction

CHAPTER 1

Control Abstraction

INTRODUCTION

Every algorithm depends on:

1. data
2. control flow

Data refers to the information manipulated by the algorithm, and **control flow** refers to the order in which instructions are executed.

Both data and control flow are the subjects of abstraction techniques. Although the principal topic of this book is data abstraction, we start with control abstraction for three reasons:

1. To emphasize the importance of abstraction in a familiar context—control flow—before moving on to data abstraction.
2. To provide a review of key topics you already may be familiar with: selection and looping structures, subprograms and parameter passage, top-down design, and software testing methods.
3. To introduce conventions of program style and documentation that we use throughout the book.

In this chapter we examine control structures (such as `if` and `while` statements) as abstractions for machine-level instructions, and we explore functions and procedures as abstractions for single actions. We describe how to develop programs using top-down design and how to integrate program testing into the design process. Additionally, we introduce the notion of assertions—special comments in a program that help us to reason about the correctness of our algorithms.

7

A Special Note: This chapter uses C++ program examples right from the start. If you have no prior background in C++, you should do the following before proceeding with this chapter.

If your experience is in Pascal or a similar language such as Modula-2 or Ada, read Appendix A and Section C.1 of Appendix C. If you have a C background, read Appendix B and Section C.1 of Appendix C.

Throughout this chapter you may need to refer to these appendices frequently until you become more comfortable with reading and understanding C++ code.

1.1   Control Structures

Apart from some experimental machines, computers cannot directly execute a program written in a high-level language such as C++. A machine's hardware circuitry only executes instructions expressed in machine language—a primitive language whose instructions are numeric, consisting of 1's and 0's. The computer must transform high-level language instructions into machine language instructions before it can execute the instructions.

Machine language instructions are relatively primitive and can perform only simple actions. A single high-level language instruction may translate into ten or more machine language instructions. In the early days of computing, everyone programmed in machine language. It was not only tedious to use numeric instructions, it was also difficult to create error-free, understandable programs because of the wealth of detail to be managed. Particularly troublesome were issues related to flow of control.

In both high-level language and machine language programs, instructions are normally executed in sequence, one after another. To alter this normal flow of control, the contemporary high-level language programmer has a variety of instructions from which to choose: if-then-else, while, for, repeat,

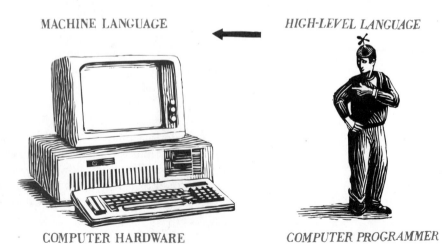

MACHINE LANGUAGE   ←   *HIGH-LEVEL LANGUAGE*

From high-level language to machine language

COMPUTER HARDWARE   *COMPUTER PROGRAMMER*

switch, function call, and so forth. In contrast, many machine languages have only three possibilities: unconditional branch, conditional branch, and subroutine call. An unconditional branch causes control to transfer immediately to some other instruction in the program. A conditional branch causes such a transfer only if some condition is found to be true. A subroutine call (corresponding to a function call or procedure call) causes transfer to a section of code that eventually concludes with a RETURN instruction, whereby control returns to the instruction following the subroutine call.

The subroutine is a form of control abstraction. By writing the body of the subroutine and putting it away somewhere, the programmer can concentrate on its use via subroutine calls without further concern for the details of its implementation. The next section of this chapter explores this abstraction mechanism further.

Early high-level languages introduced control instructions that mirror the underlying machine language instructions. For example, the GO TO instruction of the FORTRAN and BASIC languages maps directly onto machine-level unconditional branch instructions, and simple IF instructions translate into conditional branches. By the late 1960s and early 1970s it had become apparent that undisciplined use of GO TO instructions could, and often did, yield programs that were difficult to understand and debug.

More recent languages provide control abstractions such as if-then-else, while, and repeat. These are often called **control structures.** They are abstractions in the sense that they allow the programmer to take a broader view of the desired flow of control without needing to know the underlying machine language implementations. Below are two examples of high-level control structures along with their implementations using lower level branching instructions. For readability, we express the implementations in the BASIC language instead of raw machine language.

C++	**Lower level implementation**
`while (i < j)`	`160 IF I >= J GO TO 163`
`    i = i + 3;`	`161 LET I = I + 3`
`k = 5;`	`162 GO TO 160`
	`163 LET K = 5`
`if (i > j)`	`510 IF I <= J GO TO 513`
`    a = 20;`	`511 LET A = 20`
`else`	`512 GO TO 514`
`    a = 30;`	`513 LET A = 30`
`b = 2 * a;`	`514 LET B = 2 * A`

It should be evident that high-level control structures are closer to the programmer's perception of control flow than the machine's. This more abstract perspective not only makes the coding of algorithms more natural, it also eliminates errors that are completely unrelated to the algorithm itself. For example, if we erroneously wrote the instruction at line 160 as

```
IF I >= J GO TO 162
```

then the result would be an infinite loop. This error has nothing to do with the higher level while-loop algorithm; it is a detail error.

The C++ language provides control structures for selection (`if`, `if-else`, and `switch`) and for looping (`while`, `do-while`, and `for`). The `goto` statement is also available, but its primary purpose in a language with good control structures is premature exit from a loop or selection structure. The `goto` is rarely seen in C++ programs because the following features are available:

`exit`   A function that causes immediate program termination.
`return`   A statement that terminates the execution of a function.
`break`   A statement that terminates execution of a loop or `switch` statement.

In any language that offers looping structures, it is sensible to match the structure with its intended use. Counting loops, in which the number of iterations is known in advance, are inherently different from indefinite loops, in which the number of iterations is not known in advance. Although it is true that *any* loop can be expressed using a `while` statement, good programmers tend to be methodical in choosing their structures. The "Designing with Wisdom" section gives some suggestions.

Designing with Wisdom

Choosing Among Looping Structures

Choosing a looping structure should not be a matter of tossing a coin. Each has a definite purpose. Here are some guidelines.

1. The `for` loop is the natural choice for programming a pure counting loop and is compatible with many array processing algorithms.

2. For indefinite loops, the C++ programmer's choices are `while`, `do-while`, and premature exit with a `break` statement.*

   a. The `while` statement is best if the loop body might be executed no times.

   b. The `do-while` is preferable if the body is intended to be executed at least once.

   c. A loop containing a `break` statement can be difficult to read and understand; it should be chosen only after full consideration of `while` and `do-while`.

   * As explained in Appendix A, the `for` statement in C++ can be used for indefinite loops as well as for counting loops. In this book, we use the `for` statement only for counting loops.

1.2   Functional (Procedural) Abstraction

The most powerful mechanism for expressing control abstraction is the **sub-program**. Each subprogram is like a small program that performs a task on behalf of the main program. Using automobile manufacturing as an analogy,

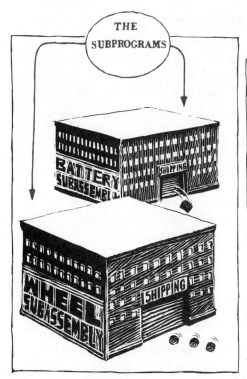

Analogy: Subprograms as automobile assembly plants

think of the main program as the main assembly plant and the subprograms as subassembly plants.

Subprograms go by various names in different languages: procedures, functions, subroutines. C++ refers to all subprograms as functions, some of which return values and some of which do not.

A function is a tool for abstraction because we can separate its behavior (what it does) from its implementation (how it does it). This separation is important for two reasons.

First, it is easier to design programs by using **functional decomposition**—decomposing a large problem into ever smaller subproblems, each expressed as a function call. With each function call, the programmer makes assumptions only about the behavior of that function, not its eventual implementation details.

Second, the separation of behavior from implementation encourages the creation of **reusable software**—pieces of software that programmers can use over and over again in different applications. Familiar examples are library functions such as sqrt and abs for computing square roots and absolute values. Instead of reinventing such routines from scratch, a programmer can simply invoke an existing library routine directly. The function's **specification,** a description of what it does, is all the programmer needs in order to use it. The particular implementation is irrelevant to the user, provided that it correctly satisfies the specification.

Functions and Procedures

Functions generally fall into two categories: those that return a single function value (in Pascal, "functions") and those that do not (in Pascal, "procedures"). A value-returning function computes exactly one value and returns this value to the expression where the function call appears:

```
y = 3 * sqrt(x);
```

In its pure form, a value-returning function mimics a mathematical function in the sense that it does not produce **side effects** (modification of variables in the parameter list or modification of global variables). In the preceding call to sqrt, we would not expect the function to compute the square root of x and then produce the side effect of adding 5 to x.

Functions in the other category (non-value-returning functions or procedures) either return no results at all:

```
PrintErrorMsg();
```

or return results implicitly by modifying their actual parameters:

```
Update(a, b);
```

Parameters and Data Flow

In designing and implementing functions, we need to pay careful attention to the **data flow** through the parameter list. By data flow we mean the flow of information from the caller to the function and from the function back to the caller. Returning to our automobile manufacturing analogy, think of data flow in a program as the flow of information and supplies between the main automobile assembly plant and the various subassembly plants.

For each parameter in a function's parameter list, there are three possibilities: a one-way flow of data *into* the function, a one-way flow *out of* the function, or a two-way flow *into and out of* the function. The direction of data flow determines the appropriate method of parameter passage. Below, we discuss these three cases. In the examples, we use the comments /* in */, /* out */, and /* inout */ to document the direction of data flow for each formal parameter.

One-way flow *into* the function

Discussion: The caller is passing a copy of the actual parameter to the function and does not want the function to modify the actual parameter. The function will inspect, but not modify, the caller's actual parameter.

Correct parameter passage method: Pass by value

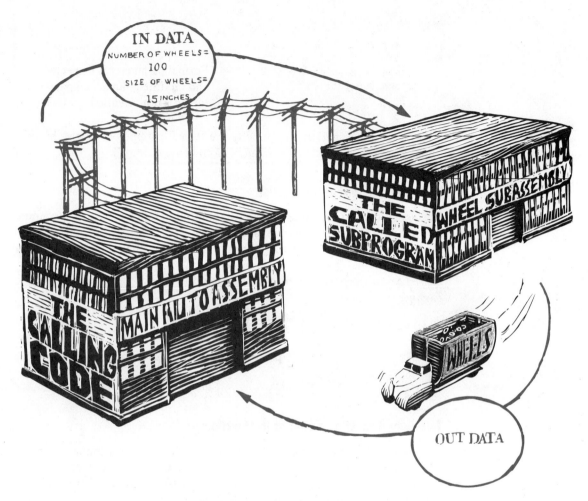

Analogy: Data flow as the transfer of information and supplies

Example 1:

```
int Trans( /* in */ int someInt )
{
    return 2*someInt + 5;          ←— Parameter is inspected but not
}                                      modified.
```

(In this example, information does, in fact, flow back to the caller by means of the function's return value. But as far as the parameter someInt is concerned, the data flow is one way, into the function.)

Example 2:

```
int Trans( /* in */ int someInt )
{
    someInt = 2*someInt + 5;          ◄— Formal parameter is inspected
    return someInt;                        and modified, but actual para-
                                           meter is not modified.
}
```

Although this function does modify the formal parameter, passing by value protects the caller's actual parameter from being changed.

One-way flow *out of* the function

Discussion: The caller is passing the location (address) of the actual parameter to the function and wants the function to modify the actual parameter. The function will not inspect the current value of the incoming parameter but will modify it.

Correct parameter passage method: Pass by reference
Example:

```
void Initialize( /* out */ float& delta,
                 /* out */ float& epsilon )
{
    delta = 1.0;           ◄— Parameters are modified but not inspected.
    epsilon = 0.002;
}
```

Two-way flow *into and out of* the function

Discussion: The caller is passing the location (address) of the actual parameter to the function and wants the function to use the parameter's current value and then possibly modify it. The function will inspect the current value of the incoming parameter and possibly modify it.

Correct parameter passage method: Pass by reference
Example:

```
void Update( /* inout */ int& alpha,
             /* inout */ int& beta  )
{
    alpha = 3 * alpha;      ◄— Parameters are both inspected and
    beta++;                     modified.
}
```

Using the Language

Passing Parameters in C++

C++ supports parameter passage by value (passing a copy of the actual parameter's value) and passage by reference (passing the memory address of the actual parameter).

Passing by value prevents the function from modifying the caller's actual parameter. There are two distinct copies of the data item, one in the calling routine and one in the function.

Passing by reference allows the function to modify the caller's actual parameter. There is only one copy of the data item, and it "belongs to" the caller.

Below is a summary of the notations C++ uses for passing by value and passing by reference. (Section A.14 of Appendix A and Section B.3 of Appendix B provide greater detail.)

1. **All data types except arrays**

    a. Passage by value—the default (assumed) method
    In the declaration of the formal parameter, no special notation is required.

    ```
    void SomeFunc( float x )
    { ... }
    ```

    b. Passage by reference
    In the declaration of the formal parameter, use an ampersand (&) after the name of the data type.

    ```
    void SomeFunc( float& x )
    { ... }
    ```

2. **Arrays**

    a. Passage by value
    It is impossible in C++ to pass an entire array by value. To prevent the function from modifying the caller's array, begin the formal parameter declaration with the word `const`.

    ```
    void SomeFunc( const float vec[] )
    { ... }
    ```

    b. Passage by reference—the default method
    In the declaration of the formal parameter, no special notation is required. (Without the word `const`, the function is free to modify the caller's actual parameter.)

    ```
    void SomeFunc( float vec[] )
    { ... }
    ```

Figure 1.1 summarizes parameter passage and data flow pictorially. It is helpful to think of a function as a sealed room with communication only possible through a window: the parameter list. (With a value-returning function, though, there is a single leak in the wall of the room: a hole where the function value is sent back via a `return` statement.)

A value-returning function:

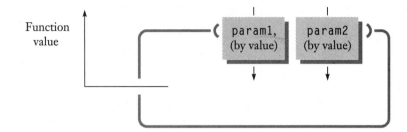

A non-value-returning function:

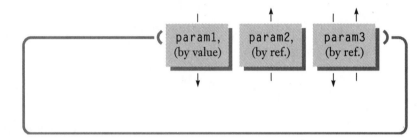

Figure 1.1 Data flow and parameter passage

Pursuing Correctness

Readable Code and Program Maintenance

Programming with readable style is not a luxury; it is a necessity. There are two reasons for writing code that is clearly understandable to readers.

First, the software developer must be able to understand his or her own code, especially when coming back to it after setting it aside for a while. Second, it is widely recognized that the original coding of a large program represents only a small fraction of the total dollars spent during its lifetime. **Program maintenance**—the repair or enhancement of existing code—costs roughly 4 to 5 times the amount of the original coding. Program maintenance often falls into the lap of a programmer different from the one who originally wrote the code. This new programmer must be able to understand how the existing program works in order to ensure correctness of the modified program.

Here are some general hints for improving program readability:

1. *Capitalize methodically.*
   Choose a convention for capitalizing identifiers and be consistent about it. Throughout this book we use the following convention:

   • For a variable name, each English word *except* the first begins with a capital letter:

   ```
   lengthInYards = 43;
   ```

- For the names of functions and programmer-defined data types, each English word *including* the first begins with a capital letter:

```
PrintValues(numPages, numWords);
```

- For identifiers representing constants, all letters are uppercase. Underscores may be used to separate English words:

```
const float AREA = 120.736;
const int   UPPER_LIMIT = 20;
```

Enumerators (the constant identifiers in enum declarations) may either use all capital letters or be capitalized in the same fashion as variable names:

```
enum CoinType {PENNY, NICKEL, DIME};
```

or

```
enum CoinType {penny, nickel, dime};
```

2. *Choose identifiers carefully.*

An identifier should immediately convey its meaning to someone reading the program for the first time.

- Names of value-returning functions should be *nouns* or *noun phrases* (or, in the case of Boolean functions, *adjectives* or *adjective phrases*).

```
Poor:    nextSum = ComputeSum(alpha, beta, gamma);
Better:  nextSum = Sum(alpha, beta, gamma);


Poor:    if (CheckIfEmpty(vector))
             ⋮
Better:  if (IsEmpty(vector))
             ⋮
```

- Names of non-value-returning functions should be *imperative verbs*. (In English, an imperative verb is one representing a command: Listen! Look! Do something!)

```
Poor:    Results(angle, length);
Better:  PrintResults(angle, length);
```

These two conventions make it easier to read aloud the statements that invoke the functions.

3. *Use comments when code is not self-documenting.*

There are many philosophies about using comments for internal documentation. The range extends from no commenting at all through commenting every single line of code. Our opinion is this: If something can be clearly stated in the language itself, do so without comment. We prefer self-documenting code to the clutter and distraction of superfluous comments:

```
int sumOfSquares;    // Sum of squares
  .
  .
Invert(matrix3);     // Invert matrix3
```

It is mandatory, though, to include comments whenever a passage of code is otherwise difficult to understand.

Additionally, all of the following (to be described later in this chapter) are candidates for comments: general assertions, loop invariants, function preconditions, and function postconditions.

4. *Use separate lines.*

   Almost every statement should appear on a separate line. For example, many programmers like to declare each variable on its own line. This facilitates adding or deleting declarations and allows on-line comments for documentation.

5. *Indent consistently.*

   C++ programmers usually indent the body of a function within the left and right braces. Bodies of `if`, `while`, and other structured statements should be indented consistently. We prefer an indentation of at least three spaces. (C++ programmers often use the Tab key, not the space bar, for indenting.) A good rule is to indent as if you were creating an outline. Indent every unit of similar importance the same distance.

   Whatever style you choose, the single most important thing is to indent the same way every time. Inconsistent indentation gives the appearance of sloppiness and raises doubts about the programmer's commitment to precision.

6. *Keep code segments short.*

   Except in unusual circumstances, it is best to limit the code for each function to about half a printed page in length.

1.3 Top-down Design

Problem Specifications

The challenge of programming is to design solutions to real-world problems that conform to the limitations imposed by a machine. Programming begins with a problem definition or **problem specification**. This is an abstract view of the program; it describes what the program does but not how to do it. The specification must ultimately be implemented by a computer program containing all of the detail abstracted in the specification.

Throughout this text we use a six-part form for problem specifications. The six parts are:

Title	A name for the problem
Description	An overview of the problem in a few sentences
Input	A detailed description of the expected input form
Output	A detailed description of the desired output form

Error Handling An extensive list of what to do with unexpected input

Example A sample execution showing input and corresponding output

Figure 1.2 displays an example of a problem specification.

Figure 1.2 Roman numeral problem specification

TITLE

Roman numeral expression evaluation

DESCRIPTION

This program prompts the user to enter Roman numeral expressions such as XXXVI + LXIII. The program prints the value of each expression as a decimal system (base 10) number. This is repeated until the user types the end-of-file keystrokes instead of an expression.

An expression consists of two operands separated by an operator (+, −, *, or /). This program uses the Roman numerals C, L, X, V, and I with decimal equivalents 100, 50, 10, 5, and 1, respectively. For simplicity, the "old Roman" system is used. In this system, no symbol precedes one of greater value; thus 9 is expressed as VIIII, not IX.

INPUT

Each input line contains the first operand, then the operator, and then the second operand. These three items are separated by one or more spaces. The expression must not continue past one input line.

Each operand may be up to 30 characters long, and Roman numerals must be uppercase letters. When prompted to enter the next expression, the user may type the end-of-file character to terminate the program. The keystrokes representing end-of-file are system dependent, examples being Ctrl/D in UNIX and Ctrl/Z in MS-DOS.

OUTPUT

The following message prompts the user to input an expression:

```
Roman numeral expression:
```

After the user types the expression, the program displays the expression value as follows:

```
Decimal value: <N>
```

where <N> denotes the value of the expression as either a decimal integer (in the case of addition, subtraction, or multiplication) or a decimal floating point number (if division was performed). The program then outputs one blank line and prompts the user for the next expression.

ERROR HANDLING

1. If the user enters an invalid operator or invalid characters within either operand, the program displays the message "BAD DATA" instead of the decimal result.

2. If a sequence of Roman numeral characters is valid but out of order (for example, VL), no special action is required. For both LV and VL, the decimal equivalent will be 55.

3. If the value of an operand or the entire expression is outside the machine's integer range, no special action is required. The results are undefined.

EXAMPLE

Below is a trace of an execution of the program. All user input is in color.

```
Roman numeral expression:
LXXXI + VIIII
Decimal value: 90

Roman numeral expression:
CXVI # XXX
BAD DATA

Roman numeral expression:
CCL / XXIII
Decimal value: 10.869565

Roman numeral expression:
L - C
Decimal value: -50

Roman numeral expression:
Xi * V
BAD DATA

Roman numeral expression:
<EOF>        ← <EOF> denotes the system's end-of-file keystrokes.
```

Top-Down Design and Stepwise Refinement

Working from the problem specification, the programmer designs a solution incorporating algorithms and data structures. A well-known technique for designing programs is **top-down design.** Top-down design is the process of decomposing a large problem into several smaller problems, each of which is further decomposed in steps. At each step, the designer refines (adds more detail to) the algorithm. This **stepwise refinement** allows the designer to manage complexity by concentrating on one subproblem at a time, proceeding gradually from the more abstract to the more detailed. Eventually the refinement process is complete when the algorithm has sufficient detail to be coded directly in a programming language. Figure 1.3 illustrates the top-down design process.

A popular method for performing top-down design is to use pencil and paper, expressing algorithms in **pseudocode**—a mixture of English words and programming language-like control structures. Here is a possible top-level algorithm for the Roman numeral problem:

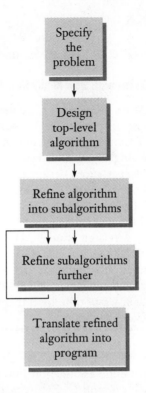

Figure 1.3 Top-down design

Level 1

1. For each input line
2.   Convert operand strings to decimal
3.   If operator and operands are all valid
4.   Print decimal value of expression
5.   else
6.   Print "BAD DATA"

A manual trace of the algorithm shows that, although most details are missing, the overall logic is correct. The actions requiring refinement are those in lines 1, 2, 3, and 4; line 6 is directly expressible in a programming language and needs no further refinement. Refinement of line 1 results in the actions of prompting the user, performing the input, and testing for loop exit. This degree of detail requires an additional action (line 7) to express the logic correctly:

Level 2

1.1 Prompt for and input string1
1.2 While input of string1 succeeded
1.3   Input operator and string2
2.   Convert operand strings to decimal
3.   If operator and operands are all valid
4.   Print decimal value of expression

5.   else
6.   Print "BAD DATA"
7.   Prompt for and input string1

Refinement: How Much? How Fast?

At each level of refinement, it is often tempting to add too much detail too fast. Psychologists suggest that humans can usefully manage only seven (plus or minus two) independent concepts at one time. Therefore, you should refine a single action into no more than seven (plus or minus two) subactions. An inexperienced designer probably should try to refine into four or fewer subactions at a time. This may take a bit longer but often saves time in the long run. The key slogan is "PRACTICE ABSTRACTION. POSTPONE DETAILS TILL LATER."

A related issue is stepwise debugging of the algorithm. The slogan here is "DEBUG AT EACH LEVEL OF REFINEMENT." Before further refinement, it is important to check for logic errors. A bug at one level will propagate throughout all lower levels, rendering them invalid. The designer will then waste time by retreating to an earlier level and restarting the refinement from that point.

From Level 2 of the Roman numeral problem, we could proceed iteratively to refine each action into increasingly detailed subactions, all the while using pseudocode. Eventually the product would be a completely detailed pseudocode program. We would then translate each line of pseudocode, line by line, into statements in an actual programming language.

Unfortunately, this two-phase process—top-down design entirely in pseudocode, followed by translation into program code—is better in principle than in practice. It is optimistic to assume that we can exhaustively debug paper-and-pencil algorithms at each level of refinement. The best programmers may be thorough, disciplined, and meticulous in analyzing algorithm logic, but they are still human. Logic errors, even though they may be rare, can still occur. Coding and running even partially refined algorithms on a machine can reveal these bugs earlier, rather than later, in the design process. The next section addresses this technique.

1.4   Top-down Testing

An alternative to designing entirely in pseudocode is to use both pseudocode and program code during the top-down design. The design begins in pseudocode. After several levels of refinement, the higher level control and data structures emerge and can be translated into program code for testing. Unrefined actions are expressed in the test program as calls to nonexistent functions.

To illustrate top-down testing, Figure 1.4 shows a C++ program corresponding to the Level 2 pseudocode algorithm for the Roman numeral problem. This program deviates slightly from the pseudocode algorithm in two

ways. First, the final statement in the program—`return 0;`—is not part of the
pseudocode algorithm. We have added this statement as a practical matter.
By convention, the `main` function returns the value 0 to the operating system
to indicate successful completion of the program.

The second deviation is the manner in which we perform the input of the
first Roman numeral string. Observe how we collapse both the input operation and the subsequent test for successful input into the `while` condition:

```
while (cin >> str1)
```

(You may wish to review the discussion of testing a C++ stream state in Section
C.1 of Appendix C.)

Figure 1.4 `main` function for the Roman numeral program

```cpp
//-----------------------------------------------------------------------------
//   roman.cpp
//   This program inputs Roman numeral expressions, one per line, and
//   outputs the decimal value of each expression.
//-----------------------------------------------------------------------------
#include <iostream.h>

typedef int Boolean;  // Define identifier Boolean as a synonym for int
const int TRUE = 1;
const int FALSE = 0;

void PrintValue( int, char, int );            // Function prototypes
void Convert( const char[], int&, Boolean& );

int main()
{
    char    str1[31];        // First Roman numeral string
    char    str2[31];        // Second Roman numeral string
    char    op;              // Operator within expression
    int     dec1;            // Decimal value of first operand
    int     dec2;            //    "      "    "  second    "
    Boolean str1Valid;       // First string valid?
    Boolean str2Valid;       // Second string valid?
    Boolean opValid;         // Operator valid?

    cout << "Roman numeral expression:\n";
    while (cin >> str1) {
        cin >> op >> str2;
        Convert(str1, dec1, str1Valid);
        Convert(str2, dec2, str2Valid);
        opValid = (op=='+' || op=='-' || op=='*' || op=='/');
        if (str1Valid && str2Valid && opValid)
            PrintValue(dec1, op, dec2);
        else
            cout << "BAD DATA\n\n";
        cout << "Roman numeral expression:\n";
    }
    return 0;
}
```

C++ Function Prototypes

In C++, every identifier must be declared before it can be used. In the case of functions, a function's declaration must physically precede any function invocation (function call).

A function declaration specifies the data type of the function's return value and the number and types of its parameters. Figure 1.4 shows a total of three function declarations. The first two declarations (for `PrintValue` and `Convert`) do not include the bodies of the functions. The third declaration (for `main`) does include its body.

In C++ terminology, a function declaration that omits the body is called a *function prototype*, and a declaration that does include the body is a *function definition*. All definitions are declarations, but not all declarations are definitions:

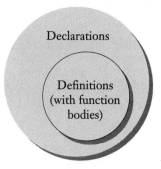

It is common for the definition of the `main` function to appear first, followed by the definitions of all other functions. To satisfy the requirement that identifiers be declared before being used, C++ programmers typically place all function prototypes near the top of the program, before the definition of `main`. Section A.14 of Appendix A and Section B.3 of Appendix B describe function prototypes and function definitions at length.

In Figure 1.4, the application of the phrase "POSTPONE DETAILS TILL LATER" is evident in the C++ source code just as in the pseudocode version. We use functional abstraction by invoking a `Convert` function before we have even written it. In other words, we assume that we eventually will write a `Convert` function but do not yet want to consider the details of how to convert Roman numeral character strings to decimal form. At this stage, we decide only what the parameter list should look like. We will send an input string to the function and expect the function to return to us two items: the decimal number that is the equivalent of the input string, and a Boolean flag that reports whether the input string was valid.

(Notice in the function prototype for `Convert` the use of the word `const` in the declaration of the first parameter. C++ arrays are always passed by reference, but we don't want the function to modify the string.)

Likewise, we practice functional abstraction by invoking a `PrintValue` function that will eventually output the result of applying the `op` operator to the two decimal operands. Although we have not yet refined either of these two actions, we are ready to machine test the high-level algorithm logic at this point—the data input, the test for end-of-file, the test for invalid data. Well, almost. We can't actually compile and run this program as it stands. The compiler will complain that the `Convert` and `PrintValue` functions are missing. We must do something more before we can run the program.

Function Stubs

Because the compiler demands function definitions for the `Convert` and `PrintValue` functions, we will supply **function stubs.** A stub is an unrefined function that "fakes" the desired action so that the rest of the program can execute. A stub performs the simplest possible task that still supplies sensible results to the calling routine. Figure 1.5 contains stubs for the `Convert` and `PrintValue` functions.

A stub typically prints a message indicating that control reached that function. The remainder of the function body contains no more than is absolutely necessary to perform the desired testing in the higher level logic—the logic in the caller. If code in the stub becomes complex, it may be less work to go ahead and design the actual function.

The stub for `Convert` ignores the incoming string parameter and prompts us to enter any integer. This input integer will masquerade as the decimal equivalent of the incoming string. The stub for `PrintValue` simply outputs the values of the incoming parameters without attempting any meaningful computation. By compiling and executing the program with stubs, we can

```cpp
void Convert( /* in */  const char str[],
              /* out */ int&      decVal,
              /* out */ Boolean&  strValid )
{
    // ***** STUB *****

    cout << "*** Convert routine entered ***\n";
    cout << "Enter an integer (nonpositive for bad data): ";
    cin >> decVal;
    strValid = (decVal > 0);
}

void PrintValue( /* in */ int  dec1,
                 /* in */ char op,
                 /* in */ int  dec2   )
{
    // ***** STUB *****

    cout << "*** PrintValue routine entered ***\n";
    cout << "dec1=" << dec1 << " op=" << op
         << " dec2=" << dec2 << "\n\n";
}
```

Figure 1.5 Function stubs

debug the higher level logic. This is called **top-down testing,** because actual machine testing proceeds concurrently with the top-down design. This technique exposes logic errors in the higher levels of design before they can filter down through lower levels.

Pursuing Correctness

Test Oracles and Code Coverage

Thorough debugging requires a **test oracle**—a collection of input values along with the predicted outputs for those inputs. The test oracle is prepared *before* executing the test program. If the actual output disagrees with the predicted output, the programmer must search the code for logic errors.

To debug the main function of Figure 1.4, we need a test oracle that causes invalid data to be trapped correctly. The main function tests for invalid operators and operands, and the stub for Convert (Figure 1.5) allows us to type a nonpositive number to signify an invalid operand. Here is a test oracle showing different combinations of input data, along with the predicted output:

Input values	Predicted output
3 + 5	dec1=3 op=+ dec2=5
3 − 5	dec1=3 op=- dec2=5
3 * 5	dec1=3 op=* dec2=5
3 / 5	dec1=3 op=/ dec2=5
3 $ 5	BAD DATA
0 + 5	BAD DATA
3 + −4	BAD DATA

Creation of a suitable test oracle is more important than may be apparent. If the oracle itself has errors, such as an incorrectly predicted output for a given input, the programmer may waste time searching the code for a nonexistent bug.

Additionally, the programmer ideally should choose input values that provide **code coverage**—the execution of every possible statement in the program. Testing for code coverage implies testing all possible paths through the control flow of the program—all of the then-clauses and else-clauses of all if statements, all of the case-clauses of all switch statements, and so forth. Realistically, code coverage is not possible for large, complex programs. For these programs, code coverage only of key portions is the best that can be attempted.

In general, then, a test oracle cannot absolutely guarantee correctness. All you can say about a program that works for one set of input values is that it succeeds or fails in that one circumstance. The program might perform differently for another set of input values. To conclude that a program is correct based on a single test is as illogical as concluding that all horses are black based on viewing a single black horse. Still, it is vital to test a program as thoroughly as possible using a well prepared test oracle, and the first few tests sometimes reveal program bugs.

Hierarchy Charts

In a top-down design, a useful aid in documenting and clarifying the relationships among functions is the **hierarchy chart** or **structure chart** (Figure 1.6). A hierarchy chart shows what lower level functions each higher level function invokes. This pictorial representation mirrors the top-down design; each function is implemented in terms of less abstract functions below it. Note that a hierarchy chart says nothing about the order in which functions are invoked. The algorithm itself specifies the order. The purpose of a hierarchy chart is to help the programmer visualize the program structure during the design process.

Further Refinement

We proceed with our design of the Roman numeral problem, assuming we have used a test oracle to debug the higher level code of Figure 1.4 along with the stubs of Figure 1.5. We now refine the `PrintValue` routine. In pseudocode, the subactions might be as follows:

```
Print "Decimal value: "
If op = '+'
    Print dec1 + dec2
else if op = '-'
    Print dec1 - dec2

        etc.
```

The simplicity of this routine suggests direct translation to basic C++ statements without further function calls (Figure 1.7). The hierarchy chart remains unaltered because `PrintValue` does not invoke other functions.

We can now substitute the complete `PrintValue` function for its corresponding stub and continue testing with only the `Convert` function still unrefined. Testing now amounts to code coverage of the new `PrintValue` function. The following is a test oracle:

Input values	Predicted output
3 + 5	Decimal value: 8
3 − 5	Decimal value: -2
3 * 5	Decimal value: 15
3 / 5	Decimal value: 0.6

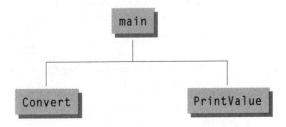

Figure 1.6 Preliminary hierarchy chart for the Roman numeral problem

```
void PrintValue( /* in */ int  dec1,
                 /* in */ char op,
                 /* in */ int  dec2 )
{
    cout << "Decimal value: ";
    switch (op) {
        case '+' : cout << dec1 + dec2;
                   break;
        case '-' : cout << dec1 - dec2;
                   break;
        case '*' : cout << dec1 * dec2;
                   break;
        case '/' : cout << float(dec1) / float(dec2);
    }
    cout << "\n\n";
}
```

Figure 1.7 PrintValue
function

Notice that we do not need to supply invalid expressions like 3$5 to test PrintValue. Our earlier test of the main function showed that main handles invalid data correctly. PrintValue receives only valid operators and operands from main.

To refine the Convert routine, observe that two actions are required: convert the string to its decimal equivalent, then set the Boolean flag strValid to indicate whether the Roman numeral characters were valid. Resisting the temptation to refine too fast, we might code these actions as shown in Figure 1.8. We assume we will write a function DecEquiv that will receive a character string and return, as the function value, either a positive integer representing the decimal equivalent or a nonpositive integer if the string contains invalid characters.

To debug this design level, we substitute this Convert function for its stub and then create a stub for the DecEquiv function. The stub for DecEquiv could ignore the incoming string and prompt for input of an integer value, thus pretending to have converted the string. Additionally, to get the program to compile correctly, we must include a function prototype for DecEquiv at the beginning of the program:

```
int DecEquiv( char[] );
```

Finally, after correcting any bugs discovered in testing the Convert function, we must refine the DecEquiv routine. Figure 1.9 displays a possible solu-

```
void Convert( /* in */  const char str[],
              /* out */ int&      decVal,
              /* out */ Boolean&  strValid )
{
    decVal = DecEquiv(str);
    strValid = (decVal > 0);
}
```

Figure 1.8 Convert
function

```
int DecEquiv( /* in */ const char str[] )
{
    Boolean dataValid = TRUE;
    int     intSum = 0;
    int     i = 0;

    while (dataValid && str[i] != '\0') {
        switch (str[i]) {
            case 'C' : intSum += 100;
                       break;
            case 'L' : intSum +=  50;
                       break;
            case 'X' : intSum +=  10;
                       break;
            case 'V' : intSum +=   5;
                       break;
            case 'I' : intSum +=   1;
                       break;
            default  : dataValid = FALSE;
        }
        i++;
    }
    return (dataValid ? intSum : 0);
}
```

Figure 1.9 DecEquiv function

tion in program code. Notice how the return statement uses the C++ conditional operator (?:) to return either the value of intSum if dataValid is nonzero (true) or the value 0 if dataValid is 0 (false).

We can now test the DecEquiv function thoroughly after substituting it for its stub. Presumably all higher level routines are already bug-free, so testing focuses only on the correct performance of this function. To test for code coverage, we should verify that all case-clauses in the switch statement (including the default clause) are exercised. Here is a test oracle for testing the DecEquiv function:

Input expression	**Predicted output**
CLXVI + I	Decimal value: 167
X5V + I	BAD DATA

The first input expression covers every one of the case-clauses except the default clause, and the second input expression covers the default clause.

After identifying and correcting any bugs in DecEquiv, we have completed the design process. No further refinement is necessary, and the final version of the hierarchy chart appears in Figure 1.10.

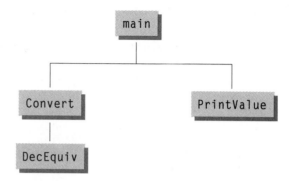

Figure 1.10 Final hierarchy chart for the Roman numeral problem

Pursuing Correctness

Top-down Testing: A Perspective

Top-down testing integrates coding and testing into the process of stepwise refinement. It is an alternative to performing stepwise refinement entirely in pseudocode and then, in a second stage, performing the coding and testing.

The Roman numeral problem is useful for demonstrating top-down testing but is overly simplistic because (a) it is a small problem, and (b) we assumed the designer and coder were the same person. Real-world projects are seldom this neat and tidy.

In larger programming shops, designers and coders are different personnel. Designers typically work with abstract tools such as specifications, hierarchy charts, and pseudocode. The coder's job, in the most narrow sense, is to take pseudocode or other abstract representations from the designer and translate them into program code. In this environment, the role of top-down testing is not always clear.

If the designer performs top-down design all the way down to the fundamental statement level, then testing is separate from the design process and becomes the coder's responsibility. On the other hand, the designer's experience may suggest that total refinement of the algorithms is unnecessary. In this case, the designer might turn over the partially refined algorithms to the coder for top-down testing and further refinement from that point. In design and testing, many variations of designer/coder interaction are possible. There are no hard and fast rules.

1.5 Bottom-up Testing

In top-down testing, unrefined functions are simulated by stubs. Using stubs allows us to debug the higher level logic before the function details are worked out.

Bottom-up testing is also useful in conjunction with top-down testing. In bottom-up testing, a newly refined function is tested individually *before* substituting it for its stub. A separate main function, called a **test driver,** is written for the express purpose of testing the new function. Before running the test driver, the programmer prepares a test oracle that anticipates all possibilities of input data, valid and invalid, and attempts code coverage.

Below is a test driver for the `Convert` routine of the Roman numeral problem. Its sole task is to repeatedly input Roman numeral strings, each time invoking the `Convert` routine and printing the result.

```
int main()
{
    char      str[31];        // Roman numeral string
    int       decVal;         // Decimal value of Roman numeral
                              // string
    Boolean strValid;         // String valid?

    while (cin >> str) {
        Convert(str, decVal, strValid);
        cout << "Decimal value: " << decVal;
        if (strValid)
            cout << " VALID\n\n";
        else
            cout << " NOT VALID\n\n";
    }
    return 0;
}
```

Bottom-up testing is the opposite of top-down testing, yet they are useful together. With top-down testing, you test the higher levels of code by supplying artificial lower level functions (stubs). With bottom-up testing, you test a lower level routine by using an artificial top level. In combination, both methods support the process of top-down design. After bottom-up testing of a function is complete, you unplug the stub, plug in the debugged function, and proceed with further top-down testing and/or design.

Combined use of top-down and bottom-up testing is especially valuable in a team programming environment. While one programmer uses stubs to test the higher level logic, another programmer can simultaneously code and test the actual lower level routines with test drivers. Performing these activities in parallel can shorten the total project time significantly.

1.6 Assertions, Invariants, and Pre/Postconditions

Many forms of internal program documentation are currently in use. One form, the **assertion,** is becoming widely accepted.

Suppose you could temporarily suspend the execution of a program. The entire collection of results produced just before the suspension is called the **state of computation.** The state of computation is like a snapshot of the contents of all variables at some instant during execution.

An assertion is a claim about the state of computation at a particular location in the program. It includes information about key portions of the execution snapshot with respect to that location.

Below is an assertion that describes the result of executing a `for` loop. The word ASSERT clarifies the purpose of the comment.

```
int trialCount[50];
int i;
```

```
for (i = 0; i < 50; i++)
    trialCount[i] = 0;
// ASSERT: All trialCount[0..49] == 0
```

An assertion is always written as a statement of fact—a fact the programmer believes to be true and wishes to emphasize. The assertion above claims that just after the `for` loop has finished, every array element with subscript from 0 through 49 contains the value 0. (The notation `trialCount[0..49]` is our shorthand for the words "`trialCount[0]` through `trialCount[49]`".) A review of this code confirms that the assertion is correct for these program statements.

Although an assertion often is written in an informal, English style, it should be phrased as a logical (Boolean) statement. That is, it is a statement with a value of true or false (true, one hopes). We explained earlier in this chapter that it is impossible, in general, to test programs exhaustively for correctness. In advanced computer science studies, principles of mathematical logic are used in **program proving**—proving that a program is correct by using its assertions. If you can prove the correctness of a program mathematically, there is no need to test it! Realistically, the current state of research is such that proofs of correctness are practical only for small programs. Although program proving is outside the scope of this book, we use assertions both to document our programs and to help us reason about the correctness of our programs.

An important thing to understand right away is that *the placement of an assertion is crucial*. It would not be correct to place the assertion about `trialCount` just above the `for` loop. In other words, you should not assert that all array elements equal zero *before* the `for` loop sets them all to zero.

Assertions are best written using English phrases and mathematical symbols that are largely independent of any particular programming language. In the assertion

```
// ASSERT: firstInt = 3 * secondInt
//         & firstInt > 0
```

the symbols = and & have their mathematical meanings of "equals" and "and". In a C++ program, though, this assertion could be confusing. The C++ operators for "equals" and "and" are == and &&, respectively. For consistency, then, we write the preceding assertion as

```
// ASSERT: firstInt == 3 * secondInt
//         && firstInt > 0
```

Loop Invariants

Assertions may be sprinkled throughout a program, wherever they improve readability. Two kinds of assertions are so commonly used that they have special names. One of these is the **loop invariant**—an assertion within a loop that must be true *every* time control reaches that position in the loop.

A loop invariant is located just prior to the test for loop exit. Here is a `while` loop for which the loop invariant is denoted by `INV`:

```
// Note: A for-loop would be more appropriate for this counting loop.
//       A while-loop is used only for demonstration purposes.

int trialCount[50];
int i = 0;

while (i < 50) {  // INV (prior to test): All trialCount[0..i-1] == 0
                  //                       && 0 <= i <= 50
    trialCount[i] = 0;
    i++;
}
// ASSERT: All trialCount[0..49] == 0
//         && i == 50
```

A loop invariant should document the task performed by the loop. The loop invariant in this example emphasizes that the loop assigns the value 0 to all elements of `trialCount`, beginning with `trialCount[0]` and ending with `trialCount[49]`.

A loop invariant must be true *every* time control reaches that position in the loop. Therefore, the loop invariant must be true

1. just before the loop body executes for the first time

2. just after the loop body has executed for the last time, and

3. after every loop iteration in between

Consider the first case. For the preceding `while` loop, i equals 0 just before the body executes for the first time. The first part of the loop invariant is trivially true because there are no subscripts from 0 through -1 in increasing order. The second part of the invariant is also true because $0 \leq 0 \leq 50$.

Now look at case 3. Suppose i equals 10 just prior to the loop test. Looking at the loop body, we can see that we have just set `trialCount[9]` to zero and then incremented i to 10. The first part of the loop invariant is therefore true: all of `trialCount[0]` through `trialCount[9]` are zero. The second part, $0 \leq 10 \leq 50$, is also true.

To show that case 2 holds, consider the final iteration of the loop. The body of the loop stores zero into `trialCount[49]` and then increments i to 50. Therefore, just prior to the final loop test the invariant is true (all array elements from 0 through 49 equal zero and $0 \leq 50 \leq 50$), after which the `while` condition is immediately false and control exits the loop.

Throughout this text, we use invariants to document loops (except for certain clearly understandable `for` loops). By becoming accustomed to reading this style of documentation you will gain important insight into the **semantics** (the meaning) of a program.

Pre- and Postconditions

The second place where assertions are especially important is in the documentation of a function. A pair of assertions known as a **precondition** and a **postcondition** precisely document the function's behavior. That is, they are part of the function's specification. The precondition describes everything the function requires to be true at the moment the caller invokes the function. The postcondition describes the state of computation at the moment the function finishes executing. Below is an example. The postcondition properly belongs at the bottom of the code but we place both the pre- and postcondition at the top so that the function's specification appears in one place.

```
void SwapChars( /* inout */ char& ch1,
                /* inout */ char& ch2 )
    //......................................................
    // PRE:  Assigned(ch1)  &&  Assigned(ch2)
    // POST: The values of ch1 and ch2 from the
    //       time of invocation have been interchanged
    //......................................................
{
    char tempCh = ch1;

    ch1 = ch2;
    ch2 = tempCh;
}
```

In the precondition, the notation Assigned(ch1) means the caller has assigned some value to the first parameter.

Preconditions and postconditions establish a contract. The contract states that if the precondition is guaranteed at the time of invocation, then the postcondition is guaranteed upon return from the function. The *caller* is responsible for ensuring the precondition, and the *function code* must ensure the postcondition. If the calling code fails to satisfy its part of the contract (the precondition), the function code is under no obligation to guarantee that the postcondition will be true.

Notation in Assertions

In this text we use PRE: and POST: to denote pre- and postconditions, respectively. In the SwapChars function the pre/postcondition contract states that SwapChars will interchange, or swap, the values of its two parameters on the condition that they have been assigned values prior to the invocation of the function. The notation Assigned(someVar) is an abbreviation we use in assertions to signify that the caller has previously assigned a value to someVar. The main purpose of the assertion Assigned(someVar) is to remind the programmer to double-check that the parameter is assigned a meaningful value before calling the function.

Preconditions implicitly refer to values of variables at the moment the function is invoked. Postconditions refer to values of variables at the moment the function returns. A postcondition also may wish to refer to values that existed at the time the function was invoked. To specify "at the time of entry to the function," we append the suffix <entry> to a variable name. Here is a more succinct version of the postcondition for Swapchars:

```
// POST: ch1 == ch2<entry>  &&  ch2 == ch1<entry>
```

```
float GradePoint( /* in */ char letterGrade )
    //......................................................
    // PRE:  'A' <= letterGrade <= 'F'
    // POST: FCTVAL == 4.0, if letterGrade == 'A'
    //             == 3.0, if letterGrade == 'B'
    //             == 2.0, if letterGrade == 'C'
    //             == 1.0, if letterGrade == 'D'
    //             == 0.0, if letterGrade == 'E'
    //             == 0.0, if letterGrade == 'F'
    //......................................................
{
    switch (letterGrade) {
        case 'A' : return 4.0;
        case 'B' : return 3.0;
        case 'C' : return 2.0;
        case 'D' : return 1.0;
        case 'E' :
        case 'F' : return 0.0;
    }
}
```

Figure 1.11 GradePoint function

Value-returning functions require a special notation to specify the single value returned. We use the word FCTVAL in a postcondition to denote the function's return value. Figure 1.11 shows a function that translates a letter grade into its corresponding numeric value, assuming a 0.0 to 4.0 grading scheme. The precondition of this GradePoint function assumes the caller will supply a letterGrade parameter from 'A' through 'F.'

Notice that the body of the GradePoint function is not required to test for an invalid character, one outside the range of 'A' through 'F'. This is because the function only guarantees the postcondition if the caller guarantees the precondition. The contract for the GradePoint function says the caller must pass a valid parameter in order to receive a valid result.

Sometimes the caller does not have to satisfy a precondition before invoking a function—the function will work regardless of the conditions that exist when it is invoked. In this case, there is no need to state any precondition. The GetNonBlank function of Figure 1.12 is an example of a function without a precondition. The caller is not required to assign any values to the parameters before invoking the function.

The GetNonBlank function illustrates a convenient abbreviation borrowed from mathematical logic. The right-arrow symbol "-->" in the postcondition denotes **logical implication**. When reading this notation, you can substitute the word "IMPLIES" for "-->". The expression

(A nonblank char exists) --> inChar == the first such char

can be read as

(A nonblank char exists) IMPLIES inChar == the first such char

or even more informally as

```
void GetNonBlank( /* out */ char& inChar,
                  /* out */ int&  blanksEaten )
  //.............................................................
  // POST: Any and all blank (' ') input chars have been consumed
  //     && blanksEaten == the number of blank chars consumed
  //     && (A nonblank char exists) --> inChar == the first such
  //                                             char
  //.............................................................
{
  blanksEaten = -1;
  do {
      blanksEaten++;
      cin.get(inChar);
          // INV: For this invocation of the function, each char
          //      prior to current inChar was a blank
          //      & blanksEaten == number of blanks consumed
          //                       prior to current input
  } while (cin && inChar == ' ');
}
```

Figure 1.12 GetNonBlank function

> IF a nonblank char exists
> THEN inChar == the first such character

Appendix D further describes the assertion notation that we use throughout this text. We recommend that you skim this appendix now, even though some of it refers to material that isn't covered until later in the book.

Pursuing Correctness

Assertions

Assertions within a program have three important uses:

- to document the semantics of sections of program code
- to provide help in arguing the correctness of programs
- to form contracts between callers and implementations of functions

Below are some suggestions for using assertions effectively.

1. Placement of assertions

   One style of internal program documentation is to place a comment like "The following code does such and such" before the code begins. However, an assertion is something quite different. It is a claim about the state of computation *at an exact moment during program execution.* Hence, an assertion is located just after the code it refers to.

   Exception: A function precondition and postcondition appear at the top of the function code for quick reference.

2. Loop invariants

   Loop invariants sometimes are difficult to write. The purpose is not to torture the programmer but to help ensure that the loop is correct. Every programmer has experienced the "off by 1" syndrome—a loop executes either one time too many or one time too few.

Because the loop invariant refers to the state of computation immediately before the test for loop exit, there is a common pattern:

a. The description of the data manipulated by the loop refers to the iteration *that has just completed*, and

b. If the loop is controlled by a variable that increases in value, the invariant states a final value *greater than* the desired upper bound for the loop. (Similarly, if the loop control variable decreases in value, the invariant states a final value less than the desired lower bound.)

You can see this pattern in the following loop, which sums the integers 1 through 10:

```
sum10 = 0;
for (i = 1; i <= 10; i++)
            // INV (prior to test):
            //     sum10 == sum of integers 1 thru i-1
            // && 1 <= i <= 11
    sum10 += i;
```

Another thing to keep in mind is that the invariant may be trivially true before the first execution of the loop body. In the preceding example, the first part of the invariant implicitly refers to the sum of the integers 1 through i-1 *in increasing order*. When i equals 1, but before the body executes, there are no integers from 1 through 0 in increasing order. Therefore, the first part of the invariant is trivially true.

3. Preconditions and postconditions

Pre- and postconditions, when well written, provide a concise but accurate description of the behavior of a function. Any reader should be able to see at a glance how to use the function by looking only at its specification (the function type, the formal parameter list, and the pre- and post-conditions) and not have to look into the code of the function body to understand what the function does.

In terms of abstraction, a postcondition states *what* the function does, not the details of *how* it does it. For this reason, the postcondition should mention (by name) what each outgoing parameter represents but should not mention any local variables. Local variables are implementation details; they are irrelevant to the function's specification.

A Study in Design

The Selection Sort

Suppose we are asked to write a program to do the following:

Input a collection of up to 100 integers from the standard input device, sort them into ascending order, and output the sorted values to the standard output device. If there are fewer than 100 numbers, the user will press the end-of-file keystrokes after the last input value.

We need to store all the input values into memory before sorting them into order, so we will use a 100-element vector (one-dimensional array):

Sorting a list of numbers

```
int vec[100];
```

By using an array, we can take advantage of algorithms that step through the data values by manipulating a subscript (index). For example, if we ignore the end-of-file issue for the moment, it is easy to input 100 numbers with a simple for loop:

```
for (i = 0; i < 100; i++)
    cin >> vec[i];
```

The Top-level Design

Having chosen a vector to store the data, we begin a top-down design for this problem. We start with a pseudocode algorithm prescribing the major actions to be performed:

1. Prompt the user to enter the input values
2. Input the data into the vector
3. Sort the vector elements
4. Output the vector

Mindful of the slogan "POSTPONE DETAILS TILL LATER," we delay thinking about how to implement any of these major actions. Remembering also the slogan "DEBUG AT EACH LEVEL OF REFINEMENT," we either can debug the logic with pencil and paper or perform top-down testing by coding the algorithm into C++ and testing as we refine.

Our top-level algorithm above is simple enough to debug with pencil and paper, but let us perform top-down testing by translating the pseudocode into program code. We will use function calls and function stubs for actions we have not yet refined.

We can code line 1 directly as a C++ output statement without need for a function:

```
cout << "This program sorts up to 100 input integers.\n"
     << "Use end-of-file to terminate the list early.\n\n"
     << "Begin input:\n";
```

The actions in lines 2, 3, and 4 need refinement, so we will translate them into function calls and refine the functions later.

Below is the main function for our problem up to this point. We have chosen to make the program more flexible by introducing a constant named MAX. Throughout the program, we use MAX instead of the "hard constant" 100. This way, if we want to change the program later to accommodate more or less than 100 numbers, we only need to change one line in the program (the declaration of MAX) instead of many.

```
#include <iostream.h>

const int MAX = 100;                    // Global constant

void InputVec( int[], int& );           // Function prototypes
void OutputVec( const int[], int );
void Sort( int[], int );

int main()
{
    int vec[MAX];       // Vector for storing input data
    int numItems;       // Number of data items entered by user

    cout << "This program sorts up to " << MAX
         << " input integers.\n"
         << "Use end-of-file to terminate the list early.\n\n"
         << "Begin input:\n";

    InputVec(vec, numItems);
    Sort(vec, numItems);
    // ASSERT: vec[0..numItems-1] are in ascending order

    cout << "\nSorted list:\n";
    OutputVec(vec, numItems);

    return 0;
}
```

The main function declares two data items: the array vec and the count of data values actually entered by the user, numItems. The call to InputVec includes both of these as parameters. The expectation is that InputVec will modify both parameters in the following way. The function will input values into the array vec, and it will (somehow) count the number of input values and return this count to main in the parameter numItems. Because the function modifies both parameters, it is appropriate to pass them by reference. Observe the function prototype for InputVec. C++ arrays are always passed by reference, so the first parameter needs no special notation to signify pass-by-reference. For the second parameter, a simple variable, the notation `int&` is required for passing by reference instead of by value.

The call to the `Sort` function also passes `vec` and `numItems` as parameters. The function prototype shows that `vec` is passed by reference but that `numItems` is passed by value. We expect `Sort` to modify the array (by re-arranging the array contents into ascending order) but not to modify `numItems`. The function uses `numItems` only to determine how many data values are present in the 100-element array.

The call to `OutputVec` once again passes `vec` and `numItems` as parameters. This time, both should be passed by value because displaying the contents of the array should not modify either the array or the count of data items. In C++ it is impossible to pass an array by value, so the function prototype for `OutputVec` declares the first parameter to be a `const` array. Remember that a function cannot modify a `const` array.

Finally, the `main` function returns the exit status 0 to the operating system, signalling successful completion of the program.

Before we can compile and test the top-level program logic, we must include function definitions for the three supporting functions. We have not yet refined the algorithms for these three, so we must create function stubs before proceeding.

Adding Stubs

For the `InputVec` function, we haven't yet considered how to input a maximum of 100 values, terminating the input early when encountering end-of-file. A suitable stub might simply use assignment statements to store three values into the array and return a value of 3 for the second parameter. It is very important at this time to give a complete and accurate function specification (complete parameter list and pre- and postconditions), even though the implementation is artificial:

```
void InputVec( /* out */ int  vec[],
               /* out */ int& size  )
    //.................................................
    // POST: size == no. of input values
    //     && vec[0..size-1] contain the input values
    //.................................................
{
    // ***** STUB *****

    cout << "*** InputVec routine entered ***\n";
    size = 3;
    vec[0] = 25;
    vec[1] = 10;
    vec[2] = 30;
}
```

Notice that the function specification does not include a precondition. As you look back at the `main` function you will see that no conditions need to be satisfied before calling the function. In particular, `main` does not need to assign any values to either the array or to `numItems`. It is the function's responsibility to assign these values.

A stub for the `Sort` routine can pretend to perform a general sort by just reassigning our three test values:

```
void Sort( /* inout */ int vec[],
           /* in */    int size  )
    //............................................................
    // PRE:  Assigned(size)  &&  Assigned(vec[0..size-1])
    // POST: vec[0..size-1] contain same values as
    //        vec[0..size-1]<entry> but are rearranged into ascending
    //        order
    //............................................................
{
    // ***** STUB *****

    cout << "*** Sort routine entered ***\n";
    vec[0] = 10;
    vec[1] = 25;
    vec[2] = 30;
}
```

For this routine, the precondition warns the caller to double-check both of the following:

- the second parameter (`size`) has been assigned some value, and
- the value of `size` indicates how many of the array elements contain valid data

Finally, the stub for the `OutputVec` function merely outputs each of the three test values:

```
void OutputVec( /* in */ const int vec[],
                /* in */       int size  )
    //............................................................
    // PRE:  Assigned(size)  &&  Assigned(vec[0..size-1])
    // POST: vec[0..size-1] have been output, one number per line
    //............................................................
{
    // ***** STUB *****

    cout << "*** OutputVec routine entered ***\n";
    cout << vec[0] << '\n';
    cout << vec[1] << '\n';
    cout << vec[2] << '\n';
}
```

We are now ready to compile the program and test for correct execution of the `main` function. Because the top-level algorithm contains no `if` or `switch` statements, we are assured of code coverage without trying a wide assortment of data values.

Refining the Functions

After successful testing of the `main` function, it is time to begin refining the three supporting functions. `OutputVec` is the easiest to refine. Given the incoming parameters `vec` and `size`, the function needs to step through the array using subscripts 0 through `size` – 1, displaying each number on a separate output line. A counting loop is most appropriate here, because the number of iterations is known in advance. Therefore, we use a `for` loop:

```
int i;

for (i = 0; i < size; i++)    // INV (prior to test):
                              //     vec[0..i-1] have been output
                              //  && i <= size
    cout << vec[i] << '\n';
```

Observe how the loop invariant states that `i <= size`, whereas the condition in the `for` loop is `i < size`. These expressions are different because the final loop iteration outputs the contents of `vec[size-1]` and then increments `i` to have the value `size`. Therefore, just prior to the final loop test the assertion `i <= size` is true, after which the loop test is false and control exits the loop.

To refine the `InputVec` routine, we must decide how to input as many as 100 numbers, stopping the input if end-of-file is encountered. Additionally, the function must count the number of input values, returning this number as the parameter `size`. Using `MAX` in place of the constant 100, the following code accomplishes the desired result:

```
size = 0;
while (size < MAX && cin >> vec[size])  // INV (prior to test):
                                        //     vec[0..size-1] have
                                        //         been input
                                        //  && size <= MAX
    size++;
```

As we did in the Roman numeral problem earlier in this chapter, we use the popular C++ technique of performing input right in the `while` condition itself. The expression

```
cin >> vec[size]
```

denotes a stream (the stream remaining after extracting an integer value), so testing the state of the stream yields a nonzero (true) value if the input succeeded. If the input failed because of end-of-file, the test yields the value zero (false) and control exits the `while` loop. If the user never presses the end-of-file keystrokes, control will exit the loop when exactly `MAX` numbers have been input.

The third function to be refined, the `Sort` function, requires the greatest effort of all. The next subsection discusses this routine.

The Selection Sort

There are many algorithms for sorting data into ascending or descending order. Later in this book we describe several of these. For this problem we use a sorting technique known as the **straight selection sort,** sometimes called more simply the *selection sort.* To demonstrate the selection sort, assume that we want to sort the following four values into ascending order:

```
vec [0]   [1]   [2]   [3]
     9  |  7  |  4  |  5
```

The selection sort makes repeated passes through the vector, moving from top to bottom (in this diagram, left to right). On the first pass, the algorithm selects the largest value in the vector (9) and swaps it with the value at the bottom (5).

```
vec [0]   [1]   [2]   [3]
     5  |  7  |  4  |  9
                        ↑
                     bottom
```

Next, it moves the bottom up by one position, creating a "false bottom" to the vector:

```
vec [0]   [1]   [2]   [3]
     5  |  7  |  4  |  9
                  ↑
               bottom
```

The algorithm makes a second pass, selecting the largest value in the now-shortened vector (7) and swapping it with the value at the new bottom (4).

```
vec [0]   [1]   [2]   [3]
     5  |  4  |  7  |  9
                  ↑
               bottom
```

At this point, the second largest value in the entire vector is in the next to last position.

The algorithm then moves the bottom up again and continues making passes until the false bottom has reached the top.

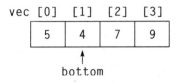

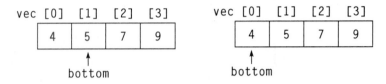

In pseudocode and C++, the algorithm for the selection sort is as follows:

```
for (bottom = size-1; bottom >= 1; bottom--) {
    Find the index of the largest value in vec[0] thru vec[bottom]—call it
        maxIndx
    If maxIndx ≠ bottom
        Swap vec[bottom] and vec[maxIndx]
}
```

The full C++ encoding of this sorting algorithm is shown in Figure 1.13 along with the entire program.

Figure 1.13 SelSort program

```
//----------------------------------------------------------------------
// selsort.cpp
// This program inputs up to MAX integer values from standard input.
// The values are sorted into ascending order and output to standard
// output.  The sorting method used is the straight selection sort.
//----------------------------------------------------------------------
#include <iostream.h>

const int MAX = 100;                    // Global constant

void InputVec( int[], int& );           // Function prototypes
void OutputVec( const int[], int );
void Sort( int[], int );
void Swap( int&, int& );

int main()
{
    int vec[MAX];       // Vector for storing input data
    int numItems;       // Number of data items entered by user

    cout << "This program sorts up to " << MAX
         << " input integers.\n"
         << "Use end-of-file to terminate the list early.\n\n"
         << "Begin input:\n";
```

```
            InputVec(vec, numItems);
            Sort(vec, numItems);
            // ASSERT: vec[0..numItems-1] are in ascending order

            cout << "\nSorted list:\n";
            OutputVec(vec, numItems);

            return 0;
        }
        //-----------------------------------------------------------------
        void InputVec( /* out */ int  vec[],
                       /* out */ int& size  )
            //.............................................................
            // POST: size == no.  of input values
            //    && vec[0..size-1] contain the input values
            //.............................................................
        {
            size = 0;
            while (size < MAX && cin >> vec[size]) // INV (prior to test):
                                                   //    vec[0..size-1] have
                                                   //         been input
                                                   // && size <= MAX
                size++;
        }
        //-----------------------------------------------------------------
        void OutputVec( /* in */ const int vec[],
                        /* in */       int size  )
            //.............................................................
            // PRE:  Assigned(size)  &&  Assigned(vec[0..size-1])
            // POST: vec[0..size-1] have been output, one number per line
            //.............................................................
        {
            int i;

            for (i = 0; i < size; i++)   // INV (prior to test):
                                         //    vec[0..i-1] have been output
                                         //    && i <= size
                cout << vec[i] << '\n';
        }
        //-----------------------------------------------------------------
        void Sort( /* inout */ int vec[],
                   /* in */    int size  )
            //.............................................................
            // PRE:  Assigned(size)  &&  Assigned(vec[0..size-1])
            // POST: vec[0..size-1] contain same values as
            //       vec[0..size-1]<entry> but are rearranged into
            //       ascending order
            //.............................................................
        {
            int maxIndx;         // Index of largest no. in each pass
            int bottom;          // "False bottom" for each pass
            int i;
```

```
        for (bottom = size-1; bottom >= 1; bottom--) {
                // INV (prior to test):
                //     All vec[0..bottom] are <= vec[bottom+1]
                //  && vec[bottom+1..size-1] are in ascending order
                //  && bottom >= 0
        maxIndx = 0;
        for (i = 1; i <= bottom; i++)   // INV (prior to test):
                                        //     vec[maxIndx] >= all
                                        //         vec[0..i-1]
                                        //  && i <= bottom+1

            if (vec[i] > vec[maxIndx])
                maxIndx = i;

        if (maxIndx != bottom)
            Swap(vec[bottom], vec[maxIndx]);
    }
}
//----------------------------------------------------------------
void Swap( /* inout */ int& int1,
           /* inout */ int& int2 )
    //..............................................................
    // PRE:  Assigned(int1)  &&  Assigned(int2)
    // POST: int1 == int2<entry>  &&  int2 == int1<entry>
    //..............................................................
{
    int temp = int1;

    int1 = int2;
    int2 = temp;
}
```

SUMMARY Programming languages support control abstraction by providing control structures and subprogram mechanisms. Control structures such as if, while, and for statements allow the programmer to focus on higher-level control flow and ignore the underlying machine language implementations. Functional abstraction—the separation of a function's behavior from its implementation—facilitates the design of new programs, the testing and modification of existing programs, and the creation of reusable software components.

Top-down design of software is permeated throughout by the notion of abstraction. Decomposition of larger problems into smaller, more manageable problems reduces complexity. Stepwise refinement produces levels of abstraction wherein inessential details are postponed to lower levels. At each level, the designer concentrates only on what a particular action is supposed to do, not on how it will eventually be implemented. In the design process, pseudocode and hierarchy charts are valuable tools.

This chapter also has discussed the strategy of performing machine testing while the design is in progress. Top-down testing (using function stubs) and bottom-up testing (using test drivers) permit error detection as early as possible in the design.

Function preconditions and postconditions are also important tools for abstraction. These assertions, together with formal parameter declarations, form a function's specification—a description of its use and behavior without mention of its implementation. By knowing only what the function does and how to use it, the user of the function does not have to depend on subtleties of its implementation. Because of the absence of implementation details in the specification, any reasonable implementation that guarantees the postcondition is allowed.

KEY TERMS

assertion (p. 31)
bottom-up testing (p. 30)
code coverage (p. 26)
control flow (p. 7)
control structures (p. 9)
data (p. 7)
data flow (p. 12)
function stub (p. 25)
functional (procedural) abstraction (p. 10)
functional decomposition (p. 11)
hierarchy chart (p. 27)
logical implication (p. 35)
loop invariant (p. 32)
postcondition (p. 33)
precondition (p. 33)
problem specification (p. 18)

program maintenance (p. 16)
program proving (p. 32)
pseudocode (p. 20)
reusable software (p. 11)
semantics (p. 33)
side effects (p. 12)
specification (p. 11)
state of computation (p. 31)
stepwise refinement (p. 20)
straight selection sort (p. 43)
structure chart (p. 27)
subprogram (p. 10)
test driver (p. 30)
test oracle (p. 26)
top-down design (p. 20)
top-down testing (p. 26)

EXERCISES

1.1 Assume that i and j are int variables. How many X's are output by each C++ code segment below? (Assume the constants TRUE and FALSE are 1 and 0, respectively.)

```
a. while ( !TRUE )
       cout << 'X';

b. do
       cout << 'X';
   while (FALSE);

c. for (i = 1; i <= 100; i++)
       if (i < 25 && i != 10)
           cout << 'X';

d. for (i = 1; i <= 100; i += 3)
       cout << 'X';

e. for (i = 10; i >= 1; i--)
       cout << 'X';

f. i = 1;
   while (i < 10) {
```

```
            i++;
            j = 1;
            do {
                cout << 'X';
                j++;
            } while (j < 77);
        }
    g.  i = -4;
        while (TRUE) {
            i += 3;
            cout << 'X';
            if (i > 10)
                break;
            i -= 2;
            cout << 'X';
            if (i > 8)
                break;
            i++;
            cout << 'X';
        }
```

1.2 For each loop below, supply a loop invariant and a loop postcondition (an assertion immediately following the loop). Here is an example:

```
sum = 0;
i = 1;
while (i <= 50) {  // INV (prior to test):
                   //     sum == 1 + 2 + ...  + (i-1)
                   //  && 1 <= i <= 51
    sum += i;
    i++;
}
// ASSERT: sum == 1 + 2 + ...  + 50  &&  i == 51
```

(Notice that the first part of the invariant is trivially true before the first execution of the loop body. There are no integers from 1 through 0 *in increasing order*.)

```
    a.  sum = 0;
        i = 0;
        while (i <= 50) {
            i++;
            sum += i;
        }
    b.  sum = 0;
        i = 0;
        while (i < 20) {
            sum += i;
```

```
        i += 2;
    }
```

c. In the following do-while loop, be sure to place the invariant just before the test at the bottom.

```
prod = 1;
i = 3;
do {
    prod *= i;
    i++;
} while (i <= 5);
```

d.
```
sum = 0;
i = 28;
while (i > 20) {
    i--;
    sum += i;
}
```

e. In the following do-while loop, be sure to place the invariant just before the test at the bottom.

```
sum = 0;
i = 33;
do {
    i++;
    sum += i;
    i++;
} while (i < 40);
```

1.3 Each part below includes a loop invariant and loop postcondition. Write a corresponding C++ loop. (Use all while loops.)

a.
```
// INV: someInt is the current input integer
//    && No input integer prior to someInt == -33

// ASSERT: someInt is the current input integer
//       && someInt == -33
//       && No input integer prior to someInt == -33
```

b.
```
// INV: maxPos == largest of all input integers that are
//                positive, if any positive numbers have been
//                input
//             == 0, otherwise

// ASSERT: maxPos == largest of all input integers that are
//                positive, if any positive numbers have been
//                input
//             == 0, otherwise
//       && End-of-file encountered
```

c. ```
// INV: oddSum == 1 + 3 + ... + (j-2)
//   && 1 <= j <= 101 && j modulo 2 == 1
```

```
// ASSERT: oddSum == 1 + 3 + ...  + 99
```

d. ```
// INV: oddSum == 1 + 3 + ... + j
//   && 0 < j < 100 && j modulo 2 == 1
```

```
// ASSERT: oddSum == 1 + 3 + ...  + 99
```

e. ```
// INV: evenSum == i + (i+2) + (i+4) + ... + 1000
//   && 0 <= i <= 1000 && i modulo 2 == 0
```

```
// ASSERT: evenSum == 0 + 2 + ...  + 1000
```

1.4   Write a C++ `for` loop to output each of the following sequences, *exactly* as shown:

a. `123456789`

b. `2  3  4  5  6  7`

c. `3 5 7 9`

d. `111 110 109 108 107 106 105 104`

e. `abcdefghijklmnop`

f. `A C E G I K M`

g. `P M J G D`

1.5   Rewrite the loops in Exercise 1.4 using `while` instead of `for`.

1.6   Rewrite the loops in Exercise 1.4 using `do-while` instead of `for`.

1.7   In the code segment below, `quizGrade` is a `char` variable and `quizScore` is an `int` variable. Assuming the initial assertion to be true, write an equivalent piece of C++ code with a `switch` statement and no `if` statements.

```
// ASSERT: 0 <= quizScore <= 10

if (quizScore >= 9)
    quizGrade = 'A';
else if (quizScore >= 7)
    quizGrade = 'B';
else if (quizScore >= 5)
    quizGrade = 'C';
else if (quizScore == 4)
    quizGrade = 'D';
else
    quizGrade = 'F';
```

1.8   For each C++ function below, document the data flow of each formal parameter with `/* in */`, `/* out */`, or `/* inout */`.
```

```
a. int Func1( int int1,
            int int2 )
   {
        return 2*int1 + int2;
   }
b. void Func2( int  int1,
            int& int2 )
   {
        switch (int2) {
            case 2:  int2 = int1;
                     break;
            case 3:  int1++;
                     int2 = 3 * int1;
                     break;
            default: int2++;
        }
   }
c. void Func3( int& int1,
            int& int2 )
   {
        cin >> int1;
        int2 *= int1;
   }
d. void Func4( const float vec[] )
   {
        cout << vec[0] << ' ' << vec[1];
   }
```

1.9 For each function in Exercise 1.8, give the function precondition and postcondition.

1.10 Write stubs for each of the following function specifications. (Remember, include only enough code to report that control reached the function and return some artificial result if necessary.)

```
a. void PrintAst( /* in */ int n )
   //...............................................
   // PRE:  n > 0
   // POST: n consecutive asterisks have been output on one line
   //...............................................
```

b. For this part, assume that you have made the declarations:

```
                              typedef int Boolean;
                              const int TRUE = 1;
                              const int FALSE = 0;

Boolean IsOdd( /* in */ int n )
   //...............................................
   // PRE:  Assigned(n)
```

```
                    // POST: FCTVAL == TRUE, if n is an odd number
                    //             == FALSE, otherwise
                    //................................................
```

c. void SomeProc(/* in */   float alpha,
                  /* inout */ float& beta,
                  /* out */   int&   anInt)

```
    //................................................
    // PRE:  Assigned(alpha)  &&  Assigned(beta)
    // POST: (alpha > 0.0) --> (beta == beta<entry> / 4.8
    //                          && NOT Assigned(anInt))
    //    && (alpha == 0.0) --> (beta == beta<entry>
    //                          && anInt == 1)
    //    && (alpha < 0.0) --> (beta == alpha && anInt == 5)
    //................................................
```

d. void GetCapLetter(/* out */ char& oneLetter)

```
    //................................................
    // POST: User has been prompted to enter a capital letter
    //    && oneLetter is a valid capital letter
    //................................................
```

e. void ClipString(/* inout */ char someStr[])

```
    //................................................
    // PRE:  someStr is a null-terminated string
    // POST: Last char of someStr (excluding \0) has been removed
    //................................................
```

f. int MaxInVec(/* in */ const int vec[],
               /* in */   int size)

```
    //................................................
    // PRE:  size > 0  &&  Assigned(vec[0..size-1])
    // POST: FCTVAL == largest integer found in vec[0..size-1]
    //................................................
```

1.11 For each function specification in Exercise 1.10, give a correct implementation of the function.

1.12 Write function pre- and postconditions for each of the following.

    a. the PrintValue routine of Figure 1.7.

    b. the Convert routine of Figure 1.8.

    c. the DecEquiv routine of Figure 1.9.

1.13 Write a test driver for the DecEquiv routine of Figure 1.9. Also, devise a comprehensive test oracle.

1.14 Improve the GetNonBlank function of Figure 1.12 by returning a Boolean flag that reports whether end-of-file occurred before a nonblank character was found. Be sure to expand the postcondition.

PROGRAMMING PROJECTS

In each of the following projects, use top-down design and maintain a hierarchy chart as you go. During the design process, make use of both top-down and bottom-up testing with stubs and test drivers. Prepare test oracles that thoroughly exercise the units you are testing.

1.1 Write and test a C++ function named `CountChars` that has exactly two parameters. The first parameter is named `puncMarks` and the second, `letterCount`. When this function is called, it reads all of the characters from the standard input, up to end-of-file. When `CountChars` completes, `puncMarks` contains the combined count of all punctuation marks encountered, defined here as period (.), comma (,), semicolon (;), colon (:), question mark (?), and exclamation mark (!). Additionally, `letterCount` contains the combined count of upper- and lowercase alphabetic letters encountered.

1.2 Write a complete C++ program to prompt for and input several lines with exactly two characters per input line. The input will terminate when the first character of some input pair is an asterisk (*). Excluding the last pair containing the asterisk, the program must count and output:

a. the total number of times a question mark character (?) was encountered.

b. the total number of pairs whose first and second characters matched. A question mark is considered a "wild card"—it matches anything.

Below is a sample execution of the desired program with all input in color.

```
Input character pairs below:
aa
xy
?a
a?
??
ww
w?
*?
Question mark count is 5
Matching pair count is 6
```

1.3 Write a C++ program to satisfy the following problem specification.

TITLE

Word length analysis

DESCRIPTION

An editor of children's books wants a program to analyze word lengths of manuscripts. This program inputs a manuscript in text form from the standard input device and analyzes the lengths of all the words encountered. For this program, only alphabetic characters and apostrophes within a word contribute to the word length.

INPUT

Input consists of natural language text with one or more whitespace characters (including newlines) separating individual words. The end-of-file condition signals the end of input data.

Although the program reads its characters from standard input, the user is unlikely to type in an entire manuscript at execution time. Command line redirection of standard input is certain to be used:

```
$ wdlength < manuscr.txt
```

(If your system does not support command line redirection, perform file input from within your program using an ifstream. You may want to review the material on basic file I/O in Section C.1 of Appendix C.)

OUTPUT

Because input is likely to come from a file, there is no prompt to the user to start typing text.

After analyzing the input text, the program produces the following output:

```
Word Length     Frequency
     1             <f1>
     2             <f2>
     .              .
     .              .
     .              .
    20            <f20>
Average word length: <a>
```

where each <fi> denotes the number of words of length i that occurred in the input, and <a> denotes the average word length.

ERROR HANDLING

If any word is longer than 20 characters, it is treated as though it were 20 characters long.

EXAMPLE

Assume a file contains the following text:

```
Did you ever wonder what happened to Dick, Jane, and Spot? As you
might expect, they lived happily ever after.  Jane is a top account
executive for a large brokerage firm.  Dick is a senior engineer for
a major computer vendor.  Spot passed away a few years ago, but he
was happy to the end.  All of his success never altered Spot's
pleasant personality.
```

From this input file, the program produces the following output:

```
Word Length    Frequency
      1             5
      2             7
      3            15
      4            12
      5             8
      6             6
      7             4
      8             4
      9             2
     10             0
     11             1
     12             0
     13             0
     14             0
     15             0
     16             0
     17             0
     18             0
     19             0
     20             0
Average word length: 4.328125
```

1.4   Write a C++ program to satisfy the following problem specification.

TITLE

Extended precision number calculator

DESCRIPTION

A scientist needs a program to add several pairs of nonnegative floating point numbers together. The difficulty is that these numbers require more digits of precision than are available in the float (single precision), double (double precision), or long double data types. In fact, the largest values can be 30 digits long. This program must input pairs of these extended precision values and output the sum of each pair.

INPUT

The user is prompted repeatedly to input pairs of nonnegative floating point numbers. The numbers are separated by whitespace characters, including newline. The end-of-file character terminates input.

A number consists of zero or more decimal digits, optionally followed by a period, then zero or more digits. The total number of digits must not exceed 30.

OUTPUT

The prompt for each pair of input numbers is:

```
Please input two numbers (EOF to quit):
```

After each pair is input, the following output occurs:

```
Sum = <s>
```

where <s> is the exact sum of the two input numbers. A blank line precedes the next input prompt.

ERROR HANDLING

All input must conform to the specifications or undefined results occur. (In other words, the program is not required to test for invalid input.)

EXAMPLE

The following is a trace of one execution of the program. All input is in color.

```
Please input two numbers (EOF to quit):
12345.12345
11111.00001
Sum = 23456.12346

Please input two numbers (EOF to quit):
99
.33
Sum = 99.33

Please input two numbers (EOF to quit):
879.5
328.6
Sum = 1208.1

Please input two numbers (EOF to quit):
7310000000000000011.2
0.111111111111111
Sum = 7310000000000000011.311111111111111

Please input two numbers (EOF to quit):
<EOF>
```
←— <EOF> denotes the system's end-of-file keystrokes

CHAPTER 2

Modules and Information Hiding

INTRODUCTION

In Chapter 1 we focused our attention on control flow, the order in which instructions are executed. A central theme was control abstraction—the separation of the behavior of a function or control structure from its implementation details.

In Chapter 3 (and in all chapters beyond it), our focus will shift to data, the information manipulated by algorithms. The central theme will be data abstraction—the separation of the behavior of a data type from its implementation details.

This chapter, Chapter 2, serves as a bridge between Chapters 1 and 3—that is, between control abstraction and data abstraction. We introduce the technique of organizing large programs into smaller, relatively self-contained units called modules. At first, we look at modules in the context of control abstraction. Then, gradually, we bring data into the picture. By the end of the chapter you will have seen examples of packaging both data and functions into modules. These examples serve as a prelude to understanding data abstraction.

2.1 Modules

When decomposing a single, large program into smaller program units, the programmer inevitably practices **modularization**. Modularization is the concept of grouping related items together into distinct software units.

A subprogram, such as a function, is a unit of modularity. That is, it can be thought of as a collection of program instructions and local data objects, all contributing to achieve the purpose of the function.

Another unit of modularity is the **module**. A module is a generalization of a function. It is a collection of related items (perhaps several functions, types,

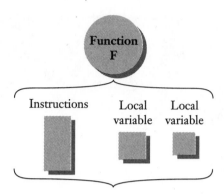

constants, and variables), packaged together into one separately compiled unit. A module is designed so that other modules or even entire programs may use all or part of its features. These other software units are called **clients** of the module.

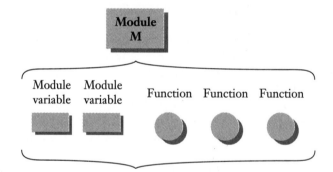

For example, a programming language's run-time library may consist of several modules. One module may provide functions for performing complicated input and output operations on files. Another module may provide mathematical routines for calculating square roots, absolute values, and trigonometric functions.

A module often specifies and implements an abstraction. The specification describes the behavior and properties of the abstraction, and the implementation contains the concrete realization in program code (Figure 2.1).

The specification is the *public* view of the module and the implementation is the *private* view. The public view serves to define the module for all clients and must therefore be visible to clients. On the other hand, only the programmer implementing the module needs access to the private view. In Figure 2.1 the public view is a description of two functions, F1 and F2, that manipulate the abstraction. The private view includes not only the implementations of F1 and F2 but also an auxiliary function F3 and, perhaps, some private data. A well-designed module **encapsulates** (groups together and hides) the function bodies and private data. Encapsulation ensures that clients do not depend on the implementation details or access the private data and code.

Specification

Implementation

```
int F1();
   // Function F1 behaves
   // as follows:
   //       .
           .
           .

int F2();
   // Function F2 behaves
   // as follows:
   //       .
           .
           .
```

```
                        .
                        .
                        .

int F1()
{
        .
        .
        .
}

int F2()
{
        .
        .
        .
}

int F3()
{
        .
        .
        .
}
```

Figure 2.1 Two views of a module

In practical terms, we can only construct modules if the programming language permits **separate compilation** of program units. Suppose that a client program, myprog.cpp, wishes to use functions supplied by three modules, mod1, mod2, and mod3. The compiler translates the modules' source code files into object code files (say, mod1.obj, mod2.obj, and mod3.obj). Although each .obj file contains machine language code, it is not in executable form. The system's *linker* program collects various object code files together to form an executable program (Figure 2.2).

Advantages of separate compilation are the following:

1. One module may be used by many clients.

2. Individual modules may be modified and recompiled without recompiling the entire program.

3. Clients of a module may be modified and recompiled without recompiling that module.

4. After a module's object file is generated, the source code file may be removed from the system to hide implementation details or proprietary information.

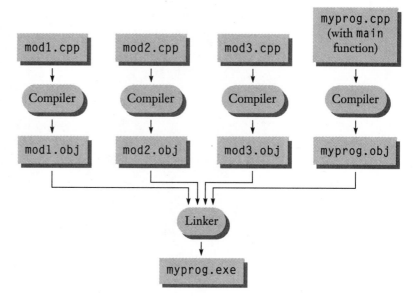

Figure 2.2 Separate
compilation and linking

This chapter explores the use of modules in structuring large programs and implementing abstractions. Throughout, it is implicit that the full benefit of modules depends on this concept of separate compilation.

2.2   Off-the-Shelf Components

A new automobile design is requested from the engineering department. A team of engineers receives the specifications for the vehicle and begins a lengthy process of planning, calculating, drawing, and testing. The efforts ultimately result in the manufacture of a new car. The engineers are able to keep the cost of this new car down by using parts such as engines and transmissions that are already in production.

A major computer vendor decides to market a new personal computer model. The engineers assigned to this project begin by reviewing computer chips and other electronic components that are already available from this company or others. In the end, the new computer incorporates existing microprocessor chips, memory chips, and other available integrated circuits. This saves considerable effort, because it is time-consuming to design and debug new circuits.

All engineers know the advantages of reusing existing components, whether the components are transmissions or computer chips. The use of such **off-the-shelf (reusable) components** is an integral part of engineering.

Effective software engineering also makes use of off-the-shelf software components in the form of modules. Examples are modules that provide collections of simple mathematical functions, statistical analysis routines, or even elaborate new data types with associated operations.

There are several advantages to using off-the-shelf modules:

- Programmers do not have to reinvent algorithms that already exist.
- The company producing the software saves money.
- Programs are generally more reliable.
- Programs are generally more efficient.

It is difficult to imagine the amount of programming time and effort wasted by different people designing the same sorting algorithm for different applications. Avoiding this duplication of effort saves money.

Assembling a product using off-the-shelf components

Using software modules also can improve the quality of programs. A company can afford to devote more effort to debugging and optimizing a module that is intended for reuse. This effort results in more efficient and reliable programs, just as using an automobile engine that has been improved and tested in other cars is likely to produce a more reliable car.

2.3 Locality

The automotive engineer who incorporates off-the-shelf engines and transmissions into the design of a new car practices abstraction. He or she depends only on the components' specifications, not their internal mechanisms. But this person is not the only one who benefits from abstraction.

Abstraction also aids the engine designer and the transmission designer. The encapsulation of implementation details results in **locality** of information and design decisions. These designers work from specification documents that dictate how the engine and transmission must interact. Beyond these stated requirements, internal design choices and mechanical implementations are localized. The engine designer can proceed without needing to know how the transmission works, and the transmission designer does not depend on the internal design of the engine.

Locality of design decisions

Designers of separate software modules enjoy this same independence. Locality of private data and algorithms within a module yields the following benefits:

1. **Division of labor**
   In a team programming environment, splitting a large program into several modules allows different team members to design and code their parts of the program simultaneously and with a minimum of interaction.

2. **Comprehensibility**
   Small program units are more understandable than an entire program taken as a whole. Furthermore, reasoning about the correctness of one module does not require knowledge of the implementation details in the others, because the modules are assumed to obey well-defined specifications.

3. **Implementation independence**
   As long as a module's specification does not change, the implementor is free to unplug one implementation and plug in another one, perhaps to correct an error or to improve efficiency. Such changes are invisible to the client, and separate compilation eliminates the need to recompile the client. (However, the client code must be relinked to the new implementation in order to use it.)

Locality is not unique to modules. A well-designed function also exhibits locality. But a function is limited in its ability to encapsulate. In many languages, functions cannot encapsulate data other than local variables, which disappear when the function returns. Some languages, including C++, cannot encapsulate functions within functions. The attraction of the module is its ability to encapsulate any number of related entities—functions, types, data objects with extended lifetimes, and so forth. Furthermore, separate compilation of modules supports implementation independence. Modifying a module's implementation has minimal effects on other components of the system.

2.4 Modules In C++

In C++, a module is represented as a pair of files: the **specification file** and the **implementation file**. The specification file describes the services the module provides. The implementation file contains the declarations and instructions that implement these services.

By convention, the names of the specification and implementation files differ only in their suffixes: `.h` and `.cpp`, respectively. For example, a module may consist of the pair of files `graphics.h` and `graphics.cpp`. The suffix `.h` suggests (correctly) that the specification file is a C++ header file containing only declarations. The suffix `.cpp` suggests that the implementation file contains executable instructions and data.

(Different systems use different file naming conventions. Using `.h` to denote C++ header files is very common, but some systems use `.hpp` or `.hxx`. Similarly, systems differ in their naming conventions for implementation files. Some use `.cpp` as we do in this text. Other examples are `.c`, `.C`, and `.cxx`.)

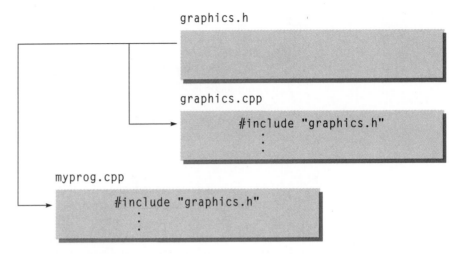

Figure 2.3 Shared access to a specification file

Specification Files

A specification file, like all C++ header files, is inserted into some other file via an #include directive. In particular, both the client and the module's implementation file must #include the specification file. Figure 2.3 pictures this shared access to the specification file. This sharing guarantees that all declarations of the features provided by the module are consistent. That is, both myprog.cpp and graphics.cpp must reference identical declarations—those located in graphics.h.

(With #include directives, recall that enclosing the file name within double quotes—#include "graphics.h"—means that the preprocessor looks for the file in the programmer's current directory. If the file name is enclosed within angle brackets—#include <iostream.h>—the preprocessor looks for the file in the standard *include directory*, a directory containing all the header files that are part of the C++ environment.)

```
//-----------------------------------------------------------------
//   SPECIFICATION FILE (powers.h)
//   This module provides exponentiation functions.
//-----------------------------------------------------------------

int PowerOfInt( /* in */ int someInt,
                /* in */ int exp       );
    // PRE:  Assigned(someInt)  &&   exp >= 0
    // POST: FCTVAL == someInt raised to the power "exp"
    //       (NOTE: Large exponents may produce overflow)

float PowerOfFloat( /* in */ float someFloat,
                    /* in */ int   exp       );
    // PRE:  Assigned(someFloat)  &&  Assigned(exp)
    //    && (exp < 0) --> someFloat != 0.0
    // POST: FCTVAL == someFloat raised to the power "exp"
    //       (NOTE: Large exponents may produce overflow)
```

Figure 2.4 Specification file for Powers

Figure 2.4 is an example of a specification file. The Powers module provides the client with functions to raise integer and floating point numbers to integer powers.

This specification file describes the items provided by the Powers module: the two functions PowerOfInt and PowerOfFloat. Specifically, this file contains function prototypes for the two functions, along with comments. The preconditions and postconditions clarify the usage of each function. As well, these assertions form a contract between the client code and the function implementation. The contract says that if the client guarantees the precondition before calling the function, then the function implementation will guarantee the postcondition.

A client program wishing to use PowerOfInt or PowerOfFloat must use the directive

```
#include "powers.h"
```

because of the C++ rule that identifiers must be declared before they are used. After the C++ preprocessor has inserted the function prototypes into the client code, the compiler can perform type checking on the client's calls to these functions.

Implementation Files

The specification file powers.h describes the behavior of the two functions but does not implement them. That is, this file contains only incomplete function declarations (function prototypes). It is the role of the implementation file to furnish the implementation details omitted from the specification file. Thus, the complete declarations (in C++, the definitions) of the functions PowerOfInt and PowerOfFloat appear in the implementation file powers.cpp. Figure 2.5 displays this file.

Figure 2.5
Implementation file for Powers

```
// -------------------------------------------------------------------
//   IMPLEMENTATION FILE (powers.cpp)
//   This module provides exponentiation functions.
// -------------------------------------------------------------------
#include "powers.h"

int PowerOfInt( /* in */ int someInt,
                /* in */ int exp     )
    //................................................................
    // PRE:  Assigned(someInt)  &&  exp >= 0
    // POST: FCTVAL == someInt raised to the power "exp"
    //       (NOTE: Large exponents may produce overflow)
    //................................................................
{
    int i;
    int partialVal = 1;
```

```
        for (i = 1; i <= exp; i++)  // INV (prior to test):
                                    //     partialVal == someInt raised
                                    //                   to power (i-1)
                                    //  && i <= exp+1
            partialVal *= someInt;
        return partialVal;
    }


    float PowerOfFloat( /* in */ float someFloat,
                        /* in */ int   exp        )
        //.............................................................
        // PRE:  Assigned(someFloat)  &&  Assigned(exp)
        //    && (exp < 0) --> someFloat != 0.0
        // POST: FCTVAL == someFloat raised to the power "exp"
        //       (NOTE: Large exponents may produce overflow)
        //.............................................................
    {
        if (exp < 0) {                     // Negative exponent means
            someFloat = 1.0/someFloat;  // repeated division
            exp = -exp;
        }
        int   i;
        float partialVal = 1.0;

        for (i = 1; i <= exp; i++) // INV (prior to test):
                                   //     partialVal == someFloat<entry>
                                   //               raised to power (i-1)
                                   //  && i <= abs(exp<entry>)+1
            partialVal *= someFloat;
        return partialVal;
    }
```

The Powers module provides two functions as abstractions. The function prototypes are in one file, the function definitions in another. It would spoil the abstraction to include the function definitions in both powers.h and powers.cpp. But even if you wanted to, the compiler would not allow it. The reason is as follows.

Near the top of Figure 2.5 is the directive #include "powers.h". If powers.h contained definitions (including bodies) of PowerOfInt and PowerOfFloat, these functions would be defined twice—once in powers.h and again in powers.cpp. The compiler would complain, because C++ allows multiple declarations of a function but only one definition.

Using the Language
· · · · · · · · · · · · · · · · · · ·

C++ Header Files

With modules, both the client code and the module's implementation file #include the same specification (.h) file. Because of the C++ rule against multiple definitions of functions and variables, specification files should not contain these items. Below are some guidelines for what may appear in a specification file (or any header file in general).

- Items that should NOT appear in C++ header (.h) files:

Function definitions (declarations with bodies)	`float Tangent( float angle)` `{ ... body ... }`
Variable definitions (declarations that allocate storage)	`float delta;`

- Items that are appropriate in C++ header (.h) files:

Constant declarations	`const char AT_SIGN = '@';`
Type declarations	`typedef long LargeInt;` `enum Error {IO, RANGE, ACCESS};`
External variable declarations	`extern float delta;`
Function prototypes (declarations without bodies)	`float Tangent( float );`
Comments	`// Some comment ...`
Preprocessor directives	`#include <math.h>` `#define DO_FOREVER while(1)`

These guidelines are not requirements of the C++ language but represent commonly accepted, safe ways to use header files.

Relationship Between Specification and Implementation Files

Implementation files contain the data and functions that implement the abstractions provided by a module. These private variables, types, and functions are invisible to the client of the module. An implementation file looks like an ordinary program file except that the main function is absent. In relation to its matching specification file, two restrictions pertain to an implementation file:

1. The implementation file must include a function definition, with body, for every function prototype in the specification file. The data types of the functions and their parameters must be identical in both files.

2. An implementation file must not redefine the meaning of any data type or the value of any constant from the specification file.

A complete C++ program often requires a combination of specification files, implementation files, and a program file (one that contains a main function). You can modify and recompile an implementation file as often as necessary, provided the specification file does not change.

If a specification file is changed in an important way (disregarding minor things like rewording of comments), then *both* the implementation file and the client of the module require modification and recompilation. For example, if we were to change the types or the parameter lists of the functions in powers.h, we would have to modify and recompile not only powers.cpp but also every client of the module.

After recompilation of any constituent files of a program, the linker must relink all the object files (even those that have not changed) to generate a new executable file (see Figure 2.2). Table 2.1 summarizes the steps that must occur after modification of any file of a multifile program. For simplicity, this table assumes a three-file program. The file myprog.cpp contains the main function, and powers.h and powers.cpp are module specification and implementation files, respectively.

Table 2.1 Recompiling and relinking

File that is modified	Recompile	Relink
myprog.cpp	myprog.cpp only	myprog.obj and powers.obj
powers.cpp	powers.cpp only	"
powers.h	powers.cpp and myprog.cpp	"

Designing with Wisdom

Specification and Implementation Files

All good programming begins with the problem specification and proceeds to the implementation. Using separate specification and implementation files for modules encourages this same pattern of specification to implementation.

Programmers should take care when designing a specification file, because it is a public specification. It is important to design this file for the benefit of the user. It must declare useful items and give precise descriptions of these items. Work on the implementation file should begin only when the specification file is in final form.

Poorly designed specification files are not only sloppy, they are also an annoyance. Whenever a specification needs changing, it forces recompilation of the implementation file as well as recompilation and relinking of every program using the module.

Compiling and Linking a Multifile Program

The mechanics of editing, compiling, linking, and executing vary from one C++ environment to another. Below we present some typical, but hypothetical, operating system commands to perform the various operations.

In these examples, we use $ as the operating system prompt for a user command. We also use cc as the name of a command that invokes either the C++ compiler or the linker or both, depending on various options given on the command line. Actual commands and file names will vary from one C++ system to another. Our discussion assumes that there are no errors in the source code.

1. `$ cc myprog.cpp`

   Action: Compile and link a single, self-contained program file (`myprog.cpp`)

   Output file: The executable file, such as `myprog.exe` or `myprog.bin` or `myprog`

   Note: The linker implicitly links in any required object files from the C++ standard library, such as I/O routines from `iostream.h`.

2. `$ cc -c graphics.cpp`

   Action: Compile only (do not link)

   Output file: The object file, such as `graphics.obj` or `graphics.o`

   Note: The object file contains machine language code but is not in executable form.

3. `$ cc myprog.cpp graphics.obj`

   Action: Compile a program file (`myprog.cpp`) and link with a previously compiled object file (`graphics.obj`)

   Output file: The executable file, say, `myprog.exe`

   Note: The linker explicitly links in the `graphics.obj` file and implicitly links in any standard library routines

4. `$ cc someprog.obj graphics.obj`

   Action: Link only (i.e., link two previously compiled object files, `someprog.obj` and `graphics.obj`)

   Output file: The executable file, say, `someprog.exe`

5. `$ cc myprog.cpp mod1.obj mod2.obj mod3.obj mod4.obj`

   Action: Compile a program file (`myprog.cpp`) and link with several object files (`mod1.obj`, ..., `mod4.obj`)

   Output file: The executable file, say, `myprog.exe`

   Note: Listing all the object files can be tedious. See items 6 and 7 for a better way.

6. `$ lib mylib.lib +mod1.obj +mod2.obj +mod3.obj +mod4.obj`

   Action: Collect several object files (`mod1.obj`, ..., `mod4.obj`) into a single **library file**

   Output file: A library file, say, `mylib.lib`

   Note: See item 7 for usage of this library file

7. `$ cc myprog.cpp mylib.lib`

   Action: Compile a program file (`myprog.cpp`) and link with object code in a library file (`mylib.lib`)

   Output file: The executable file, say, `myprog.exe`

   Note: Using a library file eliminates the need to list each object file as in item 5.

These sample commands assume that you are compiling and linking C++ programs while working at the operating system's command line. Some C++ systems provide an *integrated environment*, a program that bundles the editor, compiler, and linker into one package. Integrated environments put you back into the editor when a compile-time or link-time error occurs, pinpointing the location of the error. Some integrated environments also manage *project files*. Project files contain information about all the constituent files of a multifile program. With project files, the system automatically recompiles or relinks any files that have become out of date because of changes to other files of the program.

Whatever environment you use—the command-line environment or an integrated environment—the overall process is the same: you compile the individual source code files into object code, link the object files into an executable program, and then execute the program.

2.5   Imports and Exports

Conceptually, a module has an invisible wall around it. This wall, called the **abstraction barrier**, protects private constants, types, variables, and functions from being accessed by other modules. The barrier also prohibits the module from directly accessing data and functions outside the module. This barrier is a critical characteristic of modules.

However, a module with a totally impervious barrier would be unable to share anything with clients. Therefore, limited breaching of the barrier is desirable. A breach, known as the **module interface**, allows a module to share certain items with clients. A module and a client communicate only through the module interface.

Every module must indicate which items are available outside its barrier. These items are said to be **exported**. The kind of item exported determines how others may use it:

- If a constant is exported, a client can use its value.
- If a type is exported, a client may declare variables of that type.
- If a function is exported, a client may invoke it.

In C++, the module's specification (.h) file declares which items are exported. Every constant, type, and function declared in the specification file is available to any client. Thus, the specification file forms the public interface of the module.

A **module interface diagram** pictures the items exported from a module. Figure 2.6 shows the module interface diagram for Powers.

The outer surface represents the abstraction barrier. In the side of the barrier, the ovals represent exported functions. Figure 2.6 shows that the module interface of Powers consists of two exported functions, PowerOfInt and PowerOfFloat. These are the only two items declared in the specification file and, therefore, the only items available outside the barrier.

Figure 2.6 Powers module interface diagram

More generally, a module may export constants and types in addition to functions. In an interface diagram, we use ovals to denote exported functions and rectangles to denote exported constants and types (see Figure 2.7).

Module interface diagrams are sometimes referred to as *Booch diagrams*, named after Grady Booch, a leading figure in the field of software engineering.

To access the features exported by a module, the client uses an #include directive to include the module's specification file. The client is said to **import** the items declared in this .h file. Although every item in the specification file is implicitly imported, the client need not use every imported item. An imported identifier is global to the importing file and can be used like any other globally declared identifier.

Figure 2.8 illustrates the use of imports by a program named PowsOf2. The bottom of the figure displays the output of this program. (To review how the manipulator setw affects the format of the output, see Section C.1 of Appendix C.)

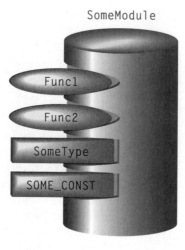

Figure 2.7 General module interface diagram

```
//-------------------------------------------------------------------
//  powsof2.cpp
//  This program outputs the powers of 2 from 1 through 10.
//  NOTE: 2^n denotes 2 raised to the nth power
//-------------------------------------------------------------------
#include <iostream.h>
#include <iomanip.h>         // For setw()
#include "powers.h"          // For PowerOfInt()

int main()
{
    int power;

    cout << "        Power    2 ^ Power \n"
         << "        -----    --------- \n";

    for (power = 1; power <= 10; power++)
                    // INV (prior to test):
                    //     2^1, 2^2, ..., 2^(power-1)
                    //        have been output
                    //     && power <= 11
        cout << setw(10) << power
             << setw(13) << PowerOfInt(2, power) << '\n';

    return 0;
}
```

Output produced by execution of the above program:

```
Power    2 ^ Power
-----    ---------
    1          2
    2          4
    3          8
    4         16
    5         32
    6         64
    7        128
    8        256
    9        512
   10       1024
```

Figure 2.8 PowsOf2 program

PowsOf2 imports items from two modules, Powers and the C++ standard library. The standard library can be thought of as one huge module with its specification file broken up into many header files: iostream.h, iomanip.h, string.h, and others. Figure 2.9 uses module interface diagrams to illustrate the relationship of PowsOf2 to these two modules.

A diagram such as Figure 2.9 pictures the complete module interfaces of the program. Each module is represented by its module interface diagram, and arrows designate the imported items.

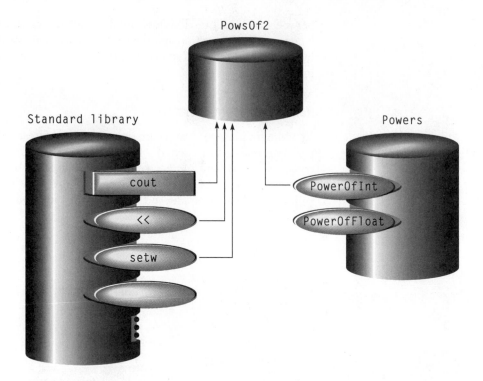

Figure 2.9 Module interfaces for `PowsOf2`

Designing with Wisdom

Thin Interfaces

As with all other program units, it is important to keep modules simple. One measure of the simplicity of a module is the "thickness" of its interface—the number of items exported to clients. Modules with thick interfaces are said to have a high **degree of coupling**. Those with thin interfaces exhibit a low degree of coupling. Experience has shown that the thinner the interface (the lower the degree of coupling), the easier it is for a programmer to understand how to use the module.

Remember, the primary goal of abstraction is to reduce complexity. The more items a module exports, the more confusing it will be to use.

2.6 Using Modules to Extend the Language

One use of modules is to extend a programming language. A programmer can add features to a programming language by specifying, implementing, and exporting the features from a module. The C++ standard library is a good example of extending the language. There are no I/O instructions built into C++, but this fact does not weaken the language because standard library modules serve the same purpose.

Some programming languages include *random number generators* as standard features. A random number generator is a function that returns an arbitrary random number with each invocation, commonly a floating point value between 0.0 and 1.0. Random number generators are not built into the C++ language. In this section and the next, we examine how to extend the language by creating a random number generator module. But first, some background information.

Random Number Generators

Random number generators are used extensively in simulations (programs that simulate real-world events). For example, a program simulating dice rolls could use a random number generator to select the result of rolling one die. Below is an algorithm for approximating the odds of various dice rolls by rolling two dice repeatedly and reporting the outcome.

```
int main()
{
    int  totalRolls;
    int  i;
    int  currentRoll;
    int  rollCount[13];     // Only elements 2..12 will be used
    int  die1;
    int  die2;

    cout << "Specify total number of dice rolls: ";
    cin >> totalRolls;

    for (i = 2; i <= 12; i++)  // INV (prior to test):
                               //      All rollCount[2..i-1]==0
                               //  && i<=13
        rollCount[i] = 0;

    for (currentRoll = 1; currentRoll <= totalRolls; currentRoll++) {
                       // INV (prior to test):
                       //      For 2<=k<=12, rollCount[k] == count
                       //          of all dice rolls totaling k out of
                       //          the first currentRoll-1 rolls
                       //  && currentRoll <= totalRolls+1
        // Simulate a roll for die1 (obtaining 1 through 6)
        // Simulate a roll for die2 (obtaining 1 through 6)
        rollCount[die1+die2]++;
    }

    cout << "\nTotal number of simulated dice rolls: "
         << totalRolls << '\n';

    for (i = 2; i <= 12; i++)   // INV (prior to test):
                                //      rollCount[2..i-1] have been
                                //      output
                                //  && i <= 13
        cout << "    Roll: " << i
             << "    Occurrences:" << rollCount[i] << '\n';

    return 0;
}
```

As you can see in the second `for` loop, this dice rolling algorithm is incomplete. The actions

```
// Simulate a roll for die1 (obtaining 1 through 6)
// Simulate a roll for die2 (obtaining 1 through 6)
```

need refinement. We need a random number generator to supply the missing code.

Suppose a `NextRand` function is available, a random number function that returns a `float` value between (but not including) 0.0 and 1.0. The following C++ expression produces a random `int` value from 1 through 6:

```
int( NextRand()*6.0 ) + 1
```

To see why this expression is correct, start with

```
0.0 < NextRand() < 1.0
```

Now multiply each of the three subexpressions by 6.0:

```
0.0 < NextRand()*6.0 < 6.0
```

Taking the integer portion of each subexpression, we get

```
0 <= int( NextRand()*6.0 ) <= 5
```

Finally, add one to each subexpression:

```
1 <= int( NextRand()*6.0 ) + 1 <= 6
```

Random number generators generally are called **pseudorandom number generators,** because the numbers they produce tend to repeat themselves after a period of time. No perfect random number generator is yet known.

A pseudorandom number generator uses some algorithm to produce a sequence of (pseudo) random numbers. The algorithm is based on a **seed**, a value that is manipulated in some way to generate each new random number. Starting with some initial seed value, the algorithm computes a random number and a new value for the seed. The value of the seed is retained between successive invocations of the generator and is used to generate the next random number and seed value.

Suppose that you execute a program and specify 5 as the initial seed value. Using this seed value, assume that the random number generator produces a sequence of numbers 0.228, 0.78634, 0.99512, and so forth. Now if you execute the program over and over again, each time specifying the same initial seed (5), the program generates exactly the same sequence of random numbers (0.228, 0.78634, 0.99512, ...). This property of random number generators facilitates testing of the program, because the results are reproducible.

Specification of a Random Number Module

To create a random number generator module, we begin with a precise description of what it does and what its public interface looks like. Figure 2.10

```
// ----------------------------------------------------------------
// SPECIFICATION FILE (rand.h)
// This module exports facilities for pseudorandom number generation.
// Machine dependency: long ints must be at least 32 bits (4 bytes).
// ----------------------------------------------------------------

void SetSeed( /* in */ long initSeed );
    // PRE:  initSeed >= 1
    // POST: Pseudorandom sequence initialized using initSeed
    // NOTE: This routine MUST be called prior to NextRand()

float NextRand();
    // PRE:  SetSeed previously invoked at least once
    // POST: FCTVAL == next pseudorandom number
    //    && 0.0 < FCTVAL < 1.0
```

Figure 2.10 The Rand specification file

shows the specification file for the module, which we have named Rand. The module exports two functions. NextRand, the function we hypothesized earlier, returns the next random number in sequence. The other function, SetSeed, initializes the seed to a value specified by the client.

As the opening comments in this specification file suggest, the module is not necessarily portable from one machine to another. It only works if the machine supports long integers of at least 32 bits. We discuss the reason for this restriction later.

A Client of the Rand Module

Before looking at how to implement the Rand module, let us revisit the dice rolling algorithm we presented earlier. The algorithm was incomplete. We needed a random number generator so we could simulate rolling a die by using the expression

```
int( NextRand()*6.0 ) + 1
```

Figure 2.11 displays the completed dice rolling algorithm, expressed as a client program named RollDice. RollDice imports the functions from Rand in order to simulate dice rolls.

Figure 2.11 The RollDice program

```
// ----------------------------------------------------------------
// rolldice.cpp
// This program investigates the odds for rolling pairs
// of dice by randomly generating such rolls.
// ----------------------------------------------------------------
#include <iostream.h>
#include <iomanip.h>      // For setw()
#include "rand.h"
```

```
int main()
{
    int   totalRolls;
    int   i;
    int   currentRoll;
    int   rollCount[13];      // Only elements 2..12 will be used
    int   die1;
    int   die2;
    long  initialSeed;

    cout << "Specify total number of dice rolls: ";
    cin >> totalRolls;
    cout << "\nSpecify an initial seed (positive integer): ";
    cin >> initialSeed;
    SetSeed( initialSeed );

    for (i = 2; i <= 12; i++)  // INV (prior to test):
                               //    All rollCount[2..i-1]==0
                               //    && i<=13
        rollCount[i] = 0;

    for (currentRoll = 1; currentRoll <= totalRolls; currentRoll++) {
                      // INV (prior to test):
                      //    For 2<=k<=12, rollCount[k] == count
                      //    of all dice rolls totaling k out of
                      //    the first currentRoll-1 rolls
                      //    && currentRoll <= totalRolls+1
        die1 = int( NextRand()*6.0 ) + 1;
        die2 = int( NextRand()*6.0 ) + 1;
        rollCount[die1+die2]++;
    }

    cout << "\nTotal number of simulated dice rolls: "
         << totalRolls << '\n';

    for (i = 2; i <= 12; i++)   // INV (prior to test):
                                //    rollCount[2..i-1] have been
                                //    output
                                //    && i <= 13
        cout << "    Roll: " << setw(2) << i
             << "    Occurrences:" << setw(5) << rollCount[i] << '\n';

    return 0;
}
```

RollDice prompts the program user to enter an initial value for the seed. Next, the program invokes SetSeed to initialize the random number generator before any invocations of NextRand.

What would happen if a client failed to invoke SetSeed before invoking NextRand? If this should happen, the precondition for NextRand would be false, and the effect of the NextRand function is undefined. Contracts in the form of pre- and postconditions rely on the cooperation of the importer and the exporter. The next chapter introduces a technique for automatic initialization of private data, a technique that eliminates dependence on the importer to do the initialization.

Having examined the public view of the Rand module as seen by its clients, we now turn to the private view: its implementation.

2.7   Information Hiding

The importer views a module from an abstract perspective. The RollDice program relies only on the public view of Rand provided by its specification file. RollDice knows nothing about how the Rand module computes random numbers or saves the seed value between successive calls to NextRand. Module interface diagrams carry this abstraction to the extreme by merely listing the exported items without elaboration. Figure 2.12 shows a module interface diagram for Rand.

Module interface diagrams treat the interior of a module as a **black box**. A programmer using the Rand module does not know what data or functions are inside the box. This black box concept is referred to as **information hiding**. Information hiding protects the user of the module from having to know all the details of its implementation. Information hiding also assures the module's implementor that the user cannot directly access any private code or data and compromise the correct functioning of the implementation.

In the preceding section, we viewed the Rand module as a black box. Now we open up the box to view the module through the implementor's eyes.

Implementation of the Rand *Module*

There are many algorithms for generating pseudorandom numbers, one of which is the *prime modulus multiplicative linear congruential generator* (PMMLCG). This intimidating name, more casually known as a **Lehmer generator**, describes a method developed by D. H. Lehmer in 1951. It is based on the formula

```
newSeed = (prevSeed * multiplier) mod max
```

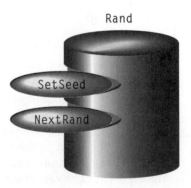

Figure 2.12 Rand module interface diagram

where mod is the modulus operator, prevSeed is the previous seed, max is a large prime number, and multiplier is an integer from 2 through max−1.

Lehmer generators produce random integers in the range 1 through max−1. The randomness of these generators depends on the values selected for multiplier and max. Computer scientists Park and Miller[1] maintain that the constants

multiplier = 16807
max = 2,147,483,647 (which is $2^{31} - 1$)

yield a statistically superior random number generator. (Park and Miller also present alternative algorithms for machines whose long integers occupy fewer than 32 bits.)

Figure 2.13 contains an implementation of the Rand module. This implementation uses a Lehmer generator with the above values for multiplier and max.

<hr>

[1] S. Park and K. Miller, "Random number generators: Good ones are hard to find," *Communications of the ACM 31*, 10 (October, 1988), pp. 1192–1201.

Figure 2.13 The Rand implementation file

```
// ------------------------------------------------------------------
//   IMPLEMENTATION FILE (rand.cpp)
//   This module exports facilities for pseudorandom number
//   generation.
//   Machine dependency: long ints must be at least 32 bits (4 bytes).
// ------------------------------------------------------------------
#include "rand.h"

static long currentSeed;              // Updated as a global variable

const long MULTIPLIER = 16807;
const long MAX =   2147483647;
const long QUOT = 127773;             // Quotient of MAX / MULTIPLIER
const long REM  = 2836;               // Remainder of MAX / MULTIPLIER

void SetSeed( /* in */ long initSeed )
    //.........................................................
    // PRE:  initSeed >= 1
    // POST: 1 <= currentSeed < MAX
    // NOTE: This routine MUST be called prior to NextRand()
    //.........................................................
{
    initSeed = initSeed % MAX;
    currentSeed = (initSeed > 0) ? initSeed : 1;
}
```

```
float NextRand()
    //................................................................
    // PRE:  1 <= currentSeed < MAX
    // POST: currentSeed ==
    //            (currentSeed<entry> * MULTIPLIER) modulo MAX
    //     && FCTVAL == currentSeed / MAX
    // NOTE: This is a prime modulus multiplicative linear
    //       congruential generator that uses the
    //       global variable currentSeed
    //................................................................
{
    long temp = MULTIPLIER*(currentSeed%QUOT) -
                REM*(currentSeed/QUOT);

    currentSeed = (temp > 0) ? temp : temp + MAX;
    return float(currentSeed) / float(MAX);
}
```

The NextRand function cannot simply calculate the next seed by multiplying currentSeed*MULTIPLIER, because the result could exceed the maximum value of a long integer. The function therefore uses the two-step algorithm shown in Figure 2.13 to avoid this multiplication. The algorithm itself is interesting but not important to this discussion.

The Rand implementation presumably hides all of the following information from the importer:

- the algorithms used by SetSeed and NextRand
- the variable currentSeed
- the values of the constants MAX, MULTIPLIER, QUOT, and REM

The global variable currentSeed is intended to be private; it is not exported by a declaration in the specification file. However, C++ does not strictly enforce information hiding in modules. The burden is on the implementor to hide currentSeed by using the declaration

```
static long currentSeed;
```

We now explain the use of the word static.

Using static *Declarations*

Suppose you have access to the source code of a module and discover the declaration of a private variable, say, modVar:

```
int modVar;
```

In your own program, you can use the declaration

```
extern int modVar;
```

to breach the module barrier and inspect and/or modify `modVar`. (Refer to Section A.11 of Appendix A or Section B.9 of Appendix B to review `extern` declarations.) Using `extern` in this manner violates the spirit of information hiding. Although such a breach is a questionable programming practice, the C++ compiler does not prevent it. Three remedies are possible:

1. Remove the implementation's source code (`.cpp`) file from the system, leaving only the compiled object (`.obj` or `.o`) file. This way an importer cannot see the source code.

2. Use a special language feature known as a *class*. We introduce this concept in the next chapter.

3. Declare a private item to be `static`.

The C++ reserved word `static` serves several purposes. One purpose is to cause the memory allocated to a local variable to persist throughout the lifetime of the entire program. (See Section A.11 of Appendix A or Section B.9 of Appendix B for discussion of this topic.)

Another purpose is to restrict the scope of an identifier to the file in which it is declared. The `Rand` implementation uses `static` for this purpose. Without the word `static`, all functions and global variables in a multifile program are visible to each other. Declaring `currentSeed` to be `static` guarantees that the compiler will prevent any access to `currentSeed` from another file.

The variable `currentSeed` is global in the sense that its declaration appears outside any function. Its storage is allocated when the client program begins execution and is deallocated only after the program completes. The functions `SetSeed` and `NextRand` both reference `currentSeed`, and its value must persist from one invocation of `NextRand` to the next. This is one case where use of global variables is beneficial.

The drawback to making any module variable an unqualified global variable is the risk that other files may access it. However, the `static` declaration eliminates this possibility.

Designing with Wisdom

How to Control Information Hiding

Any module variable declared outside a function is global to the module. Its lifetime is the lifetime of the entire program. Declaring the variable to be `static` is important, because this hides the variable from external files.

Of course, certain module identifiers *must* be exported. For example, `Rand` would be useless without export of the function `NextRand`. The best rule to follow is to *export no more than is absolutely necessary*. Granting the importer access to too much clutters the abstraction and also can be dangerous. The danger is that client code might interfere with the correct execution of the implementation code.

The `Rand` implementation in Figure 2.13 is a good illustration. The module still would work correctly if we placed the external declaration

```
extern long currentSeed;
```

in the specification file and removed the word `static` in the implementation file. But this alternative is undesirable because it allows importation of the variable. If the importer assigns new values to `currentSeed`, it may destroy the randomness of the `NextRand` generator.

When It Is Okay to Access Global Variables

Modern programming philosophy discourages the practice of inspecting, and especially modifying, global variables from within functions. Exceptions to this policy can be justified for private variables in the implementations of off-the-shelf modules. The `currentSeed` variable is such an exception.

It is still best to avoid using global variables as much as possible. If the programmer must use global variables, he or she should mark them clearly with comments.

A Study in Design

A Password Module

Consider the idea of a password, a string of characters that guards some privilege. Operating systems often use passwords to prevent unauthorized users from accessing certain resources. A user must supply the correct password to obtain access privileges.

In this section we create a module whose purpose is to store and manage a password. In designing this module, we put to use the concepts that we have discussed so far in this chapter: specification and implementation files, module interface diagrams, extending the language (to include a password as if it were a built-in feature), and enforcement of information hiding.

The Password Specification

The `Password` specification file in Figure 2.14 defines a simplified version of passwords. The module exports two functions. The first, `GetPassword`, prompts the user to establish a new password. Thereafter, the second function, `ValidUser`, verifies the password. An invocation of `ValidUser` requires the program user to type a password. If this password matches the one most recently established by `GetPassword`, then `ValidUser` returns TRUE; otherwise it returns FALSE. (The preprocessor directive `#include "bool.h"` is discussed in the Using the Language section on p. 87.)

Figure 2.14 The Password specification file

```
// -----------------------------------------------------------------
//   SPECIFICATION FILE (password.h)
//   This module provides functions to store and verify a password.
//   Note: A password is only valid during the lifetime of the
//         importing program.
// -----------------------------------------------------------------
#include "bool.h"
```

```
void GetPassword();
    // PRE:  Input is coming from the keyboard
    // POST: After a prompt, the user has supplied a password

Boolean ValidUser();
    // PRE:  GetPassword has been invoked previously
    //    && Input is coming from the keyboard
    // POST: The user has been prompted to repeat the most
    //       recently supplied password
    //    && FCTVAL == TRUE,  if the passwords are identical
    //               == FALSE, otherwise
```

The `Password` module might be a useful off-the-shelf component for an application requiring high security. Suppose that a program manipulates top secret information. When the program starts, it invokes `GetPassword` to establish the user's initial password. Thereafter, the program periodically invokes `ValidUser` to be certain the same user is still at the keyboard.

Notice in the specification file that the preconditions for both functions assume that program input is coming from the keyboard. If the user of a client program has redirected standard input to come from a file instead of the keyboard, there is no guarantee that the functions will satisfy their postconditions. The module is intended to be used with interactive I/O.

Observe also that `ValidUser`'s precondition assumes that `GetPassword` has already been invoked at least once. If this precondition is not true, the effect of executing `ValidUser` is undefined. We saw a similar situation in the `Rand` module, where the client is expected to invoke `SetSeed` before any call to `NextRand`.

The `Password` *Implementation*

Figure 2.15 displays an implementation file for `Password`. This implementation supports passwords up to ten characters long. (You may wish to review the `cin.get` and `cin.ignore` functions in Section C.1 of Appendix C.)

Figure 2.15 The Password implementation file

```
// ------------------------------------------------------------------
//   IMPLEMENTATION FILE (password.cpp)
//   This module provides functions to store and verify a password.
//   Note: A password is only valid during the lifetime of the
//         importing program.
// ------------------------------------------------------------------
#include "bool.h"
#include "password.h"
#include <iostream.h>

const  int  MAXLEN = 10;           // Max password length
static char passStr[MAXLEN+1];     // Updated as a global variable
```

```
void GetPassword()
    //.....................................................................
    // PRE:  Input is coming from the keyboard
    // POST: The user has typed a password which is, say,
    //       "len" characters long (up to '\n')
    //    && (len <= MAXLEN ) --> (passStr[0..len-1] == input string
    //                              && passStr[len] == '\0')
    //    && (len > MAXLEN )  --> (passStr[0..MAXLEN-1] == start of
    //                                                    input string
    //                              && passStr[MAXLEN] == '\0')
    //.....................................................................
{
    cout << "Establish a password of up to " << MAXLEN
         << " characters.\n"
         << "Type password then <RETURN>  --> ";

    cin.get(passStr, MAXLEN+1);
    cin.ignore(100, '\n');      // Previous "get" doesn't consume '\n'
}
Boolean ValidUser()
    //.....................................................................
    // PRE:  passStr contains a string terminated by '\0'
    //       and does not contain '\n'
    //    && Input is coming from the keyboard
    // POST: A user-input sequence of chars (thru '\n') has been read
    //    && FCTVAL == TRUE,  if the input chars up to '\n' equal
    //                        the chars of passStr up to '\0'
    //            == FALSE, otherwise
    //.....................................................................
{
    char inChar;
    int  i = 0;

    cout << "Type password then <RETURN>  --> ";
    cin.get(inChar);
    while (inChar == passStr[i]) {  // INV (prior to test):
                                    //     All passStr[0..i-1] match
                                    //     corresponding input

        i++;
        cin.get(inChar);
    }
    // ASSERT: inChar != passStr[i]

    if (inChar == '\n')
        // ASSERT: Input password may be valid
        return (passStr[i] == '\0');
    else {
        // ASSERT: Input password definitely invalid
        cin.ignore(100, '\n');              // Consume chars through '\n'
        return FALSE;
    }
}
```

The `Password` implementation is another example of information hiding. This module is practical only if it prevents the client code from gaining direct access to the password. In this implementation, `passStr` is a global array containing the password. Because `passStr` is declared as `static` in the implementation file, no other file can access it.

A Test Driver

Figure 2.16 displays a sample client of the `Password` module. The `TestPassword` program in this figure exercises the features of `Password`. Beyond being a test driver, `TestPassword` also shows the general flow of control for a client program that wants to confirm that a particular user is still at the keyboard after a period of time.

```
// ------------------------------------------------------------
//   testpass.cpp
//   Test driver for the Password module.
// ------------------------------------------------------------
#include "password.h"
#include <iostream.h>

int main()
{
    GetPassword();
    // ASSERT: User has entered an initial password

    cout << "Please verify the password:\n";
    if ( !ValidUser() ) {
        cout << "Verification failed!\n";
        return 1;
    }
    // ASSERT: User has successfully verified the password

    cout << "Busy doing important things...\n\n";

    if ( !ValidUser() ) {
        cout << "Invalid user!\n";
        return 1;
    }
    // ASSERT: The same user is still at the keyboard

    cout << "Busy some more...\n\n";

    cout << "Please specify a new password:\n";
    GetPassword();
    // ASSERT: User has established a new password

    // And so on...

    return 0;
}
```

Figure 2.16 TestPassword program

As an aside, this program is the first example that we have shown in which the main function returns a value other than zero to the operating system. The value returned by main is the program's exit status. By convention, zero indicates successful completion of the program. A nonzero value (typically 1, 2, 3, ...) means something went wrong. In the TestPassword program, if the user cannot verify the password, the main function returns immediately (hence, the program terminates) with an exit status of 1.

Module Interfaces

Figure 2.17 displays the complete set of module interfaces for the TestPassword program. These interfaces are slightly more complicated than

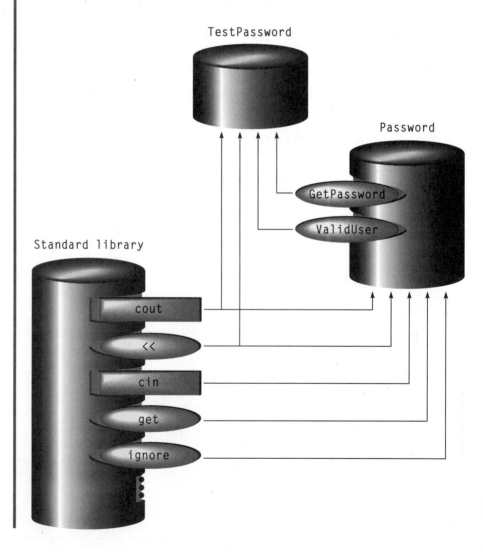

Figure 2.17 Module interfaces of TestPassword

those in earlier examples. In this program, *both* TestPassword and the Password implementation file import features from the C++ standard library.

Using the Language

Avoiding Multiple Inclusion of Header Files

The Password specification file (Figure 2.14) contains the preprocessor directive #include "bool.h". To avoid typing the lines

```
typedef int Boolean;
const int TRUE = 1;
const int FALSE = 0;
```

in every file that uses Boolean data, it is useful to put these three lines into a file named bool.h and then #include the file whenever required. But think of what happens if a program using the Password module already has included bool.h for other purposes:

```
#include "bool.h"
#include "password.h"
```

The preprocessor will insert the file bool.h, then password.h, and then bool.h again (because password.h also includes bool.h). A syntax error will result, because the identifiers Boolean, TRUE, and FALSE all are defined twice.

The widely used solution to this problem is to write bool.h this way:

```
#ifndef BOOL_H
#define BOOL_H
typedef int Boolean;
const int TRUE = 1;
const int FALSE = 0;
#endif
```

The lines beginning with "#" are directives to the preprocessor. BOOL_H (or any identifier you wish to use) is a preprocessor identifier, not a C++ program identifier. In effect, these directives say:

If the preprocessor identifier BOOL_H is not already defined, then:

1. define BOOL_H to be equal to the null string,

and

2. let the typedef and const declarations pass through to the compiler.

If a subsequent #include "bool.h" is encountered, the test #ifndef BOOL_H will fail. The typedef and const declarations will not pass through to the compiler a second time.

2.8 Standard Library Routines

C++ is a small language. Instructions for performing I/O, calculating square roots, and performing string operations are not part of the language itself. For these operations, the programmer invokes functions residing in the C++ standard library. A particular C++ environment is free to provide whatever library routines it wishes, but most routines are identical (or nearly so) from system to system.

In our discussion of C++ library routines, we use the term "module" in a figurative rather than literal sense. To speak of "the iostream module" suggests that somewhere on the system are a specification file iostream.h and its matching implementation file iostream.obj (the object code version). For convenience, however, C++ systems collect all the implementation files into one large library file named, say, cpp.lib. Therefore, only the specification (.h) files are visible by name.

The iostream module is present in all C++ environments. Appendix C describes this module in detail. Five other important modules are the math, stdlib, ctype, string, and assert modules. The specification files math.h, stdlib.h, ctype.h, string.h, and assert.h contain items such as function prototypes, constant declarations, and type declarations. The importing program should always #include the appropriate .h file to guarantee strictest type checking of calls to library functions as well as to import useful constants and types.

In this section, we describe only some of the functions available in the C++ standard library. Appendix G gives a more extensive listing.

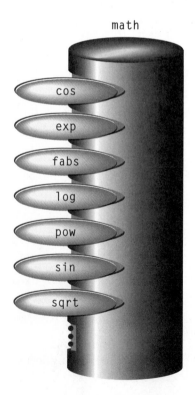

Figure 2.18 math module interface diagram

`math.h`

The `math` module exports many commonly used mathematical functions (see Figure 2.18).

Below is a list of some, but not all, of the function prototypes in `math.h`. As you survey these prototypes, keep the following in mind:

- The specifications of these functions may vary slightly from system to system.
- Error handling for incalculable results is system dependent.
- Although the formal parameters are of type `double`, the usual rules of implicit type coercion pertain. For example, the function call

  `sqrt(3)`

  is valid. The integer constant 3 is coerced to its double precision equivalent before being passed to the function.

Here are some of the prototypes in `math.h`:

```
double cos( double angle );
    // PRE:  Assigned(angle), where angle is measured in radians
    // POST: FCTVAL == trigonometric cosine of angle

double exp( double x );
    // PRE:  Assigned(x)
    // POST: FCTVAL == e (2.718...) raised to the power x

double fabs( double x );
    // PRE:  Assigned(x)
    // POST: FCTVAL == absolute value of x

double log( double x );
    // PRE:  x > 0.0
    // POST: FCTVAL == natural logarithm (base e) of x

double pow( double x, double y );
    // PRE:  (x == 0.0 --> y > 0.0)
    //    && (x <= 0.0 --> y is a whole number)
    // POST: FCTVAL == x raised to the power y

double sin( double angle );
    // PRE:  Assigned(angle), where angle is measured in radians
    // POST: FCTVAL == trigonometric sine of angle

double sqrt( double x );
    // PRE:  x >= 0.0
    // POST: FCTVAL == square root of x
```

`stdlib.h`

The `stdlib` module (Figure 2.19) provides an assortment of routines, most of which relate to material we have not yet discussed in this text.

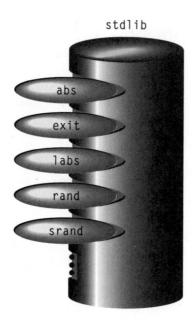

stdlib

Figure 2.19 `stdlib`
module interface
diagram

Below are the prototypes of five functions you may find useful at this point.
(The specifications of these functions may vary slightly from system to
system.)

```
int abs( int i );
    // PRE:  Assigned(i)
    // POST: FCTVAL == absolute value of i

void exit( int exitStatus );
    // PRE:  Assigned(exitStatus)
    // POST: Program has terminated immediately with all files
    //       properly closed
    // NOTE: By convention, exitStatus is 0 to signal normal program
    //       completion and is nonzero to signal some error.

long labs( long i );
    // PRE:  Assigned(i)
    // POST: FCTVAL == absolute value of i

int rand();
    // PRE:  IF srand(seed) - see below - has not previously been
    //           invoked
    //       THEN srand(1) is implicitly invoked
    // POST: FCTVAL == the next pseudorandom integer

void srand( unsigned seed );
    // PRE:  Assigned(seed)
    // POST: Random number generator rand() has been seeded with
    //       seed.
```

ctype.h

The ctype module supplies helpful routines for testing whether a given character is a letter or a digit or a whitespace character, and so on. Figure 2.20 shows the module interface diagram for ctype.

For the function prototypes below, take note of the following:

- The precondition for each function is

  ```
  // PRE: Assigned(ch)
  ```

- The postconditions are stated in terms of the ASCII character set.
- Although the formal parameters are declared to be of type int, the most common usage is to pass char values.

```
int isalpha( int ch );
    // POST: FCTVAL is nonzero, if ch is a letter: 'A'..'Z', 'a'..'z'
    //                == 0, otherwise
```

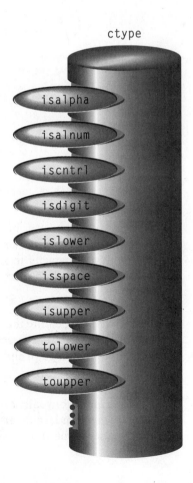

Figure 2.20 ctype module interface diagram

```
int isalnum( int ch );
    // POST: FCTVAL is nonzero, if ch is a letter or digit:
    //                            'A'..'Z', 'a'..'z', '0'..'9'
    //                == 0, otherwise

int iscntrl( int ch );
    // POST: FCTVAL is nonzero, if ch is a control char:
    //                            integer value 127 or 0..31
    //                == 0, otherwise

int isdigit( int ch );
    // POST: FCTVAL is nonzero, if ch is a digit: '0'..'9'
    //                == 0, otherwise

int islower( int ch );
    // POST: FCTVAL is nonzero, if ch is a lowercase letter: 'a'..'z'
    //                == 0, otherwise

int isspace( int ch );
    // POST: FCTVAL is nonzero, if ch is a whitespace char: blank,
    //                            tab, carriage return, newline,
    //                            form feed
    //                == 0, otherwise

int isupper( int ch );
    // POST: FCTVAL is nonzero, if ch is an uppercase letter:
    //                            'A'..'Z'
    //                == 0, otherwise

int tolower( int ch );
    // POST: FCTVAL == lowercase equivalent of ch, if ch is uppercase
    //                == ch, otherwise

int toupper( int ch );
    // POST: FCTVAL == uppercase equivalent of ch, if ch is lowercase
    //                == ch, otherwise
```

The is... functions are, in effect, Boolean functions returning an integer value that is nonzero (true) or 0 (false). These functions are efficient because they look up the character in an internal table instead of performing sequential tests. They also result in more portable programs. For instance, the test

```
if ((ch >= 'a' && ch <= 'z') || (ch >= 'A' && ch <= 'Z'))
```

will correctly include only the alphabetic characters in the ASCII character set but *not* in the EBCDIC character set. In the latter, some punctuation characters lie within the range of alphabetic characters. The test

```
if (isalpha(ch))
```

is safer (and more convenient to use).

The tolower and toupper functions are especially handy for processing interactive user input. For example, it is easier to express the test

```
if (inputChar == 'Y' || inputChar == 'y')
```

as

```
if (toupper(inputChar) == 'Y')
```

string.h

The C++ `string` module is almost indispensable for serious programming. It exports a massive collection of string-handling routines, only a few of which we discuss in this section (see Figure 2.21).

One of these routines, `strlen`, calculates the length of a character string:

```
unsigned  strlen( const char* str );
    // PRE:  str is a null-terminated string
    // POST: FCTVAL == length of str (not counting the null
    //                     character '\0')
```

The notation in this function prototype bears explanation. Recall that arrays always are passed by reference in C++. In particular, parameter passage amounts to passing the array's base address to the function. (The base address is the memory address of the first element of the array.) Thus, the declaration

```
void SomeFunc( char str[] );
```

states that `SomeFunc` receives the base address of a character array. You also could write this declaration as

```
void SomeFunc( char* str );
```

The notation `char*` means "pointer to an object of type `char`." As we will discuss at length in Chapter 8, a pointer is a variable that contains the memory

Figure 2.21 `string` module interface diagram

address, not the value, of a data object. This declaration, then, says that SomeFunc receives the memory address of a char object (specifically, the address of the first character in the string array).

In the declaration of strlen above, the precondition should more precisely state that str points to a null-terminated string, not that str *is* a null-terminated string. But to simplify the wording of the pre- and postconditions below, we take the liberty of using str to refer to the entire string that is pointed to.

Additionally, as you examine these prototypes, notice that some of the array declarations include the word const. Remember that this assures the caller that the function does not modify that array.

```
unsigned  strlen( const char* str );
    // PRE:   str is a null-terminated string
    // POST:  FCTVAL == length of str (not counting '\0')

int  strcmp( const char* str1, const char* str2 );
    // PRE:   str1 and str2 are null-terminated strings
    // POST:  FCTVAL  < 0, if str1 < str2 lexicographically
    //                == 0, if str1 == str2          "
    //                 > 0, if str1 > str2           "

char*  strcpy( char* toStr, const char* fromStr );
    // PRE:   fromStr is a null-terminated string
    //     && toStr must be large enough to hold the result
    // POST:  fromStr, including '\0', has been copied to toStr,
    //          overwriting what was there
    //     && FCTVAL == base address of toStr

char*  strcat( char* toStr, const char* fromStr );
    // PRE:   toStr and fromStr are null-terminated strings
    //     && toStr must be large enough to hold the result
    // POST:  fromStr, including '\0', is concatenated (joined)
    //          to the end of toStr
    //     && FCTVAL == base address of toStr
```

The functions strcpy and strcat achieve their results by side effect: modification of the first actual parameter. Each function also returns a function value: the base address of the destination string. In practice, the function return value usually is ignored:

```
if (i < 0)
    strcpy(msgString, "negative");
else
    strcpy(msgString, "nonnegative");
```

However, you can use the return value for **function call cascading** (or, in mathematics, **functional composition**)—the use of a function call within the parameter list of another function call. For example, you can first concatenate one string to another and then determine the new string length by doing this:

```
newLength = strlen(strcat(someStr, "now or never"));
```

Because strcat returns, as the function value, the base address of someStr, this base address becomes the parameter to strlen. Clearly, you could achieve the same effect with the sequence

```
strcat(someStr, "now or never");
newLength = strlen(someStr);
```

Many programmers avoid the practice of cascading function calls if the inner function produces side effects. The resulting code can be difficult to understand and prone to logic errors through oversights.

assert.h

The assert module exports a single item: a function named assert. (Technically, assert is not a true function but a preprocessor macro. This distinction is not important to us right now, so we'll refer to it as a function.) The assert function takes a Boolean expression as a parameter and halts the program if the expression is false. Here is its specification:

```
void assert( int boolExpr );
    // PRE:  Assigned(boolExpr)
    // POST: (boolExpr is nonzero) --> Execution just continues
    //    && (boolExpr == 0) --> Execution has terminated immediately
    //                           with a message stating the Boolean
    //                           expression, file name, and line
    //                           number in the source code
    // NOTE: If the directive #define NDEBUG is placed before the
    //       directive #include <assert.h>, all assert statements are
    //       ignored
```

So far, we have used assertions in the form of comments within our programs:

```
// ASSERT: studentCount > 0
```

All comments, of course, are ignored by the compiler. They are not executable statements; they are for humans to examine.

On the other hand, the assert function gives us the capability of writing executable assertions. Consider the following example:

```
#include <assert.h>
    ⋮
cin >> studentCount;
assert(studentCount > 0);
average = sumOfScores / studentCount;
```

The parameter to assert is a C++ logical (Boolean) expression. If its value is nonzero (true), execution continues on. If its value is zero (false), execution of the program aborts with a message similar to the following:

```
Assertion failed: studentCount > 0, file myprog.cpp, line 48
```

(This message is potentially confusing. The phrase studentCount > 0 just restates the text of the assertion that failed. The phrase is not telling you that studentCount *is* greater than zero. In fact, it is just the opposite. The assertion failed because studentCount was less than or equal to zero.)

Executable assertions have a profound advantage over assertions expressed as comments: the effect of a false assertion is highly visible (the program terminates with an error message). The assert function is therefore valuable in software testing. A program under development might be filled with calls to the assert function to help identify where errors are occurring. If an assertion is false, the error message gives the precise line number of the failed assertion.

Additionally, as we have noted in the function specification for assert, there is a way to remove the assertions without really removing them. If you place the preprocessor directive #define NDEBUG prior to including the header file assert.h:

```
#define NDEBUG
#include <assert.h>
    ⋮
```

then all calls to assert are ignored. (NDEBUG means "No debug.") During program development, programmers often like to "turn off" debugging statements yet leave them physically present in the source code in case they should need the statements later. Inserting the line #define NDEBUG turns off assertion checking without the need to remove the assertions.

A limitation of the assert function is that the assertion must be expressed as a C++ logical expression. We can make the comment

```
// ASSERT: m < 0  &&  n == 3
```

executable with the statement

```
assert(m < 0 && n == 3);
```

But there is no easy way to use the assert function and a C++ Boolean expression in place of the following comment:

```
// ASSERT: The array elements are in ascending order.
```

We will return to the assert function—both its advantages and its limitations—in later chapters.

Other Library Routines

All C++ systems contain standard library modules in addition to those we have introduced. Appendix G gives more examples but is not a comprehensive inventory. The serious C++ programmer should consult the language manuals for his or her system to survey the modules that are available "off the shelf."

Preconditions and Error Checking

Suppose that a module exports a function with the following specification:

```
float Inverse( /* in */ int n );
    // PRE:  n != 0
    // POST: FCTVAL == 1/n  (floating point)
```

A client might invoke this function in the following manner:

```
cout << Inverse(alpha) + Inverse(beta);
```

The user and the implementor both know that division by zero is possible when inverting a number. The question is, who is responsible for checking for division by zero?

The `Inverse` specification, through its precondition

```
// PRE:  n != 0
```

clearly places the responsibility on the user, not the implementor. A function precondition and postcondition form a contract between user and implementor, expressible as a logical implication:

> IF the precondition is true at function entry
> THEN the postcondition is true at function exit

According to mathematical logic, if the precondition is not true, then the postcondition may or may not be true. That is, the effect of the function is indeterminate. For the `Inverse` function, the implementor assumes that the precondition is true and does not need to test for zero:

```
float Inverse( /* in */ int n );
{
    return 1.0 / float(n);
}
```

An alternative approach is to shift the burden of error checking onto the implementor. With the `Inverse` function we could delete the precondition, let the client pass any value as a parameter, and require the function body to check for zero. A function that anticipates and traps all errors gracefully is called **robust**. Unfortunately, writing robust off-the-shelf software is a problem, because the implementor cannot always make assumptions about the client's environment. For example, the implementor of `Inverse` must decide what action to take if the incoming parameter is zero. Possible choices are as follows:

1. Just return without doing anything at all.
2. Print an error message and return.
3. Print an error message and halt the entire program.
4. Include an extra Boolean parameter that reports the error.
5. Use a global Boolean variable to report the error.

Choice 1 is clearly irresponsible. Choice 2 is often undesirable for two reasons. First, a printed error message is helpful to a human running the program, but is useless to the program itself. The program will continue executing, ignorant of the error. Second, if the output stream happens to be redirected to a file, days might elapse before someone spots the error message.

Choice 3 is usually preferable to 2, but aborting an entire program is a major decision. This decision should rest with the client, not a subservient function.

Choices 4 and 5 are wisest in most circumstances. The client, upon checking an error flag returned by the function, can decide what to do about an error. The disadvantage of choice 4 is that a value-returning function, such as Inverse, no longer behaves like a pure function. That is, the function now returns two values—the computed result and an error flag—and cannot properly be invoked several times within a single expression.

Choice 5 is common in many C++ library routines. These routines report errors by assigning some value to a global variable named errno. After invoking such a function, the client can test errno to see if anything nasty happened. The drawback is that global variables are incompatible with the principle of highly visible module interfaces. A global variable breaches the abstraction barrier in an invisible way; the variable is just "out there, somewhere."

In summary, there are two major philosophies about error checking. The first, via explicit preconditions, obligates the client to check for invalid parameters before invoking a function. The other requires the function implementation to be robust and report any errors upon return. Both philosophies have merit, but we employ the former in this book. Requiring the client to avert errors yields a simpler function implementation and a thinner module interface because there is no need to communicate error flags.

SUMMARY

Modules are separately compiled program units that specify and implement abstractions. As an abstraction tool, a module is more powerful than a function because it can encapsulate any collection of data objects and functions that implement the abstraction.

Conceptually, a module is a black box enclosed by an abstraction barrier. This barrier hides all implementation details. The client of the module depends only on the module's specification and accesses its services only through the public interface. The implementor of the module has the freedom to choose and substitute any implementation as long as it satisfies the specification and is acceptably efficient.

In C++, a module is represented as a pair of files: the specification file and the implementation file. The specification file contains declarations and assertions describing the items exported by the module. To import these items, the client #includes the specification file. The implementation file contains bodies for the functions and, possibly, private data. Declaring identifiers as static within the implementation file enforces information hiding, because the compiler prohibits access to these identifiers from other files.

Through modules, one can invent and use off-the-shelf components. Off-the-shelf software allows the creation of entire programming environments. These environments consist not only of the standard features of a programming language, but all available modules as well.

Programming environments differ from company to company and programmer to programmer. No two companies providing C++ are likely to have exactly the same environment. The act of programming can be greatly simplified by the wise inclusion of off-the-shelf components appropriate to the environment.

KEY TERMS

abstraction barrier   (p. 70)
black box   (p. 78)
client   (p. 58)
degree of coupling   (p. 73)
encapsulate   (p. 58)
export   (p. 70)
function call cascading   (p. 94)
functional composition   (p. 94)
implementation file   (p. 63)
import   (p. 71)
information hiding   (p. 78)
Lehmer generator   (p. 78)

library file   (p. 69)
locality   (p. 62)
modularization   (p. 57)
module   (p. 57)
module interface   (p. 70)
module interface diagram   (p. 70)
off-the-shelf component   (p. 60)
pseudorandom number generator   (p. 75)
robust function   (p. 97)
seed   (p. 75)
separate compilation   (p. 59)
specification file   (p. 63)

EXERCISES

2.1 Refer to Figure 2.2, an illustration of the process of compiling and linking a multifile program.

   a. If only the file myprog.cpp is modified, which files must be recompiled?

   b. If only the file myprog.cpp is modified, which files must be relinked?

   c. If only the files mod2.cpp and mod3.cpp are modified, which files must be recompiled?

   d. If only the files mod2.cpp and mod3.cpp are modified, which files must be relinked?

2.2 Which of the following do you think would make good off-the-shelf software components?

   a. A module that supplies routines for drawing various objects on a computer's video screen

   b. A module that generates weather forecasts for the town of Lander, Wyoming

   c. A module that records and analyzes the growth rates of baby penguins

   d. A module that controls the hardware circuits of ten different kinds of floppy disk drive

2.3 Consider the following declarations associated with a particular module:

```
 i. typedef int Vector[100];
ii. void Func1( int n )
    {
        Body
```

```
        ⋮
        }
iii. void Func2( float x )
     {
          Body
        ⋮
        }
iv. const int MAX = 350;
 v. void Func1( int );
vi. void Func2( float );
vii. static int temperature;
```

Suppose that the module exports everything except the variable `temperature`.

a. Which declarations should appear in the module's specification (`.h`) file?

b. Which declarations should appear in the module's implementation (`.cpp`) file?

2.4 Give an expression using a call to the `NextRand` function (Figure 2.10) that yields each of the following:

a. a `float` value greater than 5.0 and less than 10.0

b. an `int` value greater than or equal to 2 and less than or equal to 100

c. a random direction using the following type:

```
enum Direction {north, south, east, west};
```

(Recall that the first enumerator has the value 0, the second has the value 1, and so forth.)

2.5 Diagram the complete set of module interfaces for the `RollDice` program (Figure 2.11).

2.6 Below is a module named `SimpStat` that calculates simple statistics on collections of integer values. Use this module to complete parts (a) through (c).

```
// ------------------------------------------------------------------
// SPECIFICATION FILE (simpstat.h)
// This module maintains simple statistics on a collection
// of up to 100 integers.
// ------------------------------------------------------------------

// NOTE: Below, "data count" means the number of integers currently
//       in the collection

void EnterData( /* in */ int someInt );
    // PRE:   Assigned(someInt) &&  Data count < 100
    // POST:  someInt has been entered as a new data value
    //    &&  Data count == data count<entry> + 1

int Min();
    // PRE:  Data count > 0
    // POST: FCTVAL == smallest integer entered thus far
```

```
int Max();
    // PRE:  Data count > 0
    // POST: FCTVAL == largest integer entered thus far

float Mean();
    // PRE:  Data count > 0
    // POST: FCTVAL == average of all integers entered thus far


// ------------------------------------------------------------------
//   IMPLEMENTATION FILE (simpstat.cpp)
//   This module maintains simple statistics on a collection
//   of up to 100 integers.
// ------------------------------------------------------------------
#include "bool.h"
#include "simpstat.h"

static int      data[100];              // Updated as global variables
static int      count = 0;
static int      minVal;
static int      maxVal;
static float    meanVal;
static Boolean  statsValid = FALSE;

static void DoStats();

void EnterData( /* in */ int someInt )
    //.........................................................
    // PRE:  Assigned(someInt)  &&  count < 100
    // POST: data[count<entry>] == someInt
    //    && count == count<entry>+1
    //    && NOT statsValid
    //.........................................................
{
    // Code is missing here
}


static void DoStats()
    //.........................................................
    // PRE:  count > 0
    // POST: Global variables minVal, maxVal, and meanVal are the
    //       smallest, largest, and mean values in data[0..count-1]
    //    && statsValid
    //.........................................................
{
    int i;
    int sum = data[0];
```

```
        minVal = data[0];
        maxVal = data[0];
        for (i = 1; i < count; i++) {
                // INV (prior to test):
                //     minVal, maxVal == min and max
                //         values in data[0..i-1]
                //   && sum == summation of data[0..i-1]
                //   && i <= count
            if (data[i] < minVal)
                minVal = data[i];
            else if (data[i] > maxVal)
                maxVal = data[i];
            sum += data[i];
        }
        meanVal = float(sum) / float(count);
        statsValid = TRUE;
}

int Min()
    //..........................................................
    // PRE:  count > 0
    // POST: statsValid  &&  FCTVAL == minVal
    //..........................................................
{
    if ( !statsValid )
        DoStats();
    return minVal;
}

int Max()
    //..........................................................
    // PRE:  count > 0
    // POST: statsValid  &&  FCTVAL == maxVal
    //..........................................................
{

    // Code is missing here
}

float Mean()
    //..........................................................
    // PRE:  count > 0
    // POST: statsValid  &&  FCTVAL == meanVal
    //..........................................................
{
    // Code is missing here
}
```

a. List all items that SimpStat exports.

b. Provide the missing code for the EnterData, Max, and Mean functions.

c. Write a test driver for SimpStat.

2.7 Below are the abbreviated outlines of three modules: Triang, Rectang, and Polygon. Use these modules to complete parts (a) through (f).

```
// -----------------------------------------------------------------
//  SPECIFICATION FILE (triang.h)
// -----------------------------------------------------------------
#include "bool.h"

float TriangArea( /* in */ float side1,
                  /* in */ float side2,
                  /* in */ float side3 );

float TriangPerimeter( /* in */ float side1,
                       /* in */ float side2,
                       /* in */ float side3 );

Boolean IsEquilateral( /* in */ float side1,
                       /* in */ float side2,
                       /* in */ float side3 );


// -----------------------------------------------------------------
//  IMPLEMENTATION FILE (triang.cpp)
// -----------------------------------------------------------------
#include "triang.h"
#include <iostream.h>    // For cout and <<
#include <math.h>        // For sqrt()
    // Remaining code
      .
      .
      .
// -----------------------------------------------------------------
//  SPECIFICATION FILE (rectang.h)
// -----------------------------------------------------------------

float RectangArea( /* in */ float length,
                   /* in */ float width  );

float RectangPerimeter( /* in */ float length,
                        /* in */ float width  );


// -----------------------------------------------------------------
//  IMPLEMENTATION FILE (rectang.cpp)
// -----------------------------------------------------------------
#include "rectang.h"
#include <iostream.h>    // For cout and <<
    // Remaining code
      .
      .
      .
```

```
// --------------------------------------------------------------
// SPECIFICATION FILE (polygon.h)
// --------------------------------------------------------------

enum PolyType {rectangle, triangle, combined};
typedef int Dimensions[4];

float PolyArea( /* in */ PolyType   whichPoly,
                /* in */ Dimensions dim        );

float PolyPerimeter( /* in */ PolyType   whichPoly,
                     /* in */ Dimensions dim        );


// --------------------------------------------------------------
// IMPLEMENTATION FILE (polygon.cpp)
// --------------------------------------------------------------
#include "polygon.h"
#include "triang.h"    // For TriangArea() and TriangPerimeter()
#include "rectang.h"   // For RectangArea() and RectangPerimeter()
#include <iostream.h>  // For cout, cin, <<, and >>
     // Remaining code
           ⋮
```

a. Diagram the complete set of module interfaces for these declarations.

b. List all items that Polygon exports.

c. Specify one possible order in which the implementation files could be compiled in order to link all modules.

d. Suppose the implementation file for Rectang is recompiled. What other implementation files must be recompiled and/or relinked to incorporate the changes?

e. Suppose the specification file for Rectang is modified in a major way. What other implementation files must be recompiled and/or relinked to incorporate the changes?

f. Suppose the implementation of sqrt() in the math module is modified and recompiled. What other implementation files must be recompiled and/or relinked to incorporate the changes?

2.8 Using the is... functions from the standard library (header file ctype.h), rewrite each of the following code segments. (Assume that you are using the ASCII character set.)

a. ```
if (inputChar >= '0' && inputChar <= '9')
    DoSomething();
```

b. ```
if (inputChar >= 'a' && inputChar <= 'z' ||
    inputChar >= 'A' && inputChar <= 'Z'   )
    DoSomething();
```

c. ```
if (inputChar >= 'a' && inputChar <= 'z' ||
    inputChar >= 'A' && inputChar <= 'Z' ||
```
```

```
                inputChar >= '0' && inputChar <= '9'   )
                DoSomething();
```

d. `if (inputChar >= 'a' && inputChar <= 'z')`
   `inputChar = inputChar - 32;`

e. `if (inputChar >= 'A' && inputChar <= 'Z')`
   `inputChar = inputChar + 32;`

2.9 Assume that a program has the following declarations:

```
char str1[50];
char str2[50];
char str3[200];
```

Using the standard library's string-handling routines (header file `string.h`), give C++ statements to accomplish the following:

a. Store the string "Hi, there" into array `str1`.

b. Output a message that tells the length of the string currently in `str2`.

c. Copy the string that is in `str2` into `str1`.

d. Concatenate the string in `str2` to the end of the string in `str3`.

e. If the strings in `str1` and `str2` are equal, output the message "Same"; otherwise, output the message "Different".

2.10 Referring to the declarations of `str1`, `str2`, and `str3` in Exercise 2.9, what danger lies in each of the following function calls?

a. `strcpy(str1, str3);`

b. `strcat(str1, str2);`

2.11 Some C++ libraries provide a string comparison routine `stricmp`. It is identical to `strcmp` except it is *case insensitive* (upper- and lowercase letters are considered equal). Relying as much as possible on off-the-shelf routines such as `toupper`, `tolower`, and `strcmp`, write a `stricmp` body that satisfies the following specification:

```
int stricmp( const char* str1, const char* str2 );
    // PRE:  str1 and str2 are null-terminated strings
    // POST: Case-insensitive comparison of str1 and str2 yields:
    //        FCTVAL  < 0, if str1 < str2 lexicographically
    //                == 0, if str1 == str2          "
    //                 > 0, if str1 > str2           "
```

2.12 Simplify the `Password` implementation (Figure 2.15) by using off-the-shelf `string` module routines. In particular, incorporate both of the following:

- In `GetPassword`, use the extraction operator `>>` instead of `cin.get` to input a string of arbitrary length (up to, say, 80 characters). If the string length returned by `strlen` is greater than 10, truncate the length to 10 and output the message `*** Only first 10 chars retained ***`. Then copy the input string to the password string.

- In `ValidUser`, input a string of arbitrary length and use `strcmp` to compare it to the password string.

PROGRAMMING PROJECTS

2.1 Keeping in mind the desirable properties of the Rand module (Figure 2.10), write a suitable test driver. Plan a comprehensive test oracle.

2.2 Modify the Password module (Figures 2.14 and 2.15) as follows. Export a third function, named SetPassword, that creates a random password of length 10 (upper- and lowercase letters only). Generate these ten letters by using the services of the Rand module (Figure 2.10). SetPassword might either choose an arbitrary seed for the random number generator or prompt the user to supply one. After creating the random password, SetPassword displays it to the user for future verification.

Write a test driver in the style of TestPassword (Figure 2.16) to initially set a random password, verify it later, and then allow the user to specify a new password.

2.3 Modify the SimpStat module in Exercise 2.6 to export a Median() function. One way to compute the median is to sort the integers, then return the middle element. (For an even number of values, the median is the average of the two middle elements.) That is, the median of the values 20, 25, 40, 50, and 60 is 40. The median of the values 24, 26, 27, and 30 is 26.5.

For sorting, you must make some design choices. One choice is to sort the array with each invocation of DoStats. Or you could eliminate sorting altogether by having EnterData insert each new integer into the appropriate spot. Each approach has its pros and cons.

After testing your new SimpStat module, use it along with the Rand module (Figure 2.10) to solve the following problem.

TITLE

Statistical analysis of random integers

DESCRIPTION

This program generates 20 random integers in the range 0 through 1000, inclusive. It then outputs the minimum, maximum, median, and mean values of the 20 integers.

INPUT

The only input is a user-supplied positive integer to seed the random number generator.

OUTPUT

The following is the prompt for the seed input:

```
Please supply a positive integer to seed random numbers:
```

The program then outputs a blank line, a heading, and the 20 random integers in two columns as follows:

```
Random integers:
        <int>       <int>
        <int>       <int>
```

```
           .        .
           .        .
           .        .
        <int>    <int>
```

where each <int> represents a random integer.

Finally, the program outputs a blank line and the desired statistics as follows:

```
Max value = <max>
Min value = <min>
Median = <median>
Mean = <mean>
```

ERROR HANDLING

If the user enters a nonpositive seed, the program repeatedly prompts until a positive value is input.

EXAMPLE

Below is a sample execution with input in color.

```
Please supply a positive integer to seed random numbers: 0
Please supply a positive integer to seed random numbers: -4
Please supply a positive integer to seed random numbers: 7

Random integers:
            0        921
          289        210
          730        533
          329        752
          755        543
          685        636
          817        242
          374        708
          698         53
          684        468

Max value = 921
Min value = 0
Median = 589.5
Mean = 521.349976
```

2.4 Write an implementation file for the specification shown below. Then write a test driver and a comprehensive test oracle to demonstrate the correctness of your module. (In the postcondition for ReadWithCommas, recall that the right arrow "-->" means "implies".)

```
//------------------------------------------------------------------
// SPECIFICATION FILE (commaio.h)
// This module provides input and output functions for
// nonnegative integers, using the style of including a comma
// every three digits from the right.
//------------------------------------------------------------------
#include "bool.h"

void ReadWithCommas( /* out */ int&     someInt,
                     /* out */ Boolean& overflow );
    // PRE:  Apart from leading blanks, next item in the standard
    //       input stream is a string of decimal digits possibly
    //       containing commas.
    // POST: All commas in the string have been ignored
    //       && overflow == TRUE, if integer equivalent of the digit
    //                            string > maximum integer for this
    //                                     machine
    //                    == FALSE, otherwise
    //       && (NOT overflow) --> someInt contains this integer
    //                             equivalent

void WriteWithCommas( /* in */ int someInt );
    // PRE:  someInt >= 0
    // POST: Value of someInt has been output as a string
    //       with a comma every 3 digits from the right.
    //       (For example, output of 7269 is "7,269" and
    //        output of 33147 is "33,147")
```

2.5 Modify the Password module (Figures 2.14 and 2.15) to accommodate up to 100 different passwords. Each invocation of GetPassword and ValidUser must supply, as a parameter, an integer user number from 1 through 100.

Use this modified Password module to implement the following module, MultPass. In other words, the implementation file of MultPass will treat Password as an off-the-shelf module. It will use #include "password.h" and then import features from the Password module in order to provide its own services.

Write a test driver and comprehensive test oracle to demonstrate the correctness of your modules.

```
//------------------------------------------------------------------
// SPECIFICATION FILE (multpass.h)
// This module provides facilities for maintaining and verifying
// user passwords for up to 100 users.
//------------------------------------------------------------------
#include "bool.h"

int UserCount();
    // POST: FCTVAL == total number of users added via AddUser
```

```
void AddUser( /* out */ int& userID );
    // PRE:  UserCount() < 100
    // POST: userID == some value (1..100) not previously
    //                   returned by AddUser

void ChangePassword( /* in */ int userID );
    // PRE:  userID must represent a user entered via AddUser
    // POST: After a prompt, current user has supplied a password.
    //       This password is assigned to the user with number
    //       userID.

Boolean ValidPassword( /* in */ int userID );
    // PRE:  userID must represent a user entered via AddUser
    // POST: After a prompt, current user has supplied a password
    //    && FCTVAL == TRUE, if the input password matches the
    //                       password entered by the most recent
    //                       invocation of ChangePassword
    //                       for userID
    //            == FALSE, otherwise
```

CHAPTER 3

Data Abstraction Through Classes

INTRODUCTION

We began Chapter 1 by stating that every algorithm depends on two things: data and control flow. We said that data refers to the information manipulated by the algorithm and that control flow refers to the order in which instructions are executed. Within the discussion of control flow we focused on functional abstraction—the separation of a function's specification (what it does) from its implementation (how it does it).

Chapter 2 was largely about control flow and program structure, but we expanded the focus to include data. We explored the use of modules to encapsulate both data and functions in order to support information hiding and implementation independence.

Now, and for the remainder of this book, we focus on data, with control issues playing a supporting role. The central theme is **data abstraction**—the separation of the properties of a data type (its values and operations) from the implementation of that data type. Data abstraction lets us create new data types not otherwise available in a programming language. As with functional abstraction, data abstraction employs a specification and an implementation. The specification describes the properties of the data values as well as the behavior of each of the operations on those values. The user of the data abstraction needs to understand only the specification, not the implementation. Concealing the implementation details reduces complexity and also shields the user from changes to the implementation.

In this chapter, we define the notion of an abstract data type, then introduce a C++ language feature—the class—that gives direct linguistic support to the practice of data abstraction. These are important concepts; they form the foundation for the rest of the topics that follow.

3.1 Abstract Data Types

In a programming language, every built-in (standard) data type has two characteristics:

1. a set of values
2. a collection of allowable operations on those values

For example, the C++ int type consists of a finite set of whole numbers, say, −32768 through +32767, along with the operations of addition, subtraction, multiplication, division, and so forth. Because int is a data type, a program can create several **instances** (or objects) of that type:

```
int i, j, k;
```

Each of these three instances—more commonly called *variables*—must be used in a manner consistent with the values and operations defined for the int type.

Often the standard types of a language are too primitive to model real-world data. Programming languages do not have standard types like Password, AirlineSchedule, or EmployeeList. But some languages have facilities for creating **abstract data types.** An abstract data type is a *programmer-defined* type with a set of values and a collection of operations on those values. The operations must be consistent with the values of the data type. For an EmployeeList type, arithmetic operations like multiplication and division are inappropriate. It is meaningless to obtain the product or quotient of two employee lists. Allowable operations might include AddNewEmployee or DeleteEmployee or PrintList. Interface diagrams, in the style we used for module interfaces in Chapter 2, present a graphical view of the valid operations of a data type (Figure 3.1).

To implement an abstract data type, the programmer must

- choose a concrete **data representation** of the abstract data, using data types that already exist
- implement each allowable operation in terms of program instructions

At first glance it may seem that the Password module of Chapter 2 creates an abstract data type: a password, with operations GetPassword and ValidUser. The implementation file uses a concrete data representation—the string named passStr—as well as function code for the two operations. However, the Password module exports only a single password object, not a data type. It is not possible for the importer to declare and manipulate several instances of a password.

Some languages, including C++, provide a language feature called a **class.** A class is a programmer-defined type that is used for creating abstract data types. Here is an example of a C++ class declaration:

int   EmployeeList

Figure 3.1 Interface diagrams for two data types

```
class Password {
    char passStr[11];
public:
    void    GetPassword();
    Boolean ValidUser();
};
```

Data and/or functions declared after the word `public` constitute the public interface; those declared before the word `public` are hidden from clients. In this case, *hidden* does not mean hidden from the eyes of a programmer. It means that the compiler will not allow the client code to access a private item.

Alternatively, the programmer can use the reserved word `private` to be as explicit as possible:

```
class Password {
private:
    char passStr[11];
public:
    void    GetPassword();
    Boolean ValidUser();
};
```

Better yet, to highlight the public interface and deemphasize the private data representation, many programmers prefer to locate the public part first:

```
class Password {
public:
    void    GetPassword();
    Boolean ValidUser();
private:
    char passStr[11];
};
```

We use this style throughout the remainder of this book.

Because a class is a type, we can create several instances or objects of that type:

```
Password pw1, pw2, pw3;
```

With this declaration, a program can manipulate three distinct passwords. In contrast, the module approach of Chapter 2 allows importation of only one password object.

The rest of this chapter introduces and describes many of the features of the C++ class mechanism and its importance in defining abstract data types.

3.2 Classes in C++

In C++, a class is a programmer-defined type whose components are called **class members.** Class members can be variables or functions. The `Password` class in the previous section has three class members: a member function named `GetPassword`, a member function named `ValidUser`, and a member variable named `passStr`.

All class members declared `private` are inaccessible to client code. Private members can be accessed only by the class's member functions. In the `Password` class, the private variable `passStr` is accessible only to the member functions `GetPassword` and `ValidUser`, not to client code. This separation of class members into private and public parts enforces information hiding.

Visibility of public and private members

In Figure 3.2 we present the declaration of a class named JarType. This JarType class is not useful as an off-the-shelf data type, but its simplicity lets us demonstrate many features of C++ classes.

Before discussing the usage of the JarType class, we need to point out two C++ language issues. First, observe that a semicolon follows the right brace at the very end of the class declaration. The presence of the semicolon may appear to contradict the general rule that C++ compound statements (blocks) do not have a semicolon after the right brace. However, the braces in a class declaration do not define a compound statement. Their purpose is simply to mark the beginning and end of the list of class members. Class declarations, like all C++ declarations, must end in semicolons.

The second issue is the use of the word const in the declaration of the Quantity function. Briefly, the word const means that the function inspects, but does not modify, the private variable numUnits. We discuss this use of const later in the chapter.

A Class Is a Type

It is important to restate that a class is a type, not a data object. Like any type, a class is a template from which you create (or **instantiate**) many instances of that type. Think of a type as a cookie cutter and instances of that type as the cookies.

The declarations

```
JarType jar1;
JarType jar2;
```

create two instances of the JarType class. Each instance of this class has its own copy of numUnits, the private data member of the class. At a given moment during program execution, jar1's copy of numUnits might contain the value 5, and jar2's copy of numUnits might contain the value 17. Figure 3.3 is a visual image of the class instances jar1 and jar2.

(In truth, the C++ compiler does not waste memory by placing duplicate copies of a member function, say, InitToEmpty, into both jar1 and jar2. The compiler generates just one copy of InitToEmpty, and any class instance

```
class JarType {
public:
    void InitToEmpty();           // Initialize the jar to be empty
    void Add( /* in */ int n );   // Add n units to the jar
    int  Quantity() const;        // Return the current number of
                                  // units
private:
    int numUnits;
};
```

Figure 3.2 Declaration of JarType class

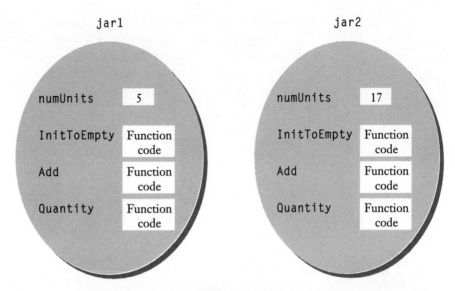

Figure 3.3 Conceptual view of two class instances

executes this one copy of the function. Nevertheless, the diagram in Figure 3.3 is a good mental picture of two different class instances.)

Be sure to distinguish between the terms *class instance (object)* and *class member*. Figure 3.3 depicts two instances (objects) of the JarType class, and each instance has four members.

Operations on Classes

In many ways, programmer-defined classes are like built-in types. You can declare as many instances of a class as you like. You can pass class instances as parameters to functions and return them as function values. Like any variable, a class instance can be automatic (created each time control reaches its declaration and destroyed when control exits its surrounding block) or static (created once when control reaches its declaration and destroyed when the program terminates). You may wish to review the concepts of static and automatic data in Section A.11 of Appendix A or Section B.9 of Appendix B.

In other ways, C++ treats classes differently from built-in types. Most of the built-in operations do not apply to classes. You cannot use the + operator to add two JarType instances, nor can you use the == operator to compare two JarType instances for equality.

Two built-in operations that are valid for class instances are member selection (.) and assignment (=). With the former, you select an individual member of the class by writing the name of the class instance, then a dot, then the member name. The statement

```
jar1.InitToEmpty();
```

invokes the InitToEmpty function, which presumably empties the first jar. The other operation, assignment, performs aggregate assignment of one class instance to another with the following semantics: If a and b are instances of the same class, then the assignment a = b copies the data members of b into a. Below are several examples using the JarType class:

```
JarType jar1;
JarType jar2;
JarType myJar;

jar1.InitToEmpty();
jar1.Add(10);
// ASSERT: jar1 contains 10 items

jar2.InitToEmpty();
jar2.Add(40);
jar2.Add(15);
// ASSERT: jar2 contains 55 items

if (jar2.Quantity() > 100)
    DoSomething();

myJar = jar2;
// ASSERT: myJar contains 55 items
```

In addition to member selection and assignment, a few other built-in operations are valid for classes. These operations require manipulating memory addresses, so we defer discussing them until later in the book. For now, think of . and = as the only valid operations.

Class Scope

The name of a class member has **class scope**—the name is local to the class. If the same name happens to be declared outside the class, the two are unrelated.

The JarType class has a member function named Add. In the same program, another class (say, SomeClass) also could have a member function named Add. Furthermore, the program might have a global Add function that is completely unrelated to any classes. If the program has statements like

```
JarType   jar1;
SomeClass someInstance;
int       n;
   :
   :
jar1.Add(32);
someInstance.Add(15);
Add(28, n);
```

then the C++ compiler has no trouble distinguishing the Add functions from one another. In the first two function calls, the dot notation denotes class member selection. The first statement will invoke the Add function of the JarType class, and the second statement will invoke the Add function of the SomeClass class. The final statement does not use dot notation, so the compiler knows that the function being called is the global Add function.

Information Hiding

Like a module, a class is enclosed by an abstraction barrier and has an interface through which data and/or functions are exported. This interface consists of the class members declared to be `public`. The creator of a class is free to choose which members are private and which are public. However, making data members public allows the importer to inspect and modify them. Because information hiding is so fundamental to data abstraction, most classes exhibit a typical pattern: the private part contains data, and the public part contains the functions that manipulate that data.

The `JarType` class exemplifies this organization. The data member `numUnits` is private, so the compiler prohibits a client from accessing `numUnits` directly. The following client statement therefore results in a syntax error:

```
myJar.numUnits = 45;        ← Prohibited
```

Because only the class's member functions can access `numUnits`, the creator of the class can offer a reliable product, knowing that external access to the private data is impossible. If it is acceptable to let the client *inspect* (but not modify) a private data member, a class might provide an **access function**. The `JarType` class has such a function, named `Quantity`. This access function simply returns the current value of `numUnits` to the client. Because `Quantity` is not intended to modify the private data, it is declared with the word `const` following the parameter list:

```
int Quantity() const;          // Return the current number of units
```

C++ refers to this kind of function as a **const member function.**

To picture a class's abstraction barrier and its public interface, we use a class interface diagram (Figure 3.4).

A class interface diagram looks just like a module interface diagram (Chapter 2). Ovals in the side of the abstraction barrier represent exported functions, and rectangles (if any) denote exported data items. In this book you

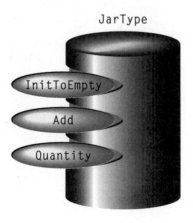

Figure 3.4 `JarType` class interface diagram

will almost never see a class interface diagram with rectangles in the side of the barrier. The abstract data types we create hide the concrete data representation and export only the operations on the data.

Specification and Implementation

As with functional abstractions, an abstract data type has a specification and an implementation. The specification describes the behavior of the data type without reference to its implementation. The implementation creates an abstraction barrier by hiding the concrete data representation as well as the code for the operations.

The JarType class declaration in Figure 3.2 serves as the specification of JarType. This declaration presents the public interface to the importer in the form of function prototypes. To implement the JarType class, we must provide function definitions (declarations with bodies) for all the member functions.

In C++, it is customary to package a class into a module. The specification (.h) file contains the class declaration as in Figure 3.2, and the implementation (.cpp) file contains the definitions of the member functions.

Let us pretend that JarType is a useful class, one that we might want to use over and over again in many programs. We create a Jar module composed of two files: jar.h and jar.cpp. Figure 3.5 displays the specification file, jar.h. The class declaration in this file is the same as in Figure 3.2, augmented with pre- and postconditions.

```
// -----------------------------------------------------------------
// SPECIFICATION FILE (jar.h)
// This module exports a JarType abstract data type
// -----------------------------------------------------------------

class JarType {
public:
    void InitToEmpty();
        // POST: Number of units in jar is 0
        // NOTE: This routine MUST be called prior to Add or Quantity

    void Add( /* in */ int n );
        // PRE:  InitToEmpty has been invoked at least once
        //    && n >= 0
        // POST: n units have been added to jar

    int Quantity() const;
        // PRE:  InitToEmpty has been invoked at least once
        // POST: FCTVAL == number of units in jar
private:
    int numUnits;
};
```

Figure 3.5 The Jar specification file

Notice the preconditions for the Add and Quantity functions. It is the responsibility of the importer to initialize a jar to be empty before adding anything to the jar or asking how many units the jar contains.

The other half of the module, the implementation file, must contain the definitions of the member functions InitToEmpty, Add, and Quantity. This implementation file is shown in Figure 3.6.

This implementation file illustrates three important points:

1. In the first line of each function definition, the class name (JarType) and the C++ **scope resolution operator** (::) must prefix the name of the member function. As we discussed earlier, it is possible for several classes to have member functions with the same name, say, Add. As well, there may be a global Add function that is not a member of any class. The scope resolution operator resolves any ambiguity about which particular function is being defined.

```
// ----------------------------------------------------------------
//   IMPLEMENTATION FILE (jar.cpp)
//   This module exports a JarType abstract data type
// ----------------------------------------------------------------
#include "jar.h"

// Private members of class:
//      int numUnits

void JarType::InitToEmpty()
    //.....................................................
    // POST: numUnits == 0
    // NOTE: This routine MUST be called prior to Add or Quantity
    //.....................................................
{
    numUnits = 0;
}

void JarType::Add( /* in */ int n )
    //.....................................................
    // PRE:  numUnits >= 0  &&  n >= 0
    // POST: numUnits == numUnits<entry> + n
    //.....................................................
{
    numUnits += n;
}

int JarType::Quantity() const
    //.....................................................
    // PRE:  numUnits >= 0
    // POST: FCTVAL == numUnits
    //.....................................................
{
    return numUnits;
}
```

Figure 3.6 The Jar implementation file

2. Although clients of a class must use the dot operator to refer to class members (for example, myJar.Empty()), members of a class always reference each other directly without using the dot operator. In Figure 3.6, the member functions all reference the member variable numUnits without using the dot operator.

3. Quantity is the only member function that does not modify the private variable numUnits. Because we have declared Quantity to be a const member function, the compiler will thwart any attempt to modify numUnits. The use of const is both an aid to the importer (as a visual signal that this function does not modify any private data) and an aid to the implementor (as a way to prevent accidental modification of the data). Notice that the word const must appear in both the function prototype and the function definition.

Compiling and Linking

After creating the jar.h and jar.cpp files, we can compile jar.cpp into object code. If we are working at the operating system's command line, we use a command similar to the following:

```
$ cc -c jar.cpp
```

The command-line switch -c means, in many systems, "compile but do not link." In other words, this command produces an object code file, say, jar.obj, but does not attempt to link this file with any other file.

A programmer wishing to import the JarType class will #include the file jar.h, then declare and use JarType instances:

```
#include "jar.h"
  ⋮
JarType someJar;

someJar.InitToEmpty();
someJar.Add(20);
  ⋮
```

If the importer's source code is in a file named myprog.cpp, an operating system command like

```
$ cc myprog.cpp jar.obj
```

will compile the importer's program into object code, link this object code with jar.obj , and produce an executable program.

The files jar.h and jar.obj must be available to importers. The importer needs to examine jar.h to see what JarType objects do and how to use them. The importer must also be able to link his or her program to jar.obj to produce an executable program. But the importer does *not* need to see jar.cpp. The main purpose of abstraction is to make the programmer's job easier by reducing complexity. Importers should not have to look at a module's implementation to see how to use it, nor should they write programs that depend on implementation details. In the latter case, any changes to the module's implementation could "break" the importer's programs.

3.3 Constructors

The `JarType` class we have just presented has a weakness. It depends on the importer to invoke `InitToEmpty` before any call to `Add` or `Quantity`. In the implementation file, the `Quantity` function's precondition is

```
numUnits >= 0
```

If the importer fails to invoke `InitToEmpty` first, this precondition may be false (because `numUnits` contains an unknown value) and the contract between the client and the function implementation is broken. Because classes nearly always encapsulate data, the creator of a class should not rely on the importer to initialize that data. The importer may forget to, or may even do it twice. Either way, unpleasant results may occur.

Guaranteed Initialization

C++ provides a mechanism, called a **constructor,** to guarantee the initialization of a class instance. A constructor is a member function that is implicitly invoked whenever a class instance is created.

A constructor function has an unusual name: the name of the class itself. Let us change the `JarType` class by removing the member function `InitToEmpty` and adding two constructors:

```
class JarType {
public:
    void Add( /* in */ int n) ;
    int  Quantity() const;
    JarType( /* in */ int n );    // Constructors
    JarType();
private:
    int numUnits;
};
```

This declaration includes two constructors, differentiated by their parameter lists. The first has a single parameter, n, and is intended to fill a jar with n units when created. The second constructor is parameterless and initializes the quantity to some default value, say, zero. A parameterless constructor is known in C++ as a **default constructor.**

Constructor declarations are unique in two ways. First, as we mentioned before, the name of the function is the same as the name of the class. Second, the data type of the function is omitted. The reason is that a constructor cannot return a function value. Its purpose is only to initialize a class instance's private data.

In the implementation file, the function definitions for the two `JarType` constructors might look like the following:

```
JarType::JarType( /* in */ int n )
    //...............................................................
    // PRE:  n >= 0
    // POST: numUnits == n
    //...............................................................

{
    numUnits = n;
}

JarType::JarType()
    //...............................................................
    // POST: numUnits == 0
    //...............................................................
{
    numUnits = 0;
}
```

Invoking a Constructor

Although a constructor is a member of a class, it is never invoked using dot notation. A constructor is invoked whenever a class instance is created. The function invocation may be either explicit or implicit. The following declaration, which creates a jar of 20 items, uses an explicit call to a constructor:

```
JarType myJar = JarType(20);
```

The expression to the right of the equal sign looks like an ordinary function call.

Alternatively, you can use an implicit constructor call by abbreviating the above form as

```
JarType myJar(20);
```

This form is more convenient and by far the more common in C++ programs. We use this form hereafter.

If there is no parameter list to a constructor, as in the declaration

```
JarType anotherJar;
```

then the default (parameterless) constructor is implicitly invoked. Here the default constructor `JarType()` initializes `anotherJar.numUnits` to zero.

Recall that a declaration in C++ is a genuine statement and can appear anywhere among executable statements. Placing declarations among executable statements is extremely useful for creating class instances whose initial values are not known until execution time:

```
cout << "Enter the initial number of items:";
cin >> itemCount;
```

```
JarType myJar(itemCount);

    ⋮

cout << "How many more items do you wish to add?";
cin >> itemCount;
myJar.Add(itemCount);
```

Using the Language

The class is an essential language feature for creating abstract data types in C++. The class mechanism is a very powerful design tool, but along with this power come rules for using classes correctly.

Semicolons and Class Declarations

As a rule of thumb, C++ statements (including declarations but *excluding* compound statements) end with semicolons:

```
int alpha;
int beta;

cin >> alpha;
if (alpha < 4) {
    beta = 3 * alpha;
    alpha = 0;
}
cout << alpha;
```

In a class declaration, the list of class members surrounded by braces is not considered to be a compound statement. Therefore, class declarations—like all declarations—end in semicolons:

```
class SomeClass {
public:

    ⋮

private:

    ⋮

};
```

Failure to terminate a class declaration with a semicolon is a very common syntax error.

Guidelines for Use of Class Constructors

A constructor is a member function that initializes a class instance at the moment the instance is created. C++ has some very intricate rules about using constructors, many of which relate to language features that we have not yet discussed. Here are some guidelines that are pertinent at this point.

1. A constructor cannot return a function value, so the function is declared without a data type.

2. The declaration

```
SomeClass anObject(param1, param2);
```

is an abbreviation for

```
SomeClass anObject = SomeClass(param1, param2);
```

3. A class may provide several constructors. When a class instance is declared, the compiler will choose the appropriate constructor according to the number and data types of the actual parameters to the constructor.

4. If a class instance is declared without a parameter list, as in

```
SomeClass anObject;
```

then the effect depends upon what constructors (if any) the class provides.

If the class has no constructors at all, memory is allocated for anObject but its private data members are in an uninitialized state.

If the class does have constructors, then the default (parameterless) constructor is invoked if there is one. If there is no default constructor, a syntax error occurs.

5. If a class has at least one constructor and a vector of class instances is declared:

```
SomeClass vec[10];
```

then one of the constructors must be the default (parameterless) constructor. This constructor will be invoked for each element of the vector. There is no way to pass a parameter to a constructor in this case.

Class Invariants

In the previous section, we modified the JarType class by adding two constructors and deleting the InitToEmpty member function. A revised module, call it Jar2, will consist of the new class declaration in the file jar2.h and the new function definitions in the file jar2.cpp. Figure 3.7 shows the contents of jar2.cpp.

Figure 3.7 The Jar2 implementation file

```
// -----------------------------------------------------------------
//    IMPLEMENTATION FILE (jar2.cpp)
//    This module exports a JarType abstract data type
// -----------------------------------------------------------------
#include "jar2.h"

// Private members of class:
//       int numUnits
//
// CLASSINV: numUnits >= 0
```

```
JarType::JarType( /* in */ int n )
    //...............................................................
    // Constructor
    // PRE:  n >= 0
    // POST: numUnits == n
    //...............................................................
{
    numUnits = n;
}

JarType::JarType()
    //...............................................................
    // Constructor
    // POST: numUnits == 0
    //...............................................................
{
    numUnits = 0;
}

void JarType::Add( /* in */ int n )
    //...............................................................
    // PRE:  n >= 0
    // POST: numUnits == numUnits<entry> + n
    //...............................................................
{
    numUnits += n;
}

int JarType::Quantity() const
    //...............................................................
    // POST: FCTVAL == numUnits
    //...............................................................
{
    return numUnits;
}
```

For the JarType class to behave as the implementor intends, the relationship

```
numUnits >= 0
```

must hold whenever the functions Add or Quantity are invoked. This relationship is described in a **class invariant,** denoted CLASSINV in the comment near the top of Figure 3.7. A class invariant is a special assertion that is a universal pre- and postcondition for a class. Each member function (except a constructor) assumes that the class invariant is true at the moment of function invocation. Furthermore, each member function (including a constructor) must ensure that the invariant is still true when the function returns. If you inspect the code in Figure 3.7, you will see that the invariant remains true upon exit from each function.

Observe that we have stated no precondition for the Quantity function in Figure 3.7. In the earlier Jar implementation file (Figure 3.6), the following was an explicit precondition:

```
PRE:  numUnits >= 0
```

In `Jar2`, this precondition would be redundant. It happens to be the same as the class invariant. We emphasize again that the class invariant is implicitly a precondition for *each* nonconstructor member function.

Pursuing Correctness

Class Invariants

A class invariant is an assertion about the current state of a class instance. The invariant typically refers only to data members of the class. In contrast, the pre- and postconditions of a member function may refer not only to data members but also to the function's particular parameters and to the function's return value.

All member functions of a class must cooperate to preserve the class invariant. The class invariant is an implicit postcondition for each member function. The invariant is also an implicit precondition for each member function (except a constructor).

Every class must provide a way to initialize its class invariant. The body of a constructor is the most appropriate location. A constructor is invoked when a class instance is created, before a client can invoke any other member function. Therefore, the statements in the body of a constructor must initialize the data of a class instance so that the class invariant is true upon return from the constructor. As a result, the class invariant is true before any subsequent calls are made to other member functions. A review of the two `JarType` constructors in Figure 3.7 shows that these constructors correctly initialize the class invariant `numUnits >= 0` to be true.

A Study in Design

A Random Number Generator Class

We have been using the `JarType` class to demonstrate C++ language features and class concepts. `JarType` is simple, but it is not very useful. We now look at a class that would make a good off-the-shelf software component: a random number generator class.

In Chapter 2, we designed a module named `Rand`. The `Rand` module exported two functions, `SetSeed` and `NextRand`, for pseudorandom number generation. The implementation file maintained a global variable `currentSeed`, declared as `static` to prevent unauthorized access from another file. Using the class concept, we can improve upon the `Rand` design in two ways:

1. The `Rand` module exports just one random number generator. By creating a random number generator class, we will see how the importer can declare any number of random number generators within a program, all of them independent of the others.

2. The `Rand` module requires the importer to invoke `SetSeed` (which initial-

izes the random number generator) before any call to the NextRand function. We will use class constructors to eliminate the reliance upon the importer for initializing the data.

The Rand2 *Specification*

Figure 3.8 shows the specification file for a new module, Rand2, that exports a random number generator class named RandGen.

The Rand2 specification uses the class mechanism to separate clearly the private data (currentSeed) from the public operations (NextRand and the class constructors). The class interface diagram for RandGen appears in Figure 3.9.

A client that #includes the header file rand2.h can declare several random number generators and invoke the public member functions for each class instance independently of the others.

By including constructors in the RandGen class, we can initialize the current seed without depending on the importer to do so. The SetSeed function from the earlier Rand module is now superfluous; we have deleted it altogether. As you can see in Figure 3.8, one of the constructors allows the client code to specify an initial seed as a parameter. The other constructor uses an initial seed chosen by the implementor. Because of these constructors, it is *impossible* for a RandGen instance to be in an uninitialized state when the client invokes

```
// ------------------------------------------------------------
// SPECIFICATION FILE (rand2.h)
// This module exports a class for pseudorandom number generation
// Machine dependency: long ints must be at least 32 bits (4 bytes).
// ------------------------------------------------------------

class RandGen {
public:
    float NextRand();
        // POST: FCTVAL == next pseudorandom number
        //     && 0.0 < FCTVAL < 1.0

//constructors:
    RandGen( /* in */ long initSeed );
        // PRE:  initSeed >= 1
        // POST: Pseudorandom sequence initialized using initSeed

    RandGen();
        // POST: Pseudorandom sequence initialized using
        //         a default initial seed
private:
    long currentSeed;
};
```

Figure 3.8 The Rand2 specification file

RandGen

Figure 3.9 RandGen class interface diagram

NextRand. Here is a sample of client code that uses two separate random number generators, one for rolling dice and the other for playing cards.

```
#include "rand2.h"
    ⋮
int  die1;
int  die2;
int  playingCard;
RandGen diceGen(359);     // Initialize using first constructor

die1 = int( diceGen.NextRand()*6.0 ) + 1;
die2 = int( diceGen.NextRand()*6.0 ) + 1;

RandGen cardGen;          // Initialize using default constructor
playingCard = int( cardGen.NextRand()*52.0 ) + 1;
```

The Rand2 *Implementation*

Figure 3.10 displays the implementation file for Rand2. This file contains the function definitions for the two class constructors and the NextRand function.

Figure 3.10 The Rand2 implementation file

```
// -----------------------------------------------------------------
//   IMPLEMENTATION FILE (rand2.cpp)
//   This module exports a class for pseudorandom number generation
//   Machine dependency: long ints must be at least 32 bits (4 bytes).
// -----------------------------------------------------------------
#include "rand2.h"

const long MULTIPLIER = 16807;
const long MAX  =  2147483647;
const long QUOT = 127773;        // Quotient of MAX / MULTIPLIER
const long REM  = 2836;          // Remainder of MAX / MULTIPLIER
```

```
// Private members of class:
//     long currentSeed
//
// CLASSINV: 1 <= currentSeed < MAX

RandGen::RandGen( /* in */ long initSeed )
    //.............................................................
    // Constructor
    // PRE:  initSeed >= 1
    // POST: 1 <= currentSeed < MAX
    //.............................................................
{
    initSeed = initSeed % MAX;
    currentSeed = (initSeed > 0) ? initSeed : 1;
}

RandGen::RandGen()
    //.............................................................
    // Default constructor
    // POST: currentSeed == 4
    //.............................................................
{
    currentSeed = 4;
}

float RandGen::NextRand()
    //.............................................................
    // POST: currentSeed ==
    //            (currentSeed<entry> * MULTIPLIER) modulo MAX
    //       && FCTVAL == currentSeed / MAX
    // NOTE: This is a prime modulus multiplicative linear
    //       congruential generator
    //.............................................................
{
    long temp = MULTIPLIER*(currentSeed%QUOT) -
                REM*(currentSeed/QUOT);

    currentSeed = (temp > 0) ? temp : temp + MAX;
    return float(currentSeed) / float(MAX);
}
```

The primary differences between this implementation file and the Rand implementation of Chapter 2 are the following:

1. The variable currentSeed is no longer a global variable in the implementation file. Instead, it is a private member of the RandGen class. The comment near the top of Figure 3.10:

```
// Private members of class:
//     long currentSeed
```

reminds the reader that any reference to currentSeed is a reference to this class member.

2. The SetSeed function has been replaced by two class constructors.

3. As the language requires, each function definition uses RandGen:: as a prefix to the function name.

Notice also the class invariant near the top of Figure 3.10:

```
1 <= currentSeed < MAX
```

Each constructor executes code that ensures the truth of this invariant. Thereafter, the invariant is implicitly a pre- and postcondition for each call to the NextRand function. All three of the member functions, therefore, cooperate to preserve the invariant.

3.4   Layered Software

One off-the-shelf component frequently is composed of other off-the-shelf components. We can use a car as an analogy. The designer of a new automobile may consider an engine to be an off-the-shelf component. In turn, the engine designer knows that the engine contains pistons and spark plugs that are themselves off-the-shelf components.

In the same way, software modules often make use of lower-level software modules. The result is called **layered software**. A module at one layer may import items from a more primitive module at a lower layer. Alternatively, we can say that a higher-level module is *implemented* by the module(s) at the next lower level. This layering yields an **implementation hierarchy**, which is often expressed with a hierarchy diagram:

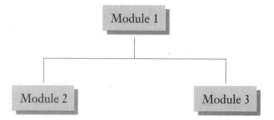

This diagram expresses the fact that Module 1 is implemented by (imports and uses the services of) both Module 2 and Module 3.

Suppose that a programmer needs an abstract data type whose private data representation consist of two items: a floating point number and a representation of a jar (as in our JarType class). Instead of devising a new jar type from scratch, the programmer decides to use Jar2 as an off-the-shelf module. The programmer's class declaration might have the following outline:

```
class NewType {
public:
    void Func( /* in */ int n );

    :

    NewType( /* in */ int jarUnits );    // Constructor
private:
    float    privateFloat;
    JarType privateJar;
};
```

The programmer now creates a module, say, NewMod. The NewType class declaration goes into the file newmod.h, and the implementations of the member functions go into the file newmod.cpp. If the NewType class makes use of standard library functions such as string routines or I/O routines, then we can picture the implementation hierarchy as follows:

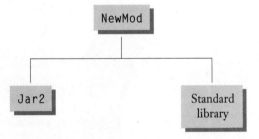

The NewType class has two private members, privateFloat and privateJar. The member privateJar is an instance of the JarType class, and all JarType operations apply to privateJar (see Figure 3.11).

Member functions of NewType must use dot notation and appropriate JarType operations when accessing privateJar. For example, the implementation of NewType's member function Func might appear as follows:

```
void NewType::Func( /* in */ int n )
{
    privateJar.Add(n);
    if (privateJar.Quantity() > 50)
        privateFloat = 3.4 * float(n);
}
```

When a NewType instance is created, its privateJar member also must be created. The parameter to the NewType constructor carries the initial quantity of jar units:

```
NewType someObject(20);
```

The question is how to pass this parameter to privateJar's constructor as well.

The answer is to use what C++ calls a **constructor initializer list**. A constructor initializer list is used whenever a class constructor needs to pass a parameter to a member's constructor. The following implementation of

An instance of `NewType`

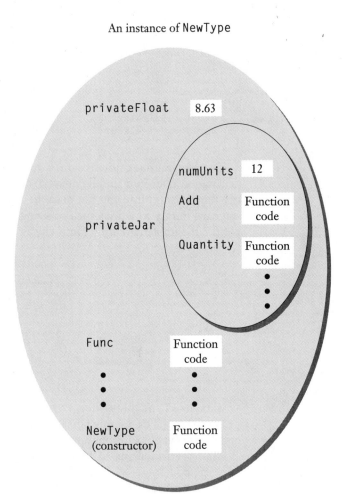

Figure 3.11 Conceptual view of a `NewType` class instance

`NewType`'s constructor shows a constructor initializer list after the right parenthesis of the parameter list:

Constructor initializer list

```
NewType::NewType( int jarUnits ) : privateJar(jarUnits)
{
    privateFloat = 0.0;
}
```

The notation is rather unusual. After `NewType`'s parameter list (but before its body), you append a colon and then a call to `privateJar`'s constructor. In this example, `NewType`'s constructor receives a parameter `jarUnits`, passes it along to `privateJar`'s constructor, and otherwise ignores it. The following rule governs the order in which the constructors are executed:

When a class instance is created, its constructor body is executed *after* all constructors for its members have been executed.

Thus, when a `NewType` instance is created, the constructor for its `privateJar` member is first invoked. After `privateJar` has been created, the body of `NewType`'s constructor is executed.

Using the Language

Class Members That Are Instances of Other Classes

Sometimes layered software results in classes whose members are instances of other classes. For example, the `NewType` class has a private member `privateJar`, an instance of type `JarType`.

When these class members have parameterized constructors, it is necessary to call their constructors using a constructor initializer list. Two rules pertain to constructor initializer lists.

1. A constructor initializer list is placed in the function definition but *not* in the function prototype.

   The prototype for `NewType`'s constructor, located in the class declaration, is simply

   ```
   NewType( int jarUnits );
   ```

   The function definition of `NewType`'s constructor must include the constructor initializer list:

   ```
   NewType::NewType( int jarUnits ) : privateJar(jarUnits)
   {
       privateFloat = 0.0;
   }
   ```

2. Suppose a class has two or more class instances as members:

   ```
   class MyClass {
   public:
          :
       MyClass( int n );    // Constructor
   private:
       int        privateVal;
       YourClass  alpha;       ←— Assume YourClass and TheirClass
       TheirClass beta;           have parameterized constructors.
   };
   ```

   Then in the definition of `MyClass`'s constructor, the constructor initializer list requires a comma to separate the calls to the member constructors:

   ```
   MyClass::MyClass( int n ) : alpha(n), beta(n+5)
   {
       privateVal = n;
   }
   ```

   In the constructor initializer list, the order in which you place the constructor calls does not matter. The constructors are executed in the order in which `alpha` and `beta` appear in the declaration of `MyClass` (namely, `alpha` and then `beta`). The final result is that `alpha` is constructed, then `beta` is constructed, and then the body of the `MyClass` constructor is executed.

A Study in Design

A Card Dealer Module

Consider designing a module that simulates the dealing of playing cards. This Dealer module would be a useful off-the-shelf component for programs that simulate card games. Because real cards are expected to be dealt randomly, we would like to incorporate random number generation into the design.

Earlier in this chapter we developed a Rand2 module for generating pseudo-random numbers. Instead of designing a new random number generator from scratch, it makes sense to view Rand2 as an off-the-shelf module and use its services for dealing cards. Therefore, we layer Dealer on top of the Rand2 module. The resulting implementation hierarchy is quite simple:

Specification of Dealer

Figure 3.12 contains the specification of the Dealer module. This specification uses C++ enumeration types to represent the face values and suits of ordinary playing cards. (For a review of enumeration types, see Section A.6 of Appendix A or Section B.5 of Appendix B.)

Figure 3.12 The Dealer specification file

```
// -------------------------------------------------------------
// SPECIFICATION FILE (dealer.h)
// This module exports CardValType, SuitType, and CardDeckType
// to randomly deal playing cards.
// Machine dependency: long ints must be at least 32 bits (4 bytes).
// -------------------------------------------------------------
#include "rand2.h"

enum CardValType { two, three, four, five, six, seven, eight,
                   nine, ten, jack, queen, king, ace };
enum SuitType    { clubs, diamonds, hearts, spades };

class CardDeckType {
public:
    void ShuffleDeck();
        // POST: All 52 cards have been returned to the deck

    void DealACard( /* out */ CardValType& cardVal,
                    /* out */ SuitType&    suit    );
        // PRE:  At least one card remains in the deck
        // POST: cardVal and suit represent a playing card not
        //       dealt since most recent ShuffleDeck
        //    && This card has been removed from the deck
```

```
      int CardsInDeck() const;
          // POST: FCTVAL == number of cards remaining in the deck

      CardDeckType( /* in */ long initSeed );
          // Constructor
          // PRE:  initSeed >= 1
          // POST: Random no. generator has been initialized with
          //          initSeed
          //       && The deck has been shuffled
private:
      RandGen cardGen;
      int     cardsRemaining;
      int     card[52];
};
```

Dealer exports three types that are useful to a program simulating card playing. The exported types CardValType and SuitType describe the face values and suits of a standard deck of playing cards. CardDeckType is an abstract data type—an abstraction of a deck of cards with related operations. Figure 3.13 shows interface diagrams for the Dealer module and the CardDeckType class. Recall that rectangles in the side of an abstraction barrier represent data-related items (usually data types and constants), whereas ovals denote operations.

The CardDeckType operations mimic real card dealing. ShuffleDeck returns all cards to the deck. DealACard selects at random and returns, through its reference parameters, the next card dealt from the deck. Its postcondition ensures that a card cannot be dealt twice without returning it to the

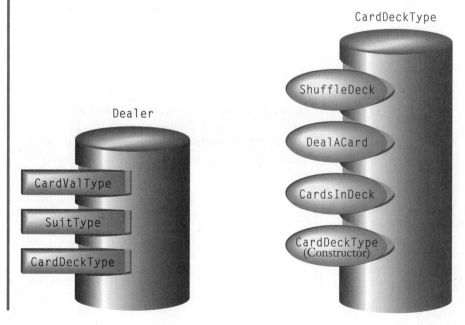

Figure 3.13 Interface diagrams for Dealer module and CardDeckType class

deck. `DealACard` also warns, through its precondition, against invocation when the deck is empty.

Through the access function `CardsInDeck`, the client can check how many cards remain in the deck. Revealing this information through an access function instead of a public variable is a better design choice. The client could alter the value of a public variable, whereas an access function merely returns a value. `CardsInDeck` is declared as a `const` member function to reinforce its role as an access function; it cannot modify the private data. Below is the outline of a program that imports and uses the types from `Dealer`.

```
// -----------------------------------------------------------------
//   carduse.cpp
//   This is an example of use of the Dealer module.
// -----------------------------------------------------------------
#include "dealer.h"

int main()
{
    SuitType     mySuit;
    CardValType  myCard;
    CardDeckType myDeck(297);    // Initialize random no. generator
                                 // with seed value 297

    myDeck.DealACard(myCard, mySuit);
    // ASSERT: myCard and mySuit represent some card dealt
        .
        .
        .
    if (myDeck.CardsInDeck() < 10)
        myDeck.ShuffleDeck();
    // ASSERT: All cards have been returned to the deck if
    //         fewer than 10 cards remained undealt
        .
        .
        .
}
```

Implementation of `Dealer`

Figure 3.14 presents a possible implementation of the `Dealer` module. `Dealer` is layered on top of the `Rand2` module. The implementation file `dealer.cpp` uses `#include` to include the specification file `dealer.h`. In turn, the file `dealer.h` (Figure 3.12) includes the file `rand2.h`. It is therefore legal for `dealer.cpp` to reference the `RandGen` class exported by `Rand2`.

Figure 3.14 An implementation file for `Dealer`

```
// -----------------------------------------------------------------
//   IMPLEMENTATION FILE (dealer.cpp)
//   This module exports CardValType, SuitType, and CardDeckType
//   to randomly deal playing cards.
//   Machine dependency: long ints must be at least 32 bits (4 bytes).
// -----------------------------------------------------------------
#include "dealer.h"
```

```
// Private members of class:
//      RandGen  cardGen
//      int      cardsRemaining
//      int      card[52]        For each card[i],
//                                    card value == card[i] modulo 13 and
//                                    suit == card[i] / 13
//
// CLASSINV: card[0..cardsRemaining-1] contain the undealt portion
//           of the deck

CardDeckType::CardDeckType( /* in */ long initSeed )
    : cardGen(initSeed)
    //..............................................................
    // Constructor
    // PRE:  initSeed >= 1
    // POST: initSeed has been passed to cardGen constructor
    //    && The deck has been shuffled
    //..............................................................
{
    ShuffleDeck();
}

void CardDeckType::ShuffleDeck()
    //..............................................................
    // POST: cardsRemaining == 52
    //    && For all i, (0<=i<=51), card[i] == i
    //       (So card[0] is two of clubs, card[1] is three of clubs,
    //        ..., card[12] is ace of clubs,
    //        card[13] is two of diamonds, ...)
    //..............................................................
{
    int i;

    for (i = 0; i < 52; i++)
        card[i] = i;
    cardsRemaining = 52;
}

void CardDeckType::DealACard( /* out */ CardValType& cardVal,
                              /* out */ SuitType&    suit    )
    //..............................................................
    // PRE:  cardsRemaining >= 1
    // POST: Some card[r] has been chosen at random from
    //       card[0..cardsRemaining<entry>-1]
    //    && cardVal == card[r] modulo 13
    //    && suit == card[r] / 13
    //    && card[r] has been "removed" by swapping it
    //       with card[cardsRemaining<entry>-1]
    //    && cardsRemaining == cardsRemaining<entry> - 1
    //..............................................................
{
    int randNo;
    int temp;
```

```
        randNo = int( cardGen.NextRand()*float(cardsRemaining-1) );

        cardVal = CardValType( card[randNo] % 13 );      // Type cast
                                                         // required
        suit = SuitType( card[randNo] / 13 );

        temp = card[randNo];
        card[randNo] = card[cardsRemaining-1];
        card[cardsRemaining-1] = temp;

        cardsRemaining--;
}

int CardDeckType::CardsInDeck() const
    //.......................................................
    // POST: FCTVAL == cardsRemaining
    //.......................................................
{
    return cardsRemaining;
}
```

CardDeckType is an abstract data type. The abstract data values are ordinary playing cards. The concrete data representation is a 52-element integer vector named card. Each element of the card array represents one card in the deck.

Data representation of a card

Instead of identifying each card by its suit and card value, we use a single integer in the range 0...51 to identify a card. We will call this number a *sequence number*. Suppose you were to take a fresh deck of playing cards arranged in the following order: two through ace of clubs, then two through ace of diamonds, then two through ace of hearts, then two through ace of spades. Now take a pencil and number each card in sequence, starting with zero. The result is that the two of clubs has sequence number 0, the three of clubs has sequence number 1, and so forth through the ace of spades, which has sequence number 51.

Given a card's sequence number, we can determine its suit and card number mathematically. Dealer exports two enumeration types, SuitType and CardValType. The SuitType enumerators clubs, diamonds, hearts, and spades have the int values 0, 1, 2, and 3, respectively. The CardValType enumerators two, three, ... ace have the int values 0 through 12. Therefore, the relationship between a card's sequence number and its suit and card value is the following:

$$\text{card value} = (\text{sequence number}) \text{ modulo } 13$$
$$\text{suit} = (\text{sequence number}) / 13$$

For example, the sequence number 0 gives

$$\left.\begin{array}{l} \text{card value} = 0 \text{ modulo } 13 = 0 \\ \text{suit} = 0 \text{ / } 13 = 0 \end{array}\right\} \text{two of clubs}$$

As another example, the sequence number 15 gives

$$\left.\begin{array}{l} \text{card value} = 15 \text{ modulo } 13 = 2 \\ \text{suit} = 15 \text{ / } 13 = 1 \end{array}\right\} \text{four of diamonds}$$

The ShuffleDeck function

The ShuffleDeck function stores the sequence number 0 into card[0], the sequence number 1 into card[1], and so forth. Quite the opposite of shuffling cards into random order, this function places all the cards into order by card value and suit, effectively forming an unopened deck of cards. The DealACard function then picks cards at random from the deck.

The class invariant

The private variable cardsRemaining represents the number of cards that remain in the deck. The array elements card[0] through card[cardsRemaining-1] represent the undealt portion of the deck. This relationship between cardsRemaining and the card array is the basis of the class invariant near the top of Figure 3.14. The class constructor initializes this invariant to true by invoking ShuffleDeck to begin with a fresh deck of playing cards. The other member functions then cooperate to preserve the class invariant.

The DealACard function

DealACard begins by obtaining a random integer in the range 0 through cardsRemaining - 1. Next, the function translates the chosen card's sequence number into a card value and suit for the benefit of the client. (It is necessary to use a type cast because C++ does not perform implicit type coercion from int to an enumeration type.) The final action is to "remove" the chosen card by doing both of the following:

1. swapping the chosen card with the card at the end of the undealt portion of the deck

2. making the undealt portion of the deck shorter (by decrementing cardsRemaining)

Constructing the cardGen object

One of the three private members of the CardDeckType class is cardGen, an instance of the RandGen class. When a CardDeckType instance is created, its cardGen member must also be created. The constructor for CardDeckType receives the initial seed value as a parameter and passes it along to cardGen's constructor by using a constructor initializer list:

```
CardDeckType::CardDeckType( long initSeed ) : cardGen(initSeed)
{
    ShuffleDeck();
}
```

According to the C++ rules governing the order of execution of constructors, the constructor for `cardGen` is first invoked, followed by execution of the body of `CardDeckType`'s constructor. Therefore, `cardGen` is created before the call to `ShuffleDeck` is executed.

Learning to use constructor initializer lists can be confusing at first, but these lists serve an important purpose. They make it possible to include instances of other classes as members of a class we are designing. The layering of software in this fashion is an important characteristic of data abstraction.

Designing with Wisdom **How to Design Software Layers**

In the design of software layers, each module should be responsible for one level of detail only. A module should have a single purpose and should rely on features provided by lower-level modules. Having a single purpose is sometimes referred to as having a high **degree of cohesion.** This means that the module's functions and data are all closely related to each other.

The `Dealer` module exhibits a high degree of cohesion. The functions and data all cooperate toward one goal: dealing cards. The module does not (and should not) know anything else about cards—rules of solitaire, bidding conventions in bridge games, and so on. High cohesion enhances understandability and therefore maintainability of the code.

Another suggestion is to keep lower levels as general purpose as possible. The `Rand2` module is more general in application than a specialized random number generator that returns only dice rolls or playing cards. `Rand2` is an effective lower layer for both `RollDice` (Chapter 2) and `Dealer`.

Special-purpose modules are important, but general-purpose modules make better off-the-shelf components. It is wise to consider generalizing a module whenever its application is likely to go beyond a very small collection of programs.

3.5 Friends

Returning to our `JarType` class, let us review the class declaration:

```
class JarType {
public:
    void Add( /* in */ int n );
    int Quantity() const;
    JarType( /* in */ int n );    // Constructors
    JarType();
private:
    int numUnits;
};
```

JarType represents an abstract data type with public operations Add, Quantity, and two constructors. The Add operation operates on a single JarType instance, say, jar1:

```
jar1.Add(34);
```

Similarly, the Quantity operation takes a single class instance as an operand.

Operations on abstract data types often require two class instances as operands. In designing a more comprehensive jar type, we may want an operation that compares two class instances for equality:

```
if (Equal(jar1, jar2))
    DoSomething();
```

The C++ equality operator (==) is not defined for programmer-defined classes, so we will have to write our own Equal function.

In this section we examine two approaches to designing operations like the Equal operation. The first approach is to make Equal a member function of the JarType class. The second is to make Equal a *friend* of the JarType class. We will see shortly what it means to be a friend of a class.

The Equal Function as a Class Member

Suppose that we revise the JarType class declaration to include an Equal function:

```
class JarType {
public:
         :
         :
    Boolean Equal( /* in */ JarType otherJar ) const;
        // POST: FCTVAL == (This jar and otherJar contain
        //                  the same number of units)
         :
         :
private:
    int numUnits;
};
```

Because Equal is a member of the JarType class, the client must use dot notation to refer to the first of the two operands:

```
if (jar1.Equal(jar2))
        :
        :
```

In the implementation file, the function definition for Equal would be written as shown in Figure 3.15.

In the body of the function, the unadorned identifier numUnits implicitly refers to the private member of the class instance for which the function is

Figure 3.15
Implementation of
Equal as a member
function

```
Boolean JarType::Equal( /* in */ JarType otherJar ) const
    // POST: FCTVAL == (This jar and otherJar contain
    //                      the same number of units)
{
    return (numUnits == otherJar.numUnits);
}
```

invoked. On the other hand, otherJar.numUnits accesses otherJar's private member. For example, suppose the client code has two JarType instances, myJar and yourJar, and uses the function invocation

```
if (myJar.Equal(yourJar))
    ⋮
```

Then within the Equal function, the plain identifier numUnits refers to myJar's private member, whereas otherJar.numUnits refers to yourJar's private member.

The Equal Function as a Friend Function

As we pointed out, a client of the JarType class invokes the member function Equal by using the dot notation:

```
if (jar1.Equal(jar2))
    ⋮
```

Many programmers prefer a more traditional syntax for invoking operations that take two operands:

```
if (Equal(jar1, jar2))
    ⋮
```

With this form, Equal could not be a JarType member function because the function call is not prefixed with the name of a class instance and a dot. But if this function is not a member of the JarType class, the function is not allowed to access the private members of its parameters jar1 and jar2.

By default, private class members can be accessed only by other members of that class. However, a class may grant permission to a *nonmember* function to access its private members by declaring that function to be a **friend** of the class:

```
class SomeClass {
public:
        ⋮
    friend SomeType SomeFunc( ... );
private:
        ⋮
};
```

Although the declaration of SomeFunc is physically located within the class declaration, SomeFunc is *not* a member of the class. The name of a friend function is not local to the class. Rather, its scope is that of the code surrounding the class declaration. Because a friend function is not a class member, a client does not use the dot operator to invoke the function. Let us examine how to make the Equal function a friend of the JarType class.

First, we declare the JarType class as follows:

```
class JarType {
public:
    ⋮
    friend Boolean Equal( /* in */ JarType firstJar,
                          /* in */ JarType secondJar );
        // POST: FCTVAL == (firstJar and secondJar contain
        //                     the same number of units)
    ⋮
private:
    int numUnits;
};
```

In this declaration, Equal is now a friend function, not a member function. In the implementation file, the function definition will be as shown in Figure 3.16.

Compare the two function definitions in Figures 3.15 and 3.16. In Figure 3.15, Equal is a member function. The first line of the function definition must name the function by using the class name and the scope resolution operator (::). In Figure 3.16, the name of the function is not prefixed this way because Equal is not a member of the class.

Observe also that both versions of the function are able to access the private class member numUnits. However, the friend function in Figure 3.16 must use dot notation for both operands because the function is not a class member.

With Equal as a friend function, a client of the JarType class executes code such as the following:

```
jar1.Add(25);
cin >> someInt;
jar2.Add(someInt);
if (Equal(jar1, jar2))
    DoSomething();
```

Because Add is a class member, the client must use dot notation to invoke the function. In contrast, Equal is a friend, not a member, of the JarType class. The client therefore does not use dot notation to invoke this function.

Figure 3.16
Implementation of
Equal as a friend
function

```
Boolean Equal( /* in */ JarType firstJar,
               /* in */ JarType secondJar )
    // POST: FCTVAL == (firstJar and secondJar contain
    //                     the same number of units)
{
    return (firstJar.numUnits == secondJar.numUnits);
}
```

Friends of a Class

The primary use of friend functions is to provide the client with a more traditional syntax for operations that have two or more class instances as operands. Some programmers are more comfortable with the notation

```
Equal(jar1, jar2)        ← Friend function
```

than with the notation required for a member function:

```
jar1.Equal(jar2)         ← Member function
```

On the surface, the use of friend functions may appear to compromise information hiding. Granting a nonmember function the right to inspect or modify a class's private data might seem to poke a hole in the abstraction barrier.

In reply to this concern, we point out that the class *creator*, not the importer, designs and writes the code for friend functions as well as member functions. A friend function should be considered just as much a part of the public interface as a member function is. The use of friend functions is a syntactic issue (giving the importer a more conventional notation for function calls), not an information-hiding issue.

3.6   Operator Overloading

An **overloaded operator** is one that has multiple meanings, depending on the data types of its operands. Consider the expression a + b. The statement "+ denotes addition" is imprecise, for there are many kinds of addition: integer addition, floating point addition, pointer addition (discussed later in this text), and others. To the hardware of a computer, these are entirely different operations; they employ different algorithms and data representations. The data types of the operands a and b determine which particular operation is required. Fortunately for the programmer, most high-level languages implicitly overload the + operator instead of requiring one symbol for integer addition, another symbol for floating point addition, and so forth.

Some languages, including Ada and C++, allow explicit operator overloading. Normally, the only operations defined for C++ class instances are assignment (=) and member selection (.). However, the programmer can overload nearly all of the built-in operators to apply to class instances.

Suppose we have a function that returns a class instance representing the sum of two other class instances:

```
SomeClass Sum( /* in */ SomeClass object1,
               /* in */ SomeClass object2 );
```

To perform the same task, we can overload the + operator by writing an **operator function.** An operator function is an ordinary C++ function, distinguished by an unusual name:

```
operator <symbol>
```

Overloaded operation:
"Shootout"

where `operator` is a reserved word and <symbol> denotes a built-in operator symbol. We modify the `Sum` function by doing one thing only—renaming it:

```
SomeClass operator+( /* in */ SomeClass object1,
                     /* in */ SomeClass object2 );
```

Only the function name has changed; the function body remains unaltered.

A client can invoke this operator function in one of two ways:

```
obj3 = operator+(obj1, obj2);      ←— Functional notation
obj3 = obj1 + obj2;                ←— Operator notation
```

The second notation is clearly what we are after. Overloading the + operator to operate on classes as well as built-in types is a good example of extending the language.

In the previous section, we wrote an `Equal` function for the `JarType` class. We did so because the built-in operator == is not defined for programmer-defined classes. First we wrote `Equal` as a member function. Then we wrote it as a friend function to give the importer a more customary syntax for invoking the function. But perhaps the best approach of all is to overload the == operator explicitly by using an operator function:

```
class JarType {
public:
    ⋮
    Boolean operator==( /* in */ JarType otherJar ) const;
        // POST: FCTVAL == (This jar and otherJar contain
        //                    the same number of units)
    ⋮
private:
    int numUnits;
};
```

Overloading the == operator results in a more natural way to compare two JarType instances:

`if (jar1.Equal(jar2))`	← Using a member function
`if (Equal(jar1, jar2))`	← Using a friend function
`if (jar1 == jar2)`	← Using an operator function

In the declaration of JarType, we declared operator== to be a member function. We could also have declared it to be a friend function, but there is no reason to do so.

The implementation of the operator== function is exactly the same as the implementation of the member function Equal, except that we rename Equal to operator==. The function body is absolutely unchanged:

```
Boolean JarType::operator==( /* in */ JarType otherJar ) const
    // POST: FCTVAL == (This jar and otherJar contain
    //                    the same number of units)
{
    return (numUnits == otherJar.numUnits);
}
```

Another example of operator overloading comes from the C++ standard library. The header file iostream.h supplies declarations for overloading the built-in operators >> and <<. (C++ defines these two operators to mean "shift right" and "shift left," respectively. Their purpose is to manipulate individual bits within a memory cell. We will discuss these low-level operations later in the text.) The input stream cin is an instance of a class that overloads the >> operator by means of an operator function named operator>>. This operator function performs input from the standard input device. Clients can call the function by using either functional notation:

```
cin.operator>>(someInt);
```

or operator notation:

```
cin >> someInt;
```

The latter is, of course, the form that we have been using and will continue to use.

Similarly, cout is an instance of a class that overloads the << operator. We can perform output by using either

```
cout.operator<<(someInt);
```

or

```
cout << someInt;
```

Later in the book we will describe how to overload the >> and << operators to perform I/O of our own programmer-defined classes.

Using the Language

Guidelines for Operator Overloading

Operator overloading is a very useful abstraction mechanism. The effect is to extend the language so that built-in operators can manipulate programmer-defined types (classes) and built-in types in a uniform way. However, there is potential for abuse. Overloading the * operator to mean division can result in unintelligible programs. The most prudent use of overloading is to mirror the conventional meaning of an operator.

As an aid to learning the syntax and semantics of operator overloading, we give the following summary:

1. All C++ operators may be overloaded, except the following four operators:

   ```
   ::    .    sizeof   ?:
   ```

2. Overloading is permitted *only* if at least one operand is a class instance. For example, you cannot overload an operator to take two ints as operands.

3. It is impossible to

   • change the standard precedence of operators (Appendix F)
   • define new operator symbols not already in the C++ language
   • change the number of operands of an operator (for example, unary / is not allowed)

4. Overloading unary operators

   Let a be of type SomeClass, and suppose that we want to overload the unary minus operator (-). Then the expression -a is equivalent to the function invocation

   ```
   a.operator-()
   ```
   if operator- is a member function
   or
   ```
   operator-(a)
   ```
   if operator- is a friend function

5. Overloading binary operators

   Let a be of type SomeClass, let b be of type AnyType, and suppose that we want to overload the addition operator (+). Then the expression a+b is equivalent to the function invocation

   ```
   a.operator+(b)
   ```
   if operator+ is a member function
   or
   ```
   operator+(a,b)
   ```
   if operator+ is a friend function

6. Overloading the ++ operator requires client code to use pre-increment form: ++someObject. There is a mechanism for allowing post-increment form as well, but we do not discuss it here. These remarks also hold for the -- operator.

7. Special rules apply to overloading the =, (), and [] operators. One restriction is that the operator functions must be class members, not friends. Chapter 7 discusses these operators further.

8. Many meanings for an operator can coexist, as long as the compiler can distinguish among the data types of the operands.

A Study in Design

A Fraction Module

In mathematics, a rational number is one that can be represented as a fraction whose numerator and denominator are both integers. 0.5 = 1/2 and 1.3125 = 21/16 are both rational numbers. However, the square root of 2 is not a rational number; you cannot express it as the ratio of two integers.

Certain computations could benefit from a fraction data type, one that preserves the numerator and denominator separately. For example, one problem inherent in all general-purpose computers is the potential for inaccuracies in floating point numbers. Because computer memory cells are finite in length, problems such as the following are legendary:

```
x = 1.0 / 3.0;        ← May yield 0.3333333.
y = 3.0 * x;          ← May yield 0.9999999, not 1.0.
```

A fraction data type could represent the fraction 1/3 as two distinct integers, 1 and 3, and the fraction 3/1 as the integers 3 and 1. Then an appropriate algorithm for multiplying these two fractions would yield *exactly* 1, not approximately 1.

The Module Specification

Figure 3.17 contains the specification of a Fraction module that extends the language to include a fraction data type.

Figure 3.17 The Fraction specification file

```
// ----------------------------------------------------------------
//   SPECIFICATION FILE (fraction.h)
//   This module exports a FracType class with two operator functions,
//   operator* and operator==.  A more general FracType class
//   might include more operations.
// ----------------------------------------------------------------
#include "bool.h"

class FracType {
public:
    void Write() const;
        // POST: The value of this fraction has been displayed as:
        //              <numerator> / <denominator>
        //          with no blanks
```

```
        float FloatEquiv() const;
            // POST: FCTVAL == float equivalent of this fraction

        void Simplify();
            // POST: Fraction is reduced to lowest terms. (No integer > 1
            //       evenly divides both the numerator and denominator)

        FracType operator*( /* in */ FracType frac2 ) const;
            // PRE:  This fraction and frac2 are in simplest terms
            // POST: FCTVAL == this fraction * frac2  (fraction
            //                     multiplication), reduced to lowest terms
            // NOTE: Numerators or denominators of large magnitude
            //       may produce overflow

        Boolean operator==( /* in */ FracType frac2 ) const;
            // PRE:  This fraction and frac2 are in simplest terms
            // POST: FCTVAL == TRUE, if this fraction == frac2
            //                     (numerically)
            //              == FALSE, otherwise

        FracType( /* in */ int initNumer,
                  /* in */ int initDenom );
            // Constructor
            // PRE:  Assigned(initNumer)  &&  initDenom > 0
            // POST: Fraction has been created and can be thought of
            //          as the fraction  initNumer / initDenom
            // NOTE: (initNumer < 0) --> fraction is a negative number
private:
    int numer;
    int denom;
};
```

The Fraction module exports a single item: a class named FracType. The public interface of FracType consists of a constructor, three functions that operate on a single fraction (Write, FloatEquiv, and Simplify), and two operator functions (operator* and operator==) for multiplying and comparing a pair of fractions. Figure 3.18 shows the interface diagram for FracType.

The member function operator== compares two fractions for equality. The first fraction is implicitly the FracType instance for which the function is invoked, and the second is the fraction in the parameter list. The operator== function overloads the == operator to give a familiar syntax for comparing fractions:

```
if (myFrac == yourFrac)
    ⋮
```

Likewise, the member function operator* has two operands, the first being the class instance for which the function is invoked. This function returns, as the function value, an entire FracType instance: the fraction representing the product of the two designated fractions. Here is a client statement that

Figure 3.18 FracType class interface diagram

invokes the function and stores the returned fraction into a FracType instance named frac3:

```
frac3 = frac1 * frac2;
```

Notice that we have declared all of the functions Write, FloatEquiv, operator*, and operator== to be const member functions. Each one accesses, but does not modify, the private data of the class.

In designing the FracType class, we need to consider a basic fact in mathematics: zero is not allowed as the denominator of a fraction. The constructor for the FracType class requires the client to supply an initial numerator and initial denominator:

```
FracType myFrac(2, 3);        ← Create the fraction 2/3.
```

If the client were to pass a zero-valued expression for the denominator, we would have to take some action. In Chapter 2, we discussed various philosophies about off-the-shelf software's response to client errors. Our design choice for FracType is to eliminate, through the constructor's precondition, the possibility of a zero-valued denominator:

```
FracType( /* in */ int initNumer,
          /* in */ int initDenom );
    // Constructor
    // PRE:  Assigned(initNumer)  &&  initDenom > 0
    // POST: Fraction has been created and can be thought of
    //       as the fraction  initNumer / initDenom
    // NOTE: (initNumer < 0) --> fraction is a negative number
```

With these pre- and postconditions, we form a contract with the client: if the client guarantees the precondition, we will guarantee the postcondition. If the client fails to guarantee the precondition (as by passing zero for the denominator), the contract is broken and we make no guarantees about what will happen. This approach may seem ruthless, but "programming by contract," as it is sometimes called, has three important advantages:

1. Programmers are much more likely to use and reuse an off-the-shelf component if it is small and lean. Filling the component with error-detection algorithms and error message strings increases memory space and decreases speed.

2. Programmers are more likely to use and reuse an off-the-shelf component if the *client*, not the component, has control over what to do with bad data. If the component announces "I will halt the program if I receive bad data," programmers may decline to use it, preferring to let the program continue after taking some action to accommodate the error.

3. Programming by contract eliminates duplication of effort. It is all too common in software systems for *both* the client and the component to perform the same error checking. This redundancy leads to inefficiency of both memory space and execution time.

We use this design philosophy throughout most of this text, although occasionally we include error checking within a component either to demonstrate a concept or because it makes good sense in a particular circumstance.

A second design decision in the FracType class is how to represent negative numbers. A fraction is negative if either its numerator or its denominator is negative, but not both. To simplify the implementation of FracType, we have chosen to require all denominators to be positive. In the constructor's specification, the precondition alerts the importer to use a positive denominator. If the importer wants to create a negative fraction, the note at the bottom of the specification tells how to do it: use a negative numerator.

A Test Driver

Below is a test driver for the Fraction module:

```
// ---------------------------------------------------------------------
// testfrac.cpp
// This is a sample test driver for the Fraction module
// ---------------------------------------------------------------------
#include <iostream.h>
#include "fraction.h"

void Print( const char[], FracType );

int main()
{
    FracType frac1(-5, 3);
    FracType frac2(-70, 1500);

    Print("Fraction 1:", frac1);
    Print("Fraction 2:", frac2);
```

```
        frac2.Simplify();
        Print("Fraction 2, simplified:", frac2);

        if (frac1 == frac2)
            cout << "The two fractions are equal\n";
        else
            cout << "The two fractions are NOT equal\n";

        Print("Their product:", frac1 * frac2);

        frac1 = frac2;
        Print("After copying, fraction 1 =", frac1);

        if (frac1 == frac2)
            cout << "The two fractions are equal\n";
        else
            cout << "The two fractions are NOT equal\n";

        return 0;
}
// -----------------------------------------------------------------
void Print( /* in */ const char  str[],
            /* in */ FracType     frac )
{
    cout << str << ' ';
    frac.Write();
    cout << "  (float value " << frac.FloatEquiv() << ") \n";
}
```

An execution of this test driver produces the following output:

```
Fraction 1: -5/3  (float value -1.666667)
Fraction 2: -70/1500  (float value -0.046667)
Fraction 2, simplified: -7/150  (float value -0.046667)
The two fractions are NOT equal
Their product: 7/90  (float value 0.077778)
After copying, fraction 1 = -7/150  (float value -0.046667)
The two fractions are equal
```

The main function in TestFrac consists of seven logical parts, separated by blank lines. The first two parts declare and output the fractions –5/3 and –70/1500. The third part simplifies frac2 and outputs the result. The fourth part finds the two fractions unequal and displays an appropriate message. The fifth part outputs the product of the two fractions. The sixth part illustrates an assignment of one entire class instance to another, and the seventh part then finds the two fractions to be equal.

This test driver is by no means comprehensive. All it demonstrates is correct execution for the two fractions –5/3 and –70/1500. A truly satisfactory test driver would use a full test oracle (Chapter 1) consisting of many different fractions—positive, negative, and zero.

The Module Implementation

Figure 3.19 displays an implementation for the Fraction module. Notice how the implementation imports, through the header file stdlib.h, the absolute value function abs. Also, the code imports I/O features by including the header file iostream.h. Every C++ program treats the C++ standard library as an off-the-shelf module. In light of our discussion of layered software, we could say that the Fraction module is layered on top of the C++ standard library.

Notice also the class invariant. Because mathematical fractions must have nonzero denominators and because we have chosen not to allow negative denominators, the class invariant is denom > 0. The class constructor initializes this invariant to true (provided the user has complied with the constructor precondition initDenom > 0).

Figure 3.19 The Fraction implementation file

```
// -----------------------------------------------------------
//   IMPLEMENTATION FILE (fraction.cpp)
//   This module exports a FracType class with two operator functions,
//   operator* and operator==.
// -----------------------------------------------------------
#include <iostream.h>
#include <stdlib.h>        // For abs() function
#include "fraction.h"

int GreatestCommonDivisor( int, int );  // Auxiliary function
                                        // prototype


// Private members of class:
//      int numer;
//      int denom;
//
// CLASSINV: denom > 0

FracType::FracType( /* in */ int initNumer,
                    /* in */ int initDenom )
    //..............................................................
    // Constructor
    // PRE:  Assigned(initNumer)  &&  initDenom > 0
    // POST: numer == initNumer  &&  denom == initDenom
    //..............................................................
{
    numer = initNumer;
    denom = initDenom;
}

void FracType::Write() const
    //..............................................................
    // POST: Fraction has been displayed as numer/denom with no
    //       blanks
    //..............................................................
{
    cout << numer << '/' << denom;
}
```

```
float FracType::FloatEquiv() const
    //...............................................................
    // POST: FCTVAL == float equivalent of this fraction
    //...............................................................
{
    return float(numer) / float(denom);
}

void FracType::Simplify()
    //...............................................................
    // POST: Fraction is reduced to lowest terms. (No integer > 1
    //       evenly divides both numer and denom)
    //...............................................................
{
    int gcd;
    int absNumer = abs(numer);

    if (numer==0 || absNumer==1 || denom==1)
        return;
    gcd = GreatestCommonDivisor(absNumer, denom);
    if (gcd > 1) {
        numer /= gcd;
        denom /= gcd;
    }
}

FracType FracType::operator*( /* in */ FracType frac2 ) const
    //...............................................................
    // PRE:  This fraction and frac2 are in simplest terms
    // POST: FCTVAL == this fraction * frac2  (fraction
    //                    multiplication)
    //       (WARNING: Overflow is possible)
    //...............................................................
{
    int resultNumer = numer * frac2.numer;
    int resultDenom = denom * frac2.denom;

    FracType resultFrac(resultNumer, resultDenom);
    // ASSERT: New fraction created

    resultFrac.Simplify();
    return resultFrac;
}

Boolean FracType::operator==( /* in */ FracType frac2 ) const
    //...............................................................
    // PRE:  This fraction and frac2 are in simplest terms
    // POST: FCTVAL == TRUE, if this fraction == frac2 (numerically)
    //               == FALSE, otherwise
    //...............................................................
{
    return (numer==frac2.numer) && (denom==frac2.denom);
}
```

```
int GreatestCommonDivisor( /* in */ int a,
                           /* in */ int b )
    //........................................................
    // PRE:  a >= 0  &&  b > 0
    // POST: FCTVAL == Greatest common divisor of a and b
    //                  (Algorithm: the Euclidean algorithm)
    //........................................................
{
    int temp = a % b;
    while (temp > 0) {  // INV (prior to test):
                        //    No integer > b evenly divides
                        //    both a<entry> and b<entry>
        a = b;
        b = temp;
        temp = a % b;
    }
    // ASSERT: b == Greatest common divisor of a<entry> and b<entry>
    return b;
}
```

The implementation code for the operator* function reflects a well-known algorithm for multiplying two fractions: multiply the numerators, then multiply the denominators, then simplify the result. In the operator* function, the statement

```
int resultNumer = numer * frac2.numer;
```

accesses the private members of two different class instances. The unadorned identifier numer implicitly refers to the private member of the class instance for which the function is invoked. On the other hand, frac2.numer accesses frac2's private member. For example, suppose the client code has two FracType instances, myFrac and yourFrac, and uses the function invocation

```
newFrac = myFrac*yourFrac;
```

Then within the operator* function, the plain identifiers numer and denom refer to myFrac's private members, whereas frac2.numer and frac2.denom refer to yourFrac's private members.

The Fraction module would make a good off-the-shelf component for programmers who need to work with rational numbers. The FracType class combines many of the features we have introduced in this chapter: public and private class members, const member functions, class constructors, and operator overloading. We will refer to the FracType class later in the book as we introduce new topics.

SUMMARY

Modules and classes are both units of modularity. Both allow the programmer to decompose a large problem into manageable subproblems, to extend the language with data types and functions not already available, to employ data abstraction, and to layer specialized software components on top of more general ones.

However, modules and classes are not interchangeable concepts. A module is an organizational mechanism, a way for the programmer to physically collect various abstractions into a separate file. In contrast, a class is a construct built into the C++ language for creating abstract data types. A class is a type, and a program can declare many instances of that type. Each instance has its own copy of the data members, which are manipulated by member functions independently of any other instances of that class.

One use of modules is simply to group several related functions together. The `Powers` module from Chapter 2 exported two functions, `PowerOfInt` and `PowerOfFloat`, but no data abstractions. Using a class to accomplish this task would be inappropriate:

```
class Powers {
public:
    int   PowerOfInt( int someInt, int exponent );
    float PowerOfFloat( float someFloat, int exponent );
};
```

The client would have to declare an instance of this class and use the dot operator just to use the functions. Using a class makes little sense and is inconvenient.

Another use of modules is to implement data abstractions, encapsulating data (as variables global to the module) and enforcing information hiding by using the word `static`. Such use of a module is certainly possible but has its disadvantages:

- The creator of the module must remember to declare each private item as `static`.
- The burden of initializing the data falls on the importer.
- Only one instance of the encapsulated data is created.

With a class, data encapsulation and information hiding are easily accomplished by specifying which members are private and which are public. The private members can be accessed by other class members or by friend functions but not by clients. The client can declare as many instances of the class as desired, and class constructors automatically guarantee initialization of each instance. Furthermore, operator overloading lends a class the appearance of a built-in type.

In summary, we give the following guidelines (with the understanding that exceptions are always possible):

1. If the goal is to provide only a related group of useful functions, export them from a module directly. A class is inappropriate.

2. If the goals are to encapsulate data and enforce information hiding, to allow multiple data objects to be declared, to guarantee initialization of those objects, and to potentially provide operator overloading, write a class and export the class from a module.

KEY TERMS

abstract data type   (p. 111)
access function   (p. 117)
class   (p. 111)
class invariant   (p. 125)
class member   (p. 113)
class scope   (p. 116)
const member function   (p. 117)
constructor   (p. 121)
constructor initializer list   (p. 131)
data abstraction   (p. 110)
data representation   (p. 111)

default constructor   (p. 121)
degree of cohesion   (p. 140)
friend   (p. 142)
implementation hierarchy   (p. 130)
instance (of a type)   (p. 111)
instantiate   (p. 114)
layered software   (p. 130)
operator function   (p. 144)
overloaded operator   (p. 144)
scope resolution operator   (p. 119)

EXERCISES

3.1   A software designer might use an abstract data type to represent each of the real-world objects below. Ignoring the concrete data representation for each, list a few abstract operations that are appropriate.

   a. a class list of students

   b. a checkbook

   c. a dictionary

   d. a radio

   e. a cornfield

   f. an automobile (from the driver's perspective)

   g. an automobile (from the auto mechanic's perspective)

   h. a grocery store (from the shopper's perspective)

   i. a grocery store (from the owner's perspective)

   j. a pizza (from the consumer's perspective)

   k. a pizza (from the cook's perspective)

3.2   To implement an abstract data type, the programmer must do two things:

   a. Choose a _____.

   b. Implement each _____.

3.3   Consider the following C++ class declaration and client code:

Class declaration
```
class SomeClass {
public:
    void Func1( int n );
    int  Func2( int n ) const;
    void Func3();
private:
    int someInt;
};
```

Client code
```
SomeClass instance1;
SomeClass instance2;
int       n;

instance1.Func1(3);
n = instance2.Func2(5);
instance1.someInt = 14; // Error
```

   a. List all the identifiers that refer to data types (both built-in and programmer-defined).

   b. List all the identifiers that are names of class members.

   c. List all the identifiers that are names of class instances.

   d. List the names of all member functions that are allowed to inspect the private data.

   e. List the names of all member functions that are allowed to modify the private data.

   f. In the last statement of the client code, the comment `// Error` is attached. Why?

   g. In the implementation of `SomeClass`, which one of the following would be the correct function definition for `Func3`?

   ```
   i. void Func3()
      { ... }
   ```

   ```
   ii. void SomeClass::Func3()
       { ... }
   ```

   ```
   iii. SomeClass::void Func3()
        { ... }
   ```

3.4   Viewing the following as abstract data types, give a C++ class declaration for each. Select suitable data representations and public interfaces for the operations. Use `const` member functions for those operations that do not modify the private data. (Do not implement the operations by giving function bodies.)

   a. Type:
      A savings account

      Operations:
      Open account (with an initial deposit), Make a deposit, Make a withdrawal, Show current balance.
      (Make the withdrawal operation robust by returning a flag stating that the withdrawal was refused due to insufficient funds.)

   b. Type:
      A countdown timer that counts off seconds, starting from an initial value. When the timer reaches zero, it beeps.

      Operations:
      Initialize to zero, Reset to some value, Tick, Display current value.

   c. Type:
      A vending machine dispensing three items: coffee, tea, and milk.

      Operations:
      Initialize machine to empty, Restock the machine, Display price of each item, Display which items are out of stock, Vend.
      (The Vend operation requires the item name and cash submitted, and it returns change.)

3.5   Which of the following C++ operators are predefined by the language to operate on programmer-defined classes?

   a. +   (Add)

   b. =   (Assign)

c. * (Multiply)

d. . (Dot)

e. == (Equals)

3.6 The following class has two constructors among its public member functions:

```
class SomeClass {
public:
    float PrivateVal() const;
        // POST: FCTVAL == value of private data

        :

    SomeClass( /* in */ float f );
        // PRE:  Assigned(f)
        // POST: Private data is initialized to f
     SomeClass();
        // POST: Private data is initialized to 3.5
private:
    float someFloat;
};
```

What output will be produced by the following client code?

```
SomeClass x;
SomeClass y(98.6);


cout << x.PrivateVal() << '\n';
cout << y.PrivateVal() << '\n';
```

3.7 The C++ compiler will signal a syntax error in the following class declaration. What is the error?

```
class SomeClass {
public:
    void Func1( int n );
    int  Func2();
    int  SomeClass();
private:
    int someInt;
};
```

3.8 In Chapter 2, Programming Project 2.4 uses a CommaIO module. Examine the module's specification. Would it make sense to rewrite the module as a class? Why or why not?

3.9 In this chapter we layered the Dealer module on top of Rand2. We could also layer a dice-rolling module on top of Rand2. Consider the following outline of a DiceType class declaration:

```
class DiceType {
public:

    :
```

```
        DiceType( /* in */ long initSeed );
            // POST: Random no. generator initialized using initSeed
            //      && The dice are both showing threes
private:
    RandGen diceGen;
    int     die1;
    int     die2;
};
```

The following implementation of the DiceType constructor is incomplete. Fill in the first line of the function definition, remembering to use a constructor initializer list to pass initSeed to diceGen's constructor.

```

┌─────────────────────────────┐
│                             │
└─────────────────────────────┘

{
    die1 = 3;
    die2 = 3;
}
```

3.10 A programmer, wishing to maintain 100 separate random number generators for a complicated simulation, imports the RandGen class from the Rand2 module (Figure 3.8).

a. Give a declaration that instantiates these 100 random number generators.

b. When creating these 100 generators, the programmer cannot specify a different initial seed for each. Why?

c. How might the RandGen implementor modify the default (parameterless) constructor to permit user initialization of the seed? (Hint: Consider I/O.)

3.11 The SimpStat module, introduced as an exercise at the end of Chapter 2, maintains a collection of integer values and computes statistics on these values. An importer may wish to maintain several collections simultaneously, but SimpStat provides only one.

a. Rewrite SimpStat as a class, exporting it from a module named StatMod. Include a class constructor to initialize count and statsValid.

b. What is the class invariant? Verify that each member function preserves this invariant upon function exit.

3.12 For the FracType class exported by the Fraction module, consider including a new operation that adds 1 to a given fraction. For instance, adding 1 to the fraction 2/3 yields the fraction 5/3. For each part below, give

i. a C++ function prototype

ii. a C++ function definition (with body)

that corresponds to the description.

a. A member function named AddOne, invoked as follows:

```
myFrac.AddOne();
```

b. A member function that overloads the ++ operator, invoked as follows:

```
++myFrac;
```

c. A friend function named AddOne, invoked as follows:

```
AddOne(myFrac);
```

d. A friend function that overloads the ++ operator, invoked as follows:

```
++myFrac;
```

3.13 An importer of the CardDeckType class (Figure 3.12) wishes to simulate a bridge tournament and needs 25 decks of cards. Unfortunately, it is not possible to declare a vector of CardDeckType instances because there is no default (parameterless) constructor. Modify the class by providing one. Give both its specification and implementation.

3.14 Rewrite the Password module of Chapter 2 as a class, exporting it from a module named PassMod. The importer can now manipulate many passwords in one program. You may wish to incorporate the changes suggested by Exercise 2.12 of Chapter 2.

   Note that the precondition for ValidUser required a prior invocation of GetPassword to initialize the password string. Eliminate this precondition by including a class constructor that initializes the password to be the empty string.

   What is the class invariant for your new class? Verify that each member function preserves this invariant upon function exit.

PROGRAMMING PROJECTS

3.1 Augment the Fraction module by including member functions operator+, operator-, and operator/ for adding, subtracting, and dividing fractions. The implementation code for each function should simplify the result before returning it.

   Be careful with division. Consider what the precondition for operator/ ought to be. Also, make sure that dividing a nonnegative fraction by a negative one results in a negative numerator, not a negative denominator.

   Test your new FracType class with the following problem.

TITLE

Fraction arithmetic

DESCRIPTION

This program prompts the user to input pairs of fractions. For each pair, the program performs a user-specified operation (addition, subtraction, multiplication, division, or equality testing) and outputs the result as a fraction.

INPUT

The program prompts the user to enter the first fraction, then an operator, then a second fraction, each on a separate line. Each fraction consists of three pieces: an integer numerator, a slash (/), and an integer denominator. Zero or more spaces separate these pieces. The operator is a single character: +, −, *, /, or =.

End of input (and end of program execution) occurs when the user supplies the machine's end-of-file keystrokes when prompted for the first fraction.

OUTPUT

The following prompts for the fractions and the operator occur in the order shown:

```
1st fraction (or <EOF> to quit):
Operation:
2nd fraction:
```

Each prompt leaves the cursor at the end of the prompt line.

The program then outputs *one* of the following lines, according to the specified operation:

```
Their sum:   <r>
Their difference:   <r>
Their product:   <r>
Their ratio:   <r>
Fractions are equal
Fractions are NOT equal
```

where <r> denotes the result in fractional form.

Finally, the program outputs a blank line and prompts for the first fraction of the next pair.

ERROR HANDLING

1. If the user enters a nonpositive denominator, the program outputs

   ```
   Denominator must be positive
   ```

   and repeatedly prompts until a positive value is input.

2. If the user enters an invalid operator, the program outputs

   ```
   Operator must be +, -, *, /, or =
   ```

   and repeatedly prompts until the operator is valid.

3. If the user attempts to divide by a zero-valued fraction, the program outputs

   ```
   Can't divide by zero
   ```

   and abandons this computation (but does not halt).

EXAMPLE

Below is a sample execution with input in color.

```
1st fraction (or <EOF> to quit): 2/0
Denominator must be positive
1st fraction (or <EOF> to quit): 2/-5
Denominator must be positive
```

```
1st fraction (or <EOF> to quit): 2/4
Operation: =
2nd fraction: 50/100
Fractions are equal

1st fraction (or <EOF> to quit): 25/23
Operation: A
Operator must be +, -, *, /, or =
Operation: +
2nd fraction: 30/78
Their sum: 440/299

1st fraction (or <EOF> to quit): 2/4
Operation: /
2nd fraction: -2/6
Their ratio: -3/2

1st fraction (or <EOF> to quit): 4/7
Operation: /
2nd fraction: 0/3
Can't divide by zero

1st fraction (or <EOF> to quit): <EOF>
```

3.2 A complex ("imaginary") number has the form $a + bi$, where i is the square root of -1. Here, a is called the real part and b is called the imaginary part. Alternatively, $a + bi$ can be expressed as the ordered pair of real numbers (a, b).

Arithmetic operations on two complex numbers (a, b) and (c, d) are as follows:

$$(a, b) + (c, d) = (a + c, b + d)$$
$$(a, b) - (c, d) = (a - c, b - d)$$
$$(a, b) * (c, d) = (a * c - b * d, a * d + b * c)$$
$$(a, b) / (c, d) = \left(\frac{a * c + b * d}{c^2 + d^2}, \frac{b * c - a * d}{c^2 + d^2} \right)$$

Also, the absolute value (or magnitude) of a complex number is defined as

$$|(a, b)| = \sqrt{a^2 + b^2}$$

Write a complex number class that represents the real and imaginary parts as `double` values (for double precision) and provides the following operations:

- operator functions to overload the operators $+$, $-$, $*$, and $/$

- a complex absolute value function `CAbs`

- two access functions, `RealPart` and `ImagPart`, that return the real and imaginary parts of a complex number

- constructors for explicit as well as default initialization. The default initial value should be (0.0, 0.0)

Be sure to document the class invariant, and ensure that each member function preserves the invariant upon function exit.

To test your class, write a problem specification similar to that of Project 3.1 above. Let the user enter each complex number as a pair of double values and specify the operations to be performed.

3.3 Use the Dealer module (Figure 3.12) to solve the following problem.

TITLE

A solitaire game

DESCRIPTION

This program simulates the following solitaire card game. The player draws eight cards from a fresh deck and turns them face up to form the bottoms of eight card stacks. Whenever the top cards on two card stacks have the same face value, the player draws two cards from the deck and places them face up on the two stacks. The game continues until all eight stacks have different card values on top. The object of the game is to draw as many cards as possible.

INPUT

The only input is a user-supplied positive integer to seed the random number generator.

OUTPUT

The following is the prompt for the seed:

```
Please supply a positive integer to seed random numbers:
```

The program then outputs a blank line, followed by a description of each card drawn:

```
Card drawn: <value> <suit>
```

where <value> is one of 2 through 10, J, Q, K, or A and <suit> is one of Hearts, Diamonds, Spades, or Clubs.

When the drawing terminates, the program displays all eight cards atop the stacks and the total number of cards drawn:

```
Total cards drawn: <n>

Stack tops:
```
<value1> <suit1>
<value2> <suit2>
<value3> <suit3>
<value4> <suit4>
<value5> <suit5>
<value6> <suit6>
<value7> <suit7>
<value8> <suit8>

ERROR HANDLING

If the user enters a nonpositive seed, the program repeatedly prompts until a positive value is input.

EXAMPLE

Below is a sample execution with input in color.

```
Please supply a positive integer to seed random numbers: 0
Please supply a positive integer to seed random numbers: -5
Please supply a positive integer to seed random numbers: 16

Card drawn: 2 Clubs
Card drawn: 7 Clubs
Card drawn: 6 Clubs
Card drawn: 5 Diamonds
Card drawn: K Diamonds
Card drawn: Q Diamonds
Card drawn: 9 Hearts
Card drawn: K Hearts
Card drawn: 7 Spades
Card drawn: 3 Spades
Card drawn: K Spades
Card drawn: A Clubs

Total cards drawn: 12

Stack tops:
    2 Clubs
    K Spades
    6 Clubs
    5 Diamonds
    A Clubs
    Q Diamonds
    9 Hearts
    3 Spades
```

3.4 First, work Exercise 3.14 above, writing a `PassMod` module that exports a `Password` class. Next, repeat Programming Project 2.5, layering the `MultPass` module on top of `PassMod`. But ignore the first sentence of that programming project—your `Password` class from Exercise 3.14 requires no modification whatsoever.

CHAPTER 4

Introduction to Data Structures

INTRODUCTION

In Chapter 3 we introduced the concept of an abstract data type. Using C++ classes, we designed and implemented three abstract data types: a random number generator type, a card deck type, and a fraction type. All of these data types have the following in common: an instance of the type represents a single item. A RandGen instance is a random number generator. A CardDeckType instance is one deck of cards. A FracType instance is a single fraction.

In this chapter, we examine data structures—data types in which one instance represents not just one item but a collection of items. Arrays are data structures familiar to most programmers. One array represents a collection of values, all related to each other in certain ways.

In addition to arrays, we look at data structures with names that may be less familiar: records, lists, stacks, queues, and sets. Using what we have learned about data abstraction in Chapter 3, for each data structure we define the abstract data values and the operations on those values.

In this chapter, we focus exclusively on the abstract properties, not the concrete implementations, of data structures. In Chapters 5 through 9 (which form Part II, *Tools for Implementation*), we will introduce additional C++ language features that allow us to implement these abstractions in different ways.

4.1 Data Types and Data Structures

Every data type has two defining characteristics:

1. the **domain** of the type (the set of all possible values)
2. a collection of allowable operations on those values

Some data types are available as built-in (standard) types in a programming language. Others must be defined as abstract data types using techniques like those we presented in Chapter 3. Definition 4.1 introduces a form that we use throughout this chapter to define the properties of a data type. We give a definition of the C++ `int` type, abbreviated by listing only a few of the permissible operations.

DATA TYPE   C++ `int` type

DOMAIN
A finite subset of the mathematical integers, where the least integer and the greatest integer are machine-dependent

OPERATIONS
```
=  Assign
+  Add
-  Subtract
*  Multiply
/  Divide, truncating result
== Test for equality
!= Test for inequality
etc.
```

Definition 4.1 The C++ `int` type

We also use this form to define abstract data types (**ADT**s). Chapter 3 introduced `FracType`, an ADT for storing and manipulating fractions. The definition of this type appears in Definition 4.2.

DATA TYPE   `FracType`

DOMAIN
All fractions in the form p/q, where p and q are `int` values and $q > 0$

OPERATIONS

`Write()`	Display fraction value in the form p/q
`FloatEquiv()`	Obtain floating point equivalent of fraction
`Simplify()`	Reduce fraction to lowest terms
`FracType(int p, int q)`	(Constructor) Create fraction p/q
`*`	Multiply two fractions
`==`	Test two fractions for equality

Definition 4.2 The `FracType` type

`FracType` is not built into the C++ language. It is a programmer-defined ADT, implemented by using the C++ `class` mechanism. The user of this abstraction depends only on the properties of the data type, not the concrete data representation of a fraction or the code that implements the operations.

Types such as `int` and `float` are called **simple data types** or **atomic data types.** A value in an atomic data type is a single data item; it cannot be broken down into constituent parts. In contrast, a **structured data type** or **data structure** has

1. component data items, each of which may be atomic or another data structure

2. rules that define how the components relate to each other and to the structure as a whole

In Definition 4.3 we define the C++ built-in array type. To describe the relationships among the components (item 2 above), the definition includes a section labeled STRUCTURE.

DATA TYPE   C++ array

DOMAIN
Each C++ array consists of

1. a collection of a fixed number of component values—each of the same type (either atomic or structured)
2. a set of index (subscript) values that are nonnegative integers

STRUCTURE
There is a one-to-one relationship between each index and an array component (array element). In particular, index 0 selects the first array element, index 1 selects the second array element, and so forth.

OPERATIONS
[i]   Retrieve the value of the array element associated with index i
[i]   Store a value into the array element associated with index i
         (The context determines whether to store or to retrieve. The assignment x=a[5] denotes retrieval, whereas the assignment a[5]=x denotes a store operation.)

Definition 4.3 The C++ built-in array type

Observe carefully that the OPERATIONS section refers to the data structure as a whole, not to individual components. For example, the OPERATIONS section in Definition 4.3 disallows the assignment operation

```
float a[20], b[20];
    ⋮
a = b;      ← No
```

because assignment is not a valid array operation. However, the assignment

```
a[i] = b[j];
```

is permissible, because subscripting is a valid operation for arrays and assignment is a valid operation for atomic float values.

Data structures are enormously powerful tools for designing and constructing programs. Real-world information often is organized into collections of related items, and programs that model real-world problems use data structures as containers for such collections. The software designer benefits from the ability to give one name to an entire collection of data values and to manipulate this collection either as a whole or in parts.

A well-chosen data structure—one that mirrors the essence of the real-world information—can simplify algorithms that would otherwise have to map information onto inadequate or inappropriate data structures. The remainder of this chapter and, indeed, most of this text explore the interplay of data structures and their associated algorithms.

4.2   Overview of Data Structures

In general, programming languages provide very few data structures as built-in types. The array, introduced in the earliest high-level languages, is by far the most common data structure. But many problems are not, by their nature, array-processing problems.

Figure 4.1 presents a classification of various data structures according to specific properties. It is important to think of these as ADTs, because no current language includes all of them as built-in types and their properties do not imply any particular form of concrete data representation.

The list of data structures in this figure—array, record, list, stack, queue, and set—is by no means comprehensive. There are many others: search tables, keyed tables, strings, priority queues, sequences, ordered sequences, and so forth. We have selected these six because (a) they are widely used, and (b) the methods of analyzing and implementing these structures are applicable to others as you encounter them.

Figure 4.1 first classifies a data structure according to whether it is linear or nonlinear. A **linear data structure** is one whose components are ordered in

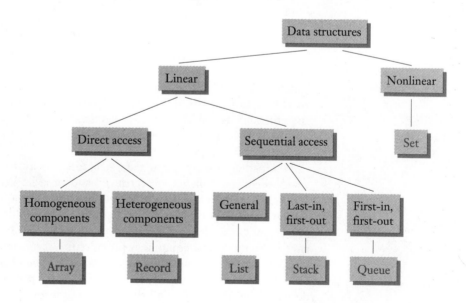

Figure 4.1 Classification of selected data structures

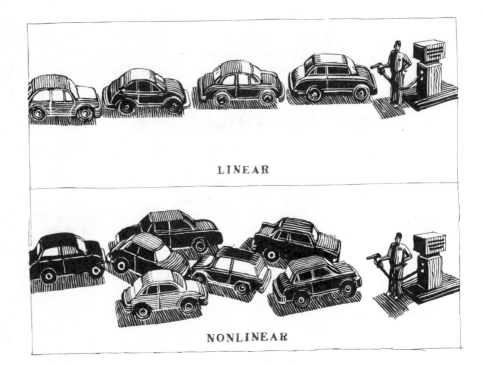

LINEAR

NONLINEAR

Linear and nonlinear
structuring

the following way. If there are two or more components, then the following
are all true:

• There is a unique first component.
• There is a unique last component.
• Every component (except the first) has a unique predecessor.
• Every component (except the last) has a unique successor.

The built-in array is an example of a linear data structure. However, the set—
an abstraction of the mathematical notion of a set—is a **nonlinear data
structure.** Sets are unordered collections of items. There is no designated
first or last element in a set, and no element precedes or succeeds another.
We will investigate sets later in the chapter.

    We further classify linear data structures by **access method,** the way in
which their components are retrieved and stored. With **direct access** data
structures, you can select component i directly without accessing the first $i - 1$
components along the way. With **sequential access** data structures, you must
pass through the first $i - 1$ components in sequence before accessing component i. Stereo sound equipment provides the classic analogy. Turntables and
compact disc players afford direct access to, say, the fifth selection on an album
or compact disc. On the other hand, a cassette player is a sequential access
device. The tape must wind through the first four selections before reaching
the fifth.

    Further subdivisions of direct and sequential access structures will unfold as
we discuss the six data structures in more detail.

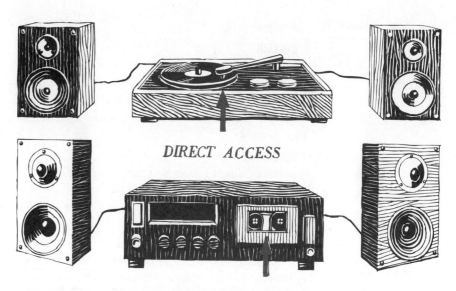

DIRECT ACCESS

SEQUENTIAL ACCESS

Direct access versus
sequential access

4.3 Arrays

The **array** is the data structure most familiar to programmers. Components are called **array elements,** and individual elements are selected by an **index** or **subscript** expression. Arrays have the following two distinguishing characteristics:

1. direct access to a component (array element) through an index expression
2. **homogeneous** components

The second characteristic means that all elements of an array must have identical type.

A more formal definition of the array—as an ADT—appears in Definition 4.4.

An array is like a
collection of P.O. boxes.

DATA TYPE   Array-as-ADT

DOMAIN

Each array consists of

1. a collection of a fixed number of component values—each of the same type (either atomic or structured)

2. a set of index values whose data type has a one-to-one correspondence with the integers

STRUCTURE

A linear, direct access structure with a one-to-one relationship between each index and an array element. The first value in the index type selects the first array element, the second value in the index type selects the second array element, and so forth.

OPERATIONS

ValueAt(i)   Retrieve the value of the array element associated with index i

Store(i, v)   Store value v into the array element associated with index i

Definition 4.4 The array as an ADT

The array as an abstraction has a common and familiar implementation: the built-in array type in a programming language. In turn, languages usually (but not always) implement built-in array types by using **contiguous allocation** of memory cells as the data representation. With contiguous allocation, the array elements are physically located one after the other in memory. The resulting implementation hierarchy has three layers of abstraction:

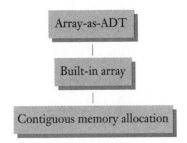

Because the bottom layer of this hierarchy is so widely used, we have come to expect that contiguous allocation is an inherent property of arrays. But Definition 4.4 defines the array as an ADT and does not restrict us to any particular data representation. We will see in subsequent chapters that contiguous allocation is only one possible representation for an array.

4.4   Records

The **record** is another direct access data structure. Components of a record usually are called **fields**, and individual fields are selected by a **field name** or

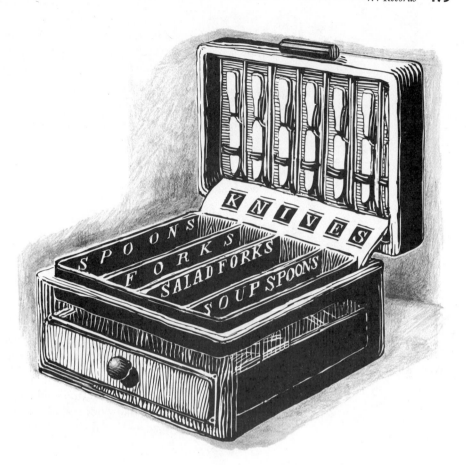

A record is like a silverware chest, storing items of different types.

field identifier. Records have the following two distinguishing characteristics:

1. direct access to a component (field) by means of the field name
2. **heterogeneous** components

The second characteristic means that the fields of a record may have different types.

In many programming languages, records are built-in types. The following type declaration, which is not C++ but a pseudolanguage notation, is typical:

```
type PatientRec = record        ←— This is not C++.
                String    patientName;
                String    patientAddress;
                Integer   patientAge;
                Floating  balanceDue;
            end record
```

In this example, the PatientRec type includes four heterogeneous fields, each selected by a field name (such as patientAge) instead of an index or subscript. Programming languages often use a dot (.) to denote field selection:

thisPatient.patientAge = 24;

Definition 4.5 presents a more formal definition of the record as an ADT.

DATA TYPE Record-as-ADT

DOMAIN
Each record consists of

1. a collection of a fixed number of component (field) values—which may be of different types (either atomic or structured)
2. a set of identifiers (field names) for selecting each component

STRUCTURE
A linear, direct access structure with a one-to-one relationship between each field name and a field of the record

OPERATIONS
ValueAt(*fname*) Retrieve the value of the field whose name is *fname*
Store(*fname, v*) Store value v into the field whose name is *fname*

Definition 4.5 The record as an ADT

Here we define the record as an ADT to avoid confusion with built-in record types. C++ is one language that does include records as standard data types. The next chapter presents details of their declaration and usage.

4.5 Lists

A **list** is a linear data structure whose components (called **list items** or **list elements**) can only be accessed sequentially, one after the other. The first item in the list is called the **head** or **front** of the list, and the last item is called the **tail, back,** or **end** of the list. Lists have the following three distinctive features:

1. Varying length. (The length of the list grows and shrinks as new items are inserted and old items are deleted.)
2. Homogeneous components.
3. Sequential access to components through an implicit **list cursor.**

Think of the list cursor as a pointer that keeps track of where you are as you sequence through the list. At any time you can reset the list cursor to the front of the list, advance it one item at a time to inspect an item, delete an item, insert an item before or after the current item, and so on.

A list is like a line of identical trucks at a weigh station, and the list cursor is like the scale.

Definition 4.6 displays the definition of the list data structure. The specifications of the operations are more comprehensive than those we gave for arrays and records. The reason is that many languages such as Pascal and C++ offer arrays and records as built-in types, but they do not offer lists. In these languages, a programmer typically implements array and record abstractions by using built-in array and record types directly. But to implement a list abstraction, the programmer must use a mechanism such as the C++ class and, therefore, needs a precise description of the pre- and postconditions for the operations.

DATA TYPE List

Definition 4.6 The list type

DOMAIN

Each list consists of

1. a collection of component values—each of the same type (either atomic or structured)

2. an implicit list cursor in the range 1 through $n + 1$, where n is the current length of the list

STRUCTURE

A linear, sequential access structure of varying length

NOTE

Conceptually, there is no upper bound on the length of a list. But in practical terms, a computer's memory size is bounded and so is the length of a list. Below, the phrase "list is full" means the maximum length has been reached.

OPERATIONS (expressed as C++ class member functions)

Create( );
    // POST: Empty list created && EndOfList( ) (See EndOfList( ) below)

Boolean IsEmpty( );
    // POST: FCTVAL == (list is empty)

Boolean IsFull( );
    // POST: FCTVAL == (list is full)

void Reset( );
    // PRE: NOT IsEmpty( )
    // POST: List cursor is at front of list

```
Boolean EndOfList( );
   // POST: FCTVAL == (list cursor is beyond end of list)

void Advance( );
   // PRE:   NOT IsEmpty( ) && NOT EndOfList( )
   // POST: List cursor has advanced to next item

ItemType CurrentItem( );
   // PRE:   NOT IsEmpty( ) && NOT EndOfList( )
   // POST: FCTVAL == item at list cursor

void InsertBefore( /* in */ ItemType someItem );
   // PRE:   Assigned(someItem) && NOT IsFull( )
   // POST: someItem inserted before list cursor
   //          (at back, if EndOfList( ))
   //       &&This is the new current item

void InsertAfter( /* in */ ItemType someItem );
   // PRE:   Assigned(someItem) && NOT IsEmpty( )
   //       &&NOT IsFull( ) && NOT EndOfList( )
   // POST: someItem inserted after list cursor
   //       &&This is the new current item

void Delete( );
   // PRE:   NOT IsEmpty( ) && NOT EndOfList( )
   // POST: Item at list cursor deleted
   //       &&Successor of deleted item is now the current item
```

The operations we have chosen are arbitrary. Some designers specify a more limited selection, such as allowing items to be inserted only at the tail of the list. Others prefer a more extensive repertoire, including operations to insert an item at the front, append an item at the tail, return the current position number (the value of the list cursor), find the ith item, delete the ith item, and so forth. Our goal for an introduction to the list data structure is to provide the most flexibility in as thin an interface as possible.

The primary advantage of lists over arrays is the ease of performing insertions and deletions. Suppose a program maintains a collection of alphabetic characters, and the programmer wants to delete the first occurrence of 'Q' from the collection. If a C++ class named CharList is available and provides operations such as those in Definition 4.6, the programmer might do the following:

```
CharList letterGroup;

   :

// ASSERT: 'Q' is definitely somewhere in the letterGroup list
letterGroup.Reset();
while (letterGroup.CurrentItem() != 'Q')
    letterGroup.Advance();
letterGroup.Delete();
```

If the programmer uses an array instead of a list to store the characters, deletion of an item requires shifting all subsequent array elements up by one position to fill in the hole. Using an abstract array type named `CharArray`, the algorithm is

```
CharArray letterGroup(200);    // Array ADT with 200 elements and
                               // indices 0 through 199
  .
  .
  .
// ASSERT: 'Q' is definitely somewhere in the array
i = 0;
while (letterGroup.ValueAt(i) != 'Q')
    i++;
for (j = i; j < 199; j++) {
    someChar = letterGroup.ValueAt(j+1);
    letterGroup.Store(j, someChar);
}
```

Both algorithms need a loop to find the character 'Q'. After that, deleting the character from a `CharList` requires only one operation (`Delete`), whereas deleting it from a `CharArray` requires a second loop to shift up all the remaining characters in the array.

The primary disadvantage of lists versus arrays is that direct access of a component is impossible. To output the 23rd list item requires sequencing through the first 22 items:

```
letterGroup.Reset();
for (count = 1; count <= 22; count++)
    letterGroup.Advance();
cout << letterGroup.CurrentItem();
```

In contrast, direct retrieval of an array element is, of course, a fundamental characteristic of arrays:

```
cout << letterGroup.ValueAt(22);
```

In summary, the list data structure is preferable when the frequency of inserting and deleting items is significantly greater than the frequency of selecting (storing and retrieving) existing items. If item selection occurs far more often than insertions and deletions, then the array, as a direct access structure, is more appropriate.

4.6   Stacks

Another sequential access data structure is the **stack.** A stack, sometimes called a **push down stack,** is a restricted form of a list in which all insertions and deletions occur at only one end. This end is called the **top** of the stack.

A stack is analogous to a box of paper. When you place a new sheet of paper into the box it goes on top of all the other sheets. You can examine or remove only the top sheet of paper. To access sheets further into the box, you must remove all of the sheets above it.

A stack is like a box of paper.

For a stack data structure, a **Push** operation places a new data item on top of the stack. Only the top item is visible at any time, and its value is examined by a **Top** operation. A **Pop** operation removes the top item from the stack. (Some definitions of a stack combine Top and Pop into a single operation. In this case, inspecting the top item also removes it.)

A stack is often referred to as a **Last-In, First-Out (LIFO)** structure, because the last item placed on top is the first item to be removed. Figure 4.2 depicts a stack and its associated operations.

There are numerous examples of stacks in the real world. Stacks of dinner plates often are stored in spring-loaded dispensers in a cafeteria. Only the top plate is accessible at any one time. A person can examine it (Top), remove it (Pop), or store a new one (Push). A driveway that is only one car wide also functions as a stack. A driver must remove the last car in the drive before removing any that was parked in the driveway earlier.

Stacks also have many applications in computer science. One example is a computer system's **run-time stack,** an area in memory that contains informa-

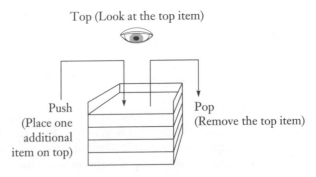

Figure 4.2 A stack and its operations

tion about the currently executing program. The current program may call functions that, in turn, call other functions. When function A calls function B, the system pushes A's **return address** (the memory address of the instruction immediately following the function call) onto the run-time stack before transferring control to B. When B returns, the system pops the top of the stack to obtain the correct return address. Control then transfers to this return address in function A.

The system stores more than return addresses on the run-time stack, but we focus only on these return addresses to simplify the discussion. Figure 4.3 illustrates the pushing and popping of return addresses during the execution of a (clumsy) program that prints the message "NOW IS THE TIME". The memory addresses shown in the left-hand margin are arbitrary, chosen for demonstration only.

As Figure 4.3 shows, the run-time stack eliminates any ambiguity about which function called another. The last-in, first-out discipline ensures that control will return to the function that most recently made a function call.

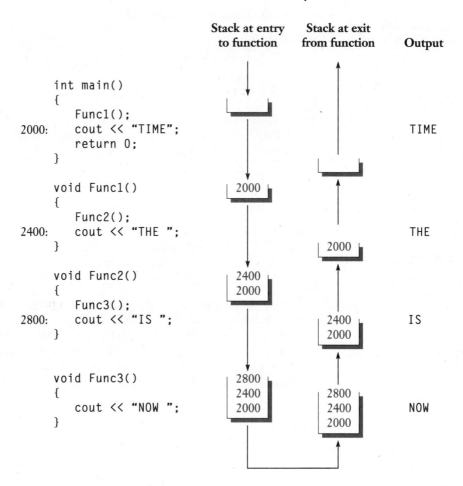

Figure 4.3 Return addresses on the run-time stack

Definition 4.7 presents a definition of the stack as an abstract data type.

DATA TYPE Stack

DOMAIN

Each stack is a collection of component values, each of the same type (either atomic or structured).

STRUCTURE

A list, maintained in LIFO order so that only the most recently inserted item is accessible

NOTE

Conceptually, there is no upper bound on the length of a stack. But in practical terms, a computer's memory size is bounded and so is the length of a stack. Below, the phrase "stack is full" means the maximum length has been reached.

OPERATIONS (expressed as C++ class member functions)

Create( );
  // POST: Empty stack created

Boolean IsEmpty( );
  // POST: FCTVAL == (stack is empty)

Boolean IsFull( );
  // POST: FCTVAL == (stack is full)

void Push(/* in */ ItemType newItem);
  // PRE: NOT IsFull( ) && Assigned(newItem)
  // POST: newItem is at top of stack

ItemType Top( );
  // PRE: NOT IsEmpty( )
  // POST: FCTVAL == item at top of stack

void Pop( );
  // PRE: NOT IsEmpty( )
  // POST: Top item removed from stack

Definition 4.7 The stack type

A simple example of using a stack within a program is to input a sequence of characters and output them in reverse order. Assume that a C++ class named CharStack is available with operations as shown in Definition 4.7. Replace ItemType with char, and assume that the Create operation is implemented as a C++ class constructor. For this algorithm, the input loop terminates when either the stack is full or the end of the file is encountered:

```
CharStack stk;
char      ch;
```

```
while ( !stk.IsFull() && cin.get(ch) ) {
    stk.Push(ch);
    if (stk.IsFull())
        cout << "Max. number of characters reached\n";
}
while ( !stk.IsEmpty() ) {
    cout << stk.Top();
    stk.Pop();
}
```

Exercises at the end of this chapter give you further opportunities to program with stacks.

4.7 Queues

The **queue,** like the stack, is a restricted form of the list data structure. With a queue, all insertions occur at the tail of the list and all deletions occur at the head. The head and tail of a queue are often called the **front** and **rear,** respectively.

At least three operations usually are defined for queues. The **Enqueue** operation appends a new item to the rear of the queue. The **Dequeue** operation removes the item at the front of the queue. The **Front** operation inspects, but does not remove, the first item in the queue. (Some interpretations of the queue structure combine the Dequeue and Front operations.)

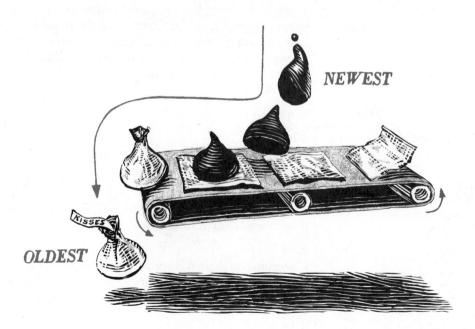

A queue is like an assembly line.

Front (Look at the front item)

Figure 4.4 A queue and
its operations

Figure 4.4 depicts a queue and its associated operations. The queue contains four values; 7 is at the front of the queue and 3 is at the rear.

Queues are **FIFO** (**First-In, First-O**ut) structures. Waiting lines and assembly lines are both examples of queues. Objects enter an assembly line from one end and exit from the opposite end in the same order in which they entered. People entering a waiting line are said to be "queued" when they go to the rear of the line. These people must wait in the queue until it is their turn to be served at the front of the queue. A well-known phrase that captures the spirit of a queue is "first come, first served."

The operating system of a computer also uses queues extensively. **Buffered input** is one example. When a user types at a computer keyboard, the characters corresponding to the keystrokes are stored in a buffer, an area of memory that functions as a queue. The operating system, instead of processing each character the moment it arrives, enqueues the characters until a carriage return character is received. The operating system then examines these characters, removing them from the queue in the same order in which they were typed.

Another example of a queue within an operating system is the printer queue. Several users may simultaneously request the use of the same printer. The operating system must enqueue and satisfy each request one at a time to prevent one user's output from being interleaved with another's.

The definition of the queue as an abstract data type appears in Definition 4.8.

DATA TYPE   Queue

Definition 4.8 The queue type

DOMAIN
Each queue is a collection of component values, each of the same type (either atomic or structured).

STRUCTURE
A list, maintained in FIFO order so that insertions take place at the rear and deletions take place at the front

NOTE
Conceptually, there is no upper bound on the length of a queue. But in practical terms, a computer's memory size is bounded and so is the length of a queue. Below, the phrase "queue is full" means the maximum length has been reached.

OPERATIONS (expressed as C++ class member functions)
Create( );
   // POST: Empty queue created

```
Boolean IsEmpty( );
   // POST: FCTVAL == (queue is empty)

Boolean IsFull( );
   // POST: FCTVAL == (queue is full)

void Enqueue( /* in */ ItemType newItem );
   // PRE:   NOT IsFull( )  &&  Assigned(newItem)
   // POST: newItem is at rear of queue

ItemType Front( );
   // PRE:   NOT IsEmpty( )
   // POST: FCTVAL == item at front of queue

void Dequeue( );
   // PRE:   NOT IsEmpty( )
   // POST: Front item removed from queue
```

A Study in Design

A Theater Simulation

It is common to find queue data structures being used in **simulation** programs, programs that model real-world events and track their behavior over time. A theater manager wants a program that simulates a line of box office customers waiting to see one of two movies, A or B. The manager knows that if the wait-

A ticket line to be simulated with a queue

ing line gets too long, newly arriving customers will turn away, perhaps to find another theater. The desired program will simulate the activity in the waiting line over a 30-minute time period, concluding with a report of the following: the number of paid customers for movie A, the number of paid customers for movie B, and the number of customers who turned away because the line was too long.

The manager's experience suggests that the average time to serve one customer is ten seconds, and during those ten seconds, the probability is 70 percent that a new customer will join the waiting line. To simulate a 30-minute time span, the program will cover 180 ten-second time intervals. In each ten-second interval, one customer will be served from the front of the line and, with 70 percent probability, one customer will join the rear of the line.

For this simulation, assume a C++ class named CharQueue is available with the operations shown in Definition 4.8. Exceptions are that ItemType is replaced by char, and the Create operation is implemented as a C++ class constructor. The simulation program, shown in Figure 4.5, imports this CharQueue class as well as the RandGen class (Chapter 3) for generating random numbers. The program simulates a customer's entering the waiting line by enqueueing the character 'A' or 'B', the customer's choice of movies. Each 'A' or 'B' is obtained by generating a random integer of 0 or 1 and then adding it to the character 'A'. (Recall that the char type is an integral type in C++. The internal representation of the ASCII character 'A' is 65. Adding 0 or 1 to 65 yields 65 or 66, the internal representations of 'A' and 'B'.)

Figure 4.5 Theater simulation program

```
// ----------------------------------------------------------------
// theater.cpp
// This program simulates a movie theater queue, where customers
// attend either movie A or movie B
// ----------------------------------------------------------------
#include "rand2.h"
#include "cqueue.h"
#include <iostream.h>

int main()
{
    CharQueue theaterQ;
    RandGen   rGen;
    int       timeUnit;
    int       turnedAway = 0;
    int       numA = 0;
    int       numB = 0;
    char      movieChoice;      // 'A' or 'B'
```

```
    for (timeUnit = 1; timeUnit <= 180; timeUnit++) {
        if ( !theaterQ.IsEmpty() ) {
            if (theaterQ.Front() == 'A')
                numA++;
            else
                numB++;
            theaterQ.Dequeue();
        }
        if (rGen.NextRand() <= 0.7)
            if (theaterQ.IsFull())
                turnedAway++;
            else {
                movieChoice = 'A' + int(rGen.NextRand()*2.0);
                theaterQ.Enqueue(movieChoice);
            }
    }
    cout << "Theater A customers: " << numA << '\n';
    cout << "Theater B customers: " << numB << '\n';
    cout << "No. turned away: " << turnedAway << '\n';

    return 0;
}
```

Below is the output produced by an execution of the above program:

```
Theater A customers: 52
Theater B customers: 64
No. turned away: 0
```

4.8   Sets

The **set** is one of the basic building blocks of mathematics. Sets are collections of objects, such as sets of numbers, sets of Boolean values, or sets of geometric points. The objects in a set are called its **elements.** A set has three important properties:

1. All elements of the set belong to some **universe** (the collection of all values that are potential elements of a set).

2. There are only two possibilities for any object from the universe—either it is an element of the set or it is not.

3. There is no particular ordering of elements within the set.

A set is like a shoebox of different items.

The second property implies that an element can appear in a set only once. Thus, both of the following denote the same set:

$$\{1, 2, 7\} = \{1, 1, 2, 7, 7, 7\}$$

The third property states that elements of a set are unordered. The value 7 neither precedes nor follows the value 2 in the set. The following sets are therefore equivalent:

$$\{1, 2, 7\} = \{7, 1, 2\} = \{7, 2, 2, 1, 7, 2\}$$

The **null set** or **empty set,** denoted by "{ }", is the set that has no elements. The **cardinality** of a set is the number of distinct elements in the set. The empty set has cardinality zero. An **infinite set,** such as the set of all even numbers, has infinitely many elements. A **finite set** has cardinality that can be expressed as a nonnegative integer. Sets used in computer programs are understandably finite sets, because the memory capacity of any computer is finite.

Binary operations on two sets S1 and S2 include **set intersection** (the set of elements common to both S1 and S2), **set union** (the set of elements that are in at least one of S1 and S2), and **set difference,** written S1 – S2 (the set of all elements of S1 that are not also elements of S2).

Relational operations on S1 and S2 include **set equality** (S1 equals S2 if they contain exactly the same elements) and **subset of** (S1 is a subset of S2 if every element of S1 is also an element of S2). Another common set operation is **set membership** (TRUE if an object x is an element of set S, FALSE otherwise).

Although set theory is the province of mathematics, sets are often good abstractions for real-world information. Doctors are concerned with the set of all illnesses that they must treat. Teachers are concerned with the set of all students in a particular class. Students are concerned with the set of all classes that are available next semester.

The ability to recognize set abstractions will help you as you decide how to represent information within a program. To decide whether an abstract collection of objects is a set, ask these two questions:

1. Is it possible for an object to appear in the collection many times?

2. Is the order of the objects in the collection important?

A set is appropriate only if the answer to both questions is no.

Pascal and Modula-2 include sets as built-in types in the language. Sets are not built-in types in C++, but the programmer can use the class mechanism to implement sets. Definition 4.9 defines the set as an abstract data type.

DATA TYPE Set

Definition 4.9 The set type

DOMAIN
Each set is a collection of component values, each of the same type (either atomic or structured).

STRUCTURE
A nonlinear collection of values corresponding to a mathematical set

NOTE
Conceptually, there is no upper bound on the size of a set. But in practical terms, a computer's memory size is bounded and so is the size of a set. Below, the phrase "set is full" means the maximum size has been reached.

OPERATIONS (expressed as C++ class member functions)
Create( );
    // POST: Set is created && set == { }

Boolean IsEmpty( );
    // POST: FCTVAL == (set == { })

Boolean IsFull( );
    // POST: FCTVAL == (set is full)

void Insert(/* in */ ElementType elt);
    // PRE: Assigned(elt) && NOT IsFull( )
    // POST: set == set<entry> UNION {elt}

void Delete(/* in */ ElementType elt);
    // PRE: Assigned(elt)
    // POST: set == set<entry> – {elt}

Boolean IsElt(/* in */ ElementType elt);
    // PRE: Assigned(elt)
    // POST: FCTVAL == (elt is an element of the set)

> **NOTE**
>
> Each of the following operations takes two entire sets as operands and returns an entire set.
>
> SetType Intersect(/* in */ SetType set2);
>   // POST: FCTVAL == (this set) INTERSECT set2
>
> SetType Union(/* in */ SetType set2);
>   // POST: FCTVAL == (this set) UNION set2

For brevity, Definition 4.9 includes a rather limited set of operations. To fully model mathematical sets, we also would include operations such as SubsetOf, Difference, Equal, and Cardinality.

Consider analyzing a stream of input characters to determine which characters were encountered. We may only want to know *if* a given character was encountered, not *how many* times it was encountered. In this case, a set whose elements are single characters is an appropriate abstraction. Upon conclusion of the input, the character 'A' is either in the set (once) or it is not. Furthermore, the order of the elements in the set is immaterial.

Suppose a C++ class named CharSet is available with the operations shown in Definition 4.9. Exceptions are that ElementType is replaced by char, and the Create operation is implemented as a C++ class constructor. The universe of CharSet is the complete set of char constants. Because this universe is small (128 constants in the ASCII character set and 256 in EBCDIC), let us assume that the class specification announces that IsFull() always returns FALSE.

In Figure 4.6, the FindChar program makes use of the CharSet class. This program inputs a passage of text and identifies all printable characters that were encountered. The figure also includes a sample run-time dialog with the user.

Notice how the program makes short work of testing for printable characters by importing the isprint function from the C++ standard library. Appendix G describes isprint and other useful character-testing routines available through the header file ctype.h.

Figure 4.6 FindChar program

```
// ---------------------------------------------------------------
//   findchar.cpp
//   This program identifies all printable characters that are read
//   from standard input
//   Note: ASCII character encoding is assumed
// ---------------------------------------------------------------
#include "cset.h"
#include <iostream.h>
#include <ctype.h>        // For isprint()
```

```
int main()
{
    char    ch;
    CharSet cSet;
    // ASSERT: cSet == {}

    cout << "Enter text below, terminated by <EOF>\n\n";

    while (cin.get(ch))      // INV (prior to test):
                             //      Each printable char prior to ch
                             //          is in cSet
                             //   && EOF not yet encountered
        if (isprint(ch))
            cSet.Insert(ch);

    cout << "\nThe set of characters found in your input is:\n\n";
    cout << '{';
    for (ch = ' '; ch <= '~'; ch++)
        if (cSet.IsElt(ch))
            cout << " '" << ch << "' ";
    cout << '}';

    return 0;
}
```

Below is a sample execution of the above program with input in color:

```
Enter text below, terminated by <EOF>

Abracadabra, she said!
<EOF>

The set of characters found in your input is:

{ ' '  '!'  ','  'A'  'a'  'b'  'c'  'd'  'e'  'h'  'i'  'r'  's' }
```

SUMMARY

The world of data types is divided into simple (atomic) data types and structured data types (data structures). Values in an atomic data type cannot be decomposed into constituent parts, whereas data structures have component data elements along with rules defining how the components relate to each other.

Real-world information often occurs as collections of related items. Data structures, along with their affiliated algorithms, are indispensable for representing and manipulating such collections within a program.

For two reasons, it is important to define data structures as abstract data types (ADTs). First, doing so allows us to focus on their properties without being distracted by implementation details. Second, many useful data structures are not built-in types in programming languages. In these cases, a programmer must implement the abstractions by choosing suitable concrete data representations and designing algorithms to implement the associated operations.

We can classify data structures broadly as linear or nonlinear. Linear data structures are those whose components are ordered by a unique-predecessor/unique-successor relationship and have a first and last component. Nonlinear data structures, such as the set, have no such ordering. A set is a collection of values from some universe, and a value from the universe is either in the set (once) or it is not.

Linear data structures are categorized by their access method: direct access or sequential access. Arrays and records are both direct access structures. Array components, which must be homogeneous, are accessed directly via an index or subscript. Record components, which may be heterogeneous, are accessed directly via the field name. Many programming languages provide arrays and records as built-in types.

Sequential access data structures include lists, stacks, and queues. Any item in a general list is accessible relative to an implicit cursor that advances one item at a time. Stacks are LIFO lists in which all insertions and deletions occur at one end, called the top. Queues are FIFO lists in which all insertions occur at the rear and all deletions occur at the front.

Lists, stacks, and queues are more appropriate than arrays and records when insertions and deletions are frequent. No special algorithms are necessary; the insert and delete operations are inherent in the data types. What is sacrificed, though, is the ability to access a component at random.

This chapter has introduced only a few of the most common data structures. The skilled programmer, through observation and experience, is familiar with many data structures and carefully chooses those that are most compatible with the problem being solved.

KEY TERMS

access method (p. 170)
ADT (p. 167)
array (p. 171)
array element (p. 171)
atomic data type (p. 167)
back (of a list) (p. 174)
buffered input (p. 182)
cardinality (p. 186)
contiguous allocation (p. 172)
data structure (p. 167)
Dequeue operation (p. 181)
direct access (p. 170)
domain (p. 166)
empty set (p. 186)
end (of a list) (p. 174)
Enqueue operation (p. 181)
field identifier (p. 173)
field name (p. 172)

FIFO (p. 182)
finite set (p. 186)
front (of a list) (p. 174)
front (of a queue) (p. 181)
Front operation (p. 181)
head (of a list) (p. 174)
heterogeneous (p. 173)
homogeneous (p. 171)
index (p. 171)
infinite set (p. 186)
LIFO (p. 178)
linear data structure (p. 169)
list (p. 174)
list cursor (p. 174)
list item (p. 174)
nonlinear data structure (p. 170)
null set (p. 186)
Pop operation (p. 178)

EXERCISES

4.1 What are the principal differences between each of the following:

a. arrays and records

b. arrays and lists

c. lists and sets

d. stacks and queues

4.2 Assume that cList is a list of type CharList (Section 4.5) with current contents (head to tail) of 'p', 'q', '#', 'A', and 'N'. We use the following symbolism to denote the list:

$$(p, q, \#, A, N)$$

Suppose, further, that the value of the list cursor is 4 so that 'A' is the current item.

Give the contents of cList after execution of each code segment below. Answer each part independently of the others, using the above initial conditions for each part.

a. `cList.InsertBefore('X');`

b. `cList.InsertAfter('X');`

c. `cList.Delete();`
`   cList.Delete();`

d. `while ( !cList.EndOfList() )`
`       cList.Advance();`
`   cList.InsertBefore('Y');`

e. `cList.Reset();`
`   while (cList.CurrentItem() != '#')`
`       cList.Advance();`
`   cList.InsertAfter('Z');`

4.3 Assume that stk1 and stk2 are stacks of type CharStack (Section 4.6), where stk1 is currently empty and stk2 currently contains 'A', 'P', and 'M' (top to bottom):

stk1

stk2

Diagram the contents of both stacks after execution of each code segment below. Answer each part independently of the others, using the above initial contents for each part.

a. ```
stk1.Push('B');
stk2.Pop();
stk2.Pop();
```

b. ```
stk1.Push(stk2.Top());
stk2.Pop();
stk1.Push('C');
stk2.Push('D');
```

c. ```
stk1.Push(stk2.Top());
stk1.Push(stk2.Top());
stk1.Push(stk2.Top());
```

d. ```
while ( !stk2.IsEmpty() ) {
    stk1.Push(stk2.Top());
    stk2.Pop();
}
```

e. ```
while (!stk2.IsEmpty()) {
    stk1.Push(stk2.Top());
    stk2.Pop();
}
while (!stk1.IsEmpty()) {
    stk2.Push(stk1.Top());
    stk1.Pop();
}
```

4.4 Assume that q1 and q2 are queues of type CharQueue (Section 4.7), where q1 is currently empty and q2 currently contains 'A', 'P', and 'M' (front to rear). We denote their contents as follows:

| q1 | q2 |
|---|---|
| () | (A, P, M) |

Give the contents of both queues after execution of each code segment below. Answer each part independently of the others, using the above initial contents for each part.

a. ```
q1.Enqueue('B');
q2.Dequeue();
q2.Dequeue();
```

b. ```
q1.Enqueue(q2.Front());
q2.Dequeue();
```
```

```
            q1.Enqueue('C');
            q2.Enqueue('D');

    c.  q1.Enqueue(q2.Front());
        q1.Enqueue(q2.Front());
        q1.Enqueue(q2.Front());

    d.  while ( !q2.IsEmpty() ) {
            q1.Enqueue(q2.Front());
            q2.Dequeue();
        }

    e.  while (q2.Front() != 'M') {
            q1.Enqueue(q2.Front());
            q2.Dequeue();
        }
        while ( !q1.IsEmpty() ) {
            q2.Enqueue(q1.Front());
            q1.Dequeue();
        }
```

4.5 Assume that s1 and s2 are sets of type CharSet (Section 4.8) with the following initial contents:

s1   **s2**
{B, e, +, c}   {m, M, e, *, A}

Give the contents of both sets after execution of each code segment below. Answer each part independently of the others, using the above initial contents for each part.

```
    a.  s1.Insert('X');
        s1.Delete('Y');

    b.  if (s2.IsElt('m'))
            s2 = s1.Intersect(s2);
        else
            s2.Delete('A');

    c.  s1 = s1.Union(s2);

    d.  for (ch = 'A'; ch <='Z'; ch++)
            if (s1.IsElt(ch))
                s2.Insert(ch);

    e.  for (count = 1; count <= 10; count++)
            s1.Insert('X');
```

4.6 One way to implement a queue is to use two stacks as the underlying data representation. Assume that you have two stacks, mainStk and auxStk, of type CharStack (Section 4.6) with their associated stack operations Push, Pop, Top, and IsEmpty. Show an algorithm for Enqueue and another for Dequeue.

  Hint: mainStk represents the queue itself and auxStk is an auxiliary stack for intermediate results.

4.7 Below is the specification of a function that takes two lists of type `CharList` (Section 4.5), concatenates (joins) the second to the end of the first, and returns the resulting list. Write the body of the function. (Recall that in assertions, the right arrow "`-->`" means "implies".)

```
void Concatenate( /* in */  CharList  list1,
                  /* in */  CharList  list2,
                  /* out */ CharList& newList,
                  /* out */ Boolean&  tooLong );
    // POST: tooLong == (resulting list would exceed max CharList
    //        length)
    //     && (tooLong) --> value of newList is undefined
    //     && (NOT tooLong) --> newList is list obtained by joining
    //                          head of list2 to tail of list1
    // NOTE: list1 and/or list2 may be empty
```

4.8 Below is the specification of a function that takes a set of type `CharSet` (Section 4.8) and returns its cardinality (the number of distinct elements in the set). Write the body of the function.

```
int Cardinality( /* in */  CharSet someSet );
    // POST: FCTVAL == cardinality of someSet
```

Caution: Some C++ compilers treat the type `char` as `unsigned char`. Others (including Turbo C++ and Borland C++) treat it as `signed char`. With the latter, the following code—designed to cycle through all ASCII characters—generates an infinite loop:

```
        char ch;
        for (ch = 0; ch < 128; ch++)
        ⋮
```

The reason is that when `ch` is incremented past 127, it becomes a negative number. The solution is to cast `ch` to type `unsigned int` in the loop test:

```
        for (ch = 0; (unsigned int) ch < 128; ch++)
```

(To review type casting, see Section A.9 of Appendix A or Section B.7 of Appendix B.)

4.9 Write a short program that uses three queues of type `CharQueue` (Sections 4.7 and 4.8). This program inputs characters from the standard input stream until end-of-file is reached, then outputs all the uppercase letters that were encountered, then all the lowercase letters that were encountered, and then all the digits that were encountered. Any other characters are ignored. For each classification, the characters must be output in FIFO order. Feel free to use the standard library routines `isupper`, `islower`, and `isdigit` (Appendix G).

PROGRAMMING PROJECTS

Note: The following projects use the `CharList`, `CharStack`, `CharQueue`, and `CharSet` classes described in this chapter. The source code files for these classes are on the disk accompanying this book. See the READ.ME file on the disk for information on how to use them.

4.1 Suppose you wish to use the CharList class (Section 4.5) to maintain a list of lowercase letters *in alphabetical order.* Duplicate letters are permitted in the list. Write function bodies for each of the following function prototypes. Write a test driver and prepare a suitable test oracle.

```
void Insert( /* inout */ CharList& cList,
             /* in    */ char       someLetter,
             /* out   */ Boolean&   inserted   );
    // PRE:  someLetter is one of 'a'..'z'
    // POST: inserted == (cList<entry> not full)
    //       && (inserted) --> (someLetter inserted into cList with
    //                          alphabetical ordering preserved
    //                          && someLetter is the new current item)
    //       && (NOT inserted) --> cList == cList<entry>

void Delete( /* inout */ CharList& cList,
             /* in    */ char       someLetter,
             /* out   */ Boolean&   found      );
    // PRE:  someLetter is one of 'a'..'z'
    // POST: found == (someLetter was found in cList)
    //       && (found) --> (First occurrence of someLetter deleted
    //                       from cList
    //                       && Successor of first occurrence of
    //                          someLetter is the new current item)
    //       && (NOT found) --> cList == cList<entry> except list
    //                          cursor is at front of list.

void PrintList( /* in */ CharList cList );
    // POST: (cList empty) --> "empty" displayed
    //       && (cList not empty) --> list items displayed, one letter
    //                                per output line
    //       && List cursor is beyond end of list
```

4.2 In computer programs as well as natural language text, certain opening and closing symbols must be balanced. To be balanced means that each opening symbol has a corresponding closing symbol. For example, the expression

$$(a + 3*(b - c)/(d + e))$$

has balanced parentheses, but the following expression does not:

$$(f - (g + (b * (i + j)))$$

A stack is a convenient data structure for checking whether opening and closing symbols are balanced. The basic algorithm is this:

Whenever an opening symbol is encountered in the input, push it on the stack. Each time a closing symbol appears, pop the stack. At the end of the input, the opening and closing symbols are balanced if and only if the stack is empty.

Write a C++ program that reads text from the standard input stream and checks for balanced braces ({ }). Use the CharStack class of Section 4.6. The program will conclude by issuing one of the following messages:

```
Braces match
More left than right braces
More right than left braces
Too many left braces in the input
```

The last message occurs if the stack becomes full.

Prepare a comprehensive test oracle. Your test oracle must include cases that produce all four of the above messages.

Notice that you can use this program to check for balanced braces in any C++ source program by redirecting input to come from a source code file.

4.3 Use the CharStack class (Section 4.6) to write and test a program for the following problem. Below the problem specification is a recommended strategy.

TITLE

Palindromes

DESCRIPTION

A *palindrome* is a string that reads the same forwards and backwards, disregarding punctuation and the distinction between uppercase and lowercase letters. Examples:

- the word LEVEL

- the sentence attributed to Napoleon when exiled to Elba:

  "Able was I, ere I saw Elba."

This program inputs several strings, one per input line, and determines whether each is a palindrome.

INPUT

The first input item, an integer constant, tells how many strings the program must analyze. After this input value, each string appears on a separate input line.

Although the program reads from standard input, it is assumed that the user has first prepared a data file containing the strings and will use command line redirection of standard input:

```
$ palind < myfile.txt
```

(If your system does not support command line redirection, perform file input from within your program using an ifstream. You may want to review the material on basic file I/O in Section C.1 of Appendix C.)

OUTPUT

Because input is likely to come from a file, there is no prompt to the user to start typing text. For each string, the program echoes the string, then prints either

```
     ** Is a palindrome **
```
or
```
     ** Is  N O T  a palindrome **
```

and then a blank line.

ERROR HANDLING

The program does not need to check for input errors.

EXAMPLE

Assume a file contains the following lines:

```
3
race car
In the twilight, I heard a nightingale.
Egad!  A base life defiles a bad age.
```

From this input file, the program produces the following output:

```
race car
** Is a palindrome **

In the twilight, I heard a nightingale.
** Is  N O T  a palindrome **

Egad!  A base life defiles a bad age.
** Is a palindrome **
```

Suggested strategy: Use two stacks and proceed as follows. As you input each character from the data line, echo it. If it's a letter, push its lowercase equivalent onto Stack 1. After the line is consumed, repeatedly pop a letter from Stack 1 and push it onto Stack 2 until half the letters have been transferred. Then determine if the two stacks are equal.

4.4 The theater manager (A Study in Design: A Theatre Simulation) now wants a more realistic simulation of the waiting queue. Expand the Theater program to accommodate the following changes:

1. Instead of starting the 30-minute simulation with an empty queue, prefill the queue with 75 customers before starting the main loop.

2. In each ten-second time interval, there is a 70 percent probability that *two* new customers, not one, will arrive.

3. The program will conclude by displaying the average queue length over all ten-second intervals, the cash receipts for movie A (at $3.50 per ticket) and movie B (at $5.00 per ticket), and the number of customers who turned away:

```
Avg queue length: 91.038889
Theater A receipts: $276.5
Theater B receipts: $505.0
No. turned away: 27
```

4.5 Use the CharSet class (Section 4.8) to write and test a program to solve the following problem:

TITLE

Character analysis

DESCRIPTION

This program inputs and analyzes a passage of text from an input file. The results of the analysis indicate the number of vowels, consonants, and punctuation marks in the passage. The program also displays the specific items in each category (apart from repetitions) that were encountered. For this program, a vowel is an uppercase or lowercase A, E, I, O, or U; a consonant is any letter other than a vowel; and a punctuation mark is a period, comma, colon, semicolon, double quotation mark, exclamation point, apostrophe, or question mark.

INPUT

Input comes from a data file containing natural language text. The end-of-file condition signals the end of input data.

The program reads its characters from standard input, so the user will redirect standard input on the command line:

```
$ analyze < myfile.txt
```

(If your system does not support command line redirection, perform file input from within your program using an ifstream. You may want to review the material on basic file I/O in Section C.1 of Appendix C.)

OUTPUT

Because input will come from a file, there is no prompt to the user to start typing text. After analyzing the input text, the program outputs the results in the following form:

```
Total vowels: <v>
Distinct vowels: <v1> <v2> ...

Total consonants: <c>
Distinct consonants: <c1> <c2> ...

Total punc. marks: <p>
Distinct punc. marks: <p1> <p2> ...
```

where \<v\> is the total number of vowels in the text, each \<vi\> is a distinct vowel encountered in the text, \<c\> is the total number of consonants, each \<ci\> is a distinct consonant, \<p\> is the number of punctuation marks, and each \<pi\> is a distinct punctuation mark.

ERROR HANDLING

The program does not need to check for input errors.

EXAMPLE

Assume that the input file contains the following text:

```
"Try," he said.
"Why?" she said.
"For two reasons: first, it's elementary; second, it's out
of the ordinary!"
```

From this input file, the program produces the following output:

```
Total vowels: 27
Distinct vowels: a  e  i  o  u

Total consonants: 48
Distinct consonants: F  T  W  c  d  f  h  l  m  n  r  s  t
w  y

Total punc. marks: 17
Distinct punc. marks: !  "  '  ,  .  :  ;  ?
```

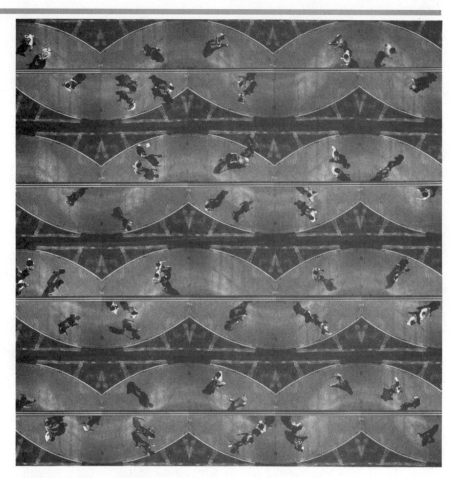

Tools For Implementation

CHAPTER 5

C++ *Records* (structs) *and Unions*

INTRODUCTION

With this chapter we begin Part II, *Tools for Implementation*. In Part I (*Abstraction*), we examined the concepts of functional abstraction and data abstraction. Chapter 4 introduced several data structures having wide application in computer science: arrays, records, lists, stacks, queues, and sets. Defining these data structures as abstract data types, we focused only on their properties and not on how we might implement them. The one exception is arrays, where it is natural to implement the array-as-ADT by using built-in arrays.

Many programming languages, including C++, offer arrays as built-in data types. Arrays are perhaps the most widely used data structures, but they must have homogeneous components. Sometimes it is more natural to represent real-world information by grouping together data components of *different*

Homogeneous and heterogeneous information

Homogeneous

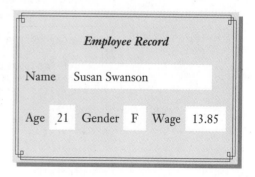

Heterogeneous

types. For example, a data structure for representing employee information might include the employee's name (a string type), age (an integer type), gender (an enumeration type), and hourly wage (a floating point type). An array cannot represent this heterogeneous information.

The **record,** introduced in Chapter 4, is a linear, direct-access data structure with heterogeneous components. Each component (**field**) has its own type (**field type**) and is accessed by specifying its **field name.** C++ provides records as built-in types but uses its own terminology. Records are called **structures,** and fields of a record are called **members** of a structure. Because the term "structure" has broader meanings throughout computer science, we use the term struct (the C++ reserved word used for declaring a record type) or "record" whenever there is a risk of ambiguity.

This chapter examines in detail the declaration and usage of structs within C++ programs. A good grounding in both arrays and structs is essential for building more complex data structures—structures that mirror real-world information that is often complex and diverse.

5.1   C++ structs

In Chapter 3 we introduced the notion of a class—a programmer-defined type for creating abstract data types (ADTs). We saw how members of a class are designated as public or private according to the principle of information hiding. Data members are usually private, and function members that represent ADT operations are declared to be public.

C++ defines a struct to be a class whose members are all, by default, public. All operations that apply to C++ classes apply also to structs. We will focus on structs whose members are all data items, even though it is possible to include member functions in a struct. Figure 5.1 displays several declarations, including a struct declaration.

In this figure, manager and worker1 are instances of the type EmployeeType. Each is a struct with five members representing a person's first initial, last initial, age, gender, and hourly wage. Figure 5.2 gives a pictorial view of worker1.

```
enum GenderType {male, female, unknown};

struct EmployeeType {
    char        firstInit;
    char        lastInit;
    int         age;
    GenderType  gender;
    float       hourlyWage;
};


EmployeeType manager;
EmployeeType worker1;
```

Figure 5.1 Example of a struct declaration

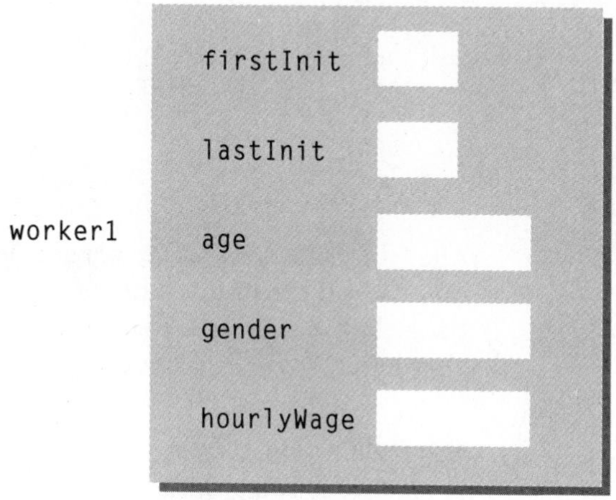

Figure 5.2 A view of an
`EmployeeType` instance

C++ uses dot notation for selecting members of classes and `structs`. To select a particular member of a `struct`, you append a dot and then the member name:

```
worker1.age
```

The following code segment, based on the declarations of Figure 5.1, demonstrates `struct` member selection:

```
// ASSERT: Assigned(worker1) && Assigned(manager)

cout << worker1.age;
// ASSERT: Value of the worker's age has been output

manager.hourlyWage = worker1.hourlyWage * 2.0;
// ASSERT: Manager's wage is double the worker's wage

if (manager.lastInit == worker1.lastInit)
    cout << "Both employees have the same last initial";

manager.age++;
// ASSERT: The manager is another year older

if (manager.gender == male)
    cout << "Manager is a male";
else if (manager.gender == female)
    cout << "Manager is a female";
else
    cout << "Manager's gender is unknown";
```

Combining Type and Instance Declarations

C++ allows you to declare instances of a `struct` as part of the type declaration itself. We could combine the three separate declarations of `EmployeeType`, `manager`, and `worker1` in Figure 5.1 into a single declaration as follows:

```
struct EmployeeType {
    char        firstInit;
    char        lastInit;
    int         age;
    GenderType gender;
    float       hourlyWage;
} manager, worker1;
```

After the right brace of the `struct` declaration, but before the semicolon, you can insert a list of instances of that type. We seldom use this form in this book, but it is a style that you might encounter when reading C++ code elsewhere.

Unnamed `struct` *Types*

In C++ it is possible to declare **unnamed `struct` types:**

```
struct {
    int    age;
    float weight;
} thisPerson;
```

Between the word `struct` and the left brace in this example, we have omitted a name for the type. This declaration creates one instance of the type, namely `thisPerson`. Because this type has no name, we cannot declare any other instances of the type later on in the program.

Unnamed `struct` types have very limited usefulness, but there sometimes are special reasons for using them. Later in this chapter we will discuss one of these reasons.

A Definition of C++ `struct`*s*

In Chapter 4 we introduced a form for defining data types. This form includes the name of the type, its domain, and the operations on values from its domain. Additionally, for structured data types the form describes the structural relationships among its components. Definition 5.1 defines the C++ `struct` type using this form.

DATA TYPE   C++ `struct` (record)

Definition 5.1 The C++ struct type

DOMAIN
Each C++ `struct` consists of

1. a collection of a fixed number of component (member) values—which may be of different types (either atomic or structured)

2. a set of identifiers (member names) for selecting each component*

STRUCTURE

A linear, direct access structure with a one-to-one relationship between each member name and a member of the struct

OPERATIONS

=	Assign one entire struct instance to another, member by member**
.membName	Retrieve the value of the member whose name is membName
.membName	Store a value into the member whose name is membName (The context determines whether to store or to retrieve. The assignment x=s.membName denotes retrieval, whereas the assignment s.membName=x denotes a store operation.)

*More precisely, C++ defines a struct to be a class whose members are all public. Therefore, struct members may be data items, functions, constructors, and so forth. This chapter confines its discussion to structs whose members are all data items.

**Assignment is valid only if the instances are of identical types or if one type is a renaming of the other.

Aggregate Operations

In a programming language, **aggregate operations** are those that manipulate an entire data structure as a whole. The OPERATIONS section of Definition 5.1 states that aggregate assignment of one struct to another of the same type is allowed. Consider the following code segment:

```
EmployeeType worker1;
EmployeeType worker2;

worker1.firstInit = 'A';
worker1.firstInit = 'G';
worker1.age = 24;
worker1.gender = female;
worker1.hourlyWage = 12.45;
worker2 = worker1;
```

The last statement in this code is an example of aggregate assignment. The statement copies worker1 into worker2 using member-by-member assignment. In contrast, recall that aggregate assignment of C++ arrays is not an allowable operation:

```
char myName[30];
char yourName[30];
  :
myName = yourName;          ⟵ Illegal
```

Table 5.1 C++ aggregate operations: Arrays versus structs

Aggregate operation	Arrays	structs
Assignment	No	Yes
Parameter passage	By reference only	By reference or by value
Return as function value	No	Yes

Passing data structures as parameters and returning data structures as function values can also be thought of as aggregate operations. Here again, C++ has different rules for arrays and structs. Table 5.1 summarizes these differences.

Although you cannot pass an array by value, it is possible to put an array into a struct and then pass the struct by value. Similarly, you can return an entire array as a function value if the array is a member of a struct that is being returned as the function value. Programmers sometimes use these "tricks" to pass arrays by value and to return arrays as function values.

Scope of Member Names

As with C++ classes, a member name is local to a struct. If the same identifier happens to be declared outside the struct, the two identifiers are unrelated. Consider the following declarations:

```
enum GenderType {male, female, unknown};

struct EmployeeType {
    char        firstInit;
    char        lastInit;
    int         age;
    GenderType  gender;
    float       hourlyWage;
};

struct PresidentType {
    int         age;
    GenderType  gender;
    float       annualWage;
};

EmployeeType  manager;
EmployeeType  worker1;
PresidentType pres;
int           age;
```

The identifier age appears three times in these declarations. It is a member name in both the EmployeeType and the PresidentType structures, and it is declared separately as an int variable. These are all valid declarations and each refers to a different entity. There is no ambiguity, because the member names of a struct are local to that struct. To reference any member, the programmer must specify, via dot notation, both the name of the struct instance and the member name:

```
worker1.age = 35;
pres.age = 62;
```

Data Structures as Members of a struct

A member of a struct may be of any built-in or previously declared type, even another structured type. Figure 5.3 declares StudentType to be a struct type whose members are name, classific, socialSecNum, gender, and gradePtAvg. (To review the use of typedef, see Section A.10 of Appendix A.)

The socialSecNum member of student is an array of 10 characters, and the notation student.socialSecNum refers to this array as an aggregate. The name member is a struct with three members: first (an array), middleInit (a simple variable), and last (an array). Figure 5.4 pictures the complete structure.

To select a member of a struct that is itself a member of another struct, you append another dot and member name:

```
student.name.middleInit = 'G';
```

Table 5.2 shows the notation required for referencing various portions of the student structure.

```
typedef char String9[10];
typedef char String15[16];
enum GenderType {male, female, unknown};
enum ClassType {
    freshman, sophomore, junior, senior, graduate, special
};
struct NameType {
    String15 first;
    char     middleInit;
    String15 last;
};
struct StudentType {
    NameType    name;
    ClassType   classific;
    String9     socialSecNum;
    GenderType  gender;
    float       gradePtAvg;
};

StudentType student;
```

Figure 5.3 Declarations of StudentType and student

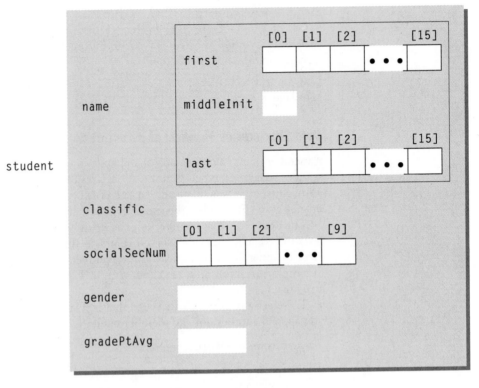

Figure 5.4 A view of a `StudentType` instance

Table 5.2 References to portions of the `student` structure

Reference	Item referenced
`student`	The entire struct (type: `StudentType`)
`student.gradePtAvg`	The `gradePtAvg` member of `student` (type: `float`)
`student.socialSecNum`	The `socialSecNum` member of `student` (type: `String9`)
`student.socialSecNum[0]`	The first character of the `socialSecNum` member of `student` (type: `char`)
`student.name`	The `name` member of `student` (type: `NameType`)
`student.name.middleInit`	The `middleInit` member of the `name` member of `student` (type: `char`)
`student.name.first`	The `first` member of the `name` member of `student` (type: `String15`)
`student.name.last[2]`	The third character of the `last` member of the `name` member of `student` (type: `char`)

Type Compatibility

Two struct instances have *compatible types* only if their types are identical or are renamings of the same type. By the latter, we mean using a typedef to give a new name to an existing type:

```
typedef ExistingType NewName;
```

In the following program code, person1 and person2 do not have compatible types, even though each of their data types has exactly the same form.

```
struct PersonType {
    char name[20];
    int  age;
};
struct  ClientType {
    char name[20];
    int  age;
};

PersonType person1;
ClientType person2;

strcpy(person1.name, "Beth Anderson");
person1.age = 20;

person2 = person1;
```
      ⟵ Not allowed; person1 and person2 have incompatible types.

To resolve this incompatibility, one possibility is to discard the ClientType declaration and declare both person1 and person2 to be of type PersonType. Or, if it is essential to retain the name ClientType for documentation purposes, we could declare ClientType to be an **alias** for the name PersonType:

```
typedef PersonType ClientType;
```

Now person1 and person2 have compatible types and can be assigned to one another. Aliasing is sometimes beneficial, but its overuse is likely to confuse the reader.

Instances of compatible struct types can be assigned, passed as parameters, and returned as function values. Additionally, the notation for initializing an array within a declaration:

```
int someVec[4] = {2, 0, 0, 23};
```

is also valid for structs:

```
PersonType person1 = {
    "Beth Anderson",
    20
};
```

Arrays and structs

The principal advantage of structs over arrays is their ability to store hetero-geneous data. But arrays have an important advantage over structs. Array components are selected by subscripts that can be arbitrary expressions. You can output a 10-element vector by using a subscript expression that varies at run time:

```
for (i = 0; i < 10; i++)
    cout << vec[i];
```

In contrast, struct components are selected by their member names. It is impossible to substitute a variable or expression for a member name. Consequently, you cannot output a 10-member struct using a for loop as above. You must name each member explicitly:

```
cout << patient.name;
cout << patient.address;
cout << patient.socSecNum;
    ⋮
```

We are not saying that arrays, therefore, are "better" than structs. Nor are we saying that structs are better than arrays. Each kind of data structure has its own purpose and is appropriate in a particular context. The knowl-edgeable programmer must recognize the advantages and disadvantages of all data structures in order to make wise design decisions.

5.2   **Arrays of** structs

The information for a single employee consists of heterogeneous data, so a struct is an appropriate data structure. But very few companies have just one employee. To store information about *several* employees, we can collect all the structs into an array. The array elements are homogeneous, because each element has the same type: a struct of employee data. Here is an example that declares such an array:

```
enum GenderType {male, female, unknown};

struct EmployeeType {
    char       firstInit;
    char       lastInit;
    int        age;
    GenderType gender;
    float      hourlyWage;
};

EmployeeType employee[100];
```

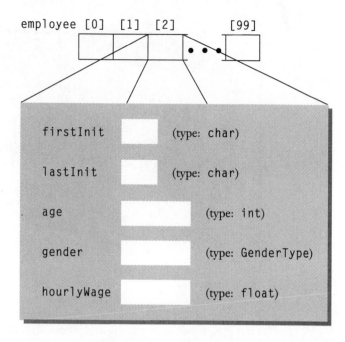

Figure 5.5 Diagram of
employee array

These statements declare employee to be a vector of 100 EmployeeType instances. Figure 5.5 shows a diagram of this structure. We have enlarged one array element, employee[2], to illustrate the element type.

When you use both dot notation and array subscripts, a reference to a portion of a data structure must be consistent with its declaration. With the employee array, the proper reference to the age member of the third employee is

```
employee[2].age
```

This reference is consistent with the declaration in the following sense. The subscript immediately follows an array name, and the member name follows a reference to a struct.

The form of the employee array—an array whose elements are structs—is extremely common. This kind of structure is appropriate for representing collections of information where each item in the collection has a nontrivial but uniform structure.

A Study in Design

A PBX Telephone Exchange

Factories and office complexes often have an on-site telephone exchange, or PBX (Private Branch eXchange). The telephone company sends an incoming call to the business's PBX, which takes over and routes the call to the internal destination. The PBX also manages the internal telephone traffic—calls placed from one location within the business to another.

A PBX (Private Branch eXchange)

Figure 5.6 contains the specification of a module named `PbxCalls`. This module is designed to control internal telephone connections for a PBX. Each phone in the exchange has a number composed of a one-digit prefix (only the digits 1 and 2 are currently allowed), followed by three more digits. This example therefore recognizes phone numbers from 1000 through 2999.

The `PbxCalls` module exports three types: `PhoneNumType`, `TimeType`, and `PbxType` (a class). `PhoneNumType` and `TimeType` are renamings of the `int` type, `typedef`ed to make the code more readable and self-documenting. The third exported type—`PbxType`—is a class from which the importer may declare any number of instances of a PBX telephone exchange. (A fourth type—the `struct` type named `OneLine`—also is declared, but the importer will not find it useful. The purpose of the declaration is to allow the private part of `PbxType` to declare an array of `OneLine` structures.)

Figure 5.6 `PbxCalls` specification file

```
// ------------------------------------------------------------
//   SPECIFICATION FILE (pbxcalls.h)
//   This module exports facilities for controlling
//   telephone calls made locally within the PBX
// ------------------------------------------------------------
#include "bool.h"

const int MAX_PREFIX = 2;
const int MAX_LINES = 200;

typedef int PhoneNumType;     // 1000..MAX_PREFIX*1000+999
typedef int TimeType;         // Time in computer minutes

struct OneLine {
    Boolean      inUse;
    PhoneNumType source;
    PhoneNumType receiver;
    TimeType     time;
};
```

```
class PbxType {
public:
    void Dial( /* in */  PhoneNumType caller,
               /* in */  PhoneNumType called,
               /* in */  TimeType     startTime,
               /* out */ Boolean&     busy      );
      // PRE:  caller and called are in PhoneNumType range
      //    && Assigned(startTime)
      // POST: busy == TRUE,  if the called phone is in use
      //           == FALSE, otherwise
      //    && NOT busy --> startTime is recorded as call
      //                          starting time

    void HangUp( /* in */ PhoneNumType caller,
                 /* in */ TimeType     endTime );
      // PRE:  caller is in PhoneNumType range
      //    && Assigned(endTime)
      // POST: IF caller currently connected THEN
      //           caller's current call terminated at time endTime
      //       ELSE
      //           no action taken

    PbxType();
      // Constructor
      // POST: Private data initialized
private:
    Boolean phoneInUse[1000*MAX_PREFIX];
    OneLine line[MAX_LINES];
};
```

The PbxType class provides two functions for handling phone calls. Dial is used to place a call and HangUp attempts to end a call. In addition, the class provides a constructor to guarantee initialization of the class's private data. Figure 5.7 illustrates the class interface diagram for PbxType.

An implementation of the PbxCalls module appears in Figure 5.8. Within the PBX hardware, only a limited number of telephone lines can carry internal calls. The PbxType class uses an array of structs, named line, to store the

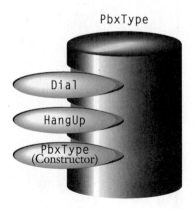

Figure 5.7 PbxType class interface diagram

current PBX internal phone calls. Each element of the line array is of type OneLine, a struct representing a PBX telephone line. The inUse member of each element represents the status of the line. (If inUse is TRUE, then this line is currently involved in a call.) The time member contains the start time of each call. Our implementation does not use this start time. A future implementation may need it for PBX statistics.

The phoneInUse array is another data structure that we use within the PbxCalls implementation. It is a Boolean array with one element for every telephone in the PBX system. An element is TRUE exactly when the associated telephone is involved in a call.

The Dial function first verifies that both the caller phone and the called phone are currently available. Next, the function searches for an unused phone line. If one of the phones is unavailable or if there are no free PBX lines, then the call cannot be completed. When this happens, busy is assigned the value TRUE. If the call can be completed, then Dial completes the call by updating both line and phoneInUse.

The HangUp function searches the line array for a currently active call involving caller. If such a call is found, the function updates the line array to show that the call has been completed. The function also updates phoneInUse to indicate that each of the phones involved in the call is no longer in use.

Figure 5.8 PbxCalls implementation file

```
// --------------------------------------------------------------
//   IMPLEMENTATION FILE (pbxcalls.cpp)
//   This module exports facilities for controlling
//   telephone calls made locally within the PBX
// --------------------------------------------------------------
#include "pbxcalls.h"

// Constant MAX_LINES is the maximum number of
// simultaneous calls
//
// Private members of class:
//     Boolean phoneInUse[1000*MAX_PREFIX];
//     OneLine line[MAX_LINES];

PbxType::PbxType()
    //..........................................................
    // Constructor
    // POST: phoneInUse[0..1000*MAX_PREFIX-1] == FALSE
    //    && line[0..MAX_LINES-1].inUse == FALSE
    //..........................................................
{
    int i;

    for (i = 0; i < 1000*MAX_PREFIX; i++)
        phoneInUse[i] = FALSE;
    for (i = 0; i < MAX_LINES; i++)
        line[i].inUse = FALSE;
}
```

```
void PbxType::Dial( /* in */  PhoneNumType caller,
                    /* in */  PhoneNumType called,
                    /* in */  TimeType     startTime,
                    /* out */ Boolean&     busy        )
    //.................................................................
    // PRE:  caller and called are in PhoneNumType range
    //    && Assigned(startTime)
    // POST: busy == TRUE, if all line[0..MAX_LINES-1].inUse == TRUE
    //                        || phoneInUse[caller-1000]<entry>
    //                        || phoneInUse[called-1000]<entry>
    //          == FALSE, otherwise
    //    && NOT busy --> There is some j, (0 <= j < MAX_LINES),
    //                  && NOT line[j].inUse<entry>
    //                  && line[j].inUse
    //                  && line[j].source == caller-1000
    //                  && line[j].receiver == called-1000
    //                  && line[j].time == startTime
    //                  && phoneInUse[caller-1000]
    //                  && phoneInUse[called-1000]
    //.................................................................
{
    caller -= 1000;
    called -= 1000;
    if (phoneInUse[caller] || phoneInUse[called]) {
        busy = TRUE;
        return;
    }
    // ASSERT: Neither phone is in use

    int lineNum = 0;
    while (lineNum < MAX_LINES && line[lineNum].inUse)
                        // INV (prior to test):
                        //     lineNum <= MAX_LINES
                        //  && line[0..lineNum-1].inUse == TRUE
        lineNum++;

    if (lineNum >= MAX_LINES)
        // ASSERT: No line available
        busy = TRUE;
    else {
        // ASSERT: A line is available
        busy = FALSE;
        line[lineNum].inUse = TRUE;
        line[lineNum].source = caller;
        line[lineNum].receiver = called;
        line[lineNum].time = startTime;
        phoneInUse[caller] = phoneInUse[called] = TRUE;
    }
}
```

```
void PbxType::HangUp( /* in */ PhoneNumType caller,
                      /* in */ TimeType    endTime )
//................................................................
// PRE:  caller is in PhoneNumType range  &&  Assigned(endTime)
// POST: IF there is some line j, (0 <= j < MAX_LINES),
//          && line[j].inUse<entry>
//          && (line[j].source == caller-1000
//              || line[j].receiver == caller-1000)
//       THEN
//             NOT line[j].inUse
//          && NOT phoneInUse[line[j].receiver]
//          && NOT phoneInUse[line[j].source]
// NOTE: endTime is intended for future use only
//................................................................
{
    caller -= 1000;
    int lineNum = 0;
    while (lineNum < MAX_LINES &&
           ( !line[lineNum].inUse ||
            (line[lineNum].source != caller &&
             line[lineNum].receiver != caller)))
                      // INV (prior to test):
                      //     lineNum <= MAX_LINES
                      // && For all j < lineNum, NOT line[j].inUse
                      //       || (   line[j].source != caller
                      //           && line[j].receiver != caller)
        lineNum++;

    if (lineNum < MAX_LINES) {
        line[lineNum].inUse  = FALSE;
        phoneInUse[line[lineNum].source] = FALSE;
        phoneInUse[line[lineNum].receiver] = FALSE;
    }
}
```

5.3   Sorting structs

Arrays of structs can be sorted just as any other array can be sorted. To sort an array of structs, the most common method is to sort according to one particular member of each struct. This is called **sorting on a member.** We could sort the line array from the PbxCalls implementation file on the source member, the receiver member, or the time member.

Figure 5.9 contains an example of a sorting function named SortLines. This function might be a useful addition to the PbxType class that we have just examined. SortLines uses a selection sort (Chapter 1) to sort the line array into ascending order on the source member. This algorithm potentially exchanges entire array elements (using the auxiliary function SwapLines) by comparing their source members.

Figure 5.9 SortLines
function

```
void SwapLines(OneLine&, OneLine&);      // Function prototype

void PbxType::SortLines()
    //..............................................................
    // PRE:  Assigned( line[0..MAX_LINES-1] )
    // POST: line[0..MAX_LINES-1] contain same values as at
    //       invocation but are rearranged into ascending order
    //       on the "source" member.
    //       (Unused elements are located at the end of the array)
    //..............................................................
{
    int minIndx;     // Index of array element with smallest source
                     //     member in each pass
    int top;         // "False top" of array for each pass
    int j;

    for (top = 0; top < MAX_LINES-1; top++) {
                    // INV (prior to test):
                    //     line[0..top-1] are in ascending order
                    //  && All in-use elements of
                    //     line[top..MAX_LINES-1]
                    //     are >= line[top-1] (by source member)
                    //  && top <= MAX_LINES-1
        minIndx = top;
        for (j = top+1; j < MAX_LINES; j++)
                    // INV (prior to test):
                    //     line[minIndx].source <= the source
                    //     member of all in-use elements of
                    //     line[top..j-1]
                    //  && j <= MAX_LINES

            if (line[j].inUse &&
                ( !line[minIndx].inUse ||
                  line[j].source < line[minIndx].source))
                minIndx = j;

        // ASSERT: line[minIndx].source is <= the source member of
        //         all in-use elements of line[top..MAX_LINES-1]
        //      OR None of line[top..MAX_LINES-1] are in use

        if (line[minIndx].inUse)
            SwapLines(line[top],line[minIndx]);
        else
            return;      // Remaining lines are not in use
    }
}
```

```
void SwapLines( /* inout */ OneLine& line1,
                /* inout */ OneLine& line2 )
   //........................................................
   // PRE:  Assigned(line1)  &&  Assigned(line2)
   // POST: line1==line2<entry>  &&  line2==line1<entry>
   //........................................................
{
    OneLine temp;

    temp = line1;
    line1 = line2;
    line2 = temp;
}
```

To add this sorting capability to the PbxCalls module, we would include a function prototype for SortLines as a public member of the PbxType class. Then in the PbxCalls implementation file we would place the function definitions of SortLines and SwapLines that appear in Figure 5.9.

5.4   Unions

In addition to structs, C++ provides a special kind of record type called the **union.** By definition, a union is a struct that holds only one of its members at a time. Memory space is allocated according to the size of the largest member. Consider the following declarations:

```
union SampleType {
    char  strMemb[10];
    int   intMemb;
    float floatMemb;
};
SampleType sampleVal;
```

When sampleVal is created, memory is *not* allocated for three distinct members. Instead, memory is allocated according to the size of the largest member (here, 10 bytes for the 10-element character array).

During program execution, the sampleVal union can hold only one of its three members at a given moment. The assumption is that the program will never need, say, sampleVal.intMemb and sampleVal.strMemb simultaneously while executing. When the program stores a new value into sampleVal, it is said to **overlay** the previous value. The following code shows statements that overlay members of the sampleVal union:

```
strcpy(sampleVal.strMemb, "Art Jones");

    ⋮

// ASSERT: Character string no longer needed
//         Memory space can be reused
```

```
sampleVal.intMemb = 35;
// ASSERT: String "Art Jones" is overlaid with int value 35
    ⋮
sampleVal.floatMemb = 248.65;
// ASSERT: Same memory space is reused.  Previous int value is lost.
```

Figure 5.10 displays the effect of executing these statements.

When working with unions, the programmer must be careful not to store a value of one type and then retrieve it as another type:

```
sampleVal.floatMemb = 98.6;
importantVar = 2 * sampleVal.intMemb;
```

The first statement stores the value 98.6 using a bit pattern unique to floating point numbers. The second statement then accesses this number, *without type coercion*, as an integer value. The bit pattern does not change, so the result is some unexpected integer number, perhaps huge or even negative.

Named and Unnamed Unions

`SampleType` is called a **named union type,** because its declaration gave it a name. As with C++ classes and `struct`s, the programmer uses dot notation to select a member of a named union. Also, the identifier of each member of a

Instruction: `strcpy(sampleVal.strMemb, "Art Jones");`
Result:

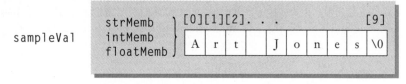

Next instruction: `sampleVal.intMemb = 35;`
Result:

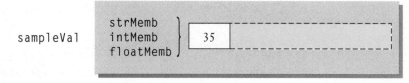

Next instruction: `sampleVal.floatMemb = 248.65;`
Result:

Figure 5.10 Union members sharing the same memory space

named union is local to the union. If the same identifier is declared outside the union, the two identifiers are not related.

Just as you can declare unnamed struct types, you can declare **unnamed union types:**

```
union {
    char ch;
    int  n;
} oneInstance;
```

This declaration omits a name for the type and creates just one instance of the type: oneInstance. As with named union types, the member names are local to the union and can only be accessed by using dot notation:

```
oneInstance.ch = 'A';
```

Anonymous Unions

C++ has a special construct known as an **anonymous union.** An anonymous union is a union that is unnamed *and* does not declare any instances after the right brace:

```
union {
    int   someInt;
    float someFloat;
};
```

With anonymous unions, member names are *not* local to the union. Here, someInt and someFloat are treated as if they were declared outside the union in the surrounding scope. Furthermore, dot notation is not used with anonymous unions:

```
someInt =  67;
```

The purpose of an anonymous union, like any union, is to force the members to share the same memory space, one at a time. It might seem at first that anonymous unions are not very useful. However, in the next section we discuss a reasonable application of anonymous unions—variant records.

A Definition of C++ Unions

Using the form for defining data types we introduced in Chapter 4, Definition 5.2 presents a definition of C++ unions.

DATA TYPE   C++ union

Definition 5.2 The C++ union type

DOMAIN

Each C++ union consists of

1. one particular value from a collection of potential component (member) values—which may be of different types (either atomic or structured)

2. a set of identifiers (member names) for selecting each component*

STRUCTURE

Logical structure:

A direct access structure with a one-to-one relationship between each member name and a member of the union

Physical structure:

None. An instance of a union is not a collection of values. It holds only one of its members at a time.

OPERATIONS (excepting anonymous unions)

=   Assign one union instance to another (of identical or renamed type)

.   Select an individual union member for storage or retrieval

*More precisely, C++ defines a union to be a class that holds only one member at a time, and these members are all public. All unions may have data members, and all unions except anonymous unions may have member functions. This chapter confines its discussion to unions whose members are all data items.

5.5   Variant Records

Suppose you are asked to design a data structure that will store 1000 numbers, some of which are integers and some of which are floating point values. A 1000-element int array is not appropriate; int arrays can store only int values. Similarly, you cannot use a 1000-element float array. The obstacle here is that arrays must have homogeneous components.

A First Approach

One approach to storing both ints and floats in the same array is to create a 1000-element array of structs, where each struct has three members:

```
enum Type {anInt, aFloat};

struct NumType {
    Type  whichType;
    int   intVal;
    float floatVal;
};
    :
    :
NumType num[1000];
```

To store an int value into num[0], you would use the intVal member of the struct and leave the floatVal member vacant:

```
num[0].intVal = 357;
```

To store a float value into num[4], you would use the floatVal member of the struct and leave the intVal member vacant:

```
num[4].floatVal = 6.8;
```

The third member of the struct, whichType, is called a **type field.** A type field serves the special purpose of recording which type of data is currently in use. For this reason, a type field is also known as a **discriminator.** Before storing a value into the num array, the program should first assign a value to the type field to designate which type of data is being stored:

```
num[0].whichType = anInt;
num[0].intVal = 357;
num[4].whichType = aFloat;
num[4].floatVal = 6.8;
```

Figure 5.11 depicts the result of executing these four statements.

Whenever the program accesses an array element, it should first check the type field to see what kind of data is stored there:

```
for (i = 0; i < 1000; i++)
    if (num[i].whichType == anInt)
        // Do something with num[i].intVal
    else
        // Do something with num[i].floatVal
```

A Second Approach

As you can see in Figure 5.11, one third of all the space in the num array is wasted. Each array element holds either an int value or a float value, but not both.

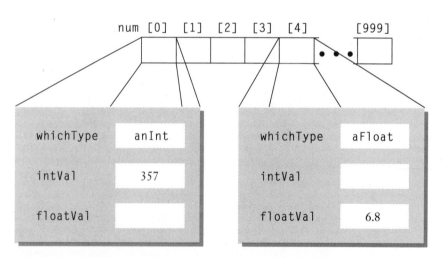

Figure 5.11 Diagram of num array (first version)

We can economize on storage by using a union to store either an int or a float in the same memory location. In particular, we redefine the NumType structure to have two members—a type field as before, and an anonymous union:

```
struct NumType {
    Type  whichType;
    union {
        int    intVal;
        float floatVal;
    };
};
```

With this approach, we force the `intVal` and `floatVal` members to share the same memory space. If we execute the same sequence of statements as in the first approach:

```
num[0].whichType = anInt;
num[0].intVal = 357;
num[4].whichType = aFloat;
num[4].floatVal = 6.8;
```

the result is that no space is wasted in the array (see Figure 5.12).

A `struct` consisting of a type field and one or more anonymous unions is called a **variant record.** In a variant record, the members of an anonymous union are called **variants.** Our second version of the `NumType` structure is an example of a variant record, and `intVal` and `floatVal` are the variants.

Variant records not only save memory space, they also increase the flexibility of a program. A variant record gives the appearance of changing its structure during program execution. In contrast, built-in arrays and nonvariant `struct`s have a form that is fixed at compile time. The precise structure is known to the compiler and does not change at execution time. When you declare an array, you must specify its size with a constant expression. When you declare a `struct`, you must fully specify the number of members, their names, and their types. On the other hand, the exact form of a variant record depends upon values that are stored while the program is executing.

Another Example of Variant Records

Figure 5.13 contains several declarations. The array `drawing`, declared at the bottom of the figure, can store information about 100 simple figures. Each

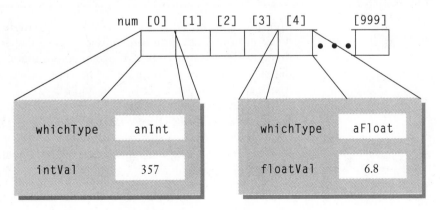

Figure 5.12 Diagram of num array (second version)

```
struct  PointType {
    int row;       // Range: 1..500
    int col;       // Range: 1..500
};
enum FigType {
    point, line, triangle, rectangle, circle
};
struct DrawingType {
    FigType whichType;
    union {
        struct {
            PointType location;
        } pt;

        struct {
            PointType leftEnd;
            PointType rightEnd;
        } ln;

        struct {
            PointType vertex1;
            PointType vertex2;
            PointType vertex3;
        } tri;

        struct {
            PointType upperLeft;
            int       length;
            int       width;
        } rect;

        struct {
            PointType center;
            int       radius;
        } circ;
    };
};

DrawingType drawing[100];
```

Figure 5.13 Declarations of DrawingType and drawing array

figure can be a point, a line segment, a triangle, a rectangle, or a circle. DrawingType is the form of a variant record that stores a single one of these figures. The five variants in the anonymous union correspond to the five different possibilities for a figure. The variants, instances of unnamed struct types, are named pt, ln, tri, rect, and circ.

The representation of each figure includes important points on a two-dimensional grid of 500 rows and 500 columns. On this grid, a single point has type PointType, a structure consisting of a row value and a column value. For example, a triangle is represented as three points, vertex1, vertex2, and vertex3.

DrawingType includes a type field named whichType. Before assigning a value to any of the variants, a program should first select which variant is in use by assigning a value to whichType. The assignment

```
drawing[2].whichType = circle;
```

states that the third element of the drawing array is to store a description of a circle. Similarly, the assignment

```
drawing[5].whichType = rectangle;
```

establishes that the sixth array element will describe a rectangle.

A program can check to see which variant is in use by testing the type field. In addition, the program can change the current variant after assigning a different value to the type field.

Below we list the five logical (conceptual) views of DrawingType:

1. If drawing[i].whichType equals point, then the logical view of drawing[i] is a struct with two members, whichType and pt:

   ```
   {
      FigType whichType;
      struct {
          PointType location;
      } pt;
   }
   ```

2. If drawing[i].whichType equals line, then the logical view of drawing[i] is a struct with two members, whichType and ln:

   ```
   {
      FigType whichType;
      struct {
          PointType leftEnd;
          PointType rightEnd;
      } ln;
   }
   ```

3. If drawing[i].whichType equals triangle, then the logical view of drawing[i] is a struct with two members, whichType and tri:

   ```
   {
      FigType whichType;
      struct {
          PointType vertex1;
          PointType vertex2;
          PointType vertex3;
      } tri;
   }
   ```

4. If drawing[i].whichType equals rectangle, then the logical view of drawing[i] is a struct with two members, whichType and rect:

```
{
  FigType whichType;
  struct {
    PointType upperLeft;
    int       length;
    int       width;
  } rect;
}
```

5. If `drawing[i].whichType` equals `circle`, then the logical view of `drawing[i]` is a `struct` with two members, `whichType` and `circ`:

```
{
  FigType whichType;
  struct {
    PointType center;
    int       radius;
  } circ;
}
```

The proper order for assigning values to a variant record is to first assign the type field and then any variant members. The following statements assign to `drawing[7]` a description of a circle of radius 75 whose center is at row 100 and column 250:

```
drawing[7].whichType = circle;
drawing[7].circ.radius = 75;
drawing[7].circ.center.row = 100;
drawing[7].circ.center.col = 250;
```

By using the concept of variant records, we are able, in a conceptual way, to escape the requirement that arrays must have homogeneous components. Although it is literally true that all elements of the `drawing` array are of the same type (`DrawingType`), conceptually the array elements can have heterogeneous structures at execution time.

Designing with Wisdom

Using Variant Records

If used wisely, a variant record enhances the pliability of structured data types. However, it is easy to abuse this technique. Below are some rules to help avoid potential pitfalls.

1. Don't overuse variant records. Variant records are always difficult to code and to maintain.

   In certain languages (such as Pascal and Modula-2, but not C++) variant records are a tightly defined language feature. In these languages, the programmer can expect the compiler and run-time system to help detect errors in their use.

   In C++, variant records are not a special language feature but are synthesized using `structs` and unions. The programmer is responsible for correctly designing and specifying variant records without any additional language support.

Our general advice is that if a suitable nonvariant alternative exists, you should use it.

2. Carefully indent all declarations to expose the form of the variant record as clearly as possible.

3. Avoid nesting variant records within variant records. This kind of nesting adds even more complexity.

4. Always use a type field in a variant record. The presence of a type field allows (and reminds) the programmer to store and retrieve values consistent with the type field, even though the C++ language does not enforce this consistency.

5. Never store data in a variant record as one type and then retrieve it as another type. This programming trick can be unreadable and nonportable; it provides a fertile climate for bugs.

SUMMARY

A programming language must incorporate data structures that are adequate for representing real-world information as program data. Arrays and records (`struct`s) are data structures built into the C++ language. If the abstract view of the information is a collection of similar objects, then an array may be a good representation. If the abstract view is a collection of dissimilar objects, a `struct` is more appropriate.

C++ provides many language features to assist with the declaration and manipulation of arrays and `struct`s. Types may be conveniently combined into arrays of arrays, arrays of `struct`s, `struct`s containing arrays, and `struct`s containing `struct`s.

Aggregate operations on `struct`s are important features supported by C++: aggregate assignment, aggregate parameter passage, and aggregate return as a function value.

Unions, which are structures in which only one member is physically present at a time, are also built-in types in C++. Variant records, constructed with unions, add pliability to the `struct` type. If used with care, variant records allow the programmer to represent information whose logical structure is not fixed prior to program execution.

Most other data structures are built from `struct`s and arrays. A thorough understanding of these types is a prerequisite for implementing more complex abstract data types.

KEY TERMS

aggregate operation   (p. 207)
alias   (p. 211)
anonymous union   (p. 222)
discriminator   (p. 224)
member (field)   (p. 204)
member (field) name   (p. 204)
member (field) type   (p. 204)
named union type   (p. 221)
overlay   (p. 220)

record   (p. 204)
sorting on a member   (p. 218)
type field   (p. 224)
union   (p. 220)
unnamed `struct` type   (p. 206)
unnamed union type   (p. 222)
variant   (p. 225)
variant record   (p. 225)

EXERCISES   **5.1**   Use the declarations below to complete parts (a) through (m).

```
typedef char String20[21];
typedef int  ValidCourseNum;  // Range: 100..799
enum ScienceDept {
    biology, chemistry, compSci, geology, math, physics
};
struct NameType {
    char     firstInit;
    String20 last;
};
struct CourseType {
    ScienceDept    dept;
    ValidCourseNum number;
};
struct CourseLoadType {
    int          count;   // Range: 1..5
    CourseType course[5];
};
struct ProfType {
    NameType       name;
    int            age;   // Range: 20..90
    ScienceDept    homeDept;
    CourseLoadType currentCourseLoad;
    long           annualSalary;
};

ProfType visitingProf;
ProfType scienceProf[50];
```

a. Give a member selector for the age member of the struct for the visiting professor.

b. Give a member selector for the first initial of the name of the visiting professor.

c. Give a member selector for the last name of the visiting professor.

d. Give a member selector for the number of courses being taught by the visiting professor.

e. Give a member selector for the department of the first course being taught by the visiting professor.

f. Give a member selector for the age member of the fifth science professor.

g. Give a member selector for the "Home department" of the science professor with index 43.

h. Give a member selector for the course number of the second course taught by the third science professor.

i. Give a sequence of assignment statements that store the following information into the visiting professor data structure:

Name: L. Clements
Age: 52
Home Department: Chemistry
Annual Salary: $31000
Current Teaching Load:
  Chemistry 100
  Chemistry 203
  Math 161

j. Give a sequence of assignment statements that assign the following information to the professor with index 31:

Name: A. Becker
Age: 35
Home Department: Computer Science
Annual Salary: $38000
Current Teaching Load:
  Computer Science 110
  Computer Science 222

k. Write a function named `WriteProf` that outputs the information for a single professor. Use the output format shown in parts (i) and (j) above. The prototype for `WriteProf` is as follows:

```
void WriteProf( /* in */ ProfType prof );
    // PRE:  Assigned(prof)
    // POST: All info for prof displayed in format
    //       shown in part (j) above
```

l. Give a sequence of statements that will output all science professors' data by repeatedly invoking `WriteProf` from part (k).

m. Write a function that swaps the information for any two science professors whose indices are passed as parameters. (The base address of the array must also be passed as a parameter.)

5.2 Give an appropriate collection of C++ declarations for each of the following.

a. A structure to store a single vegetable by storing its variety (for example, corn, bean, tomato), its growing period (number of days), and the color of its edible portion.

b. A structure to store a triangle by storing the measures of its three angles (in degrees) and the length of its longest side.

c. A structure to store up to 500 common stocks. For each stock, store the following: its name (up to 15 characters), its highest value per share, its lowest value per share, its current value per share, and its change in value per share (positive or negative) from the previous day.

d. A structure to store the typical weather for each of the past thirty days. For each day, store the average barometric pressure, average wind speed, most common wind direction, and sky condition (overcast, clear, or partly cloudy).

e. A structure to store an index for a book. This index must be capable of storing up to 1000 entries. Each entry consists of the name of the entry word (up to 20 characters) and a list of up to 15 page numbers where the word is found.

f. A structure to store the library catalog information for a single book. This information should include: a title (up to 40 characters), a catalog number (up to 25 characters), the author's name (up to 30 characters), the publisher (up to 20 characters), a brief description (up to 80 characters), and two subjects (up to 25 characters each).

g. A structure to store up to 100 invoices. Each invoice consists of a date, the original dollar amount of the invoice, the total amount paid to date on the invoice, and a list of up to 15 entries on the invoice. Each entry has a description of up to 40 characters, a dollar cost, and a quantity.

5.3 Use the personal property declarations below to complete parts (a) through (j). Observe that `PropertyInfoType` is a variant record.

```
typedef char String40[41];
struct DateType {
    int mo;    // Range: 1..12
    int day;   // Range: 1..31
    int yr;    // Range: 1900..2100
};
enum PropertyType {home, automobile, appliance, furniture, other};
enum HouseType {ranch, twoStory, split, condo};
enum ColorType {
    red, orange, yellow, green, blue, brown, purple, white, black
};
enum CarType {sedan, staWagon, van, sports, offRoad, pickup};
enum ApplianceType {range, dishwasher, washer, dryer};
enum FurnitureType {sofa, table, chair, bed, desk, cabinet};

struct PropertyInfoType {          // Variant record
    DateType     purchaseDate;
    int          hundredsVal;      // Value in units of $100
    PropertyType article;         // Type field
    union {
        struct {
            HouseType style;
            int       sqFeet;
            DateType  dateBuilt;
        } house;
        struct {
            CarType   style;
            ColorType color;
        } car;
        struct {
            ApplianceType kind;
            ColorType     color;
        } appli;
        struct {
            FurnitureType kind;
```

```
            } furn;
        struct {
            String40 descrip;
        } oth;
    };
};
```

```
PropertyInfoType majorPossession[200];
PropertyInfoType favoritePossession;
```

a. If the favorite possession is an appliance, give a member selector for the year in which the appliance was purchased.

b. If the favorite possession is an auto, give a member selector for the color of the car.

c. If the favorite possession is a home, give a member selector for the number of square feet in the home.

d. If the favorite possession is a home, give a member selector for the month in which the house was built.

e. Give an assignment statement that causes the favorite possession to use the appropriate variant for a home.

f. Give an assignment statement that causes the first element of the major possessions to use the variant appropriate for furniture.

g. Give a sequence of assignment statements that cause the favorite possession to be a desk purchased on May 9, 1951, and worth $500.

h. Give a sequence of assignment statements that cause the third element of the major possessions to be a green range purchased on Jan. 4, 1988, and valued at $900.

i. Give a sequence of assignment statements that cause the fifth element of the major possessions to be a stereo purchased on 11/29/89 and worth $2100.

j. Assume the variable possessionCount tells how many elements of the majorPossession vector are currently filled. Give a sequence of statements that search the vector for all purple possessions. For each, output its general property type and its value.

5.4 Figure 5.13 declares a vector named drawing that stores various types of drawing images. For each part below, give assignment statements that cause the third element of this array to store the indicated drawing image. The notation (R,C) denotes a point at row R and column C.

a. A point at (123,321).

b. A circle with center at (55,55) and radius of 10.

c. A line from (5,10) to (20,50).

d. A triangle with vertices at (2,2), (10,10), and (4,9).

e. A rectangle with vertices at (100,10), (100,175), (180,10), and (180,175).

5.5 Modify the SortLines function of Figure 5.9 to sort in *descending* order on the time member instead of ascending order on the source member.

PROGRAMMING PROJECTS

5.1 Write and test a program that inputs information for several professors, stores this information into the scienceProf vector of Exercise 5.1, sorts the vector into descending order on the annualSalary member, and outputs the result. You should not begin your program design until you have carefully prepared a six-part problem specification (Section 1.3).

5.2 Write and test a program that inputs personal property information, stores this information into the majorPossession vector of Exercise 5.3, sorts the vector into ascending order on the purchaseDate member, and outputs the result. You should not begin your program design until you have carefully prepared a six-part problem specification (Section 1.3).

5.3 Below is a specification file for a module named CoinMod. Write and test a corresponding implementation file. (Note: Your code must perform carries and borrows to maintain the correct value of money stored.)

```
//------------------------------------------------------------------
//  SPECIFICATION FILE (coinmod.h)
//  This module exports CoinsType and associated operations.
//  CoinsType represents a collection of coins.
//------------------------------------------------------------------
#include "bool.h"

struct CoinsType {
    int quarters;
    int dimes;
    int nickels;
    int pennies;
};

CoinsType CoinSum( /* in */ CoinsType coins1,
                   /* in */ CoinsType coins2 );
    // PRE:  Assigned(coins1) && Assigned(coins2)
    // POST: FCTVAL == coins1 + coins2  (i.e., the collection
    //                  of all coins from coins1 and coins2)

void DelCoins( /* in */  CoinsType  coins1,
               /* in */  CoinsType  coins2,
               /* out */ CoinsType& result,
               /* out */ Boolean&   suffFunds );
    // PRE:  Assigned(coins1) && Assigned(coins2)
    // POST: suffFunds == (each member of coins1 is >= the same
    //                     member of coins2)
    //     && suffFunds -->
    //        (   result.quarters == coins1.quarters -
    //                               coins2.quarters
    //         && result.dimes == coins1.dimes - coins2.dimes
    //         && result.nickels == coins1.nickels - coins2.nickels
    //         && result.pennies == coins1.pennies - coins2.pennies)
```

```
int CentValue( /* in */ CoinsType coins );
    // PRE:  Assigned(coins)
    // POST: FCTVAL == total value (in cents) of coins

void MakeChange( /* inout */ CoinsType& coins,
                 /* in */    int        cost,
                 /* out */   CoinsType& change,
                 /* out */   Boolean&   suffFunds );
    // PRE:  Assigned(coins)  &&  Assigned(Cost)
    // POST: suffFunds == (CentValue(coins<entry>) is
    //                       sufficient to cover cost)
    //     && suffFunds -->
    //         (   change == coin collection whose cent value is
    //                       CentValue(coins<entry>) - cost
    //           && coins == coins<entry> less change )
```

5.4   Below is the specification file for an automated version of a telephone book. Write and test an appropriate implementation file. You should assume that the phone book initially contains no entries and that at most 100 entries are allowed (this territory is very small).

For the LookupByName function, recall from Chapter 3 that a const member function is one that doesn't modify the private data.

```
//------------------------------------------------------------------
//  SPECIFICATION FILE (phonebk.h)
//  This module exports a PhoneBook abstract data type.
//------------------------------------------------------------------
#include "bool.h"

const int MAX_ENTRIES = 100;

typedef char String20[21];
typedef char String60[61];
struct NameType {
    String20 last;
    String20 first;
};
struct AddressType {
    String20 city;
    String60 address;
};
struct PhoneNumType {
    int areaCode;   // Range: 0..999
    int prefix;     // Range: 0..999
    int lastDigs;   // Range: 0..9999
};
```

```
class PhoneBook {
public:
    void AddPhone( /* in */  PhoneNumType number,
                   /* in */  NameType     name,
                   /* in */  NameType     spouseName,
                   /* in */  AddressType  address,
                   /* out */ Boolean&     opSuccessful );
        // PRE:  All value parameters are assigned
        // POST: opSuccessful == (At entry, phone book not full
        //                           && number not already in book)
        //      && opSuccessful --> Phone book entry made for the
        //                             info from the value parameters
        // NOTE: One phone may have two persons listed: name and
        //       spouseName

    void DelPhone( /* in */  PhoneNumType number,
                   /* out */ Boolean&     opSuccessful );
        // PRE:  Assigned(number)
        // POST: opSuccessful == (At entry, number is in
        //                          phone book)
        //      && opSuccessful --> Phone book entry for number
        //                             removed from phone book

    void LookupByName( /* in */  NameType      name,
                       /* out */ Boolean&      found,
                       /* out */ PhoneNumType& number,
                       /* out */ AddressType&  address ) const;
        // PRE:  Assigned(name)
        // POST: found == (name is in phone book)
        //      && found --> number and address are from the
        //                      phone book entry for name
        // NOTE: One phone may have two persons listed: name and
        //       spouseName

    PhoneBook();
        // Constructor
        // POST: Phone book initialized
private:
    //
    // You choose a suitable data representation
    //
};
```

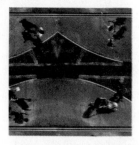

CHAPTER 6

Recursion

INTRODUCTION

Everyone gets "stuck" once in a while when trying to define a word. Sometimes it seems impossible to avoid using the word in its own definition. But circular definitions are more confusing than helpful. There is, however, an accepted form of mathematical definition that uses concepts to define themselves. Such definitions are known as **recursive** (or **inductive**) **definitions.** In this chapter we give many examples of recursive definitions and show that, when carefully worded, these definitions are surprisingly concise and thorough.

Within a computer program, a function also can be recursive. A recursive function is one that invokes itself. The thought of invoking a function recursively might seem just as circular and confusing as defining a concept in terms of itself. But we will see that recursive functions are a very powerful tool for expressing repetition without using loops.

This chapter introduces recursive definitions and recursive functions. Later chapters will demonstrate the importance of recursion in supporting data abstraction. We will see that recursive definitions are often necessary to define data and associated operations, and recursive functions are a natural means for implementing the operations on the data.

6.1 Recursive Definitions

Consider a stack of toy wooden blocks. We might define the expression "Block A is above Block B" as shown in Definition 6.1.

Definition of *"Block A is above Block B"*

Definition 6.1 Recursive definition of "Block A is above Block B"

1. If Block A is sitting directly on Block B, then Block A is above Block B.

2. If Block A is sitting directly on another block (Block C) and Block C is above Block B, then Block A is above Block B.

This definition is divided into two parts, labeled 1 and 2. For any two blocks A and B, if either Part 1 or Part 2 is satisfied (true), then the definition says that Block A is above Block B.

Part 2 of the definition is the recursive part. This part defines "A is above B" in terms of "C is above B." Hereafter, we will refer to this relationship as "is above" for convenience.

Recursive definitions may seem unnatural at first. However, they are actually an extremely powerful and precise tool. We can better understand the definition of "is above" by examining a particular example, such as Figure 6.1.

This figure shows four colored blocks in a single stack. Let us apply the definition of "is above" to the blue block and the red block. Substituting BLUE for "Block A" and RED for "Block B," our definition becomes:

Definition of *"BLUE is above RED"*

1. If BLUE is sitting directly on RED, then BLUE is above RED.

2. If BLUE is sitting directly on another block (Block C) and Block C is above RED, then BLUE is above RED.

In this case, Part 1 of the definition is satisfied, so we immediately conclude that BLUE is above RED.

Now consider the question, "Is BLUE above GREEN?" This question is a bit more difficult to answer from the definition. If we substitute BLUE and GREEN for Blocks A and B, the translated definition states:

Definition of *"BLUE is above GREEN"*

1. If BLUE is sitting directly on GREEN, then BLUE is above GREEN.

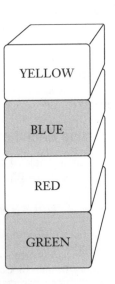

Figure 6.1 A stack of colored blocks

2. If BLUE is sitting directly on another block (Block C) and Block C is above GREEN, then BLUE is above GREEN.

Here, Part 1 of the definition is not true, so we must examine Part 2. BLUE sits directly on RED. Therefore, "Block C" in Part 2 must mean RED. Performing this substitution transforms Part 2 into the following:

2. If BLUE is sitting directly on RED, and RED is above GREEN, then BLUE is above GREEN.

To determine whether the conditions are satisfied, we must apply the definition another time to see if RED is above GREEN.

Definition of *"RED is above GREEN"*

1. If RED is sitting directly on GREEN, then RED is above GREEN.

2. If RED is sitting directly on another block (Block C) and Block C is above GREEN, then RED is above GREEN.

Part 1 of this second application is satisfied. Therefore, RED is defined to be above GREEN. This fact satisfies Part 2 of the first application of the definition, so we conclude that BLUE is above GREEN.

The process of repeatedly applying the definition to determine an answer is a characteristic of recursive definitions. Consider the question

Is YELLOW above GREEN?

This reduces to the question

Is BLUE above GREEN?

which in turn reduces to

Is RED above GREEN?

The answer to the final question, and therefore to all of the others, is "yes."

Base and Recursive Parts of a Definition

Definition 6.2 is a second recursive definition. This time we define the notion of an "odd positive integer."

Definition of *odd positive integer*

Definition 6.2 Recursive definition of odd positive integer

Base   The number one (1) is the first odd positive integer.
Recursive I is an odd positive integer if $I - 2$ is an odd positive integer.

This definition, like all recursive definitions, has two separate parts. These parts are the **base part** (or **basis**) and the **recursive part** (or **inductive part**). The base part is a nonrecursive statement establishing the definition for some fixed group of objects. In this case the base part states that the object "1" is an odd positive integer.

The recursive part of a definition is written so that with repeated applications it reduces to the base. For example, we can determine that 7 is an odd positive integer as follows. Applying the recursive part, we notice that 7 is odd if 5 is odd. A second application of the recursive part shows that 5 is odd if 3 is odd. A third application shows that 3 is odd if 1 is odd. The base part states that 1 is odd. Therefore 3, 5, and 7 also must be odd positive integers.

The earlier definition of "is above" also has a base part (the part labeled 1) and recursive part (the part labeled 2). The base part completes the definition whenever a block is directly on top of another. The recursive part defines "is above" in terms of the next lower block, so another application of the definition moves closer to the base.

In addition to the base and recursive parts, there is an implicit part to any recursive definition. The base part states one or more cases that immediately satisfy the definition. The recursive part tells how to apply the definition again to satisfy other cases. The implicit part states, "And nothing else satisfies the definition."

To see from Definition 6.2 that 4 is not an odd positive integer, we proceed as follows. The recursive part says that 4 is an odd positive integer if 2 is an odd positive integer. A second application of the recursive part states that 2 is an odd positive integer if 0 is an odd positive integer. But the base part says that 1 is the first odd positive integer. Therefore 0, 2, and 4 cannot be odd positive integers.

Fibonacci Numbers

Definition 6.3 defines a Fibonacci number. The base part of this definition says that the first and second Fibonacci numbers are both 1. Its recursive part states that each subsequent Fibonacci number is the sum of its two predecessors. The implicit part states, "No other object is a Fibonacci number."

Definition of *Fibonacci number*

Base   The first Fibonacci number is 1.
        The second Fibonacci number is also 1.
Recursive   Every Fibonacci number after the first two is the sum of the two previous Fibonacci numbers.

Definition 6.3 Recursive definition of Fibonacci number

This definition yields the following sequence of Fibonacci numbers:

2 is a Fibonacci number (it is the sum of 1 + 1).
3 is a Fibonacci number (it is the sum of 1 + 2).
5 is a Fibonacci number (it is the sum of 2 + 3).

8 is a Fibonacci number (it is the sum of 3 + 5).

$$\vdots$$

The implicit part of the definition ensures that 4 is *not* a Fibonacci number, because the sequence continues to increase in value.

Recursive definitions are essential tools for the computer scientist. They are useful for defining both data structures and algorithms. Sometimes a recursive definition is not only convenient, it is also nearly unavoidable. Try defining Fibonacci numbers without a recursive definition! (There is, in fact, a nonrecursive definition of Fibonacci numbers, but it is extremely unintuitive and difficult to understand.)

6.2   BNF—A Recursive Technique

The syntax of a programming language is a good example of the need for recursive definitions. Consider the syntax of an integer constant (Definition 6.4).

Definition of *integer constant* (decimal notation)

Definition 6.4 Recursive definition of integer constant

Base   Any decimal digit (0 through 9) is an integer constant.
Recursive   Any decimal digit followed immediately by an integer constant is an integer constant.

We can state this English definition more concisely by using a technique for defining language syntax known as **Backus–Naur Form,** abbreviated as **BNF.** BNF was developed by John Backus and Peter Naur to define the Algol 60 programming language. Since then, BNF has been used to define the syntax of virtually all programming languages.

Syntax diagrams or syntax charts (see Appendix J) belong to a class of language description techniques called **recognizers.** Given a syntax diagram and a particular program, you can trace through the syntax diagram to see if the code is "recognized" (that is, syntactically correct). BNF belongs to the second major class of description techniques, known as **generators.** A generator defines how to construct, or generate, all possible syntactically valid strings of a language, rather than how to check a particular string.

BNF consists of **rewrite rules** (or **productions**) that define how a **nonterminal symbol** can be replaced, or rewritten, by a string of symbols. Throughout this text we enclose nonterminals in angle brackets, "< >". A rewrite rule begins with a nonterminal, followed by "::=", followed by the string of symbols that can replace the left-hand nonterminal. For example, the rewrite rule below specifies that the nonterminal <Digit> can be replaced by a 7.

<Digit> ::= 7

A symbol, such as 7 above, that is not in angle brackets is called a **terminal symbol.** Terminal symbols are the literal units of the programming language being defined and cannot be rewritten further. In contrast, nonterminals are a part of the BNF notation itself.

A complete BNF definition usually consists of many rewrite rules to define all of the options. Definition 6.5 includes 10 rewrite rules with the same nonterminal, <Digit>, on the left.

Definition 6.5 Ten rewrite rules to define <Digit>

<Digit> ::= 0
<Digit> ::= 1
<Digit> ::= 2
<Digit> ::= 3
<Digit> ::= 4
<Digit> ::= 5
<Digit> ::= 6
<Digit> ::= 7
<Digit> ::= 8
<Digit> ::= 9

When the same nonterminal is on the left side of many rewrite rules, the rules represent different alternatives. In this case a digit is defined to be either a 0, or a 1, ..., or a 9.

It is easy to see how the BNF for the syntax of an entire programming language could include an enormous number of rewrite rules. One way to abbreviate the notation is to use an **alternation symbol** to separate alternative replacement strings. The BNF alternation symbol is the vertical bar "|". With this notation we can abbreviate Definition 6.5 as follows:

<Digit> ::= 0 | 1 | 2 | 3 | 4 | 5 | 6 | 7 | 8 | 9

When a BNF definition includes many different nonterminals, the **initial nonterminal** is usually the left-hand nonterminal of the first rewrite rule. This initial nonterminal represents the entire syntactic unit being defined. Definition 6.6 shows a complete BNF definition containing two nonterminals, <IntConst3> and <Digit>.

Definition 6.6 BNF definition of <IntConst3>

<IntConst3> ::= <Digit> <Digit> <Digit>
          | <Digit> <Digit>
          | <Digit>

<Digit> ::= 0 | 1 | 2 | 3 | 4 | 5 | 6 | 7 | 8 | 9

The initial nonterminal in this definition is <IntConst3>. This nonterminal can be rewritten as a string of three, two, or one consecutive <Digit> nonterminals. In turn, each <Digit> nonterminal can be rewritten as any one of the

10 decimal digits. In other words, this BNF defines <IntConst3> as any string of one to three decimal digits.

Definition 6.7 uses BNF to define the initial nonterminal <IntConst>. In this case, there are two options for <IntConst>. It can be either a single decimal digit or a decimal digit followed by an <IntConst>.

Definition 6.7 BNF definition of <IntConst>

<IntConst> ::= <Digit> | <Digit> <IntConst>

<Digit> ::= 0 | 1 | 2 | 3 | 4 | 5 | 6 | 7 | 8 | 9

This definition of <IntConst> is simply the BNF version of the English description in Definition 6.4. In BNF the "recursive part" occurs whenever a nonterminal can be rewritten by some string containing itself.

BNF descriptions, like other recursive definitions, must incorporate a base portion and a recursive portion. The base rewrite rule, allowing recursion to end for <IntConst>, is

<IntConst> ::= <Digit>

whereas the recursive part is

<IntConst> ::= <Digit> <IntConst>

Definition 6.8 includes rewrite rules that define the correct syntax for declaring a C++ enumeration type. The initial nonterminal is <EnumSpecifier>. <EnumSpecifier> is defined in terms of the terminal symbols "enum", "{", and "}" as well as the nonterminals <EnumList> and <Identifier>. <EnumList> is recursively defined as one enumerator or a sequence of several enumerators, separated by commas. Through recursion, the rewrite rule for <EnumList> permits the derivation of all such sequences of enumerators.

Definition 6.8 BNF for C++ enumeration type declaration

<EnumSpecifier> ::= enum { <EnumList> }
                  | enum <Identifier> { <EnumList> }

<EnumList> ::= <Enumerator>
             | <EnumList> , <Enumerator>

<Enumerator> ::= <Identifier>
               | <Identifier> = <ConstantExpr>

<Identifier> ::= :

These rewrite rules define only a tiny portion of the language. Appendix K contains a complete BNF definition of C++, using a modified version of the BNF notation presented here.

6.3   **Recursive Functions**

Functions can be recursive, just as definitions can. A **recursive function** is one that invokes itself either directly or indirectly. **Direct recursion** occurs when a function is invoked by a statement in its own body. **Indirect recursion** occurs when one function initiates a sequence of function invocations that eventually invokes the original. For example, A invokes B, then B invokes C, then C invokes A.

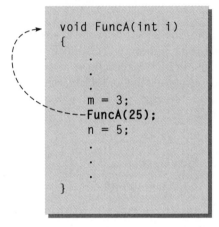

```
void FuncA(int i)
{
        .
        .
        .
        .
      m = 3;
      FuncA(25);
      n = 5;
        .
        .
        .
        .

}
```

Direct recursion

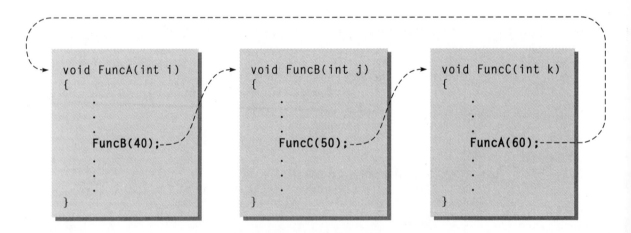

```
void FuncA(int i)        void FuncB(int j)        void FuncC(int k)
{                        {                        {
      .                        .                        .
      .                        .                        .
  FuncB(40);                 FuncC(50);                 FuncA(60);
      .                        .                        .
      .                        .                        .
      .                        .                        .
}                        }                        }
```

Indirect recursion

For many programmers, designing and reasoning about recursive algorithms does not come naturally. It takes some exposure and practice. To understand recursion better, it helps to visualize how the machine actually implements recursion.

Figure 6.2 displays a directly recursive function named EchoReversed. This function inputs a single line of characters and outputs the characters in reverse order.

When a function is invoked at execution time, it is said to be **activated.** Each individual function activation has its own **activation frame,** a collection of information maintained by the run-time system. This activation frame, which describes the **environment** of the current activation, includes:

1. the current contents of all local variables within the function (more precisely, the automatic, not static, local variables)

2. the current contents of all formal parameters within the function

3. a return address

In Chapter 4 we described how the system uses the run-time stack to push and pop return addresses at function entry and function exit. We simplified the discussion by focusing only on return addresses. More generally, the system pushes and pops entire activation frames. That is, each function invocation results in a push of an activation frame (to save the caller's environment), and each return from a function results in a pop of an activation frame (to discard the called function's environment and restore the caller's environment).

The system makes no distinction between recursive and nonrecursive functions. With recursive function invocation, the run-time stack simply contains several activation frames, one for each new activation of the recursive function.

Suppose EchoReversed is executed with the input

MUG<NL>

```
// -----------------------------------------------------------------------
void EchoReversed()
    //...........................................................
    // POST: Input chars (up to '\n') have been output in reverse
    //       order
    //...........................................................
{
    char inChar;

    cin.get(inChar);
    if (inChar == '\n')
        cout << '\n';        // Terminate previous line
    else {
        EchoReversed();
        cout << inChar;
    }
}
```

Figure 6.2 EchoReversed function

where <NL> denotes the newline character '\n'. The first invocation of EchoReversed reads the character 'M' into the local variable inChar. At this point in the execution, we can diagram the initial activation frame as Snapshot 1 of Figure 6.3.

This diagram pictures the activation frame as a rectangular window. The window displays the contents of the local inChar variable and uses an arrow to point to the currently executing instruction. This arrow in Snapshot 1 shows that the if instruction is currently executing. Because inChar is not <NL>, the else clause is executed next, producing a recursive invocation of EchoReversed.

At this moment, the system suspends execution of the first activation, pushes its activation frame onto the run-time stack, and initiates a new activation (Snapshot 2). The new activation frame is pictured as a separate window layered on top of the first. Notice that both activations have separate copies of the local inChar variable. The "?" in the inChar variable of the new activation means that this variable currently is unassigned.

Figure 6.3 Snapshot-by-snapshot trace of EchoReversed execution

Snapshot 1   input: MUG<NL>

```
inChar   'M'                                        Activation #1

      cin.get(inChar);
───►  if (inChar == '\n')
          cout << '\n';
      else {
          Ech t << inChar;
      }
}
```

Snapshot 2   input: MUG<NL>

```
inChar   'M'                                        Activation #1

      ...
───► EchoReversed();
      cout << inChar;
```

```
      inChar   ?                                    Activation #2

      ───► cin.get(inChar);
              if (inChar == ...
```

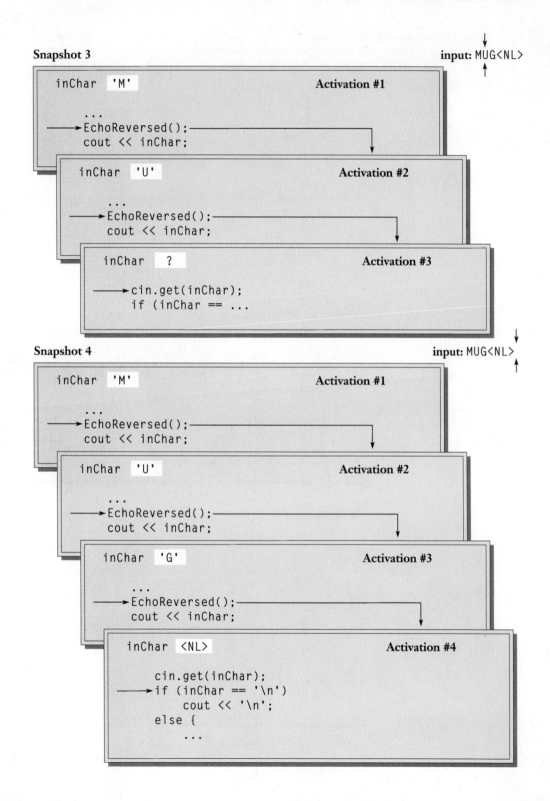

Snapshot 5   **Resulting output:** <NL>

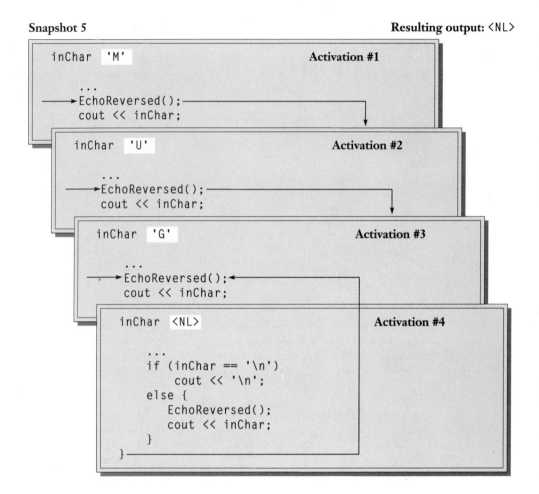

```
  inChar  'M'                                        Activation #1

    ...
  → EchoReversed();
    cout << inChar;
```

```
  inChar  'U'                                        Activation #2

    ...
  → EchoReversed();
    cout << inChar;
```

```
  inChar  'G'                                        Activation #3

    ...
  → EchoReversed();
    cout << inChar;
```

```
  inChar  <NL>                                       Activation #4

        ...
        if (inChar == '\n')
            cout << '\n';
        else {
            EchoReversed();
            cout << inChar;
        }
  }
```

Snapshot 6   **Resulting output:** `<NL>`

```
  inChar  'M'                              Activation #1

  ...
→ EchoReversed();
  cout << inChar;

     inChar  'U'                              Activation #2

     ...
  → EchoReversed();
     cout << inChar;

        inChar  'G'                              Activation #3

           ...
           EchoReversed();
     →     cout << inChar;
        }
     }
```

Snapshot 7   **Resulting output:** `<NL>G`

```
  inChar  'M'                              Activation #1

  ...
→ EchoReversed();
  cout << inChar;

     inChar  'U'                              Activation #2

     ...
  → EchoReversed();
     cout << inChar;

        inChar  'G'                              Activation #3

           ...
           EchoReversed();
           cout << inChar;
        }
     }
```

Snapshot 8   **Resulting output:** `<NL>GU`

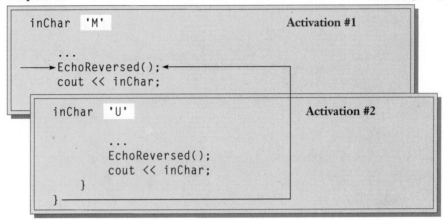

Snapshot 2 also describes the control flow at this instant. The first activation has invoked the function recursively. The first activation is now "on hold" while the second activation begins to execute. As this second activation proceeds, it reads the input character 'U' and invokes `EchoReversed` for a third time, as shown in Snapshot 3. Note how the system has pushed the frame for Activation #2 onto the top of the run-time stack.

By Snapshot 4, the third invocation has read the character 'G' and produced a fourth invocation that reads the <NL> character. At this time, there are four simultaneous activation frames, three on the run-time stack. Each frame stores the separate `inChar` value that it read.

Next, the current activation, Activation #4, executes the `cout << '\n'` instruction. Because there are no more instructions to execute, it returns as pictured in Snapshot 5. In slow motion, here is what happens. The system discards the current activation frame (for Activation #4), installs the frame at the top of the run-time stack as the new current frame, and pops the stack. These actions restore the environment of Activation #3, including its return address (Snapshot 6).

Activation #3 proceeds to output the value of its own copy of `inChar` and then it returns (Snapshot 7). Next, Activation #2 will output its local value of `inChar` and return to activation #1, as shown in Snapshot 8. When the original activation, Activation #1, of `EchoReversed` finally returns, the input characters have been output in LIFO order.

It is interesting to compare the `EchoReversed` function with the example in Chapter 4 (Section 4.6) that also showed how to output input characters in reverse order. In that example, we explicitly declared and managed a stack to store the characters. With `EchoReversed`, there is no need for an explicit stack. The function declares only a simple variable, `inChar`. It is the run-time system that manages an implicit stack—the run-time stack—to store and retrieve values in LIFO order. The resulting code is less cluttered and more concise.

Figure 6.4 shows another way to trace the complete execution of `EchoReversed`. The illustration lists the key instructions on the left in their order of execution. A trace of the data values appears on the right. Indentation signifies a recursive invocation.

Designing with Wisdom

The "One Small Step/Complete the Solution" Model

Learning to think recursively becomes easier by using the "One Small Step/Complete the Solution" model:

Each invocation of a recursive function performs one small step toward the entire solution and makes a recursive call to complete the solution.

For the `EchoReversed` function, the one small step is to echo *one* input character. To complete the solution, it echoes all the remaining input characters (via a recursive call to itself).

The order in which "One Small Step" and "Complete the Solution" take place is crucial. The sequence

```
EchoReversed();
cout << inChar;
```

Control Flow   **Data (local copies)**

```
EchoReversed();

    cin.get(inChar);---------inChar: 'M' ------------------
    EchoReversed();

        cin.get(inChar);---------inChar: 'U'-----------
        EchoReversed();

            cin.get(inChar);---------inChar: 'G'----
            EchoReversed();

                cin.get(inChar);---------inChar: NL
                cout << '\n';
                // Output '\n'
                // RETURN

            cout << inChar;----------------------
            // Output 'G'
            // RETURN

        cout << inChar;-------------------------------
        // Output 'U'
        // RETURN

    cout << inChar;-----------------------------------
    // Output 'M'
    // RETURN
```

Figure 6.4 A trace of `EchoReversed`

says to echo all the remaining characters *before* echoing the current character. This is why the input characters are output in reverse (LIFO) order. In contrast, the sequence

```
cout << inChar;
EchoReversed();
```

says to echo the current character and *then* echo all the remaining ones. This sequence will output the input characters in normal (FIFO) order.

A Study in Design

A Graphics Fill Function

This example of a recursive function comes from the field of computer graphics. Graphics programs commonly use "fill" algorithms to color regions of an image on a video screen. A region that is to be filled with a color must have a clearly defined boundary.

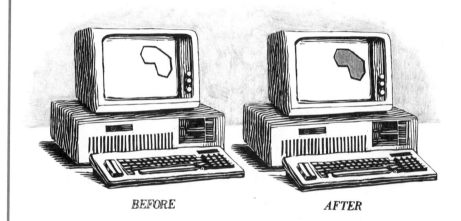

Filling a bounded region with color

BEFORE   *AFTER*

The six-part problem specification in Figure 6.5 supplies the details of a graphics fill function.

Figure 6.5 Problem specification for the Fill function

TITLE

Two-dimensional graphics fill function

DESCRIPTION

A graphics image consists of a two-dimensional grid of picture elements (pixels) representing a video display screen. Each individual pixel is referenced by its row and column location, where rows are numbered from the top and columns from the left. For this problem, each pixel can be one of eight colors (black, blue, green, cyan, red, magenta, brown, or white).

This function accepts as parameters:

1. an initial screen image as a matrix of pixel colors

2. the row and column number of a particular pixel

3. a "paint color"

The pixel addressed by the function's parameters is inside a region enclosed by a boundary of pixels with the specified paint color. The function must change all pixels within this region to the paint color. A region is said to be "bounded" when it is entirely enclosed by appropriate pixels above, below, on the left, and on the right. For example, the W's below form a boundary:

```
        WWWWWWWW
        W          W
        W          W
        W        WWWW
        WWWWW     W
            WWWWWWW
```

The following region is not completely bounded by W's because the pixel denoted by the letter O is not bounded above.

```
        WWWWWW
        W       W
        W       OW
        W      WWWW
        WWWWW     W
            WWWWWWW
```

The function assumes the following global declarations for a 200 × 400 grid:

```
const int TOP_ROW = 0;
const int BOT_ROW = 199;
const int LEFT_COL = 0;
const int RIGHT_COL = 399;

typedef int RowRange;     // Range: TOP_ROW..BOT_ROW
typedef int ColRange;     // Range: LEFT_COL..RIGHT_COL

enum Color {
    black, blue, green, cyan, red, magenta, brown, white
};

typedef Color PixMatrix[BOT_ROW+1][RIGHT_COL+1];
```

The prototype for this function is:

```
void Fill( /* inout */ PixMatrix pixel,
           /* in */    RowRange  row,
           /* in */    ColRange  col,
           /* in */    Color     paintColor );
```

INPUT

There is no external input. However, all four parameters serve to input information to the function.

OUTPUT

There is no external output. However, when the function returns, the region of the `pixel` array bounded by pixels of `paintColor` is filled in with `paintColor`.

ERROR HANDLING

If no appropriate border is found, the fill should end at the boundaries of the array.

EXAMPLE

Assume the following function invocation:

`Fill(pixel, 4, 5, white)`

Below is a portion of the `pixel` array before the invocation. The row and column numbers appear to the left and above. (Note: R is a red pixel, G is green, C is cyan, W is white, and a blank is a black pixel.)

```
                    11111111
          012345678901234567
      0
      1                    C
      2    WWWWWW          G
      3    W  WW   W       W
      4     W R  C  W
      5      W G WWWW
      6      W  G    W
      7      WWWWWWWWWWWW
      8
      9
```

Below is the same portion of the `pixel` array after the invocation:

```
                    11111111
          012345678901234567
      0
      1                    C
      2    WWWWWW          G
      3    WWWWWWWWW       W
      4     WWWWWWWW
      5      WWWWWWW
      6      WWWWWWW
      7      WWWWWWWWWWWW
      8
      9
```

A nonrecursive `Fill` function is impractical; it is extremely complicated to design. However, we can conveniently implement `Fill` with the recursive function shown in Figure 6.6. The comments to the right of the recursive invocations are for later reference when we perform a trace of the control flow.

Every invocation of this function receives a current pixel location (`row` and `col`). If this current pixel has the fill color `paintColor`, then the function returns immediately. If not, then `Fill` assigns it the fill color and repeats this algorithm for the four neighboring pixels (the ones directly above, directly to the right, directly below, and directly to the left). Thus, for this function the "One Small Step" is to store the fill color into just one pixel. To "Complete the Solution," the function makes recursive invocations on behalf of its neighbors.

Figure 6.7 displays a sample trace of the execution of the `Fill` function. This figure illustrates the effect of the invocation

```
Fill(pixel, 3, 3, white);
```

in a series of 10 snapshots. The `pixel` array appears in the upper-right corner of each snapshot.

```
void Fill( /* inout */ PixMatrix pixel,
           /* in */     RowRange   row,
           /* in */     ColRange   col,
           /* in */     Color      paintColor )
    //......................................................
    // PRE:  All parameters are assigned
    // POST: The region surrounding the pixel at (row,col), out to a
    //       boundary of color paintColor, has been filled
    //       with paintColor.
    //......................................................
{
    if (pixel[row][col] == paintColor)
        return;

    // ASSERT: pixel[row][col] is not equal to paintColor

    pixel[row][col] = paintColor;

    if (row > TOP_ROW)
        Fill(pixel, row-1, col, paintColor);     // Call 1

    if (col < RIGHT_COL)
        Fill(pixel, row, col+1, paintColor);     // Call 2

    if (row < BOT_ROW)
        Fill(pixel, row+1, col, paintColor);     // Call 3

    if (col > LEFT_COL)
        Fill(pixel, row, col-1, paintColor);     // Call 4
}
```

Figure 6.6 The `Fill` function

Figure 6.7 Snapshot-by-snapshot trace of `Fill` execution

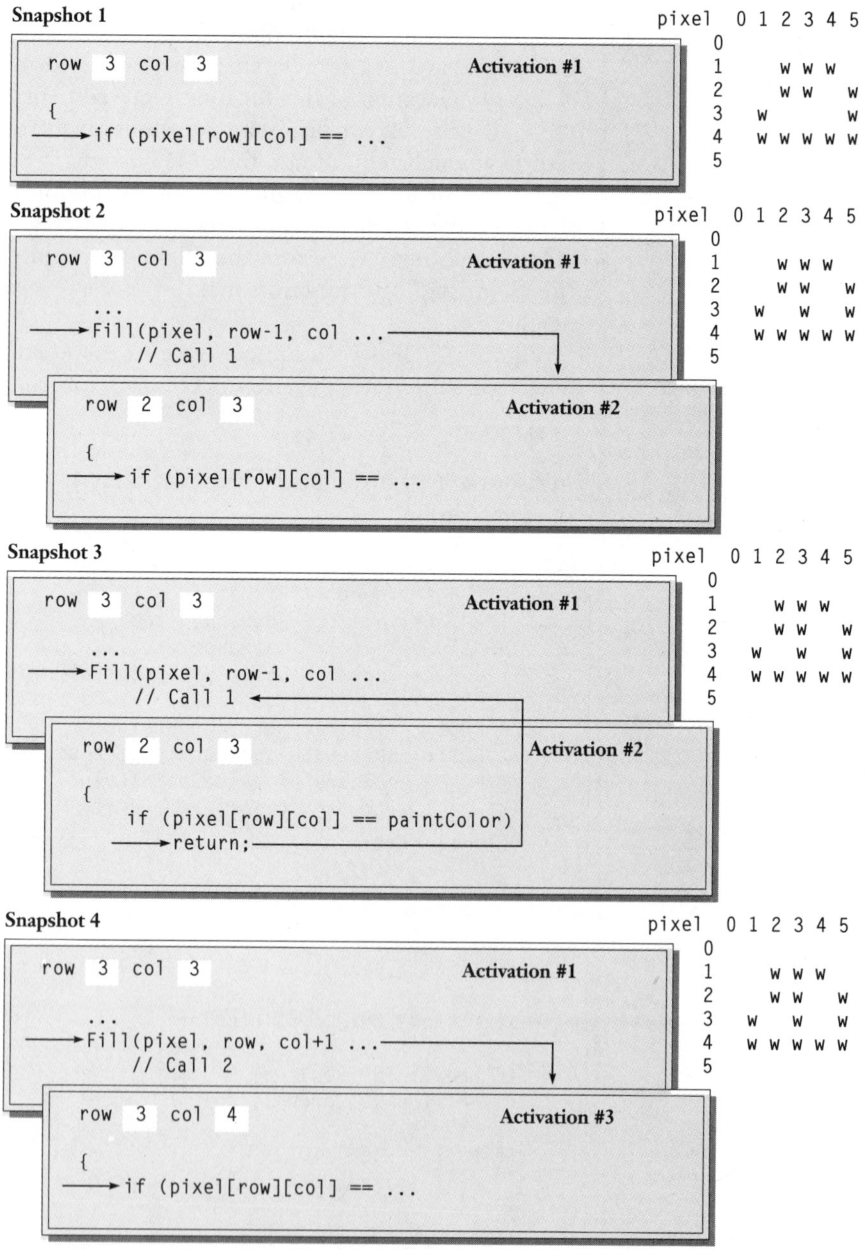

Snapshot 1

```
row  3  col  3                    Activation #1

   {
 ──────► if (pixel[row][col] == ...
```

```
pixel  0 1 2 3 4 5
0
1        w w w
2        w w   w
3      w       w
4      w w w w w
5
```

Snapshot 2

```
row  3  col  3                    Activation #1

   ...
 ──────► Fill(pixel, row-1, col ... ──────────┐
         // Call 1                            │
                                              ▼
```

```
pixel  0 1 2 3 4 5
0
1        w w w
2        w w   w
3      w   w   w
4      w w w w w
5
```

```
   row  2  col  3                 Activation #2

      {
    ──────► if (pixel[row][col] == ...
```

Snapshot 3

```
row  3  col  3                    Activation #1

   ...
 ──────► Fill(pixel, row-1, col ...
         // Call 1 ◄───────────────────┐
```

```
pixel  0 1 2 3 4 5
0
1        w w w
2        w w   w
3      w   w   w
4      w w w w w
5
```

```
   row  2  col  3                 Activation #2

      {
         if (pixel[row][col] == paintColor)
       ──────► return; ───────────────┘
```

Snapshot 4

```
row  3  col  3                    Activation #1

   ...
 ──────► Fill(pixel, row, col+1 ... ──────────┐
         // Call 2                            │
                                              ▼
```

```
pixel  0 1 2 3 4 5
0
1        w w w
2        w w   w
3      w   w   w
4      w w w w w
5
```

```
   row  3  col  4                 Activation #3

      {
    ──────► if (pixel[row][col] == ...
```

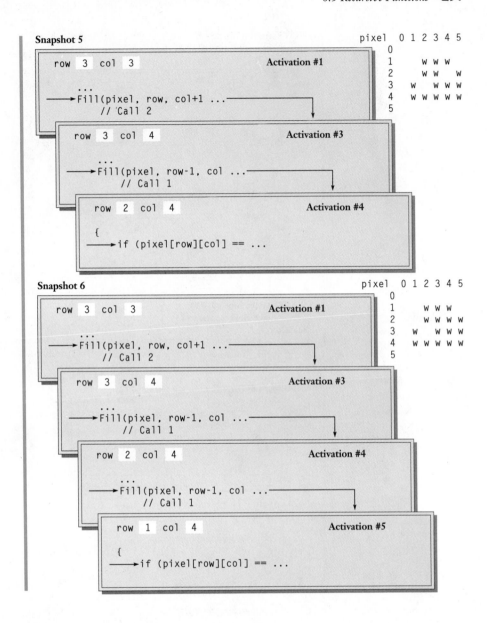

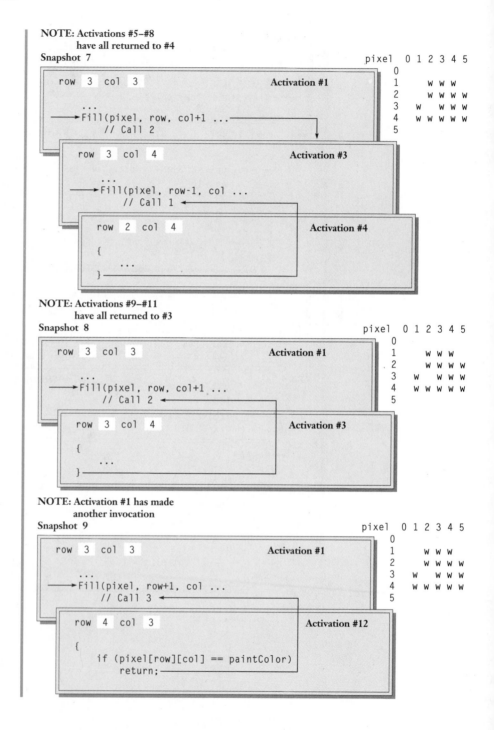

NOTE: Activations #5–#8
      have all returned to #4

Snapshot 7

pixel 0 1 2 3 4 5

```
row  3  col  3                                    Activation #1

  ...
  ──────►Fill(pixel, row, col+1 ...──────
         // Call 2


       row  3  col  4                           Activation #3

         ...
    ──────►Fill(pixel, row-1, col ...
           // Call 1 ◄


           row  2  col  4                     Activation #4

           {
               ...
           }
```

```
0
1        w w w
2        w w w w
3     w     w w w
4     w w w w w
5
```

NOTE: Activations #9–#11
      have all returned to #3

Snapshot 8

pixel 0 1 2 3 4 5

```
row  3  col  3                                    Activation #1

  ...
  ──────►Fill(pixel, row, col+1 ...
         // Call 2 ◄


       row  3  col  4                           Activation #3

       {
           ...
       }
```

```
0
1        w w w
2        w w w w
3     w     w w w
4     w w w w w
5
```

NOTE: Activation #1 has made
      another invocation

Snapshot 9

pixel 0 1 2 3 4 5

```
row  3  col  3                                    Activation #1

  ...
  ──────►Fill(pixel, row+1, col ...
         // Call 3 ◄


       row  4  col  3                          Activation #12

       {
           if (pixel[row][col] == paintColor)
               return;
       }
```

```
0
1        w w w
2        w w w w
3     w     w w w
4     w w w w w
5
```

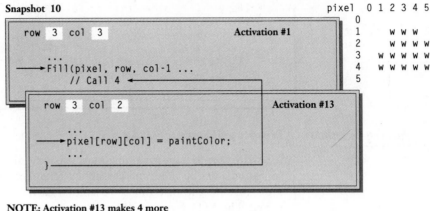

NOTE: **Activation #13 makes 4 more invocations to complete the entire process**

A total of 17 activations of Fill are required to complete this single task. Figure 6.8 traces the control flow of these invocations to further illustrate the recursive pattern.

Figure 6.8 Trace of the invocation Fill(pixel, 3, 3, white)

Initial **pixel** *array*

```
     0123456
0
1    WWW
2    WW W
3    W   W
4    WWWWW
5
```

Control Flow

```
Fill(pixel, 3, 3, white)  // Act. #1

   Fill(pixel, 2, 3, white)  // Call 1 / Act. #2
   Fill(pixel, 3, 4, white)  // Call 2 / Act. #3

      Fill(pixel, 2, 4, white)  // Call 1 / Act. #4

         Fill(pixel, 1, 4, white)  // Call 1 / Act. #5
         Fill(pixel, 2, 5, white)  // Call 2 / Act. #6
         Fill(pixel, 3, 4, white)  // Call 3 / Act. #7
         Fill(pixel, 2, 3, white)  // Call 4 / Act. #8

      Fill(pixel, 3, 5, white)  // Call 2 / Act. #9
      Fill(pixel, 4, 4, white)  // Call 3 / Act. #10
      Fill(pixel, 3, 3, white)  // Call 4 / Act. #11
```

```
Fill(pixel, 4, 3, white)   // Call 3 / Act. #12
Fill(pixel, 3, 2, white)   // Call 4 / Act. #13

 Fill(pixel, 2, 2, white)   // Call 1 / Act. #14
 Fill(pixel, 3, 3, white)   // Call 2 / Act. #15
 Fill(pixel, 4, 2, white)   // Call 3 / Act. #16
 Fill(pixel, 3, 1, white)   // Call 4 / Act. #17
```

Pursuing Correctness

Recursion and Parameter Passage

To write correct recursive functions, it is crucial to distinguish between passing parameters by value and passing by reference. Parameters passed by value are similar to automatic local variables. Each function activation has its own copy. The Fill function depends upon every activation to use its own local copy of row and col.

Parameters passed by reference do not produce local copies. There is only one copy of a reference parameter, and all activations of the recursive function are looking at that one copy.

The pixel array of Fill is a typical example of a reference parameter used in a recursive function. (Recall that C++ always passes arrays by reference.) Every activation of Fill shares the same pixel array and passes the array's base address to future activations. If the parameter passage method is changed for any of the Fill parameters, the function will not work.

6.4 From Recursive Definition to Recursive Code

Recursive functions are extremely useful for processing certain organizations of information. One example is a family tree, a collection of names of relatives and their ancestors along with their specific relationships. Figure 6.9 typifies a family tree.

This particular family tree locates children below their parents. For example, Sam Jones and Sue Smith married and had three children: Ira Jones, Ann Jones, and Mia Jones. The family tree ends at the top with "Parents Unknown" when no records exist for older ancestors.

Figure 6.9 is an abstract view of a family tree. This picture might be useful in a family album, but it must take a different form to be represented as data in a computer program.

Figure 6.10 shows one possible representation. A single enumeration type, Relative, uses an identifier for every known relative: NanBlack (represented by C++ as the int constant 0), BobHowe (represented as 1), TimHowe (represented as 2), and so on. We include an additional enumerator, Unknown, to represent family ancestors that are unknown. (For the enumerators denot-

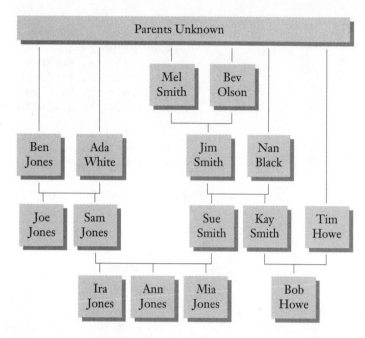

Figure 6.9 A family tree

ing people's names, we make an exception to our convention of beginning only function names and type names with capital letters. It is appropriate to capitalize a person's first name.)

The family tree is represented as two arrays, `mother` and `father`, that store the parents of all family relatives. For example, the father of Kay Smith is stored in

```
father[KaySmith]
```
or
```
father[13]
```

and the mother of Jim Smith is stored in

```
mother[JimSmith]
```
or
```
mother[11]
```

The contents of the `mother` and `father` arrays in Figure 6.10 match the abstract family tree of Figure 6.9.

Many algorithms for processing tree-structured data, like this family tree, are naturally recursive. One such algorithm counts the number of known ancestors for any given relative. The `Ancs` function, shown in Figure 6.11, implements this algorithm.

Declarations:

```
enum Relative {
    NanBlack, BobHowe,  TimHowe,  BenJones,
    IraJones, AnnJones, JoeJones, MiaJones,
    SamJones, BevOlson, JimSmith, MelSmith,
    KaySmith, SueSmith, AdaWhite, Unknown
};

Relative mother[15];
Relative father[15];
```

Contents of `mother` **and** `father` **arrays:**

father	index	mother
Unknown	[NanBlack]	Unknown
TimHowe	[BobHowe]	KaySmith
Unknown	[TimHowe]	Unknown
Unknown	[BenJones]	Unknown
SamJones	[IraJones]	SueSmith
SamJones	[AnnJones]	SueSmith
BenJones	[JoeJones]	AdaWhite
SamJones	[MiaJones]	SueSmith
BenJones	[SamJones]	AdaWhite
Unknown	[BevOlson]	Unknown
MelSmith	[JimSmith]	BevOlson
Unknown	[MelSmith]	Unknown
JimSmith	[KaySmith]	NanBlack
JimSmith	[SueSmith]	NanBlack
Unknown	[AdaWhite]	Unknown

Figure 6.10 A family tree representation with two arrays for parents

```
int Ancs( /* in */ Relative thisOne )
    //............................................................
    // PRE:  Assigned(thisOne)
    // POST: FCTVAL == count of known ancestors of thisOne
    // NOTE: The person thisOne is included in the count
    //............................................................
{
    if (thisOne == Unknown)
        return 0;
    else
        return Ancs(mother[thisOne]) + Ancs(father[thisOne]) + 1;
}
```

Figure 6.11 The Ancs function

Recursive functions often closely resemble recursive definitions. The purpose of the Ancs function is to return the count of all known ancestors. Definition 6.9 is a recursive definition of the phrase "Count of known ancestors."

Definition of "Count of known ancestors of thisOne**"**

Base   If thisOne is unknown, then the count of known ancestors of thisOne is 0.

Recursive   If thisOne is known, then the count of known ancestors of thisOne is the count of known ancestors of thisOne's mother plus the count of known ancestors of thisOne's father plus 1. (thisOne is included in the count.)

Definition 6.9 A recursive definition of "Count of known ancestors"

This definition closely parallels the program code of the Ancs function. The base part of the definition is handled by the then-clause of Ancs, and the recursive part is performed by the else-clause. For anyone accustomed to reading recursive definitions, the Ancs function is a simple and elegant algorithm. A nonrecursive version using whiles and ifs to navigate around the family tree is surprisingly difficult to write.

The Ancs function again demonstrates the "One Small Step/Complete the Solution" pattern. In the else-clause, the one small step amounts to adding 1 to the current count of ancestors. Completing the solution entails making recursive calls to count the mother's and father's ancestors.

6.5 Recursive Value-returning Functions

Ancs is the first example in this chapter of a recursive *value-returning* function. Recursive functions follow exactly the same rules of invocation as do nonrecursive functions:

- A value-returning function is invoked in an expression.
- A non-value-returning function is invoked as a separate, stand-alone statement.

Recursive invocations of value-returning functions often are embedded within `return` statements. For example, the recursion of `Ancs` is entirely expressed in the statement

```
return Ancs(mother[thisOne]) + Ancs(father[thisOne]) + 1;
```

When the machine executes this `return` statement, it first evaluates

```
Ancs(mother[thisOne])
```

by making a recursive invocation and then evaluates

```
Ancs(father[thisOne])
```

with a second recursive invocation. Each of these invocations potentially produces further invocations.

Figure 6.12 illustrates the execution of a recursive value-returning function. This figure traces the execution of `Ancs(JimSmith)` using the data structures defined in Figure 6.10.

Figure 6.12 Snapshot-by-snapshot trace of `Ancs` execution

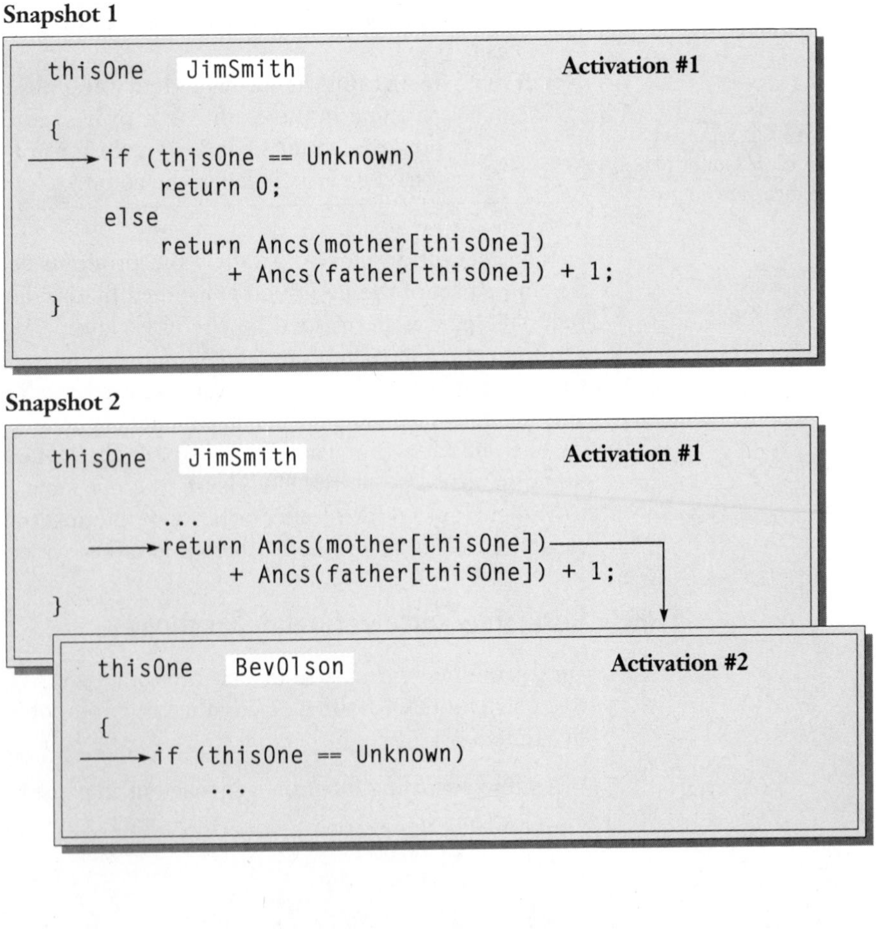

Snapshot 1

```
    thisOne   JimSmith                        Activation #1

      {
  ──────▶ if (thisOne == Unknown)
             return 0;
         else
             return Ancs(mother[thisOne])
                  + Ancs(father[thisOne]) + 1;
      }
```

Snapshot 2

```
    thisOne   JimSmith                        Activation #1

              . . .
  ──────▶ return Ancs(mother[thisOne])────────┐
               + Ancs(father[thisOne]) + 1;   │
      }                                        │
                                               ▼
         thisOne   BevOlson              Activation #2

           {
       ──────▶ if (thisOne == Unknown)
                  . . .
```

Snapshot 3

```
thisOne   JimSmith                        Activation #1

        ...
    ──► return Ancs(mother[thisOne])──────┐
            + Ancs(father[thisOne]) + 1;  │
}                                         │
                                          ▼
    thisOne   BevOlson                        Activation #2

            ...
        ──► return Ancs(mother[thisOne])──────┐
                + Ancs(father[thisOne]) + 1;  │
    }                                         │
                                              ▼
        thisOne   Unknown                         Activation #3

            {
        ──► if (thisOne == Unknown)
                ...
```

Snapshot 4

```
thisOne   JimSmith                        Activation #1

        ...
    ──► return Ancs(mother[thisOne])──────┐
            + Ancs(father[thisOne]) + 1;  │
}                                         │
                                          ▼
    thisOne   BevOlson                        Activation #2

            ...
        ──► return 0◄─────────────────────┐
                + Ancs(father[thisOne]) + 1;  │
    }                                         │
        thisOne   Unknown                     │   Activation #3

            {
                if (thisOne == Unknown)       │
            ──► return 0;─────────────────────┘
                ...
```

Snapshot 5

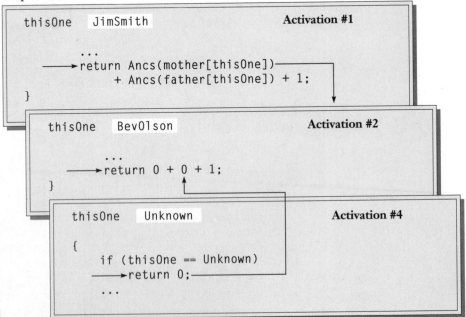

Snapshot 6

Snapshot 7

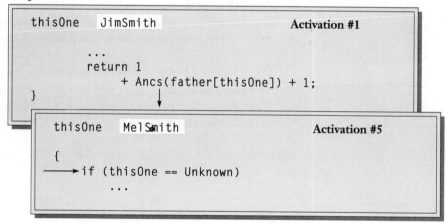

Snapshot 8

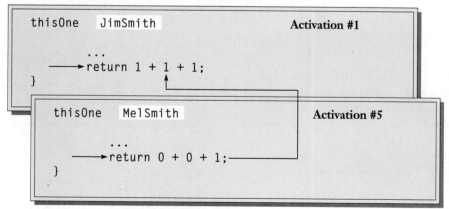

Snapshot 9

NOTE: Activation #5 also invoked Ancs
twice more. Each time 0 was returned.

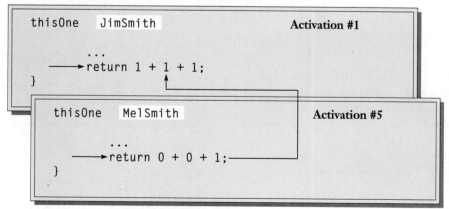

NOTE: Ancs **finally returns the value 3.**

6.6 Recursion from Repetition

The while statement is the most common C++ control structure for repetition. However, some programming languages, including FP and early versions of LISP, have recursion as the *only* repetitive control structure. When recursion is available, looping control structures are not absolutely essential. Figure 6.13 displays a general form of the while loop along with a recursive function, RecWhile, that performs the same task.

Each activation of RecWhile mimics a single iteration of the while loop. If <Condition> is true when RecWhile is invoked, then <Body> is executed. This is identical to what happens in the while loop. After executing <Body>, RecWhile invokes itself recursively to emulate the next loop iteration.

If <Condition> is false when RecWhile is invoked, the function returns immediately. When this activation of RecWhile returns, all of the earlier activations also will return without executing any more instructions. The reason is that RecWhile uses **tail recursion**—the only recursive call to RecWhile is at the very bottom of the function.

There are two important theoretical results from mathematics and computer science that summarize the relationship between recursion and looping:

1. Every loop can be replaced by recursion.
2. Not every recursion can be replaced by a loop (unless the looping algorithm explicitly manages additional data structures, such as stacks, to simulate recursive activations).

These two results further underscore the importance of recursion.

An arbitrary while *loop*	*An equivalent recursive function*
| ```
while ( <Condition> )
    <Body>
``` | ```
void RecWhile()
    // Assume <Condition> and <Body>
    // reference global variables
{
    if ( <Condition> ) {
        <Body>
        RecWhile();
    }
}
``` |

Figure 6.13 A recursive version of the while loop

6.7 Infinite Recursion

Recursion is a powerful tool that can yield elegant, concise algorithms. However, the technique is sometimes difficult to master. Even a short recursive algorithm may be mysterious.

For example, can you tell by a quick inspection of the Ancs function (Figure 6.11) whether it counts all female ancestors before males, or whether it counts all parents before grandparents? The answer to both questions happens to be "no," but the precise order in which Ancs counts ancestors is difficult to describe.

Recursive algorithms also can be tricky to debug. Seemingly minor logic bugs often result in catastrophic execution errors. One of the most common problems, **infinite recursion,** occurs when a function invokes itself recursively without end.

Suppose that we simply reverse the two statements in the then-clause of RecWhile (Figure 6.13). The resulting function, named InfWhile, appears below:

```
void InfWhile()
// WARNING - Infinite recursion below
{
    if ( <Condition> ) {
        InfWhile();
        <Body>
    }
}
```

InfWhile resembles RecWhile at first glance. More careful thought reveals that InfWhile produces infinite recursion if <Condition> is true at the first invocation. The problem is that InfWhile calls itself recursively *before* it can execute <Body>. Therefore, it never executes code that can change the value of <Condition> to false.

Infinite recursion is somewhat different from an infinite loop, because each recursive invocation pushes an additional activation frame onto the run-time stack. Eventually an execution error will occur (or the computer will just "hang") when the stack gobbles up all available memory.

The InfWhile function demonstrates blatant infinite recursion. Sometimes infinite recursion is more subtle. Figure 6.14 displays the Fill function, introduced earlier in this chapter, along with a slightly modified version.

Figure 6.14 Fill and InfFill functions

```
void Fill( /* inout */ PixMatrix pixel,
           /* in */    RowRange  row,
           /* in */    ColRange  col,
           /* in */    Color     paintColor )
{
    if (pixel[row][col] == paintColor)
        return;

    pixel[row][col] = paintColor;
```

```
        if (row > TOP_ROW)
            Fill(pixel, row-1, col, paintColor);    // Call 1
        if (col < RIGHT_COL)
            Fill(pixel, row, col+1, paintColor);    // Call 2
        if (row < BOT_ROW)
            Fill(pixel, row+1, col, paintColor);    // Call 3
        if (col > LEFT_COL)
            Fill(pixel, row, col-1, paintColor);    // Call 4
}

void InfFill( /* inout*/ PixMatrix pixel,
              /* in */    RowRange   row,
              /* in */    ColRange   col,
              /* in */    Color      paintColor )
    // WARNING - Infinite recursion below
{
    if (pixel[row][col] == paintColor)
        return;

    if (row > TOP_ROW)
        InfFill(pixel, row-1, col, paintColor);    // Call 1
    if (col < RIGHT_COL)
        InfFill(pixel, row, col+1, paintColor);    // Call 2
    if (row < BOT_ROW)
        InfFill(pixel, row+1, col, paintColor);    // Call 3
    if (col > LEFT_COL)
        InfFill(pixel, row, col-1, paintColor);    // Call 4

    pixel[row][col] = paintColor;
}
```

The Fill function is a two part algorithm:

1. Fill the current pixel, then
2. Fill the neighboring pixels through four recursive calls.

The InfFill function reverses the algorithm:

1. Fill the neighboring pixels through four recursive calls, then
2. Fill the current pixel.

The revision appears simply to change the order in which pixels are filled. However, the InfFill function results in infinite recursion whenever there are two or more unfilled neighboring pixels. During execution, the first neighbor invokes the function to fill its neighbor before it fills itself. The neighbor does likewise. The recursion is infinite, because neither neighbor can fill its own pixel until its neighbor is filled. Logic errors like this one are very hard to spot.

6.8 A Question of Efficiency: The Factorial

A second difficulty with recursive algorithms, less dramatic than infinite recursion, is the potential for inefficiency. Every recursive invocation pushes another activation frame onto the run-time stack and every return from an activation restores a frame from the top of the stack. These actions consume not only memory space but also execution time for allocating and deallocating frames. One reason for using `while` statements instead of algorithms like `RecWhile` is that loops execute faster.

Computation of the factorial function is a classic example of efficiency considerations. The factorial function, like the Fibonacci number sequence, has a recursive definition. Definition 6.10 is a recursive definition of N factorial (written $N!$).

Definition of N! (N factorial)

Base   If $N = 0$ or $N = 1$, then $N! = 1$.
Recursive   If $N > 1$ then $N! = N * (N - 1)!$

Definition 6.10 Recursive definition of $N!$

A Recursive Algorithm

The recursive definition of $N!$ suggests the use of a recursive function to calculate factorials. Figure 6.15 illustrates such a function.

The `RecFactorial` function bears a striking resemblance to the recursive definition and correctly calculates factorials. However, a more efficient, nonrecursive algorithm is also well known.

A Looping Algorithm

If $N > 0$, we can write $N!$ as $1*2*3*...*(N-1)*N$. This observation leads to the looping solution in Figure 6.16.

```
int RecFactorial( /* in */ int n )
   //..............................................................
   // PRE:  n >= 0
   // POST: FCTVAL == n!
   //..............................................................
{
   if (n <= 1)
      return 1;
   else
      return n * RecFactorial(n-1);
}
```

Figure 6.15 Recursive factorial function (`RecFactorial`)

```
int LoopFactorial( /* in */ int n )
    //...........................................................
    // PRE:  n >= 0
    // POST: FCTVAL == n!
    //...........................................................
{
    int i;
    int fact = 1;

    for (i = 1; i <= n; i++)  // INV (prior to test):
                              //    fact == (i-1)!  &&  i <= n+1
        fact = fact * i;
    return fact;
}
```

Figure 6.16 Looping factorial function (LoopFactorial)

LoopFactorial requires two local variables that are unnecessary in RecFactorial. However, it is more efficient than RecFactorial because it avoids the additional storage and execution time needed for activation frames.

Table-Driven Code

In the case of the factorial function, there is yet another algorithm that is better than either RecFactorial or LoopFactorial. This algorithm relies on the observation that factorial values grow very rapidly. Table 6.1 shows a list of all factorials from 0! through 12!

From this table it is clear that very few factorial values are less than the maximum int value in C++. For small computers, the largest factorial that can be stored as an int is 7! and nearly all C++ systems are limited to 12!

Because most factorial values are too large to be calculated and stored in memory, why write an algorithm at all? A better approach is to store the few possible alternatives in an array. Instead of recalculating a factorial each time

Table 6.1 Factorials from 0! through 12!

N	N!
0	1
1	1
2	2
3	6
4	24
5	120
6	720
7	5,040
8	40,320
9	362,880
10	3,628,800
11	39,916,800
12	439,084,800

it is needed, it is far faster to retrieve it from the array. The following is a declaration (with initialization) for storing factorials less than 8!

```
int factorial[8] = {
    1, 1, 2, 6, 24, 120, 720, 5040
};
```

This array declaration is at the heart of a programming technique known as **table-driven code** (or **table lookup**). Table-driven code replaces the execution of a sequence of instructions with a simple array (table) lookup. To obtain the value of 4!, table-driven code would replace the function invocation

```
fourFact = LoopFactorial(4);
```

with the following table lookup:

```
fourFact = factorial[4];
```

It is faster to retrieve the value from an array than to execute instructions to calculate the value. Table-driven code also can simplify algorithms. The only disadvantages are the memory space required to store the table and the execution time required to initialize it.

Designing with Wisdom

When to Use Recursion

There are no absolute rules for selecting recursive versus nonrecursive algorithms. The conciseness of many recursive functions makes them easier to read and maintain. This conciseness is, in itself, a powerful benefit of using recursion.

On the other hand, the machine implementation of recursion consumes both computer storage and time. The guidelines below should help when considering the alternatives.

1. If the problem is stated recursively and a recursive algorithm is less complex than a nonrecursive version, then recursion is likely to be preferable.

2. If both recursive and nonrecursive algorithms are of similar complexity, the nonrecursive algorithm is likely to be more efficient and therefore preferred.

3. Don't forget to consider table-driven code as an option. If this technique fits the problem, a table lookup will outperform, by far, both looping and recursive algorithms.

In many instances, the choice between recursion and looping is unclear. The classic tradeoff is the concise readability of recursion versus the efficient execution of loops. But do not get carried away with either extreme. In most cases, forcing a recursive solution onto every problem is as ill-advised as spending hours trying to shave away every last microsecond from a program's execution time. The wise designer knows when efficiency really matters and when it is less important. In Chapter 12 we examine this issue at length.

Pursuing Correctness

Debugging Recursion

A recursive algorithm can be difficult to debug. Tracing large numbers of recursive activations is often a trying experience. In addition, bugs in recursive algorithms can be very subtle, almost invisible.

Here are three basic rules to observe when designing and debugging recursive algorithms:

1. Include preconditions and postconditions in recursive routines, just as in any other routines.

2. Ensure that the recursion terminates.

3. Consider how multiple activations affect local variables and parameters.

Most errors in recursion result from failure to consider one or more of these three rules adequately. Designers should use these rules to test a design, and maintenance programmers should check these rules when debugging.

Because recursion is expressed in the form of functions, preconditions and postconditions are vital. These assertions allow the programmer to reason about the correctness of recursive routines.

Infinite recursion is a common problem. Every recursive function requires careful examination to ensure that it terminates under all cases that satisfy the precondition.

The third debugging rule addresses another major source of errors in recursive code. Each function invocation creates a unique activation frame. Every activation has its own copy of all formal parameters and locally declared automatic data. It is easy to forget that, although only one copy of a variable is visible in the *text* of the source code, there may be many copies of that variable on the run-time stack during program execution. Minimizing the number of automatic variables and parameters of recursive functions reduces the potential for bugs and increases efficiency.

With recursive functions there is also a profound difference between passing parameters by value and passing them by reference. Choosing the wrong method of parameter passage nearly always guarantees an incorrect function.

SUMMARY

Recursion is a way of thinking. Definitions can be written recursively. Programs can be written recursively. Programming language syntax can be defined recursively. This chapter has examined many aspects of recursion:

- a standard form for recursive definitions
- algorithms that model recursive definitions
- both value-returning and non-value-returning recursive functions
- Backus-Naur Form as a recursive generator for programming language syntax
- substituting recursion for looping
- numerous examples of recursive algorithms

Recursion has many advantages, but it also has weaknesses. Programmers must guard against infinite recursion. Programmers must also balance the elegance of recursive algorithms against the potential loss of run-time efficiency.

As data structures become more and more complex, the algorithms for manipulating them become correspondingly more complex. Recursion is one technique that often reduces the complexity.

KEY TERMS

activate (p. 245)	infinite recursion (p. 269)
activation frame (p. 245)	initial nonterminal (p. 242)
alternation symbol (p. 242)	nonterminal symbol (p. 241)
Backus-Naur Form (p. 241)	productions (p. 241)
base part (p. 239)	recognizers (p. 241)
basis (p. 239)	recursive definition (p. 237)
BNF (p. 241)	recursive function (p. 244)
direct recursion (p. 244)	recursive part (p. 239)
environment (p. 245)	rewrite rules (p. 241)
generators (p. 241)	table-driven code (p. 273)
indirect recursion (p. 244)	table lookup (p. 273)
inductive definition (p. 237)	tail recursion (p. 268)
inductive part (p. 239)	terminal symbol (p. 242)

EXERCISES

6.1 For each of the following, give an appropriate recursive definition:

   a. Define I^N (I to the power N), where I and N are integers and $N \geq 0$.

   b. Define $M > N$, where M and N are integers. (Hint: Use $M = N + 1$ in the base part.)

   c. Define $I * J$ (integer multiplication), where $I \geq 0$. (Hint: Define it in terms of integer addition.)

   d. Define "There are connecting airplane flights from city A to city B." (Assume that "There is a direct flight from city 1 to city 2" has already been defined.)

6.2 Section 6.1 contains a recursive definition of "Block A is above Block B." Using this definition and the stack of blocks pictured in Figure 6.1, show that the following is false: "RED is above YELLOW."

6.3 Use BNF to define each of the following:

   a. A language consisting of any string of zero or more decimal digits, followed by exactly one period, followed by one or more decimal digits.

   b. A language consisting of all strings that begin with a single 'Z', followed by one or more letters 'a' or 'b' in any order, followed by a single 'Z'.

   c. A language consisting of one or more digits '0', followed by a single 'X', followed by as many digits '0' as preceded the 'X'.

6.4 In the RecFactorial function of Figure 6.15, what is the "One Small Step/Complete the Solution" pattern?

6.5 Consider the following function specification:

```
int SumOfInts( /* in */ int m,
               /* in */ int n );
    // PRE:   m <= n
    // POST: FCTVAL == sum of the integers m thru n, inclusive
```

The following is a typical invocation:

```
cout << SumOfInts(1, 50);
```

a. Implement the function using a loop control structure.

b. Implement the function using recursion. (Before doing so, write a "One Small Step/Complete the Solution" description.)

c. Which of your two solutions is "better?" Be careful to define "better."

6.6 Using your answer to Exercise 6.1(a), write a recursive function that implements the following specification:

```
int PowerOfInt( /* in */ int someInt,
                /* in */ int exp      );
    // PRE:   Assigned(someInt)  &&  exp >= 0
    // POST: FCTVAL == someInt raised to the power "exp"
```

Compare your solution with the looping version in Section 2.4 of this text.

6.7 Your boss needs a function that returns powers of 3 according to the following specification:

```
int PowerOf3( /* in */ int exp );
    // PRE:   0 <= exp <= 9
    // POST: FCTVAL == 3 raised to the power "exp"
```

This function will be invoked so frequently that speed of execution is crucial. Implement this function with the fastest technique possible. Your boss says that your continued employment depends on it.

6.8 Consider the `Fill` function of Figure 6.6. Each part below gives an initial `pixel` grid and a `Fill` invocation. The function invocation will assign some of the `pixel` elements the value `white`. Indicate which elements these are, and specify the exact order in which the assignments occur. (Use the letters a, b, c, ... in the pixel locations to show the order in which they are painted.)

a. `Fill(pixel, 3, 4, white)`
   Below is a portion of the `pixel` array before the invocation. (Note: "W" denotes a white pixel; a blank denotes a black pixel.)

```
      0123456789
    0
    1     WWWW
    2     W  W
    3     W  W
    4     W  W
    5     WWWW
```

b. `Fill(pixel, 4, 8, white)`

   Below is a portion of the `pixel` array before the invocation. (Note: "W" denotes a white pixel; a blank denotes a black pixel.)

```
      0123456789
   0
   1
   2    WWWWWWW
   3    W     W
   4    W WWW W
   5    W WWW W
   6    W     W
   7    WWWWWWW
```

c. `Fill(pixel, 4, 8, white)`

   Below is a portion of the `pixel` array before the invocation. (Note: "W" denotes a white pixel; a blank denotes a black pixel.)

```
      0123456789
   0
   1
   2    WWWWWWW
   3    W     W
   4    WWW  W W
   5    W WWW W
   6    W     W
   7    WWWWWWW
```

d. `Fill(pixel, 4, 8, white)`

   Below is a portion of the `pixel` array before the invocation. (Note: "W" denotes a white pixel; a blank denotes a black pixel.)

```
      0123456789
   0     W  W W
   1    WWW WW W
   2    W    W W
   3    W W    W
   4    W  W W W
   5    W   WW W
   6    WWWWWWW
```

6.9   Describe the output produced by the following function:

```
void AnotherEcho()
{
    char inChar;

    cin.get(inChar);
    if (inChar == ' ')
        cout << '\n';
    else {
```

```
            cout << inChar;
            AnotherEcho();
    }
}
```

6.10 Consider the Mystery function below:

```
void Mystery( /* in */ char param1,
              /* in */ char param2 )
{
    if (param1 != param2) {
        param1++;
        param2--;
        Mystery(param1, param2);
        cout << param1;
        cout << param2;
    }
}
```

a. Show all output resulting from the following invocation:

```
Mystery('A', 'G');
```

b. Under what circumstances does Mystery result in infinite recursion?

c. Mystery uses parameter passage by value. If param1 and param2 are instead passed by reference, what output will result from the following code?

```
char1 = 'A';
char2 = 'G';
Mystery(char1, char2);
```

6.11 Consider the TermUnknown function below:

```
int TermUnknown( /* in */ int someInt )
    // This is a classic number theory problem for which
    // termination for all input is uncertain.
{
    if (someInt == 1)
        return 0;
    if (someInt % 2 == 1)
        return 1 + TermUnknown(3*someInt + 1);
    return 100 + TermUnknown(someInt / 2);
}
```

What value does each of the following invocations return?

a. TermUnknown(1)

b. TermUnknown(4)

c. TermUnknown(3)

d. TermUnknown(9)

6.12 Consider the Permute function below:

```
// Assume the following declaration:
//      typedef char String3[4];
```

```
void Permute( /* inout */ String3 str,
              /* in */    int      index )
{
    if (index == 3)
        cout << str << ' ';
    else {
        str[index] = 'X';
        Permute(str, index+1);
        str[index] = 'Y';
        Permute(str, index+1);
        str[index] = 'Z';
        Permute(str, index+1);
    }
}
```

Show all of the output produced by the following invocation:

```
String3 someStr;
Permute(someStr, 0);
```

6.13 Write a function that replaces the following loop structure with recursion. For simplicity, assume that <Condition> and <Body> reference global variables from within your function.

```
do
    <Body>
while ( <Condition> );
```

6.14 Modify the Fill function of Figure 6.6 so that it also counts the number of pixels that change color. Use an additional parameter to maintain this count. The caller must initialize this parameter to zero before invoking your function.

PROGRAMMING PROJECTS

6.1 Write and test a program to solve the following problem.

TITLE

Expression recognizer

DESCRIPTION

In programming languages, an expression such as a+b*c is inherently ambiguous. Without any precedence rules, it could mean either (a+b)*c or a+(b*c). A simple way to resolve this ambiguity without establishing precedence rules is to require *fully parenthesized expressions*. With this notation, parentheses must surround every pair of operands and their operator. The above expression must be written ((a+b)*c) or (a+(b*c)).

The following is a BNF definition of fully parenthesized expressions, with <Id>, denoting "identifier", simplified to a single letter:

> <Expr>   ::= <Id> | (<Expr> <Op> <Expr>)
> <Op>   ::= + | - | * | /

$$<Id> \quad ::= a \mid b \mid c \mid \ldots \mid z$$
$$\mid A \mid B \mid C \mid \ldots \mid Z$$

This program inputs strings and recognizes those that are valid as fully parenthesized expressions. Because the rewrite rule for <Expr> is recursive, it is natural to use a recursive algorithm. The following pseudocode algorithm, although lacking important details, should provide a starting point:

Algorithm FindAnExpression:

IF next char is a letter THEN
   it's an expression
ELSE IF next char is a '(' THEN
   FindAnExpression
   IF next char is an operator THEN
     FindAnExpression
     IF next char is a ')' THEN
       it's an expression
(For all of the above tests that fail, it's not an expression.)

INPUT

Each expression consists of a string up to 80 characters long. Successive strings are separated by whitespace characters. Therefore, an expression cannot contain embedded spaces. The end-of-file condition signals end of input.

Although the program reads from standard input, it is assumed that the user has first prepared a data file containing the strings and will use command line redirection of standard input:

```
$ recogniz < myfile.txt
```

(If your system does not support command line redirection, perform file input from within your program using an ifstream. You may want to review the material on basic file I/O in Section C.1 of Appendix C.)

OUTPUT

Because input will come from a file, there is no prompt to the user to start typing text. For each string, the program echoes the string, then prints either

```
    ** Is a valid expression **
```
or
```
    ** Is  N O T  a valid expression **
```

and then a blank line.

ERROR HANDLING

The program does not need to check for input errors.

EXAMPLE

Assume that the input file contains the following lines:

```
a
ab
(a+b)
(a)
((a+b)*c)
((a+b)*c
a+b
((a+b)/(c-d))
(((a-b)*(c+d))+(e*f))
```

From this input file, the program produces the following output:

```
a
** Is a valid expression **
ab
** Is  N O T  a valid expression **
(a+b)
** Is a valid expression **
(a)
** Is  N O T  a valid expression **
((a+b)*c)
** Is a valid expression **
((a+b)*c
** Is  N O T  a valid expression **
a+b
** Is  N O T  a valid expression **
((a+b)/(c-d))
** Is a valid expression **
(((a-b)*(c+d))+(e*f))
** Is a valid expression **
```

6.2   Write and test a function to solve the following problem.

TITLE

```
Boolean CanFlow( /* in */ int pointA,
                 /* in */ int pointB );
```

DESCRIPTION

A city engineer needs a program to analyze the city's sewer system. The program maintains the city water system connections in a global array named `connected`, whose declaration is as follows:

```
Boolean connected[100][100];
```

Whenever two water pipes join, they form a junction. These junctions are numbered from 0 through 99. The `connected` matrix specifies whether water can flow directly from one junction to another. If there is a direct connecting pipe from junction *i* to junction *j*, and water is permitted to flow from *i* to *j*, then connected[i][j] is TRUE. If there is no direct connecting pipe between *i* and *j* or if a connecting pipe exists but water may only flow from *j* to *i*, then connected[i][j] is FALSE. Below is a partial collection of pipes and the corresponding connected matrix:

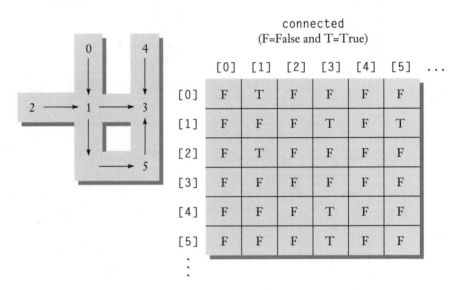

connected
(F=False and T=True)

	[0]	[1]	[2]	[3]	[4]	[5]	...
[0]	F	T	F	F	F	F	
[1]	F	F	F	T	F	T	
[2]	F	T	F	F	F	F	
[3]	F	F	F	F	F	F	
[4]	F	F	F	T	F	F	
[5]	F	F	F	T	F	F	

The invocation CanFlow(A, B) returns the value TRUE if and only if water can flow from junction A to junction B through one or more paths through the water pipes.

You may assume that no collection of water pipes forms a cycle permitting water to flow around in circles from one junction to others and back again. Also, you may access the connected matrix globally.

INPUT

There is no external input to this function. However, both pointA and pointB serve as input to the routine.

OUTPUT

There is no output to the user. However, the function returns a Boolean value to indicate the presence or absence of a path of pipes allowing water to flow from pointA to pointB.

ERROR HANDLING

If pointA, pointB, or any element of the connected matrix is unassigned, the results are undefined. If the connected matrix contains a cycle, the results are undefined.

EXAMPLE

For the example above, the following invocations return TRUE:

```
CanFlow(0, 1)
CanFlow(0, 5)
Canflow(2, 3)
```

For the example above, the following invocations return FALSE:

```
CanFlow(1, 0)
CanFlow(3, 0)
CanFlow(5, 1)
```

6.3 Using the same basic definition of `CanFlow` as in Project 6.2, write and test the following modified functions.

a. `CanFlowWithCycles` is the same as `CanFlow` except that it permits cycles in the water pipes specified by the `connected` matrix.

b. `MinPath(pointA, pointB)` returns the length of the shortest path from `pointA` to `pointB`. The shortest path is the one passing through the fewest junctions. If `NOT CanPath(A, B)` then `MinPath(A, B)` equals 0.

6.4 Write and test a program to solve the following problem.

TITLE

Maze solver

DESCRIPTION

This program inputs representations of mazes and attempts to find a path through each maze. A maze is represented as a 7 by 7 grid. Each cell of the grid is either open to pass through or filled with a barricade, making it impassable. Valid paths begin at the upper-left corner and end at the lower-right corner. Furthermore, a valid path can only pass through empty cells and may not pass through the same cell more than once. Paths proceed from one cell to the next horizontally or vertically, but not diagonally.

If the program finds a path, it displays the path graphically. Otherwise, it outputs a message stating that there is no valid path.

INPUT

The maze grids are input as seven lines with seven characters per line. Each line of input corresponds to one row of the maze. For each row, a dot (.) signifies an empty cell in the maze and an asterisk (*) signifies a barricade.

After processing a maze and producing the corresponding output, the program prompts the user to enter a 'Y' or 'y' to continue with another maze. Any input other than 'Y' or 'y' terminates the program.

OUTPUT

The program issues the following prompt prior to reading in each maze:

```
Specify maze as 7 lines of 7 chars ('.' or '*'):
```

After the user enters a maze grid, the program outputs one blank line, followed by the maze with the path indicated by consecutive lowercase letters—'a' marks the first cell of the path, 'b' marks the second, and so on. If all letters have been used, they repeat.

After output of the maze, one blank line precedes the following prompt to the user:

```
Continue? (Y or N):
```

If the user chooses to continue, one blank line precedes the prompt for input of the next maze.

ERROR HANDLING

1. If no path exists from the upper left cell to the lower right, then the following message is displayed instead of the maze and path:

   ```
   NO PATH EXISTS!
   ```

2. Any invalid input produces undefined results.

EXAMPLE

Below is a sample execution with all input in color.

```
Specify maze as 7 lines of 7 chars ('.' or '*'):
.***...
..**.**
*....**
**.*.**
.*.*.**
****...
******.

a***...
bc**.**
*defg**
**.*h**
.*.*i**
****jkl
******m

Continue? (Y or N): y

Specify maze as 7 lines of 7 chars ('.' or '*'):
```

```
..*....
..*.**.
......*.
*****.
.......
.*****.
.......

ab*hijk
.c*g**l
.def.*m
*****n
utsrqpo
v******
wxyzabc

Continue? (Y or N): y

Specify maze as 7 lines of 7 chars ('.' or '*'):
.......
..**.*.
*....*.
**.*..*
.*.*.**
**.*...
**...*.

abcde..
..**f*.
*...g*.
**.*h.*
.*.*i**
**.*jkl
**...*m

Continue? (Y or N): y

Specify maze as 7 lines of 7 chars ('.' or '*'):
.......
..**.*.
*....*.
**.*.*.
.*.*.**
**.**..
**...*.

NO PATH EXISTS!

Continue? (Y or N): y
```

```
Specify maze as 7 lines of 7 chars ('.' or '*'):
*......
.......
...*...
*..*...
...*...
*..*...
*......

NO PATH EXISTS!          ◄── This example fails because both upper-left
                             and lower-right cells must be empty.
Continue? (Y or N): n
```

6.5 The following problems are variations of Project 6.4.

   a. Write a maze path finder that differs from Project 6.4 in that it displays a separate maze with path for each possible correct path.

   b. Write a maze path finder that differs from Project 6.4 in that it displays only the shortest correct path.

CHAPTER 7

Pointers and Dynamic Data

INTRODUCTION

Every memory cell in a computer's memory unit has two characteristics:

1. a *value* (or *contents*)

and

2. a unique *address*

Just as every house in a city has a unique postal address, every memory cell has its own numeric address. The computer's central processing unit needs this memory address to know where to fetch or store data.

In a C++ program, a variable is an abstraction for one or more memory cells, and a variable name is an abstraction for a memory address. For example, we abstract the meaning of the statements

```
alpha = 20;
beta = 30;
```

to be "After execution, the variable named `alpha` contains the value 20, and the variable named `beta` contains the value 30." However, a machine-level interpretation of these statements might be as pictured in Figure 7.1.

Address	Memory cell	Program identifier
2000	20	alpha
2001	30	beta

Figure 7.1 Machine-level view of two simple variables

287

In this diagram, we have arbitrarily chosen the machine addresses 2000 and 2001 for illustration only. The key point is that *every program variable corresponds to one or more memory cells*, each uniquely identified by a numeric machine address. Furthermore, program identifiers such as `alpha` and `beta` are nothing more than symbolic synonyms for those machine addresses.

In general, the C++ programmer does not know (or need to know) the actual machine addresses of variables. It is clearly preferable to use the abstraction `alpha` throughout a program rather than the address 2000. However, many programming applications require access to addresses of data objects. C++ provides two categories of data types, *pointer types* and *reference types*, that allow a program to manipulate data objects based on their memory addresses.

In this chapter we begin by examining the details of pointer types and reference types. Thereafter, the remainder of the chapter explores a powerful application of pointers—*dynamic data*—that serves as a major tool for implementing abstract data types.

7.1   Pointer Types

Pointer Variables

A **pointer variable** is one that contains the address, not the value, of a data object. The statement

```
int* intPtr;
```

declares that `intPtr` is a variable that can point to (that is, contain the address of) an `int` object. In general, the declaration

<Type>* <Identifier>;

states that <Identifier> can hold the address of an object of type <Type>.

Using the Language

Declaring Pointer Variables

When you declare pointer variables in C++, two rules of syntax pertain:

1. *The placement of the asterisk is not important to the compiler.* The following declarations are all equivalent:

```
int*  intPtr;
int   *intPtr;
int * intPtr;
```

   The first two forms are the most common in C++ programs. We prefer the first form. Attaching the asterisk to the data type name instead of the variable name readily identifies the data type as "pointer to `int`."

2. *When you declare several pointer variables in one statement, the asterisk does* not *distribute throughout the statement.* Compare the statement

```
int* p, q;        ◄— Equivalent to int* p;
                                  int  q;
```

with the statement

```
int *p, *q;        ◄── Equivalent to int* p;
                                  int* q;
```

The best way to avoid problems is to make each declaration a separate statement.

The Address-Of Operator

Given the declaration

```
int* intPtr;
```

we can use the C++ **"address-of" operator** (&) to make `intPtr` point to `alpha` (of Figure 7.1):

```
intPtr = &alpha;
```

Here, `alpha` is called the **referent** of `intPtr`. Alternatively, we can say that `alpha` is the object pointed to by `intPtr`. If `intPtr` happens to be located at memory address 3000, this assignment statement yields the machine-level diagram shown in Figure 7.2.

Because actual numeric addresses are generally unknown to the C++ programmer, it is more common to display the relationship between a pointer and its referent by using rectangles and arrows as in Figure 7.3.

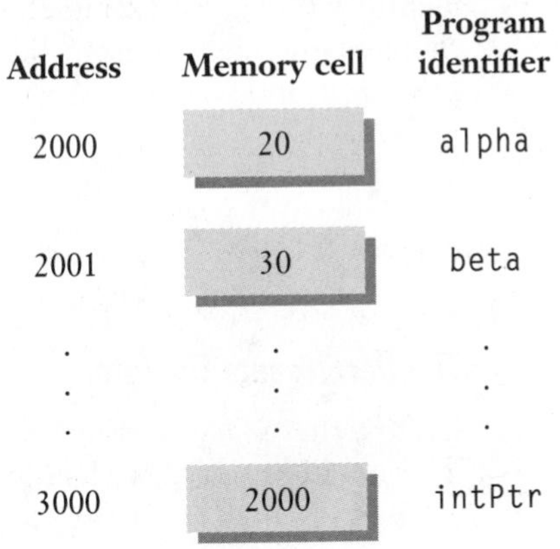

Address	Memory cell	Program identifier
2000	20	alpha
2001	30	beta
.	.	.
.	.	.
.	.	.
3000	2000	intPtr

Figure 7.2 Machine-level view of a pointer variable

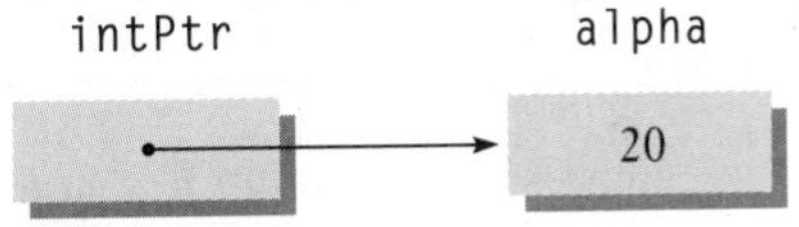

Figure 7.3 Abstract diagram of a pointer variable

The Null Pointer

During program execution, a pointer variable can be in one of the following states:

1. It is unassigned.
2. It points to some data object.
3. It contains the pointer constant 0.

The pointer constant 0 is called the **null pointer.** The null pointer does not point to any object; it is guaranteed to be distinct from any actual machine address. In particular, it is *not* the machine address 0. The null pointer is used only as a special pointer value that a program can test for:

```
if (intPtr == 0)
      .
      .
      .
```

The null pointer is compatible with all pointer types—pointer to int, pointer to char, and so forth. The following statement assigns the null pointer to somePointer:

```
somePointer = 0;
```

Figure 7.4 depicts the result of this assignment using the two most common forms for diagramming null pointers. In this text, we use the notation on the left.

Instead of using the constant 0, many feel it is better style to use a constant identifier (NULL, for example) to represent the null pointer. In fact, C++ environments define a constant identifier named NULL in the standard header file stddef.h, and programmers usually include this file when using pointers:

```
#include <stddef.h>
      .
      .
      .
somePtr = NULL;
```

The Dereference Operator

In C++ the unary operator * is the **dereference** (or **indirection**) **operator.** The notation *intPtr denotes the object pointed to by intPtr (that is, the referent of intPtr). If intPtr points to alpha as in Figure 7.3, the statement

```
*intPtr = 95;
```

assigns the value 95 to alpha. As a matter of terminology, the statement

```
alpha = 95;
```

represents **direct addressing** of alpha. At run time the machine locates alpha directly and stores 95 into it. In contrast, the statement

```
*intPtr = 95;
```

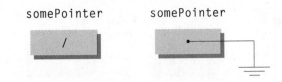

Figure 7.4 Two abstract diagrams of the null pointer

represents **indirect addressing** of alpha. At run time, the machine first locates intPtr, then uses its contents to locate alpha, and finally stores 95 into alpha.

Note the crucial distinction between the following two statements:

```
*intPtr = 34;
intPtr = 34;        ←— No!
```

The former assigns 34 to the referent of intPtr; the latter attempts to assign 34 to intPtr itself (to make it point to memory address 34). This attempt is almost certainly an error in logic and will also produce either a warning or a fatal error from the compiler.

Figure 7.5 uses four examples to illustrate dereferencing expressions. For each example, two diagrams describe the conditions before and after the instruction executes.

A Definition of C++ Pointer Types

Definition 7.1 summarizes pointer data types in C++. This definition uses the form we introduced in Chapter 4 for defining data types. The meanings of some of the allowable operations will unfold later in this chapter and the next.

Figure 7.5 Examples of dereferencing expressions

```
int* intPtrA;
int* intPtrB;
int  tempInt;
```

The code segments below use the above declarations:

Example 1:

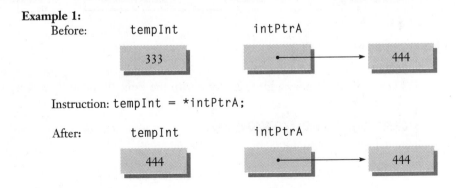

Instruction: tempInt = *intPtrA;

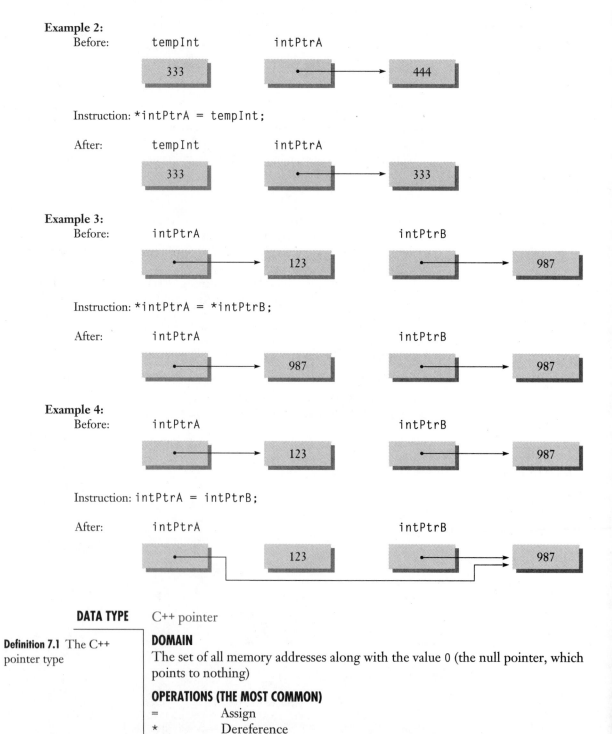

Example 2:

Before: tempInt   intPtrA

333   →   444

Instruction: `*intPtrA = tempInt;`

After: tempInt   intPtrA

333   →   333

Example 3:

Before: intPtrA   intPtrB

→ 123   → 987

Instruction: `*intPtrA = *intPtrB;`

After: intPtrA   intPtrB

→ 987   → 987

Example 4:

Before: intPtrA   intPtrB

→ 123   → 987

Instruction: `intPtrA = intPtrB;`

After: intPtrA   intPtrB

123   → 987

DATA TYPE   C++ pointer

Definition 7.1 The C++ pointer type

DOMAIN
The set of all memory addresses along with the value 0 (the null pointer, which points to nothing)

OPERATIONS (THE MOST COMMON)

=	Assign
*	Dereference
++	Pre-increment (by size of object pointed to)

++	Post-increment (by size of object pointed to)
--	Pre-decrement (by size of object pointed to)
--	Post-decrement (by size of object pointed to)
+	Add (second operand is integral)
-	Subtract (second operand is integral or pointer)
+=	Add and assign (second operand is integral)
-=	Subtract and assign (second operand is integral)
==	Test for equality
!=	Test for inequality
<	Test for less than
<=	Test for less than or equal to
>	Test for greater than
>=	Test for greater than or equal to
!	Logical NOT (result is 1 if operand is 0)
[]	Subscript
delete	Destroy (deallocate)
->	Select a member of the class, struct, or union that is pointed to

7.2 Constant Pointer Expressions and Pointer Arithmetic

The null pointer (0) is an example of a constant pointer expression. Another example is any pointer variable declared with the notation *const:

```
int *const intPtr = &someInt;
```

Once declared and initialized in this fashion, intPtr cannot be reassigned a new value.

Array names are also constant pointer expressions in C++. An array name without any subscript brackets following it is a pointer expression whose value is the beginning address (base address) of the array. Suppose that we have the declarations

```
int  vec[10];
int* vPtr;
```

and that vec[0] happens to be located at address 5000. Then the assignment statement

```
vPtr = vec;
```

has the same effect as

```
vPtr = &vec[0];
```

Both of these statements store 5000 (the base address of the vec array) into vPtr. Furthermore, Definition 7.1 says that the subscript operation is valid for *any* pointer expression, not just an array name. Therefore, we can subscript the pointer variable vPtr as follows:

```
vPtr[3] = 28;
```

This statement has the same effect as

```
vec[3] = 28;
```

because `vPtr` points to the beginning of the `vec` array.

Pointer Arithmetic

C++, unlike most other languages, allows **pointer arithmetic** on pointer variables and pointer constants. Valid operations are ++, --, +, -, +=, and -=. The statement

```
vPtr++;
```

does not necessarily increment the contents of `vPtr` by 1. Instead, it increments `vPtr` by a value that depends on the memory size of its referent. Because we declared `vPtr` to be a pointer to an `int`, this statement increments `vPtr` by the size of an `int` object. As a result, `vPtr` now points to the next element of the array.

The operators +, -, +=, and -=, which add or subtract an integer value to/from a pointer, also perform arithmetic according to the size of the pointed-to object. For instance, we could write the sequence of statements

```
vec[0] = 5;
vec[1] = 10;
vec[2] = 15;
```

as the sequence

```
vPtr = vec;
*vPtr = 5;
*(vPtr+1) = 10;
*(vPtr+2) = 15;
```

In fact, some C++ compilers automatically transform any expression `vec[i]` into `*(vec+i)` internally.

In Chapter 4 we argued that when an array is viewed as an abstract data type, contiguous allocation of memory cells is only one of several possible data representations. C++ does guarantee that, from the programmer's perspective, the built-in array types use contiguous memory allocation. Using pointer arithmetic to step through a C++ array is therefore consistent with this data representation. Figure 7.6 shows four alternative ways of zeroing out a 100-element array.

Figure 7.6 Alternatives for zeroing out an array

Each code segment below zeros out a 100-element integer array
Alternative 1:

```
// This version uses array subscripts and an index variable

int vec[100];
int i;
```

```
    i = 0;
    while (i < 100) {
        vec[i] = 0;
        i++;
    }
```

Alternative 2:

```
// This version uses a pointer variable and pointer arithmetic

int  vec[100];
int* ptr;

ptr = vec;                       // Or  ptr = &vec[0]
while (ptr < vec + 100) {
    *ptr = 0;
    ptr++;
    // ASSERT: ptr points to next array element
}
```

Alternative 3:

```
// This version uses a for-loop as shorthand for the
// while-loop of Alternative 1

int vec[100];
int i;

for (i = 0; i < 100; i++)
    vec[i] = 0;
```

Alternative 4:

```
// This version uses a for-loop as shorthand for the
// while-loop of Alternative 2

int  vec[100];
int* ptr;

for (ptr = vec; ptr < vec + 100; ptr++)
    *ptr= 0;
```

In Figure 7.6, Alternatives 3 and 4 are more likely to be seen in C++ programs than Alternatives 1 and 2. It is more straightforward to use a for loop than to set up manually the initialization, testing, and incrementing of the loop control variable.

In comparing Alternatives 3 and 4, Alternative 3 is probably more readable to a new C++ programmer. A veteran C++ programmer will find both versions equally understandable. For this particular application—zeroing out an array—there is no compelling reason to use Alternative 4. We have included it only to demonstrate pointer arithmetic in C++.

Copying Pointers

The fact that an array name is a constant pointer expression has an important consequence: aggregate array assignment is illegal in C++. We have emphasized that the following code is not permitted:

```
char str[5];
   ⋮
str = "Hi";        ←── Not allowed. Use the library function
                        strcpy(str, "Hi").
```

The unadorned array name str is a pointer *constant*, not a pointer variable, so it cannot appear to the left of the equal sign. However, the following code is legitimate:

```
char* str;
   ⋮
str = "Hi";
```

because str is now a pointer variable, not a pointer constant. A string constant, such as "Hi", implicitly has type "array of char" and storage class static. When the compiler sees this string constant, it allocates memory for the string (somewhere in the program's memory area reserved for static data) and records the base address of this string. Copying this base address into the pointer variable str is therefore a pointer copy, not a string copy. Figure 7.7 illustrates the difference between this code segment and the previous one. (Recall from Section A.7 of Appendix A or Section B.5 of Appendix B that the null character '\0' marks the end of the string in a string array.)

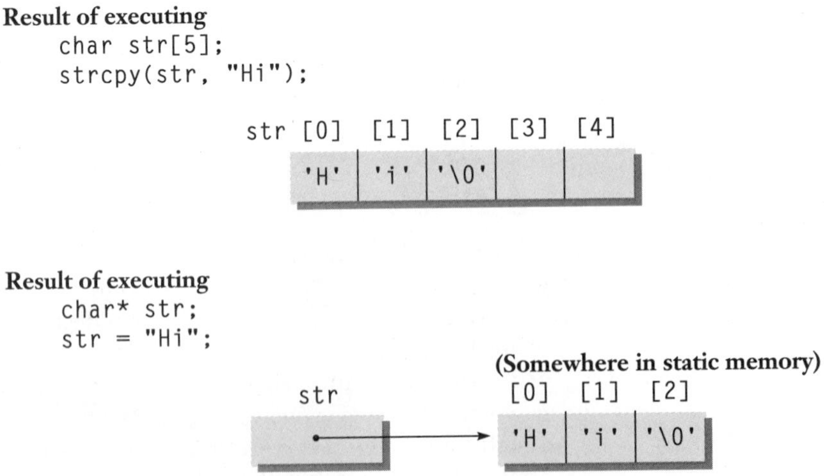

Result of executing
```
      char str[5];
      strcpy(str, "Hi");
```

str [0] [1] [2] [3] [4]

| 'H' | 'i' | '\0' | | |

Result of executing
```
      char* str;
      str = "Hi";
```

(Somewhere in static memory)

str

| | → | 'H' | 'i' | '\0' |

[0] [1] [2]

Figure 7.7 Difference between a string array and a pointer to a string

Similarly, with the following code:

```
char* str;
char* str2;

str = "Hi";
str2 = str;
```

each assignment is a pointer copy, not a string copy. As a result, both `str` and `str2` point to the same string in memory (Figure 7.8).

Passing Arrays as Parameters

Having introduced pointers, we can more precisely describe passing arrays as parameters. Recall that arrays are always passed by reference in C++. Assuming `myString` is a string array, the function invocation

```
length = StrLength(myString);
```

sends the base address of `myString` to the function `StrLength`. The function can view the formal parameter as an array

```
int StrLength( char str[] )
{ ... }
```

and use subscript notation to step through the array and calculate its length. Alternatively, because the function receives a memory address through the parameter list, the function also could view the formal parameter as a pointer

```
int StrLength( char* str )
{ ... }
```

and then use pointer arithmetic to step through the array. Figure 7.9 demonstrates alternative ways of coding the `StrLength` function.

Result of executing
```
    char* str;
    char* str2;

    str = "Hi";
    str2 = str;
```

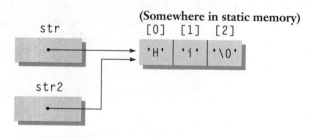

Figure 7.8 Example of assigning one pointer variable to another

Each function below returns the length, in characters, of its string parameter:

Alternative 1:

```
int StrLength( /* in */ const char str[] )
{                                // This version views the formal parameter
    int i = 0;                   // as an array

    while (str[i] != '\0')
        i++;
    return i;
}
```

Alternative 2:

```
int StrLength( /* in */ const char* str )
{                                // This version views the formal parameter
    int numChars = 0;            // as a pointer to char

    while (*str != '\0') {
        numChars++;
        str++;
        // ASSERT: str points to next array element
    }
    return numChars;
}
```

Alternative 3:

```
int StrLength( /* in */ const char* str )
{                                // This version increments the pointer as a
    int numChars = 0;            // side effect in the while condition

    while (*str++ != '\0')          ←── Unary operators group right to left,
        numChars++;                     so increment str, not the object it
    return numChars;                    points to.
}
```

Figure 7.9 Alternatives for a StrLength function

Choosing among these three versions of StrLength is largely a matter of taste. Alternative 1 will be the most familiar to those with backgrounds in Pascal-like languages. Alternatives 2 and 3 may execute slightly faster than Alternative 1, depending on the code generated by a particular compiler. However, the difference in speed will be virtually unnoticeable to the user, so speed should not play a role in your choice of style for this function.

7.3   Command-Line Arguments

In all the examples that we have looked at so far, the parameter list of the main function has been empty because main apparently is not invoked by any other

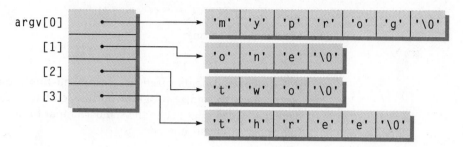

Figure 7.10 Argument vector (argv) and command-line arguments

routine. This is not quite the case. The C++ environment itself invokes the main function to begin program execution. Furthermore, the user may pass parameters to main by typing the parameters on the operating system's command line. These parameters, called **command-line arguments,** are separated by spaces and are always passed to the main function as character strings:

$ myprog one two three   ←— Assume that $ is the operating system prompt.

In this example, the user wishes to execute a program named myprog, passing three strings—"one", "two", and "three"—to the main function.

More precisely, the C++ system passes two parameters to the main function:

argc   The count of command-line arguments (including the program name)

argv   A vector of character strings, one for each command-line argument (including the program name)

To access these arguments, the main function declares them as follows:

```
int main( int argc, char* argv[] )
{
    ⋮
}
```

Here argv is declared to be a vector of pointers to char (abstractly, a vector of strings). If the user types

$ myprog one two three

then argc = 4, and

argv[0] points to the string "myprog"
argv[1] points to the string "one"
argv[2] points to the string "two"
argv[3] points to the string "three"

Figure 7.10 illustrates this relationship between argv and the command-line strings.

A program can test and manipulate argc as it would any integer variable. The program can also manipulate argv[i] as it would any character string. For example, the statement

```
cout << argv[2] << ' ' << argv[2][0];
```

outputs the following:

two t

C++ environments often use command-line arguments beginning with minus signs to signify program options or flags. For example, a program named ArgEcho might echo the standard input to the standard output with the following command-line options:

$ argecho	Pure echo of input to output
$ argecho -u	Echo, translating all lowercase to uppercase letters
$ argecho -r	Echo in reverse order of input

The program shown in Figure 7.11 satisfies this description and prints error messages in response to invalid command-line options. This program uses the C++ library routines toupper and strcmp (Appendix G) and a recursive function EchoReversed (Section 6.3).

Figure 7.11 ArgEcho program demonstrating command-line arguments

```
// --------------------------------------------------------------
//  argecho.cpp
//  This program demonstrates use of command-line arguments.
//      $ argecho       Causes pure echo of input to output
//      $ argecho -u    Translates lower- to uppercase during echo
//      $ argecho -r    Echoes in reverse order of input
// --------------------------------------------------------------
#include <iostream.h>
#include <ctype.h>      // For toupper()
#include <string.h>     // For strcmp()
#include "bool.h"

void EchoUpper( Boolean );
void EchoReversed();

int main( int argc, char* argv[] )
{
    switch (argc) {
        case 1:
            EchoUpper(FALSE);
            break;
        case 2:
            if (strcmp(argv[1], "-u") == 0)
                EchoUpper(TRUE);
            else if (strcmp(argv[1], "-r") == 0)
                EchoReversed();
            else
                cerr << "Usage: argecho [-r or -u]\n";
            break;
        default:
            cerr << "Too many args\n";
    }
    return 0;
}
```

```
// -------------------------------------------------------------
void EchoUpper( /* in */ Boolean uppercase )
{
    char ch;

    while (cin.get(ch))  // INV (prior to test):
                         //     All previous characters have been
                         //     echoed
                         //   && EOF not yet encountered
        if (uppercase)
            cout << char(toupper(ch));
        else
            cout << ch;
}
// -------------------------------------------------------------
void EchoReversed()
{
    char ch;

    if (cin.get(ch)) {
        EchoReversed();
        cout << ch;
    }
}
```

7.4   Reference Types

In addition to pointer types, C++ has a second category of data types for manipulating addresses: **reference types.** The statement

```
int& intRef;
```

declares that `intRef` is a variable that can contain the address of an int object. In general, the declaration

<Type>& <Identifier>;

states that <Identifier> can hold the address of an object of type <Type>. This description seems identical to that of pointer variables. We will clarify the difference shortly.

As with pointer variable declarations, the ampersand (&) does not distribute throughout a list of variables. Therefore, beware of the following:

```
int& p, q;        ←── Equivalent to int& p;
                                    int  q;
```

Pointer Versus Reference Variables

Although both reference variables and pointer variables store addresses of data objects, there are two essential differences. First, the dereferencing and address-of operators (* and &) are not used with reference variables. After a reference variable has been declared, the compiler *invisibly* dereferences every single appearance of that reference variable. This difference is illustrated below:

Using a reference variable	**Using a pointer variable**

```
int  someInt = 26;              int  someInt = 26;
int& intRef = someInt;          int* intPtr = &someInt;
// ASSERT: intRef points        // ASSERT: intPtr points
//          to someInt          //          to someInt

intRef = 35;                    *intPtr = 35;
// ASSERT: someInt == 35         // ASSERT: someInt == 35

intRef = intRef + 3;            *intPtr = *intPtr + 3;
// ASSERT: someInt == 38        // ASSERT: someInt == 38
```

Some programmers like to think of a reference variable as an *alias* for another variable. In the preceding code, we can regard intRef as an alias for someInt. After intRef is initialized in its declaration, everything we do to intRef is actually happening to someInt.

The second difference between reference and pointer variables is that the compiler treats a reference variable as if it were a *constant* pointer. It cannot be reassigned after being initialized. In fact, absolutely no operations apply directly to a reference variable except initialization (either explicitly in a declaration or implicitly by passing an actual parameter to a formal parameter or by returning a function value). For example, the statement

```
intRef++;
```

does not increment intRef. It increments the object intRef points to, because the compiler implicitly dereferences each appearance of the name intRef.

The principal advantage of reference variables, then, is notational convenience. The programmer is not required to continually prefix the variable with an asterisk to access the object pointed to.

Passing Variables by Reference

One use of reference variables is to pass nonarray parameters by reference instead of by value. Suppose that the programmer wants to exchange the contents of two float variables with the function call

```
Swap(alpha, beta);
```

Because C++ normally passes simple variables by value, the following code fails:

```
void Swap( float x, float y )
// Caution: This routine does not work
{
    float temp = x;
    x = y;
    y = temp;
}
```

By default, the two parameters are passed by value. Copies of alpha's and beta's values are sent to the function. Thus the local contents of x and y are exchanged within the function, but the actual parameters alpha and beta remain unchanged. To rectify this situation, the programmer has two options. The first is to send explicitly the addresses of alpha and beta by using the address-of operator (&):

```
Swap(&alpha, &beta);
```

The function must then declare the formal parameters to be pointer variables:

```
void Swap( float* px, float* py )
{
    float temp = *px;
    *px = *py;
    *py = temp;
}
```

This approach is necessary and widely used in the C language, which does not offer reference variables.

The other option is to use reference variables to eliminate the need for explicit dereferencing:

```
void Swap( float& x, float& y )
{
    float temp = x;
    x = y;
    y = temp;
}
```

In this case, the function call does not require the address-of operator (&) for the actual parameters:

```
Swap(alpha, beta);
```

The compiler implicitly generates code to pass the addresses, not the values, of alpha and beta. This method of passing (nonarray) parameters by reference is the one that we have been using all along and will continue to use throughout the book.

A Study in Design

Stream I/O of FracType **Objects**

In this section we demonstrate the use of reference types in two contexts: as data types of formal parameters and as data types of function return values. Specifically, we examine in depth the technique of overloading the insertion (<<) and extraction (>>) operators to perform stream I/O of programmer-defined classes.

The Original FracType **Class**

In Chapter 3 we developed a Fraction module that exports a class named FracType. FracType, whose specification we repeat in Figure 7.12, is an

```
// ------------------------------------------------------------
//   SPECIFICATION FILE (fraction.h)
//   This module exports a FracType class with two operator functions,
//   operator* and operator==.  A more general FracType class
//   might include more operations.
// ------------------------------------------------------------
#include "bool.h"

class FracType {
public:
    void Write() const;
        // POST: The value of this fraction has been displayed as:
        //            <numerator> / <denominator>
        //       with no blanks

    float FloatEquiv() const;
        // POST: FCTVAL == float equivalent of this fraction

    void Simplify();
        // POST: Fraction is reduced to lowest terms. (No integer > 1
        //       evenly divides both the numerator and denominator)

    FracType operator*( /* in */ FracType frac2 ) const;
        // PRE:  This fraction and frac2 are in simplest terms
        // POST: FCTVAL == this fraction * frac2  (fraction
        //                    multiplication), reduced to lowest terms
        // NOTE: Numerators or denominators of large magnitude
        //       may produce overflow

    Boolean operator==( /* in */ FracType frac2 ) const;
        // PRE:  This fraction and frac2 are in simplest terms
        // POST: FCTVAL == TRUE, if this fraction == frac2
        //                    (numerically)
        //                == FALSE, otherwise

    FracType( /* in */ int initNumer,
              /* in */ int initDenom );
        // Constructor
        // PRE:  Assigned(initNumer)  &&  initDenom > 0
        // POST: Fraction has been created and can be thought of
        //       as the fraction  initNumer / initDenom
        // NOTE: (initNumer < 0) --> fraction is a negative number
private:
    int numer;
    int denom;
};
```

Figure 7.12 Fraction
specification file

abstract data type for maintaining a fraction as a pair of numbers—a numerator and a denominator.

With the operator functions operator* and operator==, the FracType class overloads the * and == operators to permit multiplication and equality testing of class instances. The class also includes a member function named `Write`, whose purpose is to display the encapsulated data in fraction form.

Using operator functions (`operator*` and `operator==`) together with a "normal" function (`Write`) presents an inconsistency. The reason for overloading operators is to give programmer-defined types the same syntactic status as built-in types. That is, overloading extends the language by giving the illusion that a class is a built-in type. The expression

```
myFrac == yourFrac
```

looks exactly like equality testing for built-in types, and the expression

```
myFrac * yourFrac
```

has the appearance of multiplication for built-in types. In contrast, the statement

```
frac3.Write();
```

instantly identifies `frac3` as a nonstandard entity. For input and output, it would be more consistent to write statements such as

```
cout << frac3;
cin >> frac4;
```

to further the illusion that fractions are built-in types. But `cin` and `cout` can only read and write values of built-in types, not `FracType` instances.

Stream Input and Output

Let us examine `cin` and `cout` (and the error stream `cerr`) more closely. The standard header file `iostream.h` includes declarations of two classes—`istream` and `ostream`—that manage input and output. The C++ standard library declares `cin`, `cout`, and `cerr` to be instances of these classes:

```
istream cin;
ostream cout;
ostream cerr;
```

(The actual declarations are slightly different from these, but the differences are not important to this discussion.)

The `istream` class has many member functions, one of which is the `get` function:

```
cin.get(someChar);
```

The `istream` class also has several member functions named `operator>>`, one for each of the built-in simple data types: `int`, `char`, `float`, and so forth. These functions overload the `>>` operator to perform input. Clients can call `operator>>` by using either functional notation

```
cin.operator>>(someInt);
```

or the more usual operator notation

```
cin >> someInt;
```

Similarly, the ostream class includes several member functions named operator<< that overload the built-in << operator. Again, clients can use either functional notation or operator notation to invoke operator<<:

```
cout.operator<<(someInt);
cout << someInt;
```

In the istream and ostream classes, operator>> and operator<< are defined only for input and output of built-in types. We would like to overload the << and >> operators to accommodate values of the FracType class.

The NewFrac *Specification*

To allow stream I/O of FracType objects, we modify the FracType class in the following fashion:

1. Remove the Write function.
2. Introduce two friend functions, operator<< and operator>>, to overload the << and >> operators.
3. Introduce a default (parameterless) constructor FracType() so the client does not have to specify an initial value for a FracType instance before performing input.

The result of these modifications is the specification file shown in Figure 7.13. For brevity, ellipses ("...") replace the function comments that are unchanged from Figure 7.12.

Figure 7.13 NewFrac specification file

```
// ---------------------------------------------------------------
//   SPECIFICATION FILE (newfrac.h)
//   This module exports a FracType class with two operator functions,
//   operator* and operator==.
//   It also adds a default (parameterless) constructor
//   and exports operator<< and operator>> for stream I/O.
// ---------------------------------------------------------------
#include "bool.h"
#include <iostream.h>

class FracType {
public:
    float FloatEquiv() const;
        // ...

    void Simplify();
        // ...
```

```
        FracType operator*( /* in */ FracType frac2 ) const;
            // ...

        Boolean operator==( /* in */ FracType frac2 ) const;
            // ...

        FracType( /* in */ int initNumer,
                  /* in */ int initDenom );
            // Constructor
            // ...

        FracType();
            // Constructor
            // POST: Fraction has been created and can be thought of
            //       as the fraction  0 / 1

//friends:
        friend ostream& operator<<( /* inout */ ostream& someStream,
                                    /* in */    FracType frac       );
            // PRE:  someStream is a valid stream object
            // POST: The value of frac has been displayed as:
            //           <numerator> / <denominator>
            //         with no blanks
            //      && FCTVAL == address of someStream

        friend istream& operator>>( /* inout */ istream&  someStream,
                                    /* out */   FracType& frac       );
            // PRE:  someStream is a valid stream object
            //      && Client code has already prompted the user for input
            // POST: User has typed in a numerator (call it newNumer),
            //         then a slash, then a denominator (call it newDenom)
            //      && frac can be thought of as
            //           the fraction  newNumer / newDenom
            //      && newDenom > 0
            //      && FCTVAL == address of someStream
private:
    int numer;
    int denom;
};
```

Consider first the operator<< function in Figure 7.13. It has two parameters, an ostream instance named someStream and a FracType instance named frac. The function will modify someStream by appending the value of frac to the output stream, so someStream is appropriately declared as a reference parameter (type FracType&). The function returns a function value: the address of the updated ostream instance. The address is returned, though, as a reference type, not a pointer type. Therefore, the caller does not have to dereference the return value using an asterisk (*).

Returning the address of the ostream instance allows the use of cascaded function calls (function calls in parameter lists of other function calls). For example, the statement

```
cout << frac1 << frac2;
```

is equivalent to the statement

```
operator<<( operator<<(cout, frac1), frac2 );
```

In this latter statement, the inner function call returns a value—the address of cout—which then becomes the first parameter to the outer function call. The outer function call returns a value—again, the address of cout—but this return value is simply ignored.

In a similar fashion, the operator>> function in Figure 7.13 receives the address of an istream instance and returns, as the function value, the address of the modified stream. Again, we pass the parameter someStream by reference because the function modifies it (by removing the value of frac from the input stream). Notice that operator>> passes the parameter frac by reference, whereas operator<< passes frac by value. The operator>> function treats frac as an "out" parameter in order to send back the fraction to the caller.

The third new function we have added to the FracType class is the default constructor FracType(). Using the default constructor, the importer does not have to specify an initial value before performing input:

```
FracType myFrac;
cin >> myFrac;
```

The NewFrac *Implementation*

Figure 7.14 displays the implementations of all three new operations: the default constructor and the two friend functions, operator<< and operator>>. In this figure, we use ellipses in place of the function bodies that are unchanged from the Fraction module in Chapter 3.

Figure 7.14 The NewFrac implementation file

```
// -------------------------------------------------------------
//   IMPLEMENTATION FILE (newfrac.cpp)
//   This module exports FracType and two operator functions,
//   operator* and operator==.
//   It also adds a default (parameterless) constructor
//   and exports operator<< and operator>> for stream I/O.
// -------------------------------------------------------------
#include <iostream.h>
#include <stdlib.h>        // For abs() function
#include "newfrac.h"

int GreatestCommonDivisor( int, int );   // Auxiliary function
                                         // prototype


// Private members of class:
//      int numer;
//      int denom;
//
// CLASSINV: denom > 0
```

```
FracType::FracType( /* in */ int initNumer,
                    /* in */ int initDenom )
{ ... }

FracType::FracType()
    //..............................................................
    // POST: numer == 0  &&  denom == 1
    //..............................................................
{
    numer = 0;  denom = 1;
}

ostream& operator<<( /* inout */ ostream& someStream,
                     /* in */    FracType frac        )
    //..............................................................
    // Friend of the FracType class
    // PRE:  someStream is a valid stream object
    // POST: Fraction has been displayed as frac.numer/frac.denom
    //       with no blanks
    //    && FCTVAL == address of someStream
    //..............................................................
{
    someStream << frac.numer << "/" << frac.denom;
    return someStream;
}

istream& operator>>( /* inout */ istream&  someStream,
                     /* out */    FracType& frac       )
    //..............................................................
    // Friend of the FracType class
    // PRE:  someStream is a valid stream object
    // POST: User has typed in a value for frac.numer, then a slash,
    //       then a value for frac.denom
    //    && frac.denom > 0
    //    && FCTVAL == address of someStream
    //..............................................................
{
    char slash;

    do {
        someStream >> frac.numer >> slash >> frac.denom;
        if (someStream && frac.denom <= 0)
            cout << "Denominator must be positive\n"
                 << "Please re-enter fraction: ";
    } while (someStream && frac.denom <= 0);
    return someStream;
}

float FracType::FloatEquiv() const
{ ... }

void FracType::Simplify()
{ ... }
```

```
FracType FracType::operator*( /* in */ FracType frac2 ) const
{ ... }

Boolean FracType::operator==( /* in */ FracType frac2 ) const
{ ... }

int GreatestCommonDivisor( /* in */ int a,
                           /* in */ int b )
{ ... }
```

In implementing the default constructor, we must initialize the private data to guarantee the class invariant (denom > 0). Here, the zero-valued fraction is an arbitrary choice.

The operator<< function allows output of a fraction to any ostream object. If cout happens to be the actual parameter corresponding to someStream, the function code effectively executes the statement

```
cout << frac.numer << '/' << frac.denom;
```

Similarly, if cerr is the actual parameter, the code behaves the same as the statement

```
cerr << frac.numer << '/' << frac.denom;
```

Although the body of operator<< seems straightforward, there are two subtle issues. First, it might appear that this function recursively invokes itself by using << in the statement

```
someStream << frac.numer << '/' << frac.denom;
```

To see that there is no recursion here, observe the following. The ostream class overloads the << operator by defining several operator<< functions, one for each of the built-in simple types. In the above statement, there are three calls to operator<<. The data types of the values being output are int, char, and int, respectively. Therefore, the functions being called are those defined in the ostream class, not the function we are currently implementing.

The second subtlety in this operator<< implementation involves the concluding statement

```
return someStream;
```

Although it may not appear to, this statement returns the address of someStream, as required. It would be wrong to use the address-of operator (&):

```
return &someStream;      ← No
```

According to the function heading, the data type of the function return value is ostream&. The return value is therefore *implicitly* the address of someStream. Consequently, the function must not explicitly take the address of the stream object, and the caller must not explicitly dereference the returned object by using an asterisk (*).

These subtleties also pertain to the operator>> implementation in Figure 7.14. The operator>> functions invoked in the statement

```
someStream >> frac.numer >> slash >> frac.denom;
```

are those already defined by the istream class, in this case for reading int and char values. And again, the function returns the address of the stream *without* using the address-of operator.

An additional point of interest in the operator>> function is the do-while loop. In the implementation file of Figure 7.14, the class invariant is denom > 0. This invariant is a universal precondition and postcondition for member (and friend) functions. Each function (except a constructor) assumes this condition to be true prior to function invocation, and each function must ensure its truth upon function exit. The operator>> function therefore must repeatedly reject incorrect input and refuse to exit the function until it can guarantee that denom is greater than zero.

7.5   The Concept of Dynamic Data

In C++, pointer variables are heavily used in system programming. System programs, such as compilers, linkers, loaders, and operating systems, must be as compact and fast as possible. Furthermore, such programs manipulate primitive machine objects: bytes, words, addresses, and CPU registers (memory-like cells located within a computer's central processing unit). Pointers allow direct manipulation of these low-level objects, and we could devote several chapters to intricate details of programming with pointers. However, such discussion would be outside the scope of this text. Our usage of pointers hereafter will be to support a higher level notion: **dynamic data.**

There are three general classifications of program data:

- static data
- automatic data
- dynamic data

Static data objects exist throughout the entire execution of a program. Any global variable is static, as is any local variable explicitly declared as static:

```
void SomeFunc()
{
    static int someInt;        ← Retains its value from call to call
      ⋮
}
```

Automatic data objects are implicitly allocated (created) and deallocated (destroyed) automatically:

```
void SomeFunc()
{
    float someFloat;        ←— Created at entry to function
    ⋮
}                           ←— Destroyed when function exits
```

In C++, automatic variables reside within the activation frame of a function (or any block that declares local variables). An activation frame is allocated when a function is invoked and deallocated when the function returns. (To review the concepts of static and automatic data in C++, see Section A.11 of Appendix A or Section B.9 of Appendix B.)

The major limitation of static and automatic data is the inflexibility of allocation and deallocation. Even when a program no longer needs a static variable, the variable remains allocated until the program terminates. The program's control over automatic variables depends upon the control flow of function invocation and return or block entry and block exit. This limitation forces the programmer to declare all data objects that the function *might* need.

This limitation is most obvious for arrays. Programmers regularly declare arrays to have enough elements to store the *largest potential* number of data items. An airline reservation system may represent airplane seats as an array with one element per seat:

```
SeatType seat[400];
```

If the airplane flies at 60 percent of capacity, then 40 percent of this array storage is unused.

Occasionally, wasting data space is justifiable because it allows faster algorithms. However, programmers must be cautious when using this argument, because large storage requirements can also result in operating system execution overhead. A large data structure that appears to produce faster code may in fact have the opposite effect.

The requirement that the "largest potential" space be declared leads to another difficulty. What if the programmer cannot predict the maximum size? Maintenance programmers regularly have to modify programs by increasing array sizes to accommodate expanded needs. How else could the airline reservation system accommodate a new plane with twice as many seats?

One solution to the inadequacies of static and automatic data structures is to let programs explicitly allocate and deallocate data *while the program is executing*. This kind of data is known as **dynamic data.** The lifetime of a dynamic data object is completely controlled during execution by means of special program instructions. When a program requires additional storage, it allocates dynamic data. When the program no longer needs a dynamic data object, it returns the object to the computer system by deallocating it.

7.6 Allocation and Deallocation

In C++, the unary operators `new` and `delete` control allocation and deallocation of dynamic data, respectively (Figure 7.15).

Figure 7.15 The new and
delete operators

The new operator

1. Syntax (most common forms):

   new <TypeName>

   or

   new <TypeName> [<IntExpression>]   (to allocate an array)

2. Semantics (expressed as pre/postconditions):
   ```
   // POST: IF memory space is available THEN
   //                      An uninitialized object of the appropriate size is
   //                      allocated
   //            && A pointer to the object is returned
   //         ELSE
   //                      The null pointer 0 is returned
   // NOTES:
   ```

   ```
   // 1. The size of the allocated object is implicitly stored in the object
   //    so the delete operator can later deallocate it.
   ```

   ```
   // 2. The lifetime of the allocated object is the instant of creation
   //    until the delete operator destroys it.
   ```

3. Examples:

   ```
   int* intPtr = new int;
   char* str = new char[51];
   ```

The delete operator

1. Syntax (most common form):

   delete <Pointer>

2. Semantics (expressed as pre/postconditions):
   ```
   // PRE:   The value of <Pointer> was previously returned by
   //        the new operator or is 0 (the null pointer)
   // POST: IF the value of <Pointer> == 0 THEN
   //                      The delete operation has no effect
   //         ELSE
   //                      The object pointed to by <Pointer>
   //                      is deallocated
   //            && <Pointer> is considered unassigned
   ```

3. Example (using intPtr and str from the example above):

   ```
   delete intPtr;   // Single int object deallocated
   delete str;      // Entire array deallocated
   ```

The new *Operator*

Objects created by new are said to be on the **free store** (or **heap**), a region of
memory set aside for dynamic variables. The new operator obtains a chunk of
memory from the free store; the delete operator returns it to the free store. A

Result of executing
```
float* floatPtr = new float;
char*  nameStr = new char[7];
```

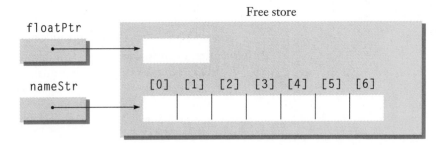

Figure 7.16 Examples of using the new operator

dynamic data object is unnamed and cannot be directly addressed. It must be indirectly addressed through the pointer returned by the new operator. Figure 7.16 illustrates two examples that use the new operator.

We have applied the new operator twice in this code. The first declaration creates a new object of type float and initializes floatPtr to contain the address of this object. The second declaration creates a 7-element char array and initializes nameStr to point to its first element.

The delete *Operator*

A dynamic object is deallocated by applying the delete operator to a pointer to that object. For example, the following statement deallocates the array pointed to by nameStr:

```
delete nameStr;
```

An execution of delete has two consequences:

1. The storage for the specified object is surrendered.

2. The pointer to that object must then be regarded as unassigned.

The statement

```
delete nameStr;
```

relinquishes the storage pointed to by nameStr. That is, the program has given up its right to use this space on the free store. The second result of this operation is that nameStr is logically left unassigned. (Depending on the particular C++ system, nameStr may or may not still physically point to the deallocated data.) Conceptually, nameStr no longer points to a valid object. Before using nameStr again, the programmer must assign it a new pointer value.

(Until you gain experience with the new and delete operators, it is important to pronounce the statement

```
delete nameStr;
```

Pointers and dynamic
data

accurately. Instead of saying "Delete `nameStr`," it is better to say "Delete the object pointed to by `nameStr`." The point is that the `delete` operation does not delete the pointer; it deletes the pointed-to object.)

It may be helpful to think of dynamic objects as lock boxes. You can access the contents of the lock box (the value of the dynamic object) only if you have the key. Pointer variables are then analogous to lock-box keys. The program cannot inspect or modify a dynamic object unless it has the key (a pointer). Furthermore, the lock for each dynamic object is different from all others. A single pointer variable can point to (serve as a key for) only one dynamic object at a time.

Dynamic Array Allocation

In Figure 7.16 we showed a 7-element character array, allocated on the free store and pointed to by `nameStr`. Using the `new` operator to create an array on the free store is known as **dynamic array allocation.**

Dynamic array allocation brings an array into existence only when it is needed at run time, and its size is specified *dynamically* (at run time):

```
int* vec = new int[someSize];
```

In contrast, the size of a built-in array must be known *statically* (at compile time):

```
int someVec[200];
```

The programmer often cannot predict the exact number of values to be stored into a built-in array. The usual strategy is to overestimate the array size, leading to wasted memory space. Dynamic array allocation alleviates this problem.

Figure 7.17 displays a program that uses dynamic array allocation. This `DynArray` program inputs an arbitrary number of integer values and outputs the values in sorted order.

Figure 7.17 `DynArray`
program

```
// -----------------------------------------------------------------
// dynarray.cpp
// This program inputs and sorts an arbitrary number of integer
// values by using dynamic array allocation.
```

```
// -------------------------------------------------------------------
#include <iostream.h>
#include <stddef.h>        // For NULL

void Sort( int[], int );

int main()
{
    int* vec;          // Pointer to dynamic vector
    int  numItems;     // Number of items to sort
    int  i;            // Index variable

    cout << "Enter the number of items to sort: ";
    cin >> numItems;

    vec = new int[numItems];
    if (vec == NULL) {
       cout << "Not enough memory for that many items\n";
       return 1;
    }

    cout << "Enter " << numItems << " integers:\n";
    for (i = 0; i < numItems; i++)
        cin >> vec[i];
    Sort(vec, numItems);
    cout << "\nSorted list:\n";
    for (i = 0; i < numItems; i++)
        cout << vec[i] << '\n';

    delete vec;        // Deallocate the dynamic vector
    return 0;
}
// -------------------------------------------------------------------
void Sort( /* inout */ int vec[],
           /* in */    int size  )
{ ... }
```

The `DynArray` program prompts the user for the number of values to be sorted, then uses the `new` operator to create an array of exactly the right size. Immediately after using `new`, the program checks the returned pointer value. If this pointer value is `NULL` (there is not enough space on the free store), the program displays an error message and terminates with a nonzero exit status.

If the `new` operator is successful, the program proceeds to input, sort, and output the data values. As we stated earlier, any pointer expression can be subscripted. In the `DynArray` program, we allocate a dynamic array and then subscript the pointer variable `vec` using exactly the same syntax we would use for a statically allocated array.

Finally, we conclude the program by using the `delete` operator to return the vector to the free store. (Remember to pronounce the statement

```
delete vec;
```

as "Delete the vector pointed to by vec," not "Delete vec.")

7.7 Inaccessible Objects, Memory Leaks, and Dangling Pointers

Working with dynamic data is more complicated than working with other structures because two separate variables are involved: the pointer and the dynamic object. Programs using dynamic data are invariably more difficult to design, read, and debug.

Storing a value into a simple variable, say `tempInt`, requires only one statement:

```
tempInt = -515;
```

Storing a value into a dynamic object requires that you first allocate it and then store a value into it:

```
intPtr = new int;
*intPtr = -515;
```

This sequence requires one more statement than the assignment to a simple variable. Moreover, it is not clear that this particular sequence of statements is the best alternative. Suppose that `intPtr` already points to an object before an assignment. The programmer now has three choices:

1. Go ahead and allocate a new object before assigning the value:

   ```
   intPtr = new int;
   *intPtr = -515;
   ```

2. Overwrite the existing object:

   ```
   *intPtr = -515;
   ```

3. Deallocate the existing object before the new allocation. (This is usually the wrong choice):

   ```
   delete intPtr;
   intPtr = new int;
   *intPtr = -515;
   ```

The first choice is best if the object currently pointed to by `intPtr` is also pointed to by a second pointer and the object is still needed by that pointer. The second choice is best if no other pointers point to the current object. In general, the third choice merely slows down execution by deallocating, then reallocating data.

The null pointer also complicates programming with pointer variables. Care must be taken not to dereference a null pointer. When `intPtr` equals NULL, the expression `*intPtr` is a logic error and may result in program termination.

Another dangerous error is to apply the `delete` operator to a pointer (other than NULL) that was not previously returned by `new`.

Two additional problems with dynamic data are so common that they have special names:

- An **inaccessible object** is a dynamic object without any pointer left pointing to it (a lock box without any key).
- A **dangling pointer** is a pointer that still points to an object that has been deallocated (a key without any lock box).

Both of these problems are well-known sources of bugs.

Inaccessible Objects and Memory Leaks

An inaccessible object usually results from one of two operations. The first is execution of the new operation; the second, an assignment to a pointer variable. Figure 7.18 shows an example of each, where the original referent of intPtrA is left inaccessible.

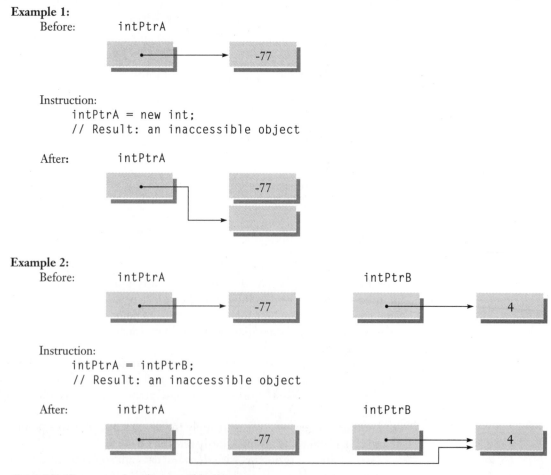

Figure 7.18 Two examples of inaccessible objects

A **memory leak** occurs when a program allocates dynamic data but never deallocates that data from the free store. Forgetfulness is one way to create a memory leak. The programmer may finish working with a dynamic object, then overlook the need to delete it. A second way to create a memory leak is to leave inaccessible objects on the free store, as in Figure 7.18. A memory leak reduces the amount of memory (specifically, dynamic memory) available to a running program. Over a period of time, the memory leak may accumulate to the point of exhausting all available free store.

Dangling Pointers

A dangling pointer results from one of two events. The first is when a function (erroneously) returns a pointer to an automatic variable:

```
int* SomeFunc()

{
    int n;
    ⋮
    return &n;
}
```

The run-time system implicitly allocates memory for automatic variables at block entry and implicitly destroys these variables at block exit. The above function returns a pointer to the local variable n, but n disappears as soon as control exits the function. The caller therefore receives a dangling pointer.

The second opportunity for dangling pointers involves the delete operation. If two pointers point to the same dynamic object and delete is applied to one of them, the other pointer is left dangling. Figure 7.19 illustrates this possibility.

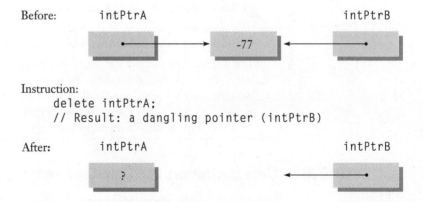

Figure 7.19 Example of a dangling pointer

Dangling pointers are significant for two reasons. First, it is easy to overlook them. In the scenario of Figure 7.19, the statement

```
delete intPtrA;
```

clearly leaves the pointer `intPtrA` unassigned. But without the pictures, it is not so obvious that `intPtrB` is left dangling.

The second reason for concern is that dangling pointers usually do *not* generate execution errors. An executing program typically cannot tell that a pointer is dangling. The result is a program that produces incorrect results with no hint of the location of the bug.

Pursuing Correctness

Using Dynamic Data

Pointers and dynamic allocation of data add complexity to a program. They can make debugging and maintaining programs a challenge. The following guidelines can help to reduce the hazards of using dynamic data.

1. *Before invoking* `new`, see if the associated pointer variable already points to an object. If so, then `delete` the old object or reuse it rather than cause a memory leak (by making the object inaccessible).

2. *After invoking* `new`, remember that `new` returns a pointer to this new object, but the object itself is still unassigned.

3. *Before dereferencing a pointer*, be sure that the pointer is assigned and not NULL. Otherwise, run-time errors are likely.

4. *Before invoking* `delete`, locate all other pointers that address the object to be deallocated. Assigning the value NULL to all these pointers, rather than leaving them to dangle, is good practice. Assigning them NULL clarifies the situation for maintenance programmers and provides a condition that is testable. (You can compare a pointer to NULL but cannot tell if a pointer is dangling.)

5. *After invoking* `delete`, remember that the associated pointer variable is now considered unassigned. (Better yet, write and use a function that *both* invokes `delete` and assigns NULL to the pointer. An exercise at the end of this chapter asks you to write such a function.)

6. *When assigning a value to a pointer variable*, be certain that it does not already point to an object that will then become inaccessible.

7. *When a function contains automatic local pointer variables*, these local pointers are destroyed when the function returns. However, dynamic data objects persist; only `delete` can deallocate them. Thus, any dynamic objects pointed to solely by local pointers become inaccessible when the function returns. The result is a memory leak.

7.8 Class Destructors and Copy-Constructors

In C++, built-in arrays are indispensable data structures but have several shortcomings:

• When declaring an array, the programmer must state its size in advance.

• Out-of-bounds subscripts are not detected at run time.

- There is no aggregate assignment of one entire array to another.
- Arrays cannot be passed by value or returned as function values.

All of these deficiencies can be overcome by using C++ class facilities along with the free store operators new and delete.

Specification of a Vector Module

Consider writing a class named IntVec that dynamically allocates an integer vector on the free store. Assuming that the class constructor allocates the array, we could pass the desired vector size as a parameter to the class constructor:

```
IntVec alpha(10);                  // 10-element vector
cout << "Input array size: ";
cin >> n;
IntVec beta(n);                    // n-element vector
```

The declaration of alpha is similar to the declaration of a built-in array: the programmer states the size of the array in advance. The declaration of beta allows greater flexibility. Its size is determined at execution time instead of being fixed in advance.

Figure 7.20 displays the specification of a Vector module that exports an IntVec class. This class allows run-time determination of a vector size and uses operator overloading for the assignment (=) and subscripting ([]) operators. The class also introduces two new C++ features: the class *destructor* and the class *copy-constructor*. One by one we will explain each of these features.

Figure 7.20 Specification file for the Vector module

```
// ---------------------------------------------------------------
//   SPECIFICATION FILE (vector.h)
//   This module exports an integer vector class that allows:
//      1. Run-time specification of vector size
//      2. Trapping of invalid subscripts
//      3. Aggregate vector assignment
//      4. Aggregate vector initialization (for parameter passage by
//         value, function value return, initialization in a
//         declaration)
// ---------------------------------------------------------------

class IntVec {
public:
    void operator=( /* in */ IntVec vec2 );
        // POST: IF size of this vector == size of vec2 THEN
        //             Each element of this vector == corresponding
        //                                           element of vec2
        //       ELSE
        //             Pgm has halted with error message
```

```
    int& operator[]( /* in */ int i ) const;
        // POST: IF 0 <= i < (declared size of vector) THEN
        //           FCTVAL == address of element i of vector
        //         ELSE
        //           Pgm has halted with error message
        // NOTE: Because return type is "int&", not "int*",
        //       the result is automatically dereferenced in the
        //       calling code.
        //       Caller uses   someVec[6] = 943;
        //               not    *(someVec[6]) = 943;

    IntVec( /* in */ int numElements );
        // Constructor
        // POST: IF numElements >= 1 THEN
        //           Uninitialized vector of size numElements is
        //           created
        //         ELSE
        //           Pgm has halted with error message

    IntVec( const IntVec& anotherVec );
        // Constructor (a "copy-constructor")
        // POST: New vector created with size and contents same
        //       as anotherVec
        // NOTE: This constructor is implicitly invoked whenever an
        //       IntVec is passed by value, is returned as a
        //       function value, or is initialized by another
        //       IntVec in a declaration.

    ~IntVec();
        // Destructor
        // POST: Vector no longer exists
private:
    int* vec;
    int  size;
};
```

The private data of IntVec consists of two variables, vec and size. The variable vec will point to an array of size size on the free store. The following is a possible implementation of the class constructor:

```
IntVec::IntVec( /* in */ int numElements )
{
    if (numElements < 1) {
        cerr << "** Vector size must be positive **\n";
        exit(1);
    }
    vec = new int[numElements];
    size = numElements;
}
```

(As described in Appendix G, the exit function—available by including the header file stdlib.h—causes immediate termination of the entire program. The function's parameter is an exit status: 0 for a normal exit, and nonzero for an abnormal exit.)

If the client-specified array size is greater than or equal to 1, the constructor allocates an integer vector of that size on the free store. Using dynamic array allocation allows the client to construct an array whose size is not known until run time. For example, consider the declaration

```
IntVec alpha(n);
```

where the value of n at run time is 5. Figure 7.21 pictures the result of executing the constructor in this declaration.

This figure illustrates an important concept: alpha does not encapsulate an array—it only encapsulates *access* to the array. The private data consists solely of two variables, one being the pointer to the array. The array itself is located externally (on the free store), not within the protective abstraction barrier. This arrangement does not violate the principle of information hiding, however. The only access to the array is through the pointer vec, which is a private class member and is therefore inaccessible to clients.

Destructors

The IntVec class of Figure 7.20 provides a **destructor** function named ~IntVec(). A class destructor, identified by a tilde (~) preceding the name of the class, can be thought of as the complement of a constructor. Just as a constructor is implicitly invoked when control reaches the declaration of a class instance, a destructor is implicitly invoked when the class instance is destroyed. A class instance is destroyed when it "goes out of scope"—that is, when control exits the block in which it is declared. The following block (which might be a function body, for example) includes remarks at the locations where the constructor and destructor are invoked:

```
{
    int n;
    ⋮
    IntVec alpha(n);        ←— Constructor is invoked here.
    ⋮
}          ←— Destructor is invoked here because alpha goes out of scope.
```

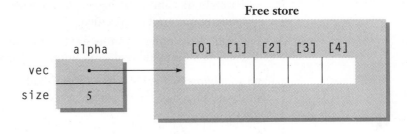

Figure 7.21 An IntVec class instance pointing to a dynamically allocated array

The implementation of the `IntVec` class destructor is very simple:

```
IntVec::~IntVec()
{
    delete vec;    // Delete the array pointed to by vec
}
```

Until now, we have not needed class destructors. In all previous examples of classes, the class data has been enclosed entirely within the abstraction barrier of the class. For example, a `FracType` class instance encapsulates all of its data:

```
                        someFrac
         numer          3
         denom          8
```

When `someFrac` goes out of scope, deallocation of `someFrac` implies deallocation of all of its data.

With the `IntVec` class, some of the data is enclosed within the class barrier and some of the data is not (Figure 7.21). Without the destructor `~IntVec()`, deallocation of a class instance would deallocate the *pointer* to the dynamic array but not the array itself. The dynamic array would remain allocated but no longer accessible.

Using the Language

Guidelines for Use of Class Destructors

A destructor is a member function that is invoked automatically when a class instance is destroyed. Below we present some guidelines for using destructors. There are some additional rules, but they pertain to language features that we have not yet discussed.

1. Whenever a class creates objects on the free store, a destructor should be provided for cleanup activity.

2. A destructor is implicitly invoked when a class instance goes out of scope. (An automatic object goes out of scope when control leaves the block in which it is declared. A static object goes out of scope when program execution terminates.)

3. Parameters cannot be passed to a destructor, and the data type of the function must not be specified.

4. A call to the library routine `exit()` should not appear in a destructor. In some cases, it could lead to an infinite recursion.

The following two rules relate to more advanced programming techniques. Until you have had more experience with C++, you may want to just skim these rules.

5. If a class X has a member that is an instance of another class, then X's destructor is executed before the member's destructor is executed.

6. Suppose that class X has a destructor and that an instance of X is allocated on the free store:

```
X* ptr = new X;
```

Then the operation

```
delete ptr;
```

implicitly invokes the class destructor before deallocating the dynamic class instance. If an *array* of class instances is allocated dynamically

```
X* ptr = new X[50];
```

then brackets are required in the `delete` operation to ensure that the destructor is called for each array element:

```
delete [] ptr;
```

(In early versions of C++, the brackets cannot be empty. The number of array elements must be specified:

```
delete [50] ptr;
```

If your compiler complains about the empty brackets, include the array size.)

Overloading the Subscript Operator

The `IntVec` class of Figure 7.20 provides a member function named `operator[]`. This function overloads the subscript operator (`[]`) to select an element of the dynamic array. If `someVec` is an instance of the `IntVec` class, the assignment statement

```
n = someVec[5];
```

is equivalent to the statement

```
n = someVec.operator[](5);
```

The first form is preferable because it lends `someVec` the appearance of a built-in array.

Because an `IntVec` instance controls access to its entire dynamic array, it is easy to control access to an individual array element as well. The following implementation of the `operator[]` function shows how we can conveniently trap invalid subscripts.

```
int& IntVec::operator[]( /* in */ int i ) const
{
    if (i < 0 || i >= size) {
        cerr << "IntVec - subscript invalid: " << i << '\n';
        exit(1);
    }
    return vec[i];                    // Implicit: return &vec[i]
}
```

The `operator[]` function returns a value of reference type `int&`. Therefore, the address of the desired array element is returned, but the caller does not dereference it with an asterisk (*). (Recall that C++ always *implicitly* dereferences an object of reference type.)

We could have chosen to return the *value* of the array element instead of its address. If so, the client statement

```
n = someVec[20];
```

would be fine. If element 20 of the dynamic array contains the value 356, then this statement would effectively be the same as

```
n = 356;
```

But if the client were to place the function call to the left of the equal sign, as in

```
someVec[20] = 10;
```

an error would result. Because the function call returns the value 356, this statement attempts to store a constant into a constant. It is as if we had written the nonsensical statement

```
356 = 10;
```

To remedy this situation, we could use a pointer type to return the address of the array element:

```
int* IntVec::operator[]( /* in */ int i ) const
{     .
      .
      .
    return &vec[i];
}
```

With this approach, it is now valid to place the function call on either side of the assignment operator:

```
n = *(someVec[20]);
*(someVec[3]) = 428;
```

However, the explicit dereferencing of the returned pointer has an unpleasant look to it.

Our preference, then, is to return a value of type `int&` instead of type `int*`. Not only do we return the address of the array element, we also provide implicit dereferencing:

```
n = someVec[20];
someVec[3] = 428;
```

Overloading the Assignment Operator

Another member of the `IntVec` class (Figure 7.20) is the `operator=` function. This function overloads the = operator to assign one class instance to another, *including their dynamic vectors.* With the built-in = operator, assignment of one class instance to another copies only the class members; it does *not* copy any data pointed to by the class members. For example, suppose that myVec and yourVec are two IntVec instances. If we had not overloaded the = operator, then the effect of the assignment statement

```
myVec = yourVec;
```

would be as shown in Figure 7.22. The result is called a **shallow copy** operation. The pointers, but not the pointed-to data, are copied.

Shallow copying is perfectly fine if none of the class members is a pointer. But if one or more members are pointers, then shallow copying may be erroneous. In Figure 7.22, the dynamic vector originally pointed to by myVec has been left inaccessible. Furthermore, suppose that the next statement in the program is

```
myVec[1] = 50;
```

Then vector element 1 will equal 50 for *both* myVec and yourVec, because they point to the same dynamic data.

What we want is a **deep copy** operation—one that duplicates not only the class members but also the pointed-to data. The operator= function of the IntVec class overloads the assignment operator to perform a deep copy. With this function, the statement (at the top of p. 328)

Before:

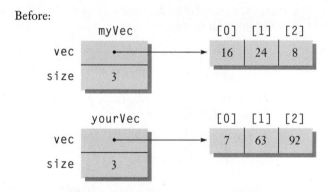

Instruction:
```
    myVec = yourVec;   // Assume built-in meaning of =
```

After:

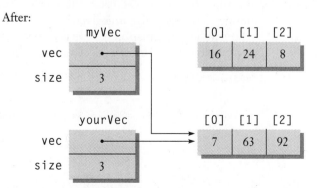

Figure 7.22 A shallow copy

```
myVec = yourVec;
```

is equivalent to the statement

```
myVec.operator=(yourVec);
```

Here is the function implementation:

```
void IntVec::operator=( /* in */ IntVec vec2 )
{
    if (size != vec2.size) {
        cerr << "IntVec assignment - sizes unequal: "
            << size << ' ' << vec2.size << '\n';
        exit(1);
    }
    int i;
    for (i = 0; i < size; i++)
        vec[i] = vec2.vec[i];
}
```

This function copies one dynamic vector to another, element by element. Figure 7.23 shows the result of executing the `operator=` function.

Copy-Constructors

The same problem with deep versus shallow copying also can appear in another context: initialization of one class instance by another. C++ defines initialization to mean:

1. initialization in a variable declaration:

   ```
   IntVec newVec = oldVec;
   ```

2. passing a copy of an actual parameter to a formal parameter (parameter passage by value)
3. returning a class instance as the value of a function:

   ```
   return someInstance;
   ```

By default, C++ performs such initializations using shallow copy semantics. In other words, the new class instance is initialized via a member-by-member copy of the old instance without regard for any data the class members may point to. For the `IntVec` class, the result would again be two class instances pointing to the same dynamic data.

To handle this situation, C++ has a special kind of constructor known as a **copy-constructor.** In a class declaration, its prototype has the following form:

```
class SomeClass {
    ⋮
    SomeClass( const SomeClass& );    // Copy-constructor
    ⋮
};
```

Before:

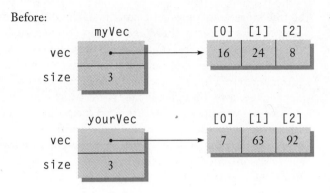

Instruction:
```
    myVec = yourVec;   // Assume overloaded assignment operator
```

After:

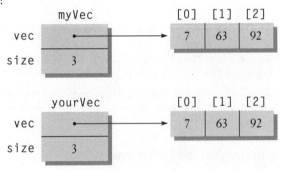

Figure 7.23 A deep copy

As with any function prototype in C++, you may optionally specify a name for the formal parameter for documentation purposes:

```
IntVec( const IntVec& anotherVec );
```

If a copy-constructor is present, the default method of initialization (member-by-member copying) is inhibited. Instead, the copy-constructor is implicitly invoked whenever one class instance is initialized by another. The following implementation of the IntVec copy-constructor shows the steps that are involved:

```
IntVec::IntVec( const IntVec& anotherVec )
{
    size = anotherVec.size;
    vec = new int[size];
    int i;
    for (i = 0; i < size; i++)
        vec[i] = anotherVec.vec[i];
}
```

First, the function copies the size of the old class instance into the size member of the new instance. Next, the function allocates a new dynamic vector on the free store and copies all elements of the old dynamic vector into the new vector. The result is therefore a deep copy—two identical class instances pointing to two identical (but *separate*) dynamic vectors.

Notice the use of the reserved word `const` in the parameter list of the copy-constructor. The word `const` ensures that the function cannot alter `anotherVec`, even though `anotherVec` is passed by reference.

As with any nonarray object in C++, a class instance can be passed to a function either by value or by reference. Because C++ defines initialization to include parameter passage by value, copy-constructors are vitally important when class instances point to dynamic data. Assume that we did not include a copy-constructor for the `IntVec` class, and assume that the following code uses parameter passage by value:

```
IntVec beta(100);
    :
    :
DoSomething(beta);
```

Without a copy-constructor, `beta` will be copied to the function's formal parameter using a shallow copy. A copy of `beta`'s dynamic vector will *not* be created for use within the function. Then both `beta` and the formal parameter will point to the same dynamic vector, a situation we saw in Figure 7.22. If the function modifies the dynamic vector (thinking it is working on a *copy* of the original), then `beta` will see a corrupted dynamic vector after the function returns.

Designing with Wisdom

Class Members That Point to Dynamic Data

Information hiding is fundamental to the concept of data abstraction. Encapsulation of implementation details prevents client code from compromising the correctness of an implementation. Encapsulation also ensures that users do not have to know how an abstraction works in order to use it.

For the C++ programmer, encapsulating the concrete data representation often means placing all the data within the abstraction barrier of a class. This arrangement works best if the number of data members is small and any data structures in the representation are of fixed size.

Sometimes concrete data representations include structures whose sizes cannot be determined in advance. In these cases, classes need to allocate memory from the free store and then keep pointers within the abstraction barrier. The default operations of assignment and initialization no longer work correctly, then. Member-by-member assignment and initialization cause only pointers to be copied, not the dynamic data on the free store.

To help with the design of classes that employ dynamic data, we offer the following suggestions.

1. If a class allocates and deallocates data on the free store, it almost certainly needs the following suite of member functions to ensure deep copying of dynamic data:

```
class SomeClass {
    :
    :
    void operator=( SomeClass anotherInstance );
        // For deep copying in assignments

    SomeClass( ... );
        // Constructor, to create data on the free store

    SomeClass( const SomeClass& anotherInstance );
        // Copy-constructor, for deep copying in initializations

    ~SomeClass();
        // Destructor, to clean up the free store
};
```

2. If a copy-constructor is provided and class instances point to large dynamic structures on the free store, parameter passage by value may be costly due to the time spent copying the large structures. In such cases, it is usually preferable to pass class instances by reference instead of by value. Passing by reference prevents the copy-constructor from being invoked.

   If this approach is taken, the function should:

   a. be very careful not to mistakenly modify the pointed-to dynamic data

   b. supply explicit documentation of the direction of information flow:

```
void SomeFunc( /* in */ IntVec& oneVec )
{ //Do not modify dynamic data here
    :
    :
}
```

3. If class members point to dynamic data and there is a class destructor but no copy-constructor, *do not pass class instances by value* to a function. Within the function, the formal parameter receives a shallow copy, not a deep copy, of the actual parameter. The actual and formal parameters then point to the same dynamic data. When the function exits, the formal parameter goes out of scope and its destructor is invoked, destroying the *caller's* dynamic data.

   To avoid this unpleasant situation, either provide a copy-constructor or pass by reference and follow the advice given in items (a) and (b) above.

The issue of deep versus shallow copying extends also to comparison operations. For example, it might be helpful to overload the == operator to test for equality of two class instances. If a class does not manipulate dynamic data, a **shallow comparison** operation, which tests the data members residing within the abstraction barrier, will suffice. But a class that creates and points to dynamic data probably needs a **deep comparison** operation to test for equality of the pointed-to data objects as well. An exercise at the end of the chapter addresses this issue.

Putting It All Together

We have used the `IntVec` class to introduce several concepts: class destructors, overloading the subscript operator, overloading the assignment operator, and class copy-constructors. For each concept, we showed an implementation of the associated class member function. Figure 7.24 displays all of these functions in the form of an implementation file for the `Vector` module, complete with a class invariant and function pre- and postconditions.

Figure 7.24
Implementation file for the `Vector` module

```
// ------------------------------------------------------------------
//   IMPLEMENTATION FILE (vector.cpp)
//   This module exports an integer vector class that allows:
//      1. Run-time specification of vector size
//      2. Trapping of invalid subscripts
//      3. Aggregate vector assignment
//      4. Aggregate vector initialization
//   Vectors are dynamically allocated on the free store.
// ------------------------------------------------------------------
#include "vector.h"
#include <iostream.h>
#include <stdlib.h>      // For exit()

// Private members of class:
//      int* vec;                Pointer to vector on free store
//      int  size;               Size of vector
//
// CLASSINV: Pgm has halted if, for some subscript i,
//              i < 0 or i >= size

IntVec::IntVec( /* in */ int numElements )
    //.......................................................
    // Constructor
    // POST: IF numElements >= 1 THEN
    //                 Uninitialized vector created on free store
    //              && vec == base address of new vector
    //              && size == numElements
    //           ELSE
    //                 Pgm has halted with error message
    //.......................................................
{
    if (numElements < 1) {
        cerr << "IntVec constructor - invalid size: "
            << numElements << '\n';
        exit(1);
    }
    vec = new int[numElements];
    size = numElements;
}
```

```
IntVec::IntVec( const IntVec& anotherVec )
    //.....................................................................
    // Constructor (copy-constructor)
    // POST: New vector created on free store
    //     && vec == base address of new vector
    //     && size == anotherVec.size
    //     && All vec[0..size-1] == anotherVec.vec[0..size-1]
    //.....................................................................
{
    size = anotherVec.size;
    vec = new int[size];
    int i;
    for (i = 0; i < size; i++)
        vec[i] = anotherVec.vec[i];
}


IntVec::~IntVec()
    //.....................................................................
    // Destructor
    // POST: Vector is no longer on the free store
    //.....................................................................
{
    delete vec;
}

void IntVec::operator=( /* in */ IntVec vec2 )
    //.....................................................................
    // POST: IF size == vec2.size THEN
    //           Each element of this vector == corresponding element
    //                                           of vec2
    //       ELSE
    //           Pgm has halted with error message
    //.....................................................................
{
    if (size != vec2.size) {
        cerr << "IntVec assignment - sizes unequal: "
            << size << ' ' << vec2.size << '\n';
        exit(1);
    }
    int i;
    for (i = 0; i < size; i++)
        vec[i] = vec2.vec[i];
}
```

```
int& IntVec::operator[]( /* in */ int i ) const
    //........................................................
    // POST: IF 0 <= i < size THEN
    //           FCTVAL == address of vec[i]
    //       ELSE
    //           Pgm has halted with error message
    //........................................................
{
    if (i < 0 || i >= size) {
        cerr << "IntVec - subscript invalid: " << i << '\n';
        exit(1);
    }
    return vec[i];                        // Implicit: return &vec[i]
}
```

As a final remark, we point out a potentially serious deficiency in the IntVec class. The member functions, by checking for invalid subscripts and array sizes, are robust but not robust enough. Both the constructor and the copy-constructor execute the new operation to allocate a vector of arbitrary size on the free store. However, both functions fail to verify that this allocation succeeded. On most systems, the size of free store is more than ample for most applications. But the free store is finite. A client of the IntVec class may create great numbers of large vectors and exhaust all available free store. A chapter exercise gives you the opportunity to correct this potential problem.

SUMMARY

In C++, memory addresses of data objects can be stored in reference variables and pointer variables. These variables can access either statically or dynamically allocated data. Pointer variables require explicit dereferencing with the * operator. Reference variables are always dereferenced implicitly and often are used for passing parameters by reference.

Manipulation of dynamic data on the free store is a powerful programming language facility. With this facility the programmer need not reserve, in advance, the maximum storage space that a data structure might potentially need. Instead, the program can allocate and deallocate, at run time, only as much memory as it requires.

Pointers go hand in hand with dynamic data. When the new operator creates dynamic data, it returns a pointer to that data. Thereafter, all access is granted only through that pointer.

When C++ classes point to data on the free store, it is important to distinguish between shallow and deep copy operations. A shallow copy of one class instance to another copies only the pointers, the result being two class instances pointing to the same dynamic object. A deep copy results in two distinct copies of the pointed-to data. Therefore, classes that manipulate dynamic data usually require a complete collection of support routines: one or more constructors, a destructor (for cleaning up the free store), a copy-constructor (for deep copying during initialization), and an overloaded assignment operator (for deep copying during assignment).

Dynamic data is an excellent example of the classic programming tradeoff between power and complexity. Pointers and dynamic data are powerful facilities, but they also are complicated to use and understand. Programming with dynamic data requires more skill than using static data, but it also offers more flexibility.

KEY TERMS

"address-of" operator   (p. 289)
automatic data   (p. 311)
command-line arguments   (p. 299)
copy-constructor   (p. 328)
dangling pointer   (p. 318)
deep comparison   (p. 331)
deep copy   (p. 327)
dereference operator   (p. 290)
destructor   (p. 323)
direct addressing   (p. 290)
dynamic array allocation   (p. 315)
dynamic data   (p. 311)
free store   (p. 313)

heap   (p. 313)
inaccessible object   (p. 318)
indirect addressing   (p. 291)
indirection operator   (p. 290)
memory leak   (p. 319)
null pointer   (p. 290)
pointer arithmetic   (p. 294)
pointer variable   (p. 288)
reference type   (p. 301)
referent   (p. 289)
shallow comparison   (p. 331)
shallow copy   (p. 327)
static data   (p. 311)

EXERCISES

7.1   Consider the following collection of declarations:

```
int  i = 34;
int* iPtr = &i;
int& iRef = i;
int v[] = {16, -4, 5};
int* vPtr = v;
int* aPtr = 0;
```

Give an abstract memory diagram showing the relationships among the six variables. Show each variable and array element as a rectangle. Each rectangle should contain a constant (for data), an arrow (for an address), or a slash (for the null pointer).

7.2   Using the declarations of Exercise 7.1, give the value of each of the following expressions. If an expression is invalid, say so.

a. *iPtr

b. iRef

c. vPtr[2]

d. *vPtr

e. *(vPtr+1)

f. *vPtr+1

g. iRef+1

h. aPtr

i. *aPtr

j. *&i

7.3 Assume that you have the following declarations:

```
typedef char* CharPtr;
CharPtr cPtr1;
CharPtr cPtr2;
CharPtr cPtr3;
```

For each code segment below, draw the resulting abstract memory diagram. Show each variable as a rectangle. Each rectangle should contain either a constant (for data) or an arrow (for an address).

a.
```
cPtr1 = new char;
*cPtr1 = 'Q';
cPtr2 = new char;
cPtr3 = cPtr2;
*cPtr3 = 'W';
```

b.
```
cPtr1 = new char;
*cPtr1 = 'T';
cPtr2 = new char;
*cPtr2 = 'F';
cPtr3 = cPtr2;
*cPtr3 = *cPtr1;
```

c.
```
cPtr1 = new char;
*cPtr1 = 'M';
cPtr2 = new char;
*cPtr2 = 'X';
cPtr3 = cPtr2;
delete cPtr2;
```

7.4 Rewrite the following function call and function definition using pointer variables instead of reference variables.

Function call:

```
Divide(x, y, quot, rem, ok);
```

Function definition:

```
void Divide( /* in */  int      dividend,
             /* in */  int      divisor,
             /* out */ int&     quotient,
             /* out */ int&     remainder,
             /* out */ Boolean& succeeded )
{
    succeeded = (divisor != 0);
    if (succeeded) {
        quotient = dividend / divisor;
        remainder = dividend % divisor;
    }
}
```

7.5 For each code segment below, give an abstract diagram of memory contents after the segment has executed. Show each variable and array element as a rectangle. Each rectangle should contain either a constant (for data) or an arrow (for an address).

a.
```
char* str = new char[5];
strcpy(str, "arf");
```

b.
```
char* someStr = new char[5];
someStr = "arf";
```

c.
```
char* myStr = new char[5];
strcpy(myStr, "arf");
char* yourStr = myStr;
delete myStr;
```

7.6   Consider the following loop:

```
int a[100];
int i;
   ⋮
// ASSERT: 5 is somewhere in the array
i = 0;
while (a[i] != 5)
     i++;
a[i] = 10;
// ASSERT: 5 replaced by 10
```

Rewrite the above loop using a pointer and pointer arithmetic instead of subscripting. Assume that you have the declaration `int* ptr` instead of `int i`.

7.7   Figure 7.9 displays three alternatives for a `StrLength` function, with Alternatives 2 and 3 using pointer arithmetic instead of subscripting. Write a string copy function, `StrCopy`, in the style of Alternative 2 or 3. This function copies the string pointed to by its second parameter to the string pointed to by its first.

7.8   Consider the `operator=` function of `IntVec` (Figures 7.20 and 7.24). In principle it is correct to pass the parameter `vec2` by value, because the function does not alter this parameter. In practice, however, it would be better to pass `vec2` by reference to prevent the class's copy-constructor from wasting time and space by creating a duplicate copy of the actual parameter's dynamic vector. Show what changes are required in both `vector.h` and `vector.cpp` to pass `vec2` by reference.

7.9   Using the concepts from the `NewFrac` module (Figures 7.13 and 7.14) as a model, add a friend function `operator<<` to the `IntVec` class (Figures 7.20 and 7.24). This function outputs all elements of the vector, one value per line, to an object of type `ostream`. Give both its specification and implementation.

7.10   When a program executes the statement

```
delete ptr;
```

the data pointed to by `ptr` is returned to the free store. Thereafter, `ptr` is logically considered to be unassigned, but physically it may still point to the deallocated data. Write a function named `Deallocate` that not only executes `delete` but also assigns the pointer the value NULL. The following is a sample of its use:

```
int* intPtr;

intPtr = new int[20];

⋮

Deallocate(intPtr);
// ASSERT: Dynamic data pointed to by intPtr has been deallocated
//         && intPtr == NULL
```

Assume that the parameter to `Deallocate` is always of type `int*`.

PROGRAMMING PROJECTS

7.1   We can define the sum of two vectors *A* and *B* as a vector *C* where $C[0] = A[0] + B[0]$, $C[1] = A[1] + B[1]$, and so forth. We can define the difference of two vectors similarly. Expand the `IntVec` class of Figures 7.20 and 7.24 by including operator functions to overload the + and - operators. Write these as member functions. Each function returns an object of type `IntVec` as the function value. You may pass the second operand either by value or by reference, the latter to save unnecessary copying of dynamic data by the copy-constructor.

Test your new functions with a suitable test driver and comprehensive test oracle.

7.2   Given two vectors *A* and *B*, we can define *A*<*B* to mean $A[0]<B[0]$ *and* $A[1]<B[1]$ *and* $A[2]<B[2]$, and so forth. We can define the other relational operators likewise. Expand the `IntVec` class of Figures 7.20 and 7.24 by including operator functions to overload the relational operators ==, !=, <, <=, >, and >=. Write these as member functions.

These Boolean functions must perform deep comparisons, because the dynamic vectors on the free store are to be compared element by element. You may pass the second operand either by value or by reference, the latter to save unnecessary copying of the dynamic data by the copy-constructor.

Test your new functions with a suitable test driver and comprehensive test oracle.

7.3   In the `IntVec` class of Figures 7.20 and 7.24, the constructor and the copy-constructor are not robust enough. Each function uses the new operator to allocate a vector on the free store but neglects to verify that this allocation succeeded. On most systems, the size of free store is large but it is finite. Make the constructor and copy-constructor more robust by halting the program with an error message if the new operation fails due to exhaustion of space in the free store.

Write a test driver that tests your constructor and copy-constructor. Make your test driver interactive. By creating `IntVec` instances of different sizes, see if you can deduce the exact size of the free store.

7.4   Write and test a program to solve the following problem.

TITLE

Character frequency counter with command-line arguments

DESCRIPTION

This program inputs natural language text from standard input and outputs the frequency of occurrence of a single character. The user specifies the desired character as a command-line argument to the program. For example, if the program is named `charfreq`, the user would enter

```
$ charfreq b
```

to count the number of occurrences of 'b' in the input text.

This argument is required. Two others are optional. The argument `-i` says to ignore the case in the search, upper- and lowercase letters to be treated the same. The argument `-1nn`, where nn denotes a two-digit decimal number, says to limit the search to the first nn occurrences of the character. The three arguments can occur in any combination, in any order. For example, the arguments b `-i` `-108` mean the same as `-108` b `-i`, and so on.

Finally, if no arguments are given at all or if too many are given, the program displays instructions about the command line format and halts.

INPUT

Input, consisting of natural language text, comes from standard input. The end-of-file condition signals end of data.

OUTPUT

If the user supplies no command-line arguments or supplies too many, the program displays the following information, then halts:

```
Usage: charfreq c [-i] [-1nn]
          c: desired char
        -i: ignore case
      -1nn: limit count to nn occurrences
```

If the user does supply command-line arguments, the program proceeds. Because the user may redirect standard input to come from a file, there is no prompt to the user to start typing text.

After the user has typed the system's end-of-file keystroke to terminate input, the program outputs a blank line and then the result:

```
Frequency of '<c>': <f>
```

where <c> is the character to be counted and <f> is its frequency as a decimal integer.

ERROR HANDLING

If any of the command-line arguments are incorrect, the program displays the message

```
Bad arg
```

and halts without reading any input. Examples of errors are: search character argument missing, duplicate arguments, unrecognized arguments, "limit" value not containing two decimal digits.

EXAMPLE

Below are several examples of execution, with operating system commands and program input in color.

```
$ charfreq
Usage: charfreq c [-i] [-lnn]
        c: desired char
       -i: ignore case
     -lnn: limit count to nn occurrences

$ charfreq a
All in a day's work,
so I say.
<EOF>

Frequency of 'a': 3

$ charfreq -i a
All in a day's work,
so I say.
<EOF>

Frequency of 'a': 4

$ charfreq -i a -i
Bad arg

$ charfreq -i g -l20
gggGGGGGGGGGGGGGggggggggggggggggggggGGGgggggggggggggggg<EOF>

Frequency of 'g': 20

$ charfreq -i g -l20 -i
Usage: charfreq c [-i] [-lnn]
        c: desired char
       -i: ignore case
     -lnn: limit count to nn occurrences
```

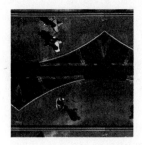

CHAPTER 8

Linked Lists

INTRODUCTION

In Chapter 4 we introduced a variety of data structures—lists, stacks, queues, and sets—as abstractions. We defined the properties of these data structures without describing how the programmer might implement them.

In this chapter, we examine an implementation tool called a *linked list*. A linked list is a low-level data structure upon which we can build higher-level data structures. Stated another way, we can implement data structures such as lists, stacks, queues, and sets by using linked lists.

This chapter explores linked lists in a specific context: a means for implementing list ADTs. In Chapter 9 we will see how we can use linked lists to implement stacks and queues as well.

8.1 Lists and Linked Lists

A program designer, working from a particular problem specification, has arrived at a decision point. This designer needs to represent a collection of integer values as program data and must choose the most suitable data structure—array, record, set, list, stack, or queue—for this collection. The designer, noting that the collection is linear and consists of homogeneous data items, immediately rules out the set and record structures. Furthermore, the designer observes that the ordering of data items does not depend on the time of insertion (for example, FIFO or LIFO) and therefore eliminates the stack and queue from consideration. This leaves the array and the list.

At this point the determining factor is direct access versus sequential access. The major benefit of the array is the ease of storing and retrieving components directly via an index or subscript. However, if the components must be maintained in, say, numeric or alphabetical order, then inserting and deleting items can require extensive data movement in the array. If a collection of 1000 integers 1, 5, 6, 8, . . . is stored in ascending order in an array, then insertion of the number 3 requires moving 999 array elements to make room for the new item.

Our designer concludes that insertions and deletions will, in fact, occur very frequently for this particular collection of data and selects the list as the most appropriate data structure. (Recall from Chapter 4 that Insert and Delete are intrinsic operations on lists.)

Lists, unlike arrays, are not built-in data types in C++. A programmer must implement the list, as an ADT, in terms of existing data types. In particular, the programmer must (1) choose a concrete data representation for the list and (2) implement the list operations. (When there is no risk of confusion, we often will use "implement" to mean both representing the data and implementing the operations on that data.)

One possibility for implementing a list is to use a built-in array. We could represent each list item as an element of the array. Then we could implement the list operations such as Reset, Advance, Insert, and Delete by using an array subscript as the list cursor and by moving list items around in the array. Unfortunately, array implementation of a list brings us back to the reason we avoided arrays in the first place: excessive data movement when insertions and deletions are frequent.

An alternative to the built-in array implementation is a data structure known as a **linked list.** A linked list is a collection of structs (records), called **nodes,** each containing at least one member that gives the location of the next node in the list. In the simplest case, each node has two members: a **data member** (the data value of the list item) and a **link member** (a value locating the successor of this node). The presence of a link member allows us to place individual nodes anywhere in memory, not necessarily in contiguous memory locations. For a list of three integers—4, 7, and 9—the following is an abstract diagram of a linked list:

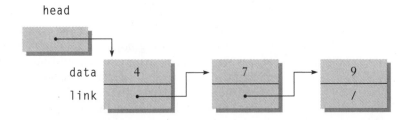

The separate variable named head is not a node in the list; its purpose is to locate the very first node. This list is known as a **singly linked list,** because each node contains only one link member. The slash in the link member of the last node signifies that this node has no successor.

The three nodes do not necessarily occupy consecutive memory locations, so inserting the integer 6 into the list involves no data movement of the existing nodes:

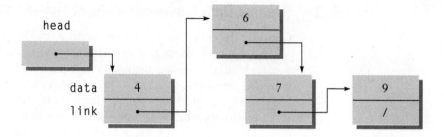

For this reason, list ADTs often are implemented with linked lists instead of built-in arrays.

Now it appears that we are implementing one ADT (the list) with another (the linked list), because linked lists are not built-in data structures in C++. This viewpoint is accurate. Linked lists are abstractions that, in turn, are implemented using built-in types. This chapter explores two popular implementations: dynamic data (with pointers) and built-in arrays. Figure 8.1 presents a perspective on this layering of abstractions, with each data type implemented by the one below it.

In the remaining sections of this chapter we begin with dynamic data implementations to illustrate various operations on linked lists and different ways of organizing linked lists. Later, we discuss how to implement a linked list using a built-in array. Finally, we present an example of a C++ class that employs a linked list to maintain information about people in an organization.

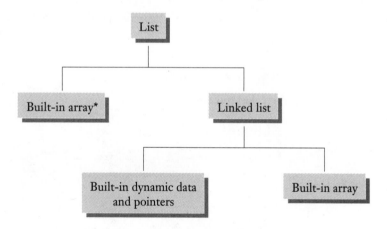

Figure 8.1
Implementation
hierarchy for a list ADT

* This implementation is very inefficient. Inserting and deleting items requires shifting all array elements up and down.

8.2   Dynamic Data Implementations of Linked Lists

Consider the collection of C++ declarations in Figure 8.2.

This figure declares two data types, NodePtr and NodeType. NodePtr is a pointer type that points to objects of type NodeType. NodeType is a struct with two members, data and link. The data member contains a value of type SomeDataType, and link contains a pointer to another NodeType structure.

The link member is of type NodeType*—that is, it can point to an instance of type NodeType. In C++, a struct or class cannot contain an instance of itself (leading to an infinitely recursive structure!) but may contain a *pointer* to an instance of itself.

The order of the declarations in Figure 8.2 is important. We have declared NodeType prior to NodePtr because of the general C++ requirement that an identifier be declared before it is referenced. However, C++ does allow **forward declarations** of structs and classes:

```
struct  NodeType;        ◄— Forward (incomplete) declaration
typedef NodeType* NodePtr;

struct  NodeType {       ◄— Complete declaration
    SomeDataType data;
    NodePtr      link;
};
```

The advantage here is that we can declare the type of link to be NodePtr instead of NodeType*.

Dynamic Allocation of List Nodes

In addition to the two type declarations, Figure 8.2 also declares two NodePtr variables, head and visitPtr. If we allocate a new dynamic object with the statement

```
head = new NodeType;
```

then the result is as follows:

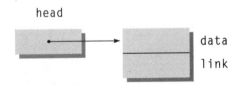

This newly allocated object is a struct with two members. If we then execute the statement

```
(*head).data = 682;
```

```
// Type declarations
struct NodeType {
    SomeDataType data;      // SomeDataType previously declared
    NodeType*    link;
};
typedef NodeType* NodePtr;

// Variable declarations
NodePtr head;
NodePtr visitPtr;
```

Figure 8.2 Declarations for a singly linked list

the resulting diagram is this:

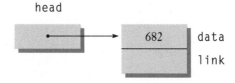

The notation (*head).data is a mixture of pointer dereferencing and struct member selection. Here *head refers to the entire struct, and (*head).data selects the data member of this struct. The parentheses are mandatory because the dot (.) has higher precedence than the asterisk (*). Without parentheses, *head.data would mean *(head.data). Whenever you are in doubt about operator precedence in C++, consult Appendix F.

Enclosing the pointer dereference within parentheses quickly becomes tedious, so C++ includes another member selection operator "->". (The operator is composed of two consecutive symbols: hyphen and greater-than sign.) By definition,

<PointerExpression> -> <MemberName>

is equivalent to

(*<PointerExpression>). <MemberName>

The expression (*head).data therefore can be written as head->data. Here is the general guideline for choosing between the two C++ member selection operators (dot and arrow):

Use the dot operator if the first operand denotes a struct, but use the arrow operator if the first operand denotes a *pointer* to a struct.

Linking Nodes Together

Using the arrow operator, the statement

head->data = 682;

gives us the following diagram, as before:

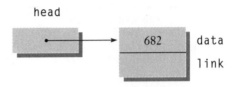

Suppose that we now execute the following statement:

```
head->link = new NodeType;
```

This statement allocates a second NodeType structure on the free store and stores its address into the link member of the struct pointed to by head. Here is the resulting picture:

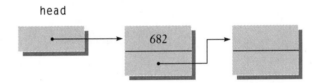

We can use the dereferencing operator to access this second struct as well, as shown in Figure 8.3. This figure contains several examples of pointer expressions, pointer dereferencing, and struct member selection. For each, the referenced object is in color.

Given the expressions in Figure 8.3, the following code assigns values to the members of the second struct:

```
head->link->data = 4;
head->link->link = NULL;
```

The resulting memory diagram is this:

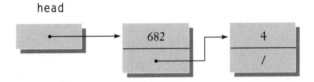

This structure exemplifies the dynamic data representation of a singly linked list. Every node except the last contains a pointer to the next node in the list, and the last node contains NULL to signal the end of the list.

Characteristics of Singly Linked Lists

The above diagram shows a separate pointer variable named head. This variable, called the **head pointer** or **list pointer,** is not a node in the list. A head pointer either points to the first node in the list or contains NULL if the list is empty.

1. Expression: `head`
   Meaning: A pointer to (that is, the address of) the first `struct`.

   head

   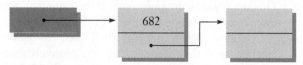

2. Expression: `*head`
   Meaning: The `struct` pointed to by `head` (the entire first `struct`).

   head

3. Expression: `head->link` or `(*head).link`
   Meaning: A pointer to (that is, the address of) the second `struct`.

   head

4. Expression: `*(head->link)` or `*((*head).link)`
   Meaning: The `struct` pointed to by `head->link` (the entire second `struct`).

   head

   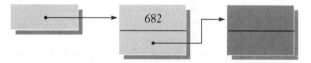

5. Expression: `head->link->data` or `*(head->link).data`
   Meaning: The `data` member of the second `struct`.

   head

Figure 8.3 Pointer dereferencing and `struct` member selection

Every node in a singly linked list includes at least two members: a link member and one or more data members. The data member(s) contain the primary value(s) of the node, and the link member contains a pointer used to connect the list.

The first and last nodes of a singly linked list are somewhat unusual. The first node is the only node pointed to by the head pointer. Some algorithms must treat the first node differently from the others because of this property. The last node is the only node that contains a null pointer. Many algorithms identify the last node (the end of the list) by this characteristic.

In abstract diagrams of linked lists, we usually draw the nodes one after another, as if they were stored consecutively in memory. At run time, however, the nodes probably are scattered throughout the free store in unknown order; each execution of the new operator obtains a piece of the free store wherever it can be found. Consequently, the only way a program can access the nodes in consecutive order is to follow the pointers stored in the link members. The next section addresses this notion of sequencing through a linked list.

8.3 Traversing Singly Linked Lists

A program that uses linked list structures is said to perform **list processing.** Several algorithms are widely used in list processing. The lock-box analogy from the previous chapter helps illustrate these algorithms.

You can think of each node of a singly linked list as a lock box containing the key to the next node. There is one key that is not locked inside another box: the head pointer. Furthermore, the last lock box contains the NULL key.

Suppose that you need to open the third lock box. Remember that the only key for this box is locked in the second box. The correct way to open the third box begins by using the head pointer key to open the first box. You can then use the key from the first box to open the second box. Finally, you can use the key from the second box to open the third.

This algorithm for opening lock boxes is very common with linked lists; it is called a **traversal algorithm.** The basic idea is to proceed from one node of a linked list to the next. As each node is reached (**visited**), its link member is used to locate the next node.

A complete traversal of a singly linked list begins by visiting the first node and finishes by visiting the last node. This algorithm, shown in Figure 8.4, uses the previous declarations from Figure 8.2.

Accessing the third node
of a linked list.

```
// PRE: "head" points to a singly linked list (or contains NULL)

visitPtr = head;
while (visitPtr != NULL) {
                    // INV (prior to test):
                    //     All list nodes preceding *visitPtr have been
                    //     visited (the entire list, if visitPtr==NULL)
                    //  && visitPtr points to a list node or == NULL
      // Do something with node *visitPtr
      visitPtr = visitPtr->link;
}

// ASSERT: (head != NULL) --> All nodes of the singly linked list
//                            beginning with *head have been visited
```

Figure 8.4 General algorithm for visiting nodes of a singly linked list

The key statement in this algorithm is

```
visitPtr = visitPtr->link;
```

Before this statement, `visitPtr` points to one node of the list; after this statement, it points to the next node. This statement for advancing a pointer from one node to the next is as common as the statement

```
index++;
```

for incrementing an array index. (*Note that it would be wrong to use* `visitPtr++` *to point to the next node of a linked list. List nodes are not necessarily contiguous in memory.*)

The list traversal loop terminates when `visitPtr` is finally assigned the value NULL, the contents of the link member of the last node in the list.

Constructing and Traversing a List

Figure 8.5 contains a program, `EchoCity`, that illustrates many list processing issues. `EchoCity` builds a singly linked list from an input file, then outputs the data from the list. Each node in this list is of type `CityNode` and contains the name, population, and number of registered voters for a single city. The link member of each node is named `next`.

The function `ReadAllCities` implements an algorithm for constructing a singly linked list. We begin by creating an empty list:

```
cityList = NULL;
```

As we input statistics for each city, we allocate another list node via

```
inNode = new CityNode;
```

and `inNode` then points to the newly created node. After assigning values to

Figure 8.5 `EchoCity` program

```
// ------------------------------------------------------------
// echocity.cpp
// This program inputs a list of city statistics from standard
// input.  (Command line redirection of standard input is likely.)
// The input information is then output.
// Provision is made for future additional processing.
// ------------------------------------------------------------
#include <iostream.h>
#include <stddef.h>        // For NULL constant definition
#include <string.h>        // For strcpy()

typedef char CityName[21];
struct  CityNode {
    CityName    name;
    int         population;     // in 1000's
    int         numVoters;      // in 1000's
    CityNode*   next;
};
typedef CityNode* CityPtr;

void ReadAllCities( CityPtr& );
void WriteAllCities( CityPtr );

int main()
{
    CityPtr cityList;

    ReadAllCities(cityList);
    // In the future, the city list could be processed at this point
    WriteAllCities(cityList);
    return 0;
}
// ------------------------------------------------------------
void WriteAllCities( /* in */ CityPtr cityList )
    //..............................................................
    // PRE:  cityList is the head pointer to a singly linked list
    // POST: All nodes of the list have been output
    //..............................................................
{
    CityPtr outNode = cityList;

    while (outNode != NULL) {
            // INV (prior to test):
            //     All nodes prior to *outNode have been output
            //  && outNode points to a list node or == NULL
        cout << outNode->name << ", "
            << outNode->population << " (in thousands), "
            << outNode->numVoters  << " (in thousands)\n";
        outNode = outNode->next;
    }
}
```

```
// -----------------------------------------------------------------
void ReadAllCities( /* out */ CityPtr& cityList )
    //................................................................
    // PRE:  NOT Assigned(cityList)
    // POST: City statistics have been input from standard input
    //    && cityList is the head pointer to a singly linked list
    //       of these statistics
    //................................................................
{
    CityPtr  inNode;
    CityName tempName;

    cityList = NULL;
    while (cin >> tempName) {
                    // INV (prior to test):
                    //     Input for each city prior to this one
                    //     has been stored in a separate list node
        inNode = new CityNode;
        strcpy(inNode->name, tempName);
        cin >> inNode->population;
        cin >> inNode->numVoters;
        inNode->next = cityList;
        cityList = inNode;
    }
}
```

the data members of *inNode, we link the new node to the front of the list with the following two statements:

```
inNode->next = cityList;
cityList = inNode;
```

Figure 8.6 illustrates the effect of these two statements.

Constructing a list by appending to the front, rather than the rear, is a common list-processing technique. The head pointer is always accessible, so locating and relinking the front of the list is uncomplicated.

The EchoCity program includes a WriteAllCities function to output the list contents. The function does this by performing a list traversal. A local pointer, outNode, points to each node in turn as it is visited.

Figure 8.6 Inserting a node at the front of a list

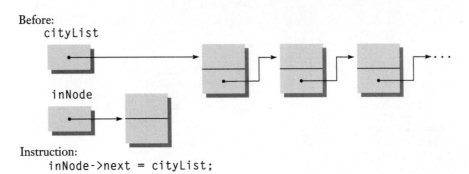

Before:
    cityList

    inNode

Instruction:
    inNode->next = cityList;

Result:

cityList

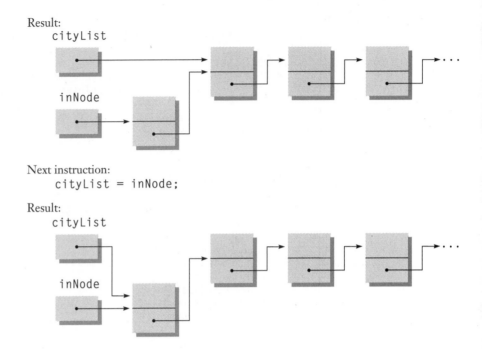

Next instruction:
    cityList = inNode;

Result:

cityList

Recursive List Traversal

It is easiest to traverse singly linked lists from the first node to the last. WriteAllCities uses this method of traversal. Notice that the output produced by this function will be in reverse order of input because the information for the *last* city is at the front of the list. Traversing the list backwards (from the last node to the first) can be accomplished through recursion. Figure 8.7 displays a recursive function that outputs the contents of the city list in reverse order (that is, in the original input order).

```
void WriteAllCitiesRev( /* in */ CityPtr outList )
    //............................................................
    // PRE:  outList points to a node in a singly linked list
    //     OR outList == NULL
    // POST: (outList != NULL) --> All nodes following *outList have
    //                             been output,
    //                             then *outList has been output
    //............................................................
{
    if (outList != NULL) {
        WriteAllCitiesRev(outList->next);
        // ASSERT: All nodes after *outList have been output
        cout << outList->name << ", "
             << outList->population << " (in thousands), "
             << outList->numVoters  << " (in thousands)\n";
    }
}
```

Figure 8.7 Recursive list traversal (WriteAllCitiesRev function)

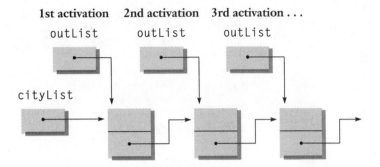

1st activation   2nd activation   3rd activation . . .

outList   outList   outList

cityList

Figure 8.8 Values of outList for consecutive activations of WriteAllCitiesRev

The pointer parameter outList contains a different node pointer for each recursive activation of WriteAllCitiesRev. For the first invocation, outList contains the same value as cityList, the list head pointer. Each consecutive activation receives an outList parameter that points to the next list node, as Figure 8.8 illustrates.

The recursion ends when WriteAllCitiesRev is invoked with outList equal to NULL. This activation returns immediately, and then all previous activations output the data from their *outList nodes and return.

8.4   Inserting and Deleting Nodes

Two fundamental operations for modifying the structure of any list are insertion and deletion. With linked lists, inserting a node amounts to placing a new node somewhere in the list without removing or rearranging any other list nodes. Deleting a node consists of removing it from the list without disturbing the remainder of the list.

Insertions

Figure 8.9 displays the general algorithm for inserting a new node *after* an existing list node. This algorithm requires two pointer variables, prevPtr and insPtr. Initially, insPtr points to the new node to be inserted and prevPtr points to the node prior to the location of the insertion.

When examining a list-processing algorithm, the programmer always should consider three separate cases:

1. The node is the first node of the list.
2. The node is an interior node (neither the first nor the last node of the list).
3. The node is the last node of the list.

This insertion algorithm works properly when *prevPtr is the first node, the last node, or any node in between. However, there is a flaw: the algorithm cannot insert a new first node into the list. The algorithm requires prevPtr to point to an existing list node and the insertion occurs after this node.

```
// Type declarations
struct NodeType {
    SomeDataType data;      // SomeDataType previously declared
    NodeType*    link;
};
typedef NodeType* NodePtr;

// Variable declarations
NodePtr head;
NodePtr prevPtr;
NodePtr insPtr;
```

The algorithm below uses the above declarations.

Before:

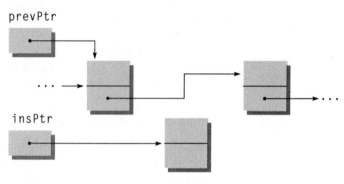

Instructions:
```
    insPtr->link = prevPtr->link;
    prevPtr->link = insPtr;
```

After:

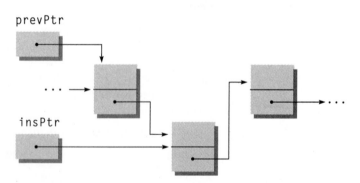

Figure 8.9 Inserting a node after *prevPtr

A slightly different algorithm is necessary to insert a new first node into a singly linked list. By replacing prevPtr->link with head in the previous algorithm, we obtain the following:

```
// ALGORITHM FOR INSERTING A NEW FIRST NODE
    insPtr->link = head;
    head = insPtr;
```

Deletions

A scheme for deleting a node from a singly linked list appears in Figure 8.10. This particular algorithm requires a pointer, named prevPtr, that points to the node prior to the one to be deleted.

This deletion algorithm works when prevPtr points to the first node or any interior node of the list. But it makes no sense if prevPtr points to the last node of the list, which has no successor. The following precondition eliminates this possibility:

```
// PRE: prevPtr points to a list node
//    && prevPtr->link != NULL
```

Just as the original insertion algorithm could not insert before the first node, this deletion algorithm cannot delete the first node. To delete the first list node, we modify the algorithm by again replacing prevPtr->link with head:

```
// ALGORITHM FOR DELETING THE FIRST NODE
    tempPtr = head;
    head = head->link;
    delete tempPtr;
```

Inserting or deleting an interior node of a singly linked list always requires a pointer to the previous node. If this pointer is immediately available, the algorithm in Figure 8.10 suffices. But if the pointer to the preceding node is not immediately available, a different algorithm is necessary. Figure 8.11 presents an algorithm for deleting the node pointed to by delPtr. It assumes that the pointer to the node preceding delPtr is not available and must be found by a list traversal.

Figure 8.10 Deleting the node after *prevPtr

```
// Type declarations
struct NodeType {
    SomeDataType data;     // SomeDataType previously declared
    NodeType*    link;
};
typedef NodeType* NodePtr;

// Variable declarations
NodePtr head;
NodePtr prevPtr;
NodePtr tempPtr;
```

Figure 8.10 (Continued)

The algorithm below uses the above declarations.

Before:

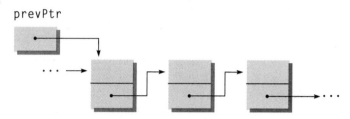

Instructions:
```
tempPtr = prevPtr->link;
prevPtr->link = tempPtr->link;
delete tempPtr;
```

After:

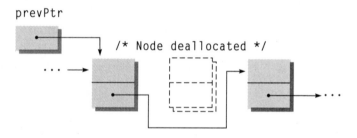

Figure 8.11 Deleting the node pointed to by delPtr

```
// Type declarations
struct NodeType {
    SomeDataType data;      // SomeDataType previously declared
    NodeType*    link;
};
typedef NodeType* NodePtr;

// Variable declarations
NodePtr head;
NodePtr prevPtr;
NodePtr delPtr;
```

The algorithm below uses the above declarations.

Before:

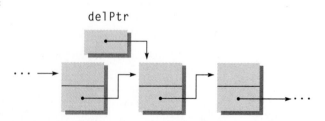

Instructions:

```
if (delPtr == head)
    head = head->link;
else {
    prevPtr = head;
    while (prevPtr->link != delPtr)
            // INV (prior to test):
            //    *prevPtr is a node somewhere
            //    before *delPtr
        prevPtr = prevPtr->link;
    prevPtr->link = delPtr->link;
}
delete delPtr;
```

After:

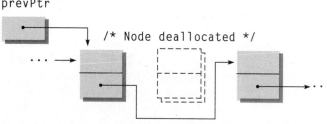

prevPtr

/* Node deallocated */

Designing with Wisdom

Advantages and Disadvantages of Dynamic Linked Lists

Using a dynamic linked list to implement a list data structure has pros and cons. It is up to the programmer to weigh the options. Below is a summary of the major advantages and disadvantages of programming with dynamic linked lists.

Advantages:

1. Wisely controlled dynamic storage can save considerable space that is wasted by other list implementations.

2. Dynamic data, unlike static and automatic data, is not declared with a fixed size. The free store for allocation of dynamic nodes is large for most systems.

3. Certain operations are simpler with linked structures. For example, the algorithm for inserting into a singly linked list consists of only two assignment statements. In contrast, inserting a new value into the middle of an array requires shifting all the remaining array elements down.

Disadvantages:

1. Algorithms involving dynamic data and pointers are sometimes more complex, harder to read, and harder to debug than similar algorithms for statically allocated structures.

2. In some cases, dynamic linked lists can waste storage space. It is possible to store many pointers and very little data. The pointer space must be considered to be overhead. This overhead is accentuated when nodes contain smaller data members. For example, a list node with a single `char` data member (one byte long) may require a 4-byte pointer as its link member. The result is 80 percent overhead (4 bytes out of 5) in each list node.

3. Allocating and deallocating dynamic data is run-time overhead. The execution time required by the `new` and `delete` operators can sometimes overshadow the time saved by simple list-processing algorithms.

But in other circumstances, this overhead is insignificant compared to the overall time saved by a list-processing algorithm. There are no hard and fast rules.

8.5   Head Nodes

The singly linked list is the most common form of linked list, but many variations have been designed to decrease the complexity or increase the efficiency of specific algorithms.

For many list-processing algorithms, the first node of the list is a special case. Both of the earlier algorithms for inserting and deleting nodes required alterations to insert or delete the first node. The first node is special because it is pointed to by the head pointer, not by another node in the list. Updating the head pointer is different from updating a link member of a node. The result is often an algorithm with the following general form:

IF the node to be processed is first in the list THEN
    Process the first node
ELSE
    Process a node other than the first

One way to eliminate this special-case code is to include a **head node** or **list header.** A head node is an extra node placed at the beginning of the list. It has the same data type as all other nodes in the list, but its data member is unused. Figure 8.12 displays a singly linked list with a head node. This diagram accurately pictures the head node as additional list overhead rather than an actual data-bearing node of the list.

Head nodes eliminate the special case for the first list node, because every "actual" list node is now pointed to by another node. Without a head node, the insertion algorithm requires a test:

```
if (/* new first node is to be inserted */) {
    insPtr->link = head;
    head = insPtr;
}
else {
    insPtr->link = prevPtr->link;
    prevPtr->link = insPtr;
}
```

head

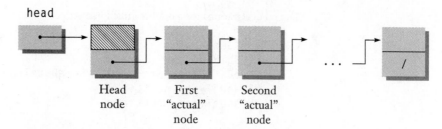

Figure 8.12 Singly linked list with a head node

Head node · First "actual" node · Second "actual" node

(This algorithm combines the two we presented earlier—one for inserting a new first node, the other for inserting any other node.)

In contrast, if a list has a head node, no test is necessary. To insert a new first node into the list, we make `prevPtr` point to the head node. Then the else-clause of the above algorithm covers all possible cases:

```
// ALGORITHM FOR INSERTING ANY NODE INTO A LIST WITH A HEAD NODE
    insPtr->link = prevPtr->link;
    prevPtr->link = insPtr;
```

There are two restrictions on the use of head nodes that are important to remember:

1. Traversal algorithms must skip the head node.
2. The head node must not be deleted.

The head node must always be present, even if the list is empty. It is good practice to allocate a head node as part of the list initialization and never to deallocate it.

Using a head node makes algorithms less complicated, but not more efficient. In fact, some algorithms are slightly less efficient because of the extra node.

8.6 Doubly Linked Lists and Circular Lists

With singly linked lists, algorithms that require the predecessor of a given node can be particularly inefficient. If you have only a pointer to a list node but need a pointer to its predecessor, you must traverse the list from the beginning. The deletion algorithm of Figure 8.11 is an example.

Doubly Linked Lists

Using a **doubly linked list** can minimize the need for list traversals. A doubly linked list consists of nodes with *two* link members. One points to the next node in the list, and the other points to the previous node. Figure 8.13 shows a set of declarations and a diagram of a doubly linked list.

In this example, a node's `nextLink` member points to its immediate successor, and its `prevLink` member points to its immediate predecessor. The two null pointers in the diagram show that the first node has no predecessor and

General declarations for a doubly linked list:

```
// Type declarations
struct DblNodeType {
    SomeDataType data;      // SomeDataType previously declared
    DblNodeType* nextLink;
    DblNodeType* prevLink;
};
typedef DblNodeType* DblNodePtr;

// Variable declaration
DblNodePtr head;
```

General form of a doubly linked list:

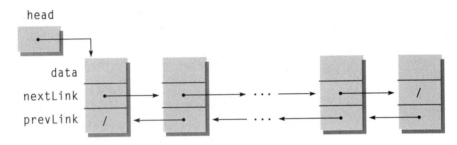

Figure 8.13 A doubly linked list

the last node has no successor. Doubly linked lists can be traversed from first node to last or from last to first.

Compared with a singly linked list, inserting and deleting nodes from a doubly linked list is a bit slower. Both of the nextLink and prevLink members must be updated. However, updating the extra link member is still much faster than doing a list traversal to find the predecessor of a node. Another potential disadvantage of doubly linked lists is the extra storage required for the second pointer in each node.

Circular Linked Lists

Still another variation of the singly linked list is the **circular linked list** or **ring**. The nodes of a circular linked list are identical to those of a singly linked list, but the link member of the last node points to the first node instead of

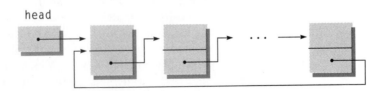

Figure 8.14 A circular linked list

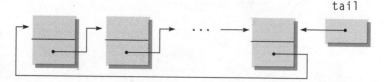

Figure 8.15 A circular linked list with a tail pointer

containing NULL. This arrangement forms the circle of nodes pictured in Figure 8.14.

Circular linked lists are useful in algorithms where there is no particular first or last item. The advantage of this structure is that you can make the head pointer point to any node without destroying the list.

Algorithms for processing circular linked lists are similar to those for singly linked lists. But identifying the last node of a circular linked list is different because there is no null pointer in the list. To find the last node, the algorithm must compare node pointers to the head pointer. (That is, you have found the last node if its `link` member points to the same node that the head pointer does.)

A convenient alternative for finding the last node is to keep a **tail pointer** to the list (Figure 8.15) instead of a head pointer. Both the first and last nodes are then accessible without traversal: `tail` points to the last node, and `tail->link` points to the first.

Circular linking often produces special cases when the list is empty. To avoid this inconvenience, many algorithms require that circular linked lists contain at least one node (for example, a head node as we described earlier).

Exercises at the end of this chapter invite further examination of doubly linked and circular lists.

8.7 Array Implementations of Linked Lists

Programmers learning about linked lists tend to associate them exclusively with dynamic data, treating the two concepts as inseparable. This perspective is not accurate. As emphasized by the implementation hierarchy of Figure 8.1, a linked list can be thought of as an abstract data type. Dynamic data and pointers are just one way to *implement* this abstraction.

Another way to implement a linked list is to use a built-in array—in particular, a vector of `struct`s. Each array element, a `struct` with a data member and a link member, represents a node in the linked list. Now, however, the link member does not contain the machine address of the next node; it contains the *array subscript* of the next node in the list. Figure 8.16 shows an abstract diagram of a linked list of characters, perhaps maintained in alphabetical order. It also shows how this list might be represented as a 100-element array of `struct`s. The integer -1 serves as a null pointer to distinguish it from any valid C++ subscript.

Whenever a node is deleted from the linked list, the corresponding array element is still physically present but logically contains unassigned data. In Figure 8.16, array elements 1, 4, and 5 contain unassigned data.

Abstract diagram:

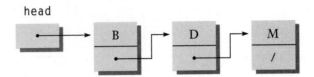

Declarations:

```
// Type declarations
struct NodeType {
    char data;
    int  link;
};
typedef int NodePtr;

// "Null pointer" constant
const int NULL_PTR = -1;

// Variable declarations
NodeType node[100];
NodePtr  head;
NodePtr  prevPtr;
NodePtr  insPtr;
NodePtr  tempPtr;
```

Array representation:

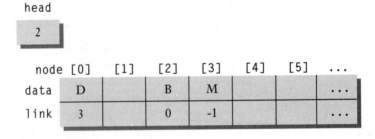

Figure 8.16 Array representation of a singly linked list

Managing a "Free Store"

In the dynamic data implementation of a linked list, we used the C++ new and delete operators to obtain and release memory from the system's free store. For the array implementation, we must maintain our own "free store."

A simple technique is to define the "free store" to be the set of all the unused elements in the node array. To keep track of which array elements are currently unused, we use a separate Boolean vector:

```
Boolean free[100];
```

At any moment during program execution, if element i of the node array is unused, then free[i] is TRUE. On the other hand, if node[i] is in use, then free[i] is FALSE. Given the linked list of Figure 8.16, the free vector would contain the following values:

free [0]	[1]	[2]	[3]	[4]	[5]	...
FALSE	TRUE	FALSE	FALSE	TRUE	TRUE	...

To emulate the C++ new and delete operators, we write our own functions NewLoc and Deallocate with the following specifications:

```
NodePtr NewLoc();
    // POST: IF there is space available on the "free store" THEN
    //           FCTVAL == index of an unused array element
    //       ELSE
    //           FCTVAL == NULL_PTR

void Deallocate( /* in */ NodePtr n );
    // PRE:  n was previously obtained by a call to NewLoc()
    // POST: Array element n has been returned to the "free store"
```

As defined in Figure 8.16, type NodePtr is a synonym for int, and NULL_PTR is the value -1. Here are the function definitions for NewLoc and Deallocate:

```
NodePtr NewLoc()
{
    int i = 0;

    while (i < 100 && !free[i] )  // INV (prior to test):
                                  //      free[0..i-1] == FALSE
                                  //   && i <= 100
        i++;
    if (i == 100)
        // ASSERT: No space available on "free store"
        return NULL_PTR;
    free[i] = FALSE;
    return i;
}

void Deallocate( /* in */ NodePtr n )
{
    free[n] = TRUE;
}
```

Insertions

Now that we have the necessary support routines to manage the "free store," let us see how to insert and delete nodes of a linked list. To insert a new node, we first create the node:

```
insPtr = NewLoc();
if (insPtr != NULL_PTR)
    node[insPtr].data = someChar;
```

Then we either insert the node after, say, node[prevPtr]:

```
node[insPtr].link = node[prevPtr].link;
node[prevPtr].link = insPtr;
```

or we insert the node at the front of the list:

```
node[insPtr].link = head;
head = insPtr;
```

The array pictured in Figure 8.16 would look like the following after inserting a node containing the data value 'P':

head

2

node	[0]	[1]	[2]	[3]	[4]	[5]	...
data	D	P	B	M			...
link	3	-1	0	1			...

Deletions

To delete the node after node[prevPtr], we can use the following code:

```
tempPtr = node[prevPtr].link;
node[prevPtr].link = node[tempPtr].link;
Deallocate(tempPtr);
```

Observe that these algorithms for insertion and deletion are very nearly the same as earlier ones for the dynamic data implementation. A quick review of those algorithms will confirm that they differ only in the syntax required to reference the various objects.

Designing with Wisdom

A Perspective on Linked Lists

Linked lists are not necessarily related to dynamic memory allocation and pointer types. A linked list is an abstraction. The programmer can represent list nodes either as dynamic structs on the free store or as structs within a C++ array. Each method has its tradeoffs.

The built-in array implementation presented in this section is likely to execute faster because "free store" management is handled by the program itself. With a dynamic data implementation, the new and delete operators typically call upon the operating system to manage the system's free store, thereby slowing down the program.

On the other hand, the array implementation is less frugal with memory space. The maximum size must be specified in advance. Because a built-in array cannot expand dynamically, the programmer must often overestimate the array size. (To escape this restriction, an alternative is to use dynamic array allocation as described in Chapter 7.) Another disadvantage of the array implementation is the need to design additional data structures and algorithms to explicitly manage the "free store" within the array.

Both the dynamic data and the array implementations of linked lists have their virtues. Choosing between the two reduces to a **space versus time** decision. A dynamic data implementation generally consumes less memory but requires more execution time. An array implementation may require more memory but is faster. The intended use of the program dictates whether space or time is more important.

A Study in Design

Implementing a List with a Linked List

Many programming applications involve the processing of personal information: name, address, social security number, marital status, personal income, and so forth. Within a program, a list data structure is a good choice for storing such information if insertions and deletions are frequent. Furthermore, the linked list is typically the preferred structure for implementing a list. In this section we design and implement a C++ class that manages a linked list for storing personal information.

Design Decisions

Suppose we have decided that a list data structure is best for storing our personal information. Suppose also that we have analyzed the intended application, concluding that memory space is more critical than execution time. Then a dynamic linked list is a suitable representation. In this example we will use a singly linked list with one list node per person. For simplicity, each node has only two data items: the person's name and the person's age.

The number of characters in people's names is highly variable. Arbitrarily choosing a 30-element char array probably is not the best way to proceed. Longer names will have to be truncated; shorter names will result in wasted storage. An alternative is to use dynamic array allocation for each person's name. (In Chapter 7 we introduced the concept of dynamic array allocation with the DynArray program.)

With this design, we cannot store a person's name in the list node itself. To do so would require a uniform array size in each node. Instead, the new operator will allocate the exact amount of free store needed for an individual's name, and we will store a *pointer* to this character array in the node. Figure 8.17 shows an abstract diagram of this linked list structure.

This figure demonstrates that not only is each list node on the free store, but also each person's name is on the free store. Thus the list nodes are small

and are all the same size. The variation in length of people's names is reflected
in varying amounts of free store occupied by the name strings.

Here is how we put a person's name onto the free store. Suppose that
newPtr points to a newly allocated list node and inputName is a char array
holding a person's name as read from the input stream. The following two
statements enlist the aid of the library routines strlen and strcpy (Appendix
G). The statements allocate free store for the dynamic string array, copy the
base address of this dynamic string into the name member of the node, and
finally copy the string from inputName onto the free store:

```
newPtr->name = new char[strlen(inputName)+1];
// ASSERT: Storage for string array is now on free store and
//          its base address is in newPtr->name
strcpy(newPtr->name, inputName);
// ASSERT: Person's name has been copied to free store.
```

Because the new operator allows run-time specification of the size of an array
(using strlen(inputName)+1 above), no memory is wasted by statically declaring the maximum size of the array.

The PersonList *Specification*

Figure 8.18 contains the specification file for a module named Person. The
type PersonNode defines the structure of each node in the linked list, but the
specification file contains only a forward declaration of this structure. The
complete declaration is hidden away in the implementation file. This strategy
promotes information hiding; the user of the class does not need to know the
implementation details.

Because PersonList is a class, the client code may declare many lists. For
example, a voter registration program could maintain three lists simultaneously
by means of the declarations

```
PersonList democrat;
PersonList republican;
PersonList independent;
```

Figure 8.18 Specification file for the Person module

```
// ----------------------------------------------------------------
//   SPECIFICATION FILE (person.h)
//   This module exports a record type for personal data and a class
//   for maintaining lists of such records
// ----------------------------------------------------------------
#include "bool.h"

struct PersonRec {
    char* name;        // Pointer to person's name
    int   age;         // Person's age
};

struct  PersonNode;     // Complete declaration hidden in
                        // implementation file
class PersonList {
public:
    Boolean IsEmpty() const;
        // POST: FCTVAL == (list is empty)

    Boolean IsFull() const;
        // POST: FCTVAL == (list is full)

    void Reset();
        // PRE:  NOT IsEmpty()
        // POST: List cursor is at front of list

    Boolean EndOfList() const;
        // POST: FCTVAL == (list cursor is beyond end of list)

    void Advance();
        // PRE:  NOT IsEmpty()  &&  NOT EndOfList()
        // POST: List cursor has advanced to next record

    PersonRec CurrentRec() const;
        // PRE:  NOT IsEmpty()  &&  NOT EndOfList()
        // POST: FCTVAL == record at list cursor

    void InsertBefore( /* in */ PersonRec someRec );
        // PRE:  Assigned(someRec)  &&  NOT IsFull()
        // POST: someRec inserted before list cursor
        //          (at back, if EndOfList())
        //       && This is the new current record

    void InsertAfter( /* in */ PersonRec someRec );
        // PRE:  Assigned(someRec)  &&  NOT IsEmpty()
        //       && NOT IsFull()  &&  NOT EndOfList()
        // POST: someRec inserted after list cursor
        //       && This is the new current record
```

```
      void Delete();
          // PRE:  NOT IsEmpty()  &&  NOT EndOfList()
          // POST: Record at list cursor deleted
          //    && Successor of deleted record is now the current
          //       record

      PersonList();
          // Constructor
          // POST: Empty list created  &&  EndOfList()

      ~PersonList();
          // Destructor
          // POST: List destroyed
private:
    PersonNode* head;
    PersonNode* currPtr;
};
```

The declaration of the PersonList class shows four const member functions: IsEmpty, IsFull, EndOfList, and CurrentRec. Recall from Chapter 3 that a const member function is one that announces to all clients that it does not modify the private data of a class.

Looking at the private part of the PersonList class, you can see that the class does not physically encapsulate a linked list. It only encapsulates *access* to the list via the private variable head, the head pointer to the linked list. Because this class allocates dynamic data, the class declaration provides a destructor, ~PersonList(), for cleaning up its portion of the free store. It would be best to provide a copy-constructor as well, but we have omitted this to keep the example simpler. Also absent, for simplicity, is an overloaded assignment operator for deep copying of one list to another (Chapter 7).

It is important to emphasize that the user's view of the PersonList class is a list, not a linked list. The public operations are the conventional list operations presented in Chapter 4: Reset, Advance, CurrentRec, InsertBefore, and so forth. For example, the following client code outputs an entire list:

```
PersonList myList;
PersonRec  pers;

:

myList.Reset();
while ( !myList.EndOfList() ) {
    pers = myList.CurrentRec();
    cout << pers.name << ' ' << pers.age << '\n';
    myList.Advance();
}
```

The user has no knowledge of dynamic nodes and node pointers. The underlying implementation—a dynamic, singly linked list—is hidden from the user. If the owner of the class decides to reimplement it with a doubly linked list or a circular linked list, the change will be transparent to the user.

The Implementation File

Figure 8.19 displays the implementation file for the Person module. The private variable currPtr keeps track of the current position in the list. That is, currPtr serves as the list cursor (Chapter 4). The auxiliary function PrevPtr is used by several member functions to obtain a pointer to the immediate predecessor of a given node. We recommend a detailed examination of the code for better understanding of dynamic data, linked lists, class constructors, and class destructors.

Figure 8.19
Implementation file for the Person module

```
// ----------------------------------------------------------------
//   IMPLEMENTATION FILE (person.cpp)
//   This module exports a record type for personal data and a class
//   for maintaining lists of such records
//   List representation: a singly linked list of dynamic nodes.
// ----------------------------------------------------------------
#include "person.h"
#include <string.h>      // For strlen() and strcpy()
#include <stddef.h>      // For NULL
#include <alloc.h>       // For coreleft()  (This function is
                         //                   nonportable)

typedef PersonNode* NodePtr;
struct PersonNode {
    char*   name;        // Pointer to person's name
    int     age;         // Person's age
    NodePtr link;        // Pointer to next node
};

// Private members of class:
//     NodePtr head;
//     NodePtr currPtr;
//
// CLASSINV:
//      (head != NULL) --> head points to front of list
//   && (head == NULL)  --> list is empty
//   && (currPtr != NULL) --> currPtr points to currently accessed
//                            node
//   && (currPtr == NULL)  --> list cursor is beyond end of list

NodePtr PrevPtr( NodePtr, NodePtr ); // Prototype for auxiliary
                                     // function


PersonList::PersonList()
    //...........................................................
    // Constructor
    // POST: head == NULL  &&  currPtr == NULL
    //...........................................................
{
    head = currPtr = NULL;
}
```

```
PersonList::~PersonList()
    //.......................................................
    // Destructor
    // POST: All free store for list has been deallocated
    //.......................................................
{
    currPtr = head;
    while ( !EndOfList() )
        Delete();
}

Boolean PersonList::IsEmpty() const
    //.......................................................
    // POST: FCTVAL == (head == NULL)
    //.......................................................
{
    return (head == NULL);
}

Boolean PersonList::IsFull() const
    //.......................................................
    // POST: FCTVAL == (there is no room on the free store for
    //                  another PersonNode object)
    //.......................................................
{
    return (coreleft() < sizeof(PersonNode));
}

void PersonList::Reset()
    //.......................................................
    // PRE:  head != NULL
    // POST: currPtr == head
    //.......................................................
{
    currPtr = head;
}

Boolean PersonList::EndOfList() const
    //.......................................................
    // POST: FCTVAL == (currPtr == NULL)
    //.......................................................
{
    return (currPtr == NULL);
}

void PersonList::Advance()
    //.......................................................
    // PRE:  head != NULL  &&  currPtr != NULL
    // POST: currPtr == (currPtr<entry>)->link
    //.......................................................
{
    currPtr = currPtr->link;
}
```

```
PersonRec PersonList::CurrentRec() const
    //.............................................................
    // PRE:  head != NULL  &&  currPtr != NULL
    // POST: FCTVAL.name == currPtr->name
    //    && FCTVAL.age == currPtr->age
    //.............................................................
{
    PersonRec rec;

    rec.name = currPtr->name;
    rec.age = currPtr->age;
    return rec;
}

void PersonList::InsertBefore( /* in */ PersonRec someRec )
    //.............................................................
    // PRE:  Assigned(someRec)
    // POST: (currPtr<entry> == NULL) --> New node is at end of list
    //    && (currPtr<entry> != NULL) --> New node inserted before
    //                                    *(currPtr<entry>)
    //    && currPtr == pointer to new node
    //.............................................................
{
    NodePtr newPtr = new PersonNode;
    // ASSERT: Storage for node is now on free store and
    //          its base address is in newPtr

    newPtr->name = new char[strlen(someRec.name)+1];
    // ASSERT: Storage for string array is now on free store and
    //          its base address is in newPtr->name

    strcpy(newPtr->name, someRec.name);
    // ASSERT: Person's name has been copied to free store

    newPtr->age = someRec.age;
    newPtr->link = currPtr;
    if (currPtr == head)
        head = newPtr;
    else {
        NodePtr p = PrevPtr(currPtr, head);
        p->link = newPtr;
    }
    currPtr = newPtr;
}
```

```
void PersonList::InsertAfter( /* in */ PersonRec someRec )
    //............................................................
    // PRE:  Assigned(someRec)  &&  head != NULL  &&  currPtr != NULL
    // POST: New node inserted after *(currPtr<entry>)
    //     && currPtr == pointer to new node
    //............................................................
{
    NodePtr newPtr = new PersonNode;
    newPtr->name = new char[strlen(someRec.name)+1];
    strcpy(newPtr->name, someRec.name);
    newPtr->age = someRec.age;

    newPtr->link = currPtr->link;
    currPtr->link = newPtr;
    currPtr = newPtr;
}

void PersonList::Delete()
    //............................................................
    // PRE:  head != NULL  &&  currPtr != NULL
    // POST: *(currPtr<entry>) deleted from list (and name string
    //        deleted from free store)
    //     && currPtr points to node after deleted node (or == NULL if
    //        last node was deleted)
    //............................................................
{
    delete currPtr->name;
    // ASSERT: Free store for name string deallocated
    NodePtr temp = currPtr;
    if (currPtr == head)
        head = currPtr = head->link;
    else {
        NodePtr p = PrevPtr(currPtr, head);
        p->link = currPtr = currPtr->link;
    }
    delete temp;
    // ASSERT: Free store for node deallocated
}

NodePtr PrevPtr( /* in */ NodePtr somePtr,
                 /* in */ NodePtr head     )
    //............................................................
    // PRE:  somePtr != head
    // POST: FCTVAL == pointer to node before *somePtr
    //............................................................
{
    NodePtr p = head;
    while (p->link != somePtr)  // INV (prior to test):
                                //    *p is a node before *somePtr
        p = p->link;
    return p;
}
```

Our implementation of the `IsFull` operation uses a library function named `coreleft`. The `coreleft` function returns, as an `unsigned int`, the number of bytes currently available on the free store. The C++ built-in operator `sizeof` yields an `unsigned int` representing the size in bytes of its operand. The `IsFull` function returns TRUE if the space remaining on the free store is less than the size of a `PersonNode` object; otherwise, it returns FALSE.

Near the top of Figure 8.19 is a preprocessor directive

```
#include <alloc.h>      // For coreleft()    (This function is
                        //                   nonportable)
```

Programs using the `coreleft` function are not portable from one C++ environment to another. Borland's Turbo C++ and Borland C++ provide this library function, imported through the header file `alloc.h`. In Microsoft C++, the equivalent function is named `_memavl` (beginning with an underscore) and is imported through `malloc.h` instead of `alloc.h`. Some C++ environments do not provide any library function analogous to `coreleft`. In these environments, it is more difficult to implement `IsFull`. One possibility would be to allocate and deallocate a `PersonNode` object, checking the pointer returned by `new` just to see if the allocation succeeded. This trial allocation and deallocation of dynamic data with every call to `IsFull` will slow down the program, but the difference in speed may not be perceptible to the user.

Finally, we again stress the importance of providing a destructor for a class such as `PersonList`. A client function may declare an automatic, local list of type `PersonList` and insert hundreds of people into the list. When the function returns, the local class instance will go out of scope and be deallocated. Unless a destructor is provided, the class instance (including the pointer to the linked list on the free store) will be deallocated, *but not the linked list itself.* The linked list will remain on the free store, allocated but inaccessible, and its storage cannot be reclaimed for use by other dynamic variables.

8.8 Debugging Dynamic Linked Lists

Programs that use dynamic linked lists can be very hard to debug. Dangling pointers, inaccessible nodes, memory leaks, and attempts to dereference null pointers are just a few of the potential complications.

With dynamic data it is often difficult to find the exact location of a bug. When dereferencing an unassigned or null pointer, one of two things can happen:

1. The run-time system is able to detect the error, and it reports an execution error.

2. The run-time system is unable to detect the error, and it references some meaningless storage.

In the first case, the system generates a message such as "Address Out of Bounds" or "Memory Violation." However, locating the origin of the error is difficult, even if the system reports the location of the dereferencing error. The real bug usually happens before this dereference, when the pointer variable is first assigned the wrong value. Tracing backward to find this error is likely to be laborious.

In the second case—the system cannot detect the invalid reference—the situation is even worse. A pointer value may be logically incorrect yet point to a valid area of the free store. Unfortunately, such undetected dereferencing errors are common, and the results can be catastrophic. Any data retrieved from an erroneously accessed node must be considered meaningless and may be in an area of the free store currently in use by other program variables. There is no limit to the interesting but dismaying execution behavior that may follow.

Because of the complexity of dynamic data and the potential for inadequate run-time error detection, good debugging techniques are critical. Here are a few suggestions for debugging dynamic linked lists.

Suggestion #1: A Picture Is Worth a Thousand Hours (of Debugging).

Drawing diagrams of linked structures is an invaluable technique. The diagrams we have used throughout this chapter are a widely accepted notation and are important tools for manual tracing of code execution.

Figure 8.20 contains an assertion and a picture. Both describe the same situation.

Suggestion #2: Check the Assertions . . . Again.

Extensive documentation with assertions is critical for dynamic data structure algorithms. Because it is so easy to make dereferencing errors, a programmer should use assertions frequently, especially as preconditions for sections of code. If these preconditions are fully specified, then locating bugs amounts to examining code for precondition violations.

```
// ASSERT: ptr1->data == 7  &&  ptr1->link == ptr2
//      && ptr2->data == 198
//      && ptr2->link->data == 175
//      && ptr2->link->link->data == 234
//      && ptr2->link->link->link == NULL
```

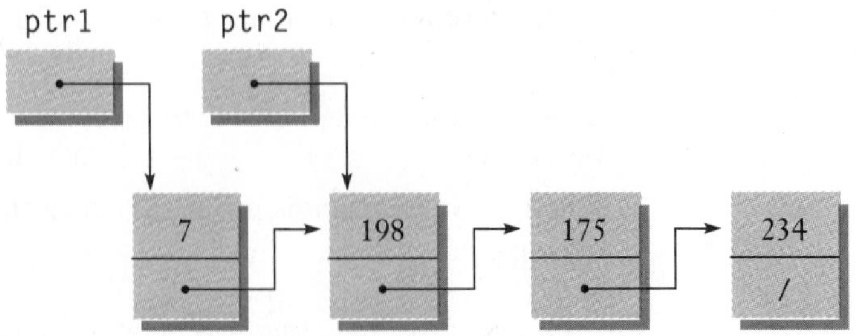

Figure 8.20 An assertion and the equivalent diagram

The following algorithm searches a singly linked list for a specific data value, searchVal, beginning at the node pointed to by prePtr:

```
// ASSERT: prePtr points to a node of a singly linked list

while (prePtr->data != searchVal && prePtr != NULL) {
                    // INV (prior to test):
                    //      No node before *prePtr contains
                    //      searchVal
                    // && prePtr points to a list node or == NULL
    prePtr = prePtr->link;
}
```

If the assertion before this algorithm is violated, several things can happen. If prePtr is unassigned or NULL, an invalid dereference will immediately occur in the first part of the loop condition. If the collection of nodes is a circular linked list and the search value is not in the list, then the result is an infinite loop. If you carefully examine code to be sure the assertions are satisfied, you can detect these bugs before they occur.

Certain assertions also lend themselves to machine checking. In Chapter 2 we discussed the assert function from the C++ standard library. During program testing it is beneficial to use this function when it is possible to express the assertion as a C++ logical expression. For the above algorithm, we could use the statements

```
#include <assert.h>
  ⋮
assert(prePtr != NULL);
while (prePtr->data != searchVal && prePtr != NULL) {

    ⋮
```

to cause abortion of the program if the pointer is NULL. However, there is no way to represent the assertions "The list is not a circular list" or "prePtr is assigned" as C++ expressions. Although assert is subject to this limitation, it can be highly valuable as a debugging tool.

Suggestion #3: Avoid Dangling Pointers.

Dangling pointers most often result from deallocating a node that is pointed to by more than one pointer. Few language implementations are able to detect invalid dereferencing of a dangling pointer. Always check for the possibility of dangling pointers before using the delete operator.

Suggestion #4: Don't Increment Pointers to Dynamic Nodes.

Incrementing a pointer variable is perfectly valid in C++, as long as its referent is an element of an array. The expression arrayPtr++ causes arrayPtr to point to the next element of the array, regardless of the size of the array elements. But incrementing a pointer to a node of a dynamic linked list is almost certain to reference meaningless data in the free store. Two separate nodes obtained from the free store are not necessarily contiguous in memory.

Suggestion #5: Use NULL.

One way to reduce the chances of undetected dereferencing errors is to make more extensive use of NULL. On some systems, dereferencing the null pointer is detected and reported as a run-time error. Debugging is easier if pointers are assigned the value NULL instead of being unassigned or dangling. An exercise at the end of Chapter 7 suggested one strategy: Write and use a function that not only invokes `delete`, but also assigns NULL to the pointer.

Suggestion #6: Dump the List.

Producing output dumps of linked lists is one possibility for locating bugs. It can be helpful to write a function that traverses a linked list, displaying the contents of the data members of each node. This function can be invoked in various locations throughout a program to pinpoint the location of a bug.

SUMMARY

As defined in Chapter 4, the list is a sequential access data structure that is most appropriate when insertions and deletions of components are frequent. Lists are not built-in types in C++ but can be implemented by built-in C++ arrays or by linked lists. The disadvantage of a direct array implementation of lists is the excessive data movement required to insert or delete list items.

A linked list implementation of a list requires a further level of implementation, because linked lists are not built-in data structures in C++. The programmer can implement linked lists by representing the nodes as `struct`s within a built-in C++ array or as dynamic `struct`s on the free store. The choice between these two implementations exemplifies a space versus time tradeoff. The array implementation is typically more efficient in terms of speed but may waste storage through overestimation of the array size. The dynamic data implementation may be somewhat slower, due to the `new` and `delete` operations, but consumes only as much memory as is needed.

Variations of linked lists include singly linked lists, doubly linked lists, circular linked lists, and lists with head nodes. Common linked list algorithms include list traversal, node insertion, and node deletion.

Advanced programming applications employ even richer varieties of linked list structures. As well, many applications use combined structures—arrays of linked lists, linked lists of linked lists, and so forth. An understanding of the fundamental forms of linked lists and the basic list processing algorithms is prerequisite to building these complex structures.

KEY TERMS

circular linked list   (p. 360)
data member (of a list node)   (p. 342)
doubly linked list   (p. 359)
forward declaration   (p. 344)

head node   (p. 358)
head pointer   (p. 346)
link member (of a list node)   (p. 342)
linked list   (p. 342)

EXERCISES   Exercises 8.1 through 8.3 refer to the following declarations:

```
typedef char String10[11];
struct StudentType {
    String10    courseName;
    char        courseGrade;    // 'A'..'F'
    StudentType* nextStu;
};
typedef StudentType* StuPtr;


StuPtr baker;
StuPtr smythe;
StuPtr tempStu;
```

8.1   What is the *data type* of each of the following expressions?

a. `baker`

b. `*tempStu`

c. `tempStu->courseName`

d. `tempStu->courseName[3]`

e. `smythe->nextStu`

f. `tempStu->nextStu->courseGrade`

8.2   Assume that each part below is the beginning of a separate program. Draw an abstract memory diagram of the pointers and dynamic data objects resulting from each.

a.
```
tempStu = new StudentType;
tempStu->nextStu = new StudentType;
strcpy(tempStu->courseName, "Bio 100");
tempStu->courseGrade = 'B';
strcpy(tempStu->nextStu->courseName, "Math 200");
tempStu->nextStu->courseGrade = 'A';
tempStu->nextStu->nextStu = NULL;
```

b.
```
tempStu = new StudentType;
tempStu->nextStu = new StudentType;
tempStu->nextStu->nextStu = new StudentType;
delete tempStu->nextStu;
```

c.
```
baker = new StudentType;
strcpy(baker->courseName, "Eng 340");
baker->courseGrade = 'C';
smythe = new StudentType;
strcpy(smythe->courseName, "Music 25");
smythe->courseGrade = 'A';
```

```
tempStu = new StudentType;
baker->nextStu = tempStu;
strcpy(baker->nextStu->courseName, "PE 100");
baker->nextStu->courseGrade = 'F';
tempStu = smythe;
smythe = baker->nextStu;
smythe->nextStu = NULL;
```

8.3 For each diagram below, write a sequence of statements that yields the given linked list structure.

a. tempStu

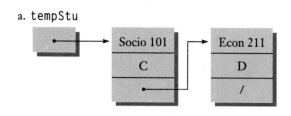

b. baker

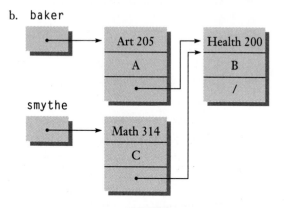

c.

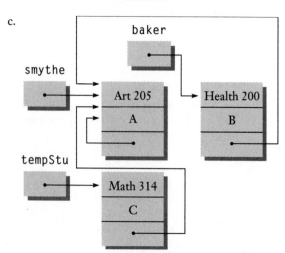

Exercises 8.4 through 8.6 refer to the following declarations for a dynamic linked list:

```
typedef char BattleName[21];
typedef char CommanderName[11];
struct DateType {
    int mo;        // 1..12
    int yr;        // 1861..1865
};
struct BattleNode;    // Forward declaration
typedef BattleNode* BattlePtr;
struct BattleNode {
    BattleName    name;
    DateType      date;
    CommanderName northCmndr;
    CommanderName southCmndr;
    int           northCasualties;
    int           southCasualties;
    BattlePtr     nextBattle;
};


BattlePtr civilWarList;
```

8.4 Assume that `civilWarList` is the head pointer to a singly linked list of 10 fully assigned `struct`s. Give a dereferencing expression for each of the following:

    a. the name of the first battle in the list

    b. the northern commander for the first battle in the list

    c. the southern casualties of the third battle in the list

    d. the southern commander of the fourth battle in the list

    e. the month of the first battle in the list

    f. the year of the second battle in the list

8.5 Give a sequence of statements to build a complete singly linked list containing the information for the following three battles. Use `civilWarList` as the head pointer.

Battle	Date	Commanders		Casualties	
		North	**South**	**North**	**South**
Bull Run	July 1861	McDowell	Beauregard	1500	2000
Gettysburg	July 1863	Meade	Lee	17500	22500
Chattanooga	Nov. 1863	Grant	Bragg	5500	2500

8.6 Assume that `listHead` is the head pointer to a singly linked list of length ≥ 1, and that all list nodes are fully assigned. Implement each function according to its specification.

    a.
```
int BattleCount( /* in */ BattlePtr listHead );
    // PRE:  listHead is the head pointer to a singly linked list
    // POST: FCTVAL == number of nodes in the list
```

    b.
```
void PrintBattleAndYear( /* in */ BattlePtr listHead );
    // PRE:  listHead is the head pointer to a singly linked list
    // POST: Battle name and year from each list node
    //       have been output in order, one per line.
```

```
c. void FindMaxCasualties( /* in */  BattlePtr listHead,
                           /* out */ int&       northMax,
                           /* out */ int&       southMax );
   // PRE:  listHead is the head pointer to a singly linked list
   // POST: northMax == Greatest northCasualties member
   //                    of all list nodes
   //    && southMax == Greatest southCasualties member
   //                    of all list nodes
```

```
d. BattlePtr SearchPtr( /* in */ BattlePtr        listHead,
                        /* in */ const BattleName battName );
   // PRE:  listHead is the head pointer to a singly linked list
   //    && Assigned(battName)
   // POST: FCTVAL == pointer to first node in list whose
   //                    name member equals battName
   //                 == NULL, if no name member equals battName
```

8.7   In Figure 8.16, a singly linked list is implemented with a built-in array instead of dynamic data. Assume that the list initially contains 'B', 'D', and 'M' as in Figure 8.16 and that the list must be maintained in alphabetical order. Diagram the contents of the head variable and the node array resulting from each pseudocode instruction below. Treat these instructions as a continuing sequence of actions, one after the other. (You may assume the NewLoc() function returns the lowest numbered subscript of all unused array elements.)

    a. Insert 'P'
    b. Insert 'J'
    c. Delete 'D'
    d. Insert 'K'
    e. Delete 'P'
    f. Delete 'B'

8.8   The EchoCity program of Figure 8.5 contains the following comment:

```
// In the future, the city list could be processed at this point.
```

For each part below, write a section of code that replaces this comment. If you need additional variables, include their declarations.

a. Output the total population of all cities in the list.

b. Output the name of the city with the largest number of registered voters.

8.9   Below is the general traversal algorithm for a dynamic singly linked list.

```
// General algorithm to visit all nodes
// PRE: "head" points to a singly linked list with node type
//       specified in Figure 8.2 (or contains NULL)
visitPtr = head;
while (visitPtr != NULL) {  // INV (prior to test):
                            //     All list nodes preceding
                            //     *visitPtr have been visited
                            //  && visitPtr points to a list node
```

```
                                        //       or == NULL
        // Visit node *visitPtr
        visitPtr = visitPtr->link;
    }
```

a. Rewrite this algorithm to traverse a doubly linked list. Use the general declarations given in Figure 8.13.

b. Rewrite this algorithm to traverse a circular linked list having a head pointer (a head pointer, not a head node).

c. Rewrite this algorithm to traverse a circular linked list having a tail pointer.

8.10 Figures 8.9 and 8.10 contain insertion and deletion algorithms for singly linked lists. Rewrite both algorithms for doubly linked lists.

8.11 Below is a collection of declarations for dynamic singly linked lists of integers. Use these declarations to implement each function according to its specification.

```
struct NodeType {
    int        data;
    NodeType* link;
};
typedef NodeType* NodePtr;
```

a. Boolean EqualLists(/* in */ NodePtr ptr1,
                       /* in */ NodePtr ptr2);
```
    // PRE:  ptr1 points to a node of one list (or == NULL)
    //    && ptr2 points to a node of another list (or == NULL)
    // POST: FCTVAL == (the two lists are identical, i.e., have
    //                  identical data members)
    // NOTE: This is a recursive function.  For the first
    //       invocation, ptr1 and ptr2 are the head pointers
    //       to two linked lists.
```

b. void Invert(/* inout */ NodePtr& head);
```
    // PRE:  head is the head pointer to a linked list
    // POST: The list is inverted such that the old list
    //       (i1, i2, ..., iN) is now (iN, ..., i2, i1)
    //    && head is the head pointer to this inverted list
```

c. void Concat(/* inout */ NodePtr& head1,
               /* in */   NodePtr head2);
```
    // PRE:  head1 points to a linked list (or == NULL)
    //    && head2 points to a linked list (or == NULL)
    // POST: The two lists are concatenated (the front of
    //       the second list joined to the tail of the first)
    //    && head1 points to this concatenated list
```

PROGRAMMING PROJECTS

8.1 Rewrite the EchoCity program of Figure 8.5 to use a doubly linked list instead of a singly linked list.

8.2 Implement an integer array with a dynamic linked list! That is, consider the one-dimensional array data structure as an abstract data type with operations

Create(n)	Create an integer vector of *n* elements
ValueAt(i)	Return the value of the array element indexed by *i*
Store(i, v)	Store value *v* into the array element indexed by *i*

In particular, begin with the `IntVec` class of Chapter 7. Make only *one* modification to the `Vector` specification file: Change the private data member `vec` so that it points to the first node of a dynamic singly linked list instead of pointing to a dynamically allocated vector. Do not alter the specification file in any other way.

The Create operation above is then handled by the class constructor, and both the ValueAt and Store operations above are taken care of by the `operator[]` function.

This is an interesting exercise, but what do you think of implementing a direct access data structure with a sequential access data structure?

8.3 In Chapter 4 (Section 4.5) a `CharList` abstract data type was hypothesized for maintaining lists of individual characters. Definition 4.6 gives representative list operations. Note that `CharList` is a general list, not a linked list. Using the C++ class mechanism, implement and test the `CharList` ADT three different ways:

a. Implement it with a built-in array.

b. Reimplement it with a singly linked list that is implemented with dynamic data.

c. Reimplement it with a singly linked list that is implemented with a built-in array.

For each version, change only the implementation, not the public interface. Also, implement the Create operation with a C++ class constructor.

8.4 Write and test a program to solve the following problem. Use a dynamic singly linked list as the major data structure.

TITLE

Convention registry

DESCRIPTION

Large conventions generally keep a registry of all people attending the conference. This program inputs and maintains a list of all conference attendees. The program then outputs two groups of data. The first is a list of all attendees, sorted alphabetically by last name. The second is a sorted list for each state with at least one person attending the conference. (Hint: It is easiest to maintain the list in sorted order as it is being input.)

INPUT

The program reads from standard input, but it is expected that standard input will be redirected to come from a data file. For each person, input consists of four lines. On the first line is the person's last name (up to 20 characters). On the second line is the first name (up to 10 characters). On the third line is the two character postal service abbreviation for the person's home state. On the fourth line is the name of the person's employer (up to 40 characters). The system's end-of-file condition signals end of input.

OUTPUT

After all input is complete, the program outputs a complete list of all conference attendees, one line per person. Across each line is the person's name (last name, first name) followed by the company name. The entire list is alphabetized by last names.

Following the complete list, another list is produced for each state that has at least one person attending the conference. These lists begin with the name of the state and they display only the last name of each person, one per line.

ERROR HANDLING

1. If any state code is invalid, that person is ignored.
2. Fewer or greater than four input lines per attendee yields undefined results.

EXAMPLE

Below is a sample execution with input in color.

```
Hume
James
MN
Control Data Corporation
Boswell
Jeffrey
MN
Minnesota Mining & Manufacturing
Carlyle
John
NY
IBM
Raeburn
John
NY
IBM
MacDonald
David
MN
Unisys

Boswell, Jeffrey  Minnesota Mining & Manufacturing
Carlyle, John  IBM
Hume, James  Control Data Corporation
MacDonald, David  Unisys
Raeburn, John  IBM
```

```
Minnesota:
---------
Boswell
Hume
MacDonald

New York:
--------
Carlyle
Raeburn
```

8.5   Write and test a program to solve the following problem. Use a dynamic singly linked list as the major data structure.

TITLE

Line editor

DESCRIPTION

Many text editors are "line oriented." This type of editor is designed to work with printing terminals, where moving about a video screen is impossible. Line oriented editors manipulate text by one line at a time. Typical commands allow inserting lines, deleting lines, and listing lines.

This program is a simple line oriented editor named LEDIT. All lines in LEDIT are up to 80 characters long. Below is the collection of valid LEDIT commands:

IN   Insert (followed by text lines and terminated by "//")
DL   Delete
MV   Move (followed by an integer)
LA   List all
XT   Exit

The editor keeps track of a "current line" at all times. The IN command inserts new input lines into the file just before the current line (the current line remains unchanged). The DL command deletes the current line; the successor of the deleted line becomes the new current line.

The MV command redefines which line is considered to be the current line. MV followed by a positive integer, n, causes the new current line to be the one n lines after the old current line. Using a negative integer, $-n$, causes the new current line to be n lines before the old current line. After repositioning, the contents of the current line are displayed. Note that MV does not create any new lines and may only be repositioned to an existing line.

A MV or DL command may cause the current line to be just beyond the final text line. This situation is permitted and allows for insertion after the final line. When the program begins, there are no edit lines and the current line is positioned just after the nonexistent final line.

An `LA` command outputs all lines from the current line through the end of the text, and the current line is unaltered. The `XT` command terminates editing.

INPUT

The user inputs a sequence of commands. Each command begins on a new line with two uppercase letters. The valid two-letter commands are `IN`, `DL`, `MV`, `LA`, and `XT`. The `MV` command is followed by one or more blanks and then an integer constant, all on the same line. The `IN` command requires one or more lines of text on subsequent lines, terminated by a line beginning with two consecutive slashes (/ /).

OUTPUT

The prompt for each editor command is the single character >, preceded by a blank line. After a `MV` command, the new current line is displayed. If the current line is positioned after the last line, then <<END>> is displayed as the current line. The `LA` command displays all lines, starting with the current line.

ERROR HANDLING

1. A negative `MV` command that attempts to reposition before the first line causes the first line to be the current line.
2. A positive `MV` past the last line or a `DL` of the last line causes the current line to be just after the last line.
3. When the current line is just beyond the last text line, the `DL` command does nothing.
4. Any invalid two-letter command is ignored.

EXAMPLE

Below is a sample execution with all input in color.

```
>LA
<<END>>

>IN
111 111 111 111 1111
222222 2222 2222 222
//

>LA
<<END>>

>MV -2
111 111 111 111 1111
```

```
>LA
111 111 111 111 1111
222222 2222 2222 222
<<END>>

>MV 1
222222 2222 2222 222

>LA
222222 2222 2222 222
<<END>>

>IN
33333333333333
44444444444444
//

>LA
222222 2222 2222 222
<<END>>

>MV -100
111 111 111 111 1111

>LA
111 111 111 111 1111
33333333333333
44444444444444
222222 2222 2222 222
<<END>>

>LA
111 111 111 111 1111
33333333333333
44444444444444
222222 2222 2222 222
<<END>>

>MV 100
<<END>>

>IN
555555555
//

>MV -999
111 111 111 111 1111

>LA
111 111 111 111 1111
33333333333333
```

```
44444444444444
222222 2222 2222 222
555555555
<<END>>

>DL

>LA
33333333333333
44444444444444
222222 2222 2222 222
555555555
<<END>>

>MV +1
44444444444444

>DL

>LA
222222 2222 2222 222
555555555
<<END>>

>MV -77
33333333333333

>LA
33333333333333
222222 2222 2222 222
555555555
<<END>>

>XT
```

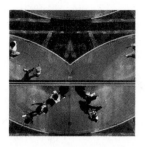

CHAPTER 9

Design and Implementation of Abstract Data Types

INTRODUCTION

This chapter ties together Parts I and II. In Part I (*Abstraction*) we introduced many of the concepts and vocabulary of control abstraction and data abstraction. Chapter 4 defined a number of data structures—general lists, stacks, queues, sets—according to their abstract properties and public interfaces without discussing how to implement these abstractions.

Part II (*Tools For Implementation*) examined both concepts and C++ language features that enable the programmer to implement abstractions in various ways. Record (struct) types, recursion, pointer and reference types, dynamically allocated data, and linked lists are all important vehicles for creating program code from abstract specifications of control and data.

This chapter integrates abstraction and implementation. Just as we considered alternative implementations of general lists in Chapter 8, in this chapter we present alternative implementations of sets, stacks, and queues. Guiding the discussion throughout are recommendations for good ADT design and the role assertions play in the correctness of implementations.

9.1 Review of Abstract Data Types

Building abstract data types is an important use of C++ classes and modules. Recall that an abstract data type (ADT) is a programmer-defined type with

- a set of data values
- a collection of allowable operations on those values

The implementation of an ADT consists of

1. a concrete representation of the abstract data in terms of existing data types

2. program code (or even hardware) that implements the allowable operations

It is possible to think of built-in types, such as int, char, and float, as ADTs that are already defined in the language. Data representations of ints and the hardware-level implementations of int operations are interesting topics in their own right. This text, however, focuses on programmer-defined ADTs—new types created with mechanisms such as C++ classes and modules to extend the language. Unless there is risk of confusion, we use ADT to mean programmer-defined ADT.

A good abstract data type has two characteristics:

1. It must be useful.

2. It must be sufficiently abstract.

"Useful" is a subjective term, but it should be clear that it is a waste of time to design and test an ADT that is not appropriate to the problem at hand. An ADT also must be abstract enough to present the important features and suppress unnecessary detail. The best abstractions emphasize the user's perspective and employ information hiding to conceal implementation details.

Suppose that a computer program controls the temperatures of all offices in a large office complex. A Thermostat ADT might be useful for such a program. The program may contain many variables of type Thermostat to represent the actual thermostats within the building. Some useful operations for this Thermostat type include:

TurnUp	Raise the current thermostat setting by one degree.
TurnDown	Lower the current thermostat setting by one degree.
UseDefault	Set the thermostat to the default setting for the building.
CheckCurrentSetting	Examine the current thermostat setting.

Using the form introduced earlier in this text, Definition 9.1 defines the Thermostat type in terms of its name, domain, and operations.

DATA TYPE   Thermostat

DOMAIN
Temperature settings from 50 degrees to 85 degrees Fahrenheit

OPERATIONS
TurnUp
TurnDown
UseDefault
CheckCurrentSetting

Definition 9.1 A Thermostat ADT

`Thermostat` incorporates both characteristics of a good ADT. First, it is a useful type. A program can declare a separate thermostat variable for each climate zone, allowing flexible control of the building's heating and cooling system. The operations provide the most desired features of a mechanical thermostat.

Second, `Thermostat` is a good abstraction. People who use a real thermostat are not concerned with how a temperature setting is stored or how the furnace is physically controlled. Similarly, the `Thermostat` ADT is not cluttered by implementation details. The operation `CheckCurrentSetting` makes a far better abstraction than `WriteInt`. The operation `TurnUp` probably activates an electromechanical system to alter the heating, but these are implementation details appropriately omitted.

ADTs should be *specified* as abstractions but must be *implemented* with standard language features and/or off-the-shelf components. The selection of an ADT and its operations is a *design* task. The implementation of the abstraction is a *coding* task.

The C++ `class` mechanism is a natural tool for building ADTs. An ADT is designed as a class declaration in a specification file. It is then implemented in the implementation file. Typically, the abstract data are concretely represented as private members of a class, and the associated operations on that data are public members and friend functions. This encapsulation of data (or pointers to data) and code for the operations within an abstraction barrier supports two fundamental benefits of ADTs:

1. The creator of the ADT is guaranteed that the user can access the encapsulated data only through the allowable operations

2. The user is guaranteed the ability to use the ADT without having to know how it is implemented.

9.2 Selecting the Operations: A Design Task

Every ADT requires two main design tasks:

1. to describe the domain of the ADT

2. to select and describe the ADT operations

The domain of the `Thermostat` ADT consists of temperature settings. This is a very simple thermostat. A more complex thermostat would include separate on/off settings for the heating system and the cooling system. The domain would be different for the more complicated thermostat.

Technically, the domain of an ADT is the set of all possible values for the type. But it is usually simpler to describe the domain in terms of a single instance of that ADT. For example, we could define the domain of the more complicated thermostat as follows:

The domain of a single thermostat is

1. a temperature setting between 50 degrees and 85 degrees Fahrenheit

2. an ON/OFF switch setting for the cooling unit

3. an ON/OFF switch setting for the heating unit

The second major task in designing an ADT is selecting operations. This task is typically the most difficult part of the design. There must be enough operations for the type to be useful, but too many operations complicate the abstraction. In addition, there are usually several different ways to accomplish the same task.

Chapters 3 and 8 presented two modules, Fraction and Person. We repeat their specification files in Figures 9.1 and 9.2, augmented with initial comments describing their domains.

Figure 9.1 Fraction specification file

```
// -----------------------------------------------------------------
// SPECIFICATION FILE (fraction.h)
// This module exports a FracType class with two operator functions,
// operator* and operator==.  A more general FracType class
// might include more operations.
// -----------------------------------------------------------------
#include "bool.h"

// DOMAIN: A FracType instance is a numeric fraction with an integer
//         numerator and a strictly positive integer denominator.

class FracType {
public:
    void Write() const;
        // POST: The value of this fraction has been displayed as:
        //             <numerator> / <denominator>
        //         with no blanks

    float FloatEquiv() const;
        // POST: FCTVAL == float equivalent of this fraction

    void Simplify();
        // POST: Fraction is reduced to lowest terms. (No integer > 1
        //       evenly divides both the numerator and denominator)

    FracType operator*( /* in */ FracType frac2 ) const;
        // PRE:  This fraction and frac2 are in simplest terms
        // POST: FCTVAL == this fraction * frac2  (fraction
        //                   multiplication), reduced to lowest terms
        // NOTE: Numerators or denominators of large magnitude
        //       may produce overflow

    Boolean operator==( /* in */ FracType frac2 ) const;
        // PRE:  This fraction and frac2 are in simplest terms
        // POST: FCTVAL == TRUE, if this fraction == frac2
        //                    (numerically)
        //               == FALSE, otherwise
```

```
        FracType( /* in */ int initNumer,
                  /* in */ int initDenom );
            // Constructor
            // PRE:  Assigned(initNumer)  &&  initDenom > 0
            // POST: Fraction has been created and can be thought of
            //       as the fraction  initNumer / initDenom
            // NOTE: (initNumer < 0) --> fraction is a negative number
private:
    int numer;
    int denom;
};
```

Figure 9.2 Person
specification file

```
// ----------------------------------------------------------------
//   SPECIFICATION FILE (person.h)
//   This module exports a record type for personal data and a class
//   for maintaining lists of such records
// ----------------------------------------------------------------
#include "bool.h"

// DOMAIN: A PersonList instance is a list of personal records, each
//         record containing a person's name and age.

struct PersonRec {
    char* name;         // Pointer to person's name
    int   age;          // Person's age
};

struct  PersonNode;     // Complete declaration hidden in
                        // implementation file
class PersonList {
public:
    Boolean IsEmpty() const;
        // POST: FCTVAL == (list is empty)

    Boolean IsFull() const;
        // POST: FCTVAL == (list is full)

    void Reset();
        // PRE:  NOT IsEmpty()
        // POST: List cursor is at front of list

    Boolean EndOfList() const;
        // POST: FCTVAL == (list cursor is beyond end of list)

    void Advance();
        // PRE:  NOT IsEmpty()  &&  NOT EndOfList()
        // POST: List cursor has advanced to next record

    PersonRec CurrentRec() const;
        // PRE:  NOT IsEmpty()  &&  NOT EndOfList()
        // POST: FCTVAL == record at list cursor
```

```
    void InsertBefore( /* in */ PersonRec someRec );
        // PRE:  Assigned(someRec)  &&  NOT IsFull()
        // POST: someRec inserted before list cursor
        //          (at back, if EndOfList())
        //      && This is the new current record

    void InsertAfter( /* in */ PersonRec someRec );
        // PRE:  Assigned(someRec)  &&  NOT IsEmpty()
        //      && NOT IsFull()  &&  NOT EndOfList()
        // POST: someRec inserted after list cursor
        //      && This is the new current record

    void Delete();
        // PRE:  NOT IsEmpty()  &&  NOT EndOfList()
        // POST: Record at list cursor deleted
        //      && Successor of deleted record is now the current
        //         record

    PersonList();
        // Constructor
        // POST: Empty list created  &&  EndOfList()

    ~PersonList();
        // Destructor
        // POST: List destroyed
private:
    PersonNode* head;
    PersonNode* currPtr;
};
```

Both the `Fraction` and `Person` modules export ADTs. The `FracType` abstraction is a numeric fraction borrowed from arithmetic. The `PersonList` ADT is a list of personal records. We will use these two modules as illustrations of many issues regarding abstract data types.

ADT-Constructors and Completeness

Every ADT must include operations to build values of the type. These operations are called **ADT-constructors.** (An ADT-constructor is a language-independent concept and is more general than the C++ class constructor function.) `FracType` contains three ADT-constructor operations:

FracType	Constructs a fraction from an integer and a positive integer
*	Constructs a new fraction by multiplying two other fractions
Simplify	Constructs a simplified version of an existing fraction

The ADT-constructor operations of `PersonList` are

PersonList	Creates an empty list
InsertBefore	Constructs a new list by inserting a record into a list

InsertAfter   Constructs a new list by inserting a record into a list

Delete   Constructs a new list by deleting a record from a list

One important rule for designing ADT operations is the following:

An ADT must include enough ADT-constructors to build all possible values of the domain.

An ADT that satisfies this property is called **complete.** FracType is complete, because the C++ class constructor FracType() can construct a fraction from any pair of integer and positive integer values. Because FracType() can construct all fractions, omission of the * and Simplify operations would not affect completeness.

PersonList also specifies a complete ADT. Any list of PersonRec records can be built using the C++ class constructor PersonList() together with InsertBefore and InsertAfter. The algorithm to build a list is first to declare a PersonList instance (implicitly invoking the PersonList() constructor), then to invoke InsertBefore or InsertAfter for each record to be included in the list.

An incomplete ADT reflects a poor design. Suppose the designer forgets to include the InsertBefore and InsertAfter operations. Then PersonList is useless; the only list to be built is the empty list.

ADT-constructor operations that create a new value for the ADT without a prior ADT value are called **initial ADT-constructors.** The two initial ADT-constructors of FracType and PersonList are the C++ class constructors FracType() and PersonList(). The PersonList() function builds an empty list without any previous list. FracType() constructs a fraction from an integer and a positive integer. The * operation, Simplify, InsertBefore, InsertAfter, and Delete are not initial ADT-constructors because they construct ADT values only from previous ADT values.

Every complete ADT contains at least one initial ADT-constructor operation, or else it is impossible to build an initial value. Fortunately, the C++ language itself provides initial ADT-constructors in the form of class constructors such as FracType() and PersonList(). If the designer of a C++ class provides a class constructor, it is impossible for a class instance to be uninitialized.

Most useful ADTs include more operations than just ADT-constructors. Some common ADT operations are

- **I/O operations** to input or output an ADT value
- **type conversion functions** to translate from an ADT value to another type or vice versa
- **test operations** to test some condition about an ADT value
- **assignment (copy) operations** to copy one ADT value to another ADT object
- **selector operations** to isolate and retrieve a portion of an ADT value
- **destructor operations** to deallocate any dynamic data created by an ADT

I/O Operations

C++ does not provide I/O operations for programmer-defined types, so designers sometimes include them in ADTs. The `Write` function of the `FracType` class is an example of an operation that outputs values of the ADT. The C++ language also provides the opportunity to overload the insertion (`<<`) and extraction (`>>`) operators for stream I/O of ADT values. In Chapter 7 we demonstrated the use of the operator functions `operator>>` and `operator<<` for input and output of `FracType` values.

I/O operations are not, and should not be, a part of every ADT. Certain special-purpose ADTs will include them, but I/O operations are not usually present in general-purpose ADTs. One reason is that I/O operations are not among those defined as fundamental operations on data structures such as lists, stacks, and queues. Another reason is the difficulty of anticipating the user's preferences for formatting the input or output. The ADT designer may output the contents of a queue across one output line, but the user may prefer just one value per output line.

Type Conversion Functions

Type conversion functions are useful, especially in a language that enforces strict type checking. Sometimes these operations permit converting ADT values to other types. An example is `FloatEquiv`, which converts a `FracType` value to a `float` value. At other times the conversion operations are really ADT-constructor operations that convert data of other types into a value of the ADT. For example, the `FracType()` class constructor converts a pair of `int` values to a fraction value.

When writing conversion routines, there is no need to provide conversions to *all* other types. The `FloatEquiv` function translates fractions to `float` values. In turn, C++ includes cast operators (and implicit type coercion) to convert from `float` to `int` and from `int` to `short`. The `FloatEquiv` function, then, indirectly provides the ability to translate fractions to `int` and `short` values.

Test Functions and Testable Preconditions

Test functions represent another group of important operations. The `operator==` function is a test function for comparing two `FracType` instances for equality. In the `PersonList` class, `IsEmpty`, `IsFull`, and `EndOfList` are test operations appropriate for lists.

A second rule for designing ADTs is the following:

An ADT must provide enough test operations for the client to check all preconditions of the ADT operations.

This rule guarantees **testable preconditions.** For example, the `Delete` operation of the `PersonList` class has the precondition that the list not be empty and that the list cursor not be beyond the end of the list. The IsEmpty and EndOfList functions allow the client to test this precondition.

An ADT that violates this rule is at best ill conceived and at worst useless. Suppose we had included the following operation in PersonList:

```
void Concat( /* in */  PersonList  someList,
             /* out */ PersonList& resultList );
  // PRE:  someList != baseList
  // POST: resultList == someList concatenated with baseList
```

This operation claims to construct a concatenated list when presented a list that is not equal to baseList. But the PersonList class does not provide any way to compare two PersonList instances. Furthermore, there is no discussion of baseList anywhere outside this new operation. Concat is a useless operation because a client cannot guarantee the precondition to be true.

Certain preconditions do not require special operations in order to be testable. For example, there is no need to provide an operation to check whether an incoming parameter is assigned. The user can identify or locate unassigned variables by examining the calling code. As another example, the precondition of the operator* function in the FracType class requires both fractions to be in simplest terms. Supplying a test function, IsSimplified(), would be unnecessary. The user can invoke the Simplify() function just before invoking operator*, thus guaranteeing the precondition.

Copy Operations

ADTs often require a copy operation. Sometimes an ADT can use the built-in assignment operator (=). In other cases, notably when an ADT creates dynamic data on the free store, the standard meaning of the assignment operator is insufficient to perform deep copying (Chapter 7). For deep copying, the ADT designer must provide a separate assignment function (preferably by overloading the = operator) and a class copy-constructor for initialization of one class instance by another.

Selector Operations (Access Functions)

Because ADTs often represent structured types, selector operations (also called access functions) may be included to retrieve components of the type. The CurrentRec operation of the PersonList class is a selector operation for accessing the current record during an iteration through the list. Selector operations could be added to FracType to return, individually, the numerator and denominator components of the type.

Destructor Operations

If a class manipulates dynamic data on the free store, it is essential for the designer to include a class destructor. Failure to deallocate dynamic data when a class instance is destroyed leads to memory leaks. The data remains on the free store but is permanently inaccessible.

Consistency

Perhaps the most important issue to keep in mind when choosing ADT operations is to keep them consistent with the intent of the abstraction. Operations such as Simplify, *, and Write are good choices for FracType because they are consistent with the fraction abstraction. A CheckSpelling operation makes no sense for fractions and should not be provided. Similarly, Delete is consistent with the abstraction of a list of personal records, but Multiply is an operation for numbers, not lists.

Designing with Wisdom

Guidelines for Selecting Abstract Data Type Operations

There are two absolute rules that must be followed when selecting the operations of an ADT:

1. Every ADT must be *complete*. (It must include enough operations to build every possible value of the domain.)

2. The *preconditions* of all ADT operations must be *testable*.

Below we give some additional guidelines for designing ADTs.

3. Consider including operations of the following kinds:

   ADT-constructor operations
   Test operations
   Type conversion operations
   I/O operations
   Copy operations (shallow and/or deep)
   Selector operations (access functions)
   A destructor operation (for classes that create dynamic data)

4. Try to keep the total number of operations to a minimum. Simple ADTs are easier to understand and therefore to use.

5. Keep the operations consistent with the abstraction.

9.3 Abstraction Versus Implementation: A Set ADT

Chapter 4 introduced the set as a data structure that reflects the mathematical notion of a set—an unordered collection of objects without duplicates. A set has a nonlinear structure. There is no designated first or last element of a set, and no element precedes or succeeds another.

Typical set operations include element insertion, element deletion, set intersection, set union, set difference, test for set equality, and test for element membership.

In Chapter 4 we wrote a program that analyzed a stream of input characters to determine which characters were encountered. A set was an appropriate data structure for this problem because we wanted to know *which* characters were encountered, not how many times each was encountered. Each character from the universe (the ASCII character set, for instance) was either in the set or it was not. Furthermore, the order of the characters in the set was irrelevant.

We now look at the design and implementation of a digit set ADT. Suppose that a program needs one or more sets whose elements are the decimal digits 0 through 9. Examples are the sets { }, {4}, and {0, 5, 8}. Creating a set of digits is straightforward in some programming languages. Pascal and Modula-2 include sets as built-in data types. C++ does not, but the programmer can extend the language by writing a set ADT and using it as though it were a built-in type.

Specification of a Set ADT

Figure 9.3 displays the specification file for a module named DigSet. This module exports a set ADT, where the 10 decimal digits constitute the universe. For brevity, we present only a few set operations. The DigitSet class overloads the operators * and + to denote set intersection and set union, respectively. Exercises at the end of the chapter give suggestions for a more general ADT.

Figure 9.3 DigSet specification file

```
// ------------------------------------------------------------
//   SPECIFICATION FILE (digset.h)
//   This module exports a digit set ADT.  A more general ADT
//   would include additional set operations.
// ------------------------------------------------------------
#include "bool.h"

// DOMAIN: A DigitSet instance is a set of single-digit integers
//            (i.e., a set from the universe 0, 1, 2, ..., 9)
//
// CLASSINV: Each integer in the set is in the range 0..9

class DigitSet {
public:
    Boolean IsEmpty() const;
        // POST: FCTVAL == (set == {})

    Boolean IsFull() const;
        // POST: FCTVAL == (set is full)

    void Insert( /* in */ int someDig );
        // PRE:  NOT IsFull()
        // POST: set == set<entry> UNION {someDig}

    void Delete( /* in */ int someDig );
        // POST: set == set<entry> - {someDig}
```

```
        Boolean IsElt( /* in */ int someDig ) const;
            // POST: FCTVAL == (someDig is an element of the set)

        void Write() const;
            // POST: Set elements have been displayed on one line

        DigitSet operator*( /* in */ DigitSet set2 ) const;
            // POST: FCTVAL == (this set) INTERSECT set2

        DigitSet operator+( /* in */ DigitSet set2 ) const;
            // POST: FCTVAL == (this set) UNION set2

        DigitSet();
            // Constructor
            // POST: Created(set)  &&  set == {}
private:
    unsigned int bitStr;
};
```

The specification file presents the abstract view of an ADT. The designer chooses and describes operations in terms that make sense to the importer. The abstract view of DigitSet is a set of digits. The following postcondition for the class constructor is entirely consistent with the abstraction:

```
// POST: Created(set)  &&  set == {}
```

This postcondition states precisely what the importer wishes to know. There is no attempt to indicate how the operation is implemented.

Writing pre- and postconditions for a specification file is similar to writing problem specifications in the following sense. The importer must be able to read and understand the specification. At the same time, the pre- and postconditions must be precise enough to remove all ambiguity for the implementor.

The operations of DigitSet are consistent with a set abstraction. The operator*, operator+, and IsElt functions reflect set intersection, set union, and element membership operations.

IsEmpty and IsFull are test operations that the client can invoke before attempting to process the contents of a set. The IsFull function ensures testable preconditions. Specifically, the only ADT operation with a precondition is Insert, which requires that the set must not be full before inserting another element. Notice that Delete has no precondition. It is all right to delete a digit that is not already in the set—it amounts to no action at all. The postcondition for Delete is true even if someDig was not in the set to begin with.

The class constructor DigitSet() and the functions Insert, operator*, and operator+ are all ADT-constructor operations that ensure completeness of the ADT. Write is an I/O operation with which the client can output the contents of the set.

From a purist's perspective, IsFull and Write are not innate operations on sets. Mathematical sets do not become full, but the inclusion of IsFull is a concession to reality. A specific implementation of DigitSet may use a data representation, such as an array, that does become full. The Write operation is also not characteristic of mathematical sets, but we have included it to exemplify I/O operations on ADTs.

The design of the DigitSet class emphasizes the two previously mentioned benefits of ADTs. First, the concrete data representation of the set is a private member of the class. Thus, access to this data is impossible except through the public interface (the allowable operations). Second, the user of the ADT does not need to know the data representation or the implementation of the operations. The collection of set operations does not imply any particular data representation, and the implementor could change the concrete representation without affecting these public operations.

The assertions in the specification file also reflect the abstraction. The postcondition for Insert does not discuss how a digit is inserted into a set. The mechanics of inserting a digit are an implementation detail to be worked out by the implementor after the design is finished.

The Implementation

The implementation file provides a completely different perspective from the specification file. In this file, the coding details are not only allowed but also required. The first detail to be considered is the concrete representation of the abstract data.

For the DigitSet ADT, we use a popular data representation for sets: a sequence of bits (a bit string) within an unsigned int variable. Suppose that our machine uses 16-bit integers and that the bit positions are numbered from 15 through 0, left to right:

Bit position: 15 14 13 12 11 10 9 8 7 6 5 4 3 2 1 0
Bit: 0 0 0 0 0 0 0 1 0 0 1 0 0 0 0 0

Bits 9 through 0 correspond to the ten values in the universe; a 1 means "Yes, this value is in the set," and a 0 means "No, this value is not in the set." (Bits 15 through 10 are unused.) In the above example, the interpretation is that the digits 4 and 7 are currently in the set. In other words, this bit string is the concrete representation of the set {4, 7}. Figure 9.4 shows additional examples.

To manipulate individual bits in a bit string, the C++ language includes an extensive collection of **bitwise operators**. Appendix H provides a detailed description of bitwise operators and bit strings. If you are not already familiar with this material, you should read Appendix H before examining the DigSet implementation file in Figure 9.5.

Abstract data (digit set)	Concrete data (bit string)
{3}	0000000000001000
{0, 5, 9}	0000001000100001
{ }	0000000000000000

Figure 9.4 Bit string representations of digit sets

Figure 9.5 `DigSet` implementation file

```
// ----------------------------------------------------------------
//   IMPLEMENTATION FILE (digset.cpp)
//   This module exports a digit set ADT.
//   Set representation: a bit string.
// ----------------------------------------------------------------
#include "digset.h"
#include <iostream.h>
#include <iomanip.h>      // For setw()

// Private members of class:
//     unsigned int bitStr;          Bit string for set
//
// CLASSINV: For all n, (0 <= n <= 9),
//           (bit n of bitStr equals 1) --> integer n is in the set
//
// NOTE: Bits are numbered such that 0 is the rightmost bit

DigitSet::DigitSet()
    //.................................................................
    // Constructor
    // POST: bitStr == 0
    //.................................................................
{
    bitStr = 0;
}

Boolean DigitSet::IsEmpty() const
    //.................................................................
    // POST: FCTVAL == (bitStr == 0)
    //.................................................................
{
    return (bitStr == 0);
}

Boolean DigitSet::IsFull() const
    //.................................................................
    // POST: FCTVAL == FALSE
    //.................................................................
{
    return FALSE;
}

void DigitSet::Insert( /* in */ int someDig )
    //.................................................................
    // POST: Bit in position someDig equals 1
    //.................................................................
{
    bitStr |= (1 << someDig);
}
```

```
void DigitSet::Delete( /* in */ int someDig )
    //.......................................................
    // POST: Bit in position someDig equals 0
    //.......................................................
{
    bitStr &= ~(1 << someDig);
}

Boolean DigitSet::IsElt( /* in */ int someDig ) const
    //.......................................................
    // POST: FCTVAL == (Bit in position someDig == 1)
    //.......................................................
{
    return ( (bitStr & (1 << someDig)) > 0 );
}

void DigitSet::Write() const
    //.......................................................
    // POST: Elements of set have been displayed on one line
    //.......................................................
{
    int i;
    for (i = 0; i < 10; i++)
        if ((bitStr & (1 << i)) > 0 )
            cout << setw(2) << i;
}

DigitSet DigitSet::operator*( /* in */ DigitSet set2 ) const
    //.......................................................
    // POST: FCTVAL == new set represented by bit string
    //                 bitStr BITWISE-AND set2.bitStr
    //.......................................................
{
    DigitSet newSet;

    newSet.bitStr = bitStr & set2.bitStr;
    return newSet;
}

DigitSet DigitSet::operator+( /* in */ DigitSet set2 ) const
    //.......................................................
    // POST: FCTVAL == new set represented by bit string
    //                 bitStr BITWISE-OR set2.bitStr
    //.......................................................
{
    DigitSet newSet;

    newSet.bitStr = bitStr | set2.bitStr;
    return newSet;
}
```

Representing a set as a bit string results in simple, efficient implementations of the ADT operations. We can use this same technique to represent other sets as well, provided that set elements are transformed into integers corresponding to bit positions. The main drawback of the bit string representation is that using only one `int` variable for the bit string limits the size of the universe to, say, 16 or 32 values (the number of bits in a particular machine's `int` location). A large universe would require several `int` or `long` variables and a mapping function to access the correct bit within the correct variable. Other alternatives might be to represent the set as a built-in array or even as a linked list of dynamic nodes, adding a new node with each insertion of a new set element. Exercises at the end of this chapter explore these possibilities.

Designing for Implementation Independence

Observe that the `IsFull` function always returns FALSE. It is reasonable to return FALSE, because an unsigned integer of 16 or 32 bits has more than enough bits to represent all ten decimal digits. For this particular data representation, we clearly could have omitted the `IsFull` operation. But the ADT designer must be very careful not to bias public operations toward a particular implementation. Selecting implementation-independent operations is especially important when designing an ADT for a general-purpose data structure such as a set. Some implementations of a set ADT will not require an `IsFull` operation, but some will. Therefore, the public interface should include `IsFull`—regardless of the specific implementation—to be consistent with the avowed goal of shielding the user from implementation details. As well, it allows reimplementation of the ADT without change to the client code. We will return to this issue later in the chapter.

9.4   Abstract Assertions Versus Implementation Assertions

The implementation file in Figure 9.5 reveals the perspective of the programmer implementing the ADT. That is, the implementor views `DigitSet` as a bit string, whereas the designer views `DigitSet` as the abstract concept of a set. The pre- and postconditions of the implementation file reflect this new perspective.

In the specification file, the postcondition for `Insert` is

```
// POST: set == set<entry> UNION {someDig}
```

The implementation file expresses this same postcondition as

```
// POST: Bit in position someDig equals 1
```

Similarly, the abstract postcondition for `operator*` is

```
// POST: FCTVAL == (this set) INTERSECT set2
```

but its implementation postcondition is

Abstract view of an operation (specification file perspective):

Implementation view of an operation:

Figure 9.6 The abstract and implementation views of an operation

```
// POST: FCTVAL == new set represented by bit string
//                 bitStr BITWISE-AND set2.bitStr
```

The assertions (preconditions, postconditions, and class invariants) in a specification file are called **abstract assertions.** These abstract assertions create a contract between the importer and the implementor. The corresponding preconditions, postconditions, and class invariants in the implementation file are called **implementation assertions.** If the class is correct, then the implementation must satisfy the contract set forth in the abstract assertions.

Figure 9.6 illustrates the two views of a single ADT operation. The importer must ensure the truth of the abstract precondition and the abstract class invariant (if present) *before invoking the operation.* After execution of the operation, the importer expects both the abstract postcondition and abstract invariant to be true.

The implementor has a slightly different perspective on an ADT operation. The implementor assumes that the implementation precondition and the implementation class invariant (if present) are true just before the function is invoked. The implementor's job is to write code that guarantees the implementation postcondition and implementation class invariant when the operation completes.

These two separate views of an ADT make it more difficult to ensure correctness. The code must be correct from the implementation perspective, and there must be agreement between the two perspectives. The implementor must be sure that the implementation file satisfies the contract published in the specification file.

Pursuing Correctness
. . . .

Agreement Between Abstract and Implementation Assertions

Preconditions, postconditions, and class invariants are assertions that may appear in either the specification file or the implementation file. The specification and implementation files usually contain different versions of these assertions.

In the specification file, assertions reflect the abstract behavior of the ADT. The language used reflects the importer's perspective. However, these assertions still must be precise and unambiguous because they serve as the specifications for the implementor.

Implementation assertions usually are written in terms of variables and functions within the implementation file. They refer to implementation details and represent the perspective of the implementor.

For the class to be correct, the programmer must be certain that for every ADT operation:

1. What the importer sees as the essential initial conditions for function invocation (the abstract precondition and class invariant) are sufficient to ensure what the implementor believes to be initially true (the implementation precondition).

2. The operation is correct in the view of the implementor (using the implementation assertions).

3. What the implementor guarantees as final conditions (the implementation postcondition and class invariant) are sufficient to ensure what the importer expects to be true afterwards (the abstract postcondition and class invariant).

9.5 Vector Implementation of a Stack

Another data structure that makes an excellent candidate for a programmer-defined ADT is the stack. Recall that a stack is a linear, sequential access structure in which all insertions and deletions occur at one end, called the top of the stack. In other words, a stack is a list maintained in LIFO order such that only the most recently inserted item is accessible.

Characteristic stack operations include Push, Pop, and Top:

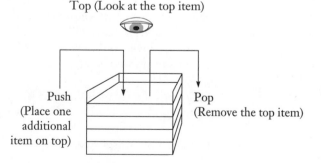

Top (Look at the top item)

Push
(Place one
additional
item on top)

Pop
(Remove the top item)

Stacks have numerous applications in computer science. In Chapter 4 we described a computer system's run-time stack, the set of activation frames created by successive function calls. As each function returns, the LIFO ordering of the activation frames ensures that control returns to the function that most recently made a function call. In Chapter 8 we saw how the run-time stack enables recursion, a powerful tool for expressing algorithms concisely and elegantly, especially when the problem to be solved is naturally defined recursively. In later chapters we will see even more examples of the uses of stacks.

Abstract Assertions

We begin the design of a stack ADT by describing the abstract operations. Describing these operations with English phrases and sentences is often unsatisfactory. It was easy to specify the DigitSet operations by building on the language of sets. We were able to give precise descriptions of operations for this ADT using the empty set, { }, and the union and intersection operations. The advantages of specifying DigitSet in terms of sets and set operations are clarity and precision. Sets are common mathematical objects understood by programmers. Both the importer and the implementor can read these assertions.

Two rules should be observed when writing abstract assertions:

1. Write the assertions in a language understandable by the implementor and all importers.
2. Write assertions that are precise.

Abstract assertions require some **universe of discourse** familiar to both the importer and the implementor. Because both importer and implementor are programmers, they certainly know about numbers, logical expressions, and sets. These mathematical systems provide an excellent universe of discourse for writing assertions. Additionally, these systems are precise and unambiguous. But for a stack ADT, there is a better universe of discourse.

Sequences

Another, less well known, mathematical system of considerable importance in computer science is the **sequence.** We can define a sequence informally as a linear collection of items with two ends, a front and a back, such that items are added or removed only at one end or the other. Figure 9.7 gives a more detailed description of a sequence and associated operations.

Figure 9.7 Description of a sequence

A *sequence* of n items is denoted by $<s1, s2, s3, ..., sn>$, where $n \geq 0$. $s1$ is the front item and sn is the back item. Every item of the sequence is of the same type.

The functions of a sequence are

Front(someSequence)	Yields a sequence item
Back(someSequence)	Yields a sequence item
AppendFront(someSequence,someItem)	Yields another sequence
AppendBack(someSequence,someItem)	Yields another sequence

RemoveFront(someSequence)   Yields another sequence
RemoveBack(someSequence)   Yields another sequence
Length(someSequence)   Yields a nonnegative integer

The values of the functions are

$\text{Front}(<s1, s2, \ldots, sn>) = s1$ for $n >= 1$
$\text{Back}(<s1, s2, \ldots, sn>) = sn$ for $n >= 1$
$\text{AppendFront}(<s1, s2, \ldots, sn>, x) = <x, s1, s2, \ldots, sn>$
$\text{AppendBack}(<s1, s2, \ldots, sn>, x) = <s1, s2, \ldots, sn, x>$
$\text{RemoveFront}(<s1, s2, \ldots, sn>) = <s2, s3, \ldots, sn>$ for $n \geq 1$
$\text{RemoveBack}(<s1, s2, \ldots, sn-1, sn>) = <s1, s2, \ldots, sn-1>$ for $n \geq 1$
$\text{Length}(<>) = 0$
$\text{Length}(<s1, s2, \ldots, sn>) = n$

Every item of a sequence is of the same type. There are sequences of integers, sequences of Booleans, sequences of sets, sequences of sequences, and so on. Below is an example of a sequence of integers:

<3, 6, –12, 0, 6, 6, 9>

Every sequence has a front (the left end) and a back (the right end). The Front function returns the value of the first (leftmost) item, and Back returns the back (rightmost) item. The operations AppendFront and AppendBack take an existing sequence and a new item and insert the item at the appropriate end of the sequence. RemoveFront and RemoveBack delete an item from one end of the sequence. The Length function returns the number of items in the sequence. Figure 9.8 displays several examples of these functions.

$\text{Front}(<3, 6, 12, 0, 6, 6, 9>) = 3$
$\text{Back}(<3, 6, 12, 0, 6, 6, 9>) = 9$
$\text{AppendFront}(<3, 6, 12, 0, 6, 6, 9>, 100) = <100, 3, 6, 12, 0, 6, 6, 9>$
$\text{AppendBack}(<3, 6, 12, 0, 6, 6, 9>, 100) = <3, 6, 12, 0, 6, 6, 9, 100>$
$\text{RemoveFront}(<3, 6, 12, 0, 6, 6, 9>) = <6, 12, 0, 6, 6, 9>$
$\text{RemoveBack}(<3, 6, 12, 0, 6, 6, 9>) = <3, 6, 12, 0, 6, 6>$
$\text{Length}(<3, 6, 12, 0, 6, 6, 9>) = 7$

$\text{Front}(<>)$ is undefined
$\text{Back}(<>)$ is undefined
$\text{AppendFront}(<>, 4) = <4>$
$\text{AppendBack}(<>, 4) = <4>$
$\text{RemoveFront}(<>)$ is undefined
$\text{RemoveBack}(<>)$ is undefined
$\text{Length}(<>) = 0$

Figure 9.8 Examples of sequence functions

Specification of a Stack ADT

With the language of sequences, we can define precisely the operations of many common ADTs, including stacks. Figure 9.9 contains a specification file to describe a stack of integers as an ADT.

The BStack module of Figure 9.9 declares an ADT named IntStack, the domain of each stack being a collection of integer items. The initial comments state that each stack can contain at most MAX_DEPTH items, where MAX_DEPTH is defined to be 200. Because of the explicit limit on the stack size, this ADT is called a **bounded stack.**

```
// ------------------------------------------------------------------
//   SPECIFICATION FILE (bstack.h)
//   This module exports an ADT for a stack of integer values.
//   The maximum stack depth is MAX_DEPTH.
//   Stacks are defined as sequences where the front of the sequence
//   is the top of the stack.
// ------------------------------------------------------------------
#include "bool.h"

// DOMAIN: An IntStack instance is a collection of integer values

const int MAX_DEPTH = 200;

class IntStack {
public:
    Boolean IsEmpty() const;
        // POST: FCTVAL == (Length(stack) == 0)

    Boolean IsFull() const;
        // POST: FCTVAL == (Length(stack) == MAX_DEPTH)

    void Push( /* in */ int newItem );
        // PRE:  Length(stack) < MAX_DEPTH  &&  Assigned(newItem)
        // POST: stack == AppendFront(stack<entry>,newItem)

    int Top() const;
        // PRE:  Length(stack) >= 1
        // POST: FCTVAL == Front(stack)

    void Pop();
        // PRE:  Length(stack) >= 1
        // POST: stack == RemoveFront(stack<entry>)

    IntStack();
        // Constructor
        // POST: Created(stack)  &&  stack == <>
private:
    int data[MAX_DEPTH];
    int top;
};
```

Figure 9.9 BStack specification file (bounded stack)

Public operations for the IntStack ADT include the usual stack operations Push, Pop, and Top. Two other operations ensure that all preconditions are testable:

IsFull   Returns TRUE if the stack is full
IsEmpty   Returns TRUE if the stack is empty

IsFull is necessary because of the precondition for the Push operation, and IsEmpty is required to satisfy the preconditions for Pop and Top.

The IntStack ADT is complete. IntStack() is an initial ADT-constructor that builds an empty stack. Thereafter, any other stack can be created from an empty stack with appropriate invocations of Push.

We have not provided a Write operation, because it is not a characteristic operation of a general-purpose data structure such as a stack. During design and testing of the ADT, the implementor probably would add a Write operation for debugging but would then remove it before offering IntStack to the public as an off-the-shelf software component.

Below is a sample of IntStack client code. Each operation is accompanied by an assertion describing the result in terms of a sequence.

```
IntStack stk;
// ASSERT: stk == <>

if (stk.IsEmpty())
    cout << "EMPTY STACK";
// ASSERT: EMPTY STACK displayed

stk.Push(123);
// ASSERT: stk == <123>

stk.Push(7);
// ASSERT: stk == <7,123>

cout << stk.Top();
// ASSERT: Value 7 displayed

stk.Pop();
// ASSERT: stk == <123>

stk.Push(455);
// ASSERT: stk == <455,123>

stk.Push(455);
// ASSERT: stk == <455,455,123>
```

Vector Representation of a Stack

It is common to use a one-dimensional array as the data representation of a bounded stack. In this representation, the item at the bottom of the stack is stored in the first vector element, the stack item second from the bottom is stored in the second vector element, and so on. A separate variable keeps track of the subscript of the current top item.

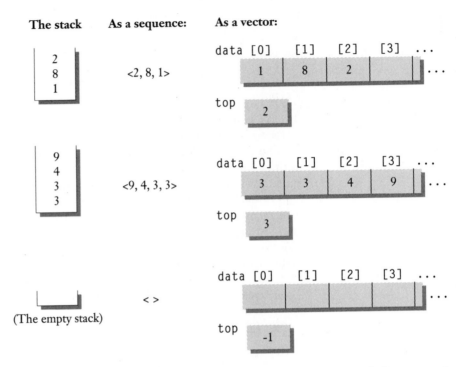

Figure 9.10 Vector
representation of a stack

Figure 9.10 shows three sample stacks (a) as sequences and (b) as stored using a vector representation. In this figure, data is the name of the vector and top is the name of the variable that subscripts the top item. If the stack is empty, top equals –1.

The Implementation of BStack

To implement the BStack module, we use the data representation pictured in Figure 9.10. The private part of the IntStack class declaration (Figure 9.9) consists of the appropriate declarations:

```
int data[MAX_DEPTH];    The vector representing the stack
int top;                The subscript of the current top item (or –1 if the
                        stack is empty)
```

The implementation file for BStack appears in Figure 9.11. The implementation of each member function is surprisingly simple, each function requiring just one statement in its body.

Figure 9.11 BStack
implementation file
(vector implementation)

```
// --------------------------------------------------------------------
//  IMPLEMENTATION FILE (bstack.cpp)
//  This module exports an ADT for a bounded stack of integer values.
//  The stack bound is MAX_DEPTH.
//  Stack representation: a vector.
// --------------------------------------------------------------------
#include "bstack.h"
```

```
// Private members of class:
//      int data[MAX_DEPTH];      // Vector representing the stack
//      int top;                  // Subscript of current top item (or
//                                //     -1 if stack is empty)
//
// CLASSINV:  -1 <= top < MAX_DEPTH

IntStack::IntStack()
    //..........................................................
    // Constructor
    // POST: top == -1
    //..........................................................
{
    top = -1;
}

Boolean IntStack::IsEmpty() const
    //..........................................................
    // POST: FCTVAL == (top == -1)
    //..........................................................
{
    return (top == -1);
}

Boolean IntStack::IsFull() const
    //..........................................................
    // POST: FCTVAL == (top == MAX_DEPTH-1)
    //..........................................................
{
    return (top == MAX_DEPTH-1);
}

void IntStack::Push( /* in */ int newItem )
    //..........................................................
    // PRE:  top < MAX_DEPTH-1  &&  Assigned(newItem)
    // POST: top == top<entry> + 1
    //     && data[top<entry>+1] == newItem
    //..........................................................
{
    data[++top] = newItem;
}

int IntStack::Top() const
    //..........................................................
    // PRE:  top >= 0
    // POST: FCTVAL == data[top]
    //..........................................................
{
    return data[top];
}
```

```
void IntStack::Pop()
    //.........................................................
    // PRE:  top<entry> >= 0
    // POST: top == top<entry> - 1
    //.........................................................
{
    top--;
}
```

Once again we see the abstract assertions of the specification file rewritten in implementation terminology. Although the specification file describes stack operations using sequences, the implementation file describes the same operations in terms of concrete data structures. In Figure 9.12 we compare the two notations by expressing sequence operations in terms of the data structures of the BStack implementation.

Sequence operation	Corresponding vector operation
Length(stack)	`top + 1`
Front(stack)	`data[top]`
AppendFront(stack,newItem)	`data[++top] = newItem`
RemoveFront(stack)	`top--`

Figure 9.12 Equivalent sequence and vector operations

Finally, it is important to verify every ADT implementation for proper initialization of the class invariant. The class invariant of this bounded stack implementation requires the subscript of the top item to be between –1 and MAX_DEPTH –1, inclusive. The class constructor guarantees this class invariant by initializing the subscript of the top item to –1.

9.6   Linked List Implementation of a Stack

Programmers are always searching for better algorithms or better data structures for a task. ADT implementors should also consider alternative implementations. Sometimes another implementation is faster or requires less storage. At other times, an implementation is selected because it is easier to understand, code, and maintain.

The major shortcoming of the vector implementation of stacks is that it limits stacks to a maximum of MAX_DEPTH items. It is possible to change the value of MAX_DEPTH and recompile the implementation file, but the size of the vector still is fixed and cannot expand at run time. An alternative that eliminates this restriction is to represent a stack as a dynamic singly linked list. For this representation, each stack item is stored within the data member of a separate list node. The front of the list corresponds to the top of the stack. Figure 9.13 shows examples of stacks represented in this manner.

The specification file for a new module, UStack, is shown in Figure 9.14. We have expanded the public interface of the IntStack class by including two additional operations:

IntStack(const IntStack&)   A copy-constructor, for initializing one stack
                                         by another

~IntStack()   A destructor, for disposing of an unneeded
                                         stack

It would be ideal if implementation issues *never* had any effect on the abstraction. Realistically, though, an implementation issue is sometimes so

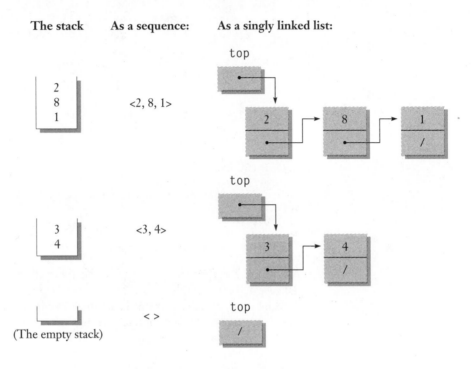

Figure 9.13 Linked list representation of a stack

Figure 9.14 UStack specification file (unbounded stack)

```
// -----------------------------------------------------------------
//   SPECIFICATION FILE (ustack.h)
//   This module exports an ADT for a stack of integer values.
//   The maximum stack depth is MAX_DEPTH, an unspecified value.
//   Stacks are defined as sequences where the front of the sequence
//   is the top of the stack.
// -----------------------------------------------------------------
#include "bool.h"

// DOMAIN: An IntStack instance is a collection of integer values

struct NodeType;    // Complete declaration hidden in
                    // implementation file

class IntStack {
public:
    Boolean IsEmpty() const;
        // POST: FCTVAL == (Length(stack) == 0)

    Boolean IsFull() const;
        // POST: FCTVAL == (Length(stack) == MAX_DEPTH)
```

```
        void Push( /* in */ int newItem );
            // PRE:  Length(stack) < MAX_DEPTH  &&  Assigned(newItem)
            // POST: stack == AppendFront(stack<entry>,newItem)

        int Top() const;
            // PRE:  Length(stack) >= 1
            // POST: FCTVAL == Front(stack)

        void Pop();
            // PRE:  Length(stack) >= 1
            // POST: stack == RemoveFront(stack<entry>)

        IntStack();
            // Constructor
            // POST: Created(stack)  &&  stack == <>

        IntStack( const IntStack& otherStk );
            // Copy-constructor
            // POST: Created(stack)  &&  stack == otherStk

        ~IntStack();
            // Destructor
            // POST: NOT Created(stack)
private:
    NodeType* top;
};
```

important that it causes a change in the abstraction. Classes that use dynamic data are a good example.

When an ADT's concrete data values reside on the free store, not within the class itself, additional public operations are necessary. A class destructor, such as ~IntStack(), must be provided to deallocate the dynamic data when the class instance is destroyed. Without this destructor, the data would remain on the free store, allocated but inaccessible.

Also, the designer would be wise to provide two additional operations:

1. an assignment operation, such as operator=, to create two distinct copies of ADT dynamic data

2. a copy-constructor, such as IntStack(const IntStack&), to allow an ADT instance to be passed by value, to be initialized by another ADT instance in a declaration, or to be returned as a function value

(We have omitted an operator= function in the IntStack class to keep the example simpler. A chapter exercise asks you to add this operation.)

An assignment operation and a copy-constructor are not necessary if the importer never copies one ADT instance to another. But if they are *not* included and the importer does perform a copy—either explicitly with the built-in assignment operator (=) or implicitly by, for example, passing an ADT instance by value—then only the *pointers* will be copied, not the dynamic data on the free store. The result will be two pointers pointing to the same data on the free store. This distinction between shallow and deep copying was discussed in detail in Chapter 7.

In the `IntStack` class, the main reason for providing a copy-constructor is to allow deep copying during parameter passage by value. It may seem wasteful to create a copy of a large stack for use by a function. But suppose that the importer writes a `PrintStack` function to output the contents of a stack for debugging purposes. If the stack is passed by value without a copy-constructor, then the pointer to the original stack is sent. `PrintStack` will then pop each item to print it and destroy the original stack!

Figure 9.15 displays an implementation file for the stack ADT implemented with a dynamic singly linked list. In this version, the private variable `top` points to the linked list on the free store, exactly as depicted in Figure 9.13. That is, `top` serves as the head pointer to the linked list.

Figure 9.15 `IntStack` implemented with a dynamic singly linked list

```
// -------------------------------------------------------------
//   IMPLEMENTATION FILE (ustack.cpp)
//   This module exports an ADT for an unbounded stack of integer
//   values.
//   Stack representation: a dynamic singly linked list.
// -------------------------------------------------------------
#include "ustack.h"
#include <stddef.h>      // For NULL
#include <alloc.h>       // For coreleft()    (This function is
                         //                    nonportable)

typedef NodeType* NodePtr;

struct NodeType {                   // List node type
    int     data;
    NodePtr link;
};

NodePtr PtrToClone( NodePtr );      // Prototype for auxiliary
                                    // function

// Private members of class:
//      NodeType* top;
//
// CLASSINV: top is the head pointer to a singly linked list
//           (or==NULL)
//      NOTE: There is no explicit bound on stack size (subject to
//            available free store memory)

IntStack::IntStack()
    //.........................................................
    // Constructor
    // POST: top == NULL
    //.........................................................
{
    top = NULL;
}
```

```
IntStack::~IntStack()
    //..............................................................
    // Destructor
    // POST: Linked list is not on free store
    //..............................................................
{
    NodePtr tempPtr;

    while (top != NULL) {  // INV (prior to test):
                           //   top points to list with previous
                           //   first node deallocated (or == NULL)
        tempPtr = top;
        top = top->link;
        delete tempPtr;
    }
}

IntStack::IntStack( const IntStack& otherStk )
    //..............................................................
    // Copy-constructor
    // POST: A clone of otherStk's linked list is on free store
    //    && top points to this new list
    //..............................................................
{
    top = PtrToClone(otherStk.top);
}

Boolean IntStack::IsEmpty() const
    //..............................................................
    // POST: FCTVAL == (top == NULL)
    //..............................................................
{
    return (top == NULL);
}

Boolean IntStack::IsFull() const
    //..............................................................
    // POST: FCTVAL == (there is no room on the free store for
    //                  another NodeType object)
    //..............................................................
{
    return (coreleft() < sizeof(NodeType));
}

void IntStack::Push( /* in */ int newItem )
    //..............................................................
    // PRE:  NOT IsFull()  &&  Assigned(newItem)
    // POST: A new node containing newItem is at front of list
    //    && top points to this node
    //..............................................................
{
    NodePtr newPtr = new NodeType;
    newPtr->data = newItem;
    newPtr->link = top;
    top = newPtr;
}
```

```
int IntStack::Top() const
    //..................................................
    // PRE:  top != NULL
    // POST: FCTVAL == top->data
    //..................................................
{
    return top->data;
}

void IntStack::Pop()
    //..................................................
    // PRE:  top != NULL
    // POST: Previous first node is not in list
    //     && top points to new first node (or == NULL)
    //..................................................
{
    NodePtr tempPtr = top;
    top = top->link;
    delete tempPtr;
}

NodePtr PtrToClone( /* in */ NodePtr currPtr )
    //..................................................
    // PRE:  Assigned(currPtr)
    // POST: A clone of sublist starting with *currPtr is on free
    //        store
    //     && FCTVAL == pointer to front of this sublist
    //..................................................
{
    NodePtr newPtr = NULL;
    if (currPtr != NULL) {
        newPtr = new NodeType;
        newPtr->data = currPtr->data;
        newPtr->link = PtrToClone(currPtr->link);
    }
    return newPtr;
}
```

This implementation file includes an auxiliary function, PtrToClone, that is invoked by the copy-constructor IntStack(const IntStack&). The function creates an identical copy of a given linked list on the free store and returns a pointer to it. Using a looping algorithm to copy a linked list is quite complicated, whereas PtrToClone employs a very simple recursive algorithm. You may find this algorithm useful in any program requiring duplication of linked lists.

The singly linked list implementation of stacks has several advantages over the vector implementation. The linked list implementation generally makes better use of storage space by allocating just enough memory to store the correct sized stack. Each Push invocation uses the new operator to create a new node, and each Pop invocation eliminates an unnecessary node via the delete operator.

The major advantage of the linked list implementation is that it does not limit the stack size. There is no explicit limit to how many nodes can be allocated. Therefore, there is no need to state a bound on the number of items the client can push onto a stack. (Clearly there will be some physical bound on the number of nodes, because computer memory is finite. But "unbounded stack" is an appropriate term from a conceptual standpoint.) The `IsFull` function checks to see if there is enough space on the free store to allocate another list node. Our implementation uses the (nonportable) library function `coreleft` as one example of how to determine the available space. If your C++ standard library does not provide the `coreleft` function, see our discussion of the `PersonList` class in Chapter 8 for alternative approaches.

Designing with Wisdom

The Effect of Implementation on Abstractions

Ideally, an ADT is first designed as an abstraction. The specification file should reflect this abstraction. Only after the design is complete should the implementation begin.

In principle, the implementor of the ADT should be able to create and change the implementation in a way that is totally transparent to the specification file and therefore to the client code. Compare this philosophy with the modular design of many consumer goods. If a module in a TV set malfunctions or is updated, it is possible to merely unplug the old module and plug in the new one. Similarly, it is desirable to simply unplug an ADT implementation file and plug in a new one with no change to the specification file.

However, examination of such implementation issues as efficiency, memory usage, flexibility, and ease of coding can sometimes lead to revising the original abstraction. Going from a vector representation of a stack to a dynamic linked list representation required us to add new public operations (a copy-constructor and a destructor). Changing an abstraction to match a specific implementation is sometimes unavoidable and must be viewed as a pragmatic necessity. But the thoughtful designer should try to keep such changes to a minimum.

9.7 Ring Buffer Implementation of a Queue

In this section and the next, we look at alternative implementations of the queue data structure. Recall that a queue is a linear, sequential access structure in which all insertions occur at the rear and all deletions occur at the front. Thus, the queue is a restricted form of a list ADT with the items maintained in FIFO order.

Queue operations include Enqueue, Dequeue, and Front:

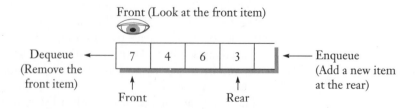

A computer's operating system makes extensive use of queues. Each I/O device typically has a queue associated with it so that multiple requests to use the device are satisfied in first-come-first-served order. The operating system also uses a queue to buffer the input data from a keyboard, processing the characters in FIFO order after the user types the Return or Enter key. Queues are also common in simulation programs, such as the theater waiting line simulation we developed in Chapter 4.

In this section, we design and implement an ADT for a queue of integer values. Figure 9.16 displays the specification file for this ADT. All assertions are written in terms of sequences.

```
// ------------------------------------------------------------------
// SPECIFICATION FILE (bqueue.h)
// This module exports an ADT for a queue of integer values.
// The maximum queue length is MAX_LENG.
// ------------------------------------------------------------------
#include "bool.h"

// DOMAIN: An IntQueue instance is a collection of integer values

const int MAX_LENG = 200;

class IntQueue {
public:
    Boolean IsEmpty() const;
        // POST: FCTVAL == (Length(queue) == 0)

    Boolean IsFull() const;
        // POST: FCTVAL == (Length(queue) == MAX_LENG)

    void Enqueue( /* in */ int newItem );
        // PRE:  Length(queue) < MAX_LENG  &&  Assigned(newItem)
        // POST: queue == AppendBack(queue<entry>,newItem)

    int Front() const;
        // PRE:  Length(queue) >= 1
        // POST: FCTVAL == Front(queue)

    void Dequeue();
        // PRE:  Length(queue) >= 1
        // POST: queue == RemoveFront(queue<entry>)

    IntQueue();
        // Constructor
        // POST: Created(queue)  &&  queue == <>
private:
    int data[MAX_LENG+1];
    int front;
    int rear;
};
```

Figure 9.16 BQueue specification file (bounded queue)

We have not included copy-constructor and destructor functions because, as we will see, IntQueue does not create dynamic data on the free store. IsFull and IsEmpty ensure that all preconditions are testable. Furthermore, the IntQueue ADT is complete. The class constructor IntQueue() is an initial ADT-constructor that creates an empty queue, from which any other can be built with successive invocations of Enqueue.

Figure 9.17 shows a possible implementation of a bounded queue that stores the queue items in a vector.

Figure 9.17 BQueue implementation file (ring buffer implementation)

```
// ----------------------------------------------------------------
//   IMPLEMENTATION FILE (bqueue.cpp)
//   This module exports an ADT for a bounded queue of integer values.
//   The maximum queue length is MAX_LENG.
//   Queue representation: a ring buffer in a vector of
//                                 size MAX_LENG + 1
// ----------------------------------------------------------------
#include "bqueue.h"

const int VEC_SIZE = MAX_LENG + 1;

// Private members of class:
//      int data[MAX_LENG+1];   // Vector representing the queue
//      int front;              // (Subscript of queue front) - 1
//      int rear;               // Subscript of queue rear
//
// CLASSINV:  At all times, at least one element of the data vector
//                 remains unused

IntQueue::IntQueue()
     //........................................................
     // Constructor
     // POST: front == 0  &&  rear == 0
     //........................................................
{
     front = rear = 0;
}

Boolean IntQueue::IsEmpty() const
     //........................................................
     // POST: FCTVAL == (rear == front)
     //........................................................
{
     return (rear == front);
}

Boolean IntQueue::IsFull() const
     //........................................................
     // POST: FCTVAL == ((rear + 1) MOD VEC_SIZE == front)
     //........................................................
{
     return ((rear + 1) % VEC_SIZE == front);
}
```

```
void IntQueue::Enqueue( /* in */ int newItem )
    //..........................................................
    // PRE:  (rear + 1) MOD VEC_SIZE != front
    //       && Assigned(newItem)
    // POST: rear == (rear<entry> + 1) MOD VEC_SIZE
    //       && data[rear] == newItem
    //..........................................................
{
    rear = (rear + 1) % VEC_SIZE;
    data[rear] = newItem;
}

int IntQueue::Front() const
    //..........................................................
    // PRE:  rear != front
    // POST: FCTVAL == data[(front + 1) MOD VEC_SIZE]
    //..........................................................
{
    return data[(front + 1) % VEC_SIZE];
}

void IntQueue::Dequeue()
    //..........................................................
    // PRE:  rear != front
    // POST: front == (front<entry> + 1) MOD VEC_SIZE
    //..........................................................
{
    front = (front + 1) % VEC_SIZE;
}
```

The private members of the IntQueue class are data (a vector that stores the items of the queue) and two integer variables, front and rear. VEC_SIZE, the size of the data vector, is declared to be one greater than MAX_LENG, the maximum length of the queue. We will discuss the reason for this discrepancy shortly.

The data representation we have chosen for the queue is known as a **ring buffer** (or **circular buffer**). The name "ring" refers to the way the vector is treated as a circular ring of items. Algorithms that manipulate the ring buffer treat the first and the last elements of the data vector as though they were adjacent (Figure 9.18).

Each time a new item is enqueued, the value of rear is incremented to index the next element in the ring, and the item is stored at this position. When rear equals VEC_SIZE - 1, the next invocation of Enqueue resets rear to 0. The statement that causes rear to rotate around the ring is

```
rear = (rear + 1) % VEC_SIZE;
```

The index front also advances around the ring. For our particular implementation, front does not index the front of the queue; it indexes the ring element *preceding* the front of the queue. The index of the front item is then given by the expression

```
(front+1) % VEC_SIZE
```

A ring buffer (the `data` **array)**

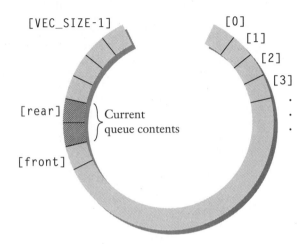

Figure 9.18 A ring buffer

Another way of characterizing `rear` and `front` is to say that `rear` designates the *last filled* slot in the vector, and `front` designates the *last emptied* slot.

Now let us see why the `data` vector is of size `MAX_LENG + 1`. When the queue is empty, `rear` equals `front`. If the length of the vector were `MAX_LENG` instead of `MAX_LENG + 1`, then filling every element in the ring would result in the same condition that signals an empty queue (`rear = front`). Therefore, the ring buffer works properly only if the vector always has at least one empty element. If there were no empty element, it would be impossible to distinguish a full queue from an empty queue.

9.8   Linked List Implementation of a Queue

The ring buffer implementation of a queue has the same limitation that we discussed earlier for the `BStack` module: the size of the vector is fixed at compile time and may be too large or too small. An alternative is to implement a queue with a dynamic linked list.

Figure 9.19 contains the specification file for an unbounded integer queue. Because the new version manipulates dynamic data, we have added to the

Figure 9.19 UQueue specification file (unbounded queue)

```
// ------------------------------------------------------------------
//   SPECIFICATION FILE (uqueue.h)
//   This module exports an ADT for an unbounded queue of integer
//   values.
//   The maximum queue length is MAX_LENG, an unspecified value.
// ------------------------------------------------------------------
#include "bool.h"
```

```
// DOMAIN: An IntQueue instance is a collection of integer values

struct NodeType;    // Complete declaration hidden in
                    // implementation file

class IntQueue {
public:
    Boolean IsEmpty() const;
        // POST: FCTVAL == (Length(queue) == 0)

    Boolean IsFull() const;
        // POST: FCTVAL == (Length(queue) == MAX_LENG)

    void Enqueue( /* in */ int newItem );
        // PRE:  Length(queue) < MAX_LENG  &&  Assigned(newItem)
        // POST: queue == AppendBack(queue<entry>,newItem)

    int Front() const;
        // PRE:  Length(queue) >= 1
        // POST: FCTVAL == Front(queue)

    void Dequeue();
        // PRE:  Length(queue) >= 1
        // POST: queue == RemoveFront(queue<entry>)

    IntQueue();
        // Constructor
        // POST: Created(queue)  &&  queue == <>

    IntQueue( const IntQueue& otherQ );
        // Copy-constructor
        // POST: Created(queue)  &&  queue == otherQ

    ~IntQueue();
        // Destructor
        // POST: NOT Created(queue)
private:
    NodeType* front;
    NodeType* rear;
};
```

original class operations a destructor and a copy-constructor. (It would also be best to include an assignment operation, operator=.)

In the UQueue module we represent a queue as a dynamic singly linked list. Each list node is of type NodeType. As we will see in the implementation file, NodeType has the same form we used in the unbounded stack ADT:

```
struct NodeType {
    int      data;
    NodeType* link;
};
```

Each queue item is stored in the data member of a list node. An Enqueue operation appends an item to the tail of the linked list, and Dequeue removes the node at the head of the list. The IntQueue private members front and

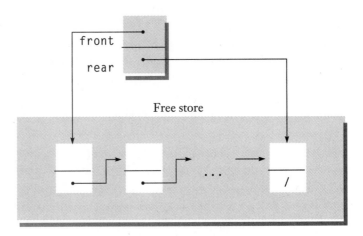

Figure 9.20 Memory diagram of IntQueue data (linked list representation)

rear point to the first and last nodes in the linked list. Figure 9.20 shows a memory diagram of this linked list representation.

The UQueue implementation file appears in Figure 9.21. The auxiliary routine CopyList is similar to PtrToClone in the UStack implementation. The difference is that CopyList must return two values—a front and a rear pointer—whereas PtrToClone returned a single pointer (the pointer to the front of the list).

Figure 9.21 UQueue implementation file (linked list implementation)

```
// ---------------------------------------------------------------
//   IMPLEMENTATION FILE (uqueue.cpp)
//   This module exports an ADT for an unbounded queue of integer
//   values.
//   Queue representation: a dynamic singly linked list with front and
//                          rear pointers.
// ---------------------------------------------------------------
#include "uqueue.h"
#include <stddef.h>     // For NULL
#include <alloc.h>      // For coreleft()   (This function is
                        //                   nonportable)


typedef NodeType* NodePtr;

struct NodeType {               // List node type
    int     data;
    NodePtr link;
};

void CopyList(NodePtr, NodePtr&, NodePtr& );   // Prototype for
                                               // auxiliary function
// Private members of class:
//      NodeType* front;
//      NodeType* rear;
//
// CLASSINV:
//      front points to first node of a singly linked list (or ==
//      NULL)
//    && rear points to last node of this list (or == NULL)
```

```
IntQueue::IntQueue()
    //...........................................................
    // Constructor
    // POST: front == NULL  &&  rear == NULL
    //...........................................................
{
    front = rear = NULL;
}

IntQueue::~IntQueue()
    //...........................................................
    // Destructor
    // POST: Linked list is not on free store
    //...........................................................
{
    NodePtr tempPtr;

    while (front != NULL) {  // INV (prior to test):
                             //    front points to list with previous
                             //    first node deallocated (or == NULL)
        tempPtr = front;
        front = tempPtr->link;
        delete tempPtr;
    }
}

IntQueue::IntQueue( const IntQueue& otherQ )
    //...........................................................
    // Copy-constructor
    // POST: A clone of otherQ's linked list is on free store
    //     && front points to front of this new list (or == NULL)
    //     && rear points to rear of this new list (or == NULL)
    //...........................................................
{
    if (otherQ.front == NULL)
        front = rear = NULL;
    else
        CopyList(otherQ.front, front, rear);
}

Boolean IntQueue::IsEmpty() const
    //...........................................................
    // POST: FCTVAL == (front == NULL)
    //...........................................................
{
    return (front == NULL);
}
```

```
Boolean IntQueue::IsFull() const
    //................................................................
    // POST: FCTVAL == (there is no room on the free store for
    //                      another NodeType object)
    //................................................................
{
    return (coreleft() < sizeof(NodeType));
}

void IntQueue::Enqueue( /* in */ int newItem )
    //................................................................
    // PRE:  NOT IsFull()  &&  Assigned(newItem)
    // POST: A new node containing newItem is at back of list
    //................................................................
{
    NodePtr newPtr = new NodeType;
    newPtr->data = newItem;
    newPtr->link = NULL;
    if (front == NULL)
        front = rear = newPtr;
    else {
        rear->link = newPtr;
        rear = newPtr;
    }
}

int IntQueue::Front() const
    //................................................................
    // PRE:  front != NULL
    // POST: FCTVAL == front->data
    //................................................................
{
    return front->data;
}

void IntQueue::Dequeue()
    //................................................................
    // PRE:  front != NULL
    // POST: Previous first node is not in list
    //    && front points to new first node (or == NULL)
    //................................................................
{
    NodePtr tempPtr = front;
    front = tempPtr->link;
    delete tempPtr;
    if (front == NULL)
        rear = NULL;
}
```

```
void CopyList( /* in */  NodePtr  currPtr,
               /* out */ NodePtr& cloneFront,
               /* out */ NodePtr& cloneRear  )
    //...............................................................
    // PRE:  Assigned(currPtr)
    // POST: A clone of sublist starting with *currPtr is on free
    //          store
    //      && cloneFront points to front of this sublist
    //      && (After recursion unwinds) cloneRear points to rear of
    //          entire clone list
    //...............................................................
{
    NodePtr newPtr = NULL;
    if (currPtr != NULL) {
        CopyList(currPtr->link, cloneFront, cloneRear);
        newPtr = new NodeType;
        newPtr->data = currPtr->data;
        newPtr->link = cloneFront;
        if (currPtr->link == NULL)       // Last node in list
            cloneRear = newPtr;
    }
    cloneFront = newPtr;
}
```

9.9   Primitive Models of Abstraction

Earlier in this chapter we defined the DigitSet ADT, in its specification file, in terms of mathematical sets. We defined the IntStack and IntQueue ADTs in terms of sequences. Both sets and sequences are well-defined mathematical concepts that constitute **primitive models.** A primitive model is a well-understood type with associated operations. Using a primitive model to describe the abstract view of an ADT lends precision and clarity to the definition.

Good primitive models are

1. commonly understood (with a good universe of discourse)

2. useful (with widespread applications)

3. precise (mathematically correct)

The numeric type known as "integer" is a good primitive model. Integers are familiar numbers. Integers are certainly useful and they include a wide range of operations, such as addition and multiplication. Integers are also precisely defined mathematical objects.

Most ADTs can be defined using only a few primitive models. Below are the four most common primitive models:

1. simple types (integer, floating point, Boolean, character, etc.)

2. sets

3. sequences

4. *N*-tuples

An *N-tuple* is denoted by $(x1, x2, \ldots, xN)$ where N is some constant and the type of each item $x1, x2, \ldots, xN$ depends upon its position in the tuple.

Form for declaring an *N*-tuple:

$$(\text{Name1: Type1, Name2: Type2}, \ldots, \text{NameN: TypeN})$$

where Name1, Name2, $\ldots$, NameN are distinct names that identify tuple positions, and Type1, Type2, $\ldots$, TypeN are primitive model types for each position.

Operations (functions on an *N*-tuple z):

Name1(z) yields the first item from *N*-tuple z.
Name2(z) yields the second item from *N*-tuple z.

$\vdots$

NameN(z) yields the *N*th item from *N*-tuple z.

Figure 9.22 The *N*-tuple primitive model

This collection of primitive models includes numerous simple (atomic) types and three widely used structured models—sets, sequences, and *N*-tuples. The only model on this list that we have not examined thus far is the **N-tuple.** Figure 9.22 describes this type and the notation we use in this text.

There are two important differences between *N*-tuples and sequences. First, an *N*-tuple is fixed in length, whereas sequences can grow and shrink. An *N*-tuple of five items is called a 5-tuple:

$$(42, 6.8 \ , \text{ 'A', } 23, 9.6)$$

and an *N*-tuple of eight items is called an 8-tuple. A 2-tuple is so common that it has a special name: **ordered pair.** Also, a 3-tuple often is called an **ordered triple.**

Second, the items in an *N*-tuple can be of different types, whereas the items in a sequence must all be of the same type. It is convenient to specify a name and a type for each *N*-tuple position in the form shown in Figure 9.22.

Figure 9.23 contains a better version of the Fraction specification file. This figure describes each fraction as an ordered pair (2-tuple) composed of a numerator and a denominator. The identifier "NumerPart" names the first item of each ordered pair, and the name "DenomPart" names the second. The assertions in this new version of Fraction are more precise through the use of the *N*-tuple model.

Figure 9.23 Fraction specification file in terms of 2-tuples

```
// ------------------------------------------------------------------
// SPECIFICATION FILE (fraction.h)
// This module exports a FracType class with two operator functions,
// operator* and operator==.  A more general FracType class
// might include more operations.
// ------------------------------------------------------------------
#include "bool.h"
```

```
// DOMAIN: Each fraction consists of an ordered pair
//         (NumerPart: Integer, DenomPart: PositiveInteger)

class FracType {
public:
    void Write() const;
        // POST: The value of this fraction has been displayed as:
        //           NumerPart(fraction) / DenomPart(fraction)
        //         with no blanks

    float FloatEquiv() const;
        // POST: FCTVAL == NumerPart(fraction) / DenomPart(fraction)

    void Simplify();
        // POST: Fraction is reduced to lowest terms. (No integer > 1
        //       evenly divides both NumerPart(fraction) and
        //       DenomPart(fraction))

    FracType operator*( /* in */ FracType frac2 ) const;
        // PRE:  This fraction and frac2 are in simplest terms
        // POST: FCTVAL ==
        //           (NumerPart(this fraction) * NumerPart(frac2),
        //            DenomPart(this fraction) * DenomPart(frac2) )
        //           reduced to lowest terms
        // NOTE: Numerators or denominators of large magnitude
        //       may produce overflow

    Boolean operator==( /* in */ FracType frac2 ) const;
        // PRE:  This fraction and frac2 are in simplest terms
        // POST: FCTVAL ==
        //           (NumerPart(this fraction) / DenomPart(this fraction)
        //            == NumerPart(frac2) / DenomPart(frac2))

    FracType( /* in */ int initNumer,
              /* in */ int initDenom );
        // Constructor
        // PRE:  Assigned(initNumer)  &&  initDenom > 0
        // POST: Fraction == (initNumer, initDenom)
        // NOTE: (initNumer < 0) --> fraction is a negative number
private:
    int numer;
    int denom;
};
```

9.10 Levels of Abstraction

Abstraction occurs at many levels. A level of abstraction is much like a layer of software. The higher the level of abstraction, the closer the algorithm or data structure comes to resembling the user's original problem. Low-level abstractions are closer to the facilities of the programming language.

Figure 9.24 displays the levels of abstraction for ADTs that we have seen in

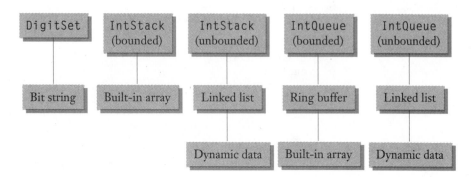

Figure 9.24
Implementation
hierarchies for
Chapter 9 ADTs

this chapter. Each higher-level abstraction is implemented by the lower-level abstraction directly below it.

Starting with a problem specification, the earliest phases of the design process generate the highest level abstractions. An architect draws homes using pictures of walls, floors, windows, and doors. In a program written to assist the architect, DoorPicture and WindowPicture may make good abstract data types:

Data type:	DoorPicture	**Data type:**	WindowPicture
Operations:	DrawDoor	**Operations:**	DrawWindow
	EraseDoor		EraseWindow
	DrawDoubleDoor		DivideIntoPanes

$\vdots$ $\vdots$

DoorPicture and WindowPicture, being close to the architect's view of the problem, are very high-level abstractions. The implementation files for DoorPicture and WindowPicture might use algorithms and data structures that display visible images on a computer screen, for example.

A drawing program for
an architect

A door usually is drawn as a rectangle with circular handles. A window is a collection of rectangles. The program designer may decide to create another level of abstraction for these objects:

Data type:	Rectangle	**Data type:**	Circle
Operations:	DrawRect	**Operations:**	DrawCircle
	EraseRect		EraseCircle
	DrawLineInRect		⋮
	⋮		

Rectangle and Circle are lower-level abstractions. They are closer to the implementation of the problem and farther from the architect's view of the problem:

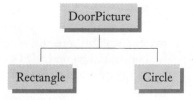

But Rectangle and Circle are still abstractions. They are not built-in types in C++.

Higher-level abstractions often are designed for a particular application. DoorPicture is designed to suit the needs of the architect. Lower-level abstractions tend to be more general in purpose. A Rectangle ADT might be useful for a number of different graphics applications. Lower-level abstractions make the best off-the-shelf software.

Top-down design works for data abstraction as well as control structures. The design of the architect's program starts with a high-level abstraction and proceeds to lower, more detailed levels. But not all data abstraction is performed top down. Most off-the-shelf components are lower-level abstractions, and higher-level design often builds upwards from these facilities.

When an ADT is designed for off-the-shelf use, the goal of the design is to extend the programming language. The availability of general purpose, off-the-shelf ADTs then changes the entire programming environment. FracType, DigitSet, IntStack, and IntQueue are all useful ADTs with applications in many contexts. Using these classes off the shelf, rather than re-inventing them, frees the programmer to work on other problems.

SUMMARY

The programmer-defined abstract data type is among the most powerful tools in modern high-level language programming. An ADT is more than data structures and functions. It is a tightly knit encapsulation of data values and related operations.

A good abstract data type is designed as an abstraction. At the design level, the domain and the operations are described in terminology that is most meaningful to a programmer importing the type. Primitive models offer precision and clarity in these descriptions.

Designing ADTs is a creative process of inventing a type and operations that match the problem to be solved. A well-designed ADT must be useful. To be useful, an ADT must be complete and must have testable preconditions. An ADT also must be described in terms that both the importer and implementor can comprehend.

Implementation of ADTs is a coding task. The implementor must supply concrete data representations and code that guarantee the behavior advertised by the specification. Every ADT has many possible implementations, and the implementor must evaluate their differences in efficiency, memory usage, flexibility, and ease of coding. Experience is invaluable in helping to make these decisions.

C++ provides useful language features to assist in creating ADTs. The class mechanism and separate specification and implementation files are important for constructing good ADTs.

Programmers often spend too much time worrying about control structures:

"Can we break the algorithm up into functions?"
"How many instructions long will your program be?"
"How deeply nested is that loop?"

Data structures sometimes get forgotten. It is important to think in terms of ADTs when designing programs. The potential benefits are more readable, maintainable, and reusable software components.

KEY TERMS

abstract assertions   (p. 404)
ADT-constructor   (p. 393)
assignment (copy) operations   (p. 394)
bitwise operators   (p. 400)
bounded stack   (p. 408)
circular buffer   (p. 421)
complete ADT   (p. 394)
destructor operations   (p. 394)
I/O operations   (p. 394)
implementation assertions   (p. 404)
initial ADT-constructor (p. 394)

N-tuple   (p. 428)
ordered pair   (p. 428)
ordered triple   (p. 428)
primitive models   (p. 427)
ring buffer   (p. 421)
selector operations   (p. 394)
sequence   (p. 406)
test operations   (p. 394)
testable preconditions   (p. 395)
type conversion functions   (p. 394)
universe of discourse   (p. 406)

EXERCISES

9.1   You are deciding among the following implementations of a general list (not linked list):

　i. built-in array

　ii. linked list implemented with a built-in array

　iii. linked list implemented with dynamic data

For each situation below, select the best of these three alternatives.

a. The maximum potential length of the list is known in advance, speed is critical, and memory space is plentiful.

b. The maximum potential length of the list is known in advance, memory space is very tight, and speed is only moderately important.

c. The maximum potential length of the list is not known in advance, speed is critical, and memory space is plentiful. (This is an unfortunate situation, but choose the best alternative.)

d. The maximum potential length of the list is not known in advance, memory space is very tight, and speed is only moderately important.

9.2 A stack is a special case of a general list. Why is it reasonable to implement a stack, but not a general list, with a built-in array?

9.3 Why is it better to implement a queue with a ring buffer than with an array whose subscripts do not "wrap around" from last to first? Why is the opposite true when implementing a stack?

9.4 The `DigSet` module implements a digit set ADT with a bit string. To implement a digit *list* ADT, why would it be inappropriate to use a bit string?

9.5 In the `DigSet` specification file (Figure 9.3), why do the `Insert`, `Delete`, and `IsElt` operations not include the following precondition?

```
// PRE: Assigned(someDig)
```

9.6 Suppose that we were to remove the `FracType` class constructor of the `Fraction` module (Figure 9.1) and replace it with the following class constructor. What is wrong with the resulting ADT?

```
FracType( /* in */ int initDenom );
    // Constructor
    // PRE:  initDenom > 0
    // POST: Fraction == 1 / initDenom
```

9.7 Suppose that we were to include the following two public functions in the class described in Exercise 9.6.

```
FracType operator+( /* in */ FracType frac2 ) const;
    // PRE:  This fraction and frac2 are in simplest terms
    // POST: FCTVAL == this fraction + frac2  (fraction
    //                    addition), reduced to lowest terms

FracType operator-( /* in */ FracType frac2 ) const;
    // PRE:  This fraction and frac2 are in simplest terms
    // POST: FCTVAL == this fraction - frac2  (fraction
    //                    difference), reduced to lowest terms
```

a. Explain why the inclusion of these two functions alleviates the problem addressed in Exercise 9.6.

b. Can either of these functions be excluded without creating the same problem as in Exercise 9.6?

9.8 The `UStack` implementation file (Figure 9.15) includes a recursive function `PtrToClone`. Describe the "One Small Step" and "Complete the Solution" parts (Chapter 6).

9.9 Suppose that a C++ class manipulates a dynamic linked list on the free store. If the ADT designer provides an assignment operation to copy one class instance B to another class instance A, this operation must begin by deallocating the entire linked list that A currently points to. Otherwise, A's original linked list would remain allocated but inaccessible.

For the `IntStack` class of the `UStack` module (Figures 9.14 and 9.15), add a new public member function: an assignment operation that copies one stack to another. In particular, overload the standard assignment operator (=) to perform a deep copy. Give both the function specification and its implementation.

Caution: Your code should watch for the possibility of assigning a stack to itself. Because the destination stack first deletes its entire linked list from the free store before the copy begins, there would be nothing left to copy. (Hint: On entry to the function, what can you conclude if the `top` members of both stacks point to the same list node?)

9.10 To the `DigitSet` ADT of the `DigSet` module (Figures 9.3 and 9.5), we wish to add the following operations: cardinality, set equality, set difference, and subset. The function specifications appear below. Implement each function. Hint: For set difference, consider using the C++ EXCLUSIVE OR operator (^).

```
int Cardinality() const;
    // POST: FCTVAL == cardinality of the set

Boolean operator==( /* in */ DigitSet set2 ) const;
    // POST: FCTVAL == (this set == set2)

Boolean operator<=( /* in */ DigitSet set2 ) const;
    // POST: FCTVAL == (this set equals or is a proper subset
    //                  of set2)

DigitSet operator-( /* in */ DigitSet set2 ) const;
    // POST: FCTVAL == this set - set2  (set difference)
```

9.11 Below is the specification of an `IntPair` abstract data type. Write the corresponding implementation file.

```
//--------------------------------------------------------------
//  SPECIFICATION FILE (ordpair.h)
//  This module exports an ADT for an ordered pair of integers.
//--------------------------------------------------------------
#include "bool.h"

// DOMAIN: Each IntPair instance is an ordered pair
//         (First: Integer, Second: Integer)
```

```
class IntPair {
public:
    int First() const;
        // POST: FCTVAL == First(pair)

    int Second() const;
        // POST: FCTVAL == Second(pair)

    void AssignFirst( /* in */ int newFirst );
        // PRE:  Assigned(newFirst)
        // POST: pair == (newFirst, Second(pair<entry>))

    void AssignSecond( /* in */ int newSecond );
        // PRE:  Assigned(newSecond)
        // POST: pair == (First(pair<entry>), newSecond)

    Boolean operator==( /* in */ IntPair pair2 ) const;
        // POST: FCTVAL == (this pair == pair2)

    IntPair();
        // Constructor
        // POST: Created(pair)  &&  pair == (0, 0)
private:
    int first;
    int second;
};
```

9.12 Make FracType a better general-purpose ADT by describing a more complete collection of operations. Using Figure 9.23 as a guide, specify each operation in terms of ordered pairs. (Do not implement these operations. Just give their specifications.)

9.13 Assume that the value of someSeq is <3, 2, 1> just prior to each sequence function below. Give the value of each function. Answer each part independently of the others. (Note: Some function values may be undefined.)

   a. Front(someSeq) = ?

   b. Back(someSeq) = ?

   c. AppendFront(someSeq, 7) = ?

   d. AppendBack(someSeq, 9) = ?

   e. RemoveFront(someSeq) = ?

   f. RemoveBack(someSeq) = ?

   g. RemoveFront(RemoveBack(someSeq)) = ?

   h. RemoveBack(AppendBack(someSeq, 12)) = ?

   i. AppendFront(AppendBack(someSeq, 1), 2) = ?

   j. RemoveBack(RemoveBack(RemoveBack(someSeq))) = ?

   k. RemoveFront(RemoveFront(RemoveFront(someSeq))) = ?

l. RemoveBack(RemoveBack(RemoveBack(RemoveBack(someSeq)))) = ?

m. Front(AppendFront(someSeq, 25)) = ?

n. Back(AppendFront(someSeq, 77)) = ?

o. Front(RemoveBack(someSeq)) = ?

p. Front(RemoveFront(RemoveFront(someSeq))) = ?

q. Front(RemoveBack(RemoveFront(someSeq))) = ?

PROGRAMMING PROJECTS

9.1 Make all necessary modifications to the bounded BStack specification and implementation files (Figures 9.9 and 9.11) to stack strings that are each 20 characters long instead of integers. Test the resulting module.

9.2 Consider the mathematical notion of a sequence and its associated functions.

  a. Design a specification file for a sequence of integers as an ADT.

  b. Write and test a suitable implementation file for this specification. Use an unbounded implementation.

  c. Rewrite and test the UStack implementation file (Figure 9.15) by layering it upon this sequence ADT.

9.3 Refer to Programming Project 3.2 of Chapter 3.

  a. Write a specification file for a module that exports this complex number class. In the operation pre- and postconditions, describe the operations in terms of ordered pairs (2-tuples). You may wish to use the Fraction specification file of Figure 9.23 as a guide.

  b. Implement and test this complex number ADT.

9.4 Reimplement the DigSet module (Figures 9.3 and 9.5) by representing a DigitSet as a Boolean array instead of a bit string. This representation takes advantage of the direct access property of arrays by using the digit itself to index the array.

  Do not alter the public part of the DigitSet class declaration in any way; change only the private data declarations. Test your new implementation.

9.5 Write and implement a bounded integer stack ADT that allows the client to declare the size of the stack:

```
IntStack stk1(100);
IntStack stk2(48);
```

Represent each stack as a dynamically allocated vector. That is, the class constructor will use the new operator to allocate a vector of the exact size on the free store. Suggestion: Use the following private class members:

int* data;	Base address of vector
int vSize;	Vector size
int top;	Subscript of current top item (or –1 if stack is empty)

Because the class creates dynamic data, be sure to include a copy-constructor and a destructor. An assignment operation might also be useful.

9.6 Write and implement a bounded integer queue ADT that allows the client to declare the size of the queue:

```
IntQueue q1(200);
IntQueue q2(125);
```

Represent each queue as a dynamically allocated ring buffer. That is, the class constructor will use the `new` operator to allocate a vector of the appropriate size on the free store for the ring buffer. Suggestion: Use the following private class members:

```
int* data;      Base address of vector
int  vSize;     Vector size
int  front;     (Subscript of queue front) – 1
int  rear;      Subscript of queue rear
```

Because the class creates dynamic data, be sure to include a copy-constructor and a destructor. An assignment operation might also be useful.

9.7 Design a `CharSet` ADT whose universe is all characters in your machine's character set (such as ASCII or EBCDIC). Implement and test your ADT with each of the following data representations:

a. a Boolean array

b. a linked list stored in a built-in array

c. a dynamic linked list

d. a bit string (which will need to span more than one integer variable)

9.8 Some instructors use seating charts to relate the names of students to their seats in a particular class. Design, implement, and test an abstract data type to automate this notion of a seating chart. Remember that a good ADT requires certain operations to be useful and consistent with the intended abstraction.

9.9 Some instructors maintain a separate gradebook for each class they teach. Design, implement, and test a gradebook ADT. Select operations that are consistent with the intent of the abstraction.

PART III

Additional Topics

Object-Oriented Design

INTRODUCTION

In modern programming practice, the development of new computer software incorporates three phases: analysis, design, and implementation. Analysis involves two parties: the user or customer who needs a new program to solve a problem, and a systems analyst who is conversant with programming. Together, the user and the systems analyst define the problem to be solved and prepare a problem specification (such as the six-part problem specification that we have used throughout this book). The problem specification describes what the program is supposed to do but not how to do it.

The design phase produces a solution to the problem without necessarily going into program-level implementation details. Working from the problem specification, the designer chooses data structures and creates algorithms that satisfy the specification. The third phase—implementation—involves coding the designer's algorithms and data structures in a programming language and then testing the resulting program.

Development of complex software is rarely this straightforward, however. The three phases do not occur in the order one, two, three. Software development is an iterative process. Unanticipated developments often lead to reanalysis, redesign, or reimplementation. Also, smaller projects may combine analysis with design or design with implementation. In this chapter, we examine the design and implementation phases, with special emphasis on design.

Currently, the most widely used design methodology is structured design (or top-down design). Structured design is the design of a problem solution by focusing on control flow. The designer identifies actions to be performed, expressing algorithms in terms of standard control structures or using functions as control abstractions. In structured design, data plays a secondary role in support of control flow.

Another software design technique, one that is rapidly gaining acceptance, is known as **object-oriented design (OOD).** Object-oriented design is the design of a problem solution by focusing on entities ("objects") and operations on those objects. The first step in object-oriented design is to identify the major objects in the problem, together with their associated operations. The final problem solution is ultimately expressed in terms of these objects and operations. In object-oriented design, data plays a leading role. Control structures are used to implement operations on the objects and to guide the interaction of objects with each other.

In this chapter, some of what we refer to as object-oriented design might more precisely be called object-oriented analysis. In the current state of research on object-oriented techniques, the boundary between analysis and design is not universally agreed upon. An in-depth discussion of their differences falls outside the scope of this book. What is important is to see the major principles of the object-oriented approach to program development.

10.1 Problem Domain and Solution Domain

Both top-down design and object-oriented design start with a statement of the problem. Neither approach can be successful without a carefully written problem specification. Figure 10.1 gives a six-part specification for a simple program that simulates the operations of an automobile parking lot. We will use this parking lot problem throughout the chapter to demonstrate the technique of object-oriented design.

Figure 10.1 Parking lot problem specification

TITLE

Parking lot simulation

DESCRIPTION

This program simulates the operations of a parking lot. This particular parking lot consists of two alleys, each of which is wide enough for only one car and is closed at one end:

Alley A ⟶ ▭

Alley B ⟶ ▭

Alley A is the primary parking location. Alley B is used only as a place to move cars out of the way when retrieving a car parked in the middle of Alley A.

Program execution starts with both alleys empty. The program repeatedly prompts the user to specify one of four commands: park a car, retrieve a car, display the contents of Alley A, or terminate the program.

To park a car, the program generates a new ticket number (1, 2, . . .), issues a ticket stub to the customer, and parks the car at the front of Alley A.

To retrieve a car, the program prompts the user for the ticket stub number and begins to search Alley A. The program moves each car at the front of

Alley A to Alley B until it finds the desired car. All of the cars that were temporarily placed in Alley B are then moved back to Alley A.

INPUT

Each input command consists of a single lowercase or uppercase letter: 'd' or 'D' to display the alley contents, 'p' or 'P' to park a car, 'r' or 'R' to retrieve a car, and 'q' or 'Q' to terminate the program. The program translates each lowercase letter into its uppercase equivalent. For the Retrieve command, the user also must enter the integer ticket stub number.

OUTPUT

The main prompt for user commands is the following:

```
D)isplay  P)ark  R)etrieve  Q)uit:
```

In response to the Park command, the program generates a ticket number and displays this number, denoted below by <t>:

```
Ticket no. = <t>
```

In response to the Retrieve command, the program displays the following prompt for the ticket stub number:

```
Ticket no.:
```

The output for the Display command is as follows, where each <t> represents the integer ticket number of a car in the alley:

```
Alley A: <t> <t> <t> ...
```

ERROR-HANDLING

1. The program ignores invalid user commands.
2. If the user tries to retrieve a car with a nonexistent ticket stub number, the program displays the message "CAR NOT PARKED IN MY LOT."
3. If Alley A is full and the user wants to park a car, the program displays the message "PARKING LOT FULL."

EXAMPLE

Below is a sample execution of this program with all input in color:

```
D)isplay  P)ark  R)etrieve  Q)uit: P
Ticket no. = 1

D)isplay  P)ark  R)etrieve  Q)uit: P
Ticket no. = 2

D)isplay  P)ark  R)etrieve  Q)uit: P
Ticket no. = 3

D)isplay  P)ark  R)etrieve  Q)uit: P
Ticket no. = 4
```

```
D)isplay  P)ark  R)etrieve  Q)uit: d
Alley A:    4   3   2   1

D)isplay  P)ark  R)etrieve  Q)uit: r
Ticket no.: 2

D)isplay  P)ark  R)etrieve  Q)uit: d
Alley A:    4   3   1

D)isplay  P)ark  R)etrieve  Q)uit: r
Ticket no.: 6
CAR NOT PARKED IN MY LOT

D)isplay  P)ark  R)etrieve  Q)uit: r
Ticket no.: 1

D)isplay  P)ark  R)etrieve  Q)uit: d
Alley A:    4   3

D)isplay  P)ark  R)etrieve  Q)uit: q
```

A computer program usually models some real-life activity or concept. The parking lot simulation models a real-life (but very simple) parking lot. A spreadsheet program models a real spreadsheet, a large paper form used by accountants and financial planners. A robotics program models human perception and human motion.

Nearly always, the aspect of the world that we are modeling (the **application domain** or **problem domain**) consists of objects—parking lot alleys, parking tickets, spreadsheet rows, spreadsheet columns, robot arms, robot legs. The computer program that solves the real-life problem also includes objects (the **solution domain**): stacks, queues, menus, windows, and so forth. Object-oriented design is based on the philosophy that programs are easier to write and understand if the objects in a program correspond closely to the objects in the problem domain. Looking ahead at the parking lot program, it seems natural to model each parking lot alley by using a stack, because cars are parked in last-in-first-out order.

Problem domain   **Solution domain**

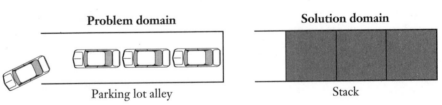

Problem-domain and solution-domain objects

Parking lot alley   Stack

There are many ways to perform object-oriented design. Different authors advocate different techniques. As a preview of what is to come, we will describe object-oriented design as a three-step process:

1. Identify the objects and operations.
2. Determine where to place the objects and operations.
3. Design the driver.

In the succeeding sections of this chapter, we explain each of these steps in detail.

10.2 Step 1: Identify the Objects and Operations

Object-oriented design (OOD) begins with identifying the major objects and the associated operations on those objects. For the parking lot problem, the designer asks questions like

"What object should I use to model the parking lot as a whole?"
"What object is the best model for an individual alley of the parking lot?"
"Do I need additional objects in my program beyond those that are apparent in the problem domain?"

To answer questions like these, we must first agree on what the terms **object** and **operation** mean. Unfortunately, not all authors and researchers agree on the meanings of these terms.

What Is an Object?

Some authors define an object to be an instance of a class—that is, an instance of a programmer-defined data type. Others define *object* more broadly as either an instance of a class or a variable of a built-in type:

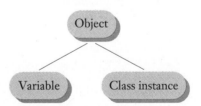

We prefer this second definition because it allows us to identify *all* important entities in the solution domain, not just entities for which we need to write or import C++ classes.

What Is an Operation?

Again, there are varied opinions about the meaning of *operation*. We define *operation* quite generally as any action that manipulates data:

With this definition, all three of the following C++ statements can be interpreted as operations on objects:

```
myObject++;          ← Built-in operation
yourObject.Write();          ← Class member function
DoSomething(myObject, yourObject);          ← Global function
```

A First Cut: Objects = Nouns, Operations = Verbs

With structured (top-down) design, we begin by identifying the major actions the program is to perform. With object-oriented design, we begin by identifying the major objects and operations we will need. In both design methods, it is often difficult to see where to start.

To identify solution-domain objects, a good way to start is to look at the problem domain. More specifically, go to the problem specification and look for important **nouns** and **verbs.** The nouns and noun phrases may suggest objects; the verbs and verb phrases may suggest operations. In the parking lot specification (Figure 10.1), the key noun phrases are

A parking lot
Alley A
Alley B
A car
A ticket
A ticket stub
A user command

Some of the operations suggested by verb phrases in the problem specification are

Park a car
Retrieve a car
Generate a new ticket number
Read a user command
Read a ticket stub number from the user
Display the contents of Alley A

Determining which nouns and verbs are significant is one of the most difficult aspects of OOD. There are no cookbook formulas for doing so, and there probably never will be. Not all nouns become objects, and not all verbs become operations. For example, we might have included

Issue a ticket stub

as an operation. But according to the problem specification, issuing a ticket stub simply amounts to displaying the new ticket number to the user. The nouns-and-verbs technique is imperfect, but it does give us a first approximation at a solution.

Object Tables

Next, we summarize the objects and operations in a table known as an **object table** (see Table 10.1). Object tables help us to organize a problem into a reasonable collection of objects and operations.

The first column of the object table lists the objects we have identified in our first approximation. (It is important to regard these objects as *candidates* for objects. We have not committed ourselves to a final decision yet.) The second column of the table lists the main characteristics of the objects. These characteristics describe in an informal way the kind of information conveyed by each object. The final column of the table lists the operations.

A single operation may apply to several different objects, in which case the operation is listed for all objects involved. For example, we have listed the Park operation for the pkgLot, alleyA, and car objects because parking a car involves all three objects. Similarly, the Display operation pertains to both the pkgLot object as a whole and to alleyA in particular.

For each object it is helpful to identify which operations can modify objects. Table 10.1 uses an asterisk (*) to signify these operations. For example, the Park operation alters the contents of pkgLot and alleyA by parking a car.

Table 10.1 Parking lot objects, characteristics, and operations (Version 1)

Object	Characteristics	Operations
pkgLot	Consists of two alleys and generates ticket numbers	Park* Retrieve* Display
alleyA	Stores cars in LIFO order	Park* Retrieve* Display
alleyB	Stores cars in LIFO order	Retrieve*
car	?	Park Retrieve
ticket	Integer 1, 2, . . .	GenNewNumber*
ticketStub	Integer 1, 2, . . .	ReadTicket* Retrieve
command	A single-letter user command	ReadCommand*

* Denotes an operation that potentially changes the value of the object.

Table 10.2 Parking lot object table (Version 2)

Object	Characteristics	Operations
pkgLot	Consists of two alleys and generates ticket numbers	Park* Retrieve* Display
alleyA	Stores ticket numbers in LIFO order	Park* Retrieve* Display
alleyB	Stores ticket numbers in LIFO order	Retrieve*
ticket	Integer 1, 2, . . .	GenNewNumber*
ticketStub	Integer 1, 2, . . .	ReadTicket* Retrieve
command	A single-letter user command	ReadCommand*

* Denotes an operation that potentially changes the value of the object.

However, there is no asterisk after the Display operation for pkgLot or alleyA because this operation leaves the parking lot unchanged.

The object table also suggests to the designer whether certain candidate objects will be meaningful in the solution. Looking at the car object, it is hard to think of any characteristics of cars in our simulation program. In real life, cars are parked and retrieved from parking lots. But in this simulation, cars have no useful properties or interesting operations. The program is actually manipulating ticket numbers, not cars. That is, "parking a car" amounts to storing a ticket number into the alleyA object so that we can later "retrieve a car" by looking for a certain ticket number. Therefore, we revise the object table by removing the car object and rewording the characteristics of the alleyA and alleyB objects. Table 10.2 displays the revised object table.

The fact that we revised the object table does not mean that we are failures at performing OOD because we did not get it right the first time. To the contrary, OOD is characterized by exploration and revision. Examining and reexamining the objects and operations usually leads to better understanding of the problem and the solution. Object tables are developed not only with pencil and paper but also with erasers!

10.3 Step 2: Determine Where to Place the Objects and Operations

After selecting the objects and operations, the next step is to examine the relationships among the objects. In particular, we want to see whether certain objects might be **subobjects** of other objects. A subobject is an object that is contained within another object. Examining the object table for the parking lot problem, we could reasonably claim that the alleyA, alleyB, and ticket objects are all subobjects of the pkgLot object. This relationship is called the **has-a** (or **contains-a**) **relationship.** The pkgLot object *has an* alleyA object, an alleyB object, and a ticket object as subobjects. However, the ticketStub and command objects are independent objects that are not part of any other objects.

By reversing the point of view, some authors refer to the has-a relationship as the **is-a-part-of relationship**—the alleyA object *is a part of* a parking lot, as are the alleyB and ticket objects. No matter what name we give to this relationship, the picture we have in mind is the following:

pkgLot

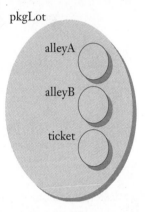

alleyA

alleyB

ticket

There are two reasons why it is important to determine the relationships among objects. First, the relationships ultimately lead to natural ways to implement the design. In other words, when we go to write the parking lot program, the above figure suggests that alleyA, alleyB, and ticket might appropriately be members of a C++ parking lot class.

The second reason is that the relationships among objects can suggest where to place the operations. For a particular operation, the key question to ask is

Which object has primary responsibility for the operation?

If you can answer this question, attach the operation to that object. Using the C++ language as a reference point, the phrase "attaching an operation to an object" means the following:

1. If the object is a class instance, make the operation a member function.

```
someObject.DoSomething();
```

2. If the object is of a built-in type, use either a built-in operator

```
someInt++;
```

or a global function.

```
DoSomething(someInt);
```

On the other hand, if you cannot assign primary responsibility to just one object, the operation is probably a global operation:

```
DoSomething(object1, object2, object3);
```

Table 10.3 Parking lot object table (Version 3)

Object	Characteristics	Operations
pkgLot	Consists of two alleys and generates ticket numbers	Park*[†] Retrieve*[†] Display[†]
alleyA	Stores ticket numbers in LIFO order	Park* Retrieve* Display
alleyB	Stores ticket numbers in LIFO order	Retrieve*
ticket	Integer 1, 2, . . .	GenNewNumber*[†]
ticketStub	Integer 1, 2, . . .	ReadTicket*[†] Retrieve
command	A single-letter user command	ReadCommand*[†]

* Denotes an operation that potentially changes the value of the object.
† Denotes an operation for which the object to the left has primary responsibility.

Referring to our object table (Table 10.2), the operations GenNewNumber, ReadTicket, and ReadCommand are each listed only once. There is no doubt that each of these operations should be attached to the designated object. However, the Park, Retrieve, and Display operations are listed for more than one object. We must decide, if possible, which object should have the primary responsibility for each of these operations.

Consider the Park operation, associated in the object table with the pkgLot and alleyA objects. Given our placement of alleyA, alleyB, and ticket as subobjects of the pkgLot object, it is probably appropriate to view Park as an operation on a parking lot rather than an operation on an alley. Similarly, Retrieve and Display are probably better as operations on parking lots than on alleys. To help us keep track of which object has primary responsibility for an operation, we make a note in the object table to this effect. Table 10.3 shows the object table with a dagger (†) noting each operation for which the associated object has primary responsibility. For example, the Park operation is listed with a dagger for the pkgLot object but is listed without a dagger for the alleyA object.

10.4 Step 3: Design the Driver

The final step in OOD is to design the driver—the top-level algorithm. In OOD, the driver is the glue that joins the objects (along with their operations) together. When we implement the design in C++, the driver becomes the `main` function.

In OOD, a driver often does little more than process user commands and delegate tasks to the objects. Below is a pseudocode driver for the parking lot problem. We express the operations as function calls whose parameters are the associated objects. This convention is only a starting point. Eventually, the C++ code will not necessarily use global functions and parameters to invoke each operation.

Top-level algorithm for the parking lot problem

```
Do
    ReadCommand(command)
    If command == 'P' then
        Park(pkgLot)
    Else if command == 'R' then
        ReadTicket(ticketStub)
        Retrieve(pkgLot, ticketStub)
    Else if command == 'D' then
        Display(pkgLot)
    Else
        Ignore command
while command != 'Q'
```

Notice that the Park operation mentions only the pkgLot object, even though the object table associates Park with both pkgLot and alleyA. The reason is that alleyA is a subobject of pkgLot, so pkgLot will manipulate alleyA when executing the Park operation. In contrast, the Retrieve operation mentions both pkgLot and ticketStub. Because ticketStub is not a subobject of pkgLot, we must send to pkgLot the value of ticketStub.

Examining the top-level algorithm gives the designer an opportunity to review the overall design. Up until now, the focus has been on data and operations on the data. At this stage, control flow becomes an issue. Tracing the control flow of our algorithm, we see immediately that we have not considered initializing any of the objects. For the algorithm to work properly, we must initialize the pkgLot object. We do not need to initialize the command or ticketStub objects; the ReadCommand and ReadTicket operations assign new values to these objects from user input.

Our review of the driver has turned up missing operations, so we go back to revise the object table one more time. Table 10.4 shows the final object table.

Table 10.4 Parking lot object table (Version 4)

Object	Characteristics	Operations
pkgLot	Consists of two alleys and generates ticket numbers	Initialize*[†] Park*[†] Retrieve*[†] Display[†]

Table 10.4 Parking lot object table (Version 4) (continued)

Object	Characteristics	Operations
alleyA	Stores ticket numbers in LIFO order	InitToEmptyA*† Park* Retrieve* Display
alleyB	Stores ticket numbers in LIFO order	InitToEmptyB*† Retrieve*
ticket	Integer 1, 2, . . .	InitTicketToZero*† GenNewNumber*†
ticketStub	Integer 1, 2, . . .	ReadTicket*† Retrieve
command	A single-letter user command	ReadCommand*†

* Denotes an operation that potentially changes the value of the object.
† Denotes an operation for which the object to the left has primary responsibility.

In Table 10.4, observe that we have included initialization operations for the alleyA, alleyB, and ticket objects. Although these three objects are not visible in the top-level algorithm, initializing the pkgLot object requires initializing all of its subobjects.

Identification of these additional operations necessitates one small change to the driver. We must precede the do-while loop with a call to the Initialize operation of the pkgLot object. Figure 10.2 displays the complete top-level algorithm.

```
Initialize(pkgLot);    // Includes InitToEmptyA(alleyA), InitToEmptyB(alleyB),
                       // and InitTicketToZero(ticket)
Do
   ReadCommand(command)
   If command == 'P' then
       Park(pkgLot)
   Else if command == 'R' then
       ReadTicket(ticketStub)
       Retrieve(pkgLot, ticketStub)
   Else if command == 'D' then
       Display(pkgLot)
   Else
       Ignore command
while command != 'Q'
```

Figure 10.2 Pseudocode driver for the parking lot problem

Designing with Wisdom

The Iterative Nature of Object-Oriented Design

Software developers, researchers, and authors have proposed many different strategies for performing OOD. Common to nearly all of these strategies are three fundamental steps:

1. Identify the objects and operations.

2. Determine where to place the objects and operations.

3. Design the driver.

Experience with large software projects has shown that these three steps are not necessarily sequential—Step 1, Step 2, Step 3, then we are done. In practice, Step 1 occurs first, but only as a first approximation. During Steps 2 and 3, we may discover new objects or operations, leading us back to Step 1 again. It is realistic to think of Steps 1 through 3 not as a sequence but as a loop.

Furthermore, each step is an iterative process within itself. Step 1 may entail working and reworking our view of the objects and operations. Similarly, Steps 2 and 3 often involve experimentation and revision. In the parking lot design, we originally included cars as candidate objects but then eliminated them. We initially conceived of alleys as holding cars, then revised our view so that alleys hold tickets. When we designed the driver, we discovered additional operations to initialize various objects.

There is never only one way to solve a problem. Iterating and reiterating through the design phase leads to insights that produce a better solution.

10.5 Implementing the Design

In OOD, when the designer identifies an object, it is an **abstract object.** The designer does not choose immediately an exact data representation for that object. The characteristics from the object table may suggest alternatives, but it usually is best to postpone decisions till later. Similarly, the operations on objects begin as **abstract operations,** because there is no initial attempt to provide algorithms for these operations.

In the software development process, the next phase after design is implementation. To implement the design, we must flesh out the objects and operations in more detail. Specifically, we must

• choose a suitable data representation for each abstract object

and

• create algorithms for the abstract operations

To select a data representation for an object, the programmer has three options:

1. Use a built-in data type of the programming language.

2. Use an off-the-shelf ADT.

3. Create a new ADT.

For a given object, a good rule of thumb is to consider these three options in the order listed. A built-in type is the most straightforward to use and understand, and operations on these types are already defined by the language. If a built-in type is not adequate to represent an object, the programmer should survey available ADTs and modules to see if any are a good match for the abstract object. If no suitable off-the-shelf ADT exists, the programmer must design and implement an ADT to represent the object.

The command Object

To implement the parking lot design, we begin by examining the object table (Table 10.4) in conjunction with the driver (Figure 10.2). The simplest object to consider is the command object. From its characteristics and operations, the most direct representation is a built-in char variable:

```
char command;
```

The ReadCommand operation is easily implemented as a global function ReadCommand, which includes a prompt to the user in accordance with the problem specification:

```
void ReadCommand( /* out */ char& command )
    //.............................................................
    // POST: User has been prompted for a single char
    //    && command == uppercase equivalent of that char
    //.............................................................
{
    cout << "\nD)isplay  P)ark  R)etrieve  Q)uit: ";
    cin >> command;
    command = toupper(command);
}
```

The toupper function, available through the header file ctype.h, is part of the C++ standard library.

The ticketStub Object

The ticketStub object requires a bit more thought. According to the object table, a ticket stub takes on the integer values 1, 2, and so forth. The built-in int type therefore seems like a reasonable data representation:

```
int ticketStub;
```

To confirm this choice, we should examine the operations associated with ticketStub. The object table lists two operations: ReadTicket and Retrieve. The first operation, ReadTicket, prompts the user for a ticket stub number and then inputs the number. For this task, the int type is a suitable representation.

The second operation, Retrieve, is a more complex operation. However, ticketStub does not have primary responsibility for the Retrieve operation. We have determined that this responsibility lies with the pkgLot object. Therefore, we do not implement the Retrieve operation at this time, and we conclude that ticketStub should indeed be an `int`. Here is the implementation of the ReadTicket operation:

```
void ReadTicket( /* out */ int& ticketStub)
    //.............................................................
    // POST: ticketStub == integer prompted for and input from user
    //.............................................................
{
    cout << "Ticket no.: ";
    cin >> ticketStub;
}
```

The pkgLot Object

According to the object table (and our earlier discussions), the pkgLot object has a complicated structure. This object has three subobjects—alleyA, alleyB, and ticket—as well as primary responsibility for four operations: Initialize, Park, Retrieve, and Display. No C++ built-in type has this kind of structure and operations, nor is there likely to be an off-the-shelf ADT that is a perfect match for a parking lot. Therefore, we must create a C++ class to implement the pkgLot object.

To begin, consider a data representation for pkgLot. This part is easy. The data representation is the three objects alleyA, alleyB, and ticket. Now we must implement each of these three objects.

For the ticket object, the built-in `int` type is appropriate. This decision is consistent with the characteristics and the operations of the object. Ticket numbers are integers in increasing order, and simple C++ statements can implement the operations InitTicketToZero and GenNewNumber:

```
ticket = 0;   // InitTicketToZero
   ⋮
ticket++;      // GenNewNumber
```

Next, consider the alleyA and alleyB objects, which store ticket numbers (that is, `int`s) in LIFO order. Because only the ticket at the front of an alley is accessible, it is natural to represent each alley as a stack of `int`s. Stacks are not built-in types in C++, so we must implement each stack using either an off-the-shelf ADT or a new ADT. Fortunately, an off-the-shelf ADT is available: the `IntStack` class developed in Chapter 9. In addition to the usual stack operations (Push, Pop, and Top), the `IntStack` class has a class constructor that initializes a stack to be empty. Therefore, there is no need to implement the InitToEmptyA and InitToEmptyB operations listed in the object table. The class constructor implicitly implements these operations.

At this point, we can give shape to the pkgLot object by writing a C++ class named, say, `PkgLotType`. The pkgLot object will be an instance of this class:

```
PkgLotType pkgLot;
```

Figure 10.3 displays the declaration of the `PkgLotType` class.

```
// -----------------------------------------------------------
//  SPECIFICATION FILE (pkglot.h)
//  This module exports an ADT for a parking lot with two alleys
// -----------------------------------------------------------
#include "bstack.h"

class PkgLotType {
public:
    void Park();
        // POST: (Alley A full) -->
        //              Car not parked  &&  Error message displayed
        //      && (NOT Alley A full) -->
        //              New ticket no. generated and displayed to
        //              user
        //          && Ticket number pushed onto Alley A stack

    void Retrieve( /* in */ int ticketStub );
        // PRE:  Assigned(ticketStub)
        // POST: Top of Alley A stack popped and pushed onto Alley B
        //       stack until ticketStub found or Alley A is empty
        //      && Error message displayed if ticketStub was not in
        //       Alley A
        //      && All tickets transferred back to Alley A from Alley B

    void Display();
        // POST: Contents of Alley A have been output in
        //       order from top to bottom

    PkgLotType();
        // Constructor
        // POST: Alleys are empty  &&  Initial ticket number == 0
private:
    IntStack alleyA;
    IntStack alleyB;
    int      ticket;
};
```

Figure 10.3 PkgLot specification file

The public member functions of PkgLotType are Park, Retrieve, Display, and a default (parameterless) constructor. In the parking lot object table, we listed an Initialize operation for the pkgLot object. With C++ classes, it is natural (and recommended) to implement such an operation by using a class constructor. It is better not to rely on the client of a class to invoke an Initialize operation. The class constructor provides guaranteed initialization of a class instance before the client can invoke any other member functions.

Having chosen a data representation for PkgLotType, we must now implement each of the four operations. Figure 10.4 shows the implementations of these operations, expressed in C++ program code.

Figure 10.4 PkgLot
implementation file

```
// --------------------------------------------------------------
//   IMPLEMENTATION FILE (pkglot.cpp)
//   This module exports an ADT for a parking lot with two alleys
// --------------------------------------------------------------
#include "pkglot.h"
#include "bool.h"
#include <iomanip.h>     // For setw()

// Private members of class:
//     IntStack alleyA;
//     IntStack alleyB;
//     int      ticket;
//
// CLASSINV:  alleyA contains ticket numbers in LIFO order
//         && alleyB is empty

PkgLotType::PkgLotType()
    //...........................................................
    // Constructor
    // POST: alleyA and alleyB are empty (by implicit calls to their
    //       class constructors)
    //    && ticket == 0
    //...........................................................
{
    ticket = 0;
}

void PkgLotType::Park()
    //...........................................................
    // POST: (Alley A full) -->
    //              Error message displayed
    //          && ticket == ticket<entry>
    //    && (NOT Alley A full) -->
    //              ticket == ticket<entry> + 1
    //          && Value of ticket displayed to user
    //          && ticket pushed onto alleyA stack
    //...........................................................
{
    if (alleyA.IsFull())
        cout << "PARKING LOT FULL\n";
    else {
        ticket++;
        cout << "Ticket no. = " << ticket << '\n';
        alleyA.Push(ticket);
    }
}
```

```
void PkgLotType::Retrieve( /* in */ int ticketStub )
    //.......................................................................
    // PRE:  Assigned(ticketStub)
    // POST: Top of alleyA popped and pushed onto alleyB until
    //       ticketStub found or alleyA is empty
    //    && Error message displayed if ticketStub was not in alleyA
    //    && All tickets transferred back to alleyA from alleyB
    //.......................................................................
{
    int     topTicket;
    Boolean found = FALSE;

    while ( !alleyA.IsEmpty() && !found ) {
        topTicket = alleyA.Top();
        alleyA.Pop();
        if (topTicket == ticketStub)
            found = TRUE;
        else
            alleyB.Push(topTicket);
    }
    if ( !found )
        cout << "CAR NOT PARKED IN MY LOT\n";
    while ( !alleyB.IsEmpty() ) {
        alleyA.Push(alleyB.Top());
        alleyB.Pop();
    }
}

void PkgLotType::Display()
    //.......................................................................
    // POST: Contents of alleyA have been output in
    //       order from top to bottom
    //.......................................................................
{
    IntStack tempStk = alleyA;  // Copy contents of alleyA into
                                // temporary stack we can destroy
    cout << "Alley A: ";
    while ( !tempStk.IsEmpty() ) {
        cout << setw(4) << tempStk.Top();
        tempStk.Pop();
    }
    cout << '\n';
}
```

The algorithms for the four operations of PkgLotType are all straightforward. Sometimes this is not the case. If an operation is extremely complex, it may be best to treat the operation as a new problem and use top-down design on the control flow. In this situation, it is appropriate to apply both top-down and object-oriented techniques iteratively. We will return to this issue later in the chapter.

Designing with Wisdom

Representing Abstract Objects and Implementing Abstract Operations

The choices of how to represent abstract objects and implement abstract operations are key design decisions. Selecting a representation for an object often requires examining the operations. Conversely, certain operations are more efficient or easier to code for particular data structures.

The designer also must keep in mind the tools at hand. If it is possible to represent an object using a simple data type, then doing so is probably the best choice. A built-in structured type or an off-the-shelf ADT is a good choice for more complex data. If none of these options is satisfactory, creating a new ADT may be in order.

Some of the most difficult decisions required of designers arise in the representation of abstract objects. There are very few right or wrong solutions. Experience helps the designer to identify the better choices.

The Driver

Now that we have chosen data representations and implemented all the operations for the parking lot objects, the final task is to implement the driver. That is, we must translate the driver pseudocode in Figure 10.2 into C++ program code.

First, we give C++ declarations for the objects used in the algorithm:

```
int main()
{
    PkgLotType pkgLot;
    char       command;
    int        ticketStub;
```

Next, we eliminate the first instruction of the pseudocode algorithm—the Initialize operation. We implemented this operation as a `PkgLotType` class constructor, so there is no explicit call to an Initialize routine.

We now proceed with the translation, paying special attention to the form used to invoke the various operations. The pseudocode instructions

ReadCommand(command)

and

ReadTicket(ticketStub)

translate into the C++ statements

```
ReadCommand(command);
```

and

```
ReadTicket(ticketStub);
```

because we implemented these two operations as global functions on the simple variables command and ticketStub.

In contrast, we implemented the Park, Retrieve, and Display operations as member functions of the PkgLotType class, not as global functions. The pseudocode instruction

Park(pkgLot)

therefore translates into C++ as

pkgLot.Park();

Similarly, we must be careful to use dot notation in the C++ calls to the Retrieve and Display functions. The result of the translation is the program file shown in Figure 10.5. With this file (and the PkgLot specification and implementation files), we have completed the design and implementation of the parking lot simulation.

Figure 10.5 Parking lot simulation program

```
// ------------------------------------------------------------------
//   parksim.cpp
//   This program simulates a parking lot.  Actions are specified by
//   user commands from standard input.
// ------------------------------------------------------------------
#include "pkglot.h"      // For PkgLotType class
#include <iostream.h>
#include <ctype.h>       // For toupper()

void ReadCommand( char& );
void ReadTicket( int& );

int main()
{
    PkgLotType  pkgLot;
    char        command;
    int         ticketStub;

    do {
        ReadCommand(command);
        switch (command) {
            case 'P':
                pkgLot.Park();
                break;
            case 'R':
                ReadTicket(ticketStub);
                pkgLot.Retrieve(ticketStub);
                break;
            case 'D':
                pkgLot.Display();
                break;
            default:
                ;
        }
    } while (command != 'Q');
```

```
        return 0;
}

void ReadCommand( /* out */ char& command )
    //......................................................
    // POST: User has been prompted for a single char
    //     && command == uppercase equivalent of that char
    //......................................................
{
    cout << "\nD)isplay  P)ark  R)etrieve  Q)uit: ";
    cin >> command;
    command = toupper(command);
}

void ReadTicket( /* out */ int& ticketStub)
    //......................................................
    // POST: ticketStub == integer prompted for and input from user
    //......................................................
{
    cout << "Ticket no.: ";
    cin >> ticketStub;
}
```

10.6   Integration of Object-Oriented Design and Structured Design

Structured (top-down) design and object-oriented design each have advantages and disadvantages. Because structured design concentrates on control structures, it works best for problems requiring complex control flow and simple data types. Conversely, OOD concentrates on data and associated operations, and it works best when the problem domain has many entities or when algorithms interact with complex data structures.

Structured design has the advantage of producing complete algorithms at each step of refinement. This gives the designer an understanding of how each piece fits into the complete fabric of the program. OOD concentrates on data objects. It is not always obvious how the objects and operations will ultimately fit together to solve the problem.

Because OOD identifies and isolates operations on objects, excellent modularity follows. Control flow is often encapsulated as separate, relatively simple ADT operations. With structured design, it is harder to obtain good modularity. It is not always easy to see how to decompose a program into functions, and it may not be clear what actions and data structures belong together. This issue of modularity is particularly important for large programs.

OOD is also consistent with the use of off-the-shelf modules. By separating a problem into objects and operations, the programmer can survey available software to save design and coding time.

The code for the parking lot program illustrates some of the benefits of OOD. The `main` function is readable because it consists of function calls that look like abstract operations. The code for each operation is short and readable because it performs a single, clearly defined task. Concentration on objects also leads to the incorporation of the IntStack class. Using an existing ADT makes the problem easier to solve.

Ease of maintenance is another asset of programs designed with the object-oriented approach. It is easier to locate and change an operation when it is localized as a single function. Suppose that we wanted to modify the parking lot program to output the alley contents in a different format. The necessary changes would be confined to the Display routine. Similarly, a change in the algorithm for retrieving cars would involve only the Retrieve function.

OOD techniques are not independent of structured design, however. The two approaches are most effective when used in concert. You may choose the objects and operations using OOD but then design the operations using structured design.

Designing with Wisdom

Combining Top-Down and Object-Oriented Design

A wise designer draws on the strengths of different design techniques when they best fit the problem. Below are some suggestions for using top-down versus object-oriented design.

- OOD produces good modularity. Use OOD as a starting point.
- If you cannot see what data structures are needed without examining the algorithms, try top-down design. (Some problems are mostly computational, involving very little data. An example is a library of mathematical routines to compute sines, cosines, square roots, and so forth.)
- If you cannot generate many algorithms without first selecting data structures, try OOD.
- In top-down design, stop after each level of refinement and decide whether it is possible to identify some objects of the subalgorithm.
- Consider each operation as a separate problem.
- When selecting objects, keep in mind any off-the-shelf components that might provide assistance.
- Consider writing a new abstract data type when designing an object and its operations.

Above all else, remember that top-down design works best for the refinement of control structures and that OOD is best for data structures and associated operations. Because every program has both control and data structures, a combination of the design techniques produces the best code.

A Study in Design

An Operating System Memory Manager

One of the roles of a computer's operating system is memory management. The operating system is responsible for allocating memory to a user's program before executing it. A fundamental service provided by many operating systems is *multiprogramming* (or *multitasking*)—the technique of holding several different programs in memory at the same time and switching the central processing unit (CPU) back and forth among them. For example, if the currently executing program must wait for a lengthy I/O operation to complete, the operating system temporarily transfers control to another program. With multiprogramming, the CPU is kept busy doing useful work on several programs instead of idly waiting for I/O transfers to complete.

To hold several programs in memory concurrently, one strategy is to divide memory into several fixed-size regions (*partitions*) and load each program (sometimes called a "job") into a different partition. For simplicity, assume that memory available to users consists of three partitions of equal size and that each job can fit entirely within one partition. When new jobs arrive in the system, they are enqueued in FIFO order in a job queue, waiting for a partition to become available:

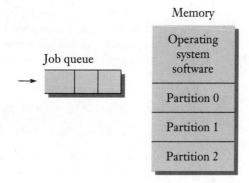

When a job in memory completes its execution and leaves the system, the job at the front of the job queue is dequeued and loaded into the vacated partition. (Although we have drawn the job queue as though it were outside the memory unit, in reality the job queue resides in the memory partition labeled "Operating system software.")

Figure 10.6 shows the problem specification for a program that simulates the memory management portion of an operating system.

Figure 10.6 Memory manager problem specification

TITLE

Operating system memory manager simulation

DESCRIPTION

This program simulates the activities of a simple memory manager. Main memory available for general use consists of three partitions (0, 1, and 2) of equal size. It is assumed that each partition is large enough to hold any job.

The simulation starts with no jobs in the system, and all partitions and the job queue are empty. The program repeatedly prompts the user to specify one of four commands: add a new job to the system, terminate a job that is currently in memory, display information about the job queue and partitions, or terminate the simulation.

To add a new job to the system, the simulation first generates a new job identification number (an integer 1, 2, . . .) and then displays this "job ID" to the user. If there is a vacant memory partition, the new job is loaded immediately into that partition. Otherwise, the simulation enqueues the ID of this new job at the rear of the job queue.

If the user selects the "Terminate a job" command, the simulation checks the job queue. If the queue is not empty, the simulation dequeues the job ID at the front of the queue and loads this job for execution.

INPUT

Each input command consists of a single lowercase or uppercase letter: 'd' or 'D' to display information about the jobs in the system, 'a' or 'A' to add a job, 't' or 'T' to terminate a job, or 'q' or 'Q' to terminate the simulation. The program translates each lowercase letter into its uppercase equivalent. For the Terminate command, the user must subsequently enter the integer job ID of the job to be terminated.

OUTPUT

The main prompt for user commands is the following:

```
A)dd job  T)erminate job  D)isplay info  Q)uit:
```

If the Add command is selected, the program generates a job ID and displays this number, denoted below by <j>:

```
Job ID: <j>
```

If the Terminate command is given, the following prompt for the job ID is displayed:

```
Job ID:
```

The output for the Display command is as follows, where <n> denotes the total number of jobs in the system, each <j> represents either an enqueued job ID or the word EMPTY, and each <cj> is either the ID of a job currently in memory or the word NONE.

```
No. of jobs in system: <n>
Job queue:    <j> <j> <j>...
Partition 0: Job <cj>
Partition 1: Job <cj>
Partition 2: Job <cj>
```

ERROR-HANDLING

1. The program ignores invalid user commands.

2. Although there is no explicit bound on the size of the job queue, it may

become full. If the user tries to add a new job when the queue is full, the program displays the message "NO ROOM FOR THIS JOB."

3. If the user tries to terminate a job that is not currently in memory, the program displays the message "THIS JOB NOT IN MEMORY."

EXAMPLE

Below is a sample execution of this program with all input in color:

```
A)dd job  T)erminate job  D)isplay info  Q)uit: a
Job ID: 1

A)dd job  T)erminate job  D)isplay info  Q)uit: a
Job ID: 2

A)dd job  T)erminate job  D)isplay info  Q)uit: a
Job ID: 3

A)dd job  T)erminate job  D)isplay info  Q)uit: a
Job ID: 4

A)dd job  T)erminate job  D)isplay info  Q)uit: a
Job ID: 5

A)dd job  T)erminate job  D)isplay info  Q)uit: d

        No. of jobs in system: 5
        Job queue:    4 5
        Partition 0: Job 1
        Partition 1: Job 2
        Partition 2: Job 3

A)dd job  T)erminate job  D)isplay info  Q)uit: t
Job ID: 6
THIS JOB NOT IN MEMORY

A)dd job  T)erminate job  D)isplay info  Q)uit: t
Job ID: 3

A)dd job  T)erminate job  D)isplay info  Q)uit: d

        No. of jobs in system: 4
        Job queue:    5
        Partition 0: Job 1
        Partition 1: Job 2
        Partition 2: Job 4

A)dd job  T)erminate job  D)isplay info  Q)uit: t
Job ID: 1
```

```
A)dd job  T)erminate job  D)isplay info  Q)uit: d

     No. of jobs in system: 3
     Job queue:   EMPTY
     Partition 0: Job 5
     Partition 1: Job 2
     Partition 2: Job 4

A)dd job  T)erminate job  D)isplay info  Q)uit: t
Job ID: 4

A)dd job  T)erminate job  D)isplay info  Q)uit: d

     No. of jobs in system: 2
     Job queue:   EMPTY
     Partition 0: Job 5
     Partition 1: Job 2
     Partition 2: NONE

A)dd job  T)erminate job  D)isplay info  Q)uit: q
```

Step 1: Identify the Objects and Operations

The first step in OOD is to identify important objects and operations, looking at the problem domain for suggestions. Examining the six-part problem specification, we use the nouns-and-verbs technique to get started. Here is a list of nouns and noun phrases drawn from the problem specification:

A job
The memory partitions (3)
The job queue
A job ID
A job to be terminated
The total number of jobs in the system
A user command

For potential operations on objects, we search for significant verbs and verb phrases:

Add a job
Generate a new job ID
Terminate a job
Display job information
Read a user command
Read a job ID from the user

Remember that the nouns-and-verbs technique is only a first cut at the solution. The objects and operations we have listed may differ from those you would have chosen. Also, we may change our minds as we proceed, perhaps adding and deleting objects and operations as we focus in on a solution.

Reviewing the list of objects we have identified, it appears that the first object—a job—is probably not an object in the solution domain. In real life, a job is a computer program to be loaded into memory and executed. Our simulation is not manipulating actual programs; rather, it is manipulating job IDs. Using job IDs to stand for real jobs, the simulation enqueues job IDs in the job queue and pretends to execute a job by associating its ID with a particular memory partition. Therefore, we delete "A job" from our list of objects.

We now construct an object table to summarize the candidate objects and operations. Table 10.5 displays this object table.

Step 2: Place the Objects and Operations

The next step in OOD is to determine where to place the objects in relation to each other. Specifically, we look for has-a (or is-a-part-of) relationships. If certain objects are naturally subobjects of others, it will be easier to decide which objects have primary responsibility for which operations.

Examining the object table, we do not find any has-a relationships among the listed objects. The job queue is not part of the memory partitions, nor are the partitions part of the job queue. The job count is not part of the job queue, and so on. These are all independent objects. Therefore, the AddJob operation, which is listed several times in the object table, is not the primary

Table 10.5 Memory manager object table (Version 1)

Object	Characteristics	Operations
jobQ	FIFO queue of job IDs	AddJob* TerminateJob* DisplayInfo
partition (numbered 0 thru 2)	Each stores the ID of the job currently in that partition (or a value representing "none")	AddJob* TerminateJob* DisplayInfo
jobCount	Total no. of jobs in system	AddJob* TerminateJob* DisplayInfo
jobID	Integer 1, 2, . . .	GenNewID* AddJob*
jobToTerminate	ID of job to be terminated	ReadJobId* TerminateJob
command	A single-letter user command	ReadCommand*

* Denotes an operation that potentially changes the value of the object.

responsibility of just one object. We can perceive of AddJob as a global operation on four equally responsible objects:

AddJob(jobID, jobCount, jobQ, partition)

Similarly, TerminateJob and DisplayInfo are operations on several independent objects.

In contrast, for each operation that is listed only once in the object table, we can assign primary responsibility to the associated object. Also, at this time we should add to the object table any operations needed to initialize the various objects. The result of these observations is the revised object table shown in Table 10.6.

Step 3: Design the Driver

For this problem, the driver has little to do but to input user commands and then call on the objects to carry out the commands. Below is a pseudocode algorithm for the driver. We express operations on objects as function calls with the objects as parameters. As we discussed in the parking lot simulation, these pseudocode function calls do not necessarily translate literally into C++ function calls when we implement the operations.

Top-level algorithm for the memory manager problem

```
InitToEmpty(jobQ)
InitPartitions(partition)
InitJobCount(jobCount)
InitJobID(jobID)
Do
   ReadCommand(command)
   If command == 'A' then
      AddJob(jobID, jobCount, jobQ, partition)
   Else if command == 'T' then
      ReadJobID(jobToTerminate)
      TerminateJob(jobToTerminate, jobQ, partition, jobCount)
   Else if command == 'D' then
      DisplayInfo(jobCount, jobQ, partition)
   Else
      Ignore command
while command != 'Q'
```

Implementing the Design

At this point in the design, all objects and operations are abstract. Now we must decide how to represent the abstract objects and implement the abstract operations.

Table 10.6 Memory manager object table (Version 2)

Object	Characteristics	Operations
jobQ	FIFO queue of job IDs	InitToEmpty*[†] AddJob* TerminateJob* DisplayInfo
partition (numbered 0 thru 2)	Each stores the ID of the job currently in that partition (or a value representing "none")	InitPartitions*[†] AddJob* TerminateJob* DisplayInfo
jobCount	Total no. of jobs in system	InitJobCount*[†] AddJob* TerminateJob* DisplayInfo
jobID	Integer 1, 2, . . .	InitJobID*[†] GenNewID*[†] AddJob*
jobToTerminate	ID of job to be terminated	ReadJobId*[†] TerminateJob
command	A single-letter user command	ReadCommand*[†]

* Denotes an operation that potentially changes the value of the object.
[†] Denotes an operation for which the object to the left has primary responsibility.

Recall that for each abstract object, we can:

1. Use a built-in data type of the programming language.
2. Use an off-the-shelf ADT.
3. Create a new ADT.

Examining the object table, we conclude that the jobCount, jobID, and jobToTerminate objects can all be represented using the built-in `int` type. For jobCount, we implement the InitJobCount operation directly as a C++ declaration with initialization:

```
int jobCount = 0;    // InitJobCount
```

For the jobID object, the InitJobID and GenNewID operations also are straightforward:

```
int jobID = 0;    // InitJobID
    :
jobID++;          // GenNewID
```

The jobToTerminate object has primary responsibility for the ReadJobID operation, which we implement in C++ as a global function:

```
void ReadJobID( /* out */ int& jobToTerminate )
    //.....................................................................
    // POST: jobToTerminate == integer prompted for and input from
    //                         user
    //.....................................................................
{
    cout << "Job ID: ";
    cin >> jobToTerminate;
}
```

For the command object, the built-in char type is appropriate. The following function implements the ReadCommand operation:

```
void ReadCommand( /* out */ char& command )
    //.....................................................................
    // POST: User has been prompted for a single char
    //    && command == uppercase equivalent of that char
    //.....................................................................
{
    cout << "\nA)dd job  T)erminate job  D)isplay info  Q)uit: ";
    cin >> command;
    command = toupper(command);
}
```

Next, the partition object is, according to the object table, not just one object but three—one for each memory partition. Each one holds an integer job ID, so the following array representation is suitable:

```
int partition[3];
```

If jobs 24, 5, and 9 currently occupy partitions 0, 1, and 2, respectively, the contents of the partition array are as follows:

```
partition [0]    [1]    [2]
          24      5      9
```

The object table mentions a special value, "none," to signify a vacant partition. Because valid job IDs are always nonnegative integers, we choose the integer -1 to represent "none":

```
const int NONE = -1;
```

That is, partition[i] = NONE means that partition *i* is currently vacant. Using this representation of "none," we can implement the InitPartitions operation as a C++ array initialization:

```
int partition[3] = {NONE, NONE, NONE};   // InitPartitions
```

(Recall that C++ allows you to initialize an array in its declaration by enclosing the initial values within braces.)

The final object, jobQ, is a FIFO queue. Queues are not built-in types in C++, so we must represent a queue using either an off-the-shelf ADT or a new ADT. Because the jobQ object enqueues integer values, it is an obvious candidate for using the IntQueue class that we developed in Chapter 9. This IntQueue class has a class constructor that initializes a queue to be empty. Therefore, we do not need to implement the abstract operation InitToEmpty; its implementation is the class constructor.

Figure 10.7 shows the complete program for the memory manager problem. In addition to the AddJob, TerminateJob, and DisplayInfo functions, we include an auxiliary routine named LoadJob. Both AddJob and TerminateJob invoke this routine to load a job into a memory partition.

Figure 10.7 Memory
manager program

```
// --------------------------------------------------------------------
// memmgr.cpp
// This program simulates an operating system memory manager.
// Actions are specified by user commands from standard input.
// --------------------------------------------------------------------
#include "uqueue.h"      // For IntQueue class
#include <iostream.h>
#include <ctype.h>        // For toupper()

void ReadCommand( char& );
void AddJob( int&, int&, IntQueue&, int[] );
void LoadJob( int, int[] );
void ReadJobID( int& );
void TerminateJob( int, IntQueue&, int[], int& );
void DisplayInfo( int, IntQueue, const int[] );

const int NONE = -1;

int main()
{
    IntQueue jobQ;
    int       partition[3] = {NONE, NONE, NONE};
    int       jobCount = 0;
    int       jobID = 0;
    int       jobToTerminate;
    char      command;
```

```
    do {
        ReadCommand(command);
        switch (command) {
            case 'A':
                AddJob(jobID, jobCount, jobQ, partition);
                break;
            case 'T':
                ReadJobID(jobToTerminate);
                TerminateJob(jobToTerminate, jobQ, partition,
                             jobCount);
                break;
            case 'D':
                DisplayInfo(jobCount, jobQ, partition);
                break;
            default:
                ;
        }
    } while (command != 'Q');

    return 0;
}

void ReadCommand( /* out */ char& command )
    //..............................................................
    // POST: User has been prompted for a single char
    //    && command == uppercase equivalent of that char
    //..............................................................
{
    cout << "\nA)dd job  T)erminate job  D)isplay info  Q)uit: ";
    cin >> command;
    command = toupper(command);
}
```

```
void AddJob( /* inout */ int&      jobID,
             /* inout */ int&      jobCount,
             /* inout */ IntQueue& jobQ,
             /* inout */ int       partition[] )
    //...............................................................
    // PRE:  All parameters assigned
    // POST: IF jobQ<entry> is full THEN
    //            Error message displayed  &&  All parameters are
    //                                         unchanged
    //        ELSE
    //            jobID == jobID<entry>+1  &&  jobID displayed to
    //                                         user
    //        && (jobCount<entry> < 3 ) --> job loaded into memory
    //        && (jobCount<entry> >= 3 ) --> jobID enqueued in jobQ
    //        && jobCount == jobCount<entry> + 1
    //...............................................................
{
    if (jobQ.IsFull()) {
        cout << "NO ROOM FOR THIS JOB\n";
        return;
    }
    jobID++;
    cout << "Job ID: " << jobID << '\n';
    if (jobCount < 3)
        LoadJob(jobID, partition);
    else
        jobQ.Enqueue(jobID);
    jobCount++;
}

void LoadJob( /* in */    int jobID,
              /* inout */ int partition[] )
    //...............................................................
    // PRE:  All parameters assigned
    //    && For some i, partition[i] == NONE
    // POST: For some i,
    //        partition[i]<entry> == NONE  &&  partition[i] == jobID
    //...............................................................
{
    int i = 0;
    while (i < 3 && partition[i] != NONE)
                        // INV (prior to test):
                        //     Partitions 0 thru i-1 are occupied
                        //  && 0 <= i <= 3
        i++;

    // ASSERT: Partition i is vacant
    partition[i] = jobID;
}
```

```
void ReadJobID( /* out */ int& jobToTerminate )
    //.............................................................
    // POST: jobToTerminate == integer prompted for and input from
    //                         user
    //.............................................................
{
    cout << "Job ID: ";
    cin >> jobToTerminate;
}

void TerminateJob( /* in */     int       jobToTerminate,
                   /* inout */ IntQueue& jobQ,
                   /* inout */ int       partition[],
                   /* inout */ int&      jobCount         )
    //.............................................................
    // PRE:  All parameters assigned
    // POST: IF for some i, partition[i]<entry>==jobToTerminate THEN
    //           jobCount == jobCount<entry> - 1
    //        && IF jobQ<entry> is not empty THEN
    //               Next job in jobQ loaded into memory
    //           ELSE
    //               partition[i] == NONE
    //        ELSE
    //           Error message displayed && All parameters are
    //                                      unchanged
    //.............................................................
{
    int i = 0;
    while (i < 3 && partition[i] != jobToTerminate)
                    // INV (prior to test):
                    //     jobToTerminate is not in
                    //     partition[0..i-1]
                    //  && 0 <= i <= 3
        i++;

    if (i == 3) {
        cout << "THIS JOB NOT IN MEMORY\n";
        return;
    }
    jobCount--;
    partition[i] = NONE;
    if ( !jobQ.IsEmpty() ) {
        int nextJob = jobQ.Front();
        jobQ.Dequeue();
        LoadJob(nextJob, partition);
    }
}
```

```
void DisplayInfo( /* in */ int       jobCount,
                  /* in */ IntQueue  q,
                  /* in */ const int partition[] )
    //.............................................................
    // PRE:  All parameters assigned
    // POST: Contents of jobCount, q, and partition displayed
    //.............................................................
{
    cout << "\n    No. of jobs in system: " << jobCount << '\n';
    cout << "    Job queue:   ";
    if (q.IsEmpty())
        cout << "EMPTY";
    else
        do {
            cout << q.Front() << ' ';
            q.Dequeue();
                // INV: All values prior to q.Front() have been
                //      displayed
        } while ( !q.IsEmpty() );
    cout << '\n';

    int i;
    for (i = 0; i < 3; i++) {
        cout << "    Partition " << i << ": ";
        if (partition[i] == NONE)
            cout << "NONE\n";
        else
            cout << "Job " << partition[i] << '\n';
    }
}
```

The `DisplayInfo` routine demonstrates the importance of copy-constructors in C++ classes that manipulate dynamic data. The importer of an off-the-shelf class like `IntQueue` should not have to depend on its implementation details, such as whether its data representation uses dynamic data or not. When writing a routine such as `DisplayInfo`, the importer expects that parameter passage by value sends to the function a *copy* of the actual queue. The function code is then free to incrementally destroy the (local) queue in order to print it. Without a copy-constructor for the `IntQueue` class (which happens to manipulate dynamic data), the `DisplayInfo` function would, in fact, destroy the caller's job queue by dequeueing the items.

SUMMARY

Object-oriented design is a data-driven design technique. Entities in the problem domain are identified and then modeled by objects within a program. The benefits of object-oriented design include the modular, readable, and maintainable code that results.

Object-oriented design begins with identifying objects and operations. Using object tables derived from the problem specification is a good way to begin the process. The next step is to discover relationships among the objects and to determine which objects are responsible for the operations. Finally, a driver algorithm is designed to coordinate the overall flow of control.

Object-oriented design typically results in layered software. Objects are layered on top of other existing objects or on top of built-in data types of the programming language. ADTs play a vital role in these layers of abstraction.

Object-oriented design and top-down design are both important approaches to problem solving. Each approach has strengths and weaknesses. Good programmers mix the techniques to draw on the strengths of each.

KEY TERMS

abstract object (p. 453)	object-oriented design (OOD) (p. 442)
abstract operation (p. 453)	object table (p. 447)
application domain (p. 444)	operation (p. 445)
contains-a relationship (p. 448)	problem domain (p. 444)
has-a relationship (p. 448)	solution domain (p. 444)
is-a-part-of relationship (p. 449)	subobject (p. 448)
nouns (p. 446)	verbs (p. 446)
object (p. 445)	

EXERCISES

10.1   Although there are many specific techniques for performing object-oriented design, this chapter uses a three-step process. What are these three steps?

10.2   True or False:

   a. Every noun and noun phrase in a problem specification becomes an object in the solution domain.

   b. For a given problem, there are usually more objects in the solution domain than in the problem domain.

   c. If an operation is associated with only one object in an object table, that object should have primary responsibility for the operation.

   d. In the three-step process for performing object-oriented design, all decisions made during each step are final.

10.3   When selecting a data representation for an object, what three choices does the programmer have?

10.4   For each of the following design methods, at what general time (beginning, middle, end) is the driver—the top-level algorithm—designed?

   a. Object-oriented design

   b. Structured (top-down) design

10.5   To see how object-oriented design makes code easier to modify, consider a program that simulates the management of five parking lots. The parking lots are all identical and have the same properties as in the simulation of Figure 10.1. For each user command, the program must prompt the user to specify a particular parking lot.

   a. What would be a good data representation of the five parking lots? (Hint: Which data structure is appropriate for storing homogeneous components and allows random access?)

b. What solution-domain objects and operations are necessary in addition to those of the original parking lot simulation?

c. Give a C++ solution to this problem. (Assume that the specification file for the PkgLotType class is available to your program.)

10.6 Below is a problem specification for a program that maintains a person's charge account balance. Create an object table showing all objects, their characteristics, and operations. Begin by identifying the key nouns and verbs in the problem specification. For this exercise, produce only an initial object table. Do not look for has-a relationships or attempt to determine which objects are responsible for which operations.

TITLE

Charge account program

DESCRIPTION

This program manages a charge account for the owner of a credit card. The program starts with an initial balance of zero. The user is repeatedly prompted to specify one of five options: display current balance due, add a charge, make a payment, add another month's interest (1.5% per month), or terminate the program.

INPUT

Each input option consists of a single lowercase or uppercase letter: 'd' or 'D' to display the current balance due, 'c' or 'C' to add a charge, 'p' or 'P' to make a payment, 'i' or 'I' to add a month's interest, and 'q' or 'Q' to terminate the program. The program translates each lowercase letter into its uppercase equivalent. For the charge and payment options, the user also must enter the amount of the transaction, in cents, as an integer.

OUTPUT

The following main prompt for user options is preceded by a blank line:

```
D)isplay  C)harge  P)ayment  I)nterestCalc  Q)uit:
```

The prompt for the value of a charge or payment is:

```
Amount (in cents):
```

The output for the Display command is as follows, where <b> represents the balance due, including '$' and decimal point:

```
Current balance due = <b>
```

ERROR HANDLING

All input errors yield undefined results.

EXAMPLE

Below is a sample execution with all input in color:

```
D)isplay  C)harge  P)ayment  I)nterestCalc  Q)uit: D
Current balance due = $0.00

D)isplay  C)harge  P)ayment  I)nterestCalc  Q)uit: C
Amount (in cents): 10000

D)isplay  C)harge  P)ayment  I)nterestCalc  Q)uit: D
Current balance due = $100.00

D)isplay  C)harge  P)ayment  I)nterestCalc  Q)uit: I

D)isplay  C)harge  P)ayment  I)nterestCalc  Q)uit: D
Current balance due = $101.50

D)isplay  C)harge  P)ayment  I)nterestCalc  Q)uit: P
Amount (in cents): 5150

D)isplay  C)harge  P)ayment  I)nterestCalc  Q)uit: D
Current balance due = $50.00

D)isplay  C)harge  P)ayment  I)nterestCalc  Q)uit: I

D)isplay  C)harge  P)ayment  I)nterestCalc  Q)uit: D
Current balance due = $50.75

D)isplay  C)harge  P)ayment  I)nterestCalc  Q)uit: Q
```

10.7 For the charge account problem of Exercise 10.6, determine where to place the objects and operations. Look for has-a relationships (if any), and modify the object table with daggers (†) to indicate which objects have primary responsibility for which operations.

10.8 Below is a problem specification for a program that simulates the operation of a vending machine. Create an object table showing all objects, their characteristics, and operations. Begin by identifying the key nouns and verbs in the problem specification. For this exercise, produce only an initial object table. Do not look for has-a relationships or attempt to determine which objects are responsible for which operations.

TITLE

Vending machine

DESCRIPTION

This program simulates the operation of a vending machine that vends three products: coffee, tea, and milk. Their prices per unit are $.35, $.30, and $.45, respectively. The program starts with an empty vending machine. The user is repeatedly prompted to specify one of five options: restock the machine, display prices of the products, display which products are out of stock, vend a product, or terminate the program.

INPUT

Each input option consists of a single lowercase or uppercase letter: 'p' or 'P' to display the prices, 'o' or 'O' to display which products are out of stock, 'r' or 'R' to restock, 'v' or 'V' to vend a product, and 'q' or 'Q' to terminate the program. The program translates each lowercase letter into its uppercase equivalent.

For the Restock option, the user also must enter (as integers) the number of units of coffee, tea, and milk to add.

For the Vend option, the user also must enter the name of the product (lowercase or uppercase 'C', 'T', or 'M' for coffee, tea, or milk) and the dollar amount tendered by the customer (in floating point representation).

OUTPUT

The following main prompt for user options is preceded by a blank line:

```
P)rices  O)utOfStock  R)estock  V)end  Q)uit:
```

The additional prompts for restocking are:

```
Units of coffee:
Units of tea:
Units of milk:
```

The additional prompts for the Vend command are:

```
C)offee  T)ea  or  M)ilk:
Amt. tendered: $
```

The output for the Prices command is as follows, where <pc>, <pt>, and <pm> denote the integer prices of coffee, tea, and milk in cents:

```
Coffee: <pc> Tea: <pt> Milk: <pm>
```

In response to the OutOfStock command, the program displays the names of any products that are out of stock, separated by commas (or the word "None," if all are in stock).

For the Vend command, the program outputs the following, where <change> denotes the customer's change from the amount tendered, using '$' and decimal point:

```
Your change: <change>
```

ERROR HANDLING

1. For the Vend command, the message "PRICE IS <price> CENTS" is displayed if the customer tenders less than the selling price of a product.

2. For the Vend command, the message "OUT OF STOCK" is displayed if the customer attempts to purchase an out-of-stock product.

3. All other input errors produce undefined results.

EXAMPLE

Below is a sample execution with all input in color:

```
P)rices  O)utOfStock  R)estock  V)end  Q)uit: P
Coffee: 35  Tea: 30  Milk: 45

P)rices  O)utOfStock  R)estock  V)end  Q)uit: O
Coffee, Tea, Milk

P)rices  O)utOfStock  R)estock  V)end  Q)uit: R
Units of coffee: 100
Units of tea: 100
Units of milk: 1

P)rices  O)utOfStock  R)estock  V)end  Q)uit: O
None

P)rices  O)utOfStock  R)estock  V)end  Q)uit: V
C)offee  T)ea  or  M)ilk: M
Amt. tendered: $.50
Your change: $.05

P)rices  O)utOfStock  R)estock  V)end  Q)uit: V
C)offee  T)ea  or  M)ilk: M
OUT OF STOCK

P)rices  O)utOfStock  R)estock  V)end  Q)uit: V
C)offee  T)ea  or  M)ilk: T
Amt. tendered: $1.00
our change: $.70

P)rices  O)utOfStock  R)estock  V)end  Q)uit: V
C)offee  T)ea  or M)ilk: C
Amt. tendered: $.25
PRICE IS 35 CENTS

P)rices  O)utOfStock  R)estock  V)end  Q)uit: Q
```

10.9 For the vending machine problem of Exercise 10.8, determine where to place the objects and operations. Look for has-a relationships (if any), and modify the object table with daggers (†) to indicate which objects have primary responsibility for which operations.

PROGRAMMING PROJECTS

10.1 Consider the vending machine problem of Exercise 10.2. Expand the problem as follows:

a. Allow many vending machine objects in one program. Each vending machine has its own prices, beverage supply, and cash supply. The user commands must specify a particular vending machine.

b. Include more comprehensive error checking of user input, including an out-of-cash condition during the Vend operation.

After expanding the design, determine suitable representations for the objects, write the code, and test your resulting program.

10.2 Modify the MemMgr program (Figure 10.7) so that job arrivals and job terminations are simulated by the program, not by interactive user input. The new program will simulate a three-minute time period and will use a random number generator to produce certain values in the simulation.

Each simulated second, a new job arrives in the system and, with a probability of .50, a second job also arrives. For each job, you must keep track of two items:

1. The total time, in seconds, required for the job (generated as a random integer in the range 1...25)

2. The job's start time (the time at which it is loaded into memory for execution)

Each simulated second, your program is to compute the length of the job queue. Every 20 simulated seconds, output the queue and partition information as in the original program. At the conclusion of the three-minute time period, output the following statistics:

1. The total number of jobs that entered the system

2. The average length of the job queue

3. The maximum length of the job queue

The following sequence is recommended at the *start* of each simulated second:

1. Terminate all jobs whose time is up, and load new jobs from the job queue
2. Add newly arrived job(s)
3. Compute the length of the job queue

For this program, the only user input is a single number: the initial seed for the random number generator. Use object-oriented design as you modify the original program. Create an expanded object table, select appropriate data representations for any new objects, and test your resulting program.

10.3 This problem considers an algorithm for calculating the value of an arithmetic expression. The expression is input as a string of characters assumed to represent a valid arithmetic expression. No blanks may appear in the input string.

An operand is a single digit 0...9, and the only operators are +, –, *, and / (the latter signifying integer division). Parentheses are permitted. The value of the expression may be any integer.

For purposes of expression evaluation, the operators * and / have the highest precedence, + and – have lower precedence, and the left parenthesis has the lowest precedence. The following is a complete BNF description (Chapter 6) for input expressions:

$$<expr> ::= <digit>$$
$$| (<expr>)$$
$$| <expr> + <expr>$$
$$| <expr> - <expr>$$
$$| <expr> * <expr>$$
$$| <expr> / <expr>$$
$$<digit> ::= 0 | 1 | 2 | 3 | 4 | 5 | 6 | 7 | 8 | 9$$

The following algorithm evaluates such expressions:

1. Create two empty stacks: an operand stack and an operator stack.
2. Push '(' onto the operator stack.
3. While more input exists, loop on the following:
   a. Input one character.
   b. If the input character is an operand, push its value onto the operand stack. If the input character is '(', push it onto the operator stack. If the input character is ')', pop and perform operations from the operator stack up to the first '(' and pop this '('. If the input character is an operator, then pop and perform operations from the operator stack up to, but not including, an operator on top of the operator stack with precedence less than the input character, and push this input character on the operator stack.
4. Pop and perform operations from the top of the operator stack until the operator stack contains only a single '('. The operand stack will now contain just one value: the value of the entire arithmetic expression.

Note: The phrase "pop and perform the operation from the top of the operator stack" translates as follows:

- Copy the top of the operand stack to `rightOperand`.
- Pop the operand stack.
- Copy the top of the operand stack to `leftOperand`.
- Pop the operand stack.
- Push onto the operand stack the value of the expression

   `leftOperand <operator> rightOperand`

   where <operator> is the one on top of the operator stack.
- Pop the operator stack.

a. Use the noun and verb identification technique to identify the key objects and operations, and create an object table.
b. Determine representations for the objects, write the code, and test the resulting program.

10.4 Using object-oriented design, write and test a program for the following problem.

TITLE

Tree marking

DESCRIPTION

Paul is an apprentice lumberjack. As part of Paul's training, he must spend time marking trees to indicate which ones should be cut. This program simulates one day's marking for Paul.

In one day, Paul typically covers a square region one thousand meters on a side. Paul starts in the northwest corner of the region. He has determined a good method for marking trees: proceed from each tree to the closest tree that is not yet marked. He repeats the process until all trees have been marked.

For this program, the location of each tree is specified by a north-south coordinate and a west-east coordinate. The north-south coordinate is given to the nearest meter, with 0 meaning the north edge and 1000 the south. Similarly, the west-east coordinate is an integer from 0 (westmost) through 1000 (eastmost). The program allows the user to specify tree locations, then outputs the order in which Paul marks the trees and the total distance traveled, to the nearest meter.

INPUT

Program input consists of one or more input lines of tree coordinates. Each line, except the last, specifies a tree location as a pair of integer constants in the range 0. . .1000. The first integer is the north-south coordinate and the second is the west-east coordinate. The last input line contains two consecutive 0s. This is not a tree location; it signifies the end of input.

OUTPUT

Prior to the input of tree coordinates, the following prompt is given:

```
Specify tree coordinates (0 0 for last):
```

After all input is read, the program outputs a blank line, then the following heading:

```
Coordinates of trees in the order marked:
```

The program outputs the coordinates (north-south, then west-east) of each tree in the order the trees were marked. The coordinates for each tree appear on a separate line. After output of all tree locations, the program outputs a blank line and then the following information:

```
Distance traveled: <d> meters
```

where <d> is the total distance Paul traveled to mark the trees, rounded to the nearest integer.

ERROR HANDLING

1. Any invalid tree coordinates are ignored and the message "INVALID TREE LOCATION" is displayed.
2. Extra input is ignored.
3. If the same tree location is input twice, it is taken to mean only a single tree.

EXAMPLE

Below is a sample execution of this program with all input in color:

```
Specify tree coordinates (0 0 for last):
100  0
530  540
100  100
500  500
500  100
0    0

Coordinates of trees in the order marked:
100     0
100    100
500    100
500    500
530    540

Distance traveled: 1050 meters
```

10.5   Using object-oriented design, write and test a program for the following problem.

TITLE

Simple language interpreter

DESCRIPTION

An interpreter is a program written in language L1 that simulates the execution of a program written in language L2. For this problem, you are to write, in C++, an interpreter for any program written in the fictitious NDPL programming language. The NDPL language has five instructions: COPY, INC, WHILENE, ENDWHILE, and END. A single program can have at most one hundred instructions. The last instruction must be an END and it must be the only END instruction in the program.

NDPL programs all use the same 10 integer variables. The names of these variables are *A, B, C, D, E, F, G, H, I,* and *J*. Whenever a program begins to execute, all 10 variables are automatically initialized to 0.

The syntax and semantics of the instructions are described below. No instruction may contain embedded blanks.

Syntax	Semantics
COPY(<d>,<s>)	Copy the value of variable <s> into variable <d>.
INC(<v>)	Increment the value of variable <v> by one.
WHILENE(<m>,<n>)	The beginning of a WHILE loop. The loop condition is that the value of variable <m> not equal the value of variable <n>. The end of the loop body is signaled by an ENDWHILE.
ENDWHILE	The end of the last unterminated loop body. The WHILENE and ENDWHILE instructions must be properly nested.
END	Terminate execution and output all variable values. This must be the last instruction of a program.

The interpreter inputs an NDPL program from the user, simulates its complete execution, and outputs the values of all variables at the end.

INPUT

The user enters from 1 through 100 lines of NDPL code. Each line contains a single instruction as described above. The END instruction is the last line input.

OUTPUT

The following is the prompt for input:

```
Please input an NDPL program of up to 100 lines:
```

After simulated execution of the NDPL program is complete, the interpreter outputs the following table of final values for variables. (Note: <value of x> denotes the integer value of variable x.)

```
Final variable values
--------------------
  A: <value of A>
  B: <value of B>
  .
  .
  .
  J: <value of J>
```

ERROR HANDLING

Any invalid NDPL instruction or invalid nesting of WHILENE loops causes the program to terminate.

EXAMPLE

Below is a sample execution with input in color.

```
Please input an NDPL program of up to 100 lines:
INC(I)
INC(C)
INC(C)
```

```
WHILENE(C,E)
INC(E)
COPY(H,A)
WHILENE(C,H)
INC(H)
INC(J)
ENDWHILE
COPY(G,H)
INC(I)
WHILENE(I,B)
INC(B)
ENDWHILE
ENDWHILE
INC(D)
END

Final variable values
----------------------
  A:  0
  B:  3
  C:  2
  D:  1
  E:  2
  F:  0
  G:  2
  H:  2
  I:  3
  J:  4
```

10.6 Using object-oriented design, write and test a program for the following problem.

TITLE

Election poll analysis

DESCRIPTION

An opinion poll is being conducted to predict the outcome of an election. This poll solicits voting preferences for three contests: for governor, for senator, and for mayor. For each contest a person may specify a preference for the Democratic, Independent, or Republican candidate or may specify no preference at all.

This program inputs the ages and genders of all respondents in addition to their preferences in all three contests. Next, it assists the user in analyzing the information. The user selects an age range and gender (male voters, female voters, or all voters). In response, the program displays the preferences of that segment of the polled individuals. The program repeats this process until the user chooses to quit.

INPUT

The user first enters the respondents' information, one line of input for each respondent. The first three characters on a line correspond to the respondent's preferences for governor, senator, and mayor, respectively. An input of 'D' signifies preference for the Democratic candidate, 'I' for the Independent, 'R' for the Republican, and 'N' for no preference. The fourth character of the line is 'M' for male or 'F' for female. After one or more spaces, the last item on the line is an integer constant denoting the respondent's age. After the final respondent's line, the next line contains a slash (/) in the first column to signify the end of input.

Following this input, the user is repeatedly asked whether more analysis is desired. If the user responds 'N', the program terminates; otherwise, another analysis is performed. For each analysis the user is prompted for the lowest age (integer) and greatest age (integer) for the age range. Then the user is prompted for a gender for the voting sample: female, male, or combined respondents. 'F' specifies female voters; 'M' specifies male voters; anything else specifies male and female voters combined.

OUTPUT

The forms of the various prompts appear below:

Prompt for respondents' data:

```
Please input respondents' data (/ to end):
```

Prompt for continued analysis:

```
Do you wish to analyze data again? (Y or N):
```

Prompt for lowest age:

```
Lowest age of age range:
```

Prompt for greatest age:

```
Greatest age of age range:
```

Prompt for gender:

```
Gender (M, F, or C):
```

Below is the output form for the results, where <d>, <i>, and <r> signify the number of respondents who preferred the Democrat, the Independent, and the Republican, and <n> denotes the number who had no preference:

```
Governor --> DEM: <d>  GOP: <r>  IND: <i>  NOPREF: <n>
Senator ---> DEM: <d>  GOP: <r>  IND: <i>  NOPREF: <n>
Mayor -----> DEM: <d>  GOP: <r>  IND: <i>  NOPREF: <n>
```

ERROR HANDLING

1. The respondents' data items are not checked for validity.

2. Any character other than 'Y' or 'N' for the "continued analysis" prompt is interpreted as 'Y'.

3. Any character other than 'M' or 'F' for the "gender" prompt is interpreted as 'C'.

4. All other invalid input produces undefined results.

EXAMPLE

Below is a sample execution with input in color.

```
Please input respondents' data (/ to end):
DDRM 21
RRRF 35
DINF 42
RRRM 25
DDNF 22
IIIM 45
DDDF 23
RRNM 27
DRDF 36
RDRM 41
DNNF 43
/

Do you wish to analyze data again? (Y or N): Y
Lowest age of age range: 25
Greatest age of age range: 25
Gender (M, F, or C): M

Governor --> DEM:   0  GOP:   1  IND:   0  NOPREF:   0
Senator ---> DEM:   0  GOP:   1  IND:   0  NOPREF:   0
Mayor -----> DEM:   0  GOP:   1  IND:   0  NOPREF:   0

Do you wish to analyze data again? (Y or N): Y
Lowest age of age range: 21
Greatest age of age range: 30
Gender (M, F, or C): C

Governor --> DEM:   3  GOP:   2  IND:   0  NOPREF:   0
Senator ---> DEM:   3  GOP:   2  IND:   0  NOPREF:   0
Mayor -----> DEM:   1  GOP:   2  IND:   0  NOPREF:   2

Do you wish to analyze data again? (Y or N): Y
Lowest age of age range: 41
Greatest age of age range: 60
Gender (M, F, or C): F
```

```
Governor --> DEM:    2  GOP:    0  IND:    0  NOPREF:    0
Senator ---> DEM:    0  GOP:    0  IND:    1  NOPREF:    1
Mayor -----> DEM:    0  GOP:    0  IND:    0  NOPREF:    2

Do you wish to analyze data again? (Y or N): N
```

10.7 Using object-oriented design, write and test a program for the following problem.

TITLE

Pattern matcher

DESCRIPTION

Pattern matching plays an important role in many algorithms. The SNOBOL programming language is built around the string data type and pattern matching operations.

This program applies a pattern to a character string in search of matches. Input to the program consists of pairs of lines. The first line contains the string and the second line, the pattern. A match occurs each time the pattern exactly matches a substring of the string, beginning with the leftmost character. A pattern consists of one or more pattern parts. The pattern matches any substring that matches the concatenation of the pattern parts. The valid pattern parts are listed below.

"<string>" where <string> is any sequence of up to 60 uppercase characters. The quotation marks are required. This pattern part matches only the exact <string>.

<n> where <n> is an integer in the range 0. . .60. This pattern part matches any string that is precisely <n> characters long.

arb This pattern matches any arbitrary string of zero or more characters.

INPUT

Input consists of an arbitrary number of pairs of lines. For each pair, the first line contains a string of from 1 through 60 uppercase letters enclosed in quotation marks. The second line consists of pattern parts separated by single blanks and will not exceed 80 characters in total length.

The user signals end of data by pressing the system's end-of-file keystroke instead of the first line of a pair.

OUTPUT

Prior to each input pair, the following prompt appears on a separate line:

```
Please input string and pattern on two lines:
```

After the input, the program outputs a blank line and then the following, where <m> denotes the number of matches:

```
Matches found: <m>
```

Two blank lines precede the next input prompt.

ERROR HANDLING

All input errors produce undefined results.

EXAMPLE

Below is a sample execution with input in color:

```
Please input string and pattern on two lines:
ABCAXCAMZWC
"A" arb "C"

Matches found: 3

Please input string and pattern on two lines:
XZXTXWXXXX
arb "X" 1 "X"

Matches found: 5

Please input string and pattern on two lines:
ABCDEFGHIJKLABCDEFGHIJKLMNOP
arb 10 "I"

Matches found: 1

Please input string and pattern on two lines:
<EOF>        ←— The system's end-of-file keystrokes
```

CHAPTER 11

Object-Oriented Programming

INTRODUCTION

In Chapter 10 we introduced object-oriented design as the technique of analyzing the problem domain, identifying the major objects and their associated operations, and then expressing the final problem solution in terms of these (and other) objects and operations.

Object-oriented design is a programming methodology, an approach to developing software. Object-oriented design is compatible with programming languages that support separate compilation of program modules and the creation of abstract data types (ADTs). These languages include C, Modula-2, Ada, and certain dialects of Pascal.

Several programming languages have been created specifically to facilitate object-oriented design: C++, Smalltalk, Simula, CLOS, Objective-C, Eiffel, Actor, Object-Pascal, Flavors, and others. These languages are known as **object-oriented programming languages,** and using them for software development is called **object-oriented programming** (abbreviated as **OOP**).

The major concepts of OOP originated as far back as the mid-1960s with a language called Simula. Much of the current terminology of OOP is due to Smalltalk, a language developed in the late 1970s at Xerox's Palo Alto Research Center. In OOP, the term **object** has a very specific meaning: it is a self-contained entity encapsulating data and operations on that data. In other words, an object is an instance of an ADT. More specifically, an object has an internal **state** (maintained by its private data or **instance variables**) and a set of **methods** (public operations), the only means by which the object's state can be inspected or modified by another object. An object-oriented program comprises a collection of objects, communicating with one another by **message passing.** If object A wants object B to perform some task, object A sends a message containing the name of the object (B) and the name of the particular method to execute. B responds by executing this method in its own way, possibly changing its state and sending messages to other objects as well.

These OOP terms have more familiar analogues in C++:

OOP	C++
Object	Class instance or class object
Instance variable	Private data member
Method	Public member function
Message passing	Function calls (to public member functions)

In addition to facilities for creating ADTs, most researchers agree that true OOP languages require two features not usually found in non-OOP languages:

1. *inheritance*

2. *dynamic binding*

The remainder of this chapter defines and explores these two important concepts.

11.1 Inheritance and Derived Classes

In the world at large, relationships among concepts range from very simple to extremely complicated. The relationship between an amoeba and a Beethoven sonata is, as far as we know, nil. But an amoeba and a horse are, in some complicated way, related. Classifying concepts by arranging them into hierarchies often helps to illuminate the similarities and differences among these concepts.

Inheritance Hierarchies

One form of hierarchical organization, an **inheritance hierarchy,** classifies each concept according to the properties that it inherits from the concept immediately above it in the hierarchy. For example, we might classify different kinds of automobiles according to the following hierarchy:

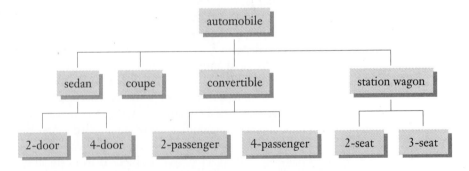

Moving down the hierarchy, each kind of automobile is more specialized than its ancestors and more general than its descendants. A convertible inherits properties common to all automobiles (four wheels, an engine, a body, and so forth) but has additional properties (such as a folding top) that make it more specialized. A two-passenger convertible inherits properties common to all convertibles but also has the more specific property of providing seating for only two people. Though it lacks defining details, this hierarchy diagram presents at a glance the relationships among various kinds of automobiles.

The above automobile hierarchy expresses **single inheritance**—each kind of automobile inherits properties from only one ancestor. Relationships also can exhibit **multiple inheritance**—inheritance from several ancestors. For example, minivans have properties common to both automobiles and trucks:

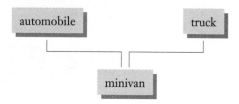

Although multiple inheritance is often useful in organizing and describing relationships, we confine our attention in this chapter to single inheritance.

In OOP languages, **inheritance** is the acquisition, by one programmer-defined class, of all the properties of another class. In these languages, inheritance hierarchies are represented by programmer-defined **class hierarchies.** With suitable mechanisms in the language, the programmer can take an existing class A and create from it a **subclass** (in C++, a **derived class**) named B. A is called a **superclass** (in C++, a **base class**) of B. B then inherits all properties of its superclass. In particular, the data and methods defined for A are now also defined for B. In OOP terminology, class B is related to class A by an **is-a relationship**—every B is also an A. The idea, next, is to specialize class B, perhaps by adding specific properties to those already inherited from A.

Deriving One Class from Another

Consider a simple example in C++. The `Jar2` module of Chapter 3 exports a class named `JarType`. We repeat its specification, without pre- and postconditions, below.

```
class JarType {
public:
    void Add( /* in */ int n );     // Add n units to jar
    int  Quantity() const;          // Return current number of units
    JarType( /* in */ int n );      // Constructor--create jar with n
                                    // units
    JarType();                      // Constructor--create empty jar
private:
    int numUnits;
};
```

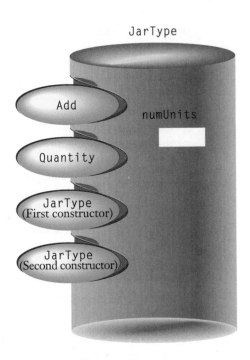

JarType

Figure 11.1 See-through
class interface diagram
for JarType

Figure 11.1 displays the class interface diagram for JarType, made transparent by showing the private class member numUnits.

Suppose that a programmer wants to modify JarType by adding, as private data, a string representing a label on a jar (such as "Cookies" or "Nails") as well as a public operation WriteLabel to output the jar's label. In conventional programming languages, the programmer would have to obtain the source code found in the Jar2 implementation file, analyze in detail how the jar type is implemented, then modify and recompile this source code.

This process has several drawbacks. If Jar2 is an off-the-shelf module on a system, the source code for the implementation is probably unavailable. Even if it is available, modifying it may introduce bugs into a previously debugged solution. Access to the source code also violates a principal benefit of abstraction: users of an abstraction should not need to know how it is implemented.

In C++, as in other OOP languages, there is a far quicker and safer way to add jar-labeling features: derive a new class from JarType and then specialize it. This new class, call it LabeledJar, inherits the members of its base class. The following is the declaration of LabeledJar:

```
class LabeledJar : public JarType {
public:
    void WriteLabel() const;
    LabeledJar( /* in */ const char* jarLabel,    // Constructor
                /* in */ int n                );
    LabeledJar( /* in */ const char* jarLabel );  // Constructor
private:
    char labelString[31];
};
```

The opening line

```
class LabeledJar : public JarType {
```

states that LabeledJar is derived from JarType. The reserved word public declares JarType to be a **public base class** of LabeledJar. This means that all public members of JarType (except constructors and destructors) are also public members of LabeledJar. In other words, JarType's member functions Add and Quantity are also valid for LabeledJar objects. The public part of LabeledJar specializes the base class by adding a new function WriteLabel and declaring its own constructors.

The private part of the LabeledJar declaration declares that a new private member is added: labelString. The private members of LabeledJar are therefore numUnits (inherited from JarType) and labelString. Figure 11.2 depicts the relationship between the LabeledJar and JarType classes.

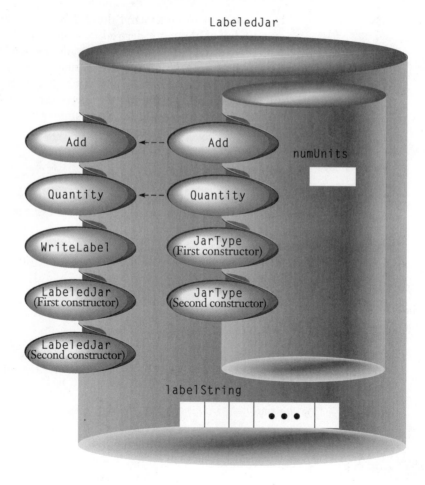

Figure 11.2 See-through class interface diagram for LabeledJar

This diagram shows that a `LabeledJar` object has a `JarType` object as a sub-object. Every `LabeledJar` is a `JarType`, and more. C++ uses the terms base class and derived class instead of superclass and subclass. The terms superclass and subclass can be confusing; the prefix *sub-* usually implies something smaller than the original (for example, subset of a mathematical set). In contrast, a subclass is often "bigger" than its superclass—it has more data and functions.

In Figure 11.2 we have drawn arrows between the ovals labeled `Add` and the ovals labeled `Quantity`. Because `JarType` is a public base class of `LabeledJar`, the public operations of `JarType` (except its constructors) are also public for `LabeledJar`. The arrows between the corresponding ovals indicate this fact. (Notice that `JarType`'s constructors are operations on `JarType`, not on `LabeledJar`. The `LabeledJar` class must have its own constructors.)

Inheritance and Accessibility

It is important to understand the difference in C++ between inheritance and accessibility. Although a derived class inherits the members of its base class, both private and public, it can access only the public members of the base class. Figure 11.2 shows the variable `numUnits` to be encapsulated within the `JarType` class. Neither external client code nor `LabeledJar` member functions can refer to `numUnits` directly. If a derived class were able to access the private members of its base class, any programmer could derive a class from another and then directly inspect or modify the private data.

Specification of `LabeledJar`

Figure 11.3 presents the fully documented specification of the `LabeledJar` class. In the specification file, the preprocessor directive

```
#include "jar2.h"
```

is necessary for the compiler to verify the consistency of the derived class with its base class.

Figure 11.3 LabJar
specification file

```
// -----------------------------------------------------------------
//   SPECIFICATION FILE (labjar.h)
//   This module exports a LabeledJar abstract data type.
//   LabeledJar is derived from the JarType class.
//   JarType is a public base class of LabeledJar, so public
//   operations of JarType are also public operations of LabeledJar.
// -----------------------------------------------------------------
#include "jar2.h"

class LabeledJar : public JarType {
public:
    void WriteLabel() const;
        // POST: Jar label has been output
```

```
      LabeledJar( /* in */ const char* jarLabel,
              /* in */ int n                );
          // Constructor
          // PRE:  Length of jarLabel is at most 30 chars
          //    && n >= 0
          // POST: Jar with n units has been created with label
          //       jarLabel

      LabeledJar( /* in */ const char* jarLabel );
          // Constructor
          // PRE:  Length of jarLabel is at most 30 chars
          // POST: Empty jar has been created with label jarLabel
private:
    char labelString[31];
};
```

With this new class, the programmer can label a jar (via a class constructor), output a jar's label (via the `WriteLabel` function), and add items to a jar or obtain the current number of items in the jar (via the inherited `Add` and `Quantity` functions):

```
#include "labjar.h"
  :

LabeledJar jar1("Nails", 25);
LabeledJar jar2("Bolts");

jar1.Add(3);
jar1.WriteLabel();
cout << ':' << jar1.Quantity() << '\n';
// ASSERT:  Nails:28 has been output

jar2.WriteLabel();
cout << ':' << jar2.Quantity() << '\n';
// ASSERT:  Bolts:0 has been output
  :
```

Implementation of LabeledJar

The implementation of the `LabeledJar` class needs to deal with only the new features that are different from `JarType`. Specifically, the programmer must write code for the `WriteLabel` function and the two constructors.

With derived classes, constructors are subject to special rules. The base class constructor is called implicitly first, before the derived class's constructor is executed. Additionally, if the base class constructor requires parameters, these parameters must be passed by the derived class's constructor. These details are exemplified in the implementation file of Figure 11.4.

```
// ----------------------------------------------------------------
//   IMPLEMENTATION FILE (labjar.cpp)
//   This module exports a LabeledJar abstract data type.
//   JarType is a public base class of LabeledJar.
// ----------------------------------------------------------------
#include "labjar.h"
#include <iostream.h>
#include <string.h>        // For strcpy()

// Additional private members of class:
//      char labelString[31];
//

LabeledJar::LabeledJar( /* in */ const char* jarLabel,
                        /* in */ int n                  ) : JarType(n)
    //..................................................................
    // Constructor
    // PRE:  Length of jarLabel is at most 30 chars
    //    && n >= 0
    // POST: Jar with n units created via call to base class
    //       constructor (passing n to that constructor)
    //    && jarLabel has been copied to labelString
    //..................................................................
{
    strcpy(labelString, jarLabel);
}

LabeledJar::LabeledJar( /* in */ const char* jarLabel )
    //..................................................................
    // Constructor
    // PRE:  Length of jarLabel is at most 30 chars
    // POST: Jar with 0 units created via implicit call to
    //       base class constructor
    //    && jarLabel has been copied to labelString
    //..................................................................
{
    strcpy(labelString, jarLabel);
}

void LabeledJar::WriteLabel() const
    //..................................................................
    // POST: labelString has been output
    //..................................................................
{
    cout << labelString;
}
```

Figure 11.4 LabJar implementation file

In the first constructor in Figure 11.4, notice the syntax by which a constructor passes parameters to its base class constructor:

```
LabeledJar::LabeledJar( /* in */ const char* jarLabel,
                        /* in */ int n                ) : JarType(n)
```

After the parameter list to the LabeledJar constructor, you place a colon and then the name of the base class along with *its* parameter list. We introduced this notation (called a *constructor initializer list*) in Chapter 3 when constructing a class object, one of whose members was itself an object of another class. The order of execution of all these constructors obeys the following rule:

First, the base class constructor is executed. Next, constructors for member objects (if any) are executed. Finally, the body of the derived class's constructor is executed.

Now the programmer can compile the file labjar.cpp into an object file, say, labjar.obj. After writing a test driver and compiling it into test.obj, the programmer can obtain an executable file by linking the three object files

```
test.obj
labjar.obj
jar2.obj
```

and can then test the resulting program.

The remarkable thing about derived classes and inheritance is that modification of the base class is unnecessary. The source code for the implementation of the JarType class may be unavailable. Yet variations of this ADT can continually be created without that source code, in ways the creator never even considered. Through the concept of inheritance, OOP languages facilitate **extensible** data abstractions. A derived class typically extends the base class by including additional private data or public operations or both.

11.2 More About Constructors and Destructors

In the previous section, we said that a base class constructor is implicitly called first, before the derived class constructor is executed. For destructors, the order is just the opposite. The derived class's destructor is executed first, followed by the base class's destructor. More generally, the rule for destructors is as follows:

First, the body of the derived class destructor is executed. Next, destructors for member objects (if any) are executed. Finally, the base class's destructor is executed.

The result is that C++ class objects are constructed inside-out and destroyed outside-in. In other words, all subobjects of an object are created before the rest of the object is created, and destruction occurs in the opposite order. We now look at an example of inheritance involving constructors and destructors.

A Named Stack Class

In Chapter 9, we created a UStack module that exports a class for an un-bounded stack of integers, IntStack. Here is the class declaration without pre- and postconditions:

```
struct NodeType;    // Complete declaration hidden in implementation
                    // file

class IntStack {
public:
    Boolean IsEmpty() const;
    Boolean IsFull() const;
    void    Push( int );
    int     Top() const;
    void    Pop();
    IntStack();                      // Constructor
    IntStack( const IntStack& );     // Copy-constructor
    ~IntStack();                     // Destructor
private:
    NodeType* top;
};
```

The reason we provided a copy-constructor and a destructor is that this class manipulates dynamic data (a linked list) on the free store. The copy-constructor provides deep copying during initialization of one class object by another, and the destructor deallocates data from the free store. (To be thorough, we might also have provided an operator= function to ensure deep copying when using the = operator to copy one stack to another.)

We want to derive a class from IntStack so that each stack stores its own name (as a character string), just as the LabeledJar class in the previous section did. This new class—call it NamedStack—will allow the client to specify a name string in the class constructor and will provide a WriteName function:

```
NamedStack stk1("First stack");

stk1.Push(5);
stk1.Push(-215);
  ⋮
stk1.WriteName();
  ⋮
```

Figure 11.5 contains the declaration of the NamedStack class derived from IntStack.

In Figure 11.5, we declare IntStack to be a public base class of NamedStack. All public operations of IntStack (except constructors and destructors) are also public operations of NamedStack—Push, Pop, Top, and so forth. Figure 11.6 illustrates how a NamedStack object has an IntStack object as a subobject.

```
// ------------------------------------------------------------------
//   SPECIFICATION FILE (namedstk.h)
//   This module exports an ADT for a stack of integer values.
//   The maximum stack depth is MAX_DEPTH, an unspecified value.
//   NamedStack is derived from the IntStack class (in the UStack
//   module).
//   IntStack is a public base class of NamedStack, so public
//   operations of IntStack are also public operations of NamedStack.
// ------------------------------------------------------------------
#include "ustack.h"

// DOMAIN: A NamedStack instance is a collection of integer values
//         along with a character string naming the stack

class NamedStack : public IntStack {
public:
    void WriteName() const;
        // POST: Name of stack has been output

    NamedStack( /* in */ const char* stackName );
        // PRE:  Assigned(stackName)
        // POST: Created(stack)  &&  stack == <>
        //     && Stack's name is stackName

    NamedStack( const NamedStack& otherStk );
        // POST: Created(stack)  &&  stack == otherStk

    ~NamedStack();
        // POST: NOT Created(stack)
private:
    char* stkName;
};
```

Figure 11.5 NamedStk specification file

Observe in the class declaration of Figure 11.5 that the private class member stkName is a pointer variable, not a character array:

```
char* stkname;
```

As we will see in the implementation file, the class constructor allocates the character array on the free store and makes stkName point to the array:

```
NamedStack::NamedStack( /* in */ const char* stackName )
{
    stkName = new char[strlen(stackName) + 1];
    strcpy(stkName, stackName);
}
```

With this technique, a NamedStack object encapsulates a pointer to a dynamically allocated string, whereas a LabeledJar object encapsulates the string itself (see p. 503):

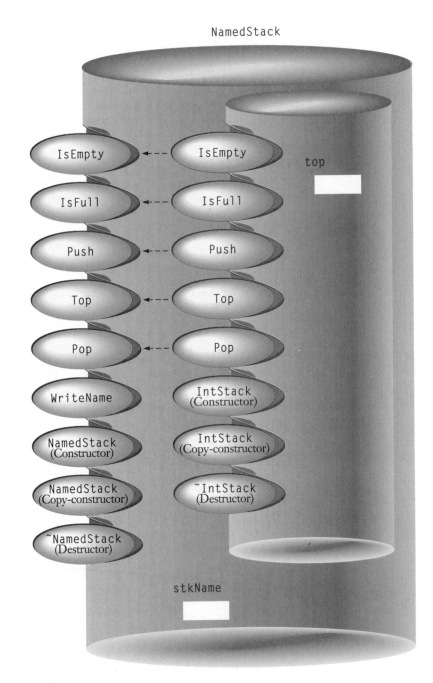

Figure 11.6 See-through class interface diagram for NamedStack

```
class LabeledJar : public JarType {
    ⋮
private:
    char labelString[31];
};
```

Using a fixed-size array for the jar label has the disadvantage of wasting storage for short strings and providing insufficient space for long strings.

Figure 11.7 displays the implementations of the NamedStack member functions. The comments in the code remind the reader that the IntStack subobject of each NamedStack object is constructed first and destroyed last.

Figure 11.7 NamedStk implementation file

```
// --------------------------------------------------------------
//   IMPLEMENTATION FILE (namedstk.cpp)
//   This module exports an ADT for an unbounded stack of integer
//   values.
//   IntStack is a public base class of NamedStack.
// --------------------------------------------------------------
#include "namedstk.h"
#include <iostream.h>
#include <string.h>        // For strcpy()

// Additional private members of class:
//      char* stkName;

NamedStack::NamedStack( /* in */ const char* stackName )
    //.............................................................
    // PRE:  Assigned(stackName)
    // POST: New stack created via implicit call to
    //       base class constructor
    //    && stkName points to duplicate of stackName on free store
    //.............................................................
{
    stkName = new char[strlen(stackName) + 1];
    strcpy(stkName, stackName);
}

NamedStack::NamedStack( const NamedStack& otherStk )
    : IntStack(otherStk)
    //.............................................................
    // POST: New stack created via call to base class copy-
    //       constructor
    //       (Incoming parameter otherStk is passed as a parameter to
    //        base class's copy-constructor)
    //    && stkName points to duplicate of otherStack.stackName
    //       on free store
    //.............................................................
{
    stkName = new char[strlen(otherStk.stkName) + 1];
    strcpy(stkName, otherStk.stkName);
}
```

```
NamedStack::~NamedStack()
    //............................................................
    // POST: stkName string deleted from free store, then stack
    //       destroyed via implicit call to base class destructor
    //............................................................
{
    delete stkName;
}

void NamedStack::WriteName() const
    //............................................................
    // POST: stkName has been output
    //............................................................
{
    cout << stkName;
}
```

When to Supply Constructors and Destructors

With the NamedStack class, it is clear that we must provide constructors and a destructor. We specialized the IntStack class by adding a private class member that points to dynamic data (the character array). The constructors allocate dynamic data, and the destructor deallocates the dynamic data. Notice carefully that the constructors and destructors of NamedStack have different responsibilities from those of IntStack. The constructors and destructors of IntStack create and destroy the linked list representing the stack, whereas the constructors and destructor of NamedStack create and destroy only the *additional* data: the character array representing the name of the stack.

If we derive a class from IntStack that does not create any additional dynamic data, we might ask whether it is necessary to provide constructors and a destructor for this new class. The answer in most cases is no. Consider the following class derived from IntStack:

```
class SillyStack : public IntStack {
public:
    void WriteHello();    // Just print "Hello"
private:
    // No additional private members
};
```

It turns out that the C++ compiler will automatically generate a default (parameterless) constructor, a copy-constructor, an operator= function, and a destructor for the SillyStack class. Each of these "invisible" *generated functions* calls the corresponding function (if it exists) in the base class. Therefore, the declaration

```
SillyStack myStack;
```

calls the generated default constructor for SillyStack, which in turn calls the IntStack default constructor. Similarly, copying and destroying SillyStack objects has the desired effect of copying and destroying the dynamic linked lists pointed to by the IntStack subobjects.

However, in certain circumstances, the C++ compiler is unable to generate functions for a derived class automatically. The rules by which the compiler creates generated functions are very complicated and are beyond the scope of this book. To always be on the safe side, we prefer to design classes according to the following guideline:

If a base class provides constructors, an operator= *function, or a destructor, it is safest for a derived class to provide exactly the same functions (even if the function bodies are empty).*

For example, because IntStack provides a default constructor, a copy-constructor, and a destructor, we prefer to declare the SillyStack class as follows:

```
class SillyStack : public IntStack {
public:
    void WriteHello();                      // Just print "Hello"
    SillyStack();                           // Constructor
    SillyStack( const SillyStack& );        // Copy-constructor
    ~SillyStack();                          // Destructor
private:
    // No additional private members
};
```

The implementations of the constructor, copy-constructor, and destructor are then empty function bodies:

```
SillyStack::SillyStack()
{
    // Nothing to do after base class constructor called
}

SillyStack::SillyStack( const SillyStack& otherStk )
    : IntStack(otherStk)
{
    // Nothing to do after base class copy-constructor called
}

SillyStack::~SillyStack()
{
    // Nothing to do before base class destructor called
}
```

By supplying these three member functions, we ensure that the corresponding member functions of IntStack are always called.

Using the Language

Derived Classes in C++

The concept of inheritance is central to object-oriented programming. In C++, the programmer specifies inheritance by using the mechanism of derived classes. Below are the basic features and rules for using derived classes in C++.

1. A derived class inherits the private and public members of its base class, then specializes the base class. A common specialization is to extend the base class with additional private data, member functions, or both.

2. If a class declaration begins with

```
class DerivedClass : public BaseClass {
```

then `BaseClass` is a public base class of `DerivedClass`. All public members of `BaseClass` (except constructors and destructors) are also public members of `DerivedClass`. That is, clients of `DerivedClass` can invoke `BaseClass` operations on `DerivedClass` objects.

3. If a class declaration omits the word `public` and begins with

```
class DerivedClass : BaseClass {
```

then `BaseClass` is a private base class of `DerivedClass`. Public members of `BaseClass` are *not* public members of `DerivedClass`. Clients of `DerivedClass` cannot invoke `BaseClass` operations on `DerivedClass` objects. Section 11.5 discusses private base classes in detail.

4. Although a derived class inherits the private and public members of its base class, it cannot directly access the inherited private members.

5. If a base class has a constructor, it will be invoked before the derived class's constructor is executed. If the base class constructor requires parameters, the derived class's constructor must pass these parameters using a constructor initializer list.

6. If a base class has a destructor, it will be invoked after the derived class's constructor has executed.

7. If a base class overloads the assignment operator with a member function named `operator=` and a derived class creates dynamic data, the derived class should supply its own version of the `operator=` function to ensure deep copying of the dynamic data it creates.

11.3   Overriding Inherited Member Functions

The purpose of deriving classes is to specialize the base class. The derived class inherits the members of its base class and may add new private variables as well as new member functions. The derived class also may redefine (or **override**) an inherited member function, customizing the function for its own purposes.

Consider a program designed to keep track of supplies in a stationery store. Objects in the problem domain are pens, pencils, rulers, paper pads, and so forth. In the object-oriented style, we can represent these problem domain objects directly as C++ program objects and define an initial class hierarchy:

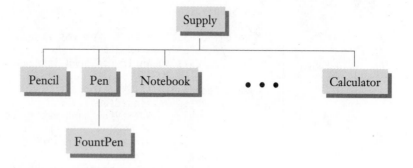

In this hierarchy, pencils, pens, notebooks, and calculators inherit properties common to all supplies but differ from each other in certain ways. Furthermore, fountain pens are pens but have more specialized characteristics.

Let us take the following as properties common to all stationery supplies:

- A verbal description of the item
- A unique stock number
- The current quantity on hand
- The current selling price

The Supply Class

Many operations on a Supply object are possible. For simplicity, we list four:

1. Increase the quantity on hand
2. Decrease the quantity on hand
3. Reprice the item
4. Display the current information (description, stock number, etc.)

Figure 11.8 shows a C++ Supply class whose public interface includes these four operations. The C++ copy-constructor and destructor are necessary because the class will create dynamic data on the free store (the descrip character string).

Figure 11.8 Supply specification file

```
// -------------------------------------------------------------------
//   SPECIFICATION FILE (supply.h)
//   This module exports an ADT for stationery store objects.
// -------------------------------------------------------------------
#ifndef SUPPLY_H
#define SUPPLY_H
```

```
class Supply {
public:
    void Increase( /* in */ int amt );
        // PRE:   Assigned(amt)
        // POST:  Quantity on hand increased by amt

    void Decrease( /* in */ int amt );
        // PRE:   Assigned(amt)
        // POST:  Quantity on hand decreased by amt

    void Reprice( /* in */ float newPrice );
        // PRE:   Assigned(newPrice)
        // POST:  Selling price is newPrice

    void Display() const;
        // POST: Item description, stock no., quantity, and price
        //       have been written to standard output

    Supply( /* in */ const char* description,
            /* in */ int         stockNumber,
            /* in */ int         initQuantity,
            /* in */ float       initPrice   );
        // PRE:  All parameters assigned
        // POST: New object created, with private data initialized
        //       by the input parameters

    Supply( const Supply& otherSupply );
        // POST: New object created, with private data initialized
        //       by otherSupply's private data

    ~Supply();
        // POST: Object destroyed
private:
    char* descrip;
    long  stockNo;
    int   quant;
    float price;
};

#endif
```

If a programmer writes a class from which someone may derive another class, it is good practice to surround the specification file with preprocessor directives such as

```
#ifndef SUPPLY_H
#define SUPPLY_H
    .
    .
    .
#endif
```

Suppose that the programmer neglects to do this. The header file for the derived class, say pen.h, will need to #include the file supply.h. Also, a program that requires both Supply and Pen objects will need the statements

```
#include "supply.h"
#include "pen.h"        ◄─── pen.h also says #include "supply.h"
```

The result—multiple inclusion of supply.h—will produce syntax errors due to multiple identifier declarations. (See Chapter 2 to review using #ifndef for this purpose.)

Although the implementation code for the Supply class is not important to this discussion, we present the constructor and destructor implementations to show how the descrip string is dynamically allocated and deallocated:

```
Supply::Supply( /* in */ const char* description,
                /* in */ int         stockNumber,
                /* in */ int         initQuantity,
                /* in */ float       initPrice   )
{
    descrip = new char[strlen(description) + 1];
    strcpy(descrip, description);
    stockNo = stockNumber;
    quant = initQuantity;
    price = initPrice;
}


Supply::~Supply()
{
    delete descrip;
}
```

We used the same technique in the NamedStack class to allocate a character array of just the right size on the free store.

Client code of the Supply class might consist of statements such as the following:

```
#include "supply.h"
#include <iostream.h>

int main()
{
    Supply clip("Paper clip", 7415, 100, .05);
    Supply ruler("12-in. ruler", 9312, 200, 1.98);
    Supply tray("Paper tray", 1045, 400, .89);

    clip.Display();
    ruler.Display();
    tray.Display();

    clip.Increase(20);
    ruler.Decrease(20);
    tray.Reprice(24.03);
       ⋮
```

To output the information for many objects, it would be convenient to declare an array of type Supply, then use a for loop to perform the output. However, the following code is erroneous:

```
Supply clip("Paper clip", 7415, 100, .05);
Supply ruler("12-in. ruler", 9312, 200, 1.98);
Supply tray("Paper tray", 1045, 400, .89);
    ⋮
Supply item[100];        ⟵── Not allowed

item[0] = clip;
item[1] = ruler;
item[2] = tray;
for (i = 0; i < 3; i++)
    item[i].Display();
```

The offending statement is the declaration of the item vector. Recall from Chapter 3 that if a class has constructors, an array of class objects can be declared only if one of the constructors is the default (parameterless) constructor. The Supply class does not have a default constructor.

One solution is to declare a vector of *pointers* to Supply objects:

```
Supply* item[100];

item[0] = &clip;
item[1] = &ruler;
item[2] = &tray;
for (i = 0; i < 3; i++)
    item[i]->Display();
```

This approach has two advantages. First, it is legal. Second, the vector occupies less memory. It contains 100 pointers instead of 100 class objects with their data members. Notice how the Display function is referenced by using the right arrow instead of dot notation. Each item[i] is a pointer to a class object, not a class object itself.

By declaring item to be a vector of pointers, it is no longer necessary to first create clip, ruler, and tray and then take their addresses. It is more straightforward to use the new operator to create them dynamically and store the resulting addresses into the item vector directly:

```
Supply* item[100];

item[0] = new Supply("Paper clip", 7415, 100, .05);
item[1] = new Supply("12-in. ruler", 9312, 200, 1.98);
item[2] = new Supply("Paper tray", 1045, 400, .89);

for (i = 0; i < 3; i++)
    item[i]->Display();
```

This scheme is very common in C++ programming and eliminates the need to invent distinct object names like clip, ruler, and tray.

Deriving a Pen *Class From* Supply

Next, consider the Pen objects from the stationery supply inheritance hierarchy. Pen objects are specializations of Supply objects, so it is appropriate to derive a new Pen class from the Supply class. Suppose that each Pen requires two additional pieces of information: the pen color and the ink color. A derived class inherits the members of its base class and can specify additional members as well. Thus, normal Supply objects have four private data members but Pen objects will have six. Figure 11.9 shows a specification for the Pen class.

The Pen module exports three items:

1. A Color type, simplified for this example as red, green, blue, and "not applicable"

2. A WriteColor function the client can use to output a color as a character string

3. The Pen class

Figure 11.9 Pen
specification file

```
// -----------------------------------------------------------------
//   SPECIFICATION FILE (pen.h)
//   This module exports a Color type, a WriteColor function, and
//   a Pen class (derived from the Supply class).  Supply is a
//   public base class of Pen, so all public operations of Supply
//   (except constructors and destructors) are also public
//   operations of Pen.
// -----------------------------------------------------------------
#ifndef PEN_H
#define PEN_H

#include "supply.h"

enum Color {red, green, blue, NA};

void WriteColor( Color c );
    // PRE:  Assigned(c)
    // POST: Value of c displayed as a character string

class Pen : public Supply {
public:
    void Display() const;
        // POST: Item description, stock no., quantity, price, pen
        //       color, and ink color have been written to standard
        //       output

    Pen( /* in */ const char* description,
         /* in */ int         stockNumber,
         /* in */ int         initQuantity,
         /* in */ float       initPrice,
         /* in */ Color       penColor,
         /* in */ Color       inkColor    );
        // PRE:  All parameters assigned
        // POST: New object created, with private data
        //       initialized by the input parameters
```

```
    Pen( const Pen& otherPen );
        // POST: New object created, with private data initialized
        //       by otherPen's private data

    ~Pen();
        // POST: Object destroyed
private:
    Color pColor;
    Color iColor;
};

#endif
```

The Pen class adds two private members—the pen color and the ink color—and declares its own constructor, copy-constructor, and destructor. Furthermore, it provides its own version of the Display function. This function overrides the Display function that Pen inherits from the Supply base class.

In C++ terminology, Display is now an overloaded function. With any overloaded function or operator, the compiler deduces by context which particular function to call. If s and p are Supply and Pen objects, respectively, then

s.Display();

outputs four pieces of information, whereas

p.Display();

outputs six.

The Pen implementation file appears in Figure 11.10.

Figure 11.10 Pen implementation file

```
// ------------------------------------------------------------
//   IMPLEMENTATION FILE (pen.cpp)
//   This module exports a Color type, a WriteColor function, and
//   a Pen class (derived from the Supply class).
// ------------------------------------------------------------
#include "pen.h"
#include <iostream.h>

void WriteColor( Color c )
    //.............................................................
    // PRE:  Assigned(c)
    // POST: Value of c displayed as a character string
    //.............................................................
{
    switch (c) {
        case red:   cout << "red";   break;
        case green: cout << "green"; break;
        case blue:  cout << "blue";  break;
        case NA:    cout << "NA";    break;
    }
}
```

```
// Additional private members of Pen class:
//     Color pColor;
//     Color iColor;

Pen::Pen( /* in */ const char* description,
          /* in */ int         stockNumber,
          /* in */ int         initQuantity,
          /* in */ float       initPrice,
          /* in */ Color       penColor,
          /* in */ Color       inkColor    )
    : Supply(description, stockNumber, initQuantity, initPrice)
    //............................................................
    // PRE:  All parameters assigned
    // POST: New object created via implicit call to base class
    //       constructor (passing the 4 required parameters to
    //       that constructor)
    //    && pColor == penColor  &&  iColor == inkColor
    //............................................................
{
    pColor = penColor;
    iColor = inkColor;
}

Pen::Pen( const Pen& otherPen ) : Supply(otherPen)
    //............................................................
    // POST: New object created via implicit call to base class
    //       copy-constructor (passing otherPen as a parameter to
    //       base class's copy-constructor)
    //    && pColor == otherPen.pColor  &&  iColor == otherPen.iColor
    //............................................................
{
    pColor = otherPen.pColor;
    iColor = otherPen.iColor;
}

Pen::~Pen()
    //............................................................
    // POST: Object destroyed via implicit call to
    //       base class destructor
    //............................................................
{
    // Nothing to do before base class destructor called
}
```

```
void Pen::Display() const
    //.................................................
    // POST: After base class's version of Display() invoked,
    //       pen and ink color have been written to standard output
    //.................................................
{
    Supply::Display();
    cout << "    Pen: ";
    WriteColor(pColor);
    cout << "  Ink: ";
    WriteColor(iColor);
    cout << '\n';
}
```

The function name Display is overloaded. There are actually two distinct functions, one a public member of the Supply class, the other a public member of the Pen class. Their full names are Supply::Display and Pen::Display. In Figure 11.10, the Pen::Display function begins by reaching up into its base class and invoking Supply::Display to output descrip, stockNo, quant, and price. Pen::Display cannot access these four variables directly; they are private to the Supply class. The function then finishes by writing Pen's private variables, the pen and ink colors.

Now consider the following test driver:

```
#include "supply.h"
#include "pen.h"
#include <iostream.h>

int main()
{
    Supply* item[100];
    int     i;

    item[0] = new Supply("Paper clip", 7415, 100, .05);
    item[1] = new Supply("12-in. ruler", 9312, 200, 1.98);
    item[2] = new Supply("Paper tray", 1045, 400, .89);
    item[3] = new Pen("Felt pen", 4593, 200, .75, red, blue);

    for (i = 0; i < 4; i++)
        item[i]->Display();

    return 0;
}
```

The assignment

```
item[3] = new Pen("Felt pen", 4593, 200, .75, red, blue);
```

involves two different data types. The left-hand side is of type Supply*, the right-hand side of type Pen*. This mixing of types across the assignment operator is permissible, governed by the following C++ rule:

A pointer to a derived class object may be converted, without a cast operation, to a pointer to an object of its base class.

The converse is not true. Conversion from a pointer to a base class object to a pointer to a derived class object requires a cast operation.

Executing the above test driver, we are likely to be dismayed by the resulting output:

```
Paper clip
      7415      100      0.05
12-in. ruler
      9312      200      1.98
Paper tray
      1045      400      0.89
Felt pen
      4593      200      0.75
```

For the felt pen, only the four basic items of information are displayed, not the additional pen and ink colors. This situation is due to the following C++ rule:

Suppose that a function Func *is overloaded and is not a virtual function (to be discussed later). With an expression* ptr->Func(), *the type of the* pointer—*not the type of the object pointed to—determines which function to invoke.*

In the above test driver, each pointer item[i] is of type Supply*. Therefore, the expression item[i]->Display() invokes Supply::Display for each array element, printing only the four data items that the Supply class knows about.

One remedy, awkward as it is, is to treat item[3] (the pointer to the felt pen) separately:

```
for (i = 0; i < 3; i++)
   item[i]->Display();

Pen* penPtr = (Pen*) item[3];
penPtr->Display();
```

We also could combine the latter two statements into one, if the cryptic notation is not too disturbing:

```
((Pen*) item[3])->Display();
```

In either version, the explicit type cast

```
(Pen*) item[3]
```

is required to convert from type Supply* to Pen*. With this modification, the output is now correct:

```
Paper clip
      7415      100      0.05
12-in. ruler
      9312      200      1.98
Paper tray
      1045      400      0.89
Felt pen
      4593      200      0.75
      Pen: red  Ink: blue
```

Later in this chapter we will see a much better approach to managing an array of objects, some of which are base class objects and some of which are derived class objects.

Deriving a FountPen *Class From* Pen

We now consider another example of deriving a class in the stationery store inheritance hierarchy. In this hierarchy, we saw that a pen has all the properties of a general supply item, plus a pen and ink color. Suppose that a fountain pen has all the properties of a pen, plus an indication of how it is filled—by ink cartridge or by direct fill from an ink bottle. We specialize the Pen class by deriving a FountPen class with one additional data member, the fill type. We also must override the Display function to accommodate this extra data member. Figure 11.11 shows the FountPen specification file.

Figure 11.11 FountPen specification file

```
// ------------------------------------------------------------------
//   SPECIFICATION FILE (fountpen.h)
//   This module exports a FountPen class (derived from the Pen
//   class).
//   Pen is a public base class of FountPen, so all public
//   operations of Pen (except constructors and destructors) are
//   also public operations of FountPen.
// ------------------------------------------------------------------
#ifndef FOUNTPEN_H
#define FOUNTPEN_H
#include "pen.h"

enum FillType {cartridge, directFill};

class FountPen : public Pen {
public:
    void Display() const;
        // POST: Item description, stock no., quantity, price, pen
        //       color, ink color, and fill type have been written
        //       to standard output

    FountPen( /* in */ const char* description,
              /* in */ int         stockNumber,
              /* in */ int         initQuantity,
              /* in */ float       initPrice,
              /* in */ Color       penColor,
              /* in */ Color       inkColor,
              /* in */ FillType    fillType    );
        // PRE:  All parameters assigned
        // POST: New object created, with private data initialized
        //       by the input parameters

    FountPen( const FountPen& otherPen );
        // POST: New object created, with private data initialized
        //       by otherPen's private data
```

```
    ~FountPen();
        // POST: Object destroyed
private:
    FillType fType;
};

#endif
```

This FountPen specification is similar to the Pen specification in the sense that each class adds additional private data to any inherited data, each introduces its own constructors and destructor, and each overrides its inherited Display function. Figure 11.12 contains the corresponding FountPen implementation.

Notice how the Display function first reaches up into its base class to invoke Pen::Display. Recall that Pen::Display also begins by reaching up into *its* base class to invoke Supply::Display.

Figure 11.12 FountPen implementation file

```
// -------------------------------------------------------------------
//   IMPLEMENTATION FILE (fountpen.cpp)
//   This module exports a FountPen class (derived from the Pen
//   class).
// -------------------------------------------------------------------
#include "fountpen.h"
#include <iostream.h>

// Additional private members of FountPen class:
//    FillType fType;

FountPen::FountPen( /* in */ const char* description,
                    /* in */ int         stockNumber,
                    /* in */ int         initQuantity,
                    /* in */ float       initPrice,
                    /* in */ Color       penColor,
                    /* in */ Color       inkColor,
                    /* in */ FillType    fillType     )
    : Pen(description, stockNumber, initQuantity,
          initPrice, penColor, inkColor)
    //................................................................
    // PRE:  All parameters assigned
    // POST: New object created via implicit call to base class
    //       constructor (passing the 6 required parameters to
    //       that constructor)
    //    && fType == fillType
    //................................................................
{
    fType = fillType;
}
```

```
FountPen::FountPen( const FountPen& otherPen ) : Pen(otherPen)
   //.................................................................
   // POST: New object created via implicit call to base class
   //       copy-constructor (passing otherPen as a parameter to
   //       base class's copy-constructor)
   //    && fType == otherPen.fType
   //.................................................................
{
   fType = otherPen.fType;
}

FountPen::~FountPen()
   //.................................................................
   // POST: Object destroyed via implicit call to
   //       base class destructor
   //.................................................................
{
   // Nothing to do before base class destructor called
}

void FountPen::Display() const
   //.................................................................
   // POST: After base class's version of Display() invoked,
   //       fill type has been written to standard output
   //.................................................................
{
   Pen::Display();
   if (fType == cartridge)
      cout << "     Uses cartridges\n";
   else
      cout << "     Direct fill\n";
}
```

Finally, we might write a simple test driver as follows:

```
#include "supply.h"
#include "pen.h"
#include "fountpen.h"
#include <iostream.h>

int main()
{
   Supply* item[100];
   int     i;

   item[0] = new Supply("Paper clip", 7415, 100, .05);
   item[1] = new Supply("12-in. ruler", 9312, 200, 1.98);
   item[2] = new Supply("Paper tray", 1045, 400, .89);
   item[3] = new Pen("Felt pen", 4593, 200, .75, red, blue);
   item[4] = new FountPen("Gold nib pen", 8734, 20, 48.39,
                          green, blue, cartridge);
   item[5] = new FountPen("Desk pen", 8825, 30, 23.39,
                          green, NA, directFill);
   for (i = 0; i < 3; i++)
      item[i]->Display();
```

```
    Pen* penPtr = (Pen*) item[3];
    penPtr->Display();

    FountPen* fPenPtr = (FountPen*) item[4];
    fPenPtr->Display();

    fPenPtr = (FountPen*) item[5];
    fPenPtr->Display();

    return 0;
}
```

This program, when executed, yields the following output:

```
Paper clip
    7415    100     0.05
12-in. ruler
    9312    200     1.98
Paper tray
    1045    400     0.89
Felt pen
    4593    200     0.75
    Pen: red  Ink: blue
Gold nib pen
    8734    20    48.39
    Pen: green  Ink: blue
    Uses cartridges
Desk pen
    8825    30    23.39
    Pen: green  Ink: NA
    Direct fill
```

11.4 Dynamic Binding: C++ Virtual Functions

For reasons we discussed in the last section, the following code does not correctly display the information for all six stationery supply objects:

```
Supply* item[100];
int     i;

item[0] = new Supply("Paper clip", 7415, 100, .05);
item[1] = new Supply("12-in. ruler", 9312, 200, 1.98);
item[2] = new Supply("Paper tray", 1045, 400, .89);
item[3] = new Pen("Felt pen", 4593, 200, .75, red, blue);
item[4] = new FountPen("Gold nib pen", 8734, 20, 48.39,
                        green, blue, cartridge);
item[5] = new FountPen("Desk pen", 8825, 30, 23.39,
                        green, NA, directFill);

for (i = 0; i < 6; i++)
    item[i]->Display();        ◄── Incorrect
```

Display is an overloaded function. The three versions are Supply::Display, Pen::Display, and FountPen::Display. The above code is faulty because the

C++ compiler uses the type of the pointer item[i] to determine which function to call. In the for loop, the base class function Supply::Display is called each time through the loop.

This code demonstrates **static** (compile-time) **binding** of a function to an object. At compile time, the compiler cannot predict what item[i] will point to *at run time*. Thus, it must associate Display with (or "bind Display to") the only type it can see: the Supply type.

Solution 1: Type Casting

Three remedies to the above situation are possible. The first, introduced in the previous section, is to use explicit type casting to convert to the correct pointer types:

```
for (i = 0; i < 3; i++)
    item[i]->Display();

Pen* penPtr = (Pen*) item[3];
penPtr->Display();

FountPen* fPenPtr = (FountPen*) item[4];
fPenPtr->Display();

fPenPtr = (FountPen*) item[5];
fPenPtr->Display();
```

Not only is this solution clumsy, it also requires the programmer to keep track of the correct object type for each item[i]. The latter severely limits the flexibility of the program.

Solution 2: Variant Records

A second solution is to rewrite the original Supply class so the private part is, in effect, a variant record (Chapter 5). This private part would consist of unions of structs for all possible supplies in the stationery store. Also required would be a type field of enumeration type

```
{generalSupply, pen, fountainPen, ... , calculator}
```

to designate which particular variant is in use. Then, in order for a general loop

```
for (i = 0; i < 6; i++)
    item[i]->Display();
```

to be feasible, there must only be one Display function, namely Supply::Display. This function would have to test the type field to know what to print:

```
switch (whichType) {
    case generalSupply:
        // Output the 4 items of info
        break;
    case pen:
        // Output the 6 items of info
        break;
    case fountainPen:
        // Output the 7 items of info
        break;
    ⋮
}
```

This solution contradicts the OOP philosophy that an object is autonomous, that it knows how to manipulate its own data. Each object should know how to display itself, yet the above solution centralizes this operation in one class: the Supply class.

Worse yet, deriving a new class now requires a programmer to rewrite the Supply class. A new variant must be included in the private part, an extra value for the type field must be added, and the switch statement in the Display routine must be expanded to test for this new type. This approach completely defeats the benefit of using derived classes: the ability to create new classes from old *without* modifying the old.

Solution 3: Virtual Functions

The third, and best, solution is to use a **virtual function.** In C++, the reserved word virtual in the declaration of a member function states that the function is expected to be redefined later in classes derived from this one. Suppose we make one small change in the Supply class declaration of Figure 11.8—we make Display a virtual function:

```
class Supply {
public:
    ⋮
    virtual void Display() const;
    ⋮
private:
    ⋮
};
```

With just this one word, virtual, our difficulties disappear entirely. (Note: The Display implementation code in supply.cpp remains unmodified. Also, in the Pen and FountPen classes, the declarations and function bodies of Display remain unchanged. The word virtual appears only in the base class declaration, not in any derived classes.)

Declaring a member function to be `virtual` instructs the compiler to generate code that guarantees **dynamic** (run-time) **binding** of a function to an object. That is, the determination of which function to call is postponed until run time. The complete C++ rule is as follows:

Consider the expression `ptr->Func()`.

If `Func` *is not a virtual function, the* type of the pointer *determines which function to call.*

If `Func` *is a virtual function, the* type of the object pointed to *determines which function to call.*

With `Display` declared as a virtual function in the `Supply` class, the code

```
for (i = 0; i < 6; i++)
    item[i]->Display();
```

now works correctly. Any of `Supply::Display`, `Pen::Display`, or `FountPen::Display` will be invoked, depending on what `item[i]` points to at run time. Deriving a new and unanticipated class presents no complications. If this new class has a `Display` function, the `Supply` class does not need to know about it. Dynamic binding ensures that each object knows how to display itself, and the appropriate version will be invoked. In OOP terminology, `Display` is a **polymorphic function**—it has multiple meanings depending on the type of the object that responds to it at run time.

Deallocating Dynamic Data

Dynamic binding is also an important issue when a program uses the `delete` operator. The test driver at the beginning of this section allocates class objects dynamically and stores their addresses into the `item` vector. In an expanded test driver it may be necessary, at some point, to deallocate the objects in the following fashion:

```
for (i = 0; i < 6; i++)
    delete item[i];
```

Before deallocating a class object from the free store, C++ guarantees that the `delete` operator first invokes the object's destructor. This is sensible, because a class object may point to other large data structures on the free store that must be deallocated by its destructor.

A potential problem with the `delete` operator is this: The default method of binding a destructor to an object is static binding. In the above `for` loop, static binding causes the base class destructor, `~Supply`, to be invoked each time, regardless of the type of the object pointed to. If `item[i]` points to a `Pen` object, the `~Pen` destructor is completely bypassed. In our particular example, no harm results. `Pen`'s destructor happens to be an empty function. In general, though, a derived class's destructor may have important cleanup activities to perform.

This situation is very subtle and is sometimes overlooked by C++ programmers. What is needed is to declare a **virtual destructor** in the base class. In our example, we declare ~Supply to be `virtual`:

```
class Supply {
    ⋮
    virtual ~Supply();
};
```

No other changes are necessary in the implementation of the Supply class or in the specifications and implementations of derived classes. This simple change results in dynamic binding when the delete operator executes. For example, if item[i] points to a FountPen object, the statement

```
delete item[i];
```

first invokes ~FountPen, then ~Pen, and then ~Supply before deallocating the object from the free store.

Using the Language

Virtual Functions in C++

Dynamic binding of functions to objects is a major characteristic of object-oriented programming languages. In C++, virtual functions are the means by which the programmer controls dynamic binding. Below is a summary of the key points and rules for using virtual functions.

1. Virtual functions are only relevant when *addresses* of class objects are involved. The function call

```
somePtr->Func()
```

is potentially ambiguous. The pointer somePtr may point to a base class object or to a derived class object. The following rule resolves this ambiguity:

> If Func *is not a virtual function, the* type of the pointer *determines which function to call—static binding.*
> If Func *is a virtual function, the* type of the object pointed to *determines which function to call—dynamic binding.*

2. Dynamic binding for pointer variables also holds for reference variables. If Display is a virtual function and the following code appears:

```
void RepriceAndDisplay( /* inout */ Supply& oneObj,
                        /* in */    float    newPrice )
{
    oneObj.Reprice(newPrice);
    oneObj.Display();
}
```

then the type of the first actual parameter (Supply, Pen, or FountPen) determines which particular Display function to call.

3. If pointer and reference types are not involved, as in the function call

```
SomeClass someObject;
    ⋮
someObject.Func();
```

it is irrelevant whether Func is virtual or not. There is no ambiguity about which function to call. The compiler knows what class someObject belongs to (namely, SomeClass) and uses the version of Func declared in that class.

4. In the declaration of a function, the word virtual appears only in the base class, not in any derived class.

5. If a base class declares a virtual function, it *must* implement that function even if the body is empty.

6. A derived class is not required to provide its own redefinition of a virtual function. In this case, the base class's version is used by default.

7. A derived class cannot redefine the return type of a virtual function.

Designing with Wisdom   Inheritance and Dynamic Binding

Taken together, inheritance and dynamic binding are two hallmarks of OOP languages that promote the creation of truly reusable software. Practitioners of OOP maintain that "truly reusable" means more than "reusable as is." It means capable of being extended, reshaped, and adapted to a specific application without copying and modifying the original source code.

A useful C++ class with virtual functions can be compiled into object code and placed in a library for others to use. Even if the source code is unavailable, the class will live on. Programmers can use the header file to derive new, more specialized classes and redefine the public functions for their particular applications.

Designing for reuse is usually harder than designing a one-time application. It requires more time and forethought to anticipate future uses of a class. Although inheritance and dynamic binding allow classes to be adapted in unforeseen ways, the class designer still must make some thoughtful decisions:

Might someone want to redefine a certain function when deriving a new class? If so, should I make the function virtual *to permit dynamic binding when pointers and references to objects are used?*

Should I make the destructor virtual, *in case pointers and references to objects are involved?*

Should I provide access functions to the private data, in case client code or derived classes need such access?

> *What if derived classes, but not client code, should have direct access to the private members? (A C++ concept—protected visibility—addresses this issue. Declaring a class member to be* protected, *rather than* private *or* public, *hides this member from client code but allows access by derived classes. The examples in this chapter are not complex enough to require* protected *class members, but you might encounter this feature in other C++ programs.)*

These, and other decisions, require a greater investment of time at the outset. But the payoff is the tremendous reduction in future effort.

11.5 Private Base Classes

In all examples of derived classes thus far, we have used public base classes. The reserved word public in a declaration such as

```
class Pen : public Supply {
    ⋮
```

states that all public members of Supply (except constructors and destructors) are also public members of Pen.

Without the word public, Supply would be a **private base class** of Pen. In this case, the public members of Supply still would be accessible to Pen but not to clients of Pen. In other words, the public members of Supply would be private members of Pen. Although public base classes are far more common in C++ programming, in this section we present an example demonstrating the usefulness of private base classes.

Consider first the relationships among stacks, queues, and sequences. Chapter 9 introduced the sequence as a primitive model of abstraction with associated functions Front, Back, AppendFront, AppendBack, RemoveFront, RemoveBack, and Length. It is convenient to describe stack and queue operations using the language of sequences, so it should not be a surprising perspective to think of stacks and queues as specializations of sequences.

Suppose a programmer has written an IntSeq class for storing sequences of integers. (Programming Project 9.2 of Chapter 9 was such an exercise.) The declaration of this class, abbreviated by omitting the pre- and postconditions, might appear as follows:

```
struct NodeType;   // Complete declaration hidden in implementation
                   // file
```

```
class IntSeq {
public:
    int     Length() const;
    Boolean IsEmpty() const;
    Boolean IsFull() const;
    int     Front() const;
    int     Back() const;
    void    AppendFront( int );
    void    AppendBack( int );
    void    RemoveFront();
    void    RemoveBack();
    IntSeq();                       // Constructor
    IntSeq( const IntSeq& );        // Copy-constructor
    ~IntSeq();                      // Destructor
private:
    NodeType* front;
    NodeType* back;
    int       len;
};
```

Deriving an integer stack class, IntStack, from this class is easy. But there are two reasons why IntSeq should not be a public base class of IntStack. First, AppendBack, RemoveBack, and Back are inappropriate operations on stacks. Second, users of IntStack will prefer the names Push, Pop, and Top to AppendFront, RemoveFront, and Front.

Below is a declaration of IntStack, derived from IntSeq. By omitting the word public, the first line declares IntSeq to be a private base class.

```
class IntStack : IntSeq {
public:
    Boolean IsEmpty() const;
    Boolean IsFull() const;
    void    Push( int );
    int     Top() const;
    void    Pop();
    IntStack();
    IntStack( const IntStack& );
    ~IntStack();
private:
    // No additional private members
};
```

Figure 11.13 shows that the public members of IntSeq are private members of IntStack. There are no arrows leading from the public operations of IntSeq to those of IntStack because no operations of IntSeq are visible to clients of IntStack.

The implementations of IntStack's member functions are very simple. They merely reach up into the base class, IntSeq, and invoke the corresponding member functions. For brevity, the following code omits the pre- and postconditions.

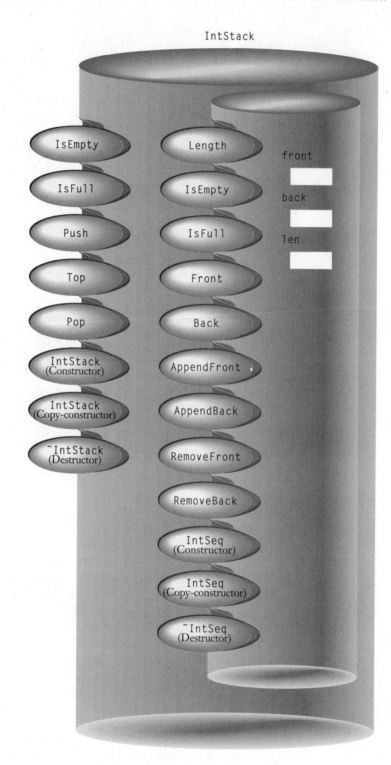

Figure 11.13 See-through class interface diagram for IntStack derived from IntSeq

```
IntStack::IntStack()
{
    // Nothing to do after IntSeq's constructor invoked
}

IntStack::IntStack( const IntStack& otherStk ) : IntSeq(otherStk)
{
    // Nothing to do after IntSeq's copy-constructor invoked
}

IntStack::~IntStack()
{
    // Nothing to do before IntSeq's destructor invoked
}

Boolean IntStack::IsEmpty() const
{
    return IntSeq::IsEmpty();
}

Boolean IntStack::IsFull() const
{
    return IntSeq::IsFull();
}

void IntStack::Push( /* in */ int newItem )
{
    IntSeq::AppendFront(newItem);
}

int IntStack::Top() const
{
    return IntSeq::Front();
}

void IntStack::Pop()
{
    IntSeq::RemoveFront();
}
```

In effect, the IntStack class is a **restricted interface** (sometimes called a **front end**) to the IntSeq class. Certain IntSeq operations are completely hidden from the IntStack client; others are renamed. Private base classes are most often used for this purpose. Deriving an IntQueue class from IntSeq is left as an exercise at the end of the chapter.

This example demonstrates again the power of inheritance. Creating an integer stack class, as a specialization of the IntSeq class, takes only minutes. The programmer does not need to obtain the source code for IntSeq, figure out how the implementation code and data structures work, modify the code to implement a stack, and introduce new bugs during the modification.

Object-oriented programming by deriving new classes from existing classes is sometimes called "programming by specialization." OOP environments often include a **browser,** a program that lets you browse through a library of off-the-shelf classes, selecting those you wish to specialize for your own application and integrating the pieces into a functioning program. The entire process takes a fraction of the time that it would take to program everything from scratch.

A Generic List and an Integer List

As another example of private base classes, consider the notion of a generic list. In a generic list, the components are homogeneous but can be of any data type. All lists—integer lists, character lists, floating point lists—have properties in common. They all permit the client to insert items, delete items, reset the list cursor, advance the list cursor, and so forth. Instead of reprogramming each kind of list from scratch, it makes sense to create a generic list class with all the common properties, then derive specialized classes as in the following class hierarchy:

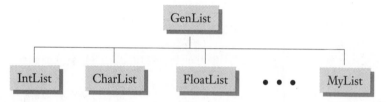

An immediate concern is that certain list operations receive parameters of fixed data types. For example, the operation `InsertBefore` receives, as a parameter, the item to insert into the list. If the data type of this parameter is `char`, it is not correct to pass an `int` to build an integer list. C++ will coerce each `int` value to a `char`. Similarly, if the parameter type is declared to be `int`, it is not possible to build a floating point list. Each `float` value will be coerced to an `int`, truncating the fractional part.

C++ does have a data type that is essentially a generic type: the pointer type `void*`. A `void*` variable can hold a pointer to anything. Using the `void*` type, we can design a generic list as a list of *pointers* to data items rather than a list of data items themselves. Each derived class will then serve as a front end, inserting and retrieving from the list the pointers to actual data items. Figure 11.14 displays the specification file for a `GenList` module.

Figure 11.14 `GenList` specification file

```
// ------------------------------------------------------------------
//   SPECIFICATION FILE (genlist.h)
//   This module exports GenList, a generic list ADT.  Each item in
//   the list is a pointer to an actual data item.
//   It is intended that specialized classes be derived from GenList
//   and that GenList will be a private base class.
// ------------------------------------------------------------------
#ifndef GENLIST_H
#define GENLIST_H
```

```
#include "bool.h"

// DOMAIN: Each list is a collection of pointers, along with an
//         implicit list cursor in the range 1..n+1, where n is
//         the current length of the list

struct NodeType;    // Complete declaration hidden in
                    // implementation file

class GenList {
public:
    Boolean IsEmpty() const;
        // POST: FCTVAL == (list is empty)

    Boolean IsFull() const;
        // POST: FCTVAL == (list is full)

    void Reset();
        // PRE:  NOT IsEmpty()
        // POST: List cursor is at front of list

    Boolean EndOfList() const;
        // POST: FCTVAL == (list cursor is beyond end of list)

    void Advance();
        // PRE:  NOT IsEmpty()  &&  NOT EndOfList()
        // POST: List cursor has advanced to next item

    void* CurrentItem() const;
        // PRE:  NOT IsEmpty()  &&  NOT EndOfList()
        // POST: FCTVAL == item at list cursor

    void InsertBefore( /* in */ void* somePtr );
        // PRE:  Assigned(somePtr)  &&  NOT IsFull()
        // POST: somePtr inserted before list cursor
        //           (at back, if EndOfList())
        //       && This is the new current item

    void InsertAfter( /* in */ void* somePtr );
        // PRE:  Assigned(somePtr)  &&  NOT IsEmpty()
        //    && NOT IsFull()  &&  NOT EndOfList()
        // POST: somePtr inserted after list cursor
        //       && This is the new current item

    void Delete();
        // PRE:  NOT IsEmpty()  &&  NOT EndOfList()
        // POST: Item at list cursor deleted
        //       && Successor of deleted item is now the current item

    GenList();
        // POST: Created(list)  &&  IsEmpty()  &&  EndOfList()

    GenList( const GenList& otherList );
        // POST: Created(list)  &&  list == otherList
        //       && EndOfList()
```

```
        ~GenList();
            // POST: List destroyed
private:
    NodeType* head;
    NodeType* currPtr;
};
#endif
```

In this class, most of the operations are ordinary housekeeping operations for list data structures. Only `InsertBefore`, `InsertAfter`, and `CurrentItem` mention the data type of the items in the list. In these functions, each list item is of type `void*`; that is, a pointer to anything. The `GenList` implementation will simply insert and delete these pointer values as it would any `int` or `char` value, so we do not examine the implementation file here.

Next, we derive a class `IntList` from `GenList`. Its specification file appears in Figure 11.15.

Figure 11.15 `IntList` specification file

```
// ---------------------------------------------------------------
//   SPECIFICATION FILE (intlist.h)
//   This module exports IntList, an ADT for maintaining lists of
//   integers.
//   GenList is a private base class of IntList.
// ---------------------------------------------------------------
#include "bool.h"
#include "genlist.h"

// DOMAIN: Each list is a collection of integer values, along with an
//         implicit list cursor in the range 1..n+1, where n is
//         the current length of the list

class IntList : GenList {
public:
    GenList::IsEmpty;
        // POST: FCTVAL == (list is empty)

    GenList::IsFull;
        // POST: FCTVAL == (list is full)

    GenList::Reset;
        // PRE:  NOT IsEmpty()
        // POST: List cursor is at front of list

    GenList::EndOfList;
        // POST: FCTVAL == (list cursor is beyond end of list)

    GenList::Advance;
        // PRE:  NOT IsEmpty()  &&  NOT EndOfList()
        // POST: List cursor has advanced to next item

    int CurrentItem() const;
        // PRE:  NOT IsEmpty()  &&  NOT EndOfList()
        // POST: FCTVAL == item at list cursor
```

```
    void InsertBefore( /* in */ int someInt );
        // PRE:  Assigned(someInt)  &&  NOT IsFull()
        // POST: someInt inserted before list cursor
        //          (at back, if EndOfList())
        //      && This is the new current item

    void InsertAfter( /* in */ int someInt );
        // PRE:  Assigned(someInt)  &&  NOT IsEmpty()
        //      && NOT IsFull()  &&  NOT EndOfList()
        // POST: someInt inserted after list cursor
        //      && This is the new current item

    void Delete();
        // PRE:  NOT IsEmpty()  &&  NOT EndOfList()
        // POST: Item at list cursor deleted
        //      && Successor of deleted item is now the current item

    IntList();
        // POST: Created(list)  &&  IsEmpty()  &&  EndOfList()

    IntList( const IntList& otherList );
        // POST: Created(list)  &&  list == otherList
        //      && EndOfList()

    ~IntList();
        // POST: List destroyed
private:
    // No additional private members
};
```

Because `GenList` is a private base class of `IntList`, public operations of `GenList` are not public operations of `IntList`. However, we have declared the first five functions using `GenList::` as a prefix. This C++ technique allows us to selectively reopen these base class functions to public access. Instead of reimplementing these functions, we simply reuse the existing implementation code supplied by the `GenList` class. (Note: *To use this technique, you must declare only the names of the functions, not their parameter lists or return value types.*)

The `CurrentItem`, `InsertBefore`, and `InsertAfter` functions differ from their counterparts in the `GenList` class by inserting and returning `int` values instead of pointers. The `IntList` implementation file in Figure 11.16 shows how `IntList` acts as an intermediary between the client, who expects `int` values, and `GenList`, which expects pointer values.

Figure 11.16 `IntList` implementation file

```
// -------------------------------------------------------------------
//   IMPLEMENTATION FILE (intlist.cpp)
//   This module exports IntList, an ADT for maintaining lists of
//   integers.
//   GenList is a private base class of IntList.
// -------------------------------------------------------------------
#include "intlist.h"
```

```
// Additional private members of class:
//      None

IntList::IntList()
    //..........................................................
    // POST: New list created via implicit call
    //       to base class constructor
    //..........................................................
{
    // Nothing to do after base class constructor called
}

IntList::IntList( const IntList& otherList ) : GenList(otherList)
    //..........................................................
    // POST: New list created via call to base class copy-constructor
    //       (Incoming parameter otherList is passed as a parameter
    //        to base class's copy-constructor)
    //..........................................................
{
    // Nothing to do after base class copy-constructor called
}

IntList::~IntList()
    //..........................................................
    // POST: List destroyed via implicit call to base class
    //       destructor
    //..........................................................
{
    // Nothing to do before base class destructor called
}

int IntList::CurrentItem() const
    //..........................................................
    // PRE:  NOT IsEmpty()  &&  NOT EndOfList()
    // POST: FCTVAL == integer pointed to by item at list cursor
    //..........................................................
{
    int* itemPtr = (int*) GenList::CurrentItem();
    return *itemPtr;
}

void IntList::InsertBefore( /* in */ int someInt )
    //..........................................................
    // PRE:  Assigned(someInt)  &&  NOT IsFull()
    // POST: Memory dynamically allocated for a copy of someInt
    //    && Its address has been inserted before list cursor
    //    && This is the new current item
    //..........................................................
{
    int* itemPtr = new int;
    *itemPtr = someInt;
    GenList::InsertBefore(itemPtr);
}
```

```
void IntList::InsertAfter( /* in */ int someInt )
    //........................................................
    // PRE:  Assigned(someInt)  &&  NOT IsEmpty()
    //    && NOT IsFull()  &&  NOT EndOfList()
    // POST: Memory dynamically allocated for a copy of someInt
    //    && Its address has been inserted after list cursor
    //    && This is the new current item
    //........................................................
{
    int* itemPtr = new int;
    *itemPtr = someInt;
    GenList::InsertAfter(itemPtr);
}

void IntList::Delete()
    //........................................................
    // PRE:  NOT IsEmpty()  &&  NOT EndOfList()
    // POST: Integer pointed to by item at list cursor
    //        deleted from free store
    //    && GenList::Delete() invoked
    //........................................................
{
    int* itemPtr = (int*) GenList::CurrentItem();
    delete itemPtr;
    GenList::Delete();
}
```

In this figure, the `InsertBefore`, `InsertAfter`, `CurrentItem`, and `Delete` functions bear close examination. `InsertBefore` receives an `int` value from the client and somehow must send a pointer value to `GenList::InsertBefore`. It does so by allocating a new integer location on the free store, copying the incoming parameter into this free store location, then passing the address of this free store location to `GenList::InsertBefore`. The `InsertAfter` function performs similar actions.

Notice that `InsertBefore` and `InsertAfter` do not need to cast their `int*` values to `void*` values before passing them to the base class:

```
GenList::InsertBefore((void*)itemPtr);        ◄── Unnecessary
```

A pointer to anything can be stored directly into a `void*` pointer. Type coercion does not occur. But going the other way, a `void*` pointer must be explicitly cast into the specific pointer type. The `CurrentItem` function in Figure 11.16 executes the following statements to return an `int` value to the client:

```
int* itemPtr = (int*) GenList::CurrentItem();
return *itemPtr;
```

The first statement casts the value returned by `GenList::CurrentItem` from `void*` to `int*`, then stores this pointer into the local variable `itemPtr`. The second statement then returns the pointed-to integer. We also could write this pair of statements more tersely as

```
return *((int*) GenList::CurrentItem());
```

Finally, the `Delete` function must perform two actions. First, it must deallocate the integer originally put onto the free store by `InsertBefore` or `InsertAfter`. Next, it must invoke `GenList::Delete` to delete the item (the pointer) from the list. We also could write the three statements shown in Figure 11.16 without the local variable `itemPtr`:

```
delete (int*) GenList::CurrentItem();
GenList::Delete();
```

Using the program code in `IntList` as a pattern, we can derive a `CharList` class or a `FloatList` class or any kind of list class in a straightforward way. The hard work, choosing a data representation and implementing the list operations, has already been done by the creator of the `GenList` class. Although deriving a class like `IntList` is a bit tricky because of the subtleties of pointer conversions, it is far less time-consuming than reinventing an entire list ADT.

SUMMARY

The single most important concept in both object-oriented design (OOD) and object-oriented programming (OOP) is encapsulation of data and associated operations via ADTs. Many languages support the creation of ADTs, but true OOP languages also have mechanisms for inheritance and dynamic binding of operations to objects.

Languages that support ADTs but not inheritance and dynamic binding (C, Modula-2, and Ada, for instance) sometimes are called "object-based" but not "object-oriented" languages.

In OOP, an object is an autonomous entity that manipulates its own data (instance variables) via a set of operations (methods). An object receives and responds to messages and may send messages to other objects. In C++, instance variables correspond to private data members, methods correspond to public member functions, and message passing corresponds to invoking member functions.

Inheritance is a vital concept in OOP. The programmer creates class hierarchies whereby a subclass (in C++: derived class) inherits data and operations from its superclass (in C++: base class). The derived class may add new private variables, add new operations, and override operations inherited from the base class. The powerful aspect of inheritance is the ability to tailor an existing class to a specific application without analyzing and modifying the implementation of the base class in any way.

Dynamic binding of member functions to objects allows objects of many different derived types to respond to a single function name, each in its own way. Without dynamic binding, one single, centralized function in the base class would need to test for all known derived classes to determine what to do. The latter solution contradicts a major benefit of inheritance—deriving new classes without modifying the base class. This solution is also incompatible with the philosophy that each object knows how to manipulate itself.

In C++, dynamic binding is achieved through the use of virtual functions and either pointers or references to class objects. With a virtual function, the type of the pointed-to object, not the type of the pointer or reference, determines which version of the function is invoked. Also, virtual destructors provide dynamic binding when the `delete` operator deallocates class objects from the free store. If the base class destructor is not declared `virtual`, the destructors for derived classes may be ignored entirely.

Together, inheritance and dynamic binding have been shown to dramatically reduce the time and effort required to customize existing ADTs. The result is truly reusable, extensible software components whose applications and lifetimes extend beyond those conceived of by the original creator.

KEY TERMS

base class   (p. 493)
browser   (p. 528)
class hierarchy   (p. 493)
derived class   (p. 493)
dynamic binding   (p. 522)
extensibility   (p. 499)
front end   (p. 528)
inheritance   (p. 493)
inheritance hierarchy   (p. 492)
instance variable   (p. 491)
is-a relationship   (p. 493)
message passing   (p. 491)
method   (p. 491)
multiple inheritance   (p. 493)
object   (p. 491)

object-oriented programming (OOP)   (p. 491)
override (an inherited function)   (p. 506)
polymorphic function   (p. 522)
private base class   (p. 525)
public base class   (p. 495)
restricted interface   (p. 528)
single inheritance   (p. 493)
state   (p. 491)
static binding   (p. 520)
subclass   (p. 493)
superclass   (p. 493)
virtual destructor   (p. 523)
virtual function   (p. 521)
void* pointer   (p. 529)

EXERCISES

11.1   Consider the following three class declarations:

```
class Abc {
public:
    void DoThis();
private:
    int alpha;
    int beta;
};

class Def : public Abc {
public:
    void DoThat();
private:
    int gamma;
};

class Ghi : Def {
public:
    void TryIt();
private:
    int delta;
};
```

For *each* class, do the following:

a. List all private data members.

b. List all private data members that the class's member functions can reference directly.

c. List all functions that the class's member functions can invoke.

d. List all member functions that a client of the class may legally invoke.

Exercises 11.2, 11.3, and 11.4 refer to the following declarations. These declarations use the Supply, Pen, and FountPen classes of this chapter.

```
Supply*    sPtr = new Supply("Desk lamp", 2844, 5, 49.95);
Pen*       pPtr = new Pen("Ballpoint", 4594, 30, 1.29, green, red);
FountPen* fpPtr = new FountPen("Executive fountain pen", 8831, 3,
                                  87.50, blue, NA, directFill);
Supply*    ptr1;
Pen*       ptr2;
FountPen* ptr3;
```

11.2 For each part below, tell whether the statement is valid. If not, correct it.

    a. ptr1 = sPtr;

    b. ptr1 = pPtr;

    c. ptr1 = fpPtr;

    d. ptr2 = pPtr;

    e. ptr2 = sPtr;

    f. ptr3 = fpPtr;

    g. ptr3 = pPtr;

11.3 For each part below, tell how many private data items get printed. Assume that Supply has declared Display to be a virtual function.

    a. sPtr->Display();

    b. pPtr->Display();

    c. fpPtr->Display();

    d. ptr1 = fpPtr;
       ptr1->Display();

    e. FountPen basicFPen("Basic fountain pen", 8897, 35, 7.35, blue,
                           blue, cartridge);
       basicFPen.Display();

    f. ptr1 = fpPtr;
       ((FountPen*) ptr1)->Display();

11.4 Repeat Exercise 11.3, assuming that Display is *not* a virtual function.

11.5   Consider the following two class declarations:

```
class Abc {                          class Def : public Abc {
public:                              public:
    void DoThis();                       void DoThat();
    Abc();                               Def();
    ~Abc();                              ~Def();
private:                             private:
    int alpha;                           int gamma;
    int beta;                        };
};
```

Let the implementation of each destructor be as follows:

```
Abc::~Abc()                          Def::~Def()
{                                    {
    cout << "Abc done\n";                cout << "Def done\n";
}                                    }
```

a. What will be the output of the following code?

```
Abc* ptr1 = new Abc;
Abc* ptr2 = new Def;
    .
    .
    .
delete ptr1;
delete ptr2;
```

b. Repeat part (a), assuming Abc's destructor is declared to be virtual:

```
virtual ~Abc();
```

11.6   We want to derive a class NamedStack2 from the NamedStack class (Section 11.2). NamedStack2 includes an additional private member: the current depth of the stack. It also adds a public function, Depth, that returns the current stack depth.

a. NamedStack could be either a public or a private base class of NamedStack2. Which is preferable, and why?

b. Give the class specification.

c. Give the class implementation.

11.7   Derive an IntQueue class from the IntSeq class (Section 11.5). Give its specification and implementation.

11.8   Derive a Pencil class from the Supply class of this chapter. It adds a private data member: a pointer to a string. This string is an advertising name, for companies that distribute personalized pencils. The Pencil class also adds the following member function:

```
void Personalize( const char* newName );
    // PRE:  Assigned(newName)
    // POST: Advertising name (if any) replaced by newName
```

When a Pencil object is constructed, the advertising name member should have the value NULL (the null pointer). Give the specification and implementation of the `Pencil` class.

11.9 Assume that `pencilPtr` points to a `Pencil` object (Exercise 11.8) and is later assigned to a pointer of type `Supply*`:

```
Supply* item[2000];
  :
item[95] = pencilPtr;
```

Then the following statement is invalid:

```
item[95]->Personalize("Barfie's Pizza Palace");
```

a. Why is the statement invalid?

b. Correct it.

<table>
<tr><td>**PROGRAMMING
PROJECTS**</td><td>**11.1**</td><td>By definition, the only accessible item in a stack is the one at the top. A *peepable stack* is one that allows inspection of any item in the stack. The following operation, which retrieves the *i*th stack item, distinguishes a peepable stack from a normal stack:</td></tr>
</table>

```
int Item( /* in */ int i );
    // PRE:  stack == <s1,s2,...,sn>, where n >= 1
    //    && 1 <= i <= n
    // POST: FCTVAL == item si
```

Derive a `PeepStack` class from the `IntStack` class of Section 11.5 (which is, itself, derived from the `IntSeq` class). Test your resulting code.

11.2 Refer to Programming Project 9.7 of Chapter 9. Write a `CharSet` class, using a Boolean vector as the data representation. Make `Insert` a virtual function. Next, derive each of the following classes:

a. a `VowelSet` class

b. a `ConsonantSet` class

c. a `PuncSet` class, for punctuation characters

For each, the `Insert` function will guarantee that if the client attempts to insert an inappropriate character into the set, the program will halt with an error message.

　　Test the resulting code by maintaining pointers to objects of all four classes (including `CharSet`) in either a vector or a list of type `CharSet*`. See what happens if you do not make `Insert` a virtual function.

11.3 a. Implement the `GenList` class (A Study in Design: A Generic List and an Integer List) using a singly- or doubly-linked list of dynamic nodes. You may wish to use the `PersonList` class of Chapter 8 as a model.

b. Use the `IntList` class, derived from `GenList` in Figure 11.15, to test your implementation of part (a).

c. Using `IntList` as a model, derive a `CharList` class from `GenList`. Test your new class.

d. From the `CharList` class of part (c), derive a new class that also includes, as a private member, the current length of the list. Provide a public function that returns the current length of the list to the client. Test your new class.

11.4 Within a program, it is common to collect class objects together into a data structure. Sometimes out of necessity and sometimes for efficiency, this data structure contains pointers to objects instead of the objects themselves.

This chapter showed examples of storing pointers to `Supply`, `Pen`, and `FountPen` objects into an array named `item`. If stationery store objects are frequently inserted and deleted, a list structure is more appropriate than an array.

a. Implement the `GenList` class of A Study in Design in this chapter. See part (a) of Programming Project 11.3 above.

b. Derive a `SupplyList` class from `GenList`. Use this list, instead of the `item` vector, to maintain pointers to stationery store objects. Test the resulting code.

11.5 Consider the `Supply`, `Pen`, and `FountPen` classes of this chapter. When creating new objects, the test drivers in this chapter used constants as parameters to constructors:

```
item[3] = new Pen("Felt pen", 4593, 200, .75, red, blue);
```

A realistic program to monitor a stationery store's inventory would *input* the object's data at run time, then pass these values as parameters to the constructor.

With this approach, it is now the program's responsibility to decide exactly how many data items to input for each kind of object. A general `Supply` object requires four items; a `Pen` object, six; and a `FountPen` object, seven. As more classes are derived, the logic in the driving program must be modified to account for all new derived classes.

A better approach, one more consistent with OOP, is to let each object input its own data. The `Supply` base class should declare a virtual function `ReadData`. Then each derived class can redefine `ReadData` according to how many and what types of data items it needs. In OOP terms, each object knows how to read its own data.

a. Redesign the `Supply` class by providing a virtual `ReadData` function and by adding a default (parameterless) constructor `Supply()`. (Retain the original parameterized constructor. It may still be useful in some cases.) Each derived class will have its own version of `ReadData` and its own default constructor. Test your new classes by supplying data from standard input, either interactively or as redirected from a data file.

b. Now derive a `Pencil` class (Exercise 11.8). Test this as well. Try both the incorrect and correct statements referred to in Exercise 11.9.

11.6 a. Create a generic stack class in the style of `GenList` (A Study in Design). A `GenStack` object will store pointers to data items rather than the data items themselves.

b. Derive an `IntStack` class from `GenStack`. Use the `IntList` class, derived from `GenList`, as a model. Use `IntStack` to test your implementation of part (a).

c. Again using `IntList` as a model, derive a `CharStack` class from `GenStack`. Test your new class.

d. From the CharStack class of part (c), derive a class that also provides a Write operation. This operation outputs the current stack contents. Test this new class.

11.7 Consider the vending machine problem of Chapter 10, Programming Project 10.1. Create a VendMach base class that stocks coffee, tea, and milk.

From VendMach, derive several classes that stock other products as well: candy bars, potato chips, soup, soda, and so forth. Write a test driver that collects pointers to various objects into a vector. Test the member functions.

Note: Be sure to determine which member functions of the VendMach base class should be made virtual. Each object should know how to restock itself, vend its own products, and so on.

11.8 Consider the Dealer module of Chapter 3 of this book. Rewrite the CardDeckType class to include not only the 52 normal cards in a deck but also a Joker.

From your new CardDeckType, derive several classes that represent more specialized card decks: a regular card deck of 52 cards but no Joker, a 500 deck with a Joker but all 2s and 3s removed, and others you might find useful in simulating card games. Write a test driver that collects pointers to various objects into a vector. Test the member functions.

Note: Be sure to determine which member functions of the CardDeckType base class should be made virtual. Each object should know how to shuffle itself, deal its own cards, and so forth.

CHAPTER 12

Algorithm Efficiency, Searching, and Sorting

INTRODUCTION

In a user's eyes, many factors contribute to the quality of a program. First and foremost, the program must be correct. In addition, convenience of the user interface, ease of maintenance, and robustness may all be important. This chapter examines another common concern of users: performance.

Many important problems exceed the capabilities of human inventions. Current supercomputers are capable of executing at speeds measured in gigaflops (one billion floating point operations per second). Yet even these machines are too slow for certain applications such as global weather forecasting.

Code performance is an important issue for problems that push the limits of technology—and for smaller problems as well. And even when performance may not be the programmer's top priority, the customer is always happier with a more efficient solution.

The run-time efficiency of a program has two main ingredients: space and time. **Space efficiency** is a measure of the amount of memory or storage a program requires. Computers have a fixed amount of available storage. If two programs perform identical functions, the one consuming less storage is more space-efficient. Sometimes conservation of storage is the dominant factor in software. However, the concern for space efficiency has diminished in recent years because of rapid decreases in the cost of computer storage hardware.

Time efficiency is a measure of how long a program takes to execute. If two programs correctly satisfy a program specification, the one that executes faster is more time-efficient.

The study of efficiency has developed into a separate field of computer science known as **complexity theory.** The main components of complexity theory are **space complexity,** the study of space issues, and **time complexity,** the study of time issues. Space and time efficiency are the most important aspects of code performance. This chapter concentrates primarily on time efficiency. Even though issues of performance must be addressed, keep in mind the larger perspective: a program's *correctness*, not its speed, is the paramount concern. It is always better to have a slower program that executes correctly than a program that executes incorrectly at lightning speed.

12.1   Big-O Notation

A programmer usually knows many alternative algorithms for accomplishing a particular task, so it is important to identify the major differences among the algorithms. A widely used technique for revealing large differences in efficiency comes from the study of **performance analysis.** Performance analysis applies to both space and time efficiency, though this chapter focuses on the latter.

The performance of an algorithm is measured in terms of some value, usually the amount of data processed. For example, the execution time of Algorithm A may depend largely upon the size, N, of some vector. That is, its execution time is proportional to N. An alternative algorithm, Algorithm B, may require time proportional to N^2. Tripling the size of the vector causes A's execution time to approximately triple, but causes B's time to increase 9-fold. Intuitively, Algorithm B has poorer time efficiency than Algorithm A because its execution time increases at a rate proportional to N^2.

Function Dominance

To define performance more formally, we use **cost functions.** A cost function is a numeric function that gives the performance of an algorithm in terms of one or more variables. (Typically, the variables capture the amount of data being processed by the algorithm.) For example, suppose that a particular program processes an array vSize cells in length. Suppose also that the cost function for the execution time of this program is

$$\text{ActualTime(vSize)} = \text{vSize}^2 + 5*\text{vSize} + 100$$

According to this cost function, the computing time for the program when given an array consisting of a single cell is ActualTime(1) = 106 time units. Similarly, the execution time of the program for an array of length 100 is ActualTime(100) = 10,600 time units. (For this discussion, the particular time units used by the cost function are not important.)

Ideally, it would be possible to capture the execution time of any algorithm in terms of simple cost functions like the preceding ActualTime function. However, in reality such cost functions are often impossible to derive and are too complicated to be truly instructional. Because of this difficulty in using actual cost functions, computer scientists generally use functions that *approximate* the actual cost.

To examine ways of approximating a cost function, we begin with the mathematical notion of **dominance.** Given two cost functions f and g, g is said to *dominate* f if there is some positive constant c such that

$$c * g(x) \geq f(x)$$

for all possible values of x.

Performance analysis uses a variation of dominance known as **asymptotic dominance.** A function g asymptotically dominates another function f if there are positive constants c and x_0 such that

$$c * g(x) \geq f(x) \text{ for all } x \geq x_0$$

In other words, g asymptotically dominates f if g dominates f for all "large" values of x. Computer scientists regularly refer to asymptotic dominance simply as "dominance." Informally, an asymptotically dominant function can be thought of as underestimating the actual cost only for small amounts of data.

For example, suppose that the following function is being considered as a possible estimate for the earlier ActualTime function:

$$\text{TimeEst(vSize)} = 1.1\text{*vSize}^2$$

Figure 12.1 shows why TimeEst is a reasonable estimate. This figure graphs the ActualTime and TimeEst functions for various values of vSize. For small values of vSize, both ActualTime and TimeEst increase in value (grow) at about the same rate. For values of vSize up to about 60, TimeEst(vSize) is less than ActualTime(vSize). When vSize > 60, TimeEst grows at a faster rate than ActualTime. TimeEst thus dominates ActualTime asymptotically. That is, for large variable values (vSize > 60), the value of TimeEst(vSize) always exceeds the value of ActualTime(vSize).

Many other functions can be shown to dominate ActualTime. A few of them are

$$\text{TimeEst1(vSize)} = 1.01\text{*vSize}^2$$
$$\text{TimeEst2(vSize)} = 1.5\text{*vSize}^2$$
$$\text{TimeEst3(vSize)} = 2\text{*vSize}^2$$
$$\text{TimeEst4(vSize)} = \text{vSize}^3$$

Among these functions it can be demonstrated that TimeEst4 dominates TimeEst3, TimeEst3 dominates TimeEst2, TimeEst2 dominates TimeEst, TimeEst dominates TimeEst1, and TimeEst1 dominates ActualTime.

Estimating Functions

The most desirable estimating function for ActualTime is a function that has three characteristics:

1. It asymptotically dominates the ActualTime function.
2. It is simple to express and understand.
3. It is as close an estimate as possible.

Function value

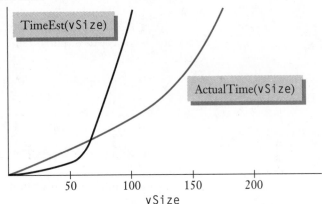

Figure 12.1 Graph of TimeEst(vSize) dominating ActualTime(vSize) asymptotically

Given the function

$$\text{ActualTime}(vSize) = vSize^2 + 5*vSize + 100$$

the following function is a good estimate of ActualTime:

$$\text{EstimateOfActualTime}(vSize) = vSize^2$$

First, EstimateOfActualTime asymptotically dominates ActualTime. Any constant c greater than 1 satisfies

$$c * vSize^2 \geq vSize^2 + 5*vSize + 100$$

for large values of vSize. Second, $vSize^2$ is simpler to express than other dominating functions we have mentioned: $1.01*vSize^2$, $1.5*vSize^2$, $2*vSize^2$. Third, the function $vSize^3$ would also satisfy the first two properties but is not as close an estimate as $vSize^2$.

To express time estimates more concisely, mathematicians and computer scientists use a concept called the **order of a function.** The order of a function f is defined as follows:

Given two nonnegative functions f *and* g, the order of f is g *if and only if* g *asymptotically dominates* f.

There are two other ways of saying "the order of f is g":

1. "f is of order g"
2. "$f = O(g)$"

The second of these is an example of **big-O notation** (or big-oh notation). The uppercase letter O stands for "Order."

At first, big-O notation may be very confusing. The statement $f = O(g)$ seems to say that the order of g is f, when in fact it means that the order of f is g. Also, with big-O notation you should think of the "=" symbol as meaning "is" rather than "equals." The best way to pronounce $f = O(g)$ is to say "f is of order g."

Applying big-O notation to our ActualTime and EstimateOfActualTime functions, we substitute ActualTime for f and EstimateOfActualTime for g to obtain

$$\text{ActualTime(vSize)} = O(\text{EstimateOfActualTime(vSize)})$$

or

$$\text{vSize}^2 + 5*\text{vSize} + 100 = O(\text{vSize}^2)$$

It is best to pronounce the last expression as "$\text{vSize}^2 + 5*\text{vSize} + 100$ is of order vSize^2."

Referring to an algorithm's running time (execution time), if we write

$$\text{ActualTime(vSize)} = O(\text{vSize}^2)$$

then it is appropriate to say that the running time "is of order vSize^2" or "is proportional to vSize^2." Also, we say that the associated algorithm "has running time $O(\text{vSize}^2)$" or that the algorithm "is an $O(\text{vSize}^2)$ algorithm."

It is important to emphasize that big-O notation expresses the *relative* speed of an algorithm, not its absolute speed. An $O(N)$ algorithm increases its running time roughly in proportion to increasing values of N. Similarly, an $O(N^2)$ algorithm increases its running time roughly in proportion to the square of N. But the precise running time cannot be determined from a big-O measure. Two algorithms that are both $O(N)$ may very well have different absolute execution times for the same value of N.

Big-O Arithmetic

To help in calculating and comparing big-O estimates, there are three important rules. Figure 12.2 summarizes these rules.

According to the first rule in Figure 12.2, constant multipliers do not affect a big-O measure. For example, $O(2*N) = O(N)$, $O(1.5*N) = O(N)$, and $O(2371*N) = O(N)$.

Let f and g be functions and k a constant. Then:

1. $O(k * f) = O(f)$
2. $O(f * g) = O(f) * O(g)$
   and
   $O(f / g) = O(f) / O(g)$
3. $O(f) \geq O(g)$ if and only if f dominates g.
4. $O(f + g) = \text{Max}[O(f), O(g)]$,
   where Max denotes the larger of the two

Figure 12.2 Rules for big-O arithmetic

Let X and Y denote variables and let a, b, n, and m denote constants. Then:

X^X	dominates	$X!$	(X factorial)
$X!$	dominates	a^X	
a^X	dominates	b^X	if $a > b$
a^X	dominates	X^n	if $a > 1$
X^n	dominates	X^m	if $n > m$
X	dominates	$\log_a X$	if $a > 1$
$\log_a X$	dominates	$\log_b X$	if $b > a > 1$
$\log_a X$	dominates	1	if $a > 1$

Any term with a single variable X neither dominates nor is dominated by a term with the single independent variable Y.

Figure 12.3 Examples of function dominance

The second rule states that the order of the product of two functions is equal to the order of the first times the order of the second. For example,

$$O((17*N)*N) = O(17*N)*O(N) = O(N)*O(N) = O(N*N) = O(N^2)$$

By the third and fourth rules in Figure 12.2, the order of the sum of functions is the order of the dominant function. For example,

$$O(N^5+N^2+N) = \text{Max}[O(N^5), O(N^2), O(N)]$$
$$= O(N^5)$$

To apply the fourth rule, it is essential to know which functions dominate others. Figure 12.3 displays several estimating functions that are common in computer science algorithms. The functions are listed from most dominant to least dominant.

We can use the rules from Figure 12.2 and the information from Figure 12.3 to determine estimating functions. For example, if

$$f(N) = 3*N^4 + 17*N^3 + 13*N + 175$$

then the order of f is

$$\text{Max}[O(3*N^4), O(17*N^3), O(13*N), O(175)] = \text{Max}[O(N^4), O(N^3), O(N), O(1)]$$
$$= O(N^4)$$

because N^4 is the dominant function. Therefore, we can say that

$$f(N) = O(N^4)$$

Below are several additional examples. For each function, its big-O order appears on the right. All identifiers are variables.

Function	Order
$53*employeeCount^2$	$O(employeeCount^2)$
$65*ordersProcessed^3 + 26*ordersProcessed$	$O(ordersProcessed^3)$
$headCount^6 + 3*headCount^5 + 5*headCount^2 + 7$	$O(headCount^6)$
$75 + 993*numberToSearch$	$O(numberToSearch)$

$4*size*(\log_2 size) + 15*size$	$O(size*\log_2 size)$
$5*count^4 + 2*3^{count} + 85$	$O(3^{count})$
7642	$O(1)$
$2*employees^2 + 3*employees + 4*managers + 6$	$O(employees^2 + managers)$

Categories of Running Time

Algorithms with running time $O(1)$ are said to take **constant time** or sometimes are referred to as **constant algorithms.** Such algorithms are very efficient and are almost always the preferred alternative. Any algorithm whose execution time never varies with the amount of the data is a constant algorithm.

Most algorithms in computer programs execute in **polynomial time,** expressed as $O(N^a)$ for some variable N (usually the number of data items processed) and some constant $a > 0$. Speeds of polynomial algorithms vary greatly. Running times $O(N)$, $O(N^2)$, and $O(N^3)$ are referred to as **linear time, quadratic time,** and **cubic time,** respectively.

Some algorithms execute in **logarithmic time.** An algorithm with running time $O(\log_a N)$ for some variable N and constant $a > 1$ will be faster than an $O(N)$ algorithm if N is large enough. Often the base of the logarithm is omitted when specifying a big-O measure. That is, $O(\log_a N)$ is often written simply as $O(\log N)$.

Algorithms of higher order than polynomial are said to be **exponential algorithms.** Exponential algorithms require time proportional to some function a^N, where N is a variable and a is a constant. Exponential algorithms are considered impractical for large values of N. Table 12.1 displays growth rates for several different estimating functions.

Table 12.2 further emphasizes the importance of big-O measures. The first column of the table displays estimating functions of various algorithms exe-

Table 12.1 Growth rates for selected functions

N	$\log_2 N$	$N*\log_2 N$	N^2	N^3	2^N	3^N
1	0	0	1	1	2	3
2	1	2	4	8	4	9
4	2	8	16	64	16	81
8	3	24	64	512	256	6,561
16	4	64	256	4,096	65,536	43,046,721
32	5	160	1,024	32,768	4,294,967,296	.
64	6	384	4,096	262,144	(Note 1)	.
128	7	896	16,384	2,097,152	(Note 2)	.
256	8	2,048	65,536	16,777,216	?????????????	

Note 1: The value here is approximately the number of machine instructions executed by a 1 gigaflop supercomputer in 5000 years.

Note 2: The value here is about 500 billion times the age of the universe in nanoseconds (billionths of a second), assuming a universe age of 20 billion years.

Table 12.2 Effect of increased computer speed

Algorithm time estimating function	Number of data collections processed on a computer 1000 times faster
N	1000.00
$N*\log_2 N$	140.22
N^2	31.62
N^3	10.00
2^N	9.97
3^N	6.29
4^N	4.98

cuted on a particular computer. Each algorithm processes one complete collection of data in a certain amount of time. The second column lists the number of complete collections that could be processed in the same length of time by a computer 1000 times faster than the existing one.

Table 12.2 shows that a linear algorithm, when executed on a machine 1000 times faster, can process 1000 times as much data. For an algorithm of order $N*\log N$, the increase in processing capability is only about 140 times. The quadratic algorithm improves by a factor of approximately 32; the cubic algorithm, by a factor of 10.

The last three rows of Table 12.2 point out the impracticality of exponential algorithms. Even when the speed of a computer improves 1000 times, the best exponential algorithm from this table processes less than 10 times as much data. Increasing the hardware speed has little effect upon the speed of exponential algorithms.

12.2 Control Structures and Run-Time Performance

A programmer needs to be able to inspect an algorithm and estimate its running time. Information about run-time performance can be drawn from control structures. Table 12.3 lists specific control structures and their corresponding big-O measures.

Table 12.3 Big-O measures of various control structures

Control structure	Running time
Single assignment statement	O(1)
Simple expression	O(1)
The sequence <statement1> <statement2>	The maximum of O(*S1*) and O(*S2*)
if (<condition>)	The maximum of O(*S1*), O(*S2*), and O(*Cond*)

Table 12.3 Big-O measures of various control structures (continued)

Control structure	Running time
<statement1> else <statement2>	(This is a worst case)
for (i=1; i<=N; i++) <statement1>	$O(N * S1)$

Note: In this table, *S1* denotes the running time of <statement1>, *S2* denotes the running time of <statement2>, and *Cond* denotes the running time for evaluating <condition>.

An algorithm without loops or recursion is not very "interesting." According to Table 12.3, such an algorithm requires constant time, O(1). Without recursion or repetition, all control structures reduce to selections among O(1) instructions. The result is therefore a constant time algorithm.

Determining the efficiency of an algorithm depends primarily on identifying loops and recursions that repeat a varying number of times. For example, the following algorithm processes every vector element exactly once:

```
for (i = 0; i < vSize; i++) { // INV (prior to test):
                              //    All vec[0..i-1] have been
                              //    processed
    // Perform some simple task on element vec[i]
    // Assume this task requires constant time
}
```

This loop requires time O(vSize), because the loop body executes vSize times and the body's computing time is O(1).

Any other loop where the number of repetitions depends solely on vSize in this way would also have running time O(vSize). The initial value of the loop control variable—here, zero—could be any other constant value without altering the big-O measure of this loop. Likewise, the kind of loop (for, while, do-while, or recursive repetition) is unimportant in determining big-O performance.

Quadratic running time occurs when one loop is nested within another and both loops depend upon the same variable. Processing each element of a square (*n*-row by *n*-column) matrix is a simple example of a quadratic algorithm:

```
for (row = 0; row < n; row++)  // INV (prior to test):
                               //    matrix[0..row-1][0..n-1]
                               //    have been processed
    for (col = 0; col < n; col++) { // INV (prior to test):
                                    //    matrix[row][0..col-1]
                                    //    have been processed
        // Perform some simple task on element matrix[row][col]
        // Assume this task requires constant time
    }
```

The running time of this algorithm is O(n^2).

Table 12.4 Forms of repetition and corresponding big-O measures

Algorithm form	Running time
Algorithm without loop or recursion	O(1)—Constant time

```
for (i=a; i<=b; i++) {                      O(1)
     // Loop body requiring
     // constant time
}
```

```
for (i=a; i<=N; i++) {                      O(N)—Linear time
        // Loop body requiring
        // constant time
}
```

```
for (i=a; i<=N; i++)                        O(N²)—Quadratic time
     for (j=b; j<=N; j++) {
           // Loop body requiring
           // constant time
}
```

```
for (i=a; i<=N; i++) {                      O(N*M)
     // Loop body requiring
     // time O(M)
}
```

Note: The lowercase letters *a* and *b* denote constants, and *N* and *M* denote variables.

Table 12.4 summarizes various forms of repetition and their corresponding big-O measures. For uniformity, we express all repetition with `for` loops.

Table 12.4 illustrates how nested repetition is the primary determinant of efficiency. Most of the execution time in an algorithm is spent within deeply nested loops. We will return to this issue in the next section.

12.3 Analyzing Run-Time Performance of an Algorithm

We now use the techniques from the last section to analyze a program. The `PythagoreanTriples` program, shown in Figure 12.4, outputs Pythagorean triples—three integers *a*, *b*, and *c* such that $a^2 + b^2 = c^2$. These represent the lengths of the sides of a right triangle. Examples of Pythagorean triples are (3, 4, 5) and (5, 12, 13). The program prompts the user to input the maximum length of a side.

Figure 12.4
PythagoreanTriples
program

```
// ------------------------------------------------------------------
//  pythag.cpp
//  This program prints all Pythagorean triples up through some user-
//  specified value.  All output triples are in increasing order.
// ------------------------------------------------------------------
#include <iostream.h>
```

```
int main()
{
    int maxLen;
    int small;
    int next;
    int last;

    cout << "Max. side length: ";
    cin >> maxLen;
    small = 1;
    while (small <= maxLen) {
                    // INV (prior to test):
                    //    All triples in the range
                    //       (1..small-1, 1..maxLen, 1..maxLen)
                    //    have been output  &&  small<=maxLen+1
        next = small;
        while (next <= maxLen) {
                        // INV (prior to test):
                        //    All triples in the range
                        //        (small, 1..next-1, 1..maxLen)
                        //    have been output  &&  next<=maxLen+1
            last = next;
            while (last <= maxLen) {
                            // INV (prior to test):
                            //    All triples in the range
                            //       (small, next, 1..last-1)
                            //    have been output
                            // && last<=maxLen+1
                if (last*last == small*small + next*next)
                    cout << small << ", " << next << ", "
                         << last << '\n';
                last++;
            }
            next++;
        }
        small++;
    }
    return 0;
}
```

For this problem there are other, more efficient algorithms, but we present this one for its simplicity. We also use while instead of for loops to give a more exhaustive demonstration of algorithm analysis.

Figure 12.5 displays the PythagoreanTriples algorithm with all comments removed and with nested code sections identified by the labels A through M.

Performance analysis can proceed either bottom-up (from inner control structures to outer) or top-down (from outer control structures to inner). We begin a bottom-up analysis of PythagoreanTriples by examining Section H:

H {cout << small << ", " << next << ", " << last << '\n';

Time for H = time to perform one output instruction
           = O(1)

```
    ⎧      ⎧  cout << "Max. side length: ";
   A⎨  cin >> maxLen;
    ⎩  small = 1;

          ⎧  while (small <= maxLen) {
       B ⎨     next = small;
          ⎩
                 ⎧  while (next <= maxLen) {
              C ⎨     last = next;
                 ⎩
                       ⎧  while (last <= maxLen) {
                    F ⎨     if (last*last == small*small + next*next)
   D⎨ E⎨ G⎨ I⎨       H ⎨        cout << small << ", " << next << ", "
                       ⎩              << last << '\n';

                    J ⎨     last++;
                       ⎩  }

              K ⎨     next++;
                 ⎩  }

       L ⎨     small++;
          ⎩  }

   M ⎨  return 0;
    ⎩
```

Figure 12.5
PythagoreanTriples
algorithm

Next, we determine the running time of F as shown below. The notation Max[*a*, *b*] denotes the maximum of *a* and *b*.

```
    ⎧ if (last*last == small*small + next*next)
  F ⎨    // Section H: O(1)
    ⎩
```

Time for F = Max[time to compute if condition, time for H]
= Max[O(1), O(1)]
= O(1)

The running time of the innermost loop, I, is determined as follows:

```
    ⎧ while (last <= maxLen) {
    ⎨    // Section F: O(1)
  I ⎨    // Section J:  O(1)
    ⎨
    ⎩ }
```

Time for I = O(maxLen) * Max[time for F, time for J]
= O(maxLen) * O(1)
= O(maxLen)

We examine next the time for the middle loop:

$$G \begin{cases} \texttt{while (next <= maxLen) \{} \\ \quad \text{// Section C: O(1)} \\ \quad \text{// Section I: O(maxLen)} \\ \quad \text{// Section K: O(1)} \\ \texttt{\}} \end{cases}$$

Time for G = O(maxLen) * Max[time for C, time for I, time for K]
= O(maxLen) * O(maxLen)
= O(maxLen^2)

The outer loop, E, is next:

$$E \begin{cases} \texttt{while (small <= maxLen) \{} \\ \quad \text{// Section B: O(1)} \\ \quad \text{// Section G: O(maxLen}^2\text{)} \\ \quad \text{// Section L: O(1)} \\ \texttt{\}} \end{cases}$$

Time for E = O(maxLen) * Max[time for B, time for G, time for L]
= O(maxLen) * O(maxLen^2)
= O(maxLen^3)

Finally, the running time of the entire algorithm unfolds as follows:

$$D \begin{cases} \text{// Section A: O(1)} \\ \text{// Section E: O(maxLen}^3\text{)} \\ \text{// Section M: O(1)} \end{cases}$$

Time for D = Max[time for A, time for E, time for M]
= O(maxLen^3)

The PythagoreanTriples algorithm therefore has cubic running time.

We could also produce the same result by analyzing the code from the top down. Figure 12.6 summarizes a top-down analysis.

Figure 12.6 Top-down determination of PythagoreanTriples running time

Running time of D
= Max[time for A,
time for E,
time for M]

= Max[O(1),
    O(maxLen)*Max[time for B, time for G, time for L],
    O(1)]

= Max[O(1),
    O(maxLen)*Max[O(1), time for G, O(1)],
    O(1)]

= Max[O(1),
    O(maxLen)*Max[O(1),
        O(maxLen)*Max[time for C, time for I, time for K],
        O(1)],
    O(1)]

= Max[O(1),
    O(maxLen)*Max[O(1),
        O(maxLen)*Max[O(1),
            O(maxLen)*Max[time for F, time for J],
            O(1)],
        O(1)],
    O(1)]

= Max[O(1),
    O(maxLen)*Max[O(1),
        O(maxLen)*Max[O(1),
            O(maxLen)*Max[O(1), O(1)],
            O(1)],
        O(1)],
    O(1)]

= Max[O(1),
    O(maxLen)*Max[O(1),
        O(maxLen)*Max[O(1),
            O(maxLen)*O(1),
            O(1)],
        O(1)],
    O(1)]

= Max[O(1),
    O(maxLen)*Max[O(1),
        O(maxLen^2),
        O(1)],
    O(1)]

= Max[O(1),
    O(maxLen^3),
    O(1)]

= O(maxLen^3)

Note: Max[a, b] denotes the maximum of a and b.

Designing with Wisdom **Code Efficiency Depends on Innermost Loops**

Empirical testing has shown that a typical program spends 90 percent of its entire execution in repetition of only 10 percent of the code. Performance analysis points out precisely where this 10 percent often lies—the innermost loops. This repetition may take the form of nested loops or nested recursion.

A programmer can use this information to improve code efficiency in two ways. First, try to reduce the levels of nested repetition if at all possible. Second, concentrate on reducing the number of instructions executed in the innermost loops. If 90 percent of all execution time occurs in the innermost loops, then a 30 percent gain in these small sections of code yields a 27 percent ($.90 \times .30$) overall improvement.

12.4 Searching Algorithms

Searching a vector for some specific value is one of the most frequently used computer algorithms. In this section we discuss two searching algorithms and compare them in terms of efficiency.

Each algorithm implements the abstract specification shown in Figure 12.7. The Lookup function accepts an integer vector, the size of that vector, and a particular value to search for (the **search key**). If Lookup finds the key in the vector, it returns the location of the key (as an array index) and reports success through the Boolean flag named found. If Lookup cannot find the key, it returns with found equal to FALSE.

(In the postcondition, recall that the right arrow "- ->" means "implies.")

Linear Search

The most straightforward implementation of Lookup is a standard **linear search** algorithm, such as the one in Figure 12.8. A linear search probes the elements of vec in order, one after the other, until it finds the key or reaches the end of the vector. The running time of a linear search is linear—in this case, O(vSize).

```
void Lookup( /* in */   const int vec[],
             /* in */   int       vSize,
             /* in */   int       key,
             /* out */  Boolean&  found,
             /* out */  int&      loc   );

    // PRE:  vSize >= 0  &&  Assigned(vec[0..vSize-1])
    //    && Assigned(key)
    // POST: (found) --> vec[loc] == key
    //    && (NOT found) --> No vec[0..vSize-1] == key
    //                       && loc is undefined
```

Figure 12.7 Specification of Lookup function

```
//  Algorithm: a linear search

void Lookup( /* in */  const int vec[],
             /* in */  int       vSize,
             /* in */  int       key,
             /* out */ Boolean&  found,
             /* out */ int&      loc   )

    // PRE:  vSize >= 0  &&  Assigned(vec[0..vSize-1])
    //    && Assigned(key)
    // POST: (found) --> vec[loc] == key
    //    && (NOT found) --> No vec[0..vSize-1] == key
    //                    && loc is undefined
{
    loc = 0;
    while (loc < vSize && vec[loc] != key)
                                    // INV (prior to test):
                                    //     vec[0..loc-1] != key
                                    //  && loc <= vSize

        loc++;
    found = (loc < vSize);
}
```

Figure 12.8 Linear search implementation of Lookup

Binary Search

If a vector is already in sorted order, a **binary search** is a more efficient algorithm for searching the vector. As an illustration of this technique, assume that each sheet in a ream of paper has a single number on top and that these numbered sheets are sorted top to bottom in increasing order. A linear search would proceed through the ream from top to bottom until the search key is either found or bypassed.

A binary search splits the ream approximately in half and examines the number on the middle sheet. If this number is greater than the search key, the entire bottom half of the ream can be eliminated from consideration. All these values must be greater than the search key. If the value of the middle sheet is less than the search key, it is not necessary to consider the top half of the ream. In other words, the examination of a single value, the middle one, eliminates half of all remaining sheets without probing them. This process of splitting the remaining sheets in half is repeated, over and over, until the value is found.

Figure 12.9 contains a binary search implementation of Lookup.

Figure 12.9 Binary search implementation of Lookup

```
//  Algorithm: a binary search
//
//  Note: The precondition differs from the linear search version.
//        vec must already be sorted into ascending order, and
//        there is a limit on vSize: half the maximum int value.
```

```
void Lookup( /* in */  const int vec[],
             /* in */   int       vSize,
             /* in */   int       key,
             /* out */  Boolean&  found,
             /* out */  int&      loc  )

    // PRE:  0 <= vSize <= (maximum int)/2  &&  Assigned(key)
    //    && vec[0..vSize-1] are in ascending order
    // POST: (found) --> vec[loc] == key
    //    && (NOT found) --> No vec[0..vSize-1] == key
    //                   && loc is undefined
{
    int lowerIndex = 0;
    int upperIndex = vSize - 1;

    loc = upperIndex / 2;
    while (lowerIndex <= upperIndex && vec[loc] != key) {
                    // INV (prior to test):
                    //    If key is in vec[0..vSize-1] then
                    //    key is in vec[lowerIndex..upperIndex]
        if (key > vec[loc])
            lowerIndex = loc + 1;
        else
            upperIndex = loc - 1;
        loc = (upperIndex + lowerIndex) / 2;
    }
    found = (lowerIndex <= upperIndex);
}
```

The binary search algorithm uses three index variables: lowerIndex, upperIndex, and loc. For each iteration of the loop, only the elements vec[lowerIndex] through vec[upperIndex] remain to be probed. The statement

```
loc = (upperIndex + lowerIndex) / 2;
```

makes loc the midpoint of this range. If vec[loc] = key, the loop terminates immediately. The loop also terminates when lowerIndex is greater than upperIndex, indicating that key is not in the vector.

The calculation of upperIndex + lowerIndex explains why the algorithm precondition restricts vSize to half the maximum int value. If key happens to reside in the last element of the vector, the sum of upperIndex and lowerIndex is approximately 2 * vSize.

Figure 12.10 shows a sample trace of the execution of this algorithm. In this trace, the values of lowerIndex, upperIndex, and loc are pictured as lines drawn to the corresponding array indices.

Analyzing the performance of a binary search reduces to analyzing its loop, because all other portions of the algorithm are O(1). This loop is not like the loops we have examined previously, because the number of executions is not a multiple of vSize. One way to study efficiency is to examine an algorithm for particular values. The binary search depends upon vSize, so we should

Assume that the search key key = 24 and the vector size vSize = 8

Conditions just prior to first loop iteration:

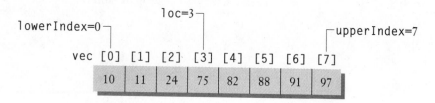

Conditions just after first loop iteration:

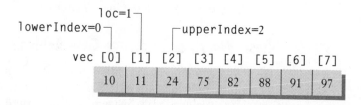

Conditions just after second loop iteration:

loc=2
lowerIndex=2 ⌐⌐upperIndex=2

vec [0] [1] [2] [3] [4] [5] [6] [7]

| 10 | 11 | 24 | 75 | 82 | 88 | 91 | 97 |

Figure 12.10 Trace of binary search

observe its behavior for different values of vSize. If vSize is 1, the while loop executes only once. If vSize is 2 or 3, the loop executes at most twice. Extending these observations leads to the values in Table 12.5.

This table suggests that 2 raised to the maximum number of loop iterations is approximately the value of the vector size, vSize. More precisely, this relationship is

$$\text{Largest vSize to ensure no more than } N \text{ loop iterations} = 2^N - 1$$

Table 12.5 Maximum loop iterations in a binary search of vectors of various sizes

Vector size	Maximum number of loop iterations
1	1
3	2
7	3

(continued...)

Table 12.5 Maximum loop iterations in a binary search of vectors of various sizes (continued)

Vector size	Maximum number of loop iterations
15	4
31	5
63	6
127	7
255	8

This behavior means that the number of loop iterations grows in direct proportion to the logarithm, base 2, of vSize. Therefore, the running time of the loop (hence, the complete binary search) is $O(\log_2 vSize)$.

12.5 Best, Worst, and Average Case Analysis

Most algorithms perform differently in different situations. A single analysis of running time may not be sufficient to capture these differences. One way to consider an algorithm's behavior is to examine its performance separately in the best possible conditions, the worst possible conditions, and conditions that lie somewhere in between.

Best Case Analysis

A **best case analysis** studies the performance of an algorithm under ideal conditions. For example, the best possible situation for both linear and binary search is to find the search key in a single probe. Therefore, we say that their best case performance is $O(1)$.

Worst Case Analysis

A best case analysis can be useful in some instances, but a **worst case analysis** is usually more informative. A worst case analysis examines the behavior of an algorithm under the worst possible conditions. Both binary search and linear search are at their worst when the search key is not in the vector at all. In this situation, a linear search makes $O(vSize)$ probes and a binary search makes $O(\log_2 vSize)$ probes.

The worst case analysis reveals a substantial contrast in efficiency between the linear search and the binary search. In the worst case, the linear search requires 1000 probes to search a vector of 1000 elements, but the binary search requires only 11 probes. The contrast is even more glaring for larger values of vSize. When vSize is 1,000,000, a linear search requires 1,000,000 probes; a binary search needs only 21. Such a dramatic difference confirms the practicality of algorithm analysis and clarifies the distinction between linear and logarithmic algorithms.

Average Case Analysis

A third type of analysis is known as **average case analysis.** An average case analysis computes the average of the individual running times of an algorithm over all possible initial arrangements of the data. To analyze the linear search, we are interested in all possible locations where the search key might be found. If the key is in the first vector position, the total count of the number of probes is one. If the key is in the second position of the vector, the probe count is two. If the key is in the last position, the probe count is vSize. If we run the algorithm once for each possible location of the search key, the average probe count is the sum of the probe counts divided by the number of runs we made:

$$\frac{(1 + 2 + \cdots + vSize)}{vSize}$$

By a well-known mathematical equality for integers, the numerator of this expression equals

$$\frac{vSize*(vSize + 1)}{2}$$

Therefore, the average probe count is

$$\frac{\left(\dfrac{vSize*(vSize + 1)}{2}\right)}{vSize} = \frac{vSize + 1}{2} = O(vSize)$$

The linear search thus has worst case and average case running times O(vSize).

For a binary search, the average case is more difficult to analyze. A proof by mathematical induction, which we do not present here, shows that the average case running time for a binary search is $O(\log_2 vSize)$.

We can improve slightly upon the earlier binary search algorithm by exploiting the knowledge that its average case and worst case performances are both $O(\log_2 vSize)$. Figure 12.11 contains a better version of the binary search algorithm.

The major difference between this binary search and the earlier version (Figure 12.9) is that the loop condition no longer tests for key being equal to the value probed. The previous binary search terminates when vec[loc] equals key. The improved binary search does not terminate until the region to be searched is reduced to a single element (that is, when lowerIndex equals upperIndex). This loop termination condition causes the big-O measures of the worst case, best case, and average case to be identical for the improved version. All are $O(\log_2 vSize)$.

Figure 12.11 A better binary search implementation of Lookup

```
//   Algorithm: an improved version of the binary search
//
//   Note: The precondition differs from the linear search version.
//         vec must already be sorted into ascending order, and
//         there is a limit on vSize: half the maximum int value.
```

```
void Lookup( /* in */   const int vec[],
             /* in */   int       vSize,
             /* in */   int       key,
             /* out */  Boolean&  found,
             /* out */  int&      loc   )

    // PRE:  0 <= vSize <= (maximum int)/2  &&  Assigned(key)
    //    && vec[0..vSize-1] are in ascending order
    // POST: (found) --> vec[loc] == key
    //    && (NOT found) --> No vec[0..vSize-1] == key
    //                    && loc is undefined
{
    int lowerIndex = 0;
    int upperIndex = vSize - 1;

    while (lowerIndex < upperIndex) {
                        // INV (prior to test):
                        //     If key is in vec[0..vSize-1] then
                        //     key is in vec[lowerIndex..upperIndex]
        loc = (upperIndex + lowerIndex) / 2;
        if (key > vec[loc])
            lowerIndex = loc + 1;
        else
            upperIndex = loc;
    }
    loc = lowerIndex;
    found = (vSize > 0 && vec[loc] == key);
}
```

The improved version, by refusing to stop when the key is found, would seem to be less efficient than the original. However, the advantage is the reduction in the amount of work performed during each loop iteration. In the first binary search, each loop iteration required

1. a test to ensure that lowerIndex ≤ upperIndex

2. a test to ensure that key ≠ vec[loc]

3. a comparison for key > vec[loc]

4. assignment of a new value to either lowerIndex or upperIndex

5. assignment of a new value to loc

The improved version eliminates one test (item 2) for each loop iteration. This improvement does not affect the algorithm's big-O measure; it is still $O(\log_2 vSize)$. But it reduces the absolute, measurable execution time of the algorithm.

Improved efficiency often has a price. The price paid for using either binary search in place of the linear search is the precondition that the vector be sorted. If a programmer wishes to search an unsorted vector, the time required to sort the vector may not be justified.

12.6 Searching with Hash Tables

We have seen that, on the average, a linear search of N data values requires $O(N)$ probes. For large values of N, the binary search yields a dramatic improvement with its $O(\log N)$ performance. We might go on to ask if it is possible to perform a search in constant time, $O(1)$. Restated, is it possible to find an algorithm where the number of probes is independent of the number of items to be searched? The answer to this question is a qualified yes.

In certain very specific cases, constant time searching algorithms exist. One example is the `DigitSet` abstraction we examined in Chapter 9, where each member of a digit set is a decimal digit in the range 0 through 9. One concrete data representation of a digit set is a Boolean vector:

```
Boolean isInSet[10];
```

If the digits 0, 4, and 7 are currently in the set, the vector conceptually looks like the following:

isInSet[0]	TRUE
[1]	FALSE
[2]	FALSE
[3]	FALSE
[4]	TRUE
[5]	FALSE
[6]	FALSE
[7]	TRUE
[8]	FALSE
[9]	FALSE

To check whether, say, the digit 6 is in the set requires exactly one probe. The expression

```
isInSet[6]
```

has the value TRUE or FALSE, and no further tests are necessary. Even if we used this data representation to maintain a set of integers in the range 0 through 5000, the number of probes would still be one. The search algorithm (in this case, a single expression) is therefore $O(1)$ because the number of probes does not depend on the length of the vector.

Hashing

The strategy for digit sets is so efficient because it exploits the direct access property of arrays. We are not forced to march through the vector looking for the search key. Instead, the search key itself is used to index the vector directly.

The physical limitations of computer memory, unfortunately, prevent us from using the above strategy for large sets. To maintain a set whose members can be *any* int value would require, on 32-bit machines, a vector of about 4 billion elements. Or consider a program for a retail company that looks up customer information by using the customer's telephone number. Suppose that each telephone number is a local number (7 digits long), and each customer's record is a struct containing an account balance, customer name, address, and so forth. Representing telephone numbers as the integers 0 through 9999999, we could use the telephone number to index the vector of customer records:

	acctBal	(Other members)
custInfo [0]	48.95	• • •
[1]	-0.58	• • •
•	•	•
•	•	•
•	•	•
[4746715]	148.38	• • •
•	•	•
•	•	•
•	•	•
[9999999]	12.95	• • •

By setting up the data this way, we can look up any customer's information in a single probe—just as with the digit set—by indexing into the vector:

```
custInfo[4746715].acctBal
```

Although the time efficiency for searching is optimal here, space efficiency is a serious problem. The vector has 10 million array elements, but if the company has only 1000 customers, 99.99 percent of the vector is unused.

To make the memory requirements more palatable, we will use a vector whose length is approximately the same as the number of customers (say 1000), and then locate a customer record by using **hashing**—the technique of mathematically transforming a search key into a vector index. For our customer information, we might extract the first three digits of the telephone number by dividing it by 10,000. This produces an array index of 0 through 999. The mapping of a data value onto an array index is called a **hash**

function, and the vector set up to accommodate this technique is called a **hash table.**

Because the array index no longer represents a complete telephone number, the hash table will contain the telephone number as one of the members of a customer record. Figure 12.12 shows this hash table.

Hash Functions and Collision Avoidance

For the customer information example, a hash function H must map a `long` integer in the range 0 through 9999999 onto an `int` value from 0 through 999. Using the previously mentioned extraction of the first three digits of the telephone number, the hash function for a search key k is

$$H(k) = \frac{k}{10000} \quad \text{(integer division)}$$

With this hash function, $H(4746715) = 474$ and $H(6851342) = 685$. If every customer's telephone number were unique in the first three digits, this hash function would be a **perfect hash function**—one that maps each potential search key onto a unique position (slot) in the hash table. With a perfect hash function, searching time is O(1) as with the digit set, since exactly one probe is required.

This particular hash function, though, is unlikely to be a perfect hash function. Because customers' telephone numbers are local numbers, it is almost certain that many customers have the same first three digits. For example, $H(4746715) = H(4742312) = H(4746876) = 474$. A **collision** occurs when two distinct keys hash to the same slot in the hash table, and the colliding keys are called **synonyms.**

	telNo	acctBal	(Other members)
custInfo [0]			• • •
[1]			• • •
• • •	• • •	• • •	• • •
[474]	4746715	148.38	• • •
• • •	• • •	• • •	• • •
[685]	6851342	-4.25	• • •
• • •	• • •	• • •	• • •
[999]			• • •

Figure 12.12 Hash table using hash function $H(k)$ = first three digits of k

If we are inserting a new record into the hash table, a collision means that the slot to which we have hashed is already occupied. We must somehow find another place in the table for this record. If we are searching for an existing record in the table, a collision means that the slot to which we have hashed may contain a record that does not match our search key. We must somehow determine where else in the table the desired record has been stored. In both situations—insertions and searching—collisions lead to additional algorithmic effort and hinder attempts to access data in a single probe. We will look at strategies for resolving collisions a bit later.

When choosing a hash function, the programmer should consider two criteria:

1. How efficient is it to compute?
2. How effectively does it avoid collisions?

The first criterion is important because the very reason for using hash tables is to support frequent search operations. If every search requires a lengthy algorithm just to generate the hash value, the benefits of using a hash table are nullified. Most hash functions are based on very simple arithmetic manipulations of the search key using addition, subtraction, multiplication, and division.

The second criterion has been the subject of much research in computer science. To minimize the chances of collisions, a hash function should disperse the data uniformly throughout the hash table. Each slot in the hash table should have equal likelihood of being selected by the hash function. In statistical terms, for a hash table of s slots we would like the probability to be $1/s$ that a random key value k hashes to slot i, for all $0 \leq i \leq s - 1$. Our hash function for the customer information table—obtaining the first three digits of the telephone number—is undoubtedly a poor one. If 70 percent of the customers have telephone numbers beginning with 474, then the probability that $H(k)$ equals 474 is 0.7 instead of the desired 0.001. Also, because no person has a phone number beginning with 000, the probability that $H(k)$ equals 0 is 0.0.

Many hash functions with good statistical properties have appeared in the research literature. Some involve separating the search key into groups of bits, then adding these groups together arithmetically to form the hash table index. Others involve multiplying or dividing certain groups of bits within the search key. One popular method, called the **midsquare technique,** is to square the key value and then extract a certain number of bits from the middle of this squared result.

The most common hash function uses what is called the **division technique.** The hash value is the remainder upon dividing the key value by the length of the hash table, s:

$$H(k) = k \; mod \; s$$

where *mod* denotes the modulus operator (in C++, the % operator). This computation yields a result in the range 0 through $s - 1$, exactly what we want as an index into the hash table. Research results have shown this method to give very good results, and it is very efficient to compute as well. To reduce the likelihood of collisions, the division technique works best if the length of the hash table is a prime number.

To use the division technique with our customer information table, we would first change the length of the table from 1000 to 1009 (a prime number), giving array indices from 0 through 1008. The hash function is then computed by the C++ expression

```
phoneNum % 1009
```

With this hash function, the following are some representative hash values:

$$H(4740997) = 715$$
$$H(4740795) = 513$$
$$H(3810993) = 0$$

Figure 12.13 displays a diagram of this version of the hash table.

Collision Resolution

With hash tables, collisions are inevitable. Even with a hash function that produces a uniform distribution of the hash values, collisions must sometimes occur because the number of possible key values is usually much greater than the number of slots in the hash table. **Collision resolution strategies** are algorithms that prescribe what to do when collisions occur.

The simplest strategy is **linear probing.** To describe this strategy, we consider inserting records and searching for records separately. To insert a new record with key value k into a hash table with s slots, compute $H(k)$. If slot

	telNo	acctBal	(Other members)
custInfo [0]	3810993	-7.23	• • •
[1]			• • •
• • •	•	•	•
[513]	4740795	12.14	• • •
• • •	•	•	•
[715]	4740997	148.38	• • •
• • •	•	•	•
[1008]			• • •

Figure 12.13 Hash table using hash function $H(k) = k \bmod 1009$

$H(k)$ is already occupied, a collision has occurred. From slot $(H(k) + 1)$ *mod s*, begin a linear search for an empty slot. (Using the modulus operation ensures a circular search, wrapping around from the end of the hash table to the beginning.) Continue searching until an empty slot is located or the table is found to be full. To prevent an infinite search when the table is full, the current probe position can be tested against the initial hash value to detect revisiting the original slot.

With linear probing, searching for a key value k proceeds as follows. If slot $H(k)$ is unoccupied, the search is over; k is not in the table. If slot $H(k)$ is already occupied, compare k against the corresponding key in the record at that slot. If they are equal, the search ends; the search key has been found in one probe. If they are unequal, a circular linear search proceeds until the key value is found at some slot in the hash table (a successful search), an empty slot is found (an unsuccessful search), or the initial hash location is revisited (an unsuccessful search of a full table).

Although linear probing is a relatively simple approach to collision resolution, it has a major drawback: the phenomenon of **clustering.** In creating a hash table, suppose the first five key values just happen to hash to the same location, slot 20. Then slots 20 through 24 form a cluster of synonyms (Figure 12.14). This occurrence is known as *primary clustering*. This cluster must be probed linearly for every subsequent synonym that hashes to slot 20. As more and more key values hashing to slot 20 are inserted, the cluster of synonyms grows longer.

A related phenomenon, *secondary clustering*, occurs when different clusters merge to form a larger cluster. This new cluster contains key values that are not all synonyms of each other. Given the primary cluster in Figure 12.14, new key values hashing initially to slot 22 get caught up in the cluster and,

	telNo	acctBal	(Other members)
•	•	•	•
•	•	•	•
•	•	•	•
[19]			• • •
[20]	3530511	12.14	• • •
[21]	3531520	0.95	• • •
[22]	8120452	129.43	• • •
[23]	3532529	10.89	• • •
[24]	7854076	1.85	• • •
[25]			• • •
•	•	•	•
•	•	•	•
•	•	•	•

Figure 12.14 Primary clustering (Linear probing with hash function $H(k) = k \bmod 1009$)

through linear probing, extend the length of the cluster. Figure 12.15 depicts this situation. The two keys hashing to slot 22 (keys 3510333 and 2540684) have been forced into the cluster, even though they are not synonyms for any of the keys in the original cluster.

As clusters grow larger and more numerous, search operations degenerate into linear searches, which, as we pointed out earlier in the chapter, are not desirable in terms of efficiency.

Several methods have been devised to reduce the likelihood of secondary clustering. Some of these are:

- *Quadratic probing*—Instead of probing linearly (adding 1 to each vector index) after a collision, probe an s-slot hash table in the order $H(k)$, $H(k) + 1^2$, $H(k) - 1^2$, $H(k) + 2^2$, $H(k) - 2^2$, . . ., $H(k) + ((s - 1)/2)^2$, $H(k) - ((s - 1)/2)^2$, all computations modulo s.

- *Random probing*—Assuming an s-slot hash table, generate a sequence of pseudorandom integers $r_1, r_2, . . ., r_{s-1}$, where each integer is unique and in the range $1 . . . s - 1$. After a collision, probe the hash table in the order $H(k)$, $H(k) + r_1$, $H(k) + r_2, . . ., H(k) + r_{s-1}$, all computations modulo s.

- *Rehashing*—Create several different hash functions, $H_1, H_2, . . ., H_m$. After a collision, probe the hash table in the order $H_1(k), H_2(k), . . . H_m(k)$.

We do not explore these methods in further detail. Although they are of theoretical interest and are useful for certain specific kinds of data distributions, we now examine a very popular technique—chained hash tables—that performs well over a wide range of programming applications.

	telNo	acctBal	(Other members)
• • •	• • •	• • •	• • •
[19]			• • •
[20]	3530511	12.14	• • •
[21]	3531520	0.95	• • •
[22]	8120452	129.43	• • •
[23]	3532529	10.89	• • •
[24]	7854076	1.85	• • •
[25]	3510333	5.95	• • •
[26]	2540684	12.64	• • •
• • •	• • •	• • •	• • •

Figure 12.15 Secondary clustering (Linear probing with hash function $H(k) = k \bmod 1009$)

Chained Hash Tables

With linear probing and, to a lesser extent, the other collision resolution techniques we have mentioned, secondary clustering is an enemy of good performance. As pictured in Figure 12.15, if a search key k hashes to a slot occupied by a nonsynonym of k, then linear probing may require many comparisons with keys that are not synonyms of k.

We can eliminate secondary clustering, and therefore many wasteful comparisons, by attaching to each slot in the hash table a separate list of all the synonyms that have collided at that slot (the primary cluster). Because we cannot know in advance how many collisions will occur, it is appropriate to implement each list as a linked list (or linked chain). This organization, known as a **chained hash table,** is shown in Figure 12.16. Notice that the hash table no longer contains any customer data; it is simply a vector of head pointers to linked lists.

With respect to time efficiency, it is important to stress that chained hash tables only help in collision resolution. The more important determinant of overall performance is still the hash function. With a perfect hash function, collisions do not occur and each linked list has length one. With a poor hash function, one that produces many collisions, chaining the synonyms leads to linear searches through the linked lists.

Performance of Hashing

The running times of most algorithms are measured in terms of N, the number of data items manipulated. We speak of linear search and binary search as being $O(N)$ and $O(\log N)$ algorithms, respectively. A direct comparison of the

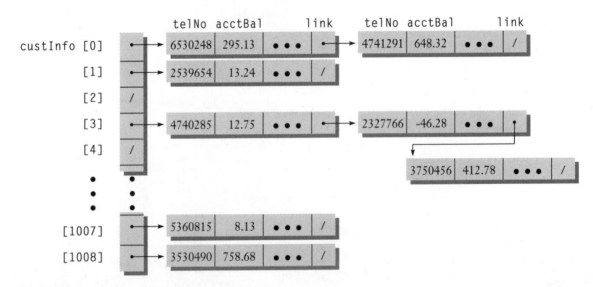

Figure 12.16 Chained hash table (Hash function $H(k) = k \bmod 1009$)

efficiency of hashing with other searching techniques is difficult because, with hashing, N is usually irrelevant. Instead, the performance of hashing depends on three factors:

1. the quality of the hash function
2. the collision resolution technique
3. the availability of space in the hash table

As we have discussed earlier, to achieve good performance, we want a uniform hash function—one that distributes the data throughout the hash table with equal probability. Studies have shown that the division method, where the divisor is a prime number, gives the best approximation to a uniform hash function for general applications. For the rest of this analysis, we will assume that a uniform hash function is in use.

As we also have discussed, the choice of collision resolution techniques plays an important role in performance. As we will see, chained hash tables give superior performance in most situations but are not *always* preferred.

The one factor we have not yet examined closely is the availability of space in the hash table. If the table is nearly empty, most search keys can be found in one probe. As more items are inserted into the table, the greater is the chance of collisions. If the table is nearly full and linear probing is used to resolve collisions, then hashing performs no better than an $O(N)$ linear search (and actually performs worse, because of the overhead of computing the hash function). A quantity called the **load factor** is a measure of how full a table is. For a hash table of s slots with n data entries currently in the table, the load factor α is defined as $\alpha = n/s$. If the hash table is empty, $\alpha = 0$. If the hash table is full and chaining is not used, $\alpha = 1$. If chaining is used, α can be arbitrarily large because there may be many data entries per slot.

In *The Art of Computer Programming: Sorting and Searching* (Addison-Wesley, 1973), Donald Knuth derives formulas for the expected number of probes required to find a value in a hash table. These formulas, shown in Table 12.6, assume a uniform hash function and a successful search (the key is present in the table).

Table 12.6 Expected number of probes for successful search of a hash table

Collision resolution method	Expected number of probes for a successful search with a uniform hash function and load factor α
Linear probing	$\frac{1}{2}\left(1 + \frac{1}{1-\alpha}\right)$
Random probing, rehashing, and quadratic probing	$\frac{1}{\alpha}\log_e\left(\frac{1}{1-\alpha}\right)$
Chaining	$1 + \frac{1}{2}\alpha$

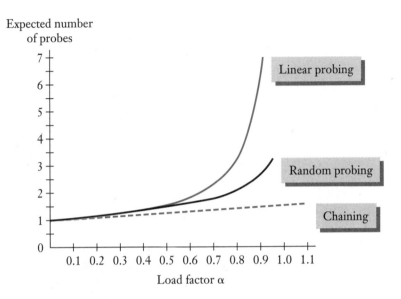

Figure 12.17 Graph of expected number of probes versus load factor

Using these formulas to graph the expected number of probes against various load factors gives a more revealing perspective (Figure 12.17).

These results show that all three collision resolution methods give comparable performance up to the point at which the hash table is about half full. Beyond that point, chaining is clearly unmatched. However, it is not true that chaining is always the method of choice. We have concentrated on time efficiency but cannot ignore space efficiency.

Suppose that a pointer occupies one word of memory and that chaining uses dynamic allocation for the linked lists. If each data value in the table is an `int` occupying one memory word, then using a vector of `int`s requires only half as much memory as chaining (which needs one word for the pointer and one for the data value). If the load factor α is typically expected to hover around 1, the superior time efficiency of chaining may outweigh its memory demand. But if α is usually small, using a vector of `int`s with linear probing is nearly as fast as chaining (see Figure 12.17) and uses only half as much memory.

If, on the other hand, the size of each data entry in the table is much larger than the size of a pointer (a `struct` with 20 members, for example), then chaining is the preferred method. In this case, only a small proportion of the total memory needed is devoted to pointer overhead.

Comparison of Searching Methods

We have seen that hashing performance spans a broad range, from $O(1)$ to $O(N)$. Best case performance is a single probe, achieved with a perfect hash function or when the table size is made large enough to accommodate every possible search key. Worst case performance is $O(N)$, arising from a poor combination of hash function, collision resolution strategy, and load factor. In such a situation, searches become, in effect, linear searches. If chaining is used with a uniform hash function, the running time is $O(1)$. Specifically, the expected number of probes is 1.5 if the load factor is 1.

In light of the benefits of hashing, it might seem that the linear search and the binary search are antiquated and should be relegated to a museum. But keep in mind that the programmer, like the mechanic or carpenter, should use the right tool for the job. If a program searches a very small list frequently or even a large list just once or twice, a linear search is perfectly reasonable. A binary search, requiring the overhead of sorting the list and using a more complicated comparison algorithm, is probably not justified. Nor is using a hash table with its overhead of computing the hash function and including algorithms for resolving collisions.

If data must be kept sorted for reasons other than searching, such as frequent output in sorted order, the binary search is preferable. A linear search of already sorted data is wasteful, and hash tables rely on random, not sorted, distributions of the data.

Hashing, then, is best for large lists of data when searching occurs frequently and the data values are rarely, if ever, to be sorted. The programmer still needs to keep all of these searching techniques in his or her toolbox and know when to use each one.

12.7 N^2 Sorting

The topic of sorting occupies a prominent position in computer science. It has been estimated that anywhere from 25 percent to 50 percent of all computing time in the commercial world is spent sorting data. Many sorting methods have been conceived. Some are more appropriate than others, depending on the nature of the data to be sorted. This section considers three sorting algorithms with different performance characteristics. Each algorithm sorts a vector of integers into ascending order. Figure 12.18 contains the specification of a general Sort routine that we will implement separately with each algorithm.

Straight Selection Sort

The **straight selection sort,** presented in Chapter 1, gets its name from the way the algorithm rearranges data. A selection sort makes repeated passes through the vector, from top to bottom. On the first pass, the algorithm finds

```
void Sort( /* inout */ int vec[],
           /* in */    int vSize );

   // PRE:  Assigned(vSize)  &&  Assigned(vec[0..vSize-1])
   // POST: vec[0..vSize-1] contain same values as
   //       vec[0..vSize-1]<entry> but are sorted into ascending
   //       order
```

Figure 12.18 Specification of Sort function

```
//  Algorithm: straight selection sort

void Sort( /* inout */ int vec[],
           /* in */    int vSize )
    //...........................................................
    // PRE:  Assigned(vSize)  &&  Assigned(vec[0..vSize-1])
    // POST: vec[0..vSize-1] contain same values as
    //       vec[0..vSize-1]<entry> but are sorted into ascending
    //       order
    //...........................................................
{
    int maxIndx;              // Index of largest no. in each pass
    int bottom;               // "False bottom" for each pass
    int i;
    int temp;

    for (bottom = vSize-1; bottom >= 1; bottom--) {
                    // INV (prior to test):
                    //     All vec[0..bottom] are <= vec[bottom+1]
                    //  && vec[bottom+1..vSize-1] are in ascending
                    //     order
                    //  && bottom >= 0
        maxIndx = 0;
        for (i = 1; i <= bottom; i++)  // INV (prior to test):
                                    //     vec[maxIndx] >= all
                                    //         vec[0..i-1]
                                    //  && i <= bottom+1

            if (vec[i] > vec[maxIndx])
                maxIndx = i;

        temp = vec[bottom];
        vec[bottom] = vec[maxIndx];
        vec[maxIndx] = temp;
    }
}
```

Figure 12.19 Straight selection version of Sort function

(hence, *selects*) the largest value in the vector and swaps it with the element at the bottom. Next, it moves the bottom up by one position, creating a "false bottom" to the vector. The algorithm makes a second pass, selecting the largest value in the now-shortened vector and swapping it with the element at the new bottom. As a result, the second largest value in the entire vector is physically in the next-to-last vector element. The algorithm then moves the bottom up again and continues making passes until the false bottom has reached the top. Figure 12.19 shows the implementation of the Sort function using a straight selection sort.

To analyze the selection sort algorithm, we rewrite the algorithm less formally as follows:

```
for (bottom = vSize-1; bottom >= 1; bottom--) {
    maxIndx = 0;
    for (i = 1; i <= bottom; i++)
        if (vec[i] > vec[maxIndx])
            maxIndx = i;

    // Swap vec[bottom] and vec[maxIndx]
}
```

In this algorithm, the outer loop iterates exactly vSize – 1 times. The first time through the outer loop, the inner loop iterates vSize – 1 times. The second time through the outer loop, the inner loop iterates vSize – 2 times, and so forth. Therefore, the total count of inner loop iterations is

$$(vSize - 1) + (vSize - 2) + \ldots + 2 + 1 = \frac{(vSize - 1)*vSize}{2} = O(vSize^2)$$

Sorting routines often are analyzed for two separate measures:

1. the number of times two array elements are *compared*
2. the number of times two array elements are *moved*

For straight selection, the number of comparisons is $O(vSize^2)$ and the number of data movements, or swaps, is $O(vSize)$. The latter is evident in the preceding algorithm because the swapping portion is within the outer loop but outside the inner loop.

The running time of the straight selection sort is largely independent of the data. The number of both comparisons and swaps remains the same regardless of the original ordering of the vector contents. The only part of the algorithm that can vary is the number of times the then-clause of the inner loop is executed. For straight selection, then, the best case and worst case number of comparisons are both $O(vSize^2)$.

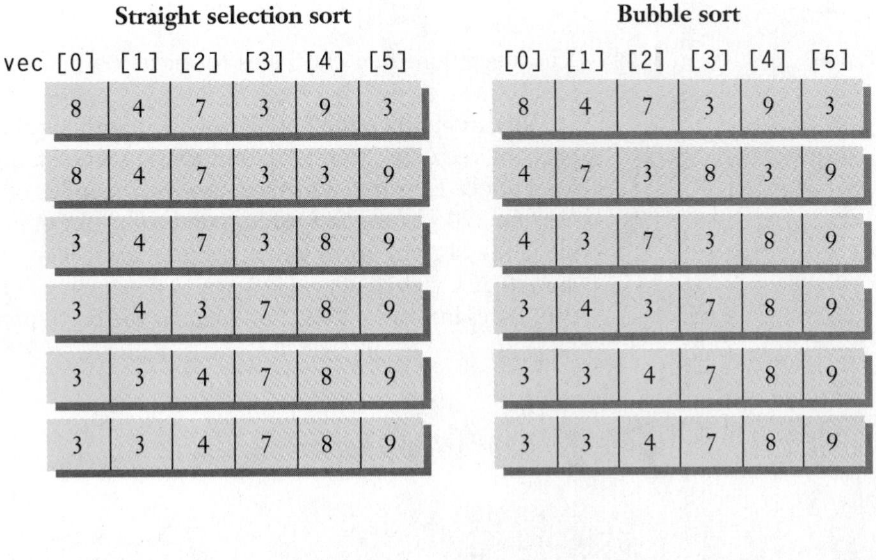

Figure 12.20 Parallel trace of straight selection and bubble sort

Bubble Sort

Another sorting algorithm, the **bubble sort,** belongs to a class of sorts known as **exchange sorts.** The bubble sort, like the selection sort, makes repeated passes through the data, each time moving the false bottom up by one. With each pass, bubble sort scans the vector from top to bottom, comparing each pair of consecutive array elements. Whenever two consecutive values are out of order (the first is greater than the second), they are swapped. At the end of the first pass, the largest value in the vector has incrementally "bubbled" its way to the bottom. (The laws of gravity are inverted for this sorting scheme!)

The false bottom then moves up by one, and the second pass bubbles the next largest value to the new bottom, and so forth. The following summarizes this algorithm:

```
// Bubble sort, Version 1

for (bottom = vSize-1; bottom > 0; bottom--)
    for (i = 0; i < bottom; i++)
        if (vec[i] > vec[i+1]) {
            // Swap vec[i] and vec[i+1]
        }
```

Figure 12.20 illustrates the operation of the bubble sort by comparing it to straight selection. Both algorithms operate on identical data. Each row, after the first, displays the contents of vec after a single execution of the algorithm's outer loop.

The bubble sort makes exactly vSize – 1 passes through the vector, regardless of the original ordering of the data. Suppose vec initially contains 1000 values and only vec[1] and vec[2] are out of order:

$$245, 270, 250, 310, 320, 330, 340, \ldots$$

After the first pass, the contents are now

$$245, 250, 270, 310, 320, 330, 340, \ldots$$

The algorithm then continues to make 998 more passes through the vector, needlessly.

We can improve the bubble sort by observing the following. After a single pass, all vector elements beyond the last one swapped *must* be in order and need not be considered further. Above, the index of the last value swapped is 1 because 270 was the last value found to be out of order. The idea, then, is to move the bottom up to index 1 in one giant leap. One more pass will determine that vec[0] and vec[1] are in order, so the algorithm terminates after two passes instead of 999. Following is the corresponding algorithm:

```
// Bubble sort, Version 2

bottom = vSize - 1;
while (bottom > 0) {
    lastSwapIndx = 0;
    for (i = 0; i < bottom; i++)
        if (vec[i] > vec[i+1]) {
            // Swap vec[i] and vec[i+1]
            lastSwapIndx = i;
        }
    bottom = lastSwapIndx;
}
```

Analyzing the bubble sort algorithm is not as easy as analyzing the straight selection sort. The efficiency of bubble sort is sensitive to the original contents of the vector. The worst case occurs when all data values are initially out of order—that is, all are in descending order. There is no opportunity for early termination using lastSwapIndx. In this case, bubble sort executes the inner loop exactly the same number of times as straight selection does: (vSize – 1)*vSize/2 times. Therefore, the worst case number of comparisons for a bubble sort is O(vSize²). The worst case number of swaps is also O(vSize²) because, unlike straight selection, the swapping statements are located within the inner loop.

A precise average case analysis of bubble sort is beyond the scope of this text. Suffice it to say that, for random data in the vector, the number of both data comparisons and data movements is O(vSize²).

The best case for bubble sort is when the vector just happens to be completely in ascending order to begin with. Using the early termination algorithm (Version 2), only one pass is necessary. The result is vSize – 1 comparisons and no swaps, so the best case performances are O(vSize) and O(1), respectively.

Many other sorting algorithms exhibit the same average case and worst case performance as straight selection sort and bubble sort: O(vSize²). These algorithms are collectively referred to as **N^2 sorts,** where N is the size of the array being sorted.

Benchmarks

Big-O is a coarse measure of efficiency. One way to obtain more precise measurements is to perform a **benchmark.** Benchmarking consists of observing the actual performance of a program under execution. Table 12.7 illustrates the results of executing the selection sort and improved bubble sort on a particular machine. This benchmark study compares the observed execution times using identical, randomly generated data for each execution.

In this study, straight selection executes in about two-thirds the time of bubble sort, even though both algorithms are N^2 sorts. The primary contributor to this difference is the number of swaps performed. The bubble sort requires O(vSize²) swaps, while straight selection performs only O(vSize) swaps.

Table 12.7 Benchmarks for bubble sort and straight selection sort

Execution time (in seconds)		
vSize	*Bubble sort*	*Straight selection*
100	1.16	0.83
200	4.95	3.25
300	11.65	7.25
400	20.65	12.90
500	32.85	20.11
1000	127.40	80.86

Benchmarks can be useful tools for comparing the performances of two different pieces of software or hardware. But three cautions are in order:

1. A benchmark must be as realistic as possible. The benchmark of Table 12.7 sorts a vector of randomly generated data. This benchmark is unrealistic for environments where the data are known to be consistently in reverse (descending) order. A benchmark using data in descending order would be more appropriate in this case.

2. A benchmark examines only one particular instance. It is a serious mistake to generalize from a single benchmark. Perhaps the particular set of data used in the sorting benchmark caused bubble sort to make an inordinately large number of swaps, whereas another set of data might yield substantially difference numbers.

3. A benchmark is highly dependent on the machine, the language, and the compiler for that language. Were the sorting benchmark to be run with a different compiler, much less another programming language or another computer, the actual numbers in the table might vary significantly. Serious benchmarking of algorithms often requires extensive combinations of machine, language, and compiler.

Like many programming tools, benchmarks are useful if kept in perspective.

Pursuing Correctness

Correctness, Code Tuning, and Profilers

As we emphasized in the introduction to this chapter, the programmer's first concern must always be the program's correctness, not its efficiency. Only after correctness is argued (by thorough testing or formal or informal correctness proofs) should the programmer worry about efficiency.

Earlier we mentioned the 90–10 phenomenon: approximately 90 percent of a large program's execution time is spent within 10 percent of the program code. A widely used practice known as **code tuning** takes advantage of this phenomenon. To improve the efficiency of a correctly executing program, code tuning amounts to locating those small portions of the program where most of the execution time occurs and replacing those portions with more efficient algorithms (and possibly data structures). Because the greatest gains in speed are made in these small "hot spots," it does not pay to peruse the entire program in search of efficiency.

An example might be a program that spends some start-up time initializing a large vector, after which the bulk of its time is spent repeatedly searching the vector for different data values. If the programmer identifies the searching routine as the origin of most of the execution time, then replacing, say, a linear search with a binary search will speed up the program.

It is often difficult to discover, by inspection or intuition, what portions of code consume the most time. A program called a **profiler** is a valuable aid. A profiler observes an executing program and produces an execution profile—a report detailing the execution time spent in each program unit. Most profilers can report which functions were called, how many times each function was called, and the total execution time spent in each function. Some can even produce these statistics down to the level of individual instructions within the program. Using the execution profile, a programmer can use code tuning to enhance the overall performance of the program.

12.8   Quicksort

N^2 sorts are too inefficient to be practical for sorting large quantities of data. The earlier bubble sort benchmark required over two minutes to sort 1000 values. This result extrapolates to more than three hours to sort 10,000 values.

One sorting algorithm with much better average case performance is the **quicksort,** created by British computer scientist C.A.R. Hoare. Quicksort rearranges the data in a vector until the vector is partitioned into two subvectors, where all values in one subvector are greater than all values in the other. The algorithm then recursively calls itself to partition each subvector into two more subvectors. This recursion continues until the vector is sorted. Below is the algorithm for sorting the elements vec[loBound] through vec[hiBound]. We will trace the execution with sample array contents shortly.

```
void Quicksort( /* inout */ int vec[],
                /* in */    int loBound,
                /* in */    int hiBound )
{
    IF there are no items or one item to sort THEN
        return;
    IF there are two items to sort THEN
        Swap vec[loBound] and vec[hiBound], if necessary;
    ELSE {
        Rearrange vec so that all values in vec[loBound..someSub-1] are
            less than all values in vec[someSub..hiBound];
        Quicksort(vec, loBound, someSub-1);
        Quicksort(vec, someSub, hiBound);
    }
}
```

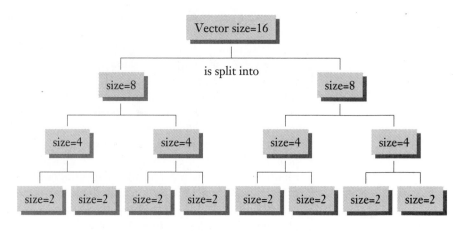

- Total number of recursive calls = 15
  (vSize = 16)

Figure 12.21 Subvector partitioning for best case of quicksort

- Average vector size = (8*2 + 4*4 +2*8 +16)/15 =4.27
  (int(log$_2$ vSize) = 4)

Quicksort performs best if it can partition a single vector into two subvectors exactly half the size of the original. In this case, each recursive invocation reduces the size of the data to be sorted by one-half. Figure 12.21 examines the invocations of quicksort for this ideal case. This figure assumes that a vector of 16 elements is to be sorted via quicksort and that each recursive invocation yields subvectors of identical size.

In this example, a 16-element vector generates a total of 15 function activations and the average vector size per activation is about 4. In general it can be shown that the best case number of activations is O(vSize) and the best case vector size per activation is O(log$_2$ vSize).

Performance

The run-time performance of this algorithm depends upon the number of function activations, multiplied by the time spent executing each activation. Other than calling itself recursively, a single activation spends most of its time rearranging the vector into subvectors. The running time is therefore

Quicksort time = Activation count * Time for one partitioning of a vector into subvectors
  = O(vSize) * Time for one partitioning

As we will see, the algorithm used by quicksort to partition a vector is linear in the size of that vector. Because the size of each vector to be partitioned averages O(log$_2$ vSize),

Quicksort time = O(vSize) * O(log$_2$ vSize)
  = O(vSize * log$_2$ vSize)

The Partitioning Algorithm

The technique for partitioning a vector into subvectors starts by selecting one of the vector elements as a **pivot,** the value against which all other vector elements are compared. Below is an algorithm for partitioning vec[loBound] through vec[hiBound]. This partitioning algorithm uses the first element of the vector as a pivot.

```
pivot = vec[loBound];
loSwap = loBound+1;
hiSwap = hiBound;
do {
    Scan forward from loSwap until encountering a value > pivot
        and set loSwap to index this value;

    Scan backward from hiSwap until encountering a value <= pivot
        and set hiSwap to index this value;

    IF loSwap and hiSwap did not cross THEN
        Swap vec[loSwap] and vec[hiSwap];
} while ( loSwap and hiSwap have not crossed );
Swap vec[loBound] (the pivot) with the vec element where
    loSwap and hiSwap crossed;
```

This algorithm is appropriate for an ascending sort. The first partition contains all values less than or equal to the pivot, and the last partition contains all values greater than the pivot. To examine this algorithm more closely, consider partitioning the following vector:

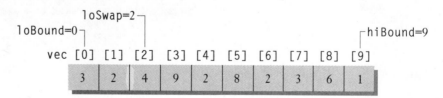

The algorithm selects vec[loBound]=vec[0]=3 as the pivot. Next, the algorithm scans the vector from vec[loBound+1] forward, looking for a value greater than the pivot. The first value greater than the pivot is vec[2], so loSwap is set to 2:

The algorithm then scans backward from vec[hiBound] until a value less than or equal to the pivot is encountered. In this case, vec[9] is immediately found to be less than the pivot, so hiSwap is set to index it:

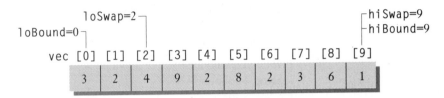

Although loSwap and hiSwap moved towards each other, they did not cross. The algorithm then swaps vec[loSwap] and vec[hiSwap], as they are out of order with respect to the pivot.

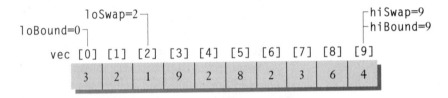

This process is repeated by first moving loSwap forward to the next value greater than the pivot and hiSwap backward to the next value less than or equal to the pivot.

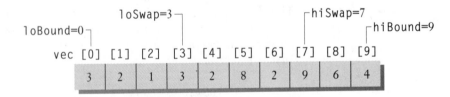

Again, the two values are interchanged.

loSwap=3 ─┐   ┌─hiSwap=7
loBound=0 ─┐   ┌─hiBound=9

vec [0] [1] [2] [3] [4] [5] [6] [7] [8] [9]

| 3 | 2 | 1 | 3 | 2 | 8 | 2 | 9 | 6 | 4 |

The next forward scan of loSwap and backward scan of hiSwap results in the following:

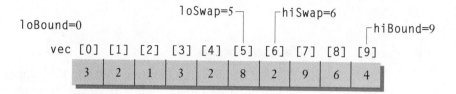

A third swap ensues:

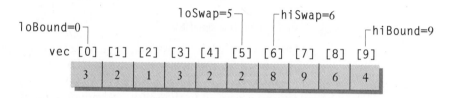

A final forward scan of loSwap and backward scan of hiSwap yields the following result:

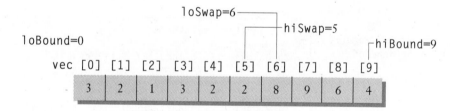

At this point, loSwap and hiSwap have crossed. The algorithm has successfully partitioned the vector, because all vector elements have been scanned. The pivot, vec[0], is the largest possible value in vec[0..hiSwap] and all values of vec[hiSwap+1..hiBound] are greater than the pivot. The algorithm now moves the pivot value to its correct, sorted position by swapping vec[5] and vec[0]. After this, vec[5] need not be considered further. The resulting vector is as follows:

loBound=0 ⌐   ⌐hiBound=9
vec [0] [1] [2] [3] [4] [5] [6] [7] [8] [9]

| 2 | 2 | 1 | 3 | 2 | 3 | 8 | 9 | 6 | 4 |

Quicksort now invokes itself recursively to sort the two resulting subvectors. These subvectors are separated by the position where the pivot is now located. For the above example, the two subvectors are `vec[0..4]` and `vec[6..9]`.

The Complete Algorithm

The entire quicksort algorithm, coded in C++, appears in Figure 12.22. This implementation differs slightly from the previous example by selecting the middle element of the vector as a pivot. This modification improves quicksort for data that are nearly sorted to begin with.

An Improved Algorithm

On most computer systems, each function invocation requires a certain amount of execution time overhead. This overhead includes pushing actual parameters onto the run-time stack, transferring control to the function, returning control to the caller, and popping the parameters off the stack. We can reduce the number of activations of `Quicksort` by checking for subvectors of length less than 2 *before* a recursive call, not after. This improvement to `QuickSort` results in the code shown in Figure 12.23.

Figure 12.22 A first version of the recursive `Quicksort` function

```
// Algorithm: quicksort

void Quicksort( /* inout */ int vec[],
                /* in */     int loBound,
                /* in */     int hiBound )
    //...............................................................
    // PRE:  Assigned(loBound) && Assigned(hiBound)
    //    && Assigned(vec[loBound..hiBound])
    // POST: vec[loBound..hiBound] contain same values as
    //       at invocation but are sorted into ascending order
    //...............................................................
{
    int pivot;
    int loSwap;
    int hiSwap;
    int temp;
```

```
    if (loBound >= hiBound)                // Zero or one item to sort
        return;
    if (hiBound-loBound == 1) {            // Two items to sort
        if (vec[loBound] > vec[hiBound]) {
            temp = vec[loBound];
            vec[loBound] = vec[hiBound];
            vec[hiBound] = temp;
        }
        return;
    }
    pivot = vec[(loBound+hiBound)/2];       // 3 or more items to sort
    vec[(loBound+hiBound)/2] = vec[loBound];
    vec[loBound] = pivot;
    loSwap = loBound + 1;
    hiSwap = hiBound;
    do {
        while (loSwap <= hiSwap && vec[loSwap] <= pivot)
                            // INV (prior to test):
                            //    All vec[loBound+1..loSwap-1]
                            //    are <= pivot && loSwap <= hiSwap+1
            loSwap++;
        while (vec[hiSwap] > pivot)
                            // INV (prior to test):
                            //    All vec[hiSwap+1..hiBound]
                            //    are > pivot && hiSwap >= loSwap-1
            hiSwap--;
        if (loSwap < hiSwap) {
            temp = vec[loSwap];
            vec[loSwap] = vec[hiSwap];
            vec[hiSwap] = temp;
        }
        // INV: All vec[loBound..loSwap-1] are <= pivot
        //    && All vec[hiSwap+1..hiBound] are > pivot
        //    && (loSwap < hiSwap) -->
        //                        vec[loSwap] <= pivot < vec[hiSwap]
        //    && (loSwap >= hiSwap) --> vec[hiSwap] <= pivot
        //    && loBound <= loSwap <= hiSwap+1 <= hiBound+1
    } while (loSwap < hiSwap);
    vec[loBound] = vec[hiSwap];
    vec[hiSwap] = pivot;
    Quicksort(vec, loBound, hiSwap-1);
    Quicksort(vec, hiSwap+1, hiBound);
}
```

```
//  Algorithm: improved version of quicksort

void Quicksort( /* inout */ int vec[],
                /* in */    int loBound,
                /* in */    int hiBound )
    //................................................................
    // PRE:  loBound < hiBound  (i.e., at least 2 items to sort)
    //    && Assigned(vec[loBound..hiBound])
    // POST: vec[loBound..hiBound] contain same values as
    //       at invocation but are sorted into ascending order
    //................................................................
{
    int pivot;
    int loSwap;
    int hiSwap;
    int temp;

    if (hiBound-loBound == 1) {              // Two items to sort
        if (vec[loBound] > vec[hiBound]) {
            temp = vec[loBound];
            vec[loBound] = vec[hiBound];
            vec[hiBound] = temp;
        }
        return;
    }
    pivot = vec[(loBound+hiBound)/2];        // 3 or more items to sort
    vec[(loBound+hiBound)/2] = vec[loBound];
    vec[loBound] = pivot;
    loSwap = loBound + 1;
    hiSwap = hiBound;
    do {
        // -----------------------------------------------------------
        // Body of loop is same as in first version
        // -----------------------------------------------------------
    } while (loSwap < hiSwap);
    vec[loBound] = vec[hiSwap];
    vec[hiSwap] = pivot;

    if (loBound < hiSwap-1)           // 2 or more items in 1st subvec
        Quicksort(vec, loBound, hiSwap-1);

    if (hiSwap+1 < hiBound)           // 2 or more items in 2nd subvec
        Quicksort(vec, hiSwap+1, hiBound);
}
```

Figure 12.23 An improved version of Quicksort

Analysis of Quicksort

The best case running time for Quicksort is O(vSize log vSize). This result assumes that the pivot always divides the vector size in half. If the pivot does not split the vector evenly, the performance of quicksort suffers. Suppose that every pivot turns out to be the smallest (or largest) value. The result is one subvector of size zero and the other of size one less than the original. This arrangement is a worst case and happens when the original data are already in sorted order and the pivot is the first element in the vector. The worst case running time of quicksort is then O(vSize^2), because the number of recursive activations is O(vSize) and the average subvector size is also O(vSize) instead of O(log vSize).

Fortunately, the average case of quicksort is more like its best case than its worst case. For this reason, it is considered to be an **N log N sort.** Quicksort is one of the best general-purpose sorting algorithms available.

Table 12.8 compares the quicksort algorithm to bubble sort and straight selection sort. Both versions of quicksort (Figures 12.22 and 12.23) are included.

The real benefits of reducing algorithm complexity are most dramatic for large quantities of data. From these benchmarks, the bubble sort would require over three hours to sort a vector of 10,000 elements. The selection sort is somewhat better, but still takes about two hours. The improved recursive quicksort was benchmarked to sort the same sized vector in 35 seconds!

Although the average case performance of bubble sort is poor, there is still one reason for considering this algorithm. Bubble sort performs very well in the best case. Bubble sort can detect when an array is sorted and will terminate prematurely. Neither selection sort nor quicksort is able to detect sorted data. Furthermore, bubble sort has the advantage of performing more like its best case for nearly sorted data. Table 12.9 shows how much better bubble sort performs in this best case.

Despite this optimistic view of bubble sort, it is rare for real-life data to be nearly sorted at the outset. Bubble sort's average case number of compari-

Table 12.8 Benchmarks for bubble sort, straight selection, and two versions of quicksort using random data

Execution time (in seconds)

vSize	Bubble	Selection	First quicksort	Improved quicksort
100	1.16	0.83	0.22	0.22
200	4.95	3.25	0.38	0.38
300	11.65	7.25	0.66	0.66
400	20.65	12.90	0.99	0.93
500	32.85	20.11	1.21	1.15
1000	127.40	80.86	2.69	2.52

Table 12.9 Benchmarks for random versus already-sorted data

Execution time (in seconds)

Benchmark	Bubble	Selection	Improved quicksort
1000 random values	127.40	80.86	2.52
1000 already sorted	0.16	85.20	1.43

Table 12.10 Running times of sorting algorithms for vectors of length N

	Best case	Average case (random data)	Worst case
Bubble sort			
1. **Comparisons**	$O(N)$	$O(N^2)$	$O(N^2)$
2. **Swaps**	Zero=$O(1)$	$O(N^2)$	$O(N^2)$
Straight selection			
1. **Comparisons**	$O(N^2)$	$O(N^2)$	$O(N^2)$
2. **Swaps**	$O(N)$	$O(N)$	$O(N)$
Quicksort	$O(N \log N)$	$O(N \log N)$	$O(N^2)$

sons and swaps are both $O(N^2)$, making it one of the least desirable sorting algorithms.

Table 12.10 summarizes the analyses of all three sorts. Big-O measures are given for the best case, worst case, and average case (using random data). To highlight the differences between bubble and selection sort, the table displays measures for both comparisons and swaps. For quicksort, the measures are for number of comparisons.

12.9   Cautions About Big-O Analysis

Big-O analysis is widely used and has many practical applications, but it is important to recognize its limitations:

- For complicated algorithms, big-O analysis may be extremely difficult or impossible.
- It is often difficult to determine a "typical case."
- Big-O is a coarse measure that cannot capture small differences in algorithms.
- Big-O says little or nothing about algorithm performance for small sets of data.

Determining big-O estimating functions is a nontrivial task. There are somewhat mechanical methods, like those shown earlier in the chapter, for estimating the running time from levels of loop nesting. These methods work for many algorithms. Optimizing compilers use similar methods to improve the efficiency of the translated machine code. However, these mechanical techniques often fail to recognize the key factors that determine performance. The binary search algorithm is efficient because of the novel way it probes data items, not because of issues related to depth of loop nesting.

Defining "typical case" is another potentially difficult problem. Little may be known about the actual conditions for the algorithm. Sometimes an algorithm is just a small portion of a large, complicated program. Sometimes the hardware or operating system, or some quirk of the compiler, will interfere with algorithm efficiency. Sometimes a single algorithm is used by many different applications.

Identifying a typical case is especially problematic with general-purpose, off-the-shelf components. Different users will have different kinds of data. One solution is to allow a choice of algorithms. For example, a general-purpose sorting module might include a parameter allowing the importer to select from a collection of different algorithms. Or the importer might specify whether the data are nearly sorted, randomly distributed, or almost in order. Although this smorgasbord approach is not without difficulties, it does provide an interesting alternative. In the absence of reliable typical case analysis, Murphy's Law ("If something can go wrong, it will") suggests that a worst case analysis may be the wisest course.

Perhaps the major shortcoming of a big-O measure is its coarseness. If algorithm A performs some task in exactly $.001*N$ seconds, while B requires $1000*N$ seconds, then A is one million times faster than B. Yet A and B both have the same big-O measure: $O(N)$.

Related to the coarseness of big-O measures is the problem of blindly applying the results to small data sets. For searching or sorting small vectors, the differences among algorithms nearly vanish. The benchmarks in this chapter showed that all algorithms were able to sort a vector of 100 values in one second or less. This performance is probably adequate for most applications. Even exponential algorithms can be reasonable on small collections of data.

Suppose an algorithm processes N data values with an execution time of exactly

$$.000001N^5 + 1000N^4$$

This execution time is $O(N^5)$ as N^5 dominates the function for all large values of N. But "large values of N" in this case means values greater than one billion. Unless the algorithm typically processes more than one billion data items, $O(N^4)$ is a better estimate.

Other factors such as correctness of code, algorithm development time, robustness of code, and ease of code maintenance are often more important than time efficiency, especially when working with small collections of data.

Because of all these limitations, augmenting a big-O analysis with benchmarks provides more confidence. The programmer should use both tools whenever possible.

12.10 Efficiency Tradeoffs: The Radix Sort

This chapter's principal focus has been the analysis of time efficiency of algorithms. However, we must not ignore two other forms of efficiency: space efficiency and **intellectual efficiency.** Space efficiency, mentioned earlier, is a measure of the amount of storage a program requires. Intellectual efficiency refers to how difficult the algorithm is to design and understand.

Space, Time, and Intellectual Efficiency

Algorithms normally demonstrate tradeoffs among the three types of efficiency. Designing an algorithm with better time efficiency often means sacrificing space or intellectual efficiency. For example, the quicksort algorithm is usually much faster than the straight selection sort. The cost of improving the time efficiency is a decrease in space and intellectual efficiency. With quicksort, the additional storage results from multiple recursive calls. Each level of recursion requires an activation frame to store the parameters and local variables.

Quicksort is also intellectually more complicated (that is, less efficient) than straight selection. If one hundred nonprogrammers were asked to sort a collection of objects, most would probably use some method similar to a straight selection sort. It is unlikely that any would intuitively come up with a quicksort. Quicksort is complicated because:

- it is difficult to describe
- it requires more lines of code than simpler algorithms do

Some might also add a third reason why quicksort is complicated:

- it is recursive

To counter this claim that recursion makes the algorithm more complicated, we should mention that a nonrecursive version of quicksort exists. It has better space efficiency, but it is far harder to comprehend than the recursive version. Once the quicksort technique is understood, recursion becomes an asset, not a complication.

A comparison of the linear search with the binary search also reveals efficiency tradeoffs. Binary search is faster, but it is more complex intellectually.

It is not always true that a gain in one efficiency measure comes at the expense of another. Straight selection sort is generally more time efficient than bubble sort, yet the space and intellectual efficiencies of these two algorithms are comparable. In fact, one could argue that straight selection is less complicated intellectually because it seems more natural for people and requires less code than the bubble sort.

Radix Sorts

The fastest sorting algorithm that we have considered is quicksort, whose average case computing time is $O(N \log N)$. There are sorting algorithms with linear—$O(N)$—computing time. One such algorithm (actually, a class of algorithms) is known as the **radix sort**. One form of radix sorting sorts unsigned integer values based on the individual decimal digits within each value.

Suppose the goal is to sort a collection of three-digit unsigned integers (values from 000 through 999). A radix sort begins by partitioning all values into 10 groups. Each value is placed into the same group as all other values with the same leftmost digit. Next, the algorithm partitions each of the 10 groups into 10 subgroups, based on the values' middle digits. Each of the resulting subgroups is further partitioned into 10 sub-subgroups according to the rightmost digits. It is then easy to order the resulting sub-subgroups.

To illustrate this algorithm, consider sorting the following sequence:

$$<572, 576, 017, 025, 064, 012, 017, 006, 045, 103, 204 >$$

The radix sort partitions this sequence into 10 sequences according to the leftmost digit. All but four of these 10 sequences are empty and do not need to be considered further. The remaining four sequences are these:

$$\begin{cases} < 017, 025, 064, 012, 017, 006, 045 > \\ < 103 > \\ < 204 > \\ < 572, 576 > \end{cases}$$

By grouping together all numbers starting with 0, then all numbers starting with 1, and so forth, the algorithm implicitly sorts the groups with respect to each other. That is, all values in one group are less than all values in lower groups and greater than all values in higher groups.

Next, each of these four sequences is partitioned according to the middle digit. Any sequence consisting of zero or one value does not need further partitioning. The result of this partitioning is as follows:

< 017, 025, 064, 012, 017, 006, 045 >
is partitioned into:

< 006 >
< 017, 012, 017 >
< 025 >
< 045 >
< 064 >

< 103 >
cannot be further partitioned

< 204 >
cannot be further partitioned

< 572, 576 >
is partitioned into:

{< 572, 576 >

At this stage of the algorithm, only two remaining sequences require partitioning. This final partitioning is based on the rightmost digit, the only digit not yet examined. The result is shown below:

< 017, 025, 064, 012, 017, 006, 045 >
is partitioned into:

< 006 >
< 017, 012, 017 >
is partitioned into:

{< 012 >
< 017, 017 >

< 025 >
< 045 >
< 064 >

< 103 >
< 204 >
< 572, 576 >
is partitioned into:

< 572, 576 >
is partitioned into:

{< 572 >
< 576 >

At this point, the algorithm concludes by joining, into a single sorted list, all sequences that were not further subdivided:

<006, 012, 017, 017, 025, 045, 064, 103, 204, 572, 576 >

Radix sorts have linear computing time because the number of times that each value is examined is fixed. The above radix sort examines every value at most three times, once for each digit. In the worst case, each value is examined three times and moved four times, regardless of the number of values to be sorted.

Radix sorts display the usual tradeoffs. Coding a radix sort is an intellectually challenging task. Keeping track of the separate groups and performing the partitioning correctly can be tricky.

Even more important is the poorer space efficiency of radix sorts. Generally, storing all of the partitioned groups into temporary locations requires considerably more storage than **in-place sorts** such as bubble sort, selection sort, and quicksort. In-place sorts are so named because the data are sorted in the original vector without need for additional temporary storage.

If memory is plentiful, it may seem desirable to sacrifice space for time by using a radix sort, which is an $O(N)$ algorithm, instead of quicksort, which is an $O(N \log N)$ algorithm. To the contrary, general-purpose radix sorts typically have slower benchmark speeds than quicksort, except for extremely large vectors. The radix sort loses its advantage by spending considerable time managing the temporary storage space.

SUMMARY

The main component of algorithm performance is referred to as time efficiency. The foremost tool for analyzing time efficiency is the study of asymptotic function dominance. Big-O notation is a concise way of expressing function dominance. Although big-O estimating functions say nothing about the absolute execution time of an algorithm, they provide a useful measure of speed relative to the amount of data processed.

Sometimes it is important to study algorithms under different conditions. Best case, worst case, and average case performance may differ drastically. All three should be considered.

The benchmark is another useful tool for determining algorithm efficiency. With well-chosen input values, a benchmark can provide representative timing information. Both big-O analysis and benchmarks have limitations. They are imprecise tools, but they are valuable if their limitations are understood.

Many problems require a compromise between space and time efficiency. A programmer can increase time efficiency by adopting an algorithm with decreased space efficiency, and vice versa. In addition, variations in space and time efficiency often are related to the intellectual efficiency of algorithms. To devise an algorithm that makes the best use of memory or that executes as rapidly as possible can increase the effort needed to design, debug, and maintain the code.

The programmer's primary responsibility is correctness of code. Efficiency of code must always be a secondary concern. Good programmers have a repertoire of algorithms that can be applied to many problems and have an understanding of efficiency.

KEY TERMS

asymptotic dominance (p. 544)
average case analysis (p. 561)
benchmark (p. 577)
best case analysis (p. 560)
big-O notation (p. 545)
binary search (p. 557)
bubble sort (p. 575)
chained hash table (p. 570)
clustering (p. 568)
code tuning (p. 578)
collision (p. 565)
collision resolution strategy (p. 567)
complexity theory (p. 542)
constant time (p. 548)
cost function (p. 543)
cubic time (p. 548)
division technique (p. 566)
dominance (p. 544)
exchange sorts (p. 575)
exponential time (p. 548)
hash function (p. 564)
hash table (p. 565)
hashing (p. 564)
in-place sorts (p. 593)
intellectual efficiency (p. 590)

linear probing (p. 567)
linear search (p. 556)
linear time (p. 548)
load factor (p. 571)
logarithmic time (p. 548)
midsquare technique (p. 566)
$N \log N$ sort (p. 587)
N^2 sorts (p. 577)
order of a function (p. 545)
perfect hash function (p. 565)
performance analysis (p. 543)
pivot (p. 581)
polynomial time (p. 548)
profiler (p. 579)
quadratic time (p. 548)
quicksort (p. 579)
radix sort (p. 591)
search key (p. 556)
space complexity (p. 543)
space efficiency (p. 542)
straight selection sort (p. 573)
synonyms (p. 565)
time complexity (p. 543)
time efficiency (p. 542)
worst case analysis (p. 560)

EXERCISES

12.1 For each pair of functions $T1$ and $T2$ below, tell whether $T1$ dominates $T2$, $T2$ dominates $T1$, or neither dominates the other. (The letter T is often used to suggest execution **T**ime of an algorithm.)

a. $T1(X) = 2{*}X^2$

   $T2(X) = 2{*}X$

b. $T1(X) = 5{*}X^2$

   $T2(X) = 2{*}X^3$

c. $T1(Y) = 55{*}Y^{15}+3{*}Y^4+7500$

   $T2(Y) = Y^{16}+2$

d. $T1(Z) = (Z + 3){*}(Z + 5)$

   $T2(Z) = 250{*}Z$

e. $T1(Z) = (Z + 7){*}(Z + 9)$

   $T2(Z) = 2{*}Z^3$

f. $T1(N) = 37{*}N^2$

   $T2(N) = N \log N$

g. $T1(N) = 37*N^2$

   $T2(N) = N^2 \log N$

h. $T1(N) = \log_2 N$

   $T2(N) = \log_3 N$

i. $T1(N) = 84$

   $T2(N) = \log_9 N$

j. $T1(X) = \dfrac{3*X + 2}{X}$

   $T2(X) = 766*X$

k. $T1(X) = \dfrac{X^4 + X^2 - 17}{X^3}$

   $T2(X) = X^2$

l. $T1(W) = W^9$

   $T2(W) = 9^W$

m. $T1(W) = W!$

   $T2(W) = 67^W$

n. $T1(V) = V^V$

   $T2(V) = 25^V$

o. $T1(X, Y) = 2*X^3*Y$

   $T2(X, Y) = 3*X*Y$

p. $T1(X, Y) = X^2 + 75$

   $T2(X, Y) = 7*Y$

q. $T1(V, W) = W^3 + W + 74$

   $T2(V, W) = V + 18$

12.2 Using big-O notation, give the order of each function in Exercise 12.1.

12.3 Rank the following big-O measures from greatest to least. (Recall that O(f) > O(g) if and only if f dominates g.)

   a. $O(N)$

   b. $O(N^3)$

   c. $O(4^N)$

   d. $O(\log_4 N)$

   e. $O(\log_5 N)$

   f. $O(N^2)$

   g. $O(1)$

   h. $O(N \log_3 N)$

   i. $O(N^2 \log_3 N)$

12.4 Classify each big-O measure of Exercise 12.3 as one (or more) of the following: constant, linear, quadratic, cubic, logarithmic, polynomial, or exponential.

12.5 Determine the order of each function below, and classify each result as constant, linear, quadratic, cubic, logarithmic, or exponential.

a. $T(N) = 3*N^2 + N$

b. $T(N) = 55*N^3 + 77*N^2 + 99$

c. $T(N) = 2^N*N^2$

d. $T(N) = 7501$

e. $T(N) = \log N + 46*N$

f. $T(N) = 3^{(N+1)}$

g. $T(N) = \dfrac{N \log N}{2 + N}$

h. $T(N) = \dfrac{3*N^4 + 4*N^3}{5*N^2 + N}$

i. $T(N) = \dfrac{17^N}{N^2}$

12.6 Using big-O notation, estimate the running time of each of the following algorithms. You may assume that all variables are of type `int`.

a.
```
for (i = 1; i <= X; i++)
    for (j = 1; j <= X; j++)
        for (k = 1; k <= X; k++) {
            // Five assignment instructions
        }
```

b.
```
for (i = 10; i <= X; i++) {
    // Two assignment instructions
    for (j = 15; j <= X; j++) {
        for (k = 1; k <= X; k++) {
            // Five assignment instructions
        }
        // Seven assignment instructions
    }
}
```

c.
```
for (i = 1; i <= X; i++) {
    for (j = 1; j <= X; j++) {
        // Twenty assignment instructions
    }
    for (j = 1; j <= X; j++)
        if (j % 2 == 1)
            for (k = 1; k <= X; k++) {
                // Five assignment instructions
            }
}
```

```
d. for (i = 1; i <= X; i++) {
       for (j = i; j <= X; j++) {
           // Six assignment instructions
       }
       if (i % 2 == 1) {
           // Four assignment instructions
       }
   }

e. for (i = 1; i <= X; i++)
       for (j = 1; j <= Y; j++)
           for (k = 1; k <= X; k++) {
               // Two assignment instructions
           }

f. i = 1;
   while (i <= X) {
       // Three assignment instructions
       j = 17;
       while (j <= 100) {
           // Two assignment instructions
           j++;
       }
       i++;
   }

g. i = X;
   do {
       // Three assignment instructions
       j = 1;
       while (j <= X) {
           // Two assignment instructions
           j++;
       }
       i--;
   } while (i >= 1);

h. i = 1;
   while (i <= X) {
       // Three assignment instructions
       j = 1;
       while (j <= X) {
           // Two assignment instructions
           j = j * 2;
       }
       i++;
   }
```

```
i. i = X;
   while (i >= 1) {
       // Three assignment instructions
       j = 1;
       while (j <= X) {
           // Two assignment instructions
           j = j + 2;
       }
       i = i / 3;
   }
```

12.7 Using big-O notation, estimate the running time of each of the following recursive functions.

a.
```
void RecA( int X )
{
    // Some task requiring constant time
    if (X > 0)
        RecA(X-1);
}
```

b.
```
void RecB( int X )
{
    int i;

    for (i = 1; i <= X; i++) {
        // Some task requiring constant time
    }
    if (X > 1)
        RecB(X-1);
}
```

c.
```
void RecC( int X )
{
    int i;

    for (i = 1; i <= X; i++) {
        // Some task requiring constant time
    }
    if (X > 1)
        RecC(X/2);
}
```

d.
```
void RecD( int X )
{
    int i;

    // Some task requiring constant time
    for (i = 1; i <= X; i++)
        if (X > 1)
            RecD(X-1);
}
```

12.8 Assume that the data values

$$358, 457, 162, 187, 24, 5, 80, 54$$

are inserted into a 10-slot hash table, in that order.

   a. Diagram the resulting hash table if the hash function is

$$H(k) = \text{the middle ("ten's") digit of } k$$

   and linear probing is used to resolve collisions.

   b. Give a C++ expression that computes the hash function of part (a).

   c. Repeat part (a) using chaining instead of linear probing to resolve collisions.

   d. Diagram the resulting hash table if the hash function is

$$H(k) = \text{the rightmost ("one's") digit of } k$$

   and linear probing is used to resolve collisions.

   e. Give a C++ expression that computes the hash function of part (d).

   f. Repeat part (d) using chaining instead of linear probing to resolve collisions.

12.9 In Exercise 12.8, the hash function of parts (d) through (f) uses the division technique (computing the remainder upon dividing by the table length). The division technique works best if the table length is a prime number. Repeat part (f) using a table length of 11 instead of 10.

12.10 Below is an informal description of the **insertion sort** algorithm for sorting an N-element integer vector.

```
for (sortHi = 0; sortHi < N-1; sortHi++) {
           // INV (prior to test):
           //      vec[0..sortHi] are in ascending order
           //   && vec[sortHi+1..N-1] are unchanged from
           //             the time of function invocation
           //   && sortHi <= N-1
     currentVal = vec[sortHi+1];


     Locate the correct place within vec[0..sortHi+1]
        to place currentVal.  Call the subscript loShift;


     For all subscripts, s, in the range loShift..sortHi,
        shift vec such that vec[s+1] == vec[s];


     vec[loShift] = currentVal;
}
```

a. A **linear insertion sort** searches for the appropriate value of loShift as follows:

```
loShift = 0;
while (loShift < sortHi+1 && currentVal > vec[loShift])
    loShift++;
```

Perform a big-O analysis of the linear insertion sort, assuming that vec is already in sorted order. Give separate measures for the number of comparisons and the number of data movements.

b. Below is another algorithm for finding loShift.

```
loShift = sortHi+1;
while (loShift > 0 && currentVal < vec[loShift-1])
    loShift--;
```

Perform the same analysis as in part (a) for this new version of the linear insertion sort, again assuming an already-sorted array.

c. Another variation of insertion sort is the **binary insertion sort.** This version uses a binary search algorithm to locate the correct value for loShift. Repeat the analysis of part (a) using binary insertion sort on an already-sorted array.

d. For the linear insertion sort and binary insertion sort, what are the worst case and average case measures? Answer for both number of comparisons and number of data movements.

12.11 For each of the bubble sort and selection sort as benchmarked in Table 12.8, compute an approximate constant of dominance (a number that when multiplied by $vecSize^2$ approximately equals the benchmark results).

12.12 Consider the following three-step algorithm:

1. Read N data items into vec[0..N-1].
2. Sort vec[0..N-1] into ascending order.
3. Perform a binary search to locate one value in vec[0..N-1] and print the result.

a. What is the worst case time running time for the entire algorithm? Consider both N^2 sorts and $N \log N$ sorts.

b. Suppose we omit step 2 and substitute a linear search for step 3. What is the resulting running time?

c. Suppose we omit step 2 and modify step 3 to be:

```
for (i = 1; i <= N; i++) {
    Perform a binary search to locate one value in vec[0..N-1] and
    print the result
}
```

What is the resulting running time?

**PROGRAMMING
PROJECTS**

12.1 Place 500 random integers into a vector. Code the linear search (Figure 12.8), binary search (Figure 12.9), improved binary search (Figure 12.11), hash table search using linear probing (Figure 12.14), and hash table search using chaining (Figure 12.16). For both hashing methods, use the division technique for the hash function, where the table length is a prime number. Benchmark each algorithm by performing 1000 different lookup operations. Compare the results.

12.2 Consider the linear insertion sort and binary insertion sort described in Exercise 12.10. Code both algorithms as alternative implementations of the Sort function (Figure 12.18).

    a. Benchmark the two algorithms for vectors of random data and vector sizes of 500, 1000, and 1500 items.

    b. Benchmark the two algorithms for vectors that are already sorted and vector sizes of 500, 1000, and 1500 items.

12.3 MergeSort is another recursive sorting algorithm. This algorithm recursively splits a vector into two halves (approximately equal in size), sorts each half, and merges the two into one. The sorting of each half is accomplished by recursively invoking MergeSort, while the merge is a separate $O(1)$ algorithm.

    a. Perform a best case, average case (using random data), and worst case performance analysis.

    b. Implement, code, and test MergeSort.

    c. Benchmark MergeSort against two other sorting algorithms.

12.4 Code a radix sort to sort unsigned integer values. Use your machine's maximum unsigned int value to determine the bounds for the sort. Sort by individual decimal digits as discussed in the chapter.

    a. Benchmark your code against two other sorts for random data.

    b. Analyze the time and space efficiencies of your algorithm, assuming a vector of 10 identical values.

    c. Analyze the time and space efficiencies of your algorithm, assuming a vector of 10 distinct values with differing leftmost decimal digits.

CHAPTER 13

Trees

INTRODUCTION

Many data structures have components arranged in **linear form.** Recall that a linear data structure has a unique first component and a unique last component, and every other component has a unique predecessor and a unique successor. The sequence is a primitive model for many linear data structures. Arrays, records, lists, stacks, and queues all have linear form.

Some data structures do not have linear form. Data and real-world information sometimes exhibit **hierarchical form.** A hierarchy is a nonlinear structure in which each component may have several successors.

A family tree is a good example of a hierarchical arrangement. The hierarchy of a family tree proceeds from ancestors to descendants. The people in a family tree are positioned below their parents and above their children. The family tree is nonlinear because each person may have several successors (children).

Another example of a hierarchical structure is the biological classification system. This system classifies every living organism according to kingdom, phylum, class, order, family, genus, species, and variety. A single kingdom contains several phyla, a single phylum contains several classes, and so forth. This system forms a hierarchy or taxonomy. As an example, the lion has the following taxonomy:

Kingdom = Animal
    Phylum = Chordata
        Subphylum = Vertebrata
           Class = Mammalia
               Order = Carnivora
                  Family = Felidae
                     Genus = Felis
                        Species = Leo

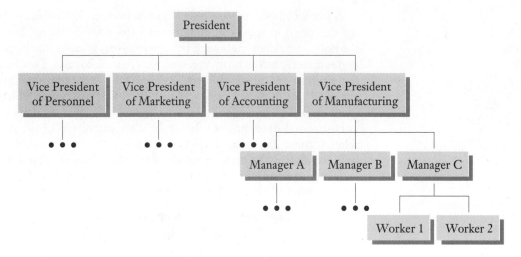

Figure 13.1 A section of a company hierarchy

The business world also has numerous examples of hierarchies. *Department, division, group,* and *subsidiary* all describe portions of business hierarchies. Figure 13.1 shows a typical business personnel hierarchy. At the top of the hierarchy is the president. Just beneath the president are several vice presidents. Each vice president is responsible for several managers. Managers oversee the work of other employees. (In Figure 13.1, only the manufacturing division and the employees under Manager C are elaborated. The other divisions could be expanded in a similar fashion.)

Most hierarchical structures take the form of **trees.** Informally, a tree is a hierarchy in which each component, except the topmost, is immediately beneath exactly one other component. That is, each component may have several successors but only one predecessor. The company hierarchy in Figure 13.1 forms a tree as long as each worker reports to a single manager, each manager reports to a single vice president, and all vice presidents report directly to the president.

The name *tree* is appropriate because of the structure's similarity to the common biological tree. In most trees, a leaf connects to a single twig, a twig to a single branch, a branch to a single limb, and all limbs ultimately connect to the tree trunk. It is conventional to diagram tree structures upside down so that all branching occurs downward, as in Figure 13.1.

13.1 The Terminology of Trees

The study of tree hierarchies uses terminology borrowed from biological trees. The **root** of a tree is the single component at the top of the hierarchical form. In Figure 13.1, the president is the root of the tree. Components having no successors (the workers in Figure 13.1) are called **leaves.** A tree must have only one root and must branch out to all the leaves.

A tree's components are referred to as **nodes.** Relationships between nodes are described in terminology borrowed from family trees. For a given node, the node immediately above it (its predecessor) is said to be its **parent,** and the nodes directly below it (its successors) are its **children.** Two nodes having the same parent are called **siblings.** In Figure 13.1, the president node is the parent of all vice president nodes, all vice president nodes are children of the president node, and all vice president nodes are siblings of each other. The **ancestor** and **descendant** relationships are extensions of the parent and child relationships. In Figure 13.1, Worker 1 is a descendant of the president node and, conversely, the president node is an ancestor of Worker 1.

A more formal definition of trees appears in Definition 13.1. A tree is also called a **general tree** to distinguish it from more specialized kinds of trees.

   i. An empty tree—one without any nodes—is a tree.

   ii. A single node by itself is a tree. (The single node is the root.)

   iii. The structure formed by taking a node R and one or more separate trees and making R the parent of all roots of the trees is a tree.

Definition 13.1 Recursive definition of tree

Part (iii) of Definition 13.1, the recursive part of the definition, states that if we take several existing trees and a new node and make the new node the par-

---

a. From part (ii) of the definition, the following is a tree:

○

b. Using three single-node trees as in (a) and a new node, part (iii) defines the following to also be a tree:

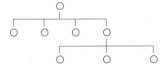

c. Using three single-node trees, the tree from (b), and a new node, part (iii) defines the following to also be a tree:

d. Using the tree from (c), one single-node tree, the tree from (b), and a new node, part (iii) defines the following to also be a tree:

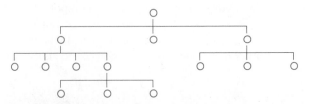

Figure 13.2 Applications of recursive definition of tree

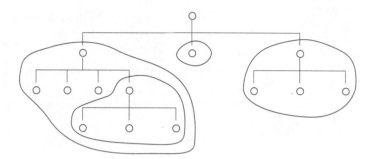

Figure 13.3 Selected subtrees of a tree

ent of all existing tree roots, the result is itself a tree. Figure 13.2 shows how we can use this recursion to construct trees. The nodes in Figure 13.2 are symbolized as circles (o).

Part (iii) of the definition of trees provides a way to construct trees from existing trees. After the construction, the new tree contains the old trees as **subtrees.** A subtree is a tree by itself but is also part of a larger tree. By convention, the empty tree is considered a subtree of every tree. Figure 13.3 illustrates some of the subtrees of a larger tree.

Two other terms associated with trees are the **level of a node** and the **height** (or **depth**) **of a tree.** The level of the root is defined to be 1, and the level of any other node is one more than the level of its parent. In Figure 13.3, the root is at level 1, its three children are at level 2, and so forth. The height of a tree is then defined in terms of the levels of its nodes. Specifically, the height of a tree is the maximum value of the levels of its leaves. The height of the tree in Figure 13.3 is 4, because the lowermost three leaves are at level 4.

Summary of Tree Terminology

Tree

    i. A collection of no nodes is a tree.

    ii. Any single node is itself a tree.

    iii. Given several trees and a separate node, the result of making each original root a child of the new node is a tree.

Empty Tree

A tree with no nodes is an empty tree.

Child

A child of a node is an immediate successor of that node. A node may have several children.

Parent

If node C is a child of node P, then P is a parent of C. A node can have at most one parent.

Descendant

    i. If node C is a child of node P, then C is a descendant of P.

ii. If node C is a child of a descendant of node D, then C is a descendant of D.

Ancestor

If node D is a descendant of node A, then A is an ancestor of D.

Root

The root of a tree is the single node having no parent.

Leaf

A leaf of a tree is a node without children.

Subtree

i. The empty tree is a subtree of any tree.

ii. Any node of a tree, together with all its descendants, is a subtree.

Level

i. The level of the root node is 1.

ii. The level of any node other than the root is one greater than the level of its parent.

Height (Depth)

The height of a tree is the maximum of the levels of its leaves.

13.2   Binary Trees

A **binary tree** is a special kind of tree of particular interest in computer science. Binary trees differ from general trees in two ways.

1. A node in a binary tree can have at most two children.

2. The two children of a node have special names: the **left child** and the **right child.**

Every node of a binary tree has zero, one, or two children. Furthermore, every child in a binary tree must be designated as the left child or the right child of its parent. A parent can have at most one left child and one right child.

Figure 13.4 shows several examples of binary trees. We have labeled each node in these trees with a letter for identification. It is customary to draw left children below and to the left of their parents and right children below and to the right.

In Figure 13.4, Binary Tree 1 consists of three nodes. The root node is the node labeled A. Node A has a left child, B, and a right child, C, both of which are leaf nodes.

Binary Tree 2 consists of eight nodes. Nodes T, R, and S are leaf nodes because they have no children. Node Z, the root node, has only a left child. Nodes X and V have only right children, and nodes Y and W have two children each.

For Binary Trees 3 and 4, every nonleaf node has a single child. In Binary Tree 3, nodes D and F each have a left child, whereas nodes E and G each

Binary Tree 1

Binary Tree 2

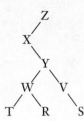

Binary Tree 3

Binary Tree 4

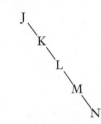

Figure 13.4 Examples of binary trees

have a right child. Every node of Binary Tree 4, except the leaf node N, has only a right child.

If we consider the two trees

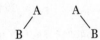

to be general trees, then they are only different drawings of the same tree. But as binary trees, these two are different trees. The left and right children of the root nodes are not the same.

A Binary Tree ADT

Just as any other data structure, a program representation of a binary tree stores data. Each node of the tree contains one or more data items. Figure 13.5 presents a specification file for a binary tree abstract data type. For the `CharTree` module of this figure, each node contains a single `char` value.

Figure 13.5 `CharTree` specification file

```
// ------------------------------------------------------------
//   SPECIFICATION FILE (chartree.h)
//   This module exports 1) CharTree, an ADT for an unbounded
//   binary tree whose nodes contain char values, 2) a pointer type
//   NodePtr for accessing nodes in a tree, and 3) operations on
//   tree nodes.
// ------------------------------------------------------------
#include "bool.h"
```

```
/*--------------------------------------------------------------*/
/*                Notation Used in Assertions                   */
/*--------------------------------------------------------------*/
/* ValidNode(n) means                                           */
/*     n is some node that has been placed in the binary tree via */
/*     BuildRoot (of CharTree class), AppendLeft, or AppendRight  */
/* Contents(n) means                                            */
/*     the data stored in node n of the tree                    */
/* HasLeftChild(n) means                                        */
/*     node n has some left child, LC, AND ValidNode(LC)        */
/* HasRightChild(n) means                                       */
/*     node n has some right child, RC, AND ValidNode(RC)       */
/* IsLeaf(n) means                                              */
/*     NOT HasLeftChild(n) AND NOT HasRightChild(n)             */
/*--------------------------------------------------------------*/

struct TreeNode;                // Complete declaration hidden in
                                // implementation file
typedef TreeNode* NodePtr;

class CharTree {
public:
    Boolean IsEmpty() const;
        // POST: FCTVAL == (tree has no nodes)

    void BuildRoot( /* in */ char someChar );
        // PRE:  IsEmpty()
        // POST: Tree has root node, call it R
        //     && Contents(R) == someChar  &&  IsLeaf(R)

    NodePtr Root() const;
        // POST: FCTVAL == NULL, if IsEmpty()
        //                 == pointer to root node, otherwise

    CharTree();
        // Constructor
        // POST: Created(tree)  &&  IsEmpty()
private:
    NodePtr rootPtr;
};

//..................................................................
// The following operations manipulate nodes indirectly
// through pointers of type NodePtr
//..................................................................

void AppendLeft( /* in */ NodePtr ptr,
                 /* in */ char    someChar );
    // PRE:  ValidNode(*ptr) &&  Assigned(someChar)
    // POST: New node, call it LC, created as left child of *ptr
    //     && ValidNode(LC) && IsLeaf(LC) && Contents(LC) == someChar
    // NOTE: Dangling pointers may occur if HasLeftChild(*ptr<entry>)
```

```
void AppendRight( /* in */ NodePtr ptr,
                  /* in */ char    someChar );
    // PRE:  ValidNode(*ptr) && Assigned(someChar)
    // POST: New node, call it RC, created as right child of *ptr
    //     && ValidNode(RC) && IsLeaf(RC) && Contents(RC) == someChar
    // NOTE: Dangling pointers may occur if
    //       HasRightChild(*ptr<entry>)

char Data( /* in */ NodePtr ptr );
    // PRE:  ValidNode(*ptr) && Assigned(Contents(*ptr))
    // POST: FCTVAL == Contents(*ptr)

void Store( /* in */ NodePtr ptr,
            /* in */ char    someChar );
    // PRE:  ValidNode(*ptr) && Assigned(someChar)
    // POST: Contents(*ptr) == someChar

NodePtr LChild( /* in */ NodePtr ptr );
    // PRE:  ValidNode(*ptr)
    // POST: FCTVAL == NULL, if NOT HasLeftChild(*ptr)
    //               == pointer to left child of *ptr, otherwise

NodePtr RChild( /* in */ NodePtr ptr );
    // PRE:  ValidNode(*ptr)
    // POST: FCTVAL == NULL, if NOT HasRightChild(*ptr)
    //               == pointer to right child of *ptr, otherwise

Boolean IsLeaf( /* in */ NodePtr ptr );
    // PRE:  ValidNode(*ptr)
    // POST: FCTVAL == IsLeaf(*ptr)

void DeleteLeaf( /* inout */ NodePtr& ptr );
    // PRE:  IsLeaf(*ptr<entry>)
    // POST: *ptr<entry> removed from tree  &&  ptr is undefined
```

The `CharTree` module exports a class, `CharTree`, for declaring binary trees and another type, `NodePtr`, for referencing nodes of a tree. The `CharTree` class constructor creates an empty tree, and the class member function `BuildRoot` creates a single root node. With these two operations and the (nonclass) functions `AppendLeft` and `AppendRight`, the importer can build any binary tree.

The `CharTree` class provides a `Root` function that returns a pointer to the root node of a tree. The `LChild` and `RChild` functions return pointers to the children of a node. For example, the left child of the root may be accessed with the expression

```
LChild(someTree.Root())
```

and the rightmost grandchild of the root of `someTree` is referenced as

```
RChild(RChild(someTree.Root()))
```

Note that the use of pointers does not necessarily imply a dynamic data implementation of binary trees. A NodePtr variable is a pointer to a TreeNode, a structure whose complete declaration is hidden in the implementation file. The user of this module does not know the data representation of a TreeNode or how the nodes are collected into a tree organization. Using pointers to the actual structures not only supports information hiding, it is also more efficient. Passing pointers from function to function is less costly than passing the nodes themselves.

Figure 13.6 illustrates the use of CharTree with a sample driver. This program constructs and outputs the contents of a binary tree of eight nodes, each containing a single character.

Figure 13.6 Driver for the CharTree module

```
// -----------------------------------------------------------------
//   testtree.cpp
//   This is a driver for the CharTree module.
// -----------------------------------------------------------------
#include "chartree.h"
#include <iostream.h>

int main()
{
    CharTree tree;

    tree.BuildRoot('r');
    AppendLeft(tree.Root(), 'h');
    AppendRight(tree.Root(), 'T');
    AppendLeft(LChild(tree.Root()), 'C');
    AppendRight(LChild(tree.Root()), 'a');
    AppendRight(RChild(tree.Root()), 'e');
    AppendLeft(RChild(RChild(tree.Root())), 'r');
    AppendRight(RChild(RChild(tree.Root())), 'e');

    /* ASSERT: tree contents appear as follows:    */
    /*                                             */
    /*                      'r'                    */
    /*                     /  \                    */
    /*                   'h'  'T'                  */
    /*                  /  \    \                  */
    /*                'C'  'a'  'e'                */
    /*                         /  \                */
    /*                       'r'  'e'              */

    cout << "Printing contents of the binary tree.\n";
    cout << "\"CharTree\" should be output: ";
    cout << Data(LChild(LChild(tree.Root())));
    cout << Data((LChild(tree.Root())));
    cout << Data(RChild(LChild(tree.Root())));
    cout << Data(tree.Root());
    cout << Data((RChild(tree.Root())));
    cout << Data(LChild(RChild(RChild(tree.Root()))));
    cout << Data(RChild(RChild(tree.Root())));
    cout << Data(RChild(RChild(RChild(tree.Root()))));
    cout << '\n';
```

```
          return 0;
    }
```

Implementing the CharTree *Module*

To implement a binary tree, one strategy is to represent each tree node as a struct with three members:

1. the data contents of the node
2. the location of the left child of the node
3. the location of the right child of the node

We can represent the entire tree by linking together these structs. In Chapter 8 we discussed two representations of a linked list. One was an array of structs, linked together by subscripts, the other a collection of dynamically allocated structs, linked together by pointers. Both alternatives are appropriate for binary trees as well. In this section we examine the dynamic data representation.

The CharTree specification file declares each tree node to be of type TreeNode. The full declaration of the TreeNode type appears in Figure 13.7, along with an abstract diagram of a TreeNode object.

The TreeNode declaration includes a constructor to simplify initializing all three members of a newly allocated node. Recall that a C++ struct is a special case of a class in which all members are public. Therefore it is possible, though not especially common, for a struct to have constructors, destructors, and other member functions.

Using this data representation, the binary tree constructed by the driver program of Figure 13.6 is pictured in Figure 13.8. The variable tree, an object of class CharTree, has private data member rootPtr that points to the root node of the tree.

```
struct TreeNode {
    char    data;                       // Data member
    NodePtr lLink;                      // Pointer to left child
    NodePtr rLink;                      // Pointer to right child
    TreeNode( char, NodePtr, NodePtr ); // Constructor
};
```

A TreeNode object:

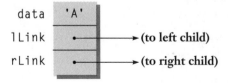

Figure 13.7 TreeNode type

Sample binary tree   **Dynamic data representation**

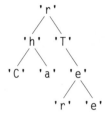

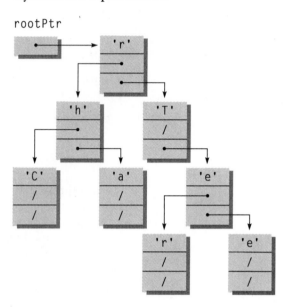

Figure 13.8 Dynamic data representation of a binary tree

Because a CharTree object manages dynamic data on the free store, a class destructor is necessary to deallocate the entire tree when the class object goes out of scope. The CharTree class declaration in Figure 13.5 is missing a destructor. Without one, destruction of a CharTree object destroys only its private data (the pointer to the root node), leaving all tree nodes still allocated on the free store but inaccessible. We have temporarily omitted a class destructor and copy-constructor because they require algorithms for traversing an entire binary tree. Later in the chapter we will write these member functions when discussing tree traversal.

The complete code for the dynamic implementation of CharTree is shown in Figure 13.9.

Figure 13.9 CharTree implementation file

```
// ------------------------------------------------------------------
// IMPLEMENTATION FILE (chartree.cpp)
// This module exports 1) CharTree, an ADT for an unbounded
// binary tree whose nodes contain char values, 2) a pointer type
// NodePtr for accessing nodes in a tree, and 3) operations on
// tree nodes.
// ------------------------------------------------------------------
#include "chartree.h"
#include <stddef.h>       // For NULL

struct TreeNode {
    char    data;                        // Data member
    NodePtr lLink;                       // Pointer to left child
    NodePtr rLink;                       // Pointer to right child
```

```
          TreeNode( char, NodePtr, NodePtr );  // Constructor
      };

      TreeNode::TreeNode( /* in */ char    someChar,
                          /* in */ NodePtr leftPtr,
                          /* in */ NodePtr rightPtr )
          //.....................................................................
          // POST: data == someChar  &&  lLink == leftPtr
          //     && rLink == rightPtr
          //.....................................................................
      {
          data = someChar;  lLink = leftPtr;  rLink = rightPtr;
      }

      // Private members of CharTree class:
      //    NodePtr rootPtr;                      Pointer to root node

      CharTree::CharTree()
          //.....................................................................
          // POST: rootPtr == NULL
          //.....................................................................
      {
          rootPtr = NULL;
      }

      Boolean CharTree::IsEmpty() const
          //.....................................................................
          // POST: FCTVAL == (rootPtr == NULL)
          //.....................................................................
      {
          return (rootPtr == NULL);
      }

      void CharTree::BuildRoot( /* in */ char someChar )
          //.....................................................................
          // PRE:  rootPtr == NULL
          // POST: rootPtr points to newly allocated node, call it N
          //     && N.data == someChar  &&  N.lLink == NULL
          //     && N.rLink == NULL
          //.....................................................................
      {
          rootPtr = new TreeNode(someChar, NULL, NULL);
      }

      NodePtr CharTree::Root() const
          //.....................................................................
          // POST: FCTVAL == rootPtr
          //.....................................................................
      {
          return rootPtr;
      }
```

```
void AppendLeft( /* in */ NodePtr ptr,
                 /* in */ char     someChar )
    //.................................................................
    // PRE:  ptr != NULL  &&  Assigned(someChar)
    // POST: ptr->lLink points to newly allocated node, call it LC
    //    && LC.data == someChar  &&  LC.lLink == NULL
    //    && LC.rLink == NULL
    //.................................................................
{
    ptr->lLink = new TreeNode(someChar, NULL, NULL);
}

void AppendRight( /* in */ NodePtr ptr,
                  /* in */ char     someChar )
    //.................................................................
    // PRE:  ptr != NULL  &&  Assigned(someChar)
    // POST: ptr->rLink points to newly allocated node, call it RC
    //    && RC.data == someChar  &&  RC.lLink == NULL
    //    && RC.rLink == NULL
    //.................................................................
{
    ptr->rLink = new TreeNode(someChar, NULL, NULL);
}

char Data( /* in */ NodePtr ptr )
    //.................................................................
    // PRE:  ptr != NULL  &&  Assigned(ptr->data)
    // POST: FCTVAL == ptr->data
    //.................................................................
{
    return ptr->data;
}

void Store( /* in */ NodePtr ptr,
            /* in */ char     someChar )
    //.................................................................
    // PRE:  ptr != NULL  &&  Assigned(someChar)
    // POST: ptr->data == someChar
    //.................................................................
{
    ptr->data = someChar;
}

NodePtr LChild( /* in */ NodePtr ptr )
    //.................................................................
    // PRE:  Assigned(ptr)
    //    && (ptr != NULL) --> Assigned(ptr->lLink)
    // POST: FCTVAL == NULL, if ptr == NULL
    //               == ptr->lLink, otherwise
    //.................................................................
{
    return (ptr==NULL) ? NULL : ptr->lLink;
}
```

```
.NodePtr RChild( /* in */ NodePtr ptr )
    //..........................................................
    // PRE:  Assigned(ptr)
    //    && (ptr != NULL) --> Assigned(ptr->rLink)
    // POST: FCTVAL == NULL, if ptr == NULL
    //             == ptr->rLink, otherwise
    //..........................................................
{
    return (ptr==NULL) ? NULL : ptr->rLink;
}

Boolean IsLeaf( /* in */ NodePtr ptr )
    //..........................................................
    // PRE:  ptr != NULL
    // POST: FCTVAL == (ptr->lLink == NULL  &&  ptr->rLink == NULL)
    //..........................................................
{
    return (ptr->lLink == NULL && ptr->rLink == NULL);
}

void DeleteLeaf( /* inout */ NodePtr& ptr )
    //..........................................................
    // PRE:  Assigned(ptr)
    // POST: *ptr deallocated
    //..........................................................
{
    delete ptr;
}
```

13.3 Binary Search Trees

A **binary search tree** is a specialized binary tree with the following properties:

1. No two nodes in the tree contain the same data value. (That is, there are no duplicate data values.)

2. The data values in the tree come from a data type for which the relations "greater than" and "less than" are defined.

3. The data value of every node in the tree is

   • greater than any data value in its left subtree

   • less than any data value in its right subtree

As we will see, binary search trees are particularly useful in searching and sorting problems.

Figure 13.10 shows five binary trees, four of which are binary search trees. Each tree node is labeled with an integer denoting the data contents of the node.

Binary Search Tree 1

Binary Search Tree 2

Binary Search Tree 3

Binary Search Tree 4

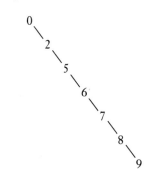

Tree 5 (Not a binary search tree)

Figure 13.10 Binary trees
containing the same
data

Each tree in Figure 13.10 contains the same five values: 0, 2, 5, 6, 7, 8, and 9. The first four trees are all binary search trees. To see that each one is a binary search tree, examine the nodes in the tree. For each node, the data in all descendants in the left subtree must be smaller than the node's data, and the data in all descendants in the right subtree must be greater than the node's data. For example, the following argument shows Binary Search Tree 1 to be a binary search tree:

For the root node (contents = 5):

- the contents of its descendants in the left subtree (0 and 2) are all less than 5

and

- the contents of its descendants in the right subtree (8, 7, 9, and 6) are all greater than 5

For the left child of the root (contents = 2):

- the contents of its single left descendant (0) are less than 2 and

- there are no right descendants

For the right child of the root (contents = 8):

- the contents of its descendants in the left subtree (6 and 7) are all less than 8

and

- the contents of its single right descendant (9) are greater than 8

For the left child of the right child of the root (contents = 7):

- the contents of its single left descendant (6) are less than 7

and

- there are no right descendants

All other nodes (those containing 0, 6, and 9) are leaf nodes and have no descendants.

The fifth binary tree in Figure 13.10 is not a binary search tree. The leaf node containing the value 6 is in the right subtree of the root. To be a binary search tree, every node in this right subtree must have a data value greater than 7, the contents of the root node.

Searching a Binary Search Tree

Binary search trees are important because they are efficient to search and maintain. The algorithm in Figure 13.11 demonstrates the process of searching for a value in a binary search tree. The algorithm searches for the value key in binSrchTree. Assume that an IntTree module exists, identical to CharTree except that tree nodes contain int data.

The algorithm in Figure 13.11 begins by selecting the root of the binary search tree as the original examination node. The loop terminates successfully if *probePtr contains the same value as key. If *probePtr contains some other value, it is compared to key to see which is greater. If key is less than the contents of *probePtr, we can ignore all values in the right subtree; they

Figure 13.11 Algorithm for searching a binary search tree

```
// PRE: binSrchTree is a binary search tree

probePtr = binSrchTree.Root();
while (probePtr != NULL && Data(probePtr) != key)
    if (key < Data(probePtr))
        probePtr = LChild(probePtr);
    else
        probePtr = RChild(probePtr);

// POST: *probePtr contains key
//    OR (key is not present in binSrchTree && probePtr == NULL)
```

binSrchTree: key: **6**

	Data(probePtr)	binSrchTree remaining
Prior to first loop iteration	5	
After first loop iteration	8	
After second loop iteration	7	
After third loop iteration.	6	6

Figure 13.12 Trace of binary search tree searching algorithm

are too large. In this case, we make probePtr point to its left child and continue the loop. Similarly, if key is greater than the value of *probePtr, we ignore the left subtree by updating probePtr to point to its right child.

The algorithm proceeds from ancestors to descendants, quitting when it locates key or when probePtr becomes NULL. In the latter case, key must not be present anywhere in the binary search tree. Figure 13.12 displays a trace of this algorithm for a particular binary search tree.

Figure 13.13 shows a second trace of this search algorithm. This time the key value being looked up, 1, is not in the binary search tree.

	Data(probePtr)	binSrchTree remaining
key: **1**		
Prior to first loop iteration	5	5 / 2 \ 8, 2: 0 / , 8: 7 / \ 9, 7: 6 /
After first loop iteration	2	2 / 0
After second loop iteration	0	0
After third loop iteration.	probePtr = NULL	none

Figure 13.13 Trace of unsuccessful search

Efficiency of Searching a Binary Search Tree

An analysis of this searching algorithm reveals that the maximum number of loop iterations equals the height of the tree. Consequently, the algorithm's computing time depends upon the shape of the tree. A tree with only a few branches is generally inefficient to search. In the worst case, every node except the single leaf node has exactly one child. This type of tree is called a **degenerate binary tree,** an example of which is Binary Search Tree 4 in Figure 13.10. A search of a degenerate binary tree cannot ignore any nodes. It is therefore equivalent to a linear search and has computing time $O(N)$.

A "bushy" binary search tree has a more desirable shape. In the best case, a tree of height k has $2^k - 1$ nodes. This type of tree is known as a **full binary tree.** Binary Search Tree 3 of Figure 13.10 is an example of a full binary tree. A bushy binary tree is said to be **balanced.** In a balanced binary tree, most nodes have two children and only a few have a single child. There are numerous types of balance and many tree balancing algorithms. A discussion of these algorithms is beyond the scope of this book.

If a binary search tree is well balanced, searching the tree requires computing time $O(\log_2 N)$. The reason is that the height of a full binary tree with N nodes is approximately $\log_2 N$, and in searching a full binary search tree, each probe descends exactly one level of the tree. Studies have shown that most binary search trees constructed from random data are somewhat balanced, so searching a binary search tree usually is considered to be a logarithmic algorithm.

Finding a value in a balanced binary search tree is similar to performing a binary search of an array. In the binary search algorithm, each probe eliminates half the remaining array elements from consideration. Correspondingly, each probe of a binary search tree eliminates either the left or right subtree. Each algorithm also requires the data to be ordered in a certain way. The binary search algorithm works only for sorted vectors, and the tree searching algorithm works only for binary trees constructed as binary search trees.

Inserting Values

Inserting an additional value into a sorted vector requires at least a linear algorithm to shift existing values down to make room for the new value. In contrast, inserting a new value into a binary search tree requires no data movement. The preferred method for insertion begins by applying a modified binary search tree search algorithm. When the search algorithm terminates at

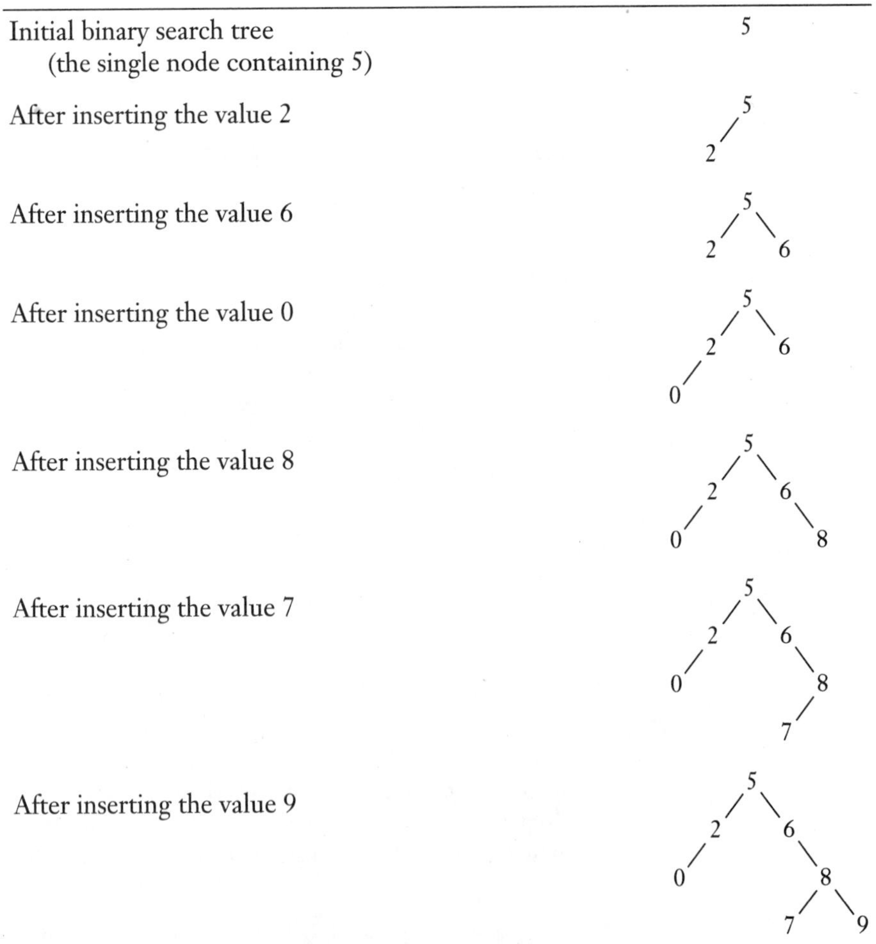

Initial binary search tree (the single node containing 5)	5
After inserting the value 2	
After inserting the value 6	
After inserting the value 0	
After inserting the value 8	
After inserting the value 7	
After inserting the value 9	

Figure 13.14 A sequence of insertions in a binary search tree

a leaf because the new value is not in the tree, we have found the correct place for the insertion. This insertion algorithm has logarithmic computing time because it uses the same basic searching algorithm that is used for looking up a value. Figure 13.14 shows a sequence of insertions and the corresponding binary search tree after each insertion.

Binary search trees often are preferred to sorted vectors because of the speed of insertions and deletions. Of course, there is a price for this improved performance. Binary trees require memory overhead: the two variables per node needed to locate the left and right children. When data values are stored directly in a vector, there is no need for these extra variables.

13.4 Binary Tree Traversal

An algorithm for processing, or visiting, every node of a tree is referred to as a **tree traversal algorithm.** Many applications require tree traversals. If data for company employees are stored in a tree, a tree traversal is necessary to issue pay checks for all employees.

Consider traversing other data structures. The two most obvious ways to traverse a vector are from least index to greatest or greatest index to least. Traversing a simple list ADT is restricted, by definition, to visiting the head through the tail. Traversing a binary tree presents a wider range of reasonable possibilities. Should ancestors be visited prior to descendants, or vice versa? Should siblings be visited left to right or right to left?

Inorder Traversal

One technique for traversing a binary tree is known as **inorder traversal.** For a tree with root R, an inorder traversal visits each node as follows. First, visit all nodes in the left subtree of R; then visit node R; finally, visit all nodes in the right subtree of R. This process sounds straightforward, but the catch is to remember that every subtree is also a tree with its own root. Therefore, visiting a subtree requires applying the algorithm again to the root of the subtree. For example, an inorder traversal of the following binary tree would visit nodes in the order G, D, B, H, E, I, A, C, F, K, L, J.

Using recursion is the best way to describe the algorithm for inorder traversal. Figure 13.15 shows a recursive C++ function that implements the algorithm.

```
void InorderTraverse( /* in */ NodePtr ptr )
    //...............................................................
    // PRE:  ptr points to the root of a binary tree (or == NULL)
    // POST: Each node in the tree has been visited
    //...............................................................
{
    if (ptr != NULL) {
        InorderTraverse(LChild(ptr));
        Visit(ptr);
        InorderTraverse(RChild(ptr));
    }
}
```

Figure 13.15 Inorder binary tree traversal algorithm

The inorder traversal algorithm performs the following sequence of steps for each non-null node pointer, `ptr`:

1. Visit each node in the left subtree of `*ptr`

2. Visit `*ptr`

3. Visit each node in the right subtree of `*ptr`

Steps 1 and 3 are accomplished through recursion.

Inorder traversal goes hand in hand with binary search trees. An inorder traversal of a binary search tree visits the nodes in ascending order of data values. For example, replace `Visit(ptr)` with

`cout << Data(ptr) << ' ';`

and apply the algorithm to the binary search tree

Then an inorder traversal outputs the data in sorted order: 0   2   5   6   7   8   9.

Preorder and Postorder Traversal

Two other well-known binary tree traversal algorithms are **preorder traversal** and **postorder traversal.** These two algorithms result from changing the sequence of the three steps in the inorder traversal algorithm. The names *preorder* and *postorder* suggest the time at which a node is visited. A preorder traversal visits the node *before* visiting its left and right subtrees. A postorder traversal visits the node *after* visiting its left and right subtrees.

Figure 13.16 shows all three traversal algorithms. To initiate the traversal of an entire binary tree, the calling code would supply the pointer to the root as an actual parameter:

`InorderTraverse(desiredTree.Root());`

```
void InorderTraverse( /* in */ NodePtr ptr )
{
    if (ptr != NULL) {
        InorderTraverse(LChild(ptr));
        Visit(ptr);
        InorderTraverse(RChild(ptr));
    }
}

void PreorderTraverse( /* in */ NodePtr ptr )
{
    if (ptr != NULL) {
        Visit(ptr);
        PreorderTraverse(LChild(ptr));
        PreorderTraverse(RChild(ptr));
    }
}

void PostorderTraverse( /* in */ NodePtr ptr )
{
    if (ptr != NULL) {
        PostorderTraverse(LChild(ptr));
        PostorderTraverse(RChild(ptr));
        Visit(ptr);
    }
}
```

Figure 13.16 Inorder, preorder, and postorder binary tree traversal algorithms

Figure 13.17 illustrates the differences among these three traversal algorithms by showing the order in which nodes are visited for a particular binary tree.

Each node of the tree is visited exactly once in a traversal. Therefore, each of the three traversal algorithms is an O(*N*) algorithm, where *N* is the number of nodes in the tree.

<u>**Binary Tree**</u>

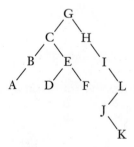

Figure 13.17 Sample traversals: inorder, preorder, and postorder

<u>**Order of visitation**</u>

Preorder traversal: G, C, B, A, E, D, F, H, I, L, J, K
Inorder traversal: A, B, C, D, E, F, G, H, I, J, K, L
Postorder traversal: A, B, D, F, E, C, K, J, L, I, H, G

A Destructor For `CharTree`

Knowing how to visit each node of a binary tree, we can now write a destructor for the `CharTree` class that we introduced earlier. When a `CharTree` object is destroyed, we must ensure that all tree nodes on the free store are deallocated. The destructor invokes a recursive function named `DeleteAll`:

```
CharTree::~CharTree()
    //......................................................
    // POST: All tree nodes deleted from free store
    //......................................................
{
    DeleteAll(rootPtr);
}
```

The `DeleteAll` routine performs a postorder traversal to deallocate each node *after* deallocating all descendants in the node's left and right subtrees:

```
void DeleteAll( /* in */ NodePtr ptr )
    //......................................................
    // PRE:  ptr points to the root of a binary tree (or == NULL)
    // POST: (ptr != NULL) --> All nodes in the left and right
    //                         subtrees of *ptr are deallocated
    //                         && *ptr is deallocated
    //......................................................
{
    if (ptr != NULL) {
        DeleteAll(LChild(ptr));
        DeleteAll(RChild(ptr));
        delete ptr;
    }
}
```

13.5 Binary Expression Trees

Another use of trees is to define the semantics of an expression. For example, the tree

describes the expression 2 + 3, and the tree

describes the expression 7 + (6*4). This kind of tree is known as an **expression tree.** If the expression uses only binary operators (operators requiring exactly

Expression: 6 * 2 + 7 + 8 * 3 – 6 / 7

Binary expression tree:

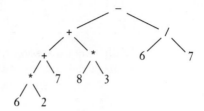

Figure 13.18 A binary
expression tree

two operands), it is known as a **binary expression tree.** The rules for a binary
expression tree are:

1. Each leaf node contains a single operand, and each nonleaf node contains
    a single operator.
2. The left and right subtrees of an operator node represent the subexpres-
    sions that must be evaluated before applying the operator at the root of
    the subtree.

Each subtree of an expression tree represents a subexpression. The interpretation is that both subtree expressions must be evaluated before performing
the operation at their root. The expression tree therefore defines the associativity (or grouping) of the operators with their operands.

Figure 13.18 illustrates a C++ expression and its corresponding binary
expression tree.

To show that this binary expression tree accurately describes the semantics
of the given expression, we start at any of the bottom subtrees—those whose
children are both leaves. Let us choose the subtree

The result of 6*2 should be added to 7, giving (6*2) + 7, as the following subtree indicates:

Next, the expression ((6*2) + 7) + (8*3) is obtained from the subtree

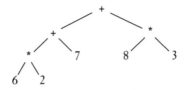

Finally, the expression tree of Figure 13.18 dictates subtracting the value of 6/7 from the current result. The complete expression, written in fully parenthesized form to show the grouping of operators and operands, is therefore

$$(((((6^*2) + 7) + (8^*3))) - (6/7))$$

Programming language compilers, when generating machine language instructions, often use expression trees to analyze the semantics of expressions. In this context the trees are called *abstract syntax trees*. Compilers also use an extension of the concept of an expression tree, known as a *derivation tree* or *parse tree*, to analyze program syntax.

Inorder, preorder, and postorder traversals of binary expression trees produce interesting results. If visiting a node means to display its contents, an inorder traversal displays the expression in **infix notation.** In infix notation, each binary operator appears immediately between its two operands. Infix notation is the "normal" expression notation that we are accustomed to using. Figure 13.19 shows the infix expression form for a particular tree.

Preorder traversal of a binary expression tree results in **prefix notation.** In prefix notation, each binary operator appears *before* its two operands. Consecutive operations must therefore be performed right to left to preserve semantic correctness. For example, the last operation to be performed is listed at the left ("–" in the example of Figure 13.19). This operation precedes its two operand subexpressions, namely "+ + * 6 2 7 * 8 3" and "/ 6 7".

A postorder traversal of an expression tree produces an expression in **postfix notation** or **reverse Polish notation (RPN).** An expression in RPN form has

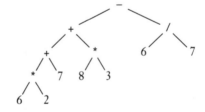

Figure 13.19 Expressions resulting from different traversals of a binary expression tree

Inorder traversal (yielding infix expression):
   6 * 2 + 7 + 8 * 3 – 6 / 7
Preorder traversal (yielding prefix expression):
   – + + * 6 2 7 * 8 3 / 6 7
Postorder traversal (yielding postfix expression):
   6 2 * 7 + 8 3 * + 6 7 / –

WHILE more tokens exist in RPNexpression {
    thisToken = next token in RPNexpression;
    IF thisToken is an operand THEN
        Push thisToken onto operand stack;
    ELSE {
        // ASSERT: thisToken is an operator
        Pop the top two values from operand stack (topmost value is the right
          operand);
        Using these two values as operands, perform operation corresponding to
          thisToken;
        Push the result onto operand stack;
    }
}
// ASSERT: Top of operand stack contains the value of RPNexpression.

Figure 13.20 Algorithm for RPN expression evaluation

the property that each binary operator comes *after* its two operands. For correct semantics, consecutive operations in an RPN expression are always performed left to right.

Some hand-held calculators allow (or even require) the user to enter RPN expressions. The algorithm for evaluating such an expression is especially efficient. This algorithm, presented in Figure 13.20, scans an RPN expression left to right and uses a stack to hold intermediate results. In the algorithm, a *token* is either an operator symbol or an individual operand.

Figure 13.21 shows a sample trace of this algorithm. This figure traces the evaluation of an expression by showing each token (highlighted on the left of the trace) and the resulting operand stack (on the right of the trace). Comments on the far right of the diagram indicate simple expressions that are evaluated.

Expression	Operand stack (top →)	
6 2 * 7 + 8 3 * + 6 7 / −	6	
6 2 * 7 + 8 3 * + 6 7 / −	6 2	
6 2 * 7 + 8 3 * + 6 7 / −	12	Value of 6 * 2
6 2 * 7 + 8 3 * + 6 7 / −	12 7	
6 2 * 7 + 8 3 * + 6 7 / −	19	Value of 12 + 7
6 2 * 7 + 8 3 * + 6 7 / −	19 8	
6 2 * 7 + 8 3 * + 6 7 / −	19 8 3	
6 2 * 7 + 8 3 * + 6 7 / −	19 24	Value of 8 * 3
6 2 * 7 + 8 3 * + 6 7 / −	43	Value of 19 + 24
6 2 * 7 + 8 3 * + 6 7 / −	43 6	
6 2 * 7 + 8 3 * + 6 7 / −	43 6 7	
6 2 * 7 + 8 3 * + 6 7 / −	43 0	Value of 6/7
6 2 * 7 + 8 3 * + 6 7 / −	43	Value of 43 − 0

Figure 13.21 Trace of RPN expression evaluation

Pursuing Correctness

Infix Notation and Semantic Correctness

One source of logic errors, especially among beginning programmers, is the evaluation of expressions in an unintended order. Without well-defined rules, the semantics of infix expressions like *a* + *b* * *c* are inherently ambiguous. If we are not told the precedence of the operators, this expression could mean either (*a* + *b*) * *c* or *a* + (*b* * *c*).

A common response is to claim that in mathematics as well as programming languages, multiplication "naturally" has higher precedence than addition. This claim is false on two counts. First, mathematics arbitrarily *defines* multiplication to have higher precedence than addition, specifically to eliminate any ambiguity. Second, it is not true that all programming languages define precedence this way. There are programming languages that do not define any precedence among operators; evaluation of expressions always takes place left to right. In such a language, the expression *a* + *b* * *c* means (*a* + *b*) * *c*. Other programming languages evaluate expressions strictly right to left, in which case *a* + *b* * *c* means *a* + (*b* * *c*).

Most programming languages do, in fact, define operator precedence to eliminate ambiguity in infix expressions. Additionally, rules for associativity (grouping) are necessary. If an expression includes two operators with the same precedence, the programmer must know whether *a* - *b* + *c* groups the operators and operands as (*a* - *b*) + *c* or *a* - (*b* + *c*). Finally, most languages allow the use of parentheses to override the default rules of precedence and associativity.

All of the rules commonly associated with infix notation—precedence, associativity, and the use of parentheses—are unnecessary with prefix and postfix notation. There is no possibility of ambiguity in these two notations. The prefix expression + *a* * *bc* has only one interpretation: *a* plus the product of *b* and *c*. Likewise, the postfix expression *abc* * + can only mean *a* plus the product of *b* and *c*.

When programming with languages that use prefix or postfix notation, there is no need to consult (or memorize) operator precedence charts. As well, these notations lessen the risk of mistakes in composing expressions. The disadvantage is having to learn how to "think prefix" or "think postfix." It usually requires some effort to overcome a lifetime of familiarity with infix notation.

13.6   Sorting with Binary Trees

In Chapter 12 we examined several algorithms for sorting data into order. Binary trees also are used for sorting. One method begins by constructing a binary search tree from the data values:

```
Initialize binSrchTree to empty;
For each data value someVal
    Insert(someVal, binSrchTree);
```

This algorithm initializes binSrchTree to be an empty tree. Each loop iteration adds one more data value as a separate node in the tree. The Insert routine is the algorithm referenced in Figure 13.14 for inserting a value into a binary search tree. After building the binary search tree, no actual sorting is necessary. The data are already sorted, in effect, because an inorder traversal will deliver the data in ascending order.

The time required to create a binary search tree is anywhere from $O(N \log N)$ to $O(N^2)$, where N is the number of data values. The loop requires $O(N)$ iterations, and inserting into the tree requires time $O(\log N)$ through $O(N)$, depending on whether the tree stays balanced or becomes unbalanced during its creation.

This method of sorting is somewhat different from earlier sorting techniques. Instead of taking data already in a vector and rearranging them into ascending order, this algorithm places the data into a binary search tree. The major disadvantage is that accessing the data in sorted order requires an inorder traversal, which is slower than iterating through a sorted vector.

The Treesort

Another sorting algorithm, the **treesort,** eliminates this problem with the binary search tree method. Treesort is a two-phase algorithm. Phase 1 begins with a full binary tree in which all data values are placed in the leaf nodes. At this time, all ancestor nodes are considered empty (shown below as "E"):

The remainder of Phase 1 consists of **promoting** the data in each pair of siblings up the tree in order to fill the empty ancestor nodes.

The promotion algorithm begins by comparing the data in each pair of leaf siblings. The smaller value in the two nodes is **promoted** by copying it into the parent node. After all leaf values have been promoted, the parent nodes are compared in sibling pairs. The smaller value is again promoted to the pair's parent (the grandparent of a leaf). This process continues by promoting values from sibling pairs of leaf grandparents, then sibling pairs of leaf great-grandparents, and so forth.

When a promotion occurs, vacancies must be filled by using additional promotions. For example, promotion from a leaf grandparent to a leaf great-grandparent leaves a **vacancy** in the leaf grandparent. This vacancy must be filled immediately by promoting a value from a child of the vacant node. This promotion causes a cascade of more vacancies and more promotions. Figure 13.22 displays an algorithm to fill a vacancy (and all resulting vacancies).

```
void FillVacancies( /* in */ NodePtr justPromoted )
    //.............................................................
    // PRE:  Value in node *justPromoted has just been promoted
    // POST: Value in *justPromoted filled in with value promoted
    //       from its left or right child
    //    && All ensuing vacancies filled in by subsequent promotions
    //    && Final vacated node contains the value EMPTY
    //.............................................................
{
    // NOTE: Below, EMPTY is a constant used to signify a node with
    //       no data contents.  The value of EMPTY compares greater
    //       than any actual data value in a tree.

    NodePtr vacantPtr = justPromoted;
    while (LChild(vacantPtr) != NULL &&
           (Data(LChild(vacantPtr)) != EMPTY ||
            Data(RChild(vacantPtr)) != EMPTY))

        if (Data(LChild(vacantPtr)) < Data(RChild(vacantPtr))) {
            Store(vacantPtr, Data(LChild(vacantPtr)));
            vacantPtr = LChild(vacantPtr);
        }
        else {          // Right child value less than left child's
            Store(vacantPtr, Data(RChild(vacantPtr)));
            vacantPtr = RChild(vacantPtr);
        }
    Store(vacantPtr, EMPTY);
}
```

Figure 13.22
FillVacancies function

Phase 1 of Treesort

To illustrate Phase 1 of the treesort algorithm, suppose that we wish to sort the values 3, 2, 5, 4, 1, 6, and 7 into ascending order. Initially, these values form the contents of the leaves of a full binary tree. Below, "E" denotes an empty node.

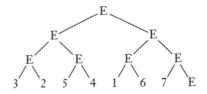

The promotion algorithm begins by comparing pairs of sibling leaves and promoting the smaller data value. Applying this algorithm to all leaf pairs, we obtain the following tree:

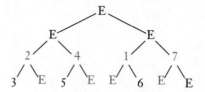

When we compare the last pair of leaf contents to create the tree above, we find the rightmost leaf is empty. Empty nodes are never promoted, so the value 7 moves up.

The promotion algorithm proceeds to compare the just-promoted parent pairs. Comparing the leftmost parents (values 2 and 4) results in the following promotion:

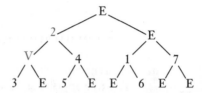

This promotion creates a vacancy (denoted by "V") where the value 2 was previously located. We then invoke the `FillVacancies` algorithm. It compares the two children of this node (values 3 and E) and promotes the smaller value:

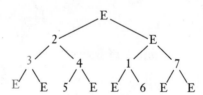

Next, we must compare the remaining pair of leaf parents (values 1 and 7) and promote the smaller. Promoting the value 1 causes a vacancy that is filled (using `FillVacancies`) by the promotion of 6:

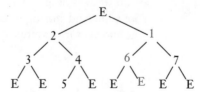

Next, the algorithm compares the only pair of leaf grandparents (values 2 and 1) and promotes the smaller:

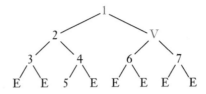

The vacant leaf grandparent must now be filled by the smaller of its children (values 6 and 7). After this promotion, the tree looks like this:

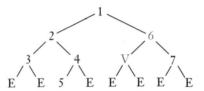

The children of the newly created vacancy are both empty, so we also designate the vacant node as empty. Phase 1 of the treesort algorithm is now complete. The tree appears as follows:

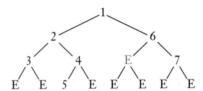

Phase 2 of Treesort

At the end of Phase 1 of treesort, the smallest value is always in the root of the tree. Phase 2 of the treesort algorithm consists of repeatedly removing the value in the root, copying this value into a separate vector, and invoking FillVacancies to handle the resulting vacancy. Each root value is smaller than all values remaining in the tree. Therefore, removing this value and placing it into the next consecutive vector element results in a sorted vector.

To illustrate Phase 2, we continue with the previous example. Removing the root value and storing it as the first element of the vector yields the following tree and vector contents:

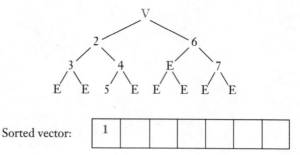

Sorted vector:

1						

Now we fill the vacancy created at the root by promoting the smaller of its two children (values 2 and 6):

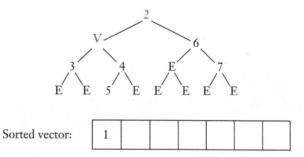

Sorted vector:

1						

This last promotion creates another vacancy that must be filled by the smaller of the node's two children (values 3 and 4). After this promotion, the result is:

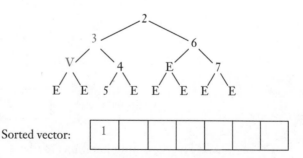

Sorted vector:

1						

The resulting vacancy is marked "E" because both its children are empty. All promotions are now complete, so the second iteration of Phase 2 begins. The algorithm removes the root value and places it into the vector:

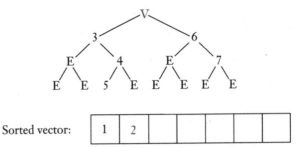

Sorted vector: 1 2

Again, the removal of the root value requires the help of `FillVacancies`. The values 3, 4, and 5 are promoted as follows:

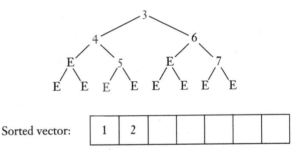

Sorted vector: 1 2

Once again, the algorithm removes the value in the root, places it into the vector and adjusts the tree through promotion. The result at this point is:

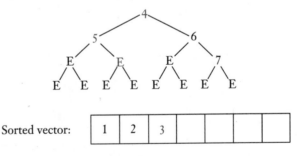

Sorted vector: 1 2 3

The remaining iterations of Phase 2 are shown consecutively as follows:

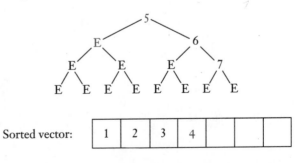

Sorted vector: 1 2 3 4

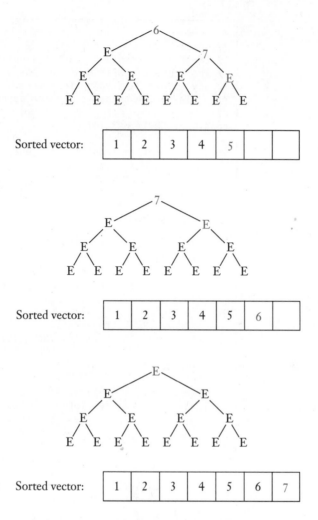

Figure 13.23 presents the complete treesort algorithm. In this code, we use an IntTree class, identical to the earlier CharTree class except that it stores int rather than char data. In this figure, observe how the recursive function PromoteSmallest implements Phase 1 of the treesort algorithm.

Each phase of the treesort algorithm requires computing time O(*N* log *N*). Because the phases occur sequentially, the time to perform the entire sort is also O(*N* log *N*).

Figure 13.23 The complete Treesort algorithm

```
// --------------------------------------------------------------------
// Note:
// EMPTY is a constant used to signify a node with no data contents.
// The value of EMPTY must be chosen to compare greater than
// any actual data value in a tree.
//     The value below is machine dependent!
// --------------------------------------------------------------------
const int EMPTY = 32767;

void Treesort( /* inout */ IntTree& someTree,
               /* out */   int      resultVec[],
               /* in */    int      vSize       )
    //............................................................
    // PRE:  vSize > 1
    //    && someTree is a full binary tree of at least 3 nodes
    //       and all nodes contain EMPTY, except for the
    //       leftmost vSize leaves
    // POST: resultVec[0..vSize-1] contain same values as the leaves
    //       of someTree<entry>, arranged in ascending order
    //    && All nodes of someTree contain EMPTY
    //............................................................
{
    // Phase 1 of treesort
    PromoteSmallest(someTree.Root());

    // Phase 2 of treesort
    int i;
    for (i = 0; i < vSize; i++) {
            // INV (prior to test):
            //     resultVec[0..i-1] contain the first i sorted
            //        values from the leaves of someTree<entry>
            //  && All values remaining in someTree
            //        are >= resultVec[i-1]
            //  && i <= vSize
        resultVec[i] = Data(someTree.Root());
        FillVacancies(someTree.Root());
    }
}
```

```
void PromoteSmallest( /* in */ NodePtr ptr )
    //.............................................................
    // PRE:  *ptr is the root of a binary tree
    // POST: The node *ptr contains the smallest data value in the
    //          tree
    //     && The root of every subtree of *ptr contains the smallest
    //          data value in that subtree
    //.............................................................
{
    if (LChild(LChild(ptr)) == NULL)
        if (Data(LChild(ptr)) <= Data(RChild(ptr))) {
            Store(ptr, Data(LChild(ptr)));
            Store(LChild(ptr), EMPTY);
        }
        else {          // Right child value less than left child's
            Store(ptr, Data(RChild(ptr)));
            Store(RChild(ptr),EMPTY);
        }
    else {              // Children have not yet been promoted to
        PromoteSmallest(LChild(ptr));
        PromoteSmallest(RChild(ptr));
        if (Data(LChild(ptr)) <= Data(RChild(ptr))) {
            Store(ptr, Data(LChild(ptr)));
            FillVacancies(LChild(ptr));
        }
        else {          // Right child value less than left child's
            Store(ptr, Data(RChild(ptr)));
            FillVacancies(RChild(ptr));
        }
    }
}

void FillVacancies( /* in */ NodePtr justPromoted )
    //.............................................................
    // PRE:  Value in node *justPromoted has just been promoted
    // POST: Value in *justPromoted filled in with value promoted
    //          from its left or right child
    //     && All ensuing vacancies filled in by subsequent promotions
    //     && Final vacated node contains the value EMPTY
    //.............................................................
{
    NodePtr vacantPtr = justPromoted;

    while (LChild(vacantPtr) != NULL &&
            (Data(LChild(vacantPtr)) != EMPTY ||
            Data(RChild(vacantPtr)) != EMPTY))
```

```
        if (Data(LChild(vacantPtr)) < Data(RChild(vacantPtr))) {
            Store(vacantPtr, Data(LChild(vacantPtr)));
            vacantPtr = LChild(vacantPtr);
        }
        else {            // Right child value less than left child's
            Store(vacantPtr, Data(RChild(vacantPtr)));
            vacantPtr = RChild(vacantPtr);
        }
    Store(vacantPtr, EMPTY);
}
```

13.7 Vector Implementation of a Binary Tree

Implementing a data abstraction (that is, choosing a suitable data representation and implementing the operations) requires a thoughtful examination of tradeoffs. Space, time, and intellectual efficiency often conflict with each other. With trees, space is a major issue. Trees have a more complicated structure than arrays, lists, or sets. A data representation of a tree must account not only for the data values in the tree but also for the shape and structure of the tree.

We have been using a linked representation of a binary tree with one dynamically allocated `struct` for every tree node. Each `struct` contains a data value and two pointers. If the storage required for a pointer is equal to the storage required for the data member, then fully two-thirds of the total tree storage is for structure rather than data.

It is possible to eliminate the child pointer overhead by packing a binary tree into a vector. This technique requires reserving space in the vector for every possible tree node. The root node is stored in the first vector element, its two children are in the next two elements, followed by its four grandchildren in the next four elements, and so forth. Figure 13.24 illustrates this data representation of a binary tree.

In this data representation, there is no need to store pointers to child nodes. Each child is located by its array index. For example, the node indexed by `nodeIndex` has left child indexed by

$$2*nodeIndex + 1$$

and right child indexed by

$$2*nodeIndex + 2$$

The vector representation also makes it easy to locate a parent in the tree. Given a node at position `nodeIndex`, its parent has index

$$(nodeIndex - 1) / 2 \quad \text{(integer division)}$$

In contrast, the dynamic data representation requires a tree traversal from the root to find the parent of a given node.

The vector representation of a tree, then, eliminates storage overhead for pointers. Data values occupy 100 percent of the total tree storage rather than,

Binary tree **Vector representation**

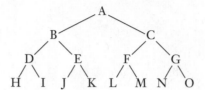

[0]	A
[1]	B
[2]	C
[3]	D
[4]	E
[5]	F
[6]	G
[7]	H
[8]	I
[9]	J
[10]	K
[11]	L
[12]	M
[13]	N
[14]	O

Figure 13.24 Vector representation of a binary tree

at worst, a small fraction. Furthermore, implementations of tree operations such as traversals are more efficient. Arithmetic manipulations of array subscripts are substantially faster than recursive function calls.

The drawback of the vector representation is the potential for unused space. A binary tree of height N needs a vector of $2^N - 1$ elements. If the tree is unbalanced, much of the vector may go unused. In the worst case, a degenerate binary tree of height 10 requires a vector of $2^{10} - 1 = 1023$ elements, yet only 10 of these 1023 elements are occupied by node data.

Another concern is how to distinguish the contents of unused vector elements from actual data. Figure 13.25 suggests two possibilities for encoding nonexistent tree nodes in a vector.

In this example, each tree node contains an integer. The first alternative uses a special integer value, 0 in this case, to denote a nonexistent node. Choosing such a value is risky and requires *a priori* knowledge of the application data. If zero happens to be the value of an actual data item, it will be forever ignored, treated as a nonexistent item.

The second alternative avoids this problem by attaching a Boolean flag to each array element. With this approach, each element is of type

```
struct ElementType {
    int     data;
    Boolean nodeExists;
}
```

	Binary tree	Vector (0 means nonexistent)		Vector of structs		

	Binary tree		Vector (0 means nonexistent)			Vector of structs	
						data	nodeExists
	101	[0]	101		[0]	101	TRUE
	201 202	[1]	201		[1]	201	TRUE
	301 302 303	[2]	202		[2]	202	TRUE
	401 402 403 404	[3]	301		[3]	301	TRUE
		[4]	302		[4]	302	TRUE
		[5]	0		[5]	?	FALSE
		[6]	303		[6]	303	TRUE
		[7]	0		[7]	?	FALSE
		[8]	401		[8]	401	TRUE
		[9]	402		[9]	402	TRUE
		[10]	0		[10]	?	FALSE
		[11]	0		[11]	?	FALSE
		[12]	0		[12]	?	FALSE
		[13]	403		[13]	403	TRUE
		[14]	404		[14]	404	TRUE

Figure 13.25 Alternatives for representing nonexistent nodes in a vector

The disadvantage of this solution is the increased storage for each array element.

A Study in Design

The Heapsort

In this section we examine in detail another tree-based sorting algorithm, **heapsort.** Heapsort combines the advantages of the treesort algorithm and vector representation of trees. The heapsort algorithm, like treesort, uses two phases. Phase 1 of heapsort rearranges the contents of tree nodes to store the *largest* value of every subtree, not the smallest, in the subtree root. Such a tree is called a **heap.** (A heap data structure is not to be confused with an unrelated concept of the same name. *Heap* is also a synonym for the free store—the area of memory available for dynamic data.)

Phase 2 of heapsort is similar to Phase 2 of treesort. This phase repeatedly removes the values from the root. Heapsort places each removed value into its proper place in the sorted vector and reconstructs the remaining tree into a heap.

Unlike treesort, which requires two data structures (one for the tree and one for the sorted results), heapsort uses only one data structure—a vector.

Heapsort starts with a vector representation of a binary tree and then sorts the data within the original vector.

Phase 1 of Heapsort

Phase 1 of heapsort treats the array as a balanced tree containing randomly arranged data. The following is a pseudocode algorithm to transform this tree into a heap:

```
FOR each tree node, thisNode, from the root to the leaves {
    originalNodeValue = Data(thisNode);
    promoteNode = thisNode;
    WHILE promoteNode != root of tree AND
            Data(Parent(promoteNode)) < originalNodeValue) {
        Store Data(Parent(promoteNode)) into promoteNode;
        promoteNode = Parent(promoteNode);
    }
    Store originalNodeValue into promoteNode;
}
```

This algorithm promotes the value in each node upward (toward the root) until reaching a new parent whose value is greater. This promotion is accomplished by repeatedly examining ancestors from parent to grandparent to great-grandparent, and so forth. Each ancestor value is **demoted** when found to be less than the value being promoted. The promotion terminates when an ancestor has value greater than the value being promoted, leaving the promotion value in the child of this ancestor.

Because heapsort uses a vector representation of the binary tree, we can represent thisNode, promoteNode, and Parent(promoteNode) as array indices. Assuming the vector to be sorted is vec[0..vSize-1], the following C++ code implements Phase 1 of the algorithm:

```
for (i = 1; i < vSize; i++) {
    originalVal = vec[i];
    promoteIndx = i;
    parentIndx = (promoteIndx-1) / 2;
    while (promoteIndx > 0 && vec[parentIndx] < originalVal) {
        vec[promoteIndx] = vec[parentIndx];
        promoteIndx = parentIndx;
        parentIndx = (promoteIndx-1) / 2;
    }
    vec[promoteIndx] = originalVal;
}
```

To illustrate Phase 1 of the algorithm, consider the following binary tree of seven values and its corresponding vector representation:

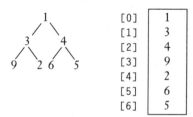

Phase 1 of the algorithm examines nodes from the root toward the leaves. Because the root has no ancestors, its value cannot be promoted. Therefore, the left child of the root (containing value 3) is the first node to consider. In the algorithm, i = 1 and originalVal = 3. This originalVal is greater than the contents of the parent node (the root). The first iteration of the while loop demotes the root contents, then updates promoteIndx to refer to its parent.

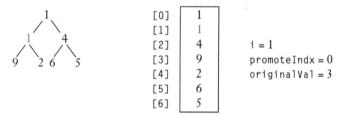

As promoteIndx now refers to the root, the while loop terminates and originalVal is stored into the final promoteIndx node.

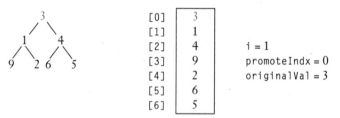

The for loop examination of the left child of the root is now complete. The second iteration of the for loop considers the right child of the root. At this point, i = 2 and originalVal = 4. The execution of the while loop proceeds as it did for the left child. The resulting tree is

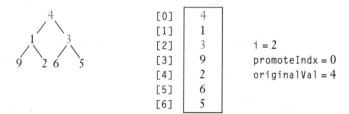

Next, the `for` loop attempts to promote the leftmost grandchild of the root. Here, `i` = 3 and `originalVal` = 9. The first iteration of the `while` loop finds the parent to contain a value (1) less than `originalVal`, so it demotes the parent and updates `promoteIndx` as shown below:

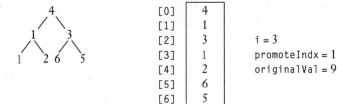

The second `while` iteration again finds the parent of the new `promoteIndx` node to contain a value (4) less than `originalVal`. We must demote this parent value also, and update `promoteIndx`.

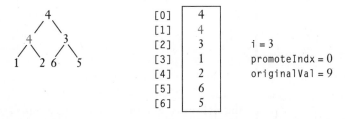

The `while` loop terminates after two iterations because `promoteIndx` = 0. The final assignment statement of the `for` loop places `originalVal` in the root, as shown below.

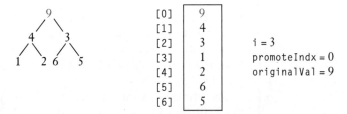

The next `for` loop iteration considers the root grandchild that is second from the left: `i` = 4 and `originalVal` = 2. In this case, `originalVal` is less than the contents of its parent (4). Therefore, this iteration of the `for` loop causes no change in the tree.

The next `for` loop iteration considers the root grandchild that is third from the left: `i` = 5 and `originalVal` = 6. This node's parent contains the value 3, less than `originalVal`, so 3 is demoted and `promoteIndx` updated.

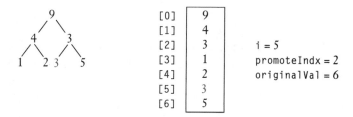

The second `while` loop iteration finds the parent of the new `promoteIndx` node to be the root with contents of 9. This value is greater than that in the `promoteIndx` node, so the `while` loop terminates and `originalVal` is stored into the `promoteIndx` node as follows:

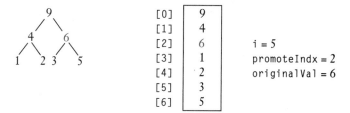

The final `for` loop iteration attempts to promote the rightmost grandchild of the root. Nothing is changed by this loop iteration, because the parent of the rightmost grandchild contains a value (6) greater than `originalVal`.

Phase 1 of the heapsort algorithm is now complete. The above structure is the resulting heap.

Phase 2 of Heapsort

Phase 2 of heapsort removes the value from the root of the heap (the largest of all the data values), places it into its correct location in the vector (the bottom, to ultimately obtain a vector in ascending order), reconstructs another heap from the remaining values, and repeats this sequence. Figure 13.26 expresses this algorithm informally.

Each time the root value is moved into its final position in the vector, the previous value in this position is displaced. Reconstructing a heap is similar to constructing the original heap, but the displaced value must also participate in the promotion of node values. Figure 13.27 contains the complete algorithm for Phase 2 of heapsort.

```
FOR bottom = vSize-1 DOWN TO 1 {
    displacedVal = vec[bottom];
    vec[bottom] = Data(root);
    Remove vec[bottom] from tree and reconstruct a heap out of the tree
        using displacedVal instead of Data(root);
}
```

Figure 13.26 Informal algorithm for Phase 2 of heapsort

```
for (bottom = vSize-1; bottom > 0; bottom--) {
    displacedVal = vec[bottom];
    vec[bottom] = vec[0];
    // ASSERT: Value in root moved to current bottom of vec

    vacantNodeIndx = 0;
    while (TRUE) {
        leftIndx = 2*vacantNodeIndx + 1;
        if (leftIndx >= bottom)
            break;
        rightIndx = 2*vacantNodeIndx + 2;
        if (rightIndx >= bottom || vec[leftIndx] > vec[rightIndx])
            maxIndx = leftIndx;
        else
            maxIndx = rightIndx;
        if (vec[maxIndx] <= displacedVal)
            break;
        vec[vacantNodeIndx] = vec[maxIndx];
        vacantNodeIndx = maxIndx;
    }
    vec[vacantNodeIndx] = displacedVal;
    // ASSERT: Heap has been recreated in vec[0..bottom-1]
}
```

Figure 13.27 Algorithm for Phase 2 of heapsort

We illustrate Phase 2 of the heapsort algorithm by continuing the example from Phase 1. The first iteration of the for loop in Phase 2 begins by saving the last vector element in displacedVal and storing the root value from the original heap into this last vector position. The result appears below:

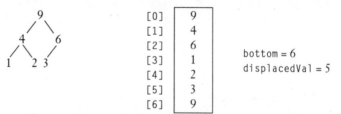

In the above tree diagram, we have pruned the rightmost leaf from the original heap to indicate that copying the value from the root into vec[bottom] has displaced the corresponding vector element.

Next, Phase 2 compares displacedVal and the two children of the root. The greatest of these three values (6) is promoted.

Now we must fill the vacated node (the node with index maxIndx). The algorithm fills this node, at the bottom of the while loop, by assigning maxIndx to vacantNodeIndx. The next loop iteration compares the single child of the vacated node with displacedVal. Because displacedVal is greater, it is copied into the vacated node.

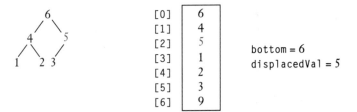

The first iteration of the for loop is now complete. The result has been to send the largest original data value, 9, to the bottom of the vector and to reconstruct the heap from the remaining six values.

Now the entire process repeats, with the false bottom of the vector moved up by one position. The current root value moves to its final position, and the displaced node is pruned from the tree.

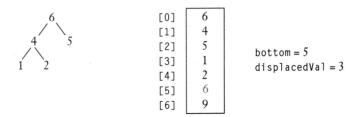

Again the algorithm compares the two children of the root to displacedVal. The right child value, being the largest of the three, is promoted.

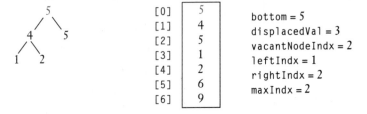

Because the vacated node has no children, displacedVal is copied into it.

[0]	5
[1]	4
[2]	3
[3]	1
[4]	2
[5]	6
[6]	9

bottom = 5
displacedVal = 3

The `for` loop has now finished. The two largest data values are in ascending order in the last two array elements, and the heap has been reconstructed.

Next, the `for` loop repeats a third time. We move the root value to `vec[4]` and prune the tree.

[0]	5
[1]	4
[2]	3
[3]	1
[4]	5
[5]	6
[6]	9

bottom = 4
displacedVal = 2

This time, the value of the left child of the root is promoted.

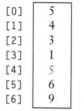

[0]	4
[1]	4
[2]	3
[3]	1
[4]	5
[5]	6
[6]	9

bottom = 4
displacedVal = 2
vacantNodeIndx = 1
leftIndx = 1
rightIndx = 2
maxIndx = 1

The only child of the newly vacated node is less than `displacedVal`, so the vacated node receives a copy of `displacedVal`, creating the following heap:

[0]	4
[1]	2
[2]	3
[3]	1
[4]	5
[5]	6
[6]	9

bottom = 4
displacedVal = 2

This process continues until all root values have been removed except the last one, which will be in the correct position following other removals.

Performance of Heapsort

The heapsort algorithm has average case and worst case computing time $O(N \log N)$ for sorting N data values. Although this big-O measure is the same as for treesort, their observed execution times may differ considerably. In Phase 2 of the algorithms, heapsort is less efficient. To fill a vacancy, treesort needs to consider only two children, but heapsort must consider two children and the displaced value. On the other hand, treesort requires as input a binary tree of dynamically allocated nodes from which to copy the root values into a vector. The initial setup time to obtain dynamic data from the free store to create this binary tree represents substantial time overhead. Therefore, in spite of the slower performance during the sort itself, heapsort often is preferred because of its lesser overall execution time and better space efficiency.

Comparing heapsort with quicksort (Chapter 12), both require average case computing time $O(N \log N)$. However, quicksort's worst case time is $O(N^2)$ compared to heapsort's $O(N \log N)$. Apart from quicksort's worst case (the input data being initially in sorted order), research studies have shown that quicksort generally outperforms heapsort in measured execution times.

13.8 Implementing General Trees

Both methods that we have presented for implementing binary trees—dynamic data and vector implementations—have pros and cons. The dynamic implementation suffers from the storage overhead of maintaining pointers to all children. For trees containing large amounts of data in a single node, this pointer overhead is minimal. However, for trees with small data content per node, the overhead of storing pointers in each node can be significant.

The vector implementation, by eliminating the need to store child pointers, is an attractive alternative. This implementation, however, reserves room for every potential child of the tree, thereby wasting space for unbalanced trees.

Both techniques for implementing binary trees are suitable for implementing general trees as well. To use these techniques, the programmer must know in advance the maximum number of children for each tree node. For example, if every tree node is known to have five or fewer children, a node can be represented as a dynamic struct of six members—one to store the data value and five to store pointers to the potential children of the node.

Extending the vector technique for such a tree requires a vector where the root is followed by its five potential children, then 25 potential grandchildren, and so forth. The parent of a node with index i is then located at index $(i - 1)/5$.

A third technique for implementing general trees uses a dynamic data representation with each node containing just two pointers: a pointer to the node's first (leftmost) child and a pointer to the node's next sibling (to the

```
struct  TreeNode;              // Forward declaration
typedef TreeNode* NodePtr;

struct TreeNode {
    SomeType data;
    NodePtr  firstChild;
    NodePtr  nextSibling;
    TreeNode( SomeType, NodePtr, NodePtr );
};
```

Figure 13.28 Declarations for nodes of a general tree

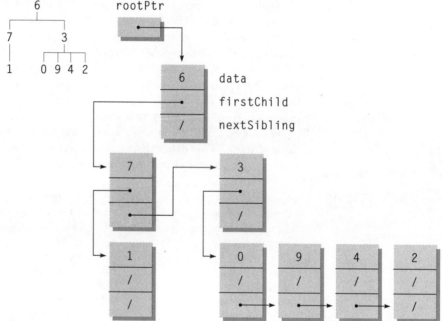

Figure 13.29 Representation of a general tree

right). This technique uses storage more efficiently for certain trees. Figure 13.28 shows the C++ declarations for this structure. The TreeNode type has its own constructor for ease of initialization.

Figure 13.29 illustrates this technique for storing a general tree. The tree in this diagram stores a single integer value in each node and has a variable number of children per node.

A major advantage of this tree implementation is that pointers are only needed for children that exist. The programmer therefore avoids wasting space when storing an unbalanced tree.

A more important advantage of this last implementation is its flexibility. It will work for any tree structure. With this technique, there is no limit to the number of children per node.

SUMMARY   Trees are important both as abstractions and as tools for implementing other abstractions. As abstractions, trees are a natural way to represent real-world hierarchies. Family trees, corporate structures, and single-elimination tournament pairings are just a few examples.

Trees are also important as implementation tools because their structure leads to efficient algorithms. Searching up through a list of ancestors or scanning down a single lineage of descendants requires computing time O(log *N*) for balanced trees. The result is efficient searching, insertion, and deletion algorithms for binary search trees. This same logarithmic computing time yields O(*N* log *N*) sorting schemes such as treesort and heapsort.

There is a variety of ways to implement trees. The most common dynamic implementation uses a single dynamic `struct` for each tree node with one pointer per child. This technique implies a fixed maximum number of children per node. A more flexible dynamic alternative uses a pointer to the node's first child and another pointer to the next sibling.

Alternatively, trees may be packed into vectors to avoid storing child pointers. This vector implementation has limitations, but it uses space efficiently when trees are nearly full. This approach also eliminates the time spent allocating and deallocating dynamic data from the free store.

The study of computer science is replete with applications and implementations of trees. This data organization is frequently acknowledged as one of the fundamental structures in computer science.

KEY TERMS

ancestor   (p. 606)
balance   (p. 619)
binary expression tree   (p. 625)
binary search tree   (p. 615)
binary tree   (p. 606)
child   (p. 605)
degenerate binary tree   (p. 619)
demotion   (p. 641)
depth   (p. 606)
descendant   (p. 605)
empty tree   (p. 605)
expression tree   (p. 625)
full binary tree   (p. 619)
general tree   (p. 604)
heap   (p. 640)
heapsort   (p. 640)
height   (p. 606)
hierarchical form   (p. 602)
infix notation   (p. 626)
inorder traversal   (p. 621)
leaf   (p. 606)

left child   (p. 606)
level (of a node)   (p. 606)
linear form   (p. 602)
node   (p. 604)
parent   (p. 605)
postfix notation   (p. 626)
postorder traversal   (p. 622)
prefix notation   (p. 626)
preorder traversal   (p. 622)
promotion   (p. 629)
reverse Polish notation   (p. 626)
right child   (p. 606)
root   (p. 606)
RPN   (p. 626)
sibling   (p. 604)
subtree   (p. 606)
tree   (p. 605)
tree traversal   (p. 621)
treesort   (p. 629)
vacancy   (p. 629)

EXERCISES   **13.1** Use the figures below to answer parts (a) through (c). In each diagram, the symbol "○" represents a node.

i.

ii.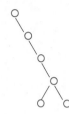

iii.

iv.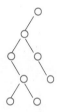

v.

vi.

a. Which of the above figures are trees?

b. For each figure that is not a tree, explain why it is not.

c. Which of the above figures are binary trees?

13.2 Use the following binary search tree to complete the remainder of this problem. Each tree node contains the integer data shown.

thisTree:

```
        5
       / \
      3   8
     / \ / \
    0  4 6  9
```

a. What data value is in the root node?

b. List the data values in all leaf nodes.

c. At what level is the node containing the value 8?

d. What is the height (depth) of this tree?

e. What is Data(RChild(thisTree.Root()))?

f. What is Data(LChild(RChild(thisTree.Root())))?

g. List the data values in all ancestors of the node containing the value 9.

h. List the data values in all descendants of the node containing the value 3.

i. For each of the following search keys, give the exact number of probes performed by the search algorithm of Figure 13.11:

5, 0, 4, and 2

j. What is the maximum number of probes performed by the search algorithm if the search key is present in the tree?

k. What is the maximum number of probes performed by the search algorithm if the search key is *not* present in the tree?

l. Is the basic structure of this binary search tree a best case, worst case, or neither a best nor worst case, for performing searches? (Explain your answer.)

m. Give the order in which nodes of this tree are visited by an inorder traversal.

n. Give the order in which nodes of this tree are visited by a preorder traversal.

o. Give the order in which nodes of this tree are visited by a postorder traversal.

13.3 Repeat Exercise 13.2 using the following binary search tree:

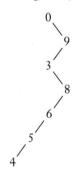

13.4 To create a binary search tree, we can repeatedly apply the binary search tree insertion algorithm until all values have been inserted (Figure 13.14). The resulting tree depends upon the order in which values are inserted. For each of the following integer sequences, show the binary search tree that results from inserting in the specified order.

a. <0, 3, 4, 5, 6, 8, 9>

b. <3, 4, 0, 8, 9, 5, 6>

c. <6, 9, 4, 8, 3, 0, 5>

d. <5, 8, 3, 6, 9, 4, 0>

13.5 To the CharTree specification file of Figure 13.5, we wish to add the following functions. Supply the body of each function, using the CharTree implementation file (Figure 13.9) as a guide.

```
a. void MovRtSubtree( /* in */ NodePtr root1,
                      /* in */ NodePtr root2 );
   // PRE:  *root1 and *root2 are roots of binary trees
   //    && *root1 has no right subtree
   // POST: Right subtree of *root2 removed and is now the
   //       right subtree of *root1
```

b. int Height(/* in */ NodePtr ptr);
```
// PRE:  ptr points to the root of a binary tree (or == NULL)
// POST: FCTVAL == 0, if ptr == NULL
//               == height of tree whose root is *ptr,
//                  otherwise
```

c. int NodeCount(/* in */ NodePtr ptr);
```
// PRE:  ptr points to the root of a binary tree (or == NULL)
// POST: FCTVAL == 0, if ptr == NULL
//               == number of nodes in tree whose
//                  root is *ptr, otherwise
```

13.6 Figure 13.16 contains the algorithms for inorder, preorder, and postorder traversal.

a. Write an algorithm for binary tree traversal that always visits nodes in the reverse of the order in which they would be visited by inorder traversal.

b. Improve the postorder traversal algorithm by eliminating recursive invocations for nonexistent nodes (that is, check for them before making another invocation).

c. Write an algorithm that outputs the data values in a binary tree by level. The algorithm outputs the root value, then the values in the children of the root, then in the grandchildren, then in the great-grandchildren, and so forth. (*Note:* The solution is more complicated than the simple recursive routines of Figure 13.16. Consider either using a vector representation of the tree or copying the data from the nodes in a dynamic data representation into a separate vector.)

13.7 Give fully parenthesized expressions for each of the following binary expression trees. (Do not bother to evaluate the expressions).

a.

b.

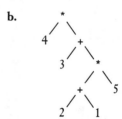

c.

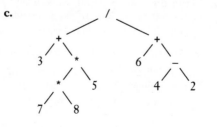

d.

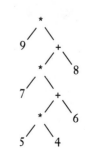

13.8 Give the infix expression (without parentheses) resulting from an inorder traversal of each tree in Exercise 13.7. (*Note:* In most cases, the semantics of the unparenthesized expressions will *not* be the same as in Exercise 13.7.)

13.9 Give the prefix expression for every tree in Exercise 13.7.

13.10 Give the postfix (RPN) expression for every tree in Exercise 13.7.

13.11 Draw a binary expression tree for each of the following fully parenthesized expressions.

    a. $(7 + (8 * (4 - 1)))$

    b. $(((6 * 3) + (8 * 7)) * (6 * 5))$

    c. $(((3 + 4) * (8 - (3 / 2))) * (9 * (7 + 4)))$

    d. $(((((5 * 2) + 3) * 4) + 5) * 6)$

    e. $(((1 + 2) * (3 + 4)) * ((5 + 6) * (7 + 8)))$

    f. $(9 + (8 * (7 + (6 * (5 + (4 * 3))))))$

13.12 Give the prefix equivalent of each expression in Exercise 13.11.

13.13 Give the postfix equivalent of each expression in Exercise 13.11.

13.14 What is the integer value of each of the following RPN expressions? (All numbers are single digits.)

    a. $3\ 4\ 5\ 6 + * +$

    b. $5\ 6 + 2 * 4 +$

    c. $3\ 4 + 3 * 1\ 1 + *$

13.15 In discussing the vector implementation of binary trees, Section 13.7 presented the following expressions for calculating child and parent indices. These formulas assume that the root value is stored in vector element 0. Rewrite each expression so that it is correct if the root value is stored in vector element 1. (Assume that element 0 is to be used for some other purpose.)

    a. `leftChildIndex = 2*nodeIndex + 1`

    b. `rightChildIndex = 2*nodeIndex + 2`

    c. `parentIndex = (nodeIndex - 1) / 2`   (integer division)

13.16 A *ternary tree* is a tree with at most three children per node and with each child designated as left, right, or middle child. (A tree node can have at most one of each type of child.)

    a. Write the type declarations, similar to those of Figure 13.7, necessary to implement a ternary tree as a linked structure with each tree node represented as a single dynamic `struct`.

    b. Write a preorder traversal algorithm for this ternary tree.

    c. Suppose that a vector implementation, like the one for binary trees, is used. In this implementation, the root value is stored in element 0, followed by the three potential children of the root, the nine potential grandchildren, and so on. Give expressions in terms of `nodeIndex` for `leftChildIndex`, `middleChildIndex`, `rightChildIndex`, and `parentIndex` to support this implementation.

13.1 Write a C++ program to construct general trees containing single char values. Use the form of tree storage described in Figure 13.29. Test your program by building the following tree as well as others.

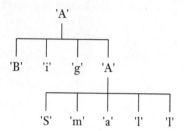

13.2 Below is the specification of a binary search tree module. Each tree node contains a single char value. The BinSrchTree class is derived from the CharTree class of Section 13.2, the latter being a public base class. (Recall from Chapter 11 that all public operations of CharTree—except constructors and destructors— are therefore public operations of BinSrchTree as well.) Write and test the corresponding implementation file.

```
//------------------------------------------------------------------
//   SPECIFICATION FILE (bst.h)
//   This module exports facilities for declaring, constructing, and
//   searching binary search trees whose nodes contain single chars.
//------------------------------------------------------------------
#include "bool.h"
#include "chartree.h"

class BinSrchTree : public CharTree {
public:
    void Insert( /* in */ char newVal );
        // PRE:  Tree is a binary search tree  &&  Assigned(newVal)
        // POST: newVal inserted into tree
        //       && Tree is still a binary search tree

    Boolean IsPresent( /* in */ char key ) const;
        // PRE:  Tree is a binary search tree  &&  Assigned(key)
        // POST: FCTVAL == TRUE, if key is present anywhere in tree
        //               == FALSE,  otherwise
        // NOTE: This is an O(log N) search

    BinSrchTree();
        // POST: Created(tree)  &&  IsEmpty()

    ~BinSrchTree();
        // POST: NOT Created(tree)
private:
    // No additional private members
};
```

13.3 Section 13.7 presents a vector implementation of binary trees. Use this technique to write and test an alternative `CharTree` module that exports the same facilities as the `CharTree` module of Section 13.2.

13.4 Implement and test the general `Sort` function from the previous chapter (Figure 12.12) using the heapsort algorithm. Benchmark the resulting code against two other sorting algorithms, using random data sets of size 500, 1000, and 1500.

13.5 Implement and test the general `Sort` function from the previous chapter (Figure 12.12) using the treesort algorithm. Benchmark the resulting code against two other sorting algorithms, using random data sets of size 500, 1000, and 1500.

13.6 Write a program to solve the following problem.

TITLE

RPN expression evaluator

DESCRIPTION

This program reads integer-valued RPN expressions and outputs the value of each expression.

Valid operators are + (addition), – (subtraction), * (multiplication) and / (integer division). Each individual operand is a single decimal digit from 0 through 9.

INPUT

Input consists of one or more lines with a single RPN expression per line. The RPN expression must not contain any internal blanks. The end-of-file condition signals the end of the input data.

OUTPUT

The program prompts the user for each input expression by printing a blank line, followed by the string `Expression:`. After each input line, the program outputs the string `Value:`, followed by the value of the RPN expression.

ERROR HANDLING

The program assumes all input to represent valid RPN expressions. Anything else produces undefined results.

EXAMPLE

In the sample execution below, all input is in color.

```
Expression: 34+
Value: 7

Expression: 52/
Value: 2

Expression: 27-4*
Value: -20
```

```
Expression: 234*57*+*
Value: 94

Expression: 6
Value: 6

Expression: <EOF>        ←— The system's end-of-file
                            keystrokes
```

13.7 Write a program to solve the problem below.

TITLE

Parenthesized tree notation

DESCRIPTION

A tree structure can be expressed by using a parenthesized notation as follows. After the name of a node, the names of all its children appear within a single set of parentheses. This notation applies recursively to any node in the tree. For example,

A(BC)

symbolizes a tree with root node A and two children B and C. Similarly,

A(B(CDE)FG)

denotes a tree whose root node A has three children, B, F, and G. Furthermore, node B also has three children, C, D, and E.

This program inputs tree structures in parenthesized form. For each tree, the program outputs the nodes as visited in a postorder traversal.

INPUT

Each parenthesized expression is on a single line. Each tree node is represented by a single alphabetic character (upper- or lowercase). The expression must not contain any internal blanks. The end-of-file condition signals the end of the input data.

OUTPUT

The user is prompted for each expression with the string Tree:. After each line of input, the program outputs the nodes in the order they are visited by a postorder traversal, followed by a blank line.

ERROR HANDLING

All input is presumed correct. Erroneous input produces undefined results.

EXAMPLE

In the sample execution below, all input is in color:

```
Tree: X
X

Tree: a(b(c)d)
cbda

Tree: X(Y(Z))
ZYX

Tree: A(B(CDE)FG)
CDEBFGA

Tree: A(B(CD)E(F(G)H(IJK(LM))))
CDBGFIJLMKHEA

Tree: <EOF>        ◄── The system's end-of-file keystrokes
```

13.8   Write a program to solve the following problem.

TITLE

Twenty questions

DESCRIPTION

This program, which learns by asking questions, is a classic artificial intelligence problem. The program uses a *decision tree* as its main data structure. The nonleaf nodes of the tree contain strings representing yes/no questions. The user must think of a single object and answer the questions based on that object.

The program starts by asking the user the question contained in the root node. If the user responds with "no," the program follows the left child branch to ask the question in the next node; with "yes," the program follows the right child branch. The program repeats this process with each new node. The leaves of the tree contain objects corresponding to the sequence of answers that led from the root to the leaf. When the program reaches a leaf, it guesses that the user is thinking of that leaf's object. If the leaf's object matches the user's object, the program wins. If the two objects do not match, the program learns by asking the user to specify a yes/no question that distinguishes the user's object from the leaf's object. The program then places this user question into the appropriate location in the tree. The user may continue to play this game for some period of time.

INPUT

Input to a program question, a program guess, or a play-again prompt is either a single 'y' or a single 'n' (either in uppercase or lowercase).

Input to an add-an-object prompt is the object that the user was thinking of while playing the game.

Input to an add-a-question prompt is a single-line question that has a "yes" answer for the user's object and a "no" answer for the object guessed by the program.

OUTPUT

All program output is double spaced. At the beginning of each game, the program begins with the following message:

```
You must think of a single object.  Please answer the
following questions about this object.
```

Each subsequent question comes from a node in the decision tree. The form is:

```
QUESTION: <question from tree node> (Y or N):
```

The program continues to ask questions from the root of the tree down through the descendants that correspond to the user's responses. When the program encounters a leaf node, it makes the following guess:

```
I guess that your object is a(n) <object>. (Y or N):
```

where <object> is the object in the leaf node. If the user responds 'Y' or 'y', the program outputs the following:

```
Notice the superior intellect of the computer!
```

If the user responds 'N' or 'n', the program outputs an add-an-object prompt, followed by an add-a-question prompt, and then a play-again prompt. The add-an-object prompt is as follows:

```
What object were you thinking of?
```

The add-a-question prompt is as follows:

```
Please specify a question that has a yes answer for
your object and a no answer for my guess:
```

The program then issues a play-again prompt:

```
Play again? (Y or N):
```

The program plays the game as many times as the user continues to respond 'Y' or 'y' to this prompt.

ERROR HANDLING

For any prompt that expects a 'Y', 'y', 'N', or 'n', erroneous input produces the error message

```
INCORRECT RESPONSE - Please type Y or N
```

and the prompt is repeated.

EXAMPLE

Suppose that the initial tree is as follows:

```
        Does it have two legs?
          /            \
        horse         bird
```

Below is a sample execution with all input in color.

```
You must think of a single object.  Please answer the
following questions about this object.

QUESTION: Does it have two legs? (Y or N): N

I guess that your object is a(n) horse. (Y or N): Y

Notice the superior intellect of the computer!

Play again? (Y or N): Y

You must think of a single object.  Please answer the
following questions about this object.

QUESTION: Does it have two legs? (Y or N): N

I guess that your object is a(n) horse. (Y or N): N

What object were you thinking of? tulip

Please specify a question that has a yes answer for
your object and a no answer for my guess:
Is it a plant?

Play again? (Y or N): A
INCORRECT RESPONSE - Please type Y or N

Play again? (Y or N): Y

You must think of a single object.  Please answer the
following questions about this object.

QUESTION: Does it have two legs? (Y or N): N

QUESTION: Is it a plant? (Y or N): n

I guess that your object is a(n) horse. (Y or N): N
```

```
What object were you thinking of? dog

Please specify a question that has a yes answer for
your object and a no answer for my guess:
Does it bark?

Play again? (Y or N): N
```

Note: The final decision tree should be as pictured below:

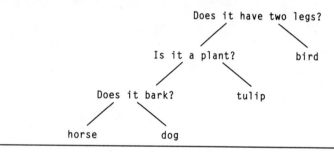

APPENDIX A

Introductory Comparison of Pascal and C++

This appendix provides an informal introduction to the C++ language for those who are familiar with Pascal. It is not a description of the entire language. We present only those features that will allow you to proceed to Appendix C (on input and output) and then on to Chapter 1 of this text.

The C++ language originated at AT&T Corporation's Bell Labs. This text is based on AT&T's Version 2.0 of the language. Because C++ is still a young and evolving language, there may be minor variations among different C++ systems.

For details about the precise syntax of various constructs, please consult Appendix J of this book.

A.1 Comments and Identifiers

Comments

Pascal comments are expressed as either

```
(* Some comment *) or { Some comment }
```

C++ comments come in two forms. The first is similar to Pascal's but uses slashes instead of parentheses:

```
/* Some comment */
```

With this form, you cannot nest comments inside others.

The other form begins with a pair of slashes (//) and extends to the end of the line:

```
// Some comment
```

Identifiers

Table A.1 summarizes the differences between Pascal and C++ identifiers. Note that C++ identifiers are **case sensitive**: uppercase letters are different

Table A.1 Identifiers in Pascal and C++

Pascal	C++
First character	
Letter	Letter or underscore*
Remaining characters	
Letters or digits	Letters, digits, or underscores
Case sensitive?	
No	Yes

* Identifiers beginning with an underscore often have special meanings in C++ environments. It is best to avoid these.

from lowercase letters. The identifiers `printtabbuffer`, `PrintTabBuffer`, and `print_tab_buffer` are three distinct names and are not interchangeable in any way.

In both Pascal and C++, an identifier may be arbitrarily long but must be unique within the first *n* characters. The value of *n* depends on each local environment.

Both Pascal and C++ include **reserved words**—identifiers like `while`, `if`, and `else` that are predefined and cannot be used for other purposes. Appendix E contains a list of all C++ reserved words.

Programmers often use capitalization as a quick, visual clue to what an identifier represents. The convention in this textbook is to begin variable names with lowercase letters:

`studentCount`

and to begin names of data types and subprograms (procedures and functions) with capital letters:

`PrintResults(alpha, beta);`

This style quickly distinguishes those identifiers representing data values in memory (variables) from those that do not (type names and subprogram names). In both cases, each subsequent English word in the identifier begins with a capital letter. (All reserved words in C++ use lowercase letters, so you cannot tamper with those.)

For identifiers representing constants (as in Pascal `const` declarations), many C++ programmers capitalize the entire identifier, again as an immediate clue to its use:

`PI`

A.2   A First Program

A C++ program consists of a collection of functions. A function may return a function value (like a Pascal function):

```
y = 3.4 * SquareRoot(x);
```

or it may not (like a Pascal procedure):

```
DoSomething(x, y, z);
```

If a function has no parameter list, you still are required to use parentheses:

```
PrintTitle();
```

We now look at a small but complete C++ program, shown in Figure A.1 with its Pascal counterpart.

Here are some observations about this C++ program:

1. There is no "main program" as in Pascal. Instead, there is a function with the distinguished name `main` (in lowercase letters). Every program must have a function named `main`, and execution always begins with this function.

2. The left brace ({) and right brace (}) are equivalent to Pascal's `begin` and `end`—they enclose a compound statement. As in Pascal, a compound statement is a group of statements that may appear wherever a single statement is allowed.

3. In C++, the semicolon is a statement terminator, not a statement separator as in Pascal. The general rule is that each statement *except* a compound statement ends with a semicolon.

4. Variable declarations seem "backwards" from those in Pascal: first the data type name, then the variable name.

5. The first line of the `main` function

```
int main()
```

Figure A.1
A small program in Pascal and C++

Pascal	C++
`program Sample (input, output);`	`#include <iostream.h>`
`   const`	`#define MONTHS_PER_YR 12`
`      monthsPerYr = 12;`	
`   var`	`int main()`
`      age : integer;`	`{`
`begin`	`   int age;`
`   write('Enter your age: ');`	
`   read(age);`	`   cout << "Enter your age: ";`
`   writeln('Your age in months: ',`	`   cin >> age;`
`           age * monthsPerYr)`	`   cout << "Your age in months: "`
`end.`	`        << age * MONTHS_PER_YR << '\n';`
	`   return 0;`
	`}`

declares that main is a function that returns an integer value. The last statement in the function body

```
return 0;
```

returns the value 0 to the operating system (UNIX, DOS, SunOS, etc.) when the program finishes executing. The value returned by main is called the program's **exit status**. By convention, an exit status of 0 signifies a normal termination of the program. We will discuss a program's exit status in more detail later.

6. For input and output, the identifiers cin (pronounced "see-in") and cout (pronounced "see-out") denote streams of characters from the standard input device and to the standard output device, respectively. The operator << (pronounced "put to") appends its next operand to the output stream, and the operator >> (pronounced "get from") inputs its next operand from the input stream. The two characters \n denote the end-of-line character for terminating the output line.

7. In the Pascal version, age is a global variable because it is declared by the main program. In the C++ version, age is a local variable because it is declared inside main. No other function can access it. In C++, a global variable is one that is declared outside any function:

```
int someInt;

int main()
{ ... }
```

8. The line saying #define MONTHS_PER_YR 12 serves the same purpose as the Pascal const declaration. It causes literal substitution of the characters 12 wherever the identifier MONTHS_PER_YR appears in the program.

9. The line specifying #include <iostream.h> says to insert the contents of an external file named iostream.h into the program. This file contains declarations needed by the program to perform stream input and output.

The #include and #define lines at the beginning of the program are not handled by the C++ compiler but by a program known as the preprocessor. The next section discusses this preprocessor program in more detail.

A.3 The Preprocessor

The **preprocessor** concept is fundamental to all C++ environments. The preprocessor is a program that acts as a filter during the compilation process. The source program passes through the preprocessor on its way to the compiler:

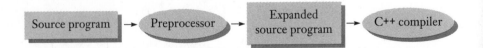

A line beginning with a pound sign (#) is *not* part of the C++ program proper (and thus is not terminated by a semicolon). It is a directive to the pre-processor. The preprocessor expands an #include directive by physically inserting the contents of the named file into the source program. Files that are #included usually have the suffix .h, meaning **header file.** In C++ environments, header files typically contain constant, type, and function declarations needed by a program.

If the file name is enclosed within double quotes:

```
#include "graphics.h"
```

the preprocessor looks for the file in the programmer's current directory. If the file name is enclosed within angle brackets:

```
#include <iostream.h>
```

the preprocessor looks for the file in the standard **include directory**—a directory containing all the header files that are part of the C++ environment. The programmer generally does not need to know where this directory is located.

The other preprocessor directive from the previous sample program is

```
#define MONTHS_PER_YR 12
```

This directive is known as a **macro definition.** It causes the preprocessor to replace every occurrence of the identifier MONTHS_PER_YR with whatever characters follow—in this case, the characters 12. The preprocessor performs the textual substitutions just as you would with a word processor.

A.4   Subprograms and Program Structure

Table A.2 describes the major differences between Pascal and C++ with respect to subprograms (procedures and functions).

Table A.2 Subprograms in Pascal and C++

Pascal	C++
Procedures versus functions	
Has both procedures and functions.	Has only functions. A "procedure" is expressed as a function that returns no value.
Function invocation *(Appears within an expression)*	
SomeFunc(a, b)	SomeFunc(a, b)

Table A.2 Subprograms in Pascal and C++ (continued)

Pascal	C++
Procedure invocation (*Appears as a separate, complete statement*)	

```
SomeProc(a, b);
```
```
SomeProc(a, b);
```

Function declaration

```
function SomeFunc( c: real ): char;
    Local declarations
begin
    .
    .
    .
    SomeFunc := resultChar;
end;
```

```
char SomeFunc( float c )
{
    Local declarations
    .
    .
    .
    return resultChar;
}
```

The major differences are:
1. The placement of local declarations
2. The mechanism for returning the single function value
   Pascal returns it by assignment to the function name.
   C++ returns it via a return statement.

Procedure declaration

```
procedure SomeProc(d:char; e:char);
    Local declarations
begin
    .
    .
    .
end;
```

```
void SomeProc( char d, char e )
    // "void" means no function
    // value returned
    {
    Local declarations
    .
    .
    .
    }
```

Pascal requires all procedures and functions to physically precede the body of the main program. In contrast, C++ functions may appear in any order. Nesting of one function within another is *not* allowed. The main function typically appears first, so the "big picture" is the first thing you see. The details then follow, tucked away in the remaining function bodies.

The next two figures illustrate this difference in the ordering of program units. Figure A.2 displays a Pascal program that inputs pairs of positive integers and determines the maximum value of each pair.

Figure A.2
Maxima program in
Pascal

```
program Maxima (input, output);
    (*----------------------------------------------------------*)
    (* This program repeatedly inputs pairs of positive integers. *)
    (* For each pair, it outputs the larger number.              *)
    (*----------------------------------------------------------*)
  var
     int1 : integer;
     int2 : integer;

  procedure PromptUser;
  begin
     write('Enter 2 positive integers');
     write(' (If first is nonpositive, I quit):')
  end;

  function Max( firstInt : integer; secondInt : integer ) : integer;
  begin
     if firstInt > secondInt then
        Max := firstInt
     else
        Max := secondInt
  end;

begin (* Main program *)
   PromptUser;
   read(int1, int2);
   while int1 > 0 do
   begin
      writeln(' The larger is: ', Max(int1, int2));
      PromptUser;
      read(int1, int2)
   end
end (* Main program *).
```

A C++ program that performs the same task appears in Figure A.3. Do not
worry about some of the language features we have not introduced yet.

Figure A.3
Maxima program in C++

```
//----------------------------------------------------------------
//  maxima.cpp
//  This program repeatedly inputs pairs of positive integers.
//  For each pair, it outputs the larger number.
//----------------------------------------------------------------

#include <iostream.h>

void PromptUser();         // Function prototypes
int  Max( int, int );

int main()
{
    int int1;
    int int2;
```

```
        PromptUser();
        cin >> int1 >> int2;
        while (int1 > 0) {
            cout << " The larger is: " << Max(int1, int2) << '\n';
            PromptUser();
            cin >> int1 >> int2;
        }
        return 0;
}

void PromptUser()
{
    cout << "Enter 2 positive integers";
    cout << " (If first is nonpositive, I quit):";
}

int Max( int firstInt, int secondInt )
{
    if (firstInt > secondInt)
        return firstInt;
    else
        return secondInt;
}
```

Both Pascal and C++ demand that you declare an identifier before you can reference it. Because C++ functions can appear in any order, a function invocation might physically precede the declaration of that function. In this case, you must use a **function prototype** near the beginning of the program. A function prototype (known as a **forward declaration** in some languages, including Pascal) specifies in advance the data types of the function parameters and the data type of the function value to be returned. In Figure A.3 the prototypes

```
void PromptUser();
int  Max( int, int );
```

declare that Max takes two int parameters and returns an int function value and that PromptUser takes no parameters and does not return a function value. You can think of a function prototype as an incomplete declaration, whereas the complete function declaration also includes the code for the body.

Notice how consistent C++ is in its "backwards" declaration syntax. Just as variable declarations require that you state the data type first, so do function declarations.

Table A.3 summarizes the differences in program structure between Pascal and C++.

Table A.3 Program structure in Pascal and C++

Pascal	C++
General structure	
Requires one main program, whose body appears last (after all declarations).	A collection of functions appearing in any order. Execution begins with a distinguished function named `main`, which often appears first.
Is nesting of subprograms allowed?	
Yes	No
Global identifiers	
Those declared by the main program.	Those declared outside all functions. (Variables declared within `main` are local to `main`.)
Order of declarations	
Fixed order required: first constants, then types, then variables, then subprograms.	No specific order required.
Must variable declarations precede executable statements?	
Yes	No. Variable declarations may be intermingled with executable statements.
Must identifiers be declared before being referenced?	
Yes	Yes

A.5 Overview of the Built-in Data Types

Figure A.4 displays the built-in data types of C++. Subsequent sections of this appendix describe each type in more detail.

Below is a list comparing the built-in types of Pascal and C++. This list is only a summary, not an explanation of the types. We will look at the various types in detail shortly.

- Integral (ordinal) types

    Pascal: `char`, `integer`, `Boolean`, enumerated (and subranges of these types)
    C++: `char`, `short`, `int`, `long`, `enum` (and `unsigned` variations)

    Notes: **1.** C++ has no subrange types, such as Pascal's `3..8` or `'A'..'Z'`.

    2. C++ has no Boolean type. Any expression with the value 0 represents *false*, and any expression with a nonzero value represents *true.* Furthermore, C++ evaluates a relational expression such as alpha > beta to 0 (false) or 1 (true).

- Floating point (real) types

  Pascal: real
  C++: float, double, long double

- Structured types

  Pascal: array, record, set, file
  C++: array, record (struct), union, class
  Notes: **1.** C++ has no set or file types.

  2. Unions and classes are introduced in the main body of this book.

- Address types

  Pascal: pointer
  C++: pointer, reference
  Note: Pointer and reference types are introduced in the main body of this book.

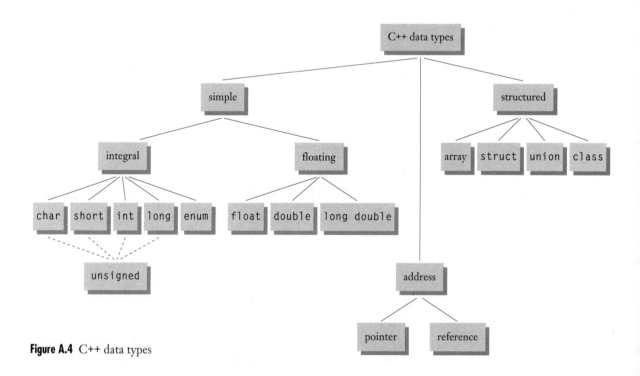

Figure A.4 C++ data types

A.6   Simple Types

The integral types char, short, int, and long all represent nothing more than integers of different sizes. Similarly, the floating types float, double (meaning double precision), and long double simply refer to floating point (real) numbers of different sizes.

In C++, sizes are measured in multiples of bytes. A byte is usually a group of eight consecutive bits (0s or 1s) in a computer's memory unit. Individual machines vary, but 8-bit bytes are most common. By definition, the size of a C++ char variable is 1 byte.

Using the notation *sizeof*(type) to denote the size in bytes of a variable of that data type, we can say that *sizeof*(char) = 1. Other than char, sizes of data objects in C++ are highly machine-dependent. On one machine it might be that

sizeof(char) = 1
sizeof(short) = 2
sizeof(int) = 4

and

sizeof(long) = 8

On another machine it might be that

sizeof(char) = 1
sizeof(short) = 2
sizeof(int) = 2

and

sizeof(long) = 4

C++ only guarantees that

$$1 = sizeof(\text{char}) \leq sizeof(\text{short}) \leq sizeof(\text{int}) \leq sizeof(\text{long})$$

and

$$sizeof(\text{float}) \leq sizeof(\text{double}) \leq sizeof(\text{long double})$$

Ranges of Values

Before looking at how sizes of data objects affect their possible values, we should point out that the word unsigned may precede an integral type name: unsigned char, unsigned short, unsigned int, unsigned long. Values of these types can be thought of as nonnegative integers with values from 0 through some machine-dependent maximum value.

Table A.4 displays sample ranges of values for C++ simple types.

Table A.4 Ranges of values for C++ simple types

C++ Type	Size (in bytes)	Range of values		
char	1	-128	through	127
unsigned char	1	0	through	255
short	2	-32,768	through	32,767
unsigned short	2	0	through	65,535
int	2	-32,768	through	32,767
unsigned int	2	0	through	65,535
long	4	-2,147,483,648	through	2,147,483,647
unsigned long	4	0	through	4,294,967,295
float	4	3.4E-38	through	3.4E+38 (absolute value)
double	8	1.7E-308	through	1.7E+308
long double	10	3.4E-4932	through	1.1E+4932

Note: The ranges of values shown are *examples only*. Those given assume an 8-bit byte and are highly machine-dependent.

Examples of Constants

In Table A.5 we present examples of various C++ constants and their Pascal equivalents. We will discuss char constants separately.

Values of Type char

Because *sizeof*(char) = 1, a char variable can store a small (one byte) integer constant:

```
char smallVal;
```

```
smallVal = 3;        ← Assignment operator is "="
```

But it is more common to use char variables to store character values, because one byte is the natural size for one character in the ASCII and EBCDIC character sets. C++ char constants come in several forms. One form, identical to Pascal's, is a single printable character enclosed in apostrophes (single quotes):

```
char someChar;
```

```
someChar = 'A';
```

Assuming a machine uses the ASCII character set, the compiler translates the constant 'A' into the integer 65, the internal representation of the letter A in the ASCII character set. (The 128 ASCII characters have internal representations 0 through 127. Appendix I contains the ASCII character chart.) Thus, we also could have written the above assignment statement as

```
someChar = 65;       ← Valid, but unclear and nonportable. (It does not
                        represent 'A' in the EBCDIC character set.)
```

Table A.5 Constants in C++ and Pascal

C++ constant	C++ type	Pascal equivalent	Remarks
1663	int	1663	Decimal (base 10) integer.
65535U	unsigned int	—	Unsigned integral constants end in U.
03177	int	—	Octal (base 8) integer. Begins with 0. Decimal equivalent is 1663.
0x67F	int	—	Hexadecimal (base 16) integer. Begins with 0, then either x or X. Decimal is 1663.
421L	long	—	Explicit long constants end in L or l.
53100	long	—	Implicit long constant, assuming machine's greatest int is, say, 32767.
—	—	maxint	Not available in C++.
6.83	double	—	Floating point constants are, by default, of type double.
6.83F	float	6.83	Explicit float constants end in F or f.
6.83L	long double	—	Explicit long double constants end in L or l.
4. or .5	double	—	Pascal requires at least one digit before and after the decimal point.
6.2E-9	double	6.2E-9	E notation same in C++ as Pascal (though this Pascal value gives single precision).

Note that execution of the statements

```
someChar = 'A';
someChar = someChar + 1;
```

causes someChar to become 66 or, abstractly, the ASCII character B. The equivalent Pascal sequence would be

```
someChar := 'A';
someChar := succ(someChar);
```

The Pascal succ function is required because integer arithmetic on char values is illegal. C++ allows such arithmetic because char is an integer type.

In C++, a char constant can be any of the following, enclosed in apostrophes (single quotes):

- A single printable character, other than an apostrophe (') or backslash (\)

- An **escape sequence**—one of the following sequences of characters starting with a backslash:

\n	Newline (line feed)
\t	Horizontal tab
\v	Vertical tab
\b	Backspace
\r	Carriage return
\f	Form feed
\a	Alert (a bell or beep)

\\	Backslash
\'	Single quote (apostrophe)
\"	Double quote (quotation mark)
\0	Null character (all zero bits)
\ddd	Bit pattern (1, 2, or 3 octal digits specifying the integer value of the desired character)
\xddd	Bit pattern (1 or more hexadecimal digits specifying the integer value of the desired character)

Despite their appearances, each escape sequence represents a single character. The "alert" character (\a) is the same as the BEL character in the ASCII character set. According to the ASCII chart, the BEL character has integer value 7 (octal as well as decimal). The statement

```
cout << '\a';
```

is equivalent to

```
cout << '\7';
```

although the former is more portable because it does not assume use of the ASCII character set. Each of these statements rings a bell (or, these days, beeps a beeper) at the terminal.

You also can use escape sequences within strings if you need to output a double quote, a backslash, or a nonprintable character. The statement

```
cout << "\aError!\n";
```

beeps the beeper, displays Error!, and terminates the output line. The statement

```
cout << "She said \"Hi\"";
```

outputs She said "Hi" and does not terminate the output line.

Choosing a Numeric Data Type

A first encounter with all the numeric data types of C++ may leave a Pascal programmer feeling overwhelmed. In choosing among the alternatives, you may feel tempted to toss a coin. You should resist this temptation, because each data type exists for a reason. Here are some guidelines:

1. In general, int is preferable.

   It is better not to use char and short for small integer values unless memory space is absolutely crucial. (Use of char for character data is appropriate, though.)

2. Use float only when absolutely necessary.

   Floating point arithmetic takes significantly longer to perform than integer arithmetic. As a rule, use float only if you need fractional values.

3. Use long only if the range of int values on your machine is too restrictive.

   Cost: Increased execution time and memory space.

4. Use double and long double only if your machine's float values do not carry enough digits of precision.

   Cost: Increased execution time and memory space.

5. The unsigned forms of integral types are best used for manipulating bit strings (see Appendix H), not for trying to obtain larger nonnegative integers. Later in this appendix we will explain why.

Enumeration Types

The final simple type in C++ is the **enumeration type** (enumerated type in Pascal). As in Pascal, an enumeration type is declared as a sequence of meaningful identifiers, not numbers, representing constants in the data type. The purpose is to encourage programmers to write self-documenting code. In C++, unlike Pascal, each constant (called an **enumerator**) has a value of type int, short, or char. Table A.6 summarizes enumeration types in C++ and Pascal.

Table A.6 Enumeration types in C++ and Pascal

Pascal	C++
Declarations and assignments	

`type FlagColor=(red,white,blue);`
`var  star : FlagColor;`
`begin`
`   star := white;`
	`enum FlagColor {red,white,blue};`
	`FlagColor star;`
	
	`star = white;`

Are the internal representations of enumerators known?	
No	Yes—red, white, and blue above are represented as the int constants 0, 1, and 2, respectively.
Can enumerators be given explicit integer values?	

No	Yes, by using "=" and an int, short, or char constant:
	
	`enum Coin {penny=1, nickel=5,`
	`                dime=10};`
	`Coin myCoin;`
	
	`myCoin = nickel;`

In this table, the `FlagColor` constants `red`, `white`, and `blue` have internal representations 0, 1, and 2. However, the compiler prevents you from storing `int` constants into a `FlagColor` variable:

```
FlagColor star;
```

```
star = white;        ← OK
star = 1;            ← Syntax error
```

This restriction is to keep you from accidentally storing an out-of-range value:

```
star = 5;
```

A.7   Structured Types

Arrays

The array is the most common structured data type. In Pascal, the subscript (index) type can be nearly any ordinal type:

```
var gradeCount : array ['A'..'F'] of integer
```

In C++, subscripts are always of type `int`. Furthermore, you cannot declare the upper and lower bounds of the subscript type. You declare only the number of elements in the array:

```
float income[100];
```

The lower bound is always zero, and the upper bound is always one less than the number of array elements. For the `income` array, the first array element is `income[0]` and the last is `income[99]`.

An array with one subscript is called a one-dimensional array or vector. An array with two subscripts is called a two-dimensional array or matrix. In C++, you must bracket the two subscripts of a matrix separately, both in the declaration and in a reference to an array element:

```
int myMatrix [3][5];
      .
      .
      .
myMatrix[0][4] = 89;
```

Note that `myMatrix[0][4]` refers to the last column (column 4) in the first row (row 0) of the matrix.

Table A.7 details the differences between Pascal and C++ arrays.

Strings

Character strings are not built-in data types in either Pascal or C++. They are special cases of one-dimensional arrays whose elements are of type `char`. In Pascal, a string array usually is declared as a `packed array` of type `char`. C++ does not have packed types.

Table A.7 Arrays in C++ and Pascal

Pascal	C++
Array declarations	
`var x, y : array [0..9] of real;`	`float x[10], y[10];`
`var y : array [1..10] of real;`	Not possible
`var z : array ['A'..'Z'] of integer;`	Not possible
`var m : array [0..5, 0..8] of integer;`	`int m[6][9];`
Subscript form	
`x[i] := 2.8;`	`x[i] = 2.8;`
`m[i,j] := 4;`	`m[i][j] = 4;`
Aggregate array assignment	
`x := y;`	Not allowed
Is there run-time checking for out-of-bound subscripts?	
With some compilers	No
Parameter passage of arrays	
By value ("value parameters") or by reference ("var parameters")	By reference only

Another difference is that C++ strings always are assumed to be terminated by the null character (`'\0'`). That is, after the last important character in the string, the programmer should store one more character, the null character. To create the string `Hi`, you could do this:

```
char myStr[3];

myStr[0] = 'H';
myStr[1] = 'i';
myStr[2] = '\0';
```

This convention of null termination, used by all C++ programmers, allows algorithms to locate the end of a string.

When you use a string constant, as in the statement

```
cout << "Hi";
```

the compiler implicitly takes care of storing the third character (`'\0'`). Table A.8 describes the differences between C++ and Pascal strings.

Table A.8 Character strings in C++ and Pascal

Pascal	C++
String constants	
'Hello' (Stored as exactly 5 characters)	"Hello" (Stored as 6 characters, including '\0'. Note: 'A' represents one character, but "A" represents two: the character A and the null character).
String array declarations	
`var str : packed array [1..10] of char;` (To hold 10 significant characters)	`char str[11];` (To hold 10 significant characters plus '\0')
Aggregate string assignment	
`str := 'Hello';`	Not allowed

Records

Record types are built into both Pascal and C++. If you are not familiar with the concept of records, you can bypass this discussion; Chapters 4 and 5 cover the material in detail.

With records, C++ and Pascal use different terminology. What Pascal calls a *record* is officially called a *structure* in C++. Pascal's reserved word `record` becomes `struct` in C++. Individual components of a Pascal record are called *fields*, whereas in C++ they are called *members*. Table A.9 summarizes the major differences between C++ and Pascal records.

Table A.9 Records in C++ and Pascal

Pascal	C++
Variable declarations using unnamed record types	

`var r1, r2 : record`
`          age : integer;`
`          height : real;`
`        end;`
	`struct {`
	`  int age;`
	`  float height;`
	`} r1, r2;`

Variable declarations using named record types	

`type RecType = record`
`          age : integer;`
`          height : real;`
`        end;`
`var r1, r2 : RecType;`
	`struct RecType {`
	`  int age;`
	`  float height;`
	`};`
	`RecType r1, r2;`

Table A.9 Records in C++ and Pascal (continued)

Pascal	C++
Record member selection	
`r1.age := 23;` `r1.height := 64.8;`	`r1.age = 23;` `r1.height = 64.8;`
The `with` *statement*	

`with r1 do begin`
`   age := 23;`
`   height := 64.8`
`end`
	Not available

Aggregate record assignment	
`r2 := r1;`	`r2 = r1;`
Parameter passage of records	
By value or by reference	By value or by reference
Arrays of records (using `RecType` *above)*	

`var r : array [0..49] of RecType;`
`begin`
`   r[0].age := 32;`
`   r[0].height := 70.0;`
	`RecType r[50];`
	
	`r[0].age = 32;`
	`r[0].height = 70.0;`

Other Structured Types

The Pascal structured types `set` and `file` are absent in C++. C++ does have two other structured types, unions and classes. These we introduce in the main body of this text.

A.8   Type Checking and Type Coercion

Both Pascal and C++ are **statically typed** languages. This term means that every value has a data type, and the compiler can determine the type compatibility of all operators and operands statically (at compile time). In both languages, the following hold true.

1. All identifiers used in a program must be declared.
2. The compiler performs **type checking** to ensure that all operations and operands have compatible data types.

Statically typed languages differ in how they define type compatibility. Pascal employs **strict type checking.** It severely limits the mixing of data types in expressions, assignment operations, and parameter passage. For example, the Pascal assignment statement

```
integerVar := realVar;
```

is prohibited. The compiler sees a type incompatibility and generates a syntax error.

C++ employs **nonstrict type checking.** The assignment statement

```
integerVar = floatVar;
```

is permissible. However, the compiler does something "under the table." It generates object code that will, at run time, temporarily convert the floating point value to integer representation (discarding the fractional part in the process) before storing the result into `integerVar`. This invisible conversion of a value from one data type to another is called **implicit type coercion.**

C++ considers integral and floating types to be compatible in the following contexts:

- Arithmetic expressions and relational expressions
- Assignment operations
- Parameter passage
- Return of a function value

When values of compatible types are mixed, implicit type coercion occurs.

Type Coercion in Arithmetic and Relational Expressions

Suppose an arithmetic expression involves one operator and two operands. Examples might be `3.4*sum` or `var1/var2`. Then implicit type coercion takes place as follows.

Step 1: Each `char`, `short`, or enumeration value is promoted (widened) to `int`. (Table A.10 describes promotion in detail.) If both operands are now `int`, the result is an `int` expression.

Step 2: If step 1 still leaves a mixed-type expression, the following precedence of types is used:

lowest $\longrightarrow$ highest

```
int, unsigned int, long, unsigned long, float, double, long double
```

The value of the operand of "lower" type is promoted to that of the "higher" type, and the result is an expression of that type.

A simple example is the expression `someFloat+2`. This expression has no `char`, `short`, or enumeration values in it, so step 1 still leaves a mixed-type expression. In step 2, `int` is a "lower" type than `float`, so the value 2 is coerced temporarily to a `float` value, say, 2.0. Then the multiplication can take place, and the type of the entire expression is `float`.

This description of type coercion also holds for relational expressions such as `someInt<someFloat`. However, the type of the result is always `int`—the value 1 (true) or 0 (false).

Table A.10 Promotion from one simple type to another

From	To	Result
`double`	`long double`	Same value occupying more memory space.
`float`	`double`	Same value occupying more memory space.
integral type	floating type	Fractional part is zero.
integral type	unsigned counterpart	No change in value in two's complement machines.
signed integral type	longer signed integral type	Sign extension occurs: leftmost byte(s) are padded with the sign bit (leftmost bit) of the shorter integer value.
unsigned integral type	longer integral type	No sign extension occurs. Leftmost byte(s) are padded with zero bits.

Note: The result of promoting a `char` to an `int` is machine-dependent. On some machines, `char` means `signed char`, so promotion of a negative value yields a negative integer. On other machines, `char` means `unsigned char`, so promotion always yields a nonnegative integer.

Promotion

Promotion (or **widening**) of a value due to type coercion follows the rules detailed in Table A.10. In this table, the phrases "two's complement" and "sign bit" refer to the most common way that machines store integers in memory. We will not go into two's complement representation here, but one characteristic is that the leftmost bit of an integer is considered the sign bit: 1 denotes a negative integer, and 0 denotes a positive integer or zero.

The note at the bottom of Table A.10 refers to a potential problem with portability of C++ programs. If you use the `char` type only to store character data, there is no problem. C++ guarantees that each character in a machine's character set (such as ASCII) is a nonnegative value.

But if you try to save memory by using the `char` type for manipulating small signed integers, then a program causing promotion of these `char`s to `int`s will produce different results on different machines! The moral is this: Unless you are squeezed to the limit for memory space, do not use `char` to manipulate small signed numbers. Use `char` only to store character data.

Type Coercion in Assignment Operations

With the exception of `char` to `int`, promoting values from one type to another does not cause unexpected results. On the other hand, **demotion** (or **narrowing**) of values can potentially cause loss of information. Demotion is possible with implicit type coercion in an assignment operation.

Consider an assignment operation

$$v = e$$

where v is a variable and e is an expression. Regarding the data types of v and e, there are three possibilities:

1. If the types of v and e are the same, no type coercion occurs.
2. If the type of v is "higher" than that of e (using the type precedence explained in the preceding discussion of promotion), then the value of e is promoted to v's type before being stored into v.
3. If the type of v is "lower" than that of e, the value of e is demoted to v's type before being stored into v.

Demotion, which you can think of as shrinking a value, may cause loss of information:

- Demotion from a longer integral type to a shorter integral type (such as `long` to `int`) results in discarding the bits on the left. The result may be a drastically different number.
- Demotion from a floating type to an integral type causes truncation of the fractional part (and an undefined result if the integer part will not fit into the destination variable).
- Demotion from a longer floating type to a shorter floating type (such as `double` to `float`) may result in loss of precision.

These rules for the assignment operation also hold for parameter passage (the mapping of actual parameters onto formal parameters) and for returning the value of a function with a `return` statement.

One consequence of implicit type coercion is the futility of declaring a variable to be `unsigned` with the hope that the compiler will prevent you from doing something like this:

```
unsignedVar = -5;
```

The compiler will not complain at all. It will generate code to perform type coercion, coercing the `int` to an `unsigned int`. The result, conceptually, will be some strange looking positive integer. Moral: Do not rely on `unsigned` types to obtain larger nonnegative numbers, thinking that the compiler will keep you from mistakenly storing a negative number. If you need larger numbers, move up from `int` to `long`, not `int` to `unsigned int`.

A.9   Type Casting

If we want to write readable and self-documenting code, it is not entirely satisfactory to rely on "invisible" implicit type coercion. C++ allows **explicit type conversion** by means of the *cast operation*. This term comes from the C++ phrase **type casting**—casting a value from one type to another.

Instead of depending on implicit type coercion in the assignment

```
intVar = floatVar;
```

we can use a cast operation, which has two possible forms:

```
intVar = (int) floatVar;
intVar = int(floatVar);
```
    ←—Prefix notation (parentheses required)
    ←—Functional notation

All three of the above statements produce identical results. The only difference is that of clarity. With the cast operation, it is perfectly clear to the programmer and to colleagues that the mixing of types was intentional, not an oversight. Countless bugs have resulted from unintentional mixing of types.

There is one restriction on using the functional notation of a cast operation. The type name must be a single identifier. If the type name consists of more than one identifier, the prefix notation is required:

```
thisChar = unsigned char(inputVal);
thisChar = (unsigned char) inputVal;
```
    ←—No
    ←—Yes

Pascal supports explicit type conversion through the functions `trunc` and `round`:

```
var someReal   : real;
    int1, int2 : integer;
begin
    .
    .
    .
    int1 := trunc(someReal);
    int2 := round(someReal);
```

The corresponding C++ code is as follows:

```
float someReal;
int   int1, int2;
.
.
.
int1 = int(someReal);
int2 = int(someReal + 0.5);
```
    ←—Assuming someReal > 0.0

Finally, we must stress a very important point about explicit type conversions. Not only are they valuable for documentation purposes, they are also mandatory in some cases for correct programming. Consider the following code:

```
int   itemSum;
int   itemCount;
float average;
.
.
.
average = itemSum / itemCount;
```
    ←—Assume itemSum contains 120
       and itemCount contains 190.

Pascal has two division operators: / for real division and div for integer division. C++ has only one: /. If both of its operands are integral expressions, it works like Pascal's div operator. Any fractional portion is discarded. Thus, the above assignment statement evaluates 120/190 to be zero and stores the value 0.0 into average. The way to express it correctly, as well as clearly, is this:

```
average = float(itemSum) / float(itemCount);
```

A.10   Constant and Type Declarations

Symbolic Constants

Both Pascal and C++ allow you to give names to constants. In Pascal, you use const declarations to create these **symbolic constants**:

```
const pi = 3.141593;
```

With const declarations, the compiler literally replaces each occurrence of a constant identifier with its corresponding constant value.

C++ provides two methods for defining symbolic constants. The first method, discussed earlier in this appendix, is to use a #define directive to the preprocessor:

```
#define PI 3.141593
```

(Recall that C++ programmers often capitalize all the letters in a constant identifier.)

Using #define to create symbolic constants has an important drawback. The preprocessor does not perform type checking or scope analysis (determination of global versus local scope) of identifiers, as the compiler does. Thus, it is preferable to use the second method—the word const along with the data type of the constant identifier:

```
const float PI = 3.141593;
```

This declaration is handled by the compiler, not the preprocessor, so that type checking and scope analysis are performed.

Below are three comparable sections of code, one in Pascal, the other two in C++.

Pascal:

```
const thisYear = 1994;
      period = '.';
      cupsPerGallon = 16;
```

C++, using preprocessor directives:

```
#define THIS_YEAR 1994
#define PERIOD '.'
#define CUPS_PER_GALLON 16
```

C++, using `const`:

```
const int  THIS_YEAR = 1994;
const char PERIOD = '.';
const int  CUPS_PER_GALLON = 16;
```

Note that if you omit a type name, C++ assumes you mean `int`:

```
const THIS_YEAR = 1994;
const CUPS_PER_GALLON = 16;
```

Sometimes you will encounter code like this, but there is no particularly good reason to omit the word `int`.

Type Declarations

In both Pascal and C++ it is possible to give names to data types. Pascal uses type declarations:

```
type Vec50 = array [1..50] of real;
```

With type declarations, you can replace the detailed form of some data type with a meaningful identifier. You can then use these identifiers to declare variables, formal parameters, and other programmer-defined types. C++ uses the reserved word `typedef` to give names to data types. Table A.11 summarizes the use of type declarations in Pascal and C++.

Armed with knowledge of `const` and `typedef`, we can see that an `enum` declaration is similar to writing a `typedef` and several `const` declarations, all of type `int`. For example,

```
enum Boolean {FALSE, TRUE};
```

is like the sequence of statements

```
typedef int Boolean;
const    int FALSE = 0;
const    int TRUE = 1;
```

However, there is an important difference. It turns out that implicit type coercion is defined for enumeration types to `int` (see Section A.8), but *not* for `int` to enumeration types. In the following code, the compiler will give either a warning or a fatal error at the assignment statement:

```
enum Boolean {FALSE, TRUE};

Boolean isGreater;
float    a, b;
.
.
.
isGreater = (a > b);
```

The data type of the relational expression `a > b` is `int` (1 for true or 0 for false). Because type coercion from `int` to enumeration types is not defined, the compiler will complain about storing an `int` value into a `Boolean` variable.

Table A.11 Type declarations in C++ and Pascal

Pascal	C++
Type declarations	

```
type Meters = integer;          typedef int   Meters;
     Vector = array [0..49] of real;   typedef float Vector[50];
     String10 = packed array [1..10]   typedef char  String10[11];
               of char;
```

Variable declarations, using the above

```
var width  : Meters;            Meters   width;
    x      : Vector;            Vector   x;
    myName : String10;          String10 myName;
    table  : array [0..19] of Vector;   Vector   table[20];
             (* a 20 x 50 matrix *)
```

We could dodge the problem by using a cast to perform explicit type conversion:

```
isGreater = Boolean(a > b);
```

But using a cast is a nuisance if we have to do it often in a program. It is simpler to define the Boolean type using a `typedef` and two `const` declarations.

A.11 Scope and Lifetime

Scope of Identifiers

In Pascal and C++, the **scope** of an identifier is the region of program code where it is legal to reference that identifier. In Pascal, an identifier declared by the main program has global scope and is visible to the main program and to all subprograms. An identifier declared within a subprogram has local scope and is visible only within that subprogram. These **scope rules** or **visibility rules** are similar in C++, but with a special twist. An identifier can be local to a **block** (another name for a compound statement):

```
if (alpha > 3) {
    int i;
    cin >> i;
    beta = beta + i;
}
```

Note that the body of a function is syntactically a block:

```
void SomeFunc()
{
    int temp;
      .
      .
      .
}
```

Thus "local to a function" is consistent with "local to a block."

C++ defines three categories of scope for any identifier:

1. **Class scope**

   This term refers to the structured type class, which is not discussed in this appendix.

2. **Local scope**

   The scope of an identifier declared inside a block extends from the point of declaration to the end of that block.

3. **File** (global) **scope**

   The scope of an identifier declared outside all functions and classes extends from the point of declaration to the end of the entire file.

Just as in Pascal, the C++ compiler prevents access to a local identifier from outside its scope.

Lifetime of a Variable

A concept related to but separate from the scope of a variable is its **lifetime**— the period of time during program execution that an identifier actually has memory allocated to it. Consider local variables in Pascal. Storage for local variables is created at the moment of procedure entry, then the variables are "alive" while the procedure is executing, and finally the storage is destroyed at procedure exit. In contrast, the lifetime of a global variable is the lifetime of the entire program. Memory is allocated only once, when the program begins executing, and is destroyed only when the entire program terminates. Observe that scope is a compile-time issue, but lifetime is a run-time issue.

In C++, each variable has a **storage class** that determines its lifetime. An **automatic variable** is one whose storage is allocated and destroyed at block entry and block exit. A **static variable** is one whose storage remains allocated for the duration of the entire program. You may specify the storage class of an identifier by prefixing its declaration with one of the reserved words auto or static.

If no storage class specifier is given, auto is assumed for any variable declared inside a block, and static is assumed for any global variable. These assumptions suffice in most cases. It would not make sense to declare a global variable auto, so the word auto is rarely seen in a C++ program. On the other hand, you might wish to give a local variable the storage class static so that its lifetime persists from function call to function call:

```
void SomeFunc()
{
    float  someFloat;        ◄— Destroyed when function exits
    static int someInt;      ◄— Retains its value from call to call
    .
    .
    .
}
```

It is usually better to declare a local variable as static than to use a global variable. A static local variable has the lifetime of a global variable, but the local scope hides the variable from other functions in the program.

Initializations in Declarations

C++, unlike standard Pascal, allows you to initialize a variable in its declaration. An automatic variable is initialized to the specified value each time control enters the block:

```
void SomeFunc( int someParam )
{
    int i = 0;                       ←— Initialized each time
    int n = 2 * someParam + 3;       ←— Initialized each time
      .
      .
      .
}
```

In contrast, initialization of a static variable (a global variable or one explicitly declared static) occurs once only, the first time control reaches its declaration. Furthermore, the initial value must be a **constant expression** (one with only constant values as operands):

```
void AnotherFunc( int aParam )
{
    static char ch = 'A';            ←— Initialized once only
    static int  n  = aParam + 1;     ←— Illegal—constant expression
                                          required
      .
      .
      .
}
```

Although an initialization gives an initial value to a variable, it is perfectly acceptable to reassign it another value during program execution.

C++ has a special syntax for initializing an array in a declaration. You separate the values of the array elements with commas and enclose the list within braces:

```
int someVec[3] = {25, 0, 4};
int someMatrix[2][3] = {
    {4, 6, 5},
    {0, 0, 12}
};
```

Table A.12 summarizes initialization of static and automatic variables.

C++ provides a shorthand notation for initializing string arrays: the string constant. The following declarations are equivalent, although the second is more likely to be used:

```
char str[3] = {'H', 'i', '\0'};
char str[3] = "Hi";
```

Table A.12 Comparison of static and automatic initializations

	Automatic variables	**Static variables**
Initialized when?	Each time control reaches the declaration	Once only, the first time control reaches the declaration
Valid initializers	Any expression (type coercion may be performed)	Constant expressions only

Caution: Initialization (in a declaration) and assignment (with an assignment statement) are two different things in C++. Different rules apply. Array initialization is legal, but recall that aggregate array assignment is not:

```
char myStr[6] = "Hello";        ← OK
    .
    .
myStr = "Howdy";                ← Illegal
```

Also, you can omit the size of an array when initializing it; the compiler will determine its size. This technique is especially useful for initializing long strings without counting the characters manually:

```
char msg[] = "Reenter last number";   ← 20 elements, including '\0'
int  vec[] = {0, 0, 0, 0, 12};        ← 5 elements
```

External Declarations

We now make a final point about variable declarations. As we discuss in the main body of this book, it is common to organize a C++ source program into many separate files. One file might contain just the main function, another file may contain some data declarations and two or three functions invoked by main, and so forth. The compiler's job is to translate the source code in each file independently, and then a program known as the linker collects all the resulting object code into a single executable program.

You can use the reserved word extern to reference a global variable located in another file. A normal declaration such as

```
int someInt;
```

causes the compiler to reserve some storage for someInt. On the other hand,

```
extern int someInt;
```

is known as an **external declaration.** It states that someInt is a global variable located in another file and that no storage should be reserved for it here. System header files such as iostream.h contain such external declarations so that user programs can access important variables located in system programs.

In C++ terminology, the statement

```
extern int someInt;
```

is merely a declaration of `someInt`. It associates a variable name with a data type so that the compiler can perform type checking. On the other hand, the statement

```
int someInt;
```

is both a declaration and a **definition** of `someInt`. In other words, a declaration is also a definition if it reserves memory for the object. In C++, you can declare an object in many locations, but you can define it only once.

A.12 Expressions

Expressions are composed of constants, variables, operators, function calls, and parentheses. C++ has a rich, sometimes bewildering, variety of operators. Table A.13 lists those C++ operators that have counterparts in Pascal.

Table A.13 Basic operators in C++ and Pascal

Pascal		C++	Remarks
:=	assignment	=	
( )	function call	( )	
[ ]	subscripting	[ ]	
.	record member selection	.	
Arithmetic operators			
+	unary plus	+	
-	unary minus	-	
+	addition	+	
-	subtraction	-	
*	multiplication	*	
/	floating point division	/	
div	integer division	/	Both operands integer; fraction truncated.
mod	modulus (remainder)	%	Both operands must be integer.
Relational operators			
=	equal	==	For C++, result is 1 (true) or 0 (false).
<>	not equal	!=	
<	less than	<	
<=	less than or equal	<=	
>	greater than	>	
>=	greater than or equal	>=	
Logical (Boolean) operators			
and	logical AND	&&	For C++, result is 1 (true) or 0 (false).
or	logical OR	||	
not	logical NOT	!	

C++ also has operators that are more specialized and seldom found in other languages. Table A.14 displays these operators. As you inspect this table, do not panic—a quick scan will do.

Tables A.13 and A.14 detail most (but not all) of the C++ operators. We will introduce other operators, when appropriate, in the main body of this book. Bitwise operators mentioned in Table A.14 are primarily for manipulating bit strings. Appendix H gives detailed coverage; we do not discuss them here.

Table A.14 Some specialized C++ operators

C++ operators		Remarks
Increment and decrement operators		
++	pre-increment	Example: ++someVar
++	post-increment	Example: someVar++
--	pre-decrement	Example: --someVar
--	post-decrement	Example: someVar--
Combined assignment operators		
+=	add and assign	
-=	subtract and assign	
*=	multiply and assign	
/=	divide and assign	
Bitwise operators (integer operands only)		
<<	left shift	
>>	right shift	
&	bitwise AND	
|	bitwise OR	
^	bitwise EXCLUSIVE OR	
~	complement (invert all bits)	
Combined assignment operators for integer operands only		
%=	modulus and assign	
<<=	shift left and assign	
>>=	shift right and assign	
&=	bitwise AND and assign	
|=	bitwise OR and assign	
^=	bitwise EXCLUSIVE OR and assign	
Others		
( )	cast (type conversion)	
sizeof	size of operand in bytes	Form: sizeof expr or sizeof(type)
?:	conditional operator	Form: expr1 ? expr2 : expr3

Assignment Operators

C++ has several assignment operators. The equal sign (=) is the basic assignment operator. When combined with its two operands, it forms an **assignment expression** (*not* an assignment statement). Every assignment expression has:

- a *value*

and

- a *side effect*: the value is stored into the object denoted by the left-hand side.

For example, the expression

```
delta = 2 * 12
```

has the value 24 and a side effect of storing this value into `delta`.

In C++, any expression becomes an **expression statement** when terminated by a semicolon. The following are all valid C++ statements, the first two doing nothing useful whatsoever:

```
23;
2 * (alpha + beta);
delta = 2 * 12;
```

The third expression statement is useful because of its side effect of storing 24 into `delta`. Because an assignment is an expression, not a statement, you can use it anywhere an expression is allowed. The following statement stores the value 20 into `firstInt`, the value 30 into `secondInt`, and the value 35 into `thirdInt`:

```
thirdInt = (secondInt = (firstInt = 20) + 10) + 5;
```

Some C++ programmers use this style of coding, but others find it hard to read and error-prone.

In addition to the = operator, C++ has several combined assignment operators (+=, *=, and so forth). These operators have the following semantics:

```
i += 5;                    ⟵── Means i = i + 5
pivotPoint *= n + 3;       ⟵── Means pivotPoint = pivotPoint*(n + 3)
```

Increment and Decrement Operators

The increment and decrement operators (++ and --) operate only on variables, not constants or arbitrary expressions. Suppose a variable `someInt` contains the value 3. With the expression ++`someInt` (denoting pre-incrementation), the side effect of incrementing `someInt` occurs first, so the resulting value of the expression is 4. With the expression `someInt`++ (denoting post-incrementation), the value of the expression is 3, and *then* the side effect of incrementing `someInt` takes place. The following code illustrates this difference:

```
int1 = 14;
int2 = ++int1;
// Now int1 and int2 both contain 15

int1 = 14;
int2 = int1++;
// Now int1 contains 15 and int2 contains 14
```

Instead of incrementing a variable with the statement

```
i = i + 1;
```

it is very common to see the statement

```
i++;
```

Here, the value of the expression is unused, but we get the desired side effect of incrementing i. In this example, pre-incrementing and post-incrementing would have the same effect; the choice is a matter of personal taste.

Logical Operators

The logical operators (!, &&, and ||) operate on expressions of any simple type, even floating types. The ! operator yields 1 (true) if its operand has the value zero (false) and yields 0 (false) if its operand has any nonzero value (true).

The && operator yields 1 if both of its operands have nonzero (true) values, otherwise it yields 0. The || operator yields 1 if either of its operands has a nonzero (true) value, otherwise it yields 0. Although the logical operators can have operands of any simple type, they typically are used with other logical (Boolean) expressions:

```
if (a == 3 && b > 5)
    .
    .
    .
```

But sometimes you will see C++ code like this:

```
int studentCount;

cin >> studentCount;
if ( !studentCount )
    cout << "There are no students";
```

where studentCount represents a numeric, not Boolean, value. Although this expression is legitimate, many consider the following to be clearer:

```
if (studentCount == 0)
    .
    .
    .
```

The logical operators && and || use **short-circuit** (or **conditional**) **evaluation.** In short-circuit evaluation of

```
expr1 && expr2
```

expr1 is evaluated first. If its value is false (zero), then the entire expression is clearly false. It is not necessary for the machine to evaluate expr2, so evaluation stops. Likewise, for

expr1 || expr2

if the evaluation of expr1 yields true (nonzero), then the entire expression is immediately true and expr2 is not evaluated.

The `sizeof` and `?:` *Operators*

The `sizeof` operator is a unary operator that yields the size, in bytes, of its operand. Its operand can be a variable name (either simple or structured), as in

```
sizeof someInt
```

Or its operand can be the name of a data type, enclosed in parentheses:

```
sizeof(float)
```

The `?:` operator is sometimes called the conditional operator. This is a ternary (three-operand) operator with the following syntax:

expr1 ? expr2 : expr3

First, expr1 is evaluated. If it is nonzero (true), then the value of the whole expression is expr2; otherwise, the value of the whole expression is expr3. Only one of expr2 and expr3 is evaluated. A classic example of its use is expressing the statement

```
if (int1 > int2)
    max = int1;
else
    max = int2;
```

as:

```
max = (int1 > int2) ? int1 : int2;
```

The parentheses around the first expression are unnecessary because, as we will see shortly, the conditional operator has very low precedence. But it is customary to include the parentheses for clarity.

Operator Precedence

Below we summarize the operator precedence of the most common C++ operators. (Appendix F contains the complete list.)

Precedence (highest to lowest)

	C++ operator	*Associativity*
	() [] .	Left to right
Unary:	++ -- ! + - (cast) sizeof	Right to left
	* / %	Left to right
	+ -	Left to right
	< <= > >=	Left to right
	== !=	Left to right
	&&	Left to right
	||	Left to right
	? :	Right to left
	= += -= etc.	Right to left

The column labeled "Associativity" describes grouping order. Within a precedence level, most operators group left to right. For example,

```
int1 - int2 + int3
```

means

```
(int1 - int2) + int3
```

and not

```
int1 - (int2 + int3)
```

The assignment operators, though, group right to left. The expression

```
int4 = int5 = 1
```

means

```
int4 = (int5 = 1)
```

This associativity makes sense because the assignment operation is naturally a right-to-left operation.

   Caution: Although operator precedence and associativity dictate the grouping of operators with their operands, C++ does not define which subexpressions are evaluated first. Thus, using side effects in expressions requires extra care. For example, if i currently contains 20, the statement

```
vec[i] = i++;
```

yields either vec[20]=20 or vec[21]=20, depending on the particular compiler being used. If you want vec[i]=i and then to increment i, you should force this ordering with two separate statements:

```
vec[i] = i;
i++;
```

Expressions: Pascal and C++

C++ provides a vast number of operators not available in Pascal. The choices may seem overwhelming at first, but they gradually become familiar. Below are some observations and cautions to help you in your transition to C++.

- In Pascal, an assignment is a statement. In C++, an assignment is an expression and can occur in other expressions. Incorporating many side effects into one statement can at times be useful but may lead to unreadable code and logic errors that are difficult to find.

- A major source of annoyance (and sometimes disastrous results) arises in confusing Pascal's relational operator = with the C++ assignment operator =. Remember, the C++ relational operator is ==, not =. (Some people pronounce == as "equals-equals" as a reminder of the difference.)

- Pascal has two division operators, / and div. In C++, the / operator is used for both integer and floating point division. If both operands are integral, the result is truncated just as with div. Thus, 25/75 equals zero.

- Although operator precedence in C++ is technically different from Pascal's, one notices little difference when actually programming. One appreciable difference is that in C++, parentheses are unnecessary when you apply a logical operator to relational expressions:

  Pascal: (a <= b) and (c = 1)
  C++: a <= b && c == 1

- C++ uses short-circuit (conditional) evaluation for the operators && and ||. Short-circuit evaluation ensures that an expression such as

  n != 0 && 7/n == 3

  cannot produce a division-by-zero execution error. Pascal does not define whether short-circuit or full evaluation is used, so an expression similar to the above will cause an execution error on some systems but not others.

- In addition to maintaining the distinction between == and =, keep in mind the difference between && and &, as well as between || and |. Although syntax errors do not result, logic bugs do. (As a memory aid, some people say "and-and" and "or-or" for these operators.)

A.13 Control Structures

The simplest statements in C++ are the **expression statement**:

expression;

the **declaration statement**:

declaration;

and the **null statement**:

;

The most common uses of expression statements are assignments and function calls. The declaration statement qualifies as a statement because C++ allows a declaration to occur anywhere an executable statement can, not just "at the top" as in Pascal. The null statement, which is rarely seen, says "Do nothing— just proceed".

A block (compound statement) consists of zero or more statements enclosed within a left brace and a right brace. A block may be used wherever a single statement is allowed.

The precise syntax rules for placement of the semicolon are rather complicated, but the simplest guideline is this: Terminate each statement (*except* a compound statement) with a semicolon.

The if *Statement*

Apart from syntax, the if statement in C++ is nearly the same as Pascal's. The primary difference is that Pascal performs its test on a Boolean expression, whereas C++ performs its test on an expression of any simple type. If this expression has a nonzero value, the then-clause is executed; otherwise the else-clause, if present, is executed. Most often the tested expression is a relational expression, which C++ evaluates to the int constant 1 (true) or 0 (false). Table A.15 displays examples of if statements. The rather unusual placement of braces in a C++ if statement is a convention originated by C language programmers.

Caution: Every C++ programmer is guaranteed to make the following error at least once:

```
alpha = 5;
if (alpha = 3)
    cout << "alpha equals 3";
else
    cout << "alpha does not equal 3";
```

This code outputs the message alpha equals 3. Why? Because

```
alpha = 3
```

is an *assignment expression*, not a relational expression. The value of this assignment expression is 3 (interpreted as "true" in the if condition), so the then-clause is executed. Worse yet, the side effect of assigning 3 to alpha destroys its previous value, 5.

Table A.15 if statements in C++ and Pascal

Pascal	C++
if *(with simple then-clause)*	

```
if alpha = beta then          if (alpha == beta)        ◄── Parentheses required
   arc := arc + 1                 arc++;
```

if *(with compound then-clause)*

```
if angle > 90 then            if (angle > 90) {
begin                            high = 90;
   high := 90;                   low++;
   low := low + 1             }
end
```

if-else *(combination)*

```
if angle <> 15 then           if (angle != 15) {
begin                            lower = 90;
   lower := 90;                  upper = 179;
   upper := 179               }
end                           else {
else                             lower = 0;
begin                            upper = 89;
   lower := 0;                }
   upper := 89
end
```

Multiway selection

```
if inVal = 1 then             if (inVal == 1)
   PrintHi                       PrintHi();
else if inVal = 3 then        else if (inVal == 3)
   PrintGreetings                PrintGreetings();
else if inVal = 4 then        else if (inVal == 4)
   PrintBye                      PrintBye();
else                          else
   PrintWhat                     PrintWhat();
```

The switch *Statement*

In Pascal, the case statement is a mechanism for multiway selection. One, and only one, of the case-clauses is chosen for execution. C++ has a similar construct—the switch statement—but it is possible, either intentionally or by accident, for several case-clauses to execute. Table A.16 compares the case and switch statements. Notice that each case-clause needs a break statement, a statement that forces immediate exit from the switch statement. Otherwise, control "falls through" to the next case-clause.

Table A.16 Pascal case statement versus C++ switch statement

Pascal	C++

An example

```
case m+n of                        switch (m+n) {
     1: (* nothing *);                  case 1:  break;        ← Don't fall through
   3, 8: alpha := 20;                   case 3:
   2, 5: begin                          case 8:  alpha = 20;
            alpha := 90;                         break;        ← Don't fall through
            beta := 40;                 case 2:
         end;                           case 5:  alpha = 90;
end                                              beta = 40;
   (No "default"                                 break;        ← Don't fall through
    clause in standard                  default: PrintError();
    Pascal)                          }
```

(No "default" clause in
standard Pascal)

Does control fall through from one case-clause to the next?

No	Yes, unless a break statement is present

Data type of the Pascal case-expression (or C++ switch-expression)

Ordinal type	Integral type (including char)

Form of a case label

One or more constants, separated by commas	The word case, followed by exactly one constant expression. Several case labels may precede one case-clause.

If a case-clause has more than one statement, are begin *and* end *(or { and })*
   required?

Yes	No

What happens if the Pascal case-expression (or C++ switch-expression) does not
   match any case label constant?

Behavior is undefined. May crash or just continue past the case statement.	The default case-clause is selected, if present. Otherwise, control continues past the switch statement.

Loops

C++ provides three looping structures: while, do-while, and for. The while statement performs its loop test at the top of the loop. The do-while test is at the bottom. As with the C++ if statement, a loop condition may be of any simple type. The do-while statement is similar to Pascal's repeat statement, but the loop condition is phrased as a *continue* condition, not an *exit* condition. Table A.17 presents examples of while and do-while.

Table A.17 while and do-while statements in C++ and Pascal

Pascal	C++
while *loop*	

```
while alpha <= 925 do          while (alpha <= 925) {
begin                              cin >> beta;
   read(beta);                     alpha += beta;
   alpha := alpha + beta       }
end
```

Infinite while *loop*

```
while true do                  while (1)
   write('Hi')                    cout << "Hi";
```

do-while *loop with single statement body*

```
repeat                         do
   read(ch)                       cin >> ch;
until ch >= 'A'                while (ch < 'A');        ←── Parentheses
                                                              required
```

do-while *loop with multiple statement body*

```
repeat                         do {
   write('Enter your age:');      cout << "Enter your age:";
   read(age)                      cin >> age;
until age > 0                  } while (age <= 0);
```

While and do-while statements are generally for **indefinite loops,** loops in which the number of loop iterations is not known in advance. If the number of iterations is known in advance, a **counting loop** is appropriate. The C++ for statement facilitates programming of counting loops. Below is a description.

- Form of the C++ for statement

  for (statement1 expression1 ; expression2)
      body
  where expression1 represents a while condition.

- Example: Print the integers 1 through 10

  ```
  for (intVal = 1; intVal <= 10; intVal++)
      cout << intVal;
  ```

- Notes

  1. The for statement is just a compact notation for a while loop. The compiler translates the above example into

  ```
  intVal = 1;
  while (intVal <= 10) {
      cout << intVal;
      intVal++;
  }
  ```

2. Most often, a for statement is written such that statement1 initializes a loop control variable and expression2 increments or decrements the loop control variable.

3. The fact that statement1 is a statement, not an expression, allows initialization within a declaration (see Section A.11 about this subject):

```
for (int i = 30; i > 0; i--)
    .
    .
    .
```

Caution: This declaration does not make the variable i local to the for loop. Its scope is taken to be the surrounding block:

```
for (int i = 0; i < 50; i++)
    a[i] = 0;
for (int i = 0; i < 75; i++)          ← Error—i is already declared.
    b[i] = 0;
```

4. Statement1 may be the null statement, and expression1 and expression2 are optional. If expression1 is omitted, the value 1 (true) is assumed. The following therefore creates an infinite loop:

```
for (;;) {
    .
    .
    .
}
```

What is unusual about C++ for loops is that they are not specialized counting loop structures as in Pascal. They are merely shorthand notations for while loops. Although you can write

```
for ( ; delta < 0.005; )
```

instead of

```
while (delta < 0.005)
```

the programs in this textbook use for statements strictly for counting loops. To express indefinite loops, we use while or do-while.

Table A.18 notes the differences between Pascal and C++ for loops

Table A.18 for statements in C++ and Pascal

Pascal	C++
Example: A for loop to input and sum 100 numbers	

```
sum := 0;                              sum = 0;
for count := 1 to 100 do               for (count = 1; count <= 100; count++) {
begin                                      cin >> inputVal;
    read(inputVal);                        sum += inputVal;
    sum := sum + inputVal
end                                    }
```

Table A.18 for statements in C++ and Pascal (continued)

Pascal	C++

Example: A for loop to zero out a 50-element vector

```
var x: array [1..50] of real;
     .
     .
     .
for i := 1 to 50 do
   x[i] := 0.0;
```

```
float x[50];           ⟵ Subscripts 0 thru 49
     .
     .
     .
for (i = 0; i < 50; i++)
    x[i] = 0.0;
```

This is a C++ idiom. It should be mastered.

Can you explicitly modify the loop control variable in the body of the loop?

No	Yes

Is the loop control variable undefined after exiting the loop?

Yes	No

The break statement, which we introduced in conjunction with the C++ switch statement, is also used with loops. A break statement causes immediate exit from the innermost switch, while, do-while, or for statement in which it appears. For premature exit from a loop, the break statement is sometimes preferable to baffling combinations of multiple Boolean flags and nested ifs. But it also can be a crutch for those who are too impatient to think carefully about the loop exit condition.

C++ also has a continue statement that causes an immediate branch to the loop test. That is, all remaining statements in the loop body are skipped, and the test for the next loop iteration immediately occurs. It is rarely used.

Figure A.5 displays five different loops that illustrate the various C++ looping statements. Each loop outputs the integers from 1 through 9.

Alternative 1 is the clear choice; this problem naturally calls for a pure counting loop. Alternative 2 represents wasted programming effort; the compiler translates Alternative 1 into this sequence anyway. Alternative 3 is also a waste of effort. Alternatives 4 and 5 are poor, but we have included them to demonstrate the possibilities in C++.

A.14 More About Functions

Recall from Section A.4 that a C++ function prototype is a declaration that only specifies the type of the function value and the number and types of its parameters:

```
void PrintProduct( int, float );
```

A complete function declaration (in C++ terminology, a **function definition**) is a declaration that also includes the body:

Figure A.5

Examples of `for`, `while`, and `do-while` in C++

Each loop below produces the output 123456789

Alternative 1

```
for (intVal = 1; intVal <= 9; intVal++)
    cout << intVal;
```

Alternative 2

```
intVal = 1;
while (intVal <= 9) {
    cout << intVal;
    intVal++;
}
```

Alternative 3

```
intVal = 1;
do {
    cout << intVal;
    intVal++;
} while (intVal <= 9);
```

Alternative 4

```
intVal = 1;
while (1) {
        if (intVal > 9)
            break;
        cout << intVal;
        intVal++;
}
```

Alternative 5

```
intVal = 1;
while (1) {
        cout << intVal;
        if (intVal == 9)
            break;
        intVal++;
}
```

```
void PrintProduct( int n, float x )
{
    cout << "Product of " << n << " and " << x
        << " is " << float(n) * x << '\n';
}
```

In our discussion of data in Section A.11, we said that a declaration becomes a definition if it reserves memory for the object. This terminology also applies to function declarations and function definitions. With a function definition, the compiler allocates memory for the instructions in the function. As with variables, you can declare a function in many locations, but you can define it only once.

The complete syntax of C++ function definitions and prototypes is very complicated, so we now look at just the basic forms.

Function Definitions

The basic form of a C++ function definition is

function-type function-name (formal-parameter-list)
{
   body
}

Here are some relevant points about function definitions:

- If function-type is the word `void`, the function does not return a value (like a Pascal procedure).
- If function-type is other than `void`, it is a value-returning function. It returns a single value of type function-type to its caller by means of a `return` statement.

- In the above definition, function-type can be any type *except* an array type.
- If function-type is omitted, `int` is assumed. (Omitting the function type is not considered good programming practice in C++.)
- In the above definition, formal-parameter-list is an optional list of formal parameter declarations. The declarations are separated by commas.

Function Prototypes

Function prototypes have the following basic form:

function-type function-name (formal-parameter-list) ;

Here are some guidelines for using function prototypes:

- A function prototype usually appears early in the program file, before its matching function definition occurs. As a result, the compiler can check every call to the function to ensure that the actual parameters and the function return value are of the appropriate types.
- No body is included, and a semicolon terminates the declaration.
- The formal parameter list must specify the data types of the formal parameters, but their names are not required:

```
int SomeFunc( int, float );
```

For documentation purposes, it is sometimes useful to supply names for the parameters. However, the names are ignored by the compiler.

- If you have not supplied a function prototype, most C++ compilers will issue an error message if a function call precedes the function definition. However, some C++ compilers proceed by assuming that the function's type is `int` and do not perform type checking of the actual parameters. It is not considered good programming practice to omit a function prototype.

The Maxima program in Section A.4 of this appendix provides a straightforward example of function prototypes and function definitions. It would be helpful for you to review this program quickly before reading further.

Parameter Passage

C++ supports both **parameter passage by value** ("value parameters" in Pascal) and **parameter passage by reference** ("var parameters" in Pascal).

With passage by value, a *copy* of the actual parameter is sent to the function. Within the function, any change to the formal parameter has no effect on the caller's actual parameter.

With passage by reference, the *memory address* of the actual parameter is sent to the function. If the function modifies the formal parameter, it is really modifying the caller's actual parameter.

By default, C++ simple variables and records (`struct`s) are always passed by value. To pass a simple variable or a record by reference, you must append an ampersand (&) to the data type name in the formal parameter list:

```
int SomeFunc( float param1,        ◄─── Passed by value
              char& param2 )       ◄─── Passed by reference
{ ... }
```

It is impossible to pass a C++ array by value; arrays are *always* passed by reference. Therefore, never use & when declaring an array as a formal parameter. When an array is passed as a parameter, its **base address**—the memory address of the first element of the array—is sent to the function. Below is a C++ function for zeroing out a `float` vector of any size.

```
void ZeroOut( float vec[],
              int   numElements )
{
    int i;

    for (i = 0; i < numElements; i++)
        vec[i] = 0.0;
}
```

In the parameter list, the declaration of the vector does not include a size within the brackets. If you include a size, the compiler will ignore it. The compiler only wants to know that it is a `float` vector, not a `float` vector of any particular size. Therefore, you must include a second parameter, the number of array elements, for this function to work correctly.

The `ZeroOut` function can be invoked for a `float` vector of any size. The following code fragment demonstrates typical function calls:

```
float velocity[30];
float refracAngle[9000];
    .
    .
    .
ZeroOut(velocity, 30);
ZeroOut(refracAngle, 9000);
```

Pascal is stricter than C++ about passing arrays as parameters. The data types of the formal and actual parameters must be identical, including their sizes. In Pascal, you cannot write just one procedure like `ZeroOut` to zero out a real vector of arbitrary size. You must write one procedure to zero out a 10-element vector, another procedure to zero out a 45-element vector, and so on.

As we have pointed out, when a C++ vector (one-dimensional array) is declared as a formal parameter, its size is not required. However, the brackets must be present to indicate that it is an array:

```
void SomeFunc( int someVec[30] )        ◄───OK, but size is ignored.
{ ... }

void AnotherFunc( int someVec[] )       ◄───Brackets are still required.
{ ... }
```

The rule for declaring a multidimensional array, such as a matrix (two-dimensional array), is somewhat trickier: the sizes of all but the first dimension must be given:

```
void ThisFunc( float someMatrix[][20] )
{ ... }

void ThatFunc( float threeDimArray[][7][15] )
{ ... }
```

Passing String Arrays as Parameters

Recall that with a C++ string array such as

```
char myName[10];
```

it is illegal to perform aggregate string assignment:

```
myName = "Al Doe";        ← Not allowed
```

One way out of this restriction is to write a `StrCopy` function to copy one string into another. Then we could invoke the function as follows:

```
StrCopy(myName, "Al Doe");    // Copy 2nd string into 1st
```

For the string constant "Al Doe", the compiler establishes an anonymous (unnamed) 7-element `char` array—six for the specified characters and one for the terminating null character. At run time, the function call passes the base address of this anonymous array to the function. Here is a possible version of the `StrCopy` function.

```
void StrCopy( char destinStr[],
              char sourceStr[] )
{
    int i = 0;

    while (sourceStr[i] != '\0') {
        destinStr[i] = sourceStr[i];
        i++;
    }
    destinStr[i] = '\0';
}
```

The `StrCopy` function does not care whether the two strings have equal lengths. It simply locates the end of the source string by testing for the null character. It also makes sure to append a null character to the end of the destination string before finishing.

Because C++ arrays are always passed by reference, there is the possibility that a function will modify the caller's actual parameter, either intentionally or by mistake. With `StrCopy`, the caller wants the function to modify the first actual parameter but not the second. When declaring an array as a formal parameter, you can use the reserved word `const` to prevent the function from modifying the parameter:

```
void StrCopy(        char destinStr[],
               const char sourceStr[] )
{ ... }
```

The word const guarantees that within StrCopy, any attempt to modify the sourceStr array will be met with a syntax error.

Although we have discussed how to write our own StrCopy routine, it is only fair to mention that a C++ programmer would not spend time writing StrCopy from scratch. Every C++ environment includes the C++ **standard library**, a large collection of previously written **library functions** that any C++ program may invoke. Among the library routines are many related to string handling. One of these, the strcpy function, performs precisely the same task as the routine we just wrote. It is invoked in exactly the same way:

```
strcpy(myName, "Al Doe");
```

To use any of the string-handling routines, you include the header file string.h at the top of your program:

```
#include <string.h>
```

The main body of this book gives detailed information about library routines.

The return *Statement*

In C++, a return statement may appear anywhere within the body of a function. This statement causes an immediate exit from the function, and control returns to the location in the caller where the function was invoked.

The return statement has two forms. The first is

```
return;
```

This form is only for functions that do not return values—that is, functions of type void. If there is no return statement, the function returns when it "falls off" the end of its body, as in Pascal. If there is a return statement and it is executed, then control returns to the caller immediately. Using return allows premature exit from a function:

```
void SomeFunc( int n )
{
    .
    .
    .
    if (3*n > 50)
        return;
    .
    .
    .
}
```

The second form of the return statement is mandatory in value-returning functions:

```
return expr ;
```

where expr is an expression whose value is returned as the function value. This value is coerced, if necessary, to match the declared function type.

Figure A.6 illustrates the use of the `return` statement. This figure presents three alternatives for a function that returns the length of a string. As is customary in C++, the code assumes that the string is terminated by the null character. We do not necessarily recommend Alternative 3; it is relatively unreadable except by seasoned C++ programmers.

Earlier we mentioned that the `main` function returns an integer value—the program's exit status—to the operating system. By convention, an exit status of 0 signifies a normal exit, and a nonzero value (typically 1, 2, and so on) signifies an error exit:

Figure A.6

Alternatives for a
`StrLength` function

Each function below returns the length, in characters, of its string parameter

Alternative 1 (This version is the most readable to a Pascal programmer.)

```
int StrLength( const char str[] )
{
    int i = 0;

    while (str[i] != '\0')
        i++;
    return i;
}
```

Alternative 2 (This version is a bit more concise.)

```
int StrLength( const char str[] )
{
    int i = 0;

    while (str[i++] != '\0')     // Post-increment i in the subscript, so
        ;                        //    there is nothing to do in the body.
    return i-1;                  // After the loop, i is one too large.
}
```

Alternative 3 (This version is even more concise.)

```
int StrLength( const char str[] )
{
    int i = 0;
                                 // Null character is all 0-bits (same as
                                 // the integer 0).  Thus, the loop says:
    while (str[i++])             // While str[i] is nonzero (true), do...
        ;
    return --i;                  // Pre-decrement i before returning it.
}
```

```
int main()
{
    .
    .
    .
    if (delta < 0) {
        cout << "Error: delta < 0";
        return 1;        ← Quit. Something is seriously wrong.
    }
    .
    .
    .
    return 0;
}
```

The operating system may wish to check the exit status and take some appropriate action.

Other Issues

A peculiarity of C++ is that the caller may choose to ignore the value returned by a value-returning function. For example, the following function effectively returns three results, one as the function value and two through the parameter list:

```
int TestFunc( int& param1,
              int& param2 )
{ ... }
```

The caller may invoke it as a value-returning function:

```
myResult = 2 * TestFunc(alpha, beta);
```

with the side effect of updating alpha and beta. Or the caller may desire only the side effect and ignore the function value:

```
TestFunc(gamma, delta);
```

Many disapprove of this practice of returning values both through the parameter list and through the function return value. But many C++ library routines do this, so it is best to understand how it works.

We have described how C++ allows premature exit from a function via the return statement. C++ also supports premature exit from an entire program by means of the **exit function**. When the exit function is invoked, the entire program immediately terminates. This function is not actually built into the C++ language; it is part of the standard C++ library. To use it, you include the header file stdlib.h at the top of your program:

```
#include <stdlib.h>
```

A call to the exit function has the form

```
exit(exit-status);
```

where exit-status is an integer exit status: 0 for a normal exit, and a nonzero value for an error exit. Usually it is the `main` function's role to return the program's exit status (as in `return 0`). But a function other than `main` can also terminate the program and report the status by using the `exit` function:

```
void SomeFunc()
{
    .
    .
    .
    if (gamma > 20) {
        PrintErrorMsg();
        exit(1);
    }
    .
    .
    .
}
```

Table A.19 summarizes the major differences between Pascal and C++ subprograms and parameters that we have discussed in this appendix.

A.15 Input and Output

We have used only the most basic features of C++ input and output (I/O) in this appendix. We have used the >> operator to input data from the standard input stream `cin` and have used the << operator to output values to the standard output stream `cout`:

```
cout << "Your 2 integers, please: ";
cin >> int1 >> int2;
cout << "Their sum is " << int1 + int2 << '\n';
```

Table A.19 Subprograms and parameters in C++ and Pascal

Pascal	C++
Kind of subprogram	
Procedure	A function whose data type is `void`
Value-returning function	A function whose data type is other than `void`
Data type of value returned from a value-returning function	
Simple type only	Any type except array
Statement that returns the function value from `SomeFunc`	
`SomeFunc := expression;`	`return expression;`
Is premature exit from a subprogram allowed?	
No	Yes, via the `return` statement

Table A.19 Subprograms and parameters in C++ and Pascal (continued)

Pascal	C++
Is an empty parameter list ( ) required for a parameterless subprogram?	
No	Yes
Methods of parameter passage	
For any type, you can pass by value or by reference	For any type except arrays, you can pass by value or by reference For arrays, you can pass by reference only
Notation for value versus reference parameters	

```
procedure Conv(    ch1 : char;        void Conv( char  ch1,
                var ch2 : char );                 char& ch2 )
                                       // But "&" is not used with arrays
```

Instead of providing more information on I/O here, we ask you to proceed now to Section C.1 of Appendix C. We have placed the I/O material in its own appendix so that all readers—not just Pascal programmers—can find it easily.

KEY TERMS

assignment expression   (p. A-32)
automatic variable   (p. A-27)
base address   (p. A-45)
block   (p. A-26)
case sensitive   (p. A-1)
constant expression   (p. A-28)
counting loop   (p. A-40)
declaration statement   (p. A-36)
declaration versus definition   (p. A-30)
demotion (or narrowing)   (p. A-21)
enumeration type   (p. A-15)
enumerator   (p. A-15)
escape sequence   (p. A-13)
exit function   (p. A-49)
exit status   (p. A-4)
explicit type conversion   (p. A-22)
expression statement   (p. A-36)
external declaration   (p. A-29)
file (global) scope   (p. A-27)
forward declaration   (p. A-8)
function definition   (p. A-42)
function prototype   (p. A-8)
header file   (p. A-5)
implicit type coercion   (p. A-20)
include directory   (p. A-5)

indefinite loop   (p. A-40)
library function   (p. A-47)
lifetime   (p. A-27)
local scope   (p. A-27)
macro definition   (p. A-5)
nonstrict type checking   (p. A-20)
null statement   (p. A-36)
parameter passage by value   (p. A-44)
parameter passage by reference   (p. A-44)
preprocessor   (p. A-4)
promotion (widening)   (p. A-21)
reserved word   (p. A-2)
scope   (p. A-26)
scope rules   (p. A-26)
short-circuit (conditional) evaluation   (p. A-33)
standard library   (p. A-47)
static variable   (p. A-27)
statically typed   (p. A-19)
storage class   (p. A-27)
strict type checking   (p. A-19)
symbolic constant   (p. A-24)
type casting   (p. A-22)
type checking   (p. A-19)
visibility rules   (p. A-26)

APPENDIX B

Introductory Comparison of C and C++

This appendix provides an informal introduction to the C++ language for those who are familiar with C. It is not a description of the entire language. We present only those features that will allow you to proceed to Appendix C (on input and output) and then on to Chapter 1 of this text.

C++ is a successor to the C language, designed to provide stricter type checking along with features for data abstraction and object-oriented programming. A primary concern in the creation of C++ was to ensure that existing C programs would compile correctly in C++. With only a few exceptions, this is the case.

This appendix mentions certain differences between C++ and C. By C we mean the original language as defined by Kernighan and Ritchie in *The C Programming Language* (first edition, Prentice-Hall, 1978). Some language extensions found in C++ also are present in ANSI C, the ANSI (American National Standards Institute) standard for the C language. If you already have an ANSI C background, some of the "differences" we discuss will not be differences.

The C++ language originated at AT&T Corporation's Bell Labs. This text is based on AT&T's Version 2.0 of the language. Because C++ is still a young and evolving language, there may be minor variations among different C++ systems.

For details about the precise syntax of various constructs, please consult Appendix J of this book.

B.1 Comments and Identifiers

Comments

C++ comments come in two forms. The first is the same as in C:

```
/* Some comment */
```

With this form, you cannot nest comments inside others.

The other form begins with a pair of slashes (//) and extends to the end of the line:

```
int   itemNo;  // Item number in inventory
float eps;     // Epsilon time units
```

Identifiers

Both C and C++ identifiers are **case sensitive:** uppercase letters are different from lowercase letters. The identifiers `printtabbuffer`, `PrintTabBuffer`, and `print_tab_buffer` are three distinct names and are not interchangeable in any way.

C++, like C, has several **reserved words**—identifiers that are predefined and cannot be used for other purposes. The reserved words in C++ are all of C's reserved words plus the following:

```
class     friend    private      this
const     inline    protected    virtual
delete    new       public       void
enum      operator  signed       volatile
```

Appendix E contains a list of all C++ reserved words.

Programmers often use capitalization as a quick, visual clue to what an identifier represents. The convention in this textbook is to begin variable names with lowercase letters:

```
studentCount
```

and to begin names of data types and functions with capital letters:

```
PrintResults(alpha, beta);
```

This style quickly distinguishes those identifiers representing data values in memory (variables) from those that do not (type names and function names). In both cases, each subsequent English word in the identifier begins with a capital letter. (All reserved words in C++ use lowercase letters, so you cannot tamper with those.)

For identifiers representing constants, many C and C++ programmers capitalize the entire identifier, again as an immediate clue to its use:

```
PI
```

B.2 A First Program

For a first look at a C++ program, consider the code in Figure B.1. This program inputs pairs of positive integers and determines the maximum value of each pair.

Figure B.1

Maxima program

```
//-----------------------------------------------------------------
//  maxima.cpp
//  This program repeatedly inputs pairs of positive integers.
//  For each pair, it outputs the larger number.
//-----------------------------------------------------------------

#include <iostream.h>

void PromptUser();        // Function prototypes
int  Max( int, int );

int main()
{
    int int1;
    int int2;

    PromptUser();
    cin >> int1 >> int2;
    while (int1 > 0) {
        cout << " The larger is: " << Max(int1, int2) << '\n';
        PromptUser();
        cin >> int1 >> int2;
    }
    return 0;
}

void PromptUser()
{
    cout << "Enter 2 positive integers";
    cout << " (If first is nonpositive, I quit):";
}

int Max( int firstInt, int secondInt )
{
    if (firstInt > secondInt)
        return firstInt;
    else
        return secondInt;
}
```

Here are some differences between this C++ program and the way you would write it in C:

1. The first line of the `main` function

```
int main()
```

declares that `main` returns an integer value. The last statement in the body of `main`

```
return 0;
```

returns the value 0 to the operating system (such as UNIX, DOS, or SunOS) when the program finishes executing. This returned value is called the program's **exit status.** By convention, an exit status of 0 signifies a normal termination of the program. We will discuss a program's exit status in more detail later.

2. For input, the identifier `cin` (pronounced "see-in") denotes a stream of characters coming from the standard input device. The C right-shift operator `>>` has an additional meaning in C++. When used with stream input, the `>>` operator (pronounced "get from") inputs its next operand from the input stream.

For output, the identifier `cout` (pronounced "see-out") denotes a stream of characters going to the standard output device. When used with stream output, the `<<` operator (pronounced "put to") appends its next operand to the output stream.

The line specifying

```
#include <iostream.h>
```

tells the C++ preprocessor to insert the contents of the header file `iostream.h` into the program. This file contains declarations needed by the program to perform stream input and output. You will become accustomed to including `iostream.h` at the beginning of your programs instead of `stdio.h`.

(As a review, when you `#include` a header file with the file name enclosed within double quotes:

```
#include "mystuff.h"
```

the preprocessor looks for the file in your current directory. If you enclose the file name within angle brackets:

```
#include <iostream.h>
```

the preprocessor looks for the file in the standard **include directory**—a directory containing all the header files that are part of the C++ environment.)

3. Unlike the C language, C++ demands that you declare every identifier before you can reference it. Because C++ functions can appear in any order, a function invocation (function call) might physically precede the declaration of that function. In this case, you must use a **function prototype** near the beginning of the program. A function prototype (known as a **forward declaration** in some languages) specifies in advance the data types of the function parameters and the data type of the function value to be returned. In Figure B.1 the prototypes

```
void PromptUser();
int  Max( int, int );
```

declare that `Max` takes two `int` parameters and returns an `int` function value and that `PromptUser` takes no parameters and does not return a function value.

In C and C++ terminology, a function declaration is also a **function definition** if it includes the body of the function. The function prototype for Max, then, is merely a declaration. It supplies data type information about the parameters and function return value. On the other hand, the complete code for Max at the bottom of Figure B.1, including the body, is not only a declaration but also a definition of the function.

4. In a C++ function definition, the data types of the formal parameters are declared within parentheses:

```
int Max( int firstInt, int secondInt )
{ ... }
```

whereas in C, their data types are declared as follows:

```
int Max( firstInt, secondInt )
    int firstInt;
    int secondInt;
{ ... }
```

The C++ programmer can still use the old style, but there is no advantage to doing so.

B.3   Functions

Recall from the previous section that a C++ function prototype is a declaration that only specifies the type of the function value and the number and types of its parameters:

```
void PrintProduct( int, int );
```

A function definition is a declaration that also includes the body:

```
void PrintProduct( int int1, int int2 )
{
    cout << "Product of " << int1 << " and " << int2
        << " is " << int1 * int2 << '\n';
}
```

The complete syntax of C++ function definitions and prototypes is very complicated, so we now look at just the basic forms.

Function Definitions

The basic form of a C++ function definition is

function-type function-name (formal-parameter-list)
```
{
    body
}
```

Here are some relevant points about function definitions:

- If function-type is the word void, the function does not return a value. If function-type is other than void, it is a value-returning function. It returns a single value of type function-type to its caller by means of a return statement.

- In the first line of the function definition, function-type can be any type *except* an array type.

- If function-type is omitted, int is assumed. (Omitting the function type is not considered good programming practice in C++.)

- Within parentheses, formal-parameter-list is an optional list of formal parameter declarations. The declarations are separated by commas.

Function Prototypes

Function prototypes have the following basic form:

function-type function-name (formal-parameter-list) ;

Here are some guidelines for using function prototypes:

- A function prototype usually appears early in the program file, before its matching function definition occurs. As a result, the compiler can check every call to the function to ensure that the actual parameters and the function return value are of the appropriate types.

- No body is included, and a semicolon terminates the declaration.

- The formal parameter list must specify the data types of the formal parameters, but their names are not required:

```
int SomeFunc( int, float );
```

For documentation purposes, it is sometimes useful to supply names for the parameters. However, the names are ignored by the compiler.

- If you have not supplied a function prototype, most C++ compilers will issue an error message if a function call precedes the function definition. C (and some C++) compilers proceed by assuming that the function's type is int and do not perform type checking of the actual parameters. It is not considered good programming practice to omit a function prototype.

The Maxima program of Figure B.1 provides a straightforward example of function prototypes and function definitions. It would be helpful for you to review this program quickly before reading further.

Parameter Passage

C++ supports both **parameter passage by value** and **parameter passage by reference**. With passage by value, a *copy* of the actual parameter is sent to the function. Within the function, any change to the formal parameter has no effect on the caller's actual parameter.

With passage by reference, the *memory address* of the actual parameter is sent to the function. If the function modifies the formal parameter, it is really modifying the caller's actual parameter.

By default, C++ simple variables and records (structs) are always passed by value. (If you are not familiar with struct types, we cover them fully in the main body of this book.) To pass a simple variable or a struct by reference, you append an ampersand (&) to the data type name in the formal parameter list:

```
void Initialize( int& m, int& n )
{
    m = 5;
    n = 7;
}
```

The caller does not need to attach any special symbols to the names of the actual parameters:

```
Initialize(alpha, beta);
```

Passing parameters this way is very different from C, where the programmer has to manipulate pointers and addresses to perform pass-by-reference. In C, the caller must explicitly pass the addresses of the actual parameters:

```
Initialize(&alpha, &beta);
```

Furthermore, the function must declare the formal parameters as pointers and then dereference the pointers throughout the function:

```
Initialize( m, n )
    int *m;
    int *n;
{
    *m = 5;
    *n = 7;
}
```

Passing Arrays as Parameters

In both C and C++ it is impossible to pass an array by value; arrays are *always* passed by reference. Therefore, you never use & when declaring a C++ array as a formal parameter. When an array is passed as a parameter, its **base address**—the memory address of the first element of the array—is sent to the function. Below is a C++ function for zeroing out a float vector (one-dimensional array) of any size.

```
void ZeroOut( float vec[],
              int   numElements )
{
    int i;
```

2D Arrays

```
    for (i = 0; i < numElements; i++)
        vec[i] = 0.0;
}
```

In the parameter list, the declaration of the vector does not include a size within the brackets. If you include a size, the compiler will ignore it. The compiler only wants to know that it is a float vector, not a float vector of any particular size. Therefore, you must include a second parameter, the number of array elements, for this function to work correctly.

The rule for declaring a multidimensional array, such as a matrix (two-dimensional array), is somewhat trickier: the sizes of all but the first dimension must be given:

```
void ThisFunc( float someMatrix[][20] )
{ ... }

void ThatFunc( float threeDimArray[][7][15] )
{ ... }
```

Declaring const Parameters

In both C and C++, aggregate assignment of one array to another is prohibited:

```
char oneVec[20];
char anotherVec[20];
    .
    .
    .
oneVec = anotherVec;        ← No
```

This rule implies that you cannot copy one character string to another:

```
char myName[10];
myName = "Al Doe";          ← Not allowed
```

The reason is that a string constant, such as "Al Doe", is stored by the compiler as a char array and, as we have just pointed out, aggregate array assignment is not allowed.

One way out of this restriction is to write our own StrCopy function. Then we could invoke the function as follows:

```
StrCopy(myName, "Al Doe");    // Copy 2nd string into 1st
```

For the string constant "Al Doe", the compiler establishes an anonymous (unnamed) 7-element char array—six for the specified characters and one for the terminating null character ('\0'). At run time, the function call passes the base address of this anonymous array to the function. Here is a possible version of the StrCopy function:

```
void StrCopy( char destinStr[],
              char sourceStr[] )
{
    int i = 0;
```

```
    while (sourceStr[i] != '\0') {
        destinStr[i] = sourceStr[i];
        i++;
    }
    destinStr[i] = '\0';
}
```

The `StrCopy` function does not care whether the two strings have equal lengths. It simply locates the end of the source string by testing for the null character. It also makes sure to append a null character to the end of the destination string before finishing.

Because C++ arrays are always passed by reference, there is the possibility that a function will modify the caller's actual parameter, either intentionally or by mistake. With `StrCopy`, the caller wants the function to modify the first actual parameter but not the second. When declaring an array as a formal parameter, you can use the reserved word `const` to prevent the function from modifying the parameter:

```
void StrCopy(        char destinStr[],
               const char sourceStr[] )
{ ... }
```

The word `const` guarantees that, within `StrCopy`, any attempt to modify the `sourceStr` array will be met with a syntax error.

Although we have discussed how to write our own `StrCopy` routine, it is only fair to mention that a C++ programmer would not spend time writing `StrCopy` from scratch. Every C++ environment includes the C++ **standard library,** a large collection of prewritten **library functions** that any C++ program may invoke. Among the library routines are many related to string handling. One of these, the `strcpy` function, performs precisely the same task as the routine we just wrote. It is invoked in exactly the same way:

```
strcpy(myName, "Al Doe");
```

To use any of the string-handling routines, you include the header file `string.h` at the top of your program:

```
#include <string.h>
```

The main body of this book gives detailed information about library routines.

A Major Incompatibility Between C and C++

In C, the forward declaration

```
float SomeFunc();
```

means that `SomeFunc` may take any number of parameters of any type. A forward declaration in C serves only to state the type of the function return value (here, `float`). The C compiler does not check function calls to verify that the actual parameters agree in number and type with the formal parameters of a function.

In contrast, the C++ compiler performs strict type checking of actual and formal parameters. The declaration

```
float SomeFunc();
```

therefore means that SomeFunc takes no parameters at all. After this declaration, any function call that includes actual parameters is a syntax error. (In ANSI C, the declaration

```
float SomeFunc( void );
```

states that SomeFunc takes no parameters, but using void this way is unnecessary in C++.)

One consequence of C++'s strict type checking of parameters is that you must be diligent about including header files for standard library routines. Consider the exit function, a library routine that terminates execution of a program. This function requires a single parameter: the program's exit status. By convention, passing the parameter 0 signifies a normal exit and passing a nonzero value (typically 1, 2, and so on) signifies an error exit:

```
  .
  .
  .
if (a > b)
    exit(0);        ←— Quit, but everything is OK
  .
  .
  .
if (delta < 0) {
    cout << "Error: delta < 0";
    exit(1);        ←— Quit. Something is seriously wrong
}
  .
  .
  .
```

If you forget the directive #include <stdlib.h> before using a call to exit, a syntax error will result. The C++ compiler needs the function prototype

```
void exit( int );
```

which is found in the header file stdlib.h.

B.4   Statements

All statements—expression statements, while statements, if statements, and so forth—carry over directly from C to C++. But there are two subtle changes.

First, C++ has what are called **declaration statements.** In C, all declarations within a block (for example, a function body) must precede all executable statements. In C++, a declaration within a block is a genuine statement and may appear anywhere an executable statement can. Thus, declarations and executable statements may be intermingled:

```
void SomeFunc( int alpha )
{
    if (alpha >= 50) {
        cout << "Bad value for alpha: " << alpha;
        exit(1);
    }
    int beta;        ←— Declaration allowed here
    cin >> beta;
    alpha = 3*alpha + beta;
    .
    .
    .
}
```

The second change is in the syntax of the `for` statement. In C, the general syntax of the `for` statement is as follows:

```
for (expression1 ; expression2 ; expression3 )
    body
```

In C++, the syntax is now

```
for (statement1 ; expression1 ; expression2 )
    body
```

Because statements naturally end in semicolons, we have omitted the semicolon after statement1 in this syntax description. The new form of the `for` statement still encompasses all familiar examples, such as

```
for (count = 1; count <= 50; count++)
    sum = sum + count;
```

because adding a semicolon to an expression like `count = 1` turns it into a statement. But the new form also allows a declaration statement to be included in the parentheses:

```
for (int i = 0; i < 50; i++)
    a[i] = 0;
```

Here, the declaration of `i` also includes its initialization.

Caution: This declaration does not make the variable `i` local to the `for` loop. Its scope is taken to be the surrounding block:

```
for (int i = 0; i < 50; i++)
    a[i] = 0;
for (int i = 0; i < 75; i++)        ←— Error—i is already declared
    b[i] = 0;
```

B.5   Built-in Data Types

Figure B.2 displays the built-in data types of C++. All of C's data types are here, plus a few new ones.

Among the simple types, both C++ and ANSI C introduce enumeration types (enum) and `long double`. We will say more about these types in this appendix.

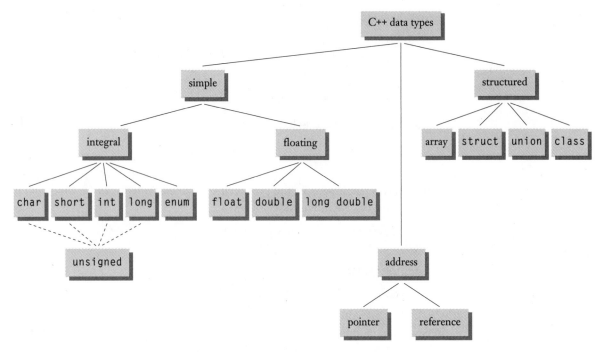

Figure B.2 C++ data types

Among the structured types, the class is new in C++. Among the address types, C++ adds to pointer types something known as reference types. The main body of this book examines all of class, pointer, and reference types in detail.

Sizes of Data Objects

The integral types char, short, int, and long all represent nothing more than integers of different sizes. Similarly, the floating types float, double (meaning double precision), and long double simply refer to floating point numbers of different sizes.

In C++, sizes are measured in multiples of bytes. A byte is usually a group of eight consecutive bits (0's or 1's) in a computer's memory unit. Individual machines vary, but 8-bit bytes are most common. By definition, the size of a C++ char variable is 1 byte.

Using the notation *sizeof*(type) to denote the size in bytes of a variable of that data type, we can say that *sizeof*(char) = 1. Other than char, sizes of data objects in C++ are highly machine-dependent. Table B.1 displays sample ranges of values for C++ simple types. Except for long double, this table is the same as you would find for data values in C.

Table B.1 Ranges of values for C++ simple types

Type	Size (in bytes)	Range of values		
char	1	-128	through	127
unsigned char	1	0	through	255
short	2	-32,768	through	32,767
unsigned short	2	0	through	65,535
int	2	-32,768	through	32,767
unsigned int	2	0	through	65,535
long	4	-2,147,483,648	through	2,147,483,647
unsigned long	4	0	through	4,294,967,295
float	4	3.4E-38	through	3.4E+38 (absolute value)
double	8	1.7E-308	through	1.7E+308
long double	10	3.4E-4932	through	1.1E+4932

Note: The ranges of values shown are *examples only.* Those shown assume an 8-bit byte and are highly machine dependent.

Numeric Constants

In Table B.2 we present examples of various C++ numeric constants. Observe how a floating point constant is, by default, of type double. To force it to be a float or a long double, you add the suffix F or L (in either uppercase or lowercase).

C and C++ differ in their assumptions about floating point arithmetic. In C, all float values in an expression are implicitly promoted (widened) to size double and arithmetic is performed in double precision. In C++, such promotion is not required by the language; arithmetic may be performed in single precision. (ANSI C also permits single precision arithmetic.)

Table B.2 Numeric constants in C++

Constant	Type	Remarks
1663	int	Decimal (base 10) integer.
65535U	unsigned int	Unsigned integral constants end in U or u.
03177	int	Octal (base 8) integer. Begins with 0. Decimal equivalent is 1663.
0x67F	int	Hexadecimal (base 16) integer. Begins with 0, then either x or X. Decimal is 1663.
421L	long	Explicit long constants end in L or l.
53100	long	Implicit long constant, assuming machine's greatest int is, say, 32767.
6.83	double	Default type of a floating point constant is double.
6.83F	float	Explicit float constants end in F or f.
6.83L	long double	Explicit long double constants end in L or l.
6.2E-9	double	Exponential (scientific) notation meaning 6.2×10^{-9}.

char *Constants*

In C++ and ANSI C, a char constant can be any of the following, enclosed in apostrophes (single quotes):

- A single printable character, other than an apostrophe (') or backslash (\)
- An **escape sequence**—one of the following sequences of characters starting with a backslash:

\n	Newline (line feed)
\t	Horizontal tab
\v	Vertical tab
\b	Backspace
\r	Carriage return
\f	Form feed
\a	Alert (a bell or beep)
\\	Backslash
\'	Single quote (apostrophe)
\"	Double quote (quotation mark)
\0	Null character (all zero bits)
\ddd	Bit pattern (1, 2, or 3 octal digits specifying the integer value of the desired character)
\xddd	Bit pattern (1 or more hexadecimal digits specifying the integer value of the desired character)

Despite their appearances, each escape sequence represents a single character. The "alert" character (\a) is the same as the BEL character in the ASCII character set. According to the ASCII chart, the BEL character has integer value 7 (octal as well as decimal). The statement

```
cout << '\a';
```

is equivalent to

```
cout << '\7';
```

although the former is more portable because it does not assume use of the ASCII character set. Each of these statements rings a bell (or, these days, beeps a beeper) at the terminal.

You also can use escape sequences within strings if you need to output a double quote, a backslash, or a nonprintable character. The statement

```
cout << "\aError!\n";
```

beeps the beeper, displays Error!, and terminates the output line. The statement

```
cout << "She said \"Hi\"";
```

outputs She said "Hi" and does not terminate the output line.

Choosing a Numeric Data Type

In choosing among the many data types available in C++, you may occasionally feel tempted to toss a coin. You should resist this temptation, because each data type exists for a reason. Here are some guidelines:

1. In general, int is preferable.

   It is better not to use char and short for small integer values unless memory space is absolutely crucial. (Use of char for character data is appropriate, though.)

2. Use float only when absolutely necessary.

   Floating point arithmetic takes significantly longer to perform than integer arithmetic. As a rule, use float only if you need fractional values.

3. Use long only if the range of int values on your machine is too restrictive.

   Cost: Increased execution time and memory space.

4. Use double and long double only if your machine's float values do not carry enough digits of precision.

   Cost: Increased execution time and memory space.

5. The unsigned forms of integral types are best used for manipulating bit strings (see Appendix H), not for trying to obtain larger nonnegative integers. Later in this appendix we will explain why.

Enumeration Types

An enumeration type is an integral type whose constants are meaningful identifiers, not numbers:

```
enum FlagColor {red, white, blue};
```

The constants red, white, and blue are called **enumerators**. You can declare variables of type FlagColor and assign them values as follows:

```
FlagColor star;
  .
  .
  .
star = white;
```

The purpose of enums is to encourage the writing of descriptive, self-documenting code. The underlying representations of the enumerators, though, are only barely concealed. They have int values in increasing order from 0, left to right. Above, red has the value 0, white has the value 1, and blue has the value 2.

You also can state an explicit value for an enumerator by using an equal sign and an `int` (or `short` or `char`) constant:

```
enum Coin {penny=1, nickel=5, dime=10};
Coin myCoin;

myCoin = nickel;
```

ANSI C also supports enumeration types, but there are two significant differences. First, in C an enumeration type is of type `int`. In C++, an enumeration is a unique type, distinct from `int`. Using `FlagColor` as an example, consider the following code:

```
star = white;      ← OK in both languages
star = 1;          ← OK in C. Syntax error in C++
```

The second assignment statement is acceptable in C because the type `FlagColor` is the same as the type `int`. But the C++ compiler prevents you from storing `int` constants into a `FlagColor` variable. The primary reason is to keep you from accidentally storing an out-of-range value:

```
star = 5;
```

The second difference between C and C++ enumeration types is that C requires you to carry along the word enum every time you declare a variable of that type:

```
enum FlagColor stripe;
```

In C++, it is unnecessary:

```
FlagColor stripe;
```

Arrays

Arrays, the most common structured type, are the same in C and C++. As a brief review, we summarize the major points about C and C++ arrays:

- Array subscripts are always of type `int`. When you declare an array, you state the number of elements in the array:

  ```
  float income[100];
  ```

  The valid subscripts are then zero through one less than the number of array elements. For the `income` array, the first array element is `income[0]` and the last is `income[99]`.

- An array with one subscript is called a one-dimensional array or vector. An array with two subscripts is called a two-dimensional array or matrix. The two subscripts of a matrix must be bracketed separately, both in the declaration and in a reference to an array element:

  ```
  int myMatrix [3][5];
     .
     .
     .
  myMatrix[0][4] = 89;
  ```

Note that myMatrix[0][4] refers to the last column (column 4) in the first row (row 0) of the matrix.

- There is no run-time checking for out-of-bound subscripts. The *programmer* is responsible for ensuring that wild subscripts do not run off the end of the array into other data.

- Character strings are arrays of type char, terminated by the null character ('\0'). The presence of the null character allows algorithms to locate the end of a string.

- As parameters to functions, arrays are always passed by reference. It is impossible to pass an array by value.

- An array cannot be returned as the value of a value-returning function.

Structures (structs)

The struct is another widely used structured type in C and C++. If you are not familiar with the concept of structs, you can bypass this discussion; Chapters 4 and 5 cover the material in detail.

A struct (structure) is a collection of components called *members*, all of which can have different data types. Among programming languages, this terminology is unique to C and C++. In many other languages a struct is called a *record*, and the individual components of a record are called *fields* of the record.

There are several differences between C and C++ with respect to structs. The first difference is that after you have defined a struct type such as

```
struct PatientType {
    int    age;
    float height;
};
```

C requires you to supply the word struct whenever you declare a variable of that type:

```
struct PatientType patient1;
```

In C++, the word struct is unnecessary:

```
PatientType patient1;
```

Another difference is that C++ allows an entire struct object to be passed as a parameter or returned as a function value. This contrasts with some versions of C that allow only *pointers* to structs to be passed as parameters or returned as function values.

Finally, C++ has made a major change by defining a struct to be a special case of a class, a brand new category of structured types. We do not describe the class in this appendix. The relationship between structs and classes is described in Chapters 3 through 5 of this book.

B.6 Type Checking and Type Coercion

Many programming languages employ **strict type checking**—they severely limit the mixing of data types in expressions, assignment operations, and parameter passage. For example, the Pascal assignment statement

```
integerVar := floatVar;
```

is prohibited. The compiler sees a type incompatibility and generates a syntax error.

C and C++ employ **nonstrict type checking** in many situations. The assignment statement

```
integerVar = floatVar;
```

is permissible. However, the compiler does something "under the table." It generates object code that will, at run time, temporarily convert the floating point value to integer representation (discarding the fractional part in the process) before storing the result into `integerVar`. This invisible conversion of a value from one data type to another is called **implicit type coercion**.

C and C++ consider integral and floating types to be compatible in the following contexts:

• Arithmetic expressions and relational expressions
• Assignment operations
• Parameter passage
• Return of a function value

When values of compatible types are mixed, implicit type coercion occurs.

The remainder of this section discusses type coercion, promotion, and demotion. C and C++ handle these actions the same way. If you are thoroughly familiar with type coercion in C, you might wish to read the following as a review or else skip to the next section.

Type Coercion in Arithmetic and Relational Expressions

Suppose an arithmetic expression involves one operator and two operands. Examples might be `3.4*sum` or `var1/var2`. Then implicit type coercion takes place as follows.

Step 1: Each `char`, `short`, or enumeration value is promoted (widened) to `int`. (Table B.3 describes promotion in detail.) If both operands are now `int`, the result is an `int` expression.

Step 2: If step 1 still leaves a mixed-type expression, the following precedence of types is used:

$$\text{lowest} \longrightarrow \text{highest}$$

```
int, unsigned int, long, unsigned long, float, double, long double
```

The value of the operand of "lower" type is promoted to that of the "higher" type, and the result is an expression of that type.

A simple example is the expression `someFloat+2`. This expression has no `char`, `short`, or enumeration values in it, so step 1 still leaves a mixed-type expression. In step 2, `int` is a "lower" type than `float`, so the value 2 is coerced temporarily to a `float` value, say 2.0. Then the multiplication can take place, and the type of the entire expression is `float`.

This description of type coercion also holds for relational expressions such as `someInt<someFloat`. However, the type of the result is always `int`—the value 1 (true) or 0 (false).

Promotion

Promotion (or **widening**) of a value due to type coercion follows the rules detailed in Table B.3. In this table, the phrases "two's complement" and "sign bit" refer to the most common way that machines store integers in memory. We will not go into two's complement representation here, but one characteristic is that the leftmost bit of an integer is considered the sign bit: 1 denotes a negative integer, and 0 denotes a positive integer or zero.

The note at the bottom of Table B.3 refers to a potential problem with portability of C++ programs. If you use the `char` type only to store character data, there is no problem. C++ guarantees that each character in a machine's character set (such as ASCII) is a nonnegative value.

But if you try to save memory by using the `char` type for manipulating small signed integers, then a program causing promotion of these `char`s to `int`s will produce different results on different machines! The moral is this: Unless you are squeezed to the limit for memory space, do not use `char` to manipulate small signed numbers. Use `char` only to store character data.

Table B.3 Promotion from one simple type to another

From	To	Result
`double`	`long double`	Same value occupying more memory space.
`float`	`double`	Same value occupying more memory space.
integral type	floating type	Fractional part is zero.
integral type	unsigned counterpart	No change in value in two's complement machines.
signed integral type	longer signed integral type	Sign extension occurs: leftmost byte(s) are padded with the sign bit (leftmost bit) of the shorter integer value.
unsigned integral type	longer integral type	No sign extension occurs. Leftmost byte(s) are padded with zero bits.

Note: The result of promoting a `char` to an `int` is machine-dependent. On some machines, `char` means `signed char`, so promotion of a negative value yields a negative integer. On other machines, `char` means `unsigned char`, so promotion always yields a nonnegative integer.

Type Coercion in Assignment Operations

With the exception of char to int, promoting values from one type to another does not cause unexpected results. On the other hand, **demotion** (or narrowing) of values can potentially cause loss of information. Demotion is possible with implicit type coercion in an assignment operation.

Consider an assignment operation

$$v = e$$

where v is a variable and e is an expression. Regarding the data types of v and e, there are three possibilities:

1. In the types of v and e are the same, no type coercion occurs.
2. If the type of v is "higher" than that of e (using the type precedence explained in the preceding discussion of promotion), then the value of e is promoted to v's type before being stored into v.
3. If the type of v is "lower" than that of e, the value of e is demoted to v's type before being stored into v.

Demotion, which you can think of as shrinking a value, may cause loss of information:

* Demotion from a longer integral type to a shorter integral type (such as long to int) results in discarding the bits on the left. The result may be a drastically different number.
* Demotion from a floating type to an integral type causes truncation of the fractional part (and an undefined result if the integer part will not fit into the destination variable).
* Demotion from a longer floating type to a shorter floating type (such as double to float) may result in loss of precision.

These rules for the assignment operation also hold for parameter passage (the mapping of actual parameters onto formal parameters) and for returning the value of a function with a return statement.

One consequence of implicit type coercion is the futility of declaring a variable to be unsigned with the hope that the compiler will prevent you from doing something like this:

```
unsignedVar = -5;
```

The compiler will not complain at all. It will generate code to perform type coercion, coercing the int to an unsigned int. The result, conceptually, will be some strange looking positive integer. Moral: Do not rely on unsigned types to obtain larger nonnegative numbers, thinking that the compiler will keep you from mistakenly storing a negative number. If you need larger numbers, move up from int to long, not int to unsigned int.

B.7   Type Casting

If we want to write readable and self-documenting code, it is not entirely satis-factory to rely on "invisible" implicit type coercion. C and C++ allow **explicit type conversion** by means of the *cast operation*. This term comes from the phrase **type casting**—casting a value from one type to another.

Instead of depending on implicit type coercion in the assignment

```
intVar = floatVar;
```

we can use a cast operation. C uses a prefix notation for the cast operator. C++ adds a functional notation:

```
intVar = (int) floatVar;        ◄— Prefix notation (parentheses required)
intVar = int(floatVar);         ◄— Functional notation
```

All three of the above statements produce identical results. The only differ-ence is that of clarity. With the cast operation, it is perfectly clear to the pro-grammer and to colleagues that the mixing of types was intentional, not an oversight. Countless bugs have resulted from unintentional mixing of types.

There is one restriction on using the functional notation of a cast operation. The type name must be a single identifier. If the type name consists of more than one identifier, the prefix notation is required:

```
thisChar = unsigned char(inputVal);     ◄— No
thisChar = (unsigned char) inputVal;    ◄— Yes
```

We must stress a very important point about explicit type conversions. Not only are they valuable for documentation purposes, they are also mandatory in some cases for correct programming. Consider the following code:

```
int   itemSum;
int   itemCount;
float average;
   .
   .
   .
average = itemSum / itemCount;     ◄— Assume itemSum contains 120
                                       and itemCount contains 190.
```

Recall that if both operands of the / operator are integral expressions, the frac-tional portion of the result is discarded. Thus, the above assignment statement evaluates 120/190 to be zero and stores the value 0.0 into average. The way to express it correctly, as well as clearly, is this:

```
average = float(itemSum) / float(itemCount);
```

B.8   Symbolic Constants

C++ provides two methods for defining **symbolic constants** (or **named con-stants**). The first method, as in the C language, is to use a #define directive to the preprocessor:

```
#define PI 3.141593
```

The C++ preprocessor literally replaces each occurrence of the identifier PI with its corresponding constant value. (Recall that C and C++ programmers often capitalize all the letters in a constant identifier.)

Using #define to create symbolic constants has an important drawback. The preprocessor does not perform type checking or scope analysis (determination of global versus local scope) of identifiers, as the compiler does. Thus, it is preferable to use the second method: attach the word const to the declaration and initialization of PI:

```
const float PI = 3.141593;
```

This declaration is handled by the compiler, not the preprocessor, so that type checking and scope analysis are performed. The preprocessor directives

```
#define THIS_YEAR 1994
#define PERIOD '.'
#define CUPS_PER_GALLON 16
```

are better written using the const declarations

```
const int  THIS_YEAR = 1994;
const char PERIOD = '.';
const int  CUPS_PER_GALLON = 16;
```

Note that if you omit a type name, C++ assumes you mean int:

```
const THIS_YEAR = 1994;
const CUPS_PER_GALLON = 16;
```

Sometimes you will encounter code like this, but there is no particularly good reason to omit the word int.

You may use symbolic constants in places where constant expressions are required. For example, in the declaration of an array it is required that the declared size be a constant or an expression containing only constant values. Such expressions may include declared constants:

```
const int MAX_LEN = 50;
   .
   .
   .
char myString[MAX_LEN+1];
```

Having introduced const declarations, we now make an observation about C++ enumeration types. It would seem that an enum declaration is the same as writing a typedef and several const declarations, all of type int. For example,

```
enum Boolean {FALSE, TRUE};
```

is like the sequence of statements

```
typedef int Boolean;
const    int FALSE = 0;
const    int TRUE = 1;
```

However, there is an important difference. It turns out that implicit type coercion is defined for enumeration types to int (see Section B.5), but *not* for int to enumeration types. In the following code, the compiler will give either a warning or a fatal error at the assignment statement:

```
enum Boolean {FALSE, TRUE};

Boolean isGreater;
float   a, b;
 .
 .
 .
isGreater = (a > b);
```

The data type of the relational expression a > b is int (1 for true or 0 for false). Because type coercion from int to enumeration types is not defined, the compiler will complain about storing an int value into a Boolean variable.

We could dodge the problem by using a cast to perform explicit type conversion:

```
isGreater = Boolean(a > b);
```

But using a cast is a nuisance if we have to do it often in a program. It is simpler to define the Boolean type using a typedef and two const declarations.

B.9 Scope and Lifetime

Scope of Identifiers

In C and C++, the **scope** of an identifier is the region of program code where it is legal to reference that identifier. An identifier declared outside all functions has global scope and is visible to any function, including main. An identifier declared within a function has local scope and is visible only within that function. More precisely, an identifier can be local to a **block** (another name for a compound statement):

```
if (alpha > 3) {
    int i;
    cin >> i;
    beta = beta + i;
}
```

Note that the body of a function is syntactically a block:

```
void SomeFunc()
{
    int temp;
     .
     .
     .
}
```

Thus "local to a function" is consistent with "local to a block."

These two **scope rules** or **visibility rules** are the same in C and C++, but the comprehensive scope rules in C++ are far more elaborate than in C. C++ defines three categories of scope for any identifier:

1. **Class scope**
   This term refers to the structured type `class`, which is not discussed in this appendix.

2. **Local scope**
   The scope of an identifier declared inside a block extends from the point of declaration to the end of that block.

3. **File** (global) **scope**
   The scope of an identifier declared outside all functions and classes extends from the point of declaration to the end of the entire file.

We will not say any more about class scope in this appendix. For now, global and local scope are of interest. Chapter 3 provides a detailed introduction to classes.

Lifetime of a Variable

A concept related to but separate from the scope of a variable is its **lifetime**— the period of time during program execution that an identifier actually has memory allocated to it. Consider local variables within a function. Storage for local variables is created at the moment of function entry, then the variables are "alive" while the function is executing, and finally the storage is destroyed at function exit. In contrast, the lifetime of a global variable is the lifetime of the entire program. Memory is allocated only once, when the program begins executing, and is destroyed only when the entire program terminates. Observe that scope is a compile-time issue, but lifetime is a run-time issue.

In C and C++, each variable has a **storage class** that determines its lifetime. An **automatic variable** is one whose storage is allocated and destroyed at block entry and block exit. A **static variable** is one whose storage remains allocated for the duration of the entire program. You may specify the storage class of an identifier by prefixing its declaration with one of the reserved words `auto` or `static`.

If no storage class specifier is given, `auto` is assumed for any variable declared inside a block, and `static` is assumed for any global variable. These assumptions suffice in most cases. It would not make sense to declare a global variable `auto`, so the word `auto` is rarely seen in a program. On the other hand, you might wish to give a local variable the storage class `static` so that its lifetime persists from function call to function call:

```
void SomeFunc()
{
    float   someFloat;          ←— Destroyed when function exits
    static int someInt;         ←— Retains its value from call to call
        .
        .
        .
}
```

It is usually better to declare a local variable as static than to use a global variable. A static local variable has the lifetime of a global variable, but the local scope hides the variable from other functions in the program.

Initializations in Declarations

Both C and C++ allow you to initialize a variable in its declaration. An automatic variable is initialized to the specified value each time control enters the block:

```
void SomeFunc( int someParam )
{
    int i = 0;                          ←—— Initialized each time
    int n = 2 * someParam + 3;          ←—— Initialized each time
        .
        .
        .
}
```

In contrast, initialization of a static variable (a global variable or one explicitly declared static) occurs once only, the first time control reaches its declaration. Furthermore, the initial value must be a constant expression (one with only constant values as operands):

```
void AnotherFunc( int aParam )
{
    static char ch = 'A';               ←—— Initialized once only
    static int  n  = aParam + 1;        ←—— Illegal—constant expression
        .                                       required
        .
        .
}
```

Although an initialization gives an initial value to a variable, it is perfectly acceptable to reassign it another value during program execution.

C and C++ have a special syntax for initializing an array in a declaration. You separate the values of the array elements with commas and enclose the list within braces:

```
int someVec[3] = {25, 0, 4};
int someMatrix[2][3] = {
    {4, 6, 5},
    {0, 0, 12}
};
```

A difference between C and C++ in array initializations is that C requires the array to be static (either global or explicitly declared static). This restriction is removed in ANSI C and C++.

Table B.4 summarizes initialization of static and automatic variables.

Table B.4 Comparison of static and automatic initializations

	Automatic variables	**Static variables**
Initialized when?	Each time control reaches declaration	Once only, the first time control reaches the declaration
Valid initializers	Any expression (type coercion may be performed)	Constant expressions only

C and C++ provide a shorthand notation for initializing string arrays: the string constant. The following declarations are equivalent, although the second is more likely to be used:

```
char str[3] = {'H', 'i', '\0'};
char str[3] = "Hi";
```

Caution: Initialization (in a declaration) and assignment (with an assignment statement) are two different things. Different rules apply. Array initialization is legal, but recall that aggregate array assignment is not:

```
char myStr[6] = "Hello";        ← OK
   .
   .
   .
myStr = "Howdy";                ← Illegal
```

Also, you can omit the size of an array when initializing it; the compiler will determine its size. This technique is especially useful for initializing long strings without counting the characters manually:

```
char msg[] = "Reenter last number";     ← 20 elements, including '\0'
int  vec[] = {0, 0, 0, 0, 12};          ← 5 elements
```

External Declarations

We now make a final point about variable declarations. As we discuss in the main body of this book, it is common to organize a C++ source program into many separate files. One file might contain just the main function, another file may contain some data declarations and two or three functions invoked by main, and so forth. The compiler's job is to translate the source code in each file independently, and then a program known as the linker collects all the resulting object code into a single executable program.

You can use the reserved word extern to reference a global variable located in another file. A normal declaration such as

```
int someInt;
```

causes the compiler to reserve some storage for someInt. On the other hand,

```
extern int someInt;
```

is known as an **external declaration**. It states that someInt is a global variable located in another file and that no storage should be reserved for it here.

System header files such as `iostream.h` contain such external declarations so that user programs can access important variables located in system programs.

In C++ terminology, the statement

```
extern int someInt;
```

is merely a declaration of `someInt`. It associates a variable name with a data type so that the compiler can perform type checking. On the other hand, the statement

```
int someInt;
```

is both a declaration and a **definition** of `someInt`. In other words, a declaration is also a definition if it reserves memory for the object. With functions, we earlier made this same distinction between function prototypes and function definitions. In C++, you can declare an object in many locations, but you can define it only once.

B.10 Input and Output

We have used only the most basic features of C++ input and output (I/O) in this appendix. We have used the `>>` operator to input data from the standard input stream `cin` and have used the `<<` operator to output values to the standard output stream `cout`:

```
cout << "Your 2 integers, please: ";
cin >> int1 >> int2;
cout << "Their sum is " << int1 + int2 << '\n';
```

Instead of providing more information on I/O here, we ask you to proceed now to Section C.1 of Appendix C. We have placed the I/O material in its own appendix so that all readers—not just C programmers—can find it easily.

KEY TERMS

automatic variable   (p. A-76)
base address   (p. A-59)
block   (p. A-75)
case sensitive   (p. A-54)
declaration statement   (p. A-62)
declaration versus definition   (p. A-79)
demotion (narrowing)   (p. A-72)
enumerator   (p. A-67)
escape sequence   (p. A-66)
exit status   (p. A-56)
explicit type conversion   (p. A-73)
external declaration   (p. A-78)
file (global) scope   (p. A-76)
forward declaration   (p. A-56)
function definition   (p. A-57)
function prototype   (p. A-56)
implicit type coercion   (p. A-70)
include directory   (p. A-56)

library function   (p. A-61)
lifetime   (p. A-76)
local scope   (p. A-76)
nonstrict type checking   (p. A-70)
parameter passage by value   (p. A-58)
parameter passage by reference   (p. A-58)
promotion (widening)   (p. A-71)
reserved word   (p. A-54)
scope   (p. A-75)
scope rules   (p. A-75)
standard library   (p. A-61)
static variable   (p. A-76)
storage class   (p. A-76)
strict type checking   (p. A-70)
symbolic constant   (p. A-73)
type casting   (p. A-73)
visibility rules   (p. A-75)

APPENDIX C

C++ *Stream I/O*

This appendix describes many of the features of input and output (I/O) in Version 2.0 of the C++ programming environment. However, it is not intended to be comprehensive—a discussion of all I/O operations would be beyond the scope of this text.

C.1   Fundamentals of Stream I/O

In many languages, I/O operations such as Pascal's readln and writeln are built into the language. In C++, I/O facilities are not part of the language itself. To perform I/O, a C++ program must invoke a function that is located in an external library.

A typical C++ environment has a wealth of library routines for performing I/O to and from console terminals, disk files, tape files, communication ports, and other devices. Many of these routines, carried over from the C language environment, are available to any C++ program because C++ is a superset of the C language. This appendix, however, focuses on an innovative I/O concept unique to C++: the **stream.** You can think of a stream as an endless sequence of characters, such as ASCII characters. An istream is a data type representing a stream of input characters coming from some I/O device, and an ostream represents an output stream going to some I/O device.

To use stream I/O, a program must begin with the preprocessor directive

```
#include <iostream.h>
```

The header file iostream.h contains, among other things, declarations that are approximately as follows:

```
extern istream cin;
extern ostream cout;
extern ostream cerr;
```

(We say "approximately" because the actual declarations are slightly different in a way that is not important right now.) The first line declares cin (pronounced "see-in") to be a variable of type istream, and extern states that the

definition of cin occurs in another file. The next two lines declare cout and
cerr (pronounced "see-out" and "see-air") to be variables of type ostream. By
default, cin is associated with the **standard input device** (usually the keyboard), cout is associated with the **standard output device** (usually the display screen), and cerr is associated with the **standard error output device**
(usually the same display screen).

The Extraction (>>) and Insertion (<<) Operators

Only certain operations on istreams and ostreams are permissible. For
istream input, the **extraction operator** >> (sometimes pronounced "get
from") takes a stream as its first operand and a simple variable or a string vector as its second:

```
cin >> someInt;
```

The second operand can be of any built-in data type. The effect is to extract
one or more characters from the input stream and convert them into a single
value of the appropriate data type.

When performing input, >> consumes and discards any leading **whitespace**
characters: blank, tab, line feed, form feed, or carriage return. For numeric
data, input stops at the first character that is inappropriate for the specified
data type. For the above input of someInt, if the input stream initially consists
of bbb158ABC, where b denotes a blank, then execution of the instruction stores
the value 158 into someInt and leaves the input stream as ABC. For string data,
input stops at the first trailing whitespace character (which is not consumed—
it remains as the first character waiting in the input stream).

For output to an ostream, the **insertion operator** << (sometimes pronounced "put to") takes two operands. The first is a stream and the second is
either an expression of simple type or a string:

```
cout << "The coefficient is ";
cout << 3.8 * alpha;
       .
       .
       .
cerr << "Invalid denominator in Division routine!";
```

The insertion operator converts its second operand to a sequence of characters
and inserts them into (or, more precisely, appends them to) the output stream.

You can input (or output) several data items with successive applications of
the >> (or <<) operator. For example, the statement

```
cout << "Hi" << "There";
```

outputs

```
HiThere
```

The reason is as follows. Any operation on a stream can be thought of as a
function that not only has a side effect (performing the I/O) but also returns a
value: the stream as modified by the I/O. For example, think of

```
cout << "Hi";
```

as performing the output and then returning a stream: the previous stream with Hi appended to it. Thus, you can interpret the notation

```
cout << "Hi" << "There";
```

as

```
(cout << "Hi") << "There";
```

That is, we are appending the string "There" to a stream: the stream obtained by appending "Hi" to the previous stream.

Similarly, think of

```
cin >> int1 >> int2;
```

as meaning

```
(cin >> int1) >> int2;
```

That is, we are removing the value for int2 from an input stream: the stream obtained by removing the value for int1 from the previous stream.

Note that the newline (end-of-line) character '\n' must be sent explicitly to cout to terminate a line. You can embed the newline character within a string:

```
cout << "Welcome\n";
```

or append it separately:

```
cout << "delta = " << 3*(alpha-5) << '\n';
```

The get, getline, ignore, put, *and* putback *Functions*

As we discussed earlier, the extraction operator >> skips leading whitespace characters when performing input. Sometimes a program needs to treat all characters as important characters, even blanks and other whitespace characters. For istream input, the get function inputs a single character or a string *without* skipping whitespace. The function is invoked by giving the name of the istream variable (for example, cin), followed by a dot, followed by the function name and parameter list:

```
cin.get(someChar);
cin.get(stringVec, charCount+1);
```

The first version above inputs the very next character waiting in the input stream, even if it is a whitespace character such as a blank, and stores it into someChar. The second version, used for reading a character string, does not skip leading whitespace characters and continues until it either has read charCount characters or it reaches the newline character '\n'. It then appends the null character '\0' to the end of the string vector.

Using get is especially useful for reading character strings that may contain embedded blanks. With the statements

```
char oneLine[81];    // Room for 80 characters plus '\0'
    .
    .
    .
cin.get(oneLine, 81);
```

the get function reads and stores an entire input line (up to 80 characters), blanks and all. Note that reading stops at '\n' but does not consume it. The newline character is now the first one waiting in the input stream. To read two consecutive lines worth of strings, it is necessary to consume the newline character:

```
char dummy;
    .
    .
    .
cin.get(string1, 81);
cin.get(dummy);         // Eat newline before next "get"
cin.get(string2, 81);
```

The first invocation reads characters up to, but not including, '\n'. If the input of dummy were omitted, then the input of string2 would read *no* characters because '\n' would immediately be the first character waiting in the stream.

A simpler way to consume '\n' is to use the getline function. This function is like get, but they differ in what happens if '\n' is encountered. The get function does not consume the '\n', whereas getline does. The statement

```
cin.getline(string1, 81);
```

does consume the newline if fewer than 80 characters are read.

For string input, it is also possible to supply a third parameter that specifies a terminating character other than '\n':

```
cin.get(myString, 41, '\t');
```

or

```
cin.getline(myString, 41, '\t');
```

Here, each function stops reading when either 40 characters have been read or the tab character, '\t', is encountered. In the latter case, get does not consume the tab character, but getline does.

Another useful function for istream input is the ignore function. When supplied with one int parameter *n*, the function inputs and discards the next *n* characters in the input stream. The statement

```
cin.ignore(5);
```

discards the next five input characters. If supplied with two parameters—an int *n* and a char *c*—the ignore function stops reading when either *n* characters have been read or the character *c* was read in. The statement

```
cin.ignore(100, '\n');
```

says to consume at most 100 characters, but stop if a newline was read. (Note that the newline character *is* consumed by the function.) If a program inputs a long string from the user but only wants to retain the first four characters of the response, here is a way to do it:

```
char response[5];    // Room for 4 characters plus '\0'

cin.get(response, 5);    // Input at most 4 characters
cin.ignore(100, '\n');   // Skip remaining chars up to and
                         // including '\n'
```

The value 100 in the last statement is arbitrary. Any "large enough" number will do.

For ostream output of single characters, there is a function named put:

```
cout.put(someChar);
```

This function is seldom used because, in all but very rare situations, it produces the same output as

```
cout << someChar;
```

Its primary use is to provide compatibility with older versions of the stream I/O library.

Finally, there is a putback function for istream input:

```
cin.putback(someChar);
```

This function puts a character back into the input stream after it has been read. The effect is to "peek" at the next character in the stream. A program may need to read a character, inspect it, then put it back into the input stream for later consumption.

Manipulators

Manipulators are function-like operations that may appear in the midst of a series of extractions and insertions. The programmer uses them to control input and output formatting. The header file iostream.h provides seven manipulators: dec, hex, oct, ws, flush, endl, and ends (see Table C.1).

The manipulators dec, hex, and oct control the number base when performing I/O of integral types. The statements

```
i = 49;
cout << i << ' ' << hex << i << ' ' << i+1 << dec << i+1;
```

produce the output

```
49 31 32 50
```

(If you are not familiar with hexadecimal numbers, do not worry about the meaning of this sample output.) The number base remains in effect until a subsequent manipulator changes it.

Table C.1 Manipulators declared in iostream.h

Manipulator	Usage	Action
dec	inStrm >> dec	Interpret subsequent input as decimal (base 10).
	outStrm << dec	Output in decimal (base 10) representation.
hex	inStrm >> hex	Interpret subsequent input as hexadecimal (base 16).
	outStrm << hex	Output in hexadecimal (base 16) representation.
oct	inStrm >> oct	Interpret subsequent input as octal (base 8).
	outStrm << oct	Output in octal (base 8) representation.
ws	inStrm >> ws	Extract and discard whitespace characters.
flush	outStrm << flush	Flush an ostream (output any characters that have accumulated, waiting to be output).
endl	outStrm << endl	Append a newline ('\n') and flush an ostream.
ends	outStrm << ends	Append a terminating null character ('\0') to an ostream.

Note: In the table, inStrm is assumed to be of type istream and outStrm is assumed to be of type ostream.

The ws manipulator is usually unnecessary because the >> operator discards leading whitespace anyway. The flush and ends manipulators are important only in advanced applications, so we will not discuss them further. Finally, the endl manipulator can be useful as an alternative to '\n' for those who do not like typing apostrophes and backslashes. The following two statements yield the same output:

```
cout << "Result = " << 3*alpha << '\n';
cout << "Result = " << 3*alpha << endl;
```

In addition to the above manipulators, the header file iomanip.h declares several parameterized manipulators. Each of these, described in Table C.2, requires a single parameter enclosed in parentheses.

The setbase manipulator is an alternative to using the previously described dec, hex, and oct manipulators. The setprecision manipulator controls how many digits to the right of the decimal point are displayed. On many systems, the default is 6 digits. The output for the statements

```
x = 24.93468;
cout << setprecision(2) << x << ' ' << setprecision(4) << x;
```

is

```
24.93 24.9347
```

Table C.2 Parameterized manipulators declared in iomanip.h

Manipulator	Usage	Action
setbase(b)	outStrm << setbase(b)	Set number base to b (8, 10, or 16).
setfill(ch)	outStrm << setfill(ch)	Set fill character to ch.
setprecision(n)	outStrm << setprecision(n)	Set floating-point precision to n.
setw(w)	outStrm << setw(w) inStrm >> setw(w)	Set field width to w. (setw is only for numbers and strings, not for char data. Also, the field width is reset to 0 after the very next insertion or extraction.)

Notes: 1. To use these manipulators, you must use the preprocessor directive #include <iomanip.h>.
2. All parameters to the manipulators are of type int.
3. In the table above, inStrm is assumed to be of type istream and outStrm is assumed to be of type ostream.

(The effect of setprecision may vary from one C++ environment to another. Your system may produce different output from that shown above.)

The setw manipulator, when used with ostreams, allows control over horizontal spacing of the output. Suppose three variables i, j, and k contain the values 12, 3, and 4, respectively. The statement

```
cout << "Results:" << i << j << k;
```

outputs the characters

```
Results:1234
```

Without spacing between the numbers, this output is difficult to interpret. Although it is possible to control the horizontal spacing by inserting strings of blanks, the code is tedious to write and hard to read:

```
cout << "Results:    " << i << "    " << j << "    " << k;
```

Instead, it is more convenient to use setw. Its parameter specifies a minimum field width—the minimum number of print positions the next numeric value or string should occupy. If the field width is specified as zero or is too small to hold the result, no harm is done. The result will occupy exactly as many print positions as are needed anyway. If the field width is larger than needed to hold the result, the result is right-justified (filled with blanks on the left). The statement

```
cout << "Results:" << setw(6) << i << setw(6) << j << setw(6) << k;
```

therefore gives the following output:

```
Results:    12     3     4
```

Setting the field width is a one-time action. It holds only for the very next item to be output using the << operator. After this output, the field width is reset to zero (meaning "use as many print positions as needed").

When values are right-justified using setw, the default fill character is the blank. The purpose of the setfill manipulator is to change the fill character (and leave it changed until the next call to setfill):

```
i = 25;
cout << setfill('#') << setw(4) << i << setw(8) << 2*i;
```

These statements yield the output

```
##25######50
```

Finally, the setw manipulator, when used with istreams, dictates the maximum number of characters to input when reading into a character string. For an array someString, the statement

```
cin >> setw(5) >> someString;
```

says to input at most four (not five) characters from the standard input device and store them into someString, followed by a fifth character: the null character ('\0'). For input, using setw has no effect when reading data of any type other than a character string.

Testing the State of a Stream

An important stream operation is that of **testing the state** of the stream. When a stream is tested, as in an if or while condition, it either returns a nonzero value if the last I/O operation succeeded or it returns zero if it failed (due to an attempt to read beyond end-of-file or any other I/O error).

To test for end-of-file, the programmer can choose between two styles of while loops. The first style consists of the following pattern: the first data item is read just before the loop begins (the *priming read*), and the body of the loop consists of processing the data and performing the next read at the very bottom:

```
cin >> someInt;
while (cin) {                    // While the previous input succeeded ...
    Process(someInt);
    cin >> someInt;
}
```

In this example, the while condition tests the stream cin. If the most recent input operation succeeded, the value returned is nonzero (true), so the loop will continue. Eventually, when end-of-file occurs, the input statement at the bottom of the loop will fail. The while condition will then have the value zero (false), so the loop will terminate.

Caution: For rather complicated reasons, the nonzero and zero values returned by testing a stream state are not compatible with the int constant 0. Tests such as if (cin != 0) and if (cin == 0) will yield syntax errors. Instead, use tests like if (cin) and if (!cin).

Just as the identifier cin denotes a stream, so does an expression such as cin >> someInt. The latter denotes the stream that remains after extracting the value of someInt from the previous stream. The fact that cin >> someInt denotes a stream leads to a second style of testing for end-of-file. It eliminates the need for two separate input operations (the priming read and the next read at the bottom of the loop):

```
while (cin >> someInt)    // While input of someInt succeeded ...
    Process(someInt);
```

This style of performing the input and testing for success, all within the while condition, seems very unusual to people first learning C++.

You also can use this second approach when using the get operation, as shown in the program in Figure C.1. All this program does is echo each input character to cout until the user types the end-of-file keystrokes, such as Ctrl/D in UNIX or Ctrl/Z in MS-DOS.

A Turbo C++ Note: Testing a Stream State

If you have Borland International's Turbo C++ Version 1.0 or 1.01 (2nd Edition), the technique for testing a stream state does not behave as we have just described. Using a statement like

```
while (cin >> someInt)
        .
        .
        .
```

results in an infinite loop. Borland has issued an update to the iostream library that conforms to this popular manner of testing a stream state. The update, in a compressed file named TCPPT3.ZIP, is available on request from Customer Service at Borland or can be found on various electronic bulletin boards. (Note that versions of Turbo C++ later than Version 1.01 are not involved in this update, nor is Borland's professional compiler, Borland C++. With these compilers, testing a stream state does behave as described.)

Figure C.1 EchoFile program

```
//---------------------------------------------------------------------
//  echofile.cpp
//  This program copies its input to its output.
//---------------------------------------------------------------------
#include <iostream.h>

int main()
{
    char ch;

    while (cin.get(ch))    // While this input of ch succeeded ...
        cout << ch;

    return 0;
}
```

An alternative to obtaining Borland's update is to do the following. To test a stream state, add a dot and then a call to the function good():

```
if (cin.good())
    .
    .
    .
```

If the stream being tested involves the insertion or extraction operator, put parentheses around the entire expression before adding the dot and the call to good():

```
while ((cin >> someInt).good())
    .
    .
    .
```

This solution is somewhat messy, but it does work.

Comparison of Pascal and C++ Techniques

For Pascal programmers, we present in Table C.3 some examples of C++ stream I/O operations and their equivalents in Pascal.

Table C.3 C++ stream I/O and Pascal equivalents

Pascal	C++
read(anInt, aReal);	cin >> anInt >> aReal;
read(anInt, aChar, aReal); (* Pascal: reading a char *)	cin >> anInt; cin.get(aChar);
(* doesn't skip whitespace *)	cin >> aReal;
readln; (* Skip remaining chars, *) (* including newline char *)	cin.ignore(100, '\n');
writeln(int1, int2, int3);	cout << int1 << int2 << int3 << '\n';
writeln('My', age, ' years');	cout << "My" << age << " years\n";
write(char1, ' and ', char2);	cout << char1 << " and " << char2;

write(ord(char1));	cout << int(char1); // Cast to an
	                      // int

write(int1:5, int2:7);	cout << setw(5) << int1 << setw(7) << int2;

Table C.3 C++ stream I/O and Pascal equivalents (continued)

Pascal	C++
`writeln;`	`cout << '\n';   or   cout << endl;`

`while not eof do`
`   begin`
`      read(int1, int2);`
`      Process(int1, int2)`
`   end`
	Either
	`cin >> int1 >> int2;`
	`while (cin) {`
	`    Process(int1, int2);`
	`    cin >> int1 >> int2;`
	`}`
	or
	`while (cin >> int1 >> int2)`
	`    Process(int1, int2);`

A Note to C Programmers

In C++ the use of stream I/O is not mandatory. All the usual I/O routines from the C library, such as `scanf` and `printf`, are still available by including the relevant header files, such as `stdio.h`. However, we strongly urge you to accustom yourself to the C++ stream I/O model.

If you do mix C++ stream I/O and C-style I/O within the same program, you may get garbled input or output. This problem occurs in some systems that use one memory area to manage the characters involved in C++ stream I/O and a different memory area for C-style I/O. To remedy this situation, try invoking the function

```
ios::sync_with_stdio();
```

at the beginning of your program. (Do not worry about what the prefix "`ios::`" means.) This function usually takes care of the problem.

Command Line Redirection of I/O

On the surface, the `EchoFile` program of Figure C.1 may not seem very useful. Reading each character from the standard input device (usually the keyboard) and echoing it to the standard output device (usually the display screen) may not make sense, especially for those systems that automatically echo each keystroke anyway. However, many C++ environments permit **command line redirection** of standard input and standard output. Assume that the operating system prompt is $ and the standard input and output devices are the keyboard and screen, respectively. If we execute the `EchoFile` program by typing

```
$ echofile
```

then the program reads from the keyboard and writes to the screen. With command line redirection, we can redirect the input as follows:

```
$ echofile < oldfile.dat
```

This command redirects the input to come from the file `oldfile.dat`, not the keyboard. Now the `EchoFile` program becomes useful. It can display, character by character, the contents of any text file in our directory. In a similar fashion, we can redirect the output:

```
$ echofile > newfile.dat
```

Here, we create a new file by typing text on the keyboard and echoing it to `newfile.dat`, not to the screen. Finally, we can create a copy of an existing file by redirecting both input and output:

```
$ echofile < oldfile.dat > newfile.dat
```

C++ also has a rich variety of methods for manipulating files from *within* a C++ program, but you can write very sophisticated programs before learning how to use them. Many, if not most, applications simply input from `cin` and output to `cout`, then rely on command line redirection to specify source and destination files.

An obvious problem with redirecting standard output is the inability of a program to write messages to the screen if `cout` output is redirected to a file. In C++, this problem is resolved easily by sending some output to `cout` and sending other output to `cerr`, the error output stream. The `cerr` stream often is used for displaying important error messages but may be used for any purpose:

```
cerr << "Still processing your data.  Hang on ...\n";
```

Figure C.2 displays a program that uses several of the C++ stream facilities. It is a **filter** program (one that copies its entire input to the output, massaging certain characters along the way). The input stream is presumed to contain characters that cause corresponding parts of the output stream to be underlined. In particular, underlining is toggled on and off by the appearance of backslash (\) characters in the input stream.

Figure C.2 Filter program

```
//--------------------------------------------------------------------------
// filter.cpp
// This program copies standard input to standard output with
// underlining.  Underlining is toggled on and off by input of the
// character '\'. Command line redirection of standard input is likely.
//--------------------------------------------------------------------------
#include <iostream.h>

typedef int Boolean;
const int TRUE = 1;
const int FALSE = 0;

int main()
{
    const char TOGGLE_CHAR = '\\';
    const char BACKSPACE = '\b';
    const char UNDERLINE = '_';
```

```
char    inChar;
Boolean underlining = FALSE;

cerr << "This program filters an input file with underlining,\n"
     << "which is toggled on/off by backslash (\\) chars.\n\n";

while (cin.get(inChar))          // Don't skip whitespace
    switch (inChar) {
        case '\n':               // Don't underline a newline
            cout << '\n';
            break;
        case TOGGLE_CHAR:
            underlining = !underlining;
            break;
        default:
            cout << inChar;
            if (underlining) {
                cout << BACKSPACE;
                cout << UNDERLINE;
            }
    }
cerr << "\nFinished.\n";
return 0;
}
```

Basic File I/O

Despite the simplicity of manipulating files via command line redirection, it is important to know how to perform file I/O from within a program. Some C++ environments do not support command line redirection. Even when command line redirection is available, a program may need to read and write to many files at once.

Through the header file `fstream.h`, the C++ library supplies two stream types for file I/O: `ifstream` (for "input file stream") and `ofstream` (for "output file stream"). All operations defined for `istream`s also are defined for `ifstream`s: `>>`, `get`, `getline`, `ignore`, `putback`, and testing the stream state. Similarly, all operations defined for `ostream`s—`<<`, `put`, and testing the stream state—are defined for `ofstream`s. Thus, after opening a file, you can perform I/O operations just as if input were coming from `cin` or output were going to `cout`.

To open an existing file for input, declare a variable of type `ifstream` and supply, in parentheses, a character string giving the file name as it exists in your directory:

```
ifstream inputFile("somefile.dat");
```

This file name can be either a string constant, as above, or the name of a string array containing the file name:

```
ifstream inputFile(someString);
```

Immediately after this statement, it is important to check the state of `inputFile` to see if the file was opened successfully:

```
ifstream inputFile("somefile.dat");
if ( !inputFile ) {
    PrintErrorMsg();
    exit(1);
}
```

Recall that testing a stream yields a nonzero value if the most recent I/O operation succeeded or zero if it failed.

In Figure C.1 we wrote a program, EchoFile, that copies all characters from cin to cout. We showed how to use command line redirection to create a new file and copy an existing file to this new file. In Figure C.3 we modify the EchoFile program so that it opens an input and output file from within the program, then copies all characters from one to the other. This program prompts the user to supply the file names at run time.

Figure C.3 CopyFile program

```
//----------------------------------------------------------------
// copyfile.cpp
// This program copies all characters from an existing input file to a
// new output file.  The user is prompted for the names of the input
// and output files.
//----------------------------------------------------------------
#include <iostream.h>
#include <fstream.h>

int main()
{
    char fileName[20];

    cout << "Name of input file: ";
    cin >> fileName;

    ifstream inFile(fileName);
    if ( !inFile ) {
        cerr << "Can't open input file\n";
        return 1;
    }

    cout << "Name of output file: ";
    cin >> fileName;

    ofstream outFile(fileName);
    if ( !outFile ) {
        cerr << "Can't open output file\n";
        return 1;
    }

    char ch;
    while (inFile.get(ch))
        outFile << ch;

    return 0;
}
```

Notice how, after the initial housekeeping work of opening the input and output files, most of the program's work is accomplished in two lines:

```
while (inFile.get(ch))
    outFile << ch;
```

Compare this loop with the EchoFile program's main loop:

```
while (cin.get(ch))
    cout << ch;
```

These two loops differ only in the names of the source and destination streams. What is nice about C++ stream I/O is that the programmer has a uniform syntax for performing I/O operations, regardless of whether input and output are related to the keyboard, the screen, or files.

Summary

This section has described the basic features of stream I/O:

- The use of istreams and ostreams
- The insertion and extraction operators (<< and >>)
- The get, getline, ignore, put, and putback functions
- Manipulators
- Testing a stream state
- Command line redirection of I/O
- File I/O using ifstreams and ofstreams

The next section of this appendix introduces more advanced features but requires further knowledge of C++ for full understanding. You should postpone reading the next section until you have read through Chapter 7 and, better yet, Chapter 11 of this book.

C.2 Additional Features

This section of the appendix discusses some more of the many features of stream I/O. It is optional reading, because the main body of this text does not reference any of this material. It is assumed that you have read through Chapter 7 as well as Appendix H (machine-level data and bitwise operators). Preferably, you also have read Chapter 11 on object-oriented programming.

Class Inheritance Hierarchy

The types istream, ostream, ifstream, and ofstream are all classes declared in the header file iostream.h. They all share common characteristics, yet are different from each other in certain ways. The characteristics they all share in common—such as the ability to have their error states tested for success or failure—are centralized in a class named ios. The class istream is said to be **derived from** the class ios. Alternatively, ios is said to be a **base class** of istream. Therefore, data members and function members of the ios class are also members of the istream class. In object-oriented programming terminology, istream **inherits** the members of ios. In addition to the class members inherited from ios, the istream class also adds new data and/or functions appropriate to its purposes. Again from object-oriented programming terminology, ios and istream are related by an **is-a relationship**—every istream is also an ios (with additional properties as well).

The ostream class also is derived from ios. So every ostream is also an ios, but with additional data and functions appropriate to performing output. This section of the appendix discusses several stream I/O classes that are related according to the inheritance hierarchy shown in Figure C.4.

This diagram shows that every istream is also an ios, and more. Also, every ifstream (input file stream) is also an istream, and more. In particular, an ifstream inherits the characteristics of an istream and is specialized with additional data and operations pertaining to file operations. We could make an analogous statement for ostreams and ofstreams.

Notice that the iostream class is derived from both istream and ostream. This is an example of multiple inheritance. An iostream can be read from *and* written to. Furthermore, iostream is the base class of fstream, a file-oriented specialization of an iostream. We will discuss these classes later in this appendix.

Formatting Flags

Every object of type ios (and classes derived from ios) contains a variable, call it flags, that regulates the format (visual appearance) of the input or output. Each bit in this flags variable controls one aspect of formatting—whether the output should be right-justified or left-justified, whether whitespace should be

Note: This inheritance diagram shows a simplified portion of the complete inheritance hierarchy defined by iostream.h.

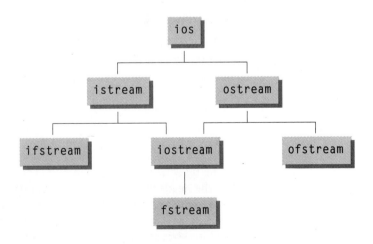

Figure C.4 Stream I/O class hierarchy

skipped on input, and so forth. Think of each of these bits as a Boolean value (or "Boolean flag"), where 1 means true and 0 means false. In the header file iostream.h, the public part of the ios class includes an enumeration type that defines these flags:

```
class ios {
public:
        .
        .
        .
    enum {
        skipws      = 0x0001,  // Skip whitespace on input
        left        = 0x0002,  // Left-justify the output
        right       = 0x0004,  // Right-justify the output
        internal    = 0x0008,  // Left-justify the sign or base
                               //     indicator, and right-justify
                               //     the number
        dec         = 0x0010,  // Decimal conversion
        oct         = 0x0020,  // Octal conversion
        hex         = 0x0040,  // Hexadecimal conversion
        showbase    = 0x0080,  // Show base indicator (0 or 0x) on
                               //     output
        showpoint   = 0x0100,  // Show dec. pt. on whole-numbered
                               //     floating pt. values
                               //     (2.000000 versus 2)
        uppercase   = 0x0200,  // Use uppercase X for hex output and
                               //     uppercase E for scientific
                               //     notation
        showpos     = 0x0400,  // Show '+' with positive integers
        scientific  = 0x0800,  // For floating pt. values, use
                               //     scientific notation (9.365E2)
        fixed       = 0x1000   // For floating pt. values, use
                               //     "normal" notation (936.5)
    };
        .
        .
        .
};
```

The specific hexadecimal values for these enumeration constants are from Borland's Turbo C++ and Borland C++ and may vary from system to system. From the values shown above, the bit that controls whitespace skipping is the rightmost bit in the flags variable, the bit that controls left-justification of output is the second bit from the right, and so forth. By default, the following flags are on (that is, 1): skipws, right, dec, and fixed. All others are off (0).

Because these enumeration constants are declared public, client code can access them directly. However, they are defined inside the class declaration, so client code must use the class name and scope resolution operator (::) to reference them: ios::skipws, ios::left, and so forth.

The flags variable is *not* declared public; it is not directly accessible to client programs. Instead, the ios class and all classes derived from it provide the following public operations and constants:

```
class ios {
public:
    .
    .
    .
    long setf( long flagBits );
    long setf( long flagBits, long field );
    long unsetf( long flagBits );

    // Constants for second parameter of setf():
    static const long basefield;    // For dec, oct, hex
    static const long adjustfield;  // For left, right, internal
    static const long floatfield;   // For scientific, fixed
    .
    .
    .
};
```

The first form of the setf function—the one with a single parameter—
sets the specified flag(s) and leaves the other flags unaltered. To set the
ios::showbase flag so that hexadecimal numbers are printed with a prefix
of 0x, we can do the following:

```
cout << hex << 25 << ' ';
cout.setf(ios::showbase);
cout << 25;
```

This sequence produces the output

```
19 0x19
```

The setf function returns a long value—the value of the flags variable
before the new flag bit is set—but most often the programmer ignores this
return value, as in the preceding example.

To set more than one flag in a call to setf, you can use a bitwise OR of the
desired constants:

```
cout.setf(ios::showbase | ios::uppercase);
cout << hex << 25;
```

For this example, the output is

```
0X25
```

The second form of the setf function, the one taking two parameters,
addresses the following potential problem. Among the formatting flags
ios::left, ios::right, and ios::internal, only one should be set at a
time. If ios::right is currently set and the programmer specifies
cout.setf(ios::left), then both left- and right-justification would be in
effect simultaneously. This situation is a contradiction; the result is unpredictable. The safe way to proceed is to use the two-parameter form of setf,
where the second parameter is the constant ios::adjustfield:

```
cout.setf(ios::left, ios::adjustfield);
```

The implementation code for this version of setf not only sets the ios::left bit but also clears the ios::right and ios::internal bits. This same discussion holds true for ios::scientific and ios::fixed. For these, use the two-parameter version of setf with a second parameter of ios::floatfield. Likewise, for ios::dec, ios::oct, and ios::hex, use the two-parameter version of setf with the second parameter being ios::basefield. (Note that in the last case, it is really easier to use the dec, oct, and hex manipulators described in the first part of this appendix.)

Finally, the unsetf function clears the specified flag bit(s), leaving all the others unchanged:

```
cout.unsetf(ios::showpoint);
```

Stream States

At any moment, a C++ stream object has an associated state, recorded in a nonpublic variable named state. Bits in this variable are set or cleared according to whether the last I/O operation succeeded or failed. The ios class and all classes derived from it provide an enumeration type describing the bits within the state variable, as well as public functions for querying the stream's state:

```
class ios {
public:
    .
    .
    .
    enum io_state {
        goodbit = 0x00,     // No bits set. Previous I/O operation
                            //      succeeded. Next operation may
                            //      succeed.
        eofbit  = 0x01,     // Previous read succeeded and input
                            //      stream is empty.  Next read
                            //      will fail.
        failbit = 0x02,     // Previous I/O operation failed, but no
                            //      characters were lost from stream.
        badbit  = 0x04,     // Previous I/O operation failed, and
                            //      characters were lost.
    };                          .

    int  good() const;      // Returns nonzero if no state bits set
    int  eof()  const;      // Returns nonzero if eofbit=1
    int  fail() const;      // Returns nonzero if failbit=1 or
                            //      badbit=1
    int  bad()  const;      // Returns nonzero if badbit=1
```

```
        void clear();              // Resets the stream state to
                                   //    good
        void clear( int stateBits );  // Sets the stream state
                                      //    according to stateBits

        .
        .
        .
};
```

If a stream is not in the "good" state—that is, if any bits in the state variable are set—a subsequent I/O operation is considered a null operation. The operation is ignored and failbit is set (or if badbit was already set, it remains set).

The failbit bit is most commonly set in three circumstances. The first is an attempt to read past end-of-file. The second is an attempt to open a nonexistent input file. The third is when a format error occurs on input, such as the user's typing the character 'A' when an int is expected. The badbit bit signals some serious problem with an I/O device. The difference between failbit and badbit is of interest primarily to system programmers. Most C++ applications simply treat failure as general failure.

Once failbit or badbit is set, it remains set. Any further I/O operations on the stream are silently ignored. It is possible to reset the stream state using the clear function shown in the preceding class declaration, but doing so can be dangerous unless the programmer is absolutely certain what caused failbit or badbit to be set.

The ios member functions good(), eof(), fail(), and bad() allow detailed testing of the state bits. These can be considered Boolean functions that return true or false. Code such as

```
if (someStream.eof())
    .
    .
    .
if (someStream.fail())
    .
    .
    .
```

can be useful in very intricate situations, especially in low-level system programs. But by far the most common way to test the stream state is to test the entire stream itself, as in the statement

```
while (someStream)
    .
    .
    .
```

This test yields either a nonzero value (if its state is "good" or if only eofbit is set) or the value 0 (if failbit or badbit is set). Both of the following loops serve to detect end-of-file or an I/O error:

```
someStream >> someInt;
while (someStream) {
    Process(someInt);
    someStream >> someInt;
}
```

and

```
while (someStream >> someInt)
    Process(someInt);
```

In each case, the `while` loop exits only when the value of the condition becomes zero—that is, when the input operation fails.

Finally, the `ios` class and all classes derived from it provide an operator function `operator!` as a public member:

```
int operator!();    // Returns nonzero if failbit or badbit is set
```

This function allows stream testing to be phrased in a complementary way:

```
if ( !(someStream >> someVal) )
  :     // I/O error or attempt to read past end-of-file
  .
```

All of these methods for testing stream states are useful in different contexts. Some programmers need to distinguish between `failbit` and `badbit` to know if an I/O device experienced a "soft error" or "hard error." Other programmers might want to know whether it was end-of-file or an I/O error that caused a reading loop to terminate. But for most applications, simply testing for overall success or failure of an I/O operation is the customary approach.

Opening and Closing Files

Two fundamental operations on any file are

- opening a file
- closing a file

A file must be opened before any file I/O takes place. If the file already exists, the operating system checks the directory on the I/O device, locates the file on the device, and loads information about that file into internal tables. If the programmer is creating a new file for output, the open operation adds a new entry to the directory and initializes a new empty file.

The close operation signals completion of I/O for the given file. The operating system performs various wrap-up activities. For example, it must update the directory, write an end-of-file marker at the end of an output file, and flush an output file's I/O buffer. Flushing an output buffer means to output any unwritten characters that have been accumulating in a temporary memory area known as a buffer. Failure to close a file, especially an output file, may have unpleasant consequences.

In Section C.1, we described how to establish and use input and output file streams—ifstreams and ofstreams—declared in the header file fstream.h. Consider the following code:

```
void ReadData( char* fileName )
{
    int        int1, int2;
    ifstream iFile(fileName);

    if ( !iFile ) {
        cerr << "Can't open " << fileName;
        exit(1);
    }
    while (iFile >> int1 >> int2)
        DoSomething(int1, int2);
}
```

The declaration

```
ifstream iFile(fileName);
```

serves two purposes. First, it introduces the name iFile as an object of type ifstream. Second, passing an actual file name as a parameter to the class constructor causes the file to be opened, if possible. To close the file, no explicit statement is required. The ifstream class has a destructor (Chapter 7) that automatically closes the file when execution leaves the scope in which iFile is declared.

Alternatively, file streams have member functions named open and close that allow finer control over these operations. Here is an example of using the open function:

```
char      command;
ifstream myFile;

cin >> command;
if (command == 'C')
    myFile.open("customer.dat");
else
    myFile.open("inventory.dat");
```

Observe that the declaration of myFile calls a parameterless (default) constructor and makes no attempt to actually open a file.

The close member function is only needed if it is necessary to close a file while the name of the stream object is still in scope:

```
ofStream outFile;

outFile.open("arizona.dat");
:
:              // Write to file arizona.dat
:
outFile.close();
```

```
outFile.open("wisconsin.dat");
   :                  // Write to file wisconsin.dat
   .
```

File Opening Modes

In C++ stream I/O, you may open a file for input only, for output only, or for both input and output. We will discuss the last option—both reading from and writing to the same file—in an upcoming subsection.

The ios class, from which all the other stream classes are derived, defines the following enumeration type pertaining to file opening modes. The specific hexadecimal values may vary from system to system.

```
class ios {
public:
    .
    .
    .
    enum open_mode {
        in        = 0x01,    // Open for reading
        out       = 0x02,    // Open for writing
        ate       = 0x04,    // Advance to end of file after opening
        app       = 0x08,    // Append mode. All output is at end of
                             //    file
        trunc     = 0x10,    // Truncate existing file to 0 length
        nocreate  = 0x20,    // Open fails if file does not exist
        noreplace = 0x40     // Open fails if file already exists
    };
    .
    .
    .
};
```

When you open a file, either through the stream class constructor or through a call to open, you can supply a second parameter in addition to the file name. This second parameter is one of the above open_mode constants. The declaration

```
ifstream file1("student.dat");
```

also could be expressed as

```
ifstream file1("student.dat", ios::in);
```

It is unnecessary to do the latter, though. The ifstream class assumes ios::in as the default opening mode. Similarly, the declaration

```
ofstream file2("sales.dat");
```

could be expressed (unnecessarily) as

```
ofstream file2("sales.dat", ios::out);
```

This file, file2, can only receive output. If the file does not exist, the operating system creates it for you. If the file does exist, its current contents are discarded. In either case, the current file position (marked by what is called a **file pointer**) is at the end of the empty file. After this, each successive write operation advances the file pointer to add data to the end of the file.

When you open a file, you can specify a combination of open_mode constants by using the bitwise OR operator (|). For file2 above, if you want to guard against destroying the contents of sales.dat in case it already exists, you can do this:

```
ofstream file2("sales.dat", ios::out | ios::noreplace);

if ( !file2 )
    :              // Take some alternative action
    :
```

Sometimes it is necessary to add data to the end of an existing file. Using the append mode, an existing file is opened and the file pointer is advanced to the end of the file, after which writing takes place:

```
ofstream file3("clients.dat", ios::app);
```

In this case, you may wish to guarantee that the file already exists before opening it. The ios::nocreate constant is what you need:

```
ofstream file3("clients.dat", ios::app | ios::nocreate);
```

As always, it is essential that you subsequently test the state of the file3 stream to check whether opening the file succeeded.

Random Access Files

Operating systems usually provide several access methods for files, the two most common being **sequential access** and **random** (or **direct**) **access.** A sequential access file is analogous to a sequential access data structure such as a list. To access the ith component in the file requires passing through the first i-1 components. A random access file is similar to a direct access data structure such as an array. You may process file components in any order, not only in sequential order.

I/O devices such as keyboards and tape drives are inherently sequential access devices. It is impossible to jump directly to a data item in the middle of a magnetic tape without moving the tape through all preceding data values. Other I/O devices, such as disk drives, are suited to either sequential or random access of file components.

C++ stream I/O supports both sequential and random access of files from within a C++ program. File I/O used in the main body of this book and in the first section of this appendix is sequential access I/O, reading successive values from an input file, one at a time, or writing values to an output file, always progressing forward. We now examine how to access values in a file in random order, jumping directly to arbitrary locations in the file.

In C++, a file can be viewed at a rather low level as a collection of bytes, regardless of the information the bytes represent. An input file has an invisible file pointer—we will call it the **get-pointer**—that indicates the position in the file where the next input will occur. When an input file is opened, the get-pointer is initialized to 0, meaning the first byte (byte number 0) is the next byte available for input. If you read a single char value, where one character occupies one byte, the get-pointer is incremented to 1. As you continue to read values sequentially from the file, the get-pointer is invisibly incremented to indicate the current position in the file.

In a similar fashion, a file opened for output has a **put-pointer** that is incremented after every write operation. Observe that with sequential access of an output file, the put-pointer always indicates the end of the file.

At any moment you can jump to a different position in the file by changing the file pointer. Moving directly to a position in a file is called a **seek** operation. Before describing how to do this, here are some relevant declarations from iostream.h:

```
typedef long streampos;     // Data type for absolute position
                            //     within a stream
typedef long streamoff;     // Data type for relative position
                            //     (offset from the current position)


class ios {
public:
    .
    .
    .
    // Stream seek direction
    enum seek_dir {
        beg = 0,      // From beginning of file
        cur = 1,      // From current position in file
        end = 2       // From end of file
    };
    .
    .
    .
};
```

The following declarations from iostream.h are also pertinent. In the declarations for istream and ostream, do not worry about the meaning of virtual public ios. This declaration refers to a certain form of inheritance that does not matter in this discussion.

```
class istream : virtual public ios {
public:
    .
    .
    .
    // Set/inspect the get-pointer
    istream&   seekg( streampos pos );
    istream&   seekg( streamoff offset, seek_dir dir );
    streampos tellg();
    .
    .
    .
};
```

```
class ostream : virtual public ios {
public:
    .
    .
    .
    // Set/inspect the put-pointer
    ostream&  seekp( streampos pos );
    ostream&  seekp( streamoff offset, seek_dir dir );
    streampos tellp();
    .
    .
    .
};
```

The seekg and seekp functions have suffixes p and g to refer to the get- and put-pointers, respectively. We will see later that a file can be open for both input and output simultaneously, in which case both a get-pointer and a put-pointer will be active. The first form of seekg takes a parameter representing an absolute position within the stream. The statement

```
inFile.seekg(124);
```

means to move directly to byte number 124 in the input file. The second form of the seekg function takes two parameters, the first being an offset relative to the second parameter. The statement

```
inFile.seekg(2, ios::cur);
```

says to move 2 bytes beyond the current get-pointer position, and the statement

```
inFile.seekg(-10, ios::end);
```

says to move to a position 10 bytes prior to the end of the file. Each version of seekg returns a value—the address of the stream object as a reference value (Chapter 7)—but it is most common to ignore the return value, as in the examples above.

The tellg function returns the current position in the input file. It might be that a program is reading data sequentially and needs to jump somewhere else, read some other data, then return to the original position. The following code shows how to get back to the original position:

```
ifstream  inputFile(fileName);
streampos originalPos;
    .
    .
    .
inputFile >> someInfo;
originalPos = tellg();             // Where are we?
inputFile.seekg(300);             // Go somewhere else
inputFile >> otherInfo;
inputFile.seekg(originalPos);     // Resume where we left off
```

Another use we can make of seekg and tellg is to write a program that computes the size in bytes of any file in our directory. Instead of reading each character of the file and counting the characters until running into end-of-file, we can seek directly to the end of the file and then ask for the file position.

Here is a complete program to do this:

```
#include <iostream.h>
#include <fstream.h>

int main()
{
    char fName[20];

    cout << "File name: ";
    cin >> fName;

    ifstream inFile(fName);
    if ( !inFile ) {
        cout << "Can't open file\n";
        return 1;
    }
    inFile.seekg(0, ios::end);
    cout << "Length of file: " << inFile.tellg();
    return 0;
}
```

We have given examples of random access operations on input files, but the seekp and tellp functions work analogously on output files.

Note that, although the seek and tell operations are members of the istream and ostream classes, it would make no sense to use them for the standard istream and ostream objects cin and cout. The keyboard and screen are naturally sequential access, not random access, devices. However, ifstream and ofstream are derived from istream and ostream, respectively (see Figure C.4). So file streams, where random access is meaningful, inherit the seek and tell operations.

A final example of random access is shown in Figure C.5. This program allows the user to enter a file position (0, 1, 2, . . .) and then displays the character at that position. This process is inside a loop, and the user can enter file positions in any order. By using the seekg function, the program can access any character in the file at random.

Figure C.5 FilePos program

```
//-------------------------------------------------------------------
// filepos.cpp
// This program prompts the user for a file name, then prompts for the
// position (0, 1, 2, ...) of any character in the file. It then
// displays the character found at that position and prompts the user
// for another position. This continues until the user types a
// negative number for the position. If the specified position is
// greater than the size of the file, the results are undefined.
//-------------------------------------------------------------------
#include <iostream.h>
#include <fstream.h>

int main()
{
    char      fName[20];
    streampos position;
    char      ch;
```

```
    cout << "File name: ";
    cin >> fName;

    ifstream inFile(fName);
    if ( !inFile ) {
        cout << "Can't open file\n";
        return 1;
    }

    do {
        cout << "Char at which position (0, 1, 2, ...) ? ";
        cin >> position;
        if (position >= 0) {
            inFile.seekg(position);
            inFile.get(ch);
            cout << "Char: " << ch << '\n';
        }
    } while (position >= 0);

    return 0;
}
```

A Turbo C++ Note: The `tellg` Function

With Borland's Turbo C++ Version 1.0 and 1.01 (2nd Edition), the `tellg` function sometimes returns unpredictable values. Try using the `open_mode` constant `ios::binary`, a constant specific to Borland's C++ products and not mentioned earlier in this appendix:

```
ifstream someFile("myfile.dat", ios::in | ios::binary);
```

The `fstream` Class

In the inheritance diagram of Figure C.4 there is a stream class named `iostream`. This class is derived from both `istream` and `ostream`, so it inherits the characteristics and operations of both classes. In particular, a program may both read from and write to an `iostream`. Figure C.4 also shows a class `fstream`, which is derived from `iostream` and includes extra properties pertaining to file I/O. Because every `fstream` is also an `iostream`, we can both read from and write to an `fstream` object.

Suppose that we want to open an existing file, read all the way through it while processing the input data, and then write some additional information at the end of the file. If only sequential file access were permitted, we would need two files. We would have to open the existing file for input only, create a new output file, copy all the input data to the new output file, and then write the additional information at the end of the output file. With the `fstream` class, we can open a single file as follows:

```
fstream dataFile("stats.dat", ios::in | ios::app | ios::nocreate);
```

The three open_mode constants say that we want to read from the file, that we want to write to the file (at the end), and that we want to be sure that the file already exists.

After testing the state of dataFile to see that it was opened successfully, we want to read and process all the information until we hit end-of-file, and then write some new information:

```
while (dataFile >> someValue) {
    :
    :                    // Process someValue
}
dataFile << newValue1;
dataFile << newValue2;
```

By using an fstream, we have avoided the use of two separate files, one for input only and another for output only. Unfortunately, the above code does not work properly. If we inspect the new contents of the file stat.dat, we will find that the two new values we thought we had written at the end of the file are missing. Only the original data are present.

What we have forgotten is that when a stream state becomes "non-good," it *remains* that way. We have correctly programmed the reading loop to terminate on end-of-file, after which the dataFile stream is in a fail state. Remember that if a stream is in a fail state, any further I/O operations are considered null operations—they are ignored silently. So the two final output operations in the above code are not carried out.

What we need to do is reset the state to "good" after leaving the reading loop. The clear function is exactly what we need. This function clears all error bits in the stream state so that we can perform subsequent I/O:

```
while (dataFile >> someValue) {
    :
    :                    // Process someValue
}
dataFile.clear();           // Crucial
dataFile << newValue1;
dataFile << newValue2;
```

Using a file for both input and output also simplifies a technique that is common in the world of data processing: updating information within a file. If only sequential access is allowed, updating the information on one employee—say, Smith—in an employee information file requires creating a new output file, reading all employee information up to Smith's and copying it to the output file, writing Smith's new information to the output file, then reading and copying all employee information after Smith's.

With an fstream, information can be updated in-place within a single file. Because fstreams allow both input and output, there are two independent file pointers: the get-pointer and the put-pointer. To perform an update, the strategy is to use `seekp` to move the put-pointer to the desired file position and then perform the output, overwriting the data that was there. Sometimes locating the correct position entails reading until some information is found and then using the `tellg` function to determine where to move the put-pointer for output. We use this approach in the program in Figure C.6. This program performs a search-and-replace operation on a text file, replacing all occurrences of one string with another string. For example, the user might want to replace all occurrences of Smyth with Smith or replace each single blank in the file with a tab character. To keep the example less complex and therefore shorter, the program requires the old string and the new string to be the same length.

Figure C.6 Change program

```
//--------------------------------------------------------------------------
// change.cpp
// This program replaces all occurrences of one string with another
// string within a text file. The user is prompted for the file name,
// the old string, and the new string.
// The old and new strings must be the same length.
//--------------------------------------------------------------------------
#include <iostream.h>
#include <fstream.h>
#include <string.h>     // For strlen() and strcmp()

const int MAX_LEN = 100;     // Max. length of search string

int main()
{
    char fName[51];                  // Assume file name is at most 50 chars

    cout << "File name: ";
    cin >> fName;
    cin.ignore(100, '\n');           // Eat newline

    fstream theFile(fName, ios::in | ios::out | ios::nocreate);
    if ( !theFile ) {
        cerr << "Can't open file\n";
        return 1;
    }

    char      oldStr[MAX_LEN+1];
    char      newStr[MAX_LEN+1];
    char      fileStr[MAX_LEN+1];
    int       strLength;
    streampos savedPos = 0;          // Last search position

    cout << "Old string (max. 100 chars): ";
    cin.get(oldStr, MAX_LEN+1);                    // Don't skip whitespace
    cin.ignore(100, '\n');                         // Eat newline

    cout << "New string (same length as old string): ";
    cin.get(newStr, MAX_LEN+1);
```

```
    strLength = strlen(oldStr);
    if (strLength != strlen(newStr)) {
        cerr << "Strings not the same length\n";
        return 1;
    }

    while (theFile.get(fileStr, strLength+1))  // Read strLength chars

        if (strcmp(fileStr, oldStr) == 0) {
            // ASSERT: Old string is found
            theFile.seekp(savedPos);        // Move the put-pointer
            theFile << newStr;              // Overwrite old string
            savedPos = theFile.tellg();     // Continue input at
                                            //    current position
        }
        else {
            savedPos++;
            theFile.seekg(savedPos);    // Retreat to previous
        }                               //    search position + 1
    return 0;
}
```

APPENDIX D

Assertion Notation

D.1   Introduction

Assertions are logical (Boolean) statements describing the state of computation at specific locations within a program. An assertion states what the programmer believes to be true at a precise location at a given moment during program execution. An assertion is expressed as a comment within the program, so the notation is more flexible than the code of a programming language.

D.2   Types of Assertions

ASSERT (general assertion)
This comment describes the state of computation at one particular program location.

```
Sort(vec1, size);
// ASSERT: Elements of vec1 are in ascending order
```

Notice that the location of an assertion is crucial. Above, it would be wrong to place the assertion *before* the call to Sort. The assertion is true only after the vector is sorted.

INV (loop invariant)
A loop invariant is an assertion that is always true with respect to its position within a loop.
Note: In the code below, *X*! means *X* factorial. $X! = 1*2*3*\ldots*X$ if $X > 0$, and $0! = 1$.

```
// ASSERT: n >= 0
fact = 1;
i = 1;
while (i <= n) {  // INV (prior to test):
                  //     fact == (i-1)!  &&  i <= n+1
    fact = fact * i;
    i++;
}
// ASSERT: fact == n!
```

Loop invariant for a do-while loop:

```
// ASSERT: n >= 1
fact = 1;
i = 1;
do {
    fact = fact * i;
    i++;
    // INV:  fact == (i-1)!  &&  i <= n+1
} while (i <= n);
// ASSERT: fact == n!
```

Loop invariant for a for loop:

```
// ASSERT: n >= 0
fact = 1;
for (i = 1; i <= n; i++)    // INV (prior to test):
                            //    fact == (i-1)!  &&  i <= n+1
    fact = fact * i;

// ASSERT: fact == n!
```

PRE (function precondition)

A function precondition is an assertion that is assumed to be true at the moment the function is invoked. Therefore, the *caller* is responsible for guaranteeing the precondition before invoking the function.

```
void WriteAve( /* in */ float sum,
               /* in */ int count )
    //...............................................
    // PRE:  sum is assigned  AND  count > 0
    // POST: sum/count has been output
    //...............................................
{
    cout << "Average is " << sum / float(count) << '\n';
}
```

If the caller does not need to satisfy any precondition before invoking a function, then the precondition can either be omitted or written as the value TRUE.

POST (function postcondition)

A function postcondition states what is true at the moment the function finishes executing.

```
void Read2Chars( /* out */ char& firstChar,
                 /* out */ char& secondChar )
    //...............................................
    // POST: User has been prompted to input two chars
    //    && firstChar == the first input char
    //    && secondChar == the second input char
    //...............................................
{
    cout << "Please type two characters: ";
    cin.get(firstChar);
    cin.get(secondChar);
}
```

A postcondition should describe all parameters that are altered by the function. If the postcondition states nothing about a particular parameter, it is implicitly stating that the parameter did not change during execution of the function.
Postconditions only describe changes that are important to the calling routine. Changes to local variables should not be mentioned in a postcondition.

CLASSINV (class invariant)

A class invariant states what is true about the environment of a class instance before and after any operation of that class is invoked. A user can expect the class invariant to be true *after* any class operation has executed, but it is the user's responsibility to ensure that the class invariant is true *before* using any class operation. (Examples of class invariants are introduced in Chapter 3.)

D.3 Notation Within Assertions

"**&&**" is an alternative to the logical AND operator.

```
i = 3;
j = 4;
// ASSERT: i == 3  &&  j == 4
```

"**-->**" denotes the logical implication operator. The expression "*P* --> *Q*" means "*P* implies *Q*" or "If *P* then *Q*."

```
if (bal == 0) {
    amtNeeded = 100;
    interest = 0;
}
// ASSERT: (bal == 0) --> (amtNeeded == 100  &&  interest == 0)
```

Assigned(X) means the variable X has been assigned some value. The purpose of this assertion is to remind the caller to double-check that the parameter has been assigned a meaningful value before calling the function.

```
void Write2Ints( /* in */ int int1,
                 /* in */ int int2 )
    //..................................................
    // PRE:  Assigned(int1)  &&  Assigned(int2)
    // POST: int1 and int2 have been output on one line
    //..................................................
{
    cout << int1 << ' ' << int2 << '\n';
}
```

<entry> denotes a value at the moment of function invocation. This notation is used as a suffix to some parameter. It is not always needed. It is included only when the parameter's value might otherwise be unclear.

```
void Discount( /* inout */ float& cost,
               /* in */    float  discountRate )
    //.................................................
    // PRE:  Assigned(cost)  &&  Assigned(discountRate)
    // POST: cost == cost<entry> * (1.0 - discountRate)
    //.................................................
{
    cost = cost * (1.0 - discountRate);
}
```

FCTVAL denotes the single value returned by a function (via a `return` statement).

```
float Smaller( /* in */ float float1,
               /* in */ float float2 )
    //.................................................
    // PRE:  Assigned(float1)  &&  Assigned(float2)
    // POST: (float1 < float2)  --> FCTVAL == float1
    //    && (float1 >= float2) --> FCTVAL == float2
    //.................................................
{
    if (float1 < float2)
        return float1;
    return float2;
}
```

Alternative to the Implication Operator

Sometimes it is convenient to use a notation such as

```
result == X, if someCondition
       == Y, otherwise
```

as an alternative to:

```
   (someCondition) --> result == X
&& (NOT someCondition) --> result == Y
```

For example:

```
float Larger( /* in */ float float1,
              /* in */ float float2 )
    //.................................................
    // PRE:  Assigned(float1)  &&  Assigned(float2)
    // POST: FCTVAL == float1, if float1 > float2
    //               == float2, otherwise
    //.................................................
{
    if (float1 > float2)
        return float1;
    return float2;
}
```

Abbreviation for a Range of Array Elements

Sometimes it is necessary to refer to a range of consecutive array elements. The notation

```
arrayName[lower]..arrayName[upper]
```

or

```
arrayName[lower..upper]
```

denotes such a range. For example:

```
avg = (a[3] + a[4] + a[5] + a[6] + a[7]) / 5.0;
// ASSERT: avg == the average of a[3..7]
```

APPENDIX E

C++ Reserved Words

Below is a list of identifiers that are C++ *reserved words*—identifiers with predefined meanings in the C++ language. The programmer cannot declare them for other uses in a C++ program.

asm	delete	goto	public	this
auto	do	if	register	typedef
break	double	inline	return	union
case	else	int	short	unsigned
char	enum	long	signed	virtual
class	extern	new	sizeof	void
const	float	operator	static	volatile
continue	for	private	struct	while
default	friend	protected	switch	

APPENDIX F

Operator Precedence in C++

Precedence (highest to lowest)

	Operator	Associativity
	`( ) [ ] -> . ::`	Left to right
Unary:	`++ -- ~ ! + - & * new delete (cast) sizeof`	Right to left
	`->* .*`	Left to right
	`* / %`	Left to right
	`+ -`	Left to right
	`<< >>`	Left to right
	`< <= > >=`	Left to right
	`== !=`	Left to right
	`&`	Left to right
	`^`	Left to right
	`|`	Left to right
	`&&`	Left to right
	`||`	Left to right
	`?:`	Right to left
	`= += -=` etc.	Right to left
	`,` (the operator, not the separator)	Left to right

Notes

1. This book does not discuss the comma operator listed at the bottom of the chart or the `->*` and `.*` operators (pointer-to-member selection operators). For a description, see Stroustrup's *The C++ Programming Language* (Addison-Wesley, 1991).

2. Although the compiler will not violate the above precedence rules, it may rearrange expressions involving associative and commutative operators (`*`, `+`, `&`, `^`, `|`). Usually the order makes no difference: `x = a+b` means the same as `x = b+a`.

   However, if side effects are involved, as in

```
x = Func1() + Func2();
```

where `Func1` and `Func2` inspect and modify global variables, then the order does make a difference. Here, one should use explicit temporary variables to force the desired ordering:

```
temp = Func1();
x = temp + Func2();
```

3. C++ does not dictate the order in which function parameters are evaluated. The statement

```
Print(++n, Power(2, n));
```

can give different results with different compilers. The safe way to do the above is:

```
++n;
Print(n, Power(2, n));
```

APPENDIX G

C++ *Library Routines*

C++ environments provide a multitude of standard library routines. This appendix details some of the most widely used of these routines. Be aware of the fact that these functions may vary slightly from one system to the next. It is always best to consult the manual for your particular system.

To ensure strictest type checking of parameters and function types, the importing program should always #include the appropriate header file before referencing a library function:

```
#include <math.h>
    .
    .
    .
y = sqrt(x);
```

In the postconditions for the functions below, we use the following notations:

- FCTVAL means the value returned by the function
- "-->" means "implies"

G.1   The Header File assert.h

```
void assert( int boolExpr );
    // PRE:  Assigned(boolExpr)
    // POST: (boolExpr is nonzero) --> Execution just continues
    //     && (boolExpr == 0) --> Execution has terminated
    //                              immediately with a
    //                              message stating  the Boolean
    //                              expression, file name, and
    //                              line number in the source code
    // NOTE: If the directive #define NDEBUG is placed before the
    //       directive #include <assert.h>,
    //       all assert statements are ignored
```

G.2   **The Header File** ctype.h

Notes:

1. Each function below has the following precondition:

```
// PRE: Assigned(ch)
```

2. The wording of the postconditions is based on the ASCII character set.

```
int isalnum( int ch );
    // POST: FCTVAL is nonzero, if ch is a letter or digit:
    //                         'A'..'Z', 'a'..'z', '0'..'9'
    //              == 0, otherwise

int isalpha( int ch );
    // POST: FCTVAL is nonzero, if ch is a letter: 'A'..'Z',
    //                         'a'..'z'
    //              == 0, otherwise

int iscntrl( int ch );
    // POST: FCTVAL is nonzero, if ch is a control char:
    //                           integer value 127 or 0..31
    //              == 0, otherwise

int isdigit( int ch );
    // POST: FCTVAL is nonzero, if ch is a digit: '0'..'9'
    //              == 0, otherwise

int isgraph( int ch );
    // POST: FCTVAL is nonzero, if ch is a nonblank printable
    //                           char:
    //                             '!'..'~'
    //              == 0, otherwise

int islower( int ch );
    // POST: FCTVAL is nonzero, if ch is a lowercase letter:
    //                             'a'..'z'
    //              == 0, otherwise

int isprint( int ch );
    // POST: FCTVAL is nonzero, if ch is a printable char
    //                           (including the blank):
    //                             ' '..'~'
    //              == 0, otherwise

int ispunct( int ch );
    // POST: FCTVAL is nonzero, if ch is a punctuation char
    //                           (isgraph(ch) && !isalnum(ch))
    //              == 0, otherwise
```

```
int isspace( int ch );
    // POST: FCTVAL is nonzero, if ch is a whitespace char:
    //                          blank, tab, carriage return,
    //                          newline, form feed
    //              == 0, otherwise

int isupper( int ch );
    // POST: FCTVAL is nonzero, if ch is an uppercase letter:
    //                          'A'..'Z'
    //              == 0, otherwise

int isxdigit( int ch );
    // POST: FCTVAL is nonzero, if ch is a hexadecimal digit:
    //                          '0'..'9', 'A'..'F', 'a'..'f'
    //              == 0, otherwise

int tolower( int ch );
    // POST: FCTVAL == lowercase equivalent of ch, if ch is
    //                 uppercase
    //              == ch, otherwise

int toupper( int ch );
    // POST: FCTVAL == uppercase equivalent of ch, if ch is
    //                 lowercase
    //              == ch, otherwise
```

G.3   The Header File `math.h`

Note:

In the following `math` routines, error handling for incalculable or out-of-range results is system dependent.

```
double acos( double x );
    // PRE:  -1.0 <= x <= 1.0
    // POST: FCTVAL == arc cosine of x, in the range 0.0 through pi

double asin( double x );
    // PRE:  -1.0 <= x <= 1.0
    // POST: FCTVAL == arc sine of x, in the range -pi/2
    //                 through pi/2

double atan( double x );
    // PRE:  Assigned(x)
    // POST: FCTVAL == arc tangent of x, in the range -pi/2
    //                 through pi/2

double ceil( double x );
    // PRE:  Assigned(x)
    // POST: FCTVAL == "ceiling" of x (i.e., smallest whole
    //                 number >= x)
```

```
double cos( double angle );
    // PRE:  Assigned(angle)  &&  angle is measured in radians
    // POST: FCTVAL == trigonometric cosine of angle

double cosh( double x );
    // PRE:  Assigned(x)
    // POST: FCTVAL == hyperbolic cosine of x

double exp( double x );
    // PRE:  Assigned(x)
    // POST: FCTVAL == e (2.718...) raised to the power x

double fabs( double x );
    // PRE:  Assigned(x)
    // POST: FCTVAL == absolute value of x

double floor( double x );
    // PRE:  Assigned(x)
    // POST: FCTVAL == "floor" of x (i.e., largest whole
    //                 number <= x)

double log( double x );
    // PRE:  x > 0.0
    // POST: FCTVAL == natural logarithm (base e) of x

double log10( double x );
    // PRE:  x > 0.0
    // POST: FCTVAL == common logarithm (base 10) of x

double pow( double x, double y );
    // PRE:  (x == 0.0) --> y > 0.0
    //    && (x <= 0.0) --> y is a whole number
    // POST: FCTVAL == x raised to the power y

double sin( double angle );
    // PRE:  Assigned(angle)  &&  angle is measured in radians
    // POST: FCTVAL == trigonometric sine of angle

double sinh( double x );
    // PRE:  Assigned(x)
    // POST: FCTVAL == hyperbolic sine of x

double sqrt( double x );
    // PRE:  x >= 0.0
    // POST: FCTVAL == square root of x

double tan( double angle );
    // PRE:  Assigned(angle)  &&  angle is measured in radians
    // POST: FCTVAL == trigonometric tangent of angle

double tanh( double x );
    // PRE:  Assigned(x)
    // POST: FCTVAL == hyperbolic tangent of x
```

G.4   **The Header File** stddef.h

This header file defines constants and types related to the particular machine on which the C++ environment runs. From this header file, the only item we use in this book is the following symbolic constant:

    NULL   The system-dependent null pointer constant (usually 0)

G.5   **The Header File** stdlib.h

```
int abs( int i );
    // PRE:  Assigned(i)
    // POST: FCTVAL == absolute value of i

double atof( const char* str );
    // PRE:  str points to a null-terminated string representing a
    //       floating point number, possibly preceded by whitespace
    //       chars and a '+' or '-'
    // POST: FCTVAL == floating point equivalent of the characters
    //                     in str
    // NOTE: Conversion stops at the first character in str that is
    //       inappropriate for a floating point number.  If no
    //       appropriate characters were found, FCTVAL is
    //       system dependent.

int atoi( const char* str );
    // PRE:  str points to a null-terminated string representing an
    //       integer, possibly preceded by whitespace chars
    //       and a '+' or '-'
    // POST: FCTVAL == integer equivalent of the characters in str
    // NOTE: Conversion stops at the first character in str that is
    //       inappropriate for an integer number.  If no
    //       appropriate characters were found, FCTVAL is
    //       system dependent.

long atol( const char* str );
    // PRE:  str points to a null-terminated string representing a
    //       long integer, possibly preceded by whitespace chars
    //       and a '+' or '-'
    // POST: FCTVAL == long integer equivalent of the characters in
    //                     str
    // NOTE: Conversion stops at the first character in str that is
    //       inappropriate for a long integer number. If no
    //       appropriate characters were found, FCTVAL is
    //       system dependent.

void exit( int exitStatus );
    // PRE:  Assigned(exitStatus)
    // POST: Program has terminated immediately with all files
    //       properly closed
    // NOTE: By convention, exitStatus is 0 to signal normal
    //       program completion and is nonzero to signal
    //       some error
```

```
long labs( long i );
    // PRE:  Assigned(i)
    // POST: FCTVAL == absolute value of i

int rand();
    // PRE:  IF srand(seed) - see below - has not previously been
    //              invoked
    //          THEN srand(1) is implicitly invoked
    // POST: FCTVAL == the next pseudorandom integer

void srand( unsigned seed );
    // PRE:  Assigned(seed)
    // POST: Random number generator rand() has been seeded with
    //          seed

int system( const char* str );
    // PRE:  str points to a null-terminated string representing an
    //          operating system command, exactly as it would be typed
    //          by a user on the operating system command line
    // POST: Operating system command represented by str has been
    //          executed
    //      && FCTVAL is system dependent
```

G.6   The Header File `string.h`

Note:

In the functions below, a formal parameter such as `char* str` means the variable `str` points to the first character of a string. To simplify the wording of the pre- and postconditions, we take the liberty of using `str` to refer to the entire string that is pointed to.

```
char* strcat( char* toStr, const char* fromStr );
    // PRE:  toStr and fromStr are null-terminated strings
    //      && toStr must be large enough to hold the result
    // POST: fromStr, including '\0', is concatenated (joined)
    //          to the end of toStr
    //      && FCTVAL == base address of toStr

char* strchr( const char* str, int someChar );
    // PRE:  str is a null-terminated string
    //      && Assigned(someChar)
    // POST: FCTVAL == pointer to first occurrence of someChar in
    //                  str, if someChar is present in str
    //              == NULL, otherwise

int strcmp( const char* str1, const char* str2 );
    // PRE:  str1 and str2 are null-terminated strings
    // POST: FCTVAL < 0, if str1 < str2 lexicographically
    //              == 0, if str1 == str2       "
    //              > 0, if str1 > str2         "
```

```
char* strcpy( char* toStr, const char* fromStr );
    // PRE:  fromStr is a null-terminated string
    //    && toStr must be large enough to hold the result
    // POST: fromStr, including '\0', has been copied to toStr,
    //       overwriting what was there
    //    && FCTVAL == base address of toStr

unsigned int strlen( const char* str );
    // PRE:  str is a null-terminated string
    // POST: FCTVAL == length of str (not counting '\0')

char* strncat(char* toStr, const char* fromStr, unsigned numChars);
    // PRE:  toStr and fromStr are null-terminated strings
    //    && toStr must be large enough to hold the result
    //    && Assigned(numChars)
    // POST: (Length of fromStr <= numChars) -->
    //           fromStr, including '\0', is appended to the end of
    //           toStr
    //    && (Length of fromStr > numChars) -->
    //           First numChars chars of fromStr, then '\0', are
    //           appended to the end of toStr
    //    && FCTVAL == base address of toStr

int strncmp(const char* str1, const char* str2, unsigned numChars);
    // PRE:  str1 and str2 are null-terminated strings
    //    && Assigned(numChars)
    // POST: (numChars > 0) -->
    //           First numChars chars of str1 and str2 are
    //           compared (comparison stops at the first '\0'
    //           if str1 and/or str2 has fewer than
    //           numChars chars)
    //        && FCTVAL  < 0, if str1 < str2 lexicographically
    //                   == 0, if str1 == str2          "
    //                    > 0, if str1 > str2            "
    //    && (numChars == 0) --> FCTVAL == 0

char* strncpy(char* toStr, const char* fromStr, unsigned numChars);
    // PRE:  fromStr is a null-terminated string
    //    && toStr must be large enough to hold the result
    // POST: (Length of fromStr <= numChars) -->
    //           fromStr has been copied to toStr, overwriting
    //           what was there
    //        && toStr has been padded to length numChars with
    //           '\0' chars
    //    && (Length of fromStr > numChars) -->
    //           First numChars chars of fromStr have been copied
    //           to toStr, overwriting what was there
    //        && toStr is NOT terminated with a '\0'
    //    && FCTVAL == base address of toStr
```

```
char* strrchr( const char* str, int someChar );
    // PRE:  str is a null-terminated string
    //      && Assigned(someChar)
    // POST: FCTVAL == pointer to last occurrence of someChar in
    //                  str, if someChar is present in str
    //               == NULL, otherwise

char* strstr( const char* str, const char* subStr );
    // PRE:  str and subStr are null-terminated strings
    // POST: (Length of subStr > 0) -->
    //            FCTVAL == pointer to first occurrence of subStr
    //                       within str, if subStr is present in str
    //                    == NULL, otherwise
    //      && (Length of subStr == 0) -->
    //            FCTVAL == base address of str
```

APPENDIX H

Machine-level Data and Bitwise Operators

H.1   Binary Numbers

Modern digital computers store information by using the **binary** (base 2) number system, which has only the digits 0 and 1. Humans are more accustomed to using **decimal** (base 10) numbers with digits 0 through 9.

Consider first the decimal number system. Decimal numbers are written in **positional notation**: the value of each digit depends on its position in the number. Each position represents some power of ten. Moving from right to left, each successive position represents the next higher power of ten. The number 4071 can be expressed as:

$$4071 = 4*(10^3) + 0*(10^2) + 7*(10^1) + 1*(10^0)$$
$$= 4*1000 + 0*100 + 7*10 + 1*1$$
$$= 4000 + 70 + 1$$

Binary numbers also are written in positional notation, but now each position represents a power of two. Moving from right to left, each consecutive position represents the next higher power of two. The binary number 10011 can be expressed as:

$$10011 = 1*(2^4) + 0*(2^3) + 0*(2^2) + 1*(2^1) + 1*(2^0)$$
$$= 1*16 + 0*8 + 0*4 + 1*2 + 1*1$$
$$= 16 + 2 + 1$$
$$= 19 \text{ (as a decimal value)}$$

Table H.1 displays the decimal numbers from 0 through 16 and the corresponding binary numbers.

Table H.1 Decimal and binary equivalents

Decimal	Binary	Decimal	Binary
0	0	8	1000
1	1	9	1001
2	10	10	1010
3	11	11	1011
4	100	12	1100
5	101	13	1101
6	110	14	1110
7	111	15	1111
		16	10000

H.2 Bits, Bytes, and Words

A **bit** is the smallest unit of information in a computer's memory unit. *Bit* is short for "binary digit." Thus a bit is simply a 0 or 1, and a computer's memory is essentially an enormous sequence of bits.

A single bit represents very little data, so bits are grouped together into **bytes** and **words.** A byte is typically a group of 6, 7, 8, or 9 consecutive bits. The size of a byte is machine-dependent, but the 8-bit byte is by far the most common. On nearly all machines, a byte is capable of representing a single character, such as an ASCII character. A word is an even larger grouping of bits and is even more machine-dependent. A popular word size for small computers is 16 bits (2 bytes). Another common word size is 32 bits (4 bytes).

Every data value in memory has a unique **memory address** that identifies where it is located. It is not practical to assign each bit its own memory address, so only bytes or words have memory addresses. A **word-addressable memory** is one in which the smallest addressable unit of storage is the word. A **byte-addressable** memory is one in which the smallest addressable unit is the byte.

H.3 Octal and Hexadecimal Notations

To the computer's hardware, a word or byte of memory is just a **bit string**, a generic sequence of bits with no particular meaning. Depending on how the bit string 1001001001110101 is *used* by a program, we could view this bit string as an unsigned integer, a signed integer, a floating point number, or even a machine language instruction. But these are all just human, abstract interpretations of what a bit string represents. The computer hardware knows nothing of the semantics—it sees only a string of 1's and 0's.

Because of their length, bit strings can be cumbersome for humans to read and write. An alternative is to express a bit string in either **octal notation** or **hexadecimal notation.**

Octal Notation

An octal (base 8) digit is one of the digits 0 through 7. We can parcel a bit string into groups of three consecutive bits, with each group symbolized by an octal digit:

Bit string: 010111101

Octal form: 2   7   5

This grouping must begin with the **least significant** (rightmost) bits. A single octal digit then replaces each group of three bits. Table H.2 shows several 16-bit bit strings and their corresponding octal representations.

Hexadecimal Notation

A disadvantage of octal notation is that bits are grouped three per digit. Three is an awkward number of bits, because it does not evenly divide most popular word sizes. In a 16-bit word, the rightmost 15 bits are represented by five octal digits and the leftmost single bit requires a sixth octal digit.

This inconvenience is alleviated by using hexadecimal (base 16) notation. The 16 hexadecimal digits are 0, 1, 2, 3, 4, 5, 6, 7, 8, 9, A, B, C, D, E, and F (decimal values 0 through 15). In a hexadecimal number, the position of each hexadecimal digit from the right represents an increasing power of 16.

Conversion between bit strings and hexadecimal form is similar to conversion between bit strings and octal, except that groups of four bits are used instead of three. Table H.3 shows the same bit strings as in Table H.2, expressed in hexadecimal notation.

In C++, the programmer can specify an integer constant in decimal, octal, or hexadecimal form. Octal form consists of the digit 0 (zero) followed by a sequence of octal digits. For example, we can express the decimal value 47 as 057, because $47 = 5*8 + 7$. Constants in hexadecimal form are written as a 0 (zero), then x or X, then a sequence of hexadecimal digits. For example, 0x2F is equivalent to the decimal value 47, because $47 = 2*16 + 15$.

Table H.2 Bit strings and their octal equivalents

Bit string (16 bits)	Octal form
0 000 000 000 000 000	000000
0 000 000 000 000 001	000001
0 000 000 101 001 011	000513
0 111 110 111 000 011	076703
0 010 011 111 110 100	023764
1 000 000 000 000 001	100001
1 111 111 111 111 111	177777

Table H.3 Bit strings and their hexadecimal equivalents

Bit string (16 bits)	Hexadecimal form
0000 0000 0000 0000	0000
0000 0000 0000 0001	0001
0000 0001 0100 1011	014B
0111 1101 1100 0011	7DC3
0010 0111 1111 0100	27F4
1000 0000 0000 0001	8001
1111 1111 1111 1111	FFFF

H.4 Bitwise Operators

Some programs need to access individual bits in memory. Although bits within a word or byte do not have their own addresses, C++ provides several **bitwise operators** for manipulating bits:

Operator	Semantics
&	Bit-by-bit AND
|	Bit-by-bit OR
^	Bit-by-bit EXCLUSIVE OR
~	Complement
<<	Left shift
>>	Right shift

These operators require *integral* operands (char, short, int, or long). Because the operands are most often viewed as bit strings rather than signed integer values, it is customary to add the qualifier unsigned when declaring such variables:

```
unsigned int someVal;
```

The Complement Operator

The complement operator has a single operand and yields the value obtained by **inverting** (or **toggling**) each bit of this operand: each 1 becomes a 0 and each 0 becomes a 1. The operand itself is unchanged. If int1 contains the 16-bit binary value 0010010011101111, then the expression

```
~int1
```

has the binary value 1101101100010000. The contents of int1 are unaltered.

Bitwise AND, OR, and EXCLUSIVE OR

Given two bits, b1 and b2, the operations AND, OR, and EXCLUSIVE OR are defined as follows:

b1	*b2*	**b1 AND b2**	**b1 OR b2**	**b1 EXCLUSIVE OR b2**
0	*0*	0	0	0
0	*1*	0	1	1
1	*0*	0	1	1
1	*1*	1	1	0

EXCLUSIVE OR differs from OR as follows. OR yields a 1 if either bit is a 1, or if both are 1. EXCLUSIVE OR yields a 1 if either bit is a 1, but not both.

The bitwise operators &, |, and ^ are applied to their two operands, one pair of corresponding bits at a time. As an example, assume that int1 and int2 are 16-bit unsigned ints. The table below shows the effect of applying each bitwise operator to the two variables.

```
          int1    1000110001111001  (binary)
          int2    1110000100001000

int1 & int2    1000000000001000
int1 | int2    1110110101111001
int1 ^ int2    0110110101110001
```

To see how the result for int1 & int2 was obtained, look first at the most significant (leftmost) bit of int1 and int2. Each is a 1, so the bitwise AND of 1 and 1 (which is 1) becomes the leftmost bit of the result. Next, look at the second bit from the left in int1 and int2. The bitwise AND of 0 and 1 (which is 0) becomes the second bit from the left in the result. Continuing in this fashion, a total of 16 AND operations take place.

Masks

Suppose that the bit positions in a 16-bit quantity are numbered from 15 through 0, left to right. We can **set** ("turn on") bits 4 and 1 of an arbitrary bit string stored in int1 by doing the following:

```
int1 = int1 | 0x12;
```

0x12 is called a **mask**. Its binary equivalent is 0000000000010010. Because the OR of any bit with a 0 yields no change, all bits of int1 except bits 4 and 1 remain unaltered. Bits 4 and 1 of int1 are set to 1 because the OR of any bit with a 1 yields 1.

To **clear** ("turn off") bits 4 and 1 of an arbitrary bit string, there are two methods. First, we can explicitly establish a mask value of 1111111111101101 and perform a bitwise AND:

```
int1 = int1 & 0xFFED;
```

The AND of any bit with a 1 yields no change, whereas the AND of a bit with 0 yields 0. Therefore, bits 4 and 1 of int1 are cleared to 0 but the others remain unchanged.

An easier method is to use the original mask value of 0x12 and complement it:

```
int1 = int1 & ~0x12;
```

Observe that toggling all the bits of 0x12 yields 0xFFED. This second method is by far the more common.

Shift Operators

The left shift operator << shifts an integral value left by *n* bit positions, where *n* is the operator's second operand:

```
    int1      0110110001111001  (binary)
int1 << 5     1000111100100000
```

The high-order (leftmost) bits that are shifted out are discarded. Zeros are filled into the vacated low-order bits. If the second operand, the number of bit positions, is negative or is greater than or equal to the number of bits in the first operand, the result is undefined.

The right shift operator >> is similar, but the values filled into the high-order bits depend on the data type of the first operand. If the first operand is unsigned or is a nonnegative value, the high-order bits are always zero-filled. Otherwise, the result is machine dependent. Some machines fill these bits with copies of the original high-order bit. Others fill with zero.

Combined Assignment Operators

As with many of the arithmetic operators, bitwise operations (other than ~) can be combined with assignment:

&=   Bit-by-bit AND and assign
|=   Bit-by-bit OR and assign
^=   Bit-by-bit EXCLUSIVE OR and assign
<<=   Shift left and assign
>>=   Shift right and assign

For example, int1 |= 0x12 has the same effect as int1 = int1 | 0x12.

Operator Precedence

The programmer must exercise special care when writing expressions with bit-wise operators. As the C++ operator precedence table in Appendix F shows, the bitwise operators &, |, and ^ have higher precedence than the operators && and || but lower precedence than the relational operators ==, <, >, and so forth. Therefore, parentheses are often mandatory. The test

```
if ((int1 & int2) > 0)
```

is entirely different from the test

```
if (int1 & int2 > 0)
```

The former performs a bitwise AND of int1 and int2, then compares the result with 0. The latter first compares int2 with 0, yielding 1 (true) or 0 (false), and *then* performs a bitwise AND of int1 and this 1 or 0.

APPENDIX I

ASCII Conversion Table

In the table on p. A-140, the decimal, octal, and hexadecimal representations of ASCII characters are shown.

- The *Char* column shows the name or symbol of each ASCII character.
- The *Dec*, *Oct*, and *Hex* columns show the character's internal representation in decimal (base 10), octal (base 8), and hexadecimal (base 16), respectively.
- SPACE (decimal 32) is the single space (blank) character.
- Unprintable characters (decimal 0–31 and 127) are described separately in the section Unprintable Characters following the table.

Dec	Oct	Hex	Char	Dec	Oct	Hex	Char	Dec	Oct	Hex	Char
0	000	00	NUL	43	053	2B	+	86	126	56	V
1	001	01	SOH	44	054	2C	,	87	127	57	W
2	002	02	STX	45	055	2D	-	88	130	58	X
3	003	03	ETX	46	056	2E	.	89	131	59	Y
4	004	04	EOT	47	057	2F	/	90	132	5A	Z
5	005	05	ENQ	48	060	30	0	91	133	5B	[
6	006	06	ACK	49	061	31	1	92	134	5C	\
7	007	07	BEL	50	062	32	2	93	135	5D	]
8	010	08	BS	51	063	33	3	94	136	5E	^
9	011	09	HT	52	064	34	4	95	137	5F	_
10	012	0A	LF	53	065	35	5	96	140	60	`
11	013	0B	VT	54	066	36	6	97	141	61	a
12	014	0C	FF	55	067	37	7	98	142	62	b
13	015	0D	CR	56	070	38	8	99	143	63	c
14	016	0E	SO	57	071	39	9	100	144	64	d
15	017	0F	SI	58	072	3A	:	101	145	65	e
16	020	10	DLE	59	073	3B	;	102	146	66	f
17	021	11	DC1	60	074	3C	<	103	147	67	g
18	022	12	DC2	61	075	3D	=	104	150	68	h
19	023	13	DC3	62	076	3E	>	105	151	69	i
20	024	14	DC4	63	077	3F	?	106	152	6A	j
21	025	15	NAK	64	100	40	@	107	153	6B	k
22	026	16	SYN	65	101	41	A	108	154	6C	l
23	027	17	ETB	66	102	42	B	109	155	6D	m
24	030	18	CAN	67	103	43	C	110	156	6E	n
25	031	19	EM	68	104	44	D	111	157	6F	o
26	032	1A	SUB	69	105	45	E	112	160	70	p
27	033	1B	ESC	70	106	46	F	113	161	71	q
28	034	1C	FS	71	107	47	G	114	162	72	r
29	035	1D	GS	72	110	48	H	115	163	73	s
30	036	1E	RS	73	111	49	I	116	164	74	t
31	037	1F	US	74	112	4A	J	117	165	75	u
32	040	20	SPACE	75	113	4B	K	118	166	76	v
33	041	21	!	76	114	4C	L	119	167	77	w
34	042	22	"	77	115	4D	M	120	170	78	x
35	043	23	#	78	116	4E	N	121	171	79	y
36	044	24	$	79	117	4F	O	122	172	7A	z
37	045	25	%	80	120	50	P	123	173	7B	{
38	046	26	&	81	121	51	Q	124	174	7C		
39	047	27	'	82	122	52	R	125	175	7D	}
40	050	28	(	83	123	53	S	126	176	7E	~
41	051	29	)	84	124	54	T	127	177	7F	DEL
42	052	2A	*	85	125	55	U				

Unprintable Characters

In the table below, the *Keystroke* column indicates the keyboard combinations that, on most systems, produce the associated ASCII characters. The notation "Ctrl-A" means to hold down the Ctrl key and tap the A key at the same time. Many of these unprintable characters have special purposes that differ from one computer system to another.

Unprintable Char	Keystroke	Meaning
NUL	Ctrl-@	Null character
SOH	Ctrl-A	Start of header
STX	Ctrl-B	Start of text
ETX	Ctrl-C	End of text
EOT	Ctrl-D	End of transmission
ENQ	Ctrl-E	Enquiry
ACK	Ctrl-F	Acknowledge
BEL	Ctrl-G	Bell character (audible beep)
BS	Ctrl-H	Back space
HT	Ctrl-I	Horizontal tab
LF	Ctrl-J	Line feed
VT	Ctrl-K	Vertical tab
FF	Ctrl-L	Form feed
CR	Ctrl-M	Carriage return
SO	Ctrl-N	Shift out
SI	Ctrl-O	Shift in
DLE	Ctrl-P	Data link escape
DC1	Ctrl-Q	Device control one (resume transmission)
DC2	Ctrl-R	Device control two
DC3	Ctrl-S	Device control three (stop transmission)
DC4	Ctrl-T	Device control four
NAK	Ctrl-U	Negative acknowledge
SYN	Ctrl-V	Synchronous idle
ETB	Ctrl-W	End of transmitted block
CAN	Ctrl-X	Cancel
EM	Ctrl-Y	End of medium
SUB	Ctrl-Z	Substitute
ESC	Ctrl-[	Escape
FS	Ctrl-\	File separator
GS	Ctrl-]	Group separator
RS	Ctrl-^	Record separator
US	Ctrl-_	Unit separator
DEL	Del	Delete

APPENDIX J

Syntax Diagrams for C++

This appendix describes Version 2.0 of the C++ programming language through syntax diagrams. These diagrams refer to all of C++, including several language features not discussed in the body of this textbook.

Each syntax diagram is labeled with a name. Within a syntax diagram, high-lighted symbols and identifiers refer to literal symbols in the C++ language, and nonhighlighted identifiers refer to other syntax diagrams.

Note: Some constructions allowed by the syntax diagrams may still be rejected by the compiler. For example, the syntax diagrams for PostfixExpr, PrimaryExpr, LiteralConstant, and IntConstant allow a constant to be incremented using "++":

25++

However, the compiler will not permit this expression. The syntax is valid, but not the semantics.

Table of Syntax Diagrams

Table of Syntax Diagrams (continued)

Program

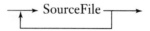

SourceFile

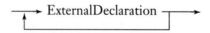

ExternalDeclaration

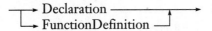

FunctionDefinition

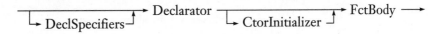

FctBody

⟶ Block ⟶

Block

Statement

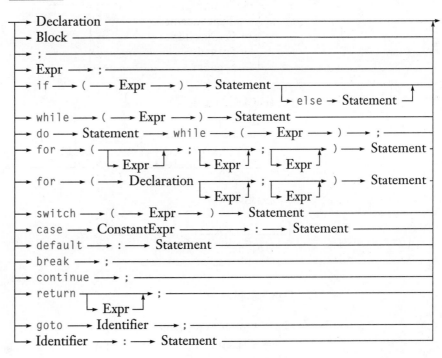

Identifier

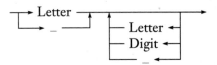

Letter

Any uppercase or lowercase alphabetic character

Declaration

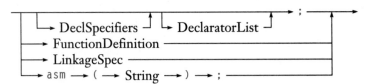

DeclSpecifiers

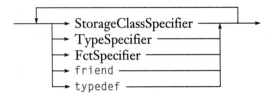

StorageClassSpecifier

FctSpecifier

TypeSpecifier

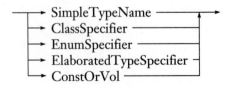

SimpleTypeName

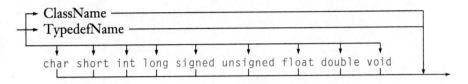

ClassName

→ Identifier →   *(An identifier declared as the name of a class, struct, or union)*

TypedefName

→ Identifier →   *(An identifier introduced in a typedef declaration)*

ElaboratedTypeSpecifier

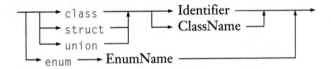

EnumName

→ Identifier →   *(An identifier declared as the name of an enum)*

EnumSpecifier

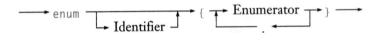

Enumerator

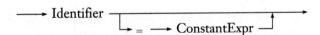

ConstantExpr

⟶ ConditionalExpr ⟶

LinkageSpec

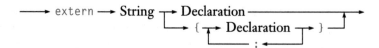

DeclaratorList

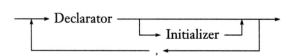

Declarator

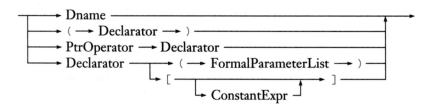

PtrOperator

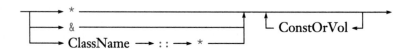

ConstOrVol

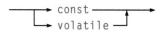

Dname

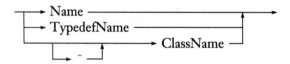

Name

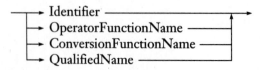

OperatorFunctionName

⟶ operator ⟶ Operator ⟶

Operator

UnaryOperator   BinaryOperator   ()   []   new   delete

BinaryOperator

AssignmentOperator

+   -   *   /   %   <<   >>   <   >   <=   >=

==   !=   &   ^ | && || ,   ->   ->*   .*

ConversionFunctionName

⟶ operator ⟶ TypeSpecifier ⟶ PtrOperator

QualifiedName

⟶ ClassName ⟶ :: ⟶ Identifier
⟶ OperatorFunctionName
⟶ ConversionFunctionName
~ ⟶ ClassName

FormalParameterList

⟶ FormalParamDeclaration , ...
⟶ FormalParamDeclaration , ...

FormalParamDeclaration

⟶ DeclSpecifiers ⟶ Declarator ⟶ = ⟶ Expr
⟶ AbstractDeclarator

AbstractDeclarator

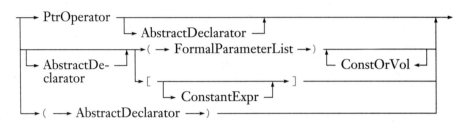

Initializer

InitializerList

ClassSpecifier

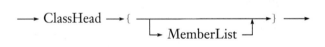

ClassHead

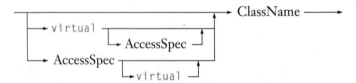

BaseSpecifier

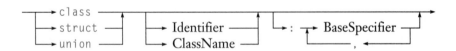

AccessSpec

MemberList

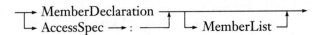

MemberDeclaration

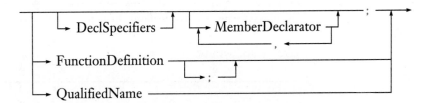

MemberDeclarator

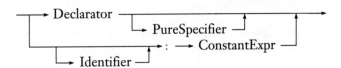

PureSpecifier

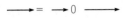

CtorInitializer

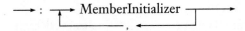

MemberInitializer

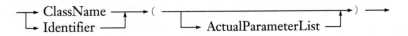

ActualParameterList

→ ExpressionList →

ExpressionList

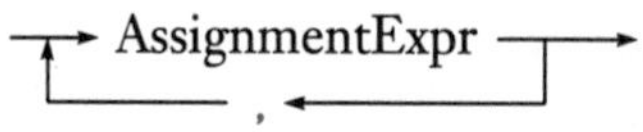

Expr

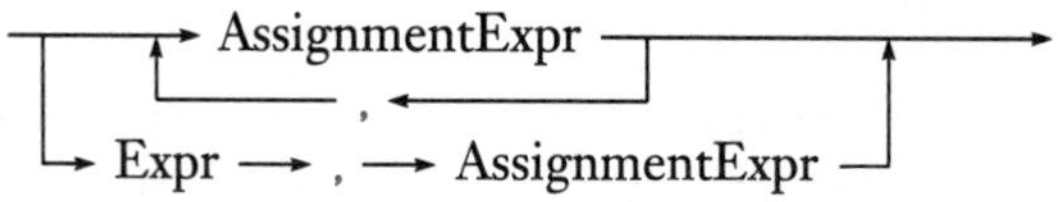

AssignmentExpr

AssignmentOperator

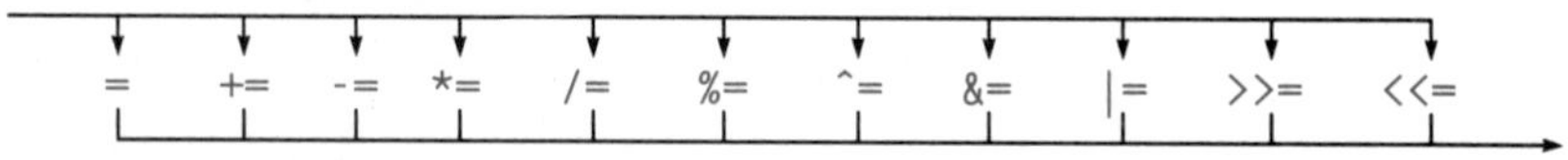

ConditionalExpr

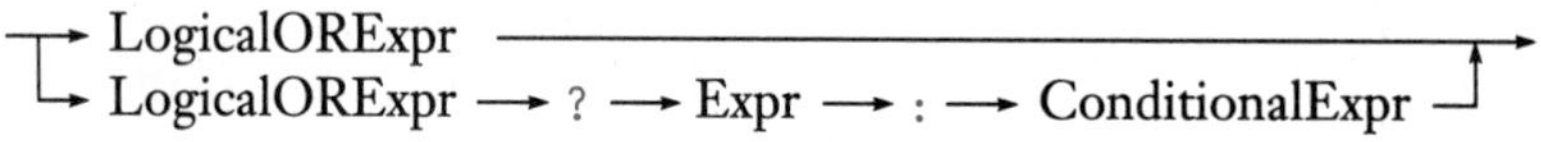

LogicalORExpr

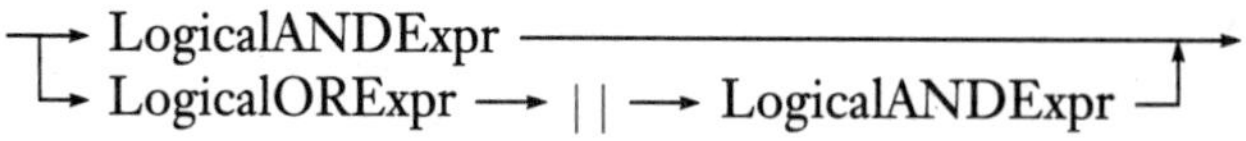

LogicalANDExpr

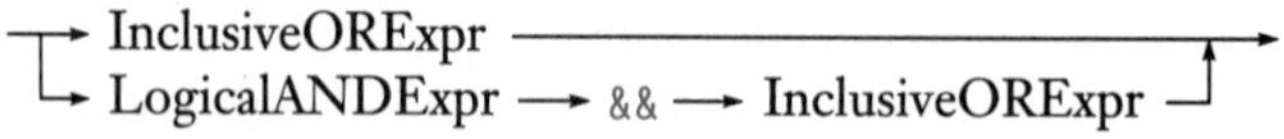

InclusiveORExpr

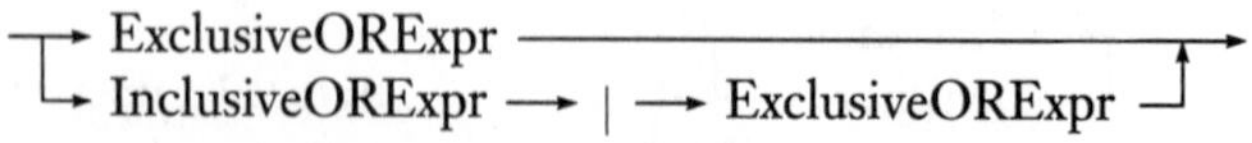

ExclusiveORExpr

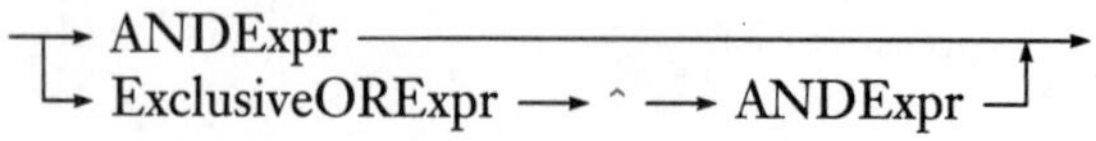

ANDExpr

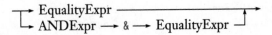

EqualityExpr

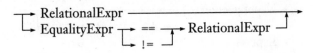

RelationalExpr

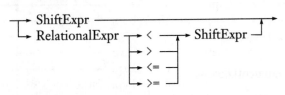

ShiftExpr

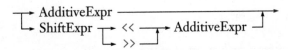

AdditiveExpr

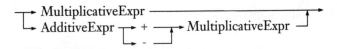

MultiplicativeExpr

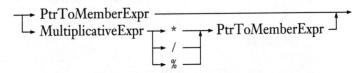

PtrToMemberExpr

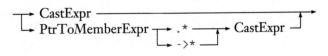

CastExpr

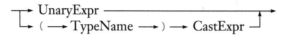

TypeName

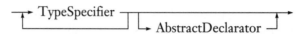

UnaryExpr

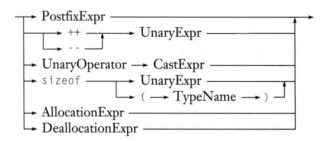

UnaryOperator

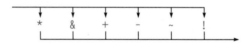

AllocationExpr

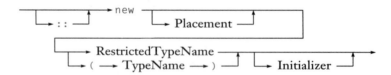

Placement

$\longrightarrow$ ($\longrightarrow$ ExpressionList $\longrightarrow$) $\longrightarrow$

RestrictedTypeName

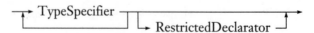

RestrictedDeclarator

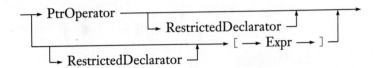

DeallocationExpr

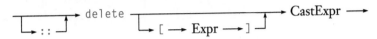

PostfixExpr

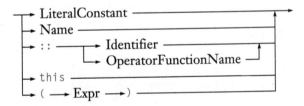

PrimaryExpr

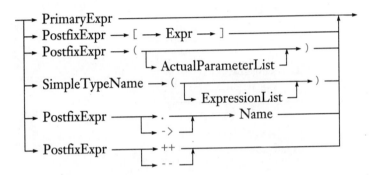

LiteralConstant

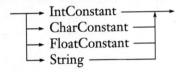

IntConstant

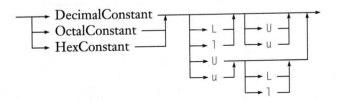

DecimalConstant

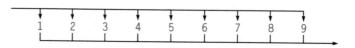

NonzeroDigit

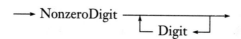

Digit

OctalConstant

OctalDigit

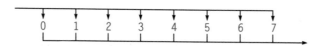

HexConstant

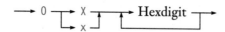

HexDigit

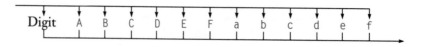

FloatConstant

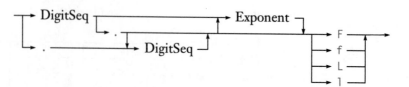

Exponent

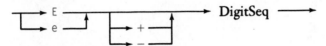

DigitSeq

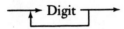

CharConstant

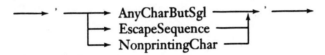

AnyCharButSgl

Any printable character except a single quote (') or backslash(\)

EscapeSequence

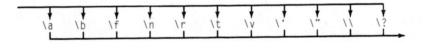

NonprintingChar

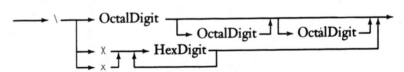

String

AnyCharButDble

Any printable character except a double quote (") or backslash(\)

APPENDIX K

Extended BNF for C++

This appendix describes Version 2.0 of the C++ programming language using an extended Backus-Naur Form (BNF). This BNF defines all of C++, including several language features not discussed in the body of this textbook.

 Note: Some constructions allowed by this BNF may still be rejected by the compiler. For example, the BNF rules for PostfixExpr, PrimaryExpr, LiteralConstant, and IntConstant allow a constant to be incremented using "++":

 25++

However, the compiler will not permit this expression. The syntax is valid, but not the semantics.

 The syntactic description of C++ below uses BNF, extended by the following metasymbols:

Metasymbol	Description
" "	All terminal symbols (literal units in the language) are enclosed in quotation marks (") and are in color. For example, "+" denotes a plus sign character, and " ' " denotes an apostrophe character.
< >	All identifiers enclosed within angle brackets denote non-terminal symbols (symbols that are not literal units in the language).
|	The vertical bar denotes alternation. For example, <Letter> | <Digit> denotes either a <Letter> or a <Digit>.
[ ]	Square brackets denote an optional expression. For example, <Letter> [<Digit>] denotes either a <Letter> or a <Letter> followed by a <Digit>.
{ }	When braces surround an expression, the expression may be repeated zero or more times. For example, <Letter> {<Digit>} denotes <Letter> or <Letter><Digit> or <Letter><Digit><Digit> and so forth.
( )	Parentheses are used for grouping. For example, (<Letter> | <Digit>) <Digit> means <Letter><Digit> or <Digit><Digit>.

Below, the definitions of all nonterminal symbols appear in alphabetical order. The initial nonterminal is <Program>.

<AbstractDeclarator> ::=
  <PtrOperator> [<AbstractDeclarator>]
| [<AbstractDeclarator>] "(" <FormalParameterList> ")" { <ConstOrVol> }
| [<AbstractDeclarator>] "[" [<ConstantExpr>] "]"
| "(" <AbstractDeclarator> ")"

<AccessSpec> ::= "public" | "private" | "protected"

<ActualParameterList> ::= <ExpressionList>

<AdditiveExpr> ::= <MultiplicativeExpr>
                | <AdditiveExpr> ("+" | "-") <MultiplicativeExpr>

<AllocationExpr> ::=
        ["::"] "new" [<Placement>] <RestrictedTypeName> [<Initializer>]
        | ["::"] "new" [<Placement>] "(" <TypeName> ")" [<Initializer>]

<ANDExpr> ::= <EqualityExpr>
            | <ANDExpr> "&" <EqualityExpr>

<AnyCharButDble>   is any printable character except a double quote (") or
                    backslash (\)

<AnyCharButSgl>   is any printable character except a single quote (') or
                   backslash (\)

<AssignmentExpr> ::= <ConditionalExpr>
                | <UnaryExpr> <AssignmentOperator> <AssignmentExpr>

<AssignmentOperator> ::= "=" | "+=" | "-=" | "*=" | "/=" | "%="
                | "^=" | "&=" | "|=" | ">>=" | "<<="

<BaseSpec> ::= ":" <BaseSpecifier> { "," <BaseSpecifier> }

<BaseSpecifier> ::= <ClassName>
                | "virtual" [<AccessSpec>] <ClassName>
                | <AccessSpec> ["virtual"] <ClassName>

<BinaryOperator> ::= "+" | "-" | "*" | "/" | "%" | "<<" | ">>" | "<" | ">"
                | "<=" | ">=" | "==" | "!=" | "&" | "^" | "|" | "&&" | "||"
                | "," | "->" | "->*" | ".*" | <AssignmentOperator>

<Block> ::= "{" { <Statement> } "}"

<CastExpr> ::= <UnaryExpr>
     | "(" <TypeName> ")" <CastExpr>

<CharConstant> ::=
    " ' " (<AnyCharButSgl> | <EscapeSequence> | <NonprintingChar>) " ' "

<ClassHead> ::= <ClassStructUnion> [<Identifier>] [<BaseSpec>]
    | <ClassStructUnion> <ClassName> [<BaseSpec>]

<ClassName> ::= <Identifier> /* An identifier declared as the name of
    a class, struct, or union */

<ClassSpecifier> ::= <ClassHead> "{" [<MemberList>] "}"

<ClassStructUnion> ::= "class" | "struct" | "union"

<ConditionalExpr> ::= <LogicalORExpr>
    | <LogicalORExpr> "?" <Expr> ":" <ConditionalExpr>

<ConstantExpr> ::= <ConditionalExpr>

<ConstOrVol> ::= "const" | "volatile"

<ConversionFunctionName> ::=
    "operator" <TypeSpecifier> { <TypeSpecifier> } [<PtrOperator>]

<CtorInitializer> ::= ":" <MemberInitializer> { "," <MemberInitializer> }

<DeallocationExpr> ::= ["::"] "delete" <CastExpr>
    | ["::"] "delete" "[" <Expr> "]" <CastExpr>

<DecimalConstant> ::= <NonzeroDigit> { <Digit> }

<Declaration> ::= [<DeclSpecifiers>] [<DeclaratorList>] ";"
    | <FunctionDefinition>
    | <LinkageSpec>

<Declarator> ::= <Dname>
    | <PtrOperator> <Declarator>
    | "(" <Declarator> ")"
    | ("*" | "&") ["const"] <Declarator>
    | <Declarator> "(" <FormalParameterList> ")" { <ConstOrVol> }
    | <Declarator> "[" [<ConstantExpr>] "]"

<DeclaratorList> ::=
    <Declarator> [<Initializer>] { " ," <Declarator> [<Initializer>] }

<DeclSpecifier> ::= <StorageClassSpecifier>
    | <TypeSpecifier> | <FctSpecifier>
    | " friend" | " typedef"

<DeclSpecifiers> ::= <DeclSpecifier> { <DeclSpecifier> }

<Digit> ::= " 0" | <NonzeroDigit>

<DigitSeq> ::= <Digit> { <Digit> }

<Dname> ::= <Name>
    | <TypedefName>
    | [" ~"] <ClassName>

<ElaboratedTypeSpecifier> ::= <ClassStructUnion> <Identifier>
    | <ClassStructUnion> <ClassName>
    | " enum" <EnumName>

<Enumerator> ::= <Identifier> [" =" <ConstantExpr>]

<EnumName> ::= <Identifier> /* An identifier declared as the name of
    an enum */

<EnumSpecifier> ::=
    " enum" [<Identifier>] " {" <Enumerator> { " ," <Enumerator> } " }"

<EqualityExpr> ::= <RelationalExpr>
    | <EqualityExpr> (" ==" | " !=") <RelationalExpr>

<EscapeSequence> ::= " \a" | " \b" | " \f" | " \n" | " \r" | " \t"
    | " \v" | " \'" | " \"" | " \\" | " \?"

<ExclusiveORExpr> ::= <ANDExpr>
    | <ExclusiveORExpr> " ^" <ANDExpr>

<Exponent> ::= (" E" | " e") [" +" | " -"] <DigitSeq>

<Expr> ::= <AssignmentExpr> { " ," <AssignmentExpr> }
    | <Expr> " ," <AssignmentExpr>

<ExpressionList> ::= <AssignmentExpr> { " ," <AssignmentExpr> }

<ExternalDeclaration> ::= <Declaration> | <FunctionDefinition>

<FctBody> ::= <Block>

<FctSpecifier> ::= " inline" | " virtual"

<FloatConstant> ::= (<DigitSeq> <Exponent>
      | <DigitSeq> " ." [<DigitSeq>] [<Exponent>]
      | " ." <DigitSeq> [<Exponent>]
) [" F" | " f" | " L" | " l"]

<FormalParamDeclaration> ::=
      <DeclSpecifiers> <Declarator> [" =" <Expr>]
     | <DeclSpecifiers> [<AbstractDeclarator>] [" =" <Expr>]

<FormalParameterList> ::=
 [<FormalParamDeclaration> { " ," <FormalParamDeclaration> }] [" . . ."]
 | <FormalParamDeclaration> { " ," <FormalParamDeclaration> } " ," " . . ."

<FunctionDefinition> ::=
    [<DeclSpecifiers>] <Declarator> [<CtorInitializer>] <FctBody>

<HexConstant> ::= " 0" (" X" | " x") <HexDigit> { <HexDigit> }

<HexDigit> ::= <Digit> | " A" | " B" | " C" | " D" | " E" | " F"
     | " a" | " b" | " c" | " d" | " e" | " f"

<Identifier> ::= (<Letter> | " _") { <Letter> | <Digit> | " _" }

<InclusiveORExpr> ::= <ExclusiveORExpr>
      | <InclusiveORExpr> " |" <ExclusiveORExpr>

<Initializer> ::= " =" <AssignmentExpr>
    | " =" " {" <InitializerList> [" ,"] " }"
    | " (" <ExpressionList> ")"

<InitializerList> ::= <AssignmentExpr>
     | <InitializerList> " ," <AssignmentExpr>
     | " {" <InitializerList> [" ,"] " }"

<IntConstant> ::= <DecimalConstant> [" L" | " l"] [" U" | " u"]
     | <DecimalConstant> [" U" | " u"] [" L" | " l"]
     | <OctalConstant> [" L" | " l"] [" U" | " u"]
     | <OctalConstant> [" U" | " u"] [" L" | " l"]
     | <HexConstant> [" L" | " l"] [" U" | " u"]
     | <HexConstant> [" U" | " u"] [" L" | " l"]

<Letter> is any upper- or lowercase alphabetic character

<LinkageSpec> ::=
        "extern" <String> <Declaration>
    | "extern" <String> "{" <Declaration> { ";" <Declaration> } "}"

<LiteralConstant> ::= <IntConstant> | <CharConstant>
        | <FloatConstant> | <String>

<LogicalANDExpr> ::= <InclusiveORExpr>
        | <LogicalANDExpr> "&&" <InclusiveORExpr>

<LogicalORExpr> ::= <LogicalANDExpr>
        | <LogicalORExpr> "||" <LogicalANDExpr>

<MemberDeclaration> ::=
  [<DeclSpecifiers>] [<MemberDeclarator> { "," <MemberDeclarator> }] ";"
 | <FunctionDefinition> [";"]
 | <QualifiedName>

<MemberDeclarator> ::= <Declarator> [<PureSpecifier>]
        | [<Identifier>] ":" <ConstantExpr>

<MemberInitializer> ::= <ClassName> "(" [ActualParameterList] ")"
        | <Identifier> "(" [ActualParameterList] ")"

<MemberList> ::= <MemberDeclaration> [<MemberList>]
        | <AccessSpec> ":" [<MemberList>]

<MultiplicativeExpr> ::=
        <PtrToMemberExpr>
    | <MultiplicativeExpr> ("*" | "/" | "%") <PtrToMemberExpr>

<Name> ::= <Identifier> | <OperatorFunctionName>
    | <ConversionFunctionName> | <QualifiedName>

<NonprintingChar> ::= "\" <OctalDigit> [<OctalDigit>] [<OctalDigit>]
        | "\" ("X" | "x") <HexDigit> { <HexDigit> }

<NonzeroDigit> ::= "1" | "2" | "3" | "4" | "5" | "6" | "7" | "8" | "9"

<OctalConstant> ::= "0" { <OctalDigit> }

<OctalDigit> ::= "0" | "1" | "2" | "3" | "4" | "5" | "6" | "7"

<Operator> ::= <UnaryOperator> | <BinaryOperator> | "()" | "[]"
        | "new" | "delete"

<OperatorFunctionName> ::= "operator" <Operator>

<Placement> ::= "(" <ExpressionList> ")"

<PostfixExpr> ::= <PrimaryExpr>
        | <PostfixExpr> "[" <Expr> "]"
        | <PostfixExpr> "(" [<ActualParameterList>] ")"
        | <SimpleTypeName> "(" [<ExpressionList>] ")"
        | <PostfixExpr> ("." | "->") <Name>
        | <PostfixExpr> ("++" | "--")

<PrimaryExpr> ::= <LiteralConstant>
        | <Name>
        | "::" (<Identifier> | <OperatorFunctionName>)
        | "this"
        | "(" <Expr> ")"

<Program> ::= <SourceFile> { <SourceFile> }

<PtrOperator> ::= ("*" | "&" | <ClassName> "::" "*") { <ConstOrVol> }

<PtrToMemberExpr> ::= <CastExpr>
        | <PtrToMemberExpr> (".*" | "->*") <CastExpr>

<PureSpecifier> ::= "=" "0"

<QualifiedName> ::= <ClassName> "::" (<Identifier>
                        | <OperatorFunctionName>
                        | <ConversionFunctionName>
                        | ["~"] <ClassName>
)

<RelationalExpr> ::= <ShiftExpr>
        | <RelationalExpr> ("<" | ">" | "<=" | ">=") <ShiftExpr>

<RestrictedDeclarator> ::= <PtrOperator> [<RestrictedDeclarator>]
        | [<RestrictedDeclarator>] "[" <Expr> "]"

<RestrictedTypeName> ::=
        <TypeSpecifier> { <TypeSpecifier> } [<RestrictedDeclarator>]

<ShiftExpr> ::= <AdditiveExpr>
     | <ShiftExpr> ("<<" | ">>") <AdditiveExpr>

<SimpleTypeName> ::= <ClassName> | <TypedefName>
     | "char" | "short" | "int" | "long" | "signed"
     | "unsigned" | "float"
     | "double" | "void"

<SourceFile> ::= <ExternalDeclaration> { <ExternalDeclaration> }

<Statement> ::=
     <Declaration>
     | <Block>
     | ";"
     | <Expr> ";"
     | "if" "(" <Expr> ")" <Statement> ["else" <Statement>]
     | "while" "(" <Expr> ")" <Statement>
     | "do" <Statement> "while" "(" <Expr> ")" ";"
     | "for" "(" [<Expr>] ";" [<Expr>] ";" [<Expr>] ")" <Statement>
     | "for" "(" <Declaration> [<Expr>] ";" [<Expr>] ")" <Statement>
     | "switch" "(" <Expr> ")" <Statement>
     | "case" <ConstantExpr> ":" <Statement>
     | "default" ":" <Statement>
     | "break" ";"
     | "continue" ";"
     | "return" [<Expr>] ";"
     | "goto" <Identifier> ";"
     | <Identifier> ":" <Statement>

<StorageClassSpecifier> ::= "auto" | "extern" | "register" | "static"

<String> ::=
     " " " { <AnyCharButDbl> | <EscapeSequence> | <NonprintingChar> } " " "

<TypedefName> ::= <Identifier> /* An identifier introduced in
     a typedef declaration */

<TypeName> ::= <TypeSpecifier> { <TypeSpecifier> } [<AbstractDeclarator>]

<TypeSpecifier> ::= <SimpleTypeName> | <ClassSpecifier>
     | <EnumSpecifier> | <ElaboratedTypeSpecifier>
     | <ConstOrVol>

```
<UnaryExpr> ::= <PostfixExpr>
            | ( "++" | "--" ) <UnaryExpr>
            | <UnaryOperator> <CastExpr>
            | "sizeof" <UnaryExpr>
            | "sizeof" "(" <TypeName> ")"
            | <AllocationExpr>
            | <DeallocationExpr>

<UnaryOperator> ::= "*" | "&" | "+" | "-" | "~" | "!"
```

SOLUTIONS TO SELECTED EXERCISES

Chapter 1

1.1 a. 0
   c. 23
   e. 10
   g. 19

1.2 a.
```
sum = 0;
i = 0;
while (i <= 50) {  // INV (prior to test):
                   //     sum == 1 + 2 + ... + i
                   // && 0 <= i <= 51

    i++;
    sum += i;
}
// ASSERT: sum == 1 + 2 + ... + 51  &&  i == 51
```
   c.
```
prod = 1;
i = 3;
do {
    prod *= i;
    i++;
    // INV: prod == 3 * 4 * ... * (i-1)
    //     && 4 <= i <= 6
} while (i <= 5);
// ASSERT: prod == 3 * 4 * 5  &&  i == 6
```

1.3 a.
```
cin >> someInt;
while (someInt != -33)
                    // INV (prior to test):
                    //     someInt is the current input integer
                    // && No input integer prior to someInt == -33

    cin >> someInt;

// ASSERT: someInt is the current input integer
//     && someInt == -33
//     && No input integer prior to someInt == -33
```

```
c. oddSum = 0;
   j = 1;
   while (j <= 99) {  // INV (prior to test):
                      //    oddSum == 1 + 3 + ... + (j-2)
                      //    && 1 <= j <= 101  &&  j modulo 2 == 1
       oddSum += j;
       j += 2;
   }
   // ASSERT: oddSum == 1 + 3 + ... + 99
```

1.4 a.
```
for (someInt = 1; someInt <= 9; someInt++)
    cout << someInt;
```
c.
```
for (someInt = 3; someInt <= 9; someInt += 2)
    cout << someInt << ' ';
```

Note: The following solution assumes use of the ASCII character set.

f.
```
for (someChar = 'A'; someChar <= 'M'; someChar += 2)
    cout << someChar << ' ';
```

1.5 a.
```
someInt = 1;
while (someInt <= 9) {
    cout << someInt;
    someInt++;
}
```
c.
```
someInt = 3;
while (someInt <= 9) {
    cout << someInt << ' ';
    someInt += 2;
}
```

Note: The following solution assumes use of the ASCII character set.

f.
```
someChar = 'A';
while (someChar <= 'M') {
    cout << someChar << ' ';
    someChar += 2;
}
```

1.6 a.
```
someInt = 1;
do {
    cout << someInt;
    someInt++;
} while (someInt <= 9);
```
c.
```
someInt = 3;
do {
    cout << someInt << ' ';
    someInt += 2;
} while (someInt <= 9);
```

Note: The following solution assumes use of the ASCII character set.

f.
```
someChar = 'A';
do {
    cout << someChar << ' ';
    someChar += 2;
} while (someChar <= 'M');
```

1.7
```
switch (quizScore) {
    case 9:
    case 10: quizGrade = 'A';
            break;
    case 7:
    case 8:  quizGrade = 'B';
            break;
    case 5:
    case 6:  quizGrade = 'C';
            break;
    case 4:  quizGrade = 'D';
            break;
    default: quizGrade = 'F';
}
```

1.8
a.
```
int Func1( /* in */ int int1,
           /* in */ int int2 )
```
c.
```
void Func3( /* out */   int& int1,
            /* inout */ int& int2 )
```

1.9
a.
```
// PRE:  Assigned(int1)  &&  Assigned(int2)
// POST: FCTVAL == 2*int1 + int2
```
c.
```
// PRE:  Assigned(int2)
// POST: int1 == value input from standard input
//    && int2 == int2<entry> * int1
```

1.10
a.
```
{
    cout << "*** PrintAst entered ***\n";
}
```
c.
```
{
    cout << "*** SomeProc entered ***\n";
    anInt = 1;
}
```
e.
```
{
    cout << "*** ClipString entered ***\n";
}
```

1.11
a.
```
{
    int i;

    for (i = 1; i <= n; i++)
        cout << '*';
}
```
c.
```
{
    if (alpha > 0.0)
        beta /= 4.8;
    else if (alpha == 0.0)
        anInt = 1;
    else {
        beta = alpha;
        anInt = 5;
    }
}
```
e.
```
{
    int i = 0 ;
    while (someStr[i] != '\0')
        i++;
    if (i > 0)
        someStr[i-1] = '\0';
}
```

1.12 a. `// PRE:  Assigned(dec1)  &&  Assigned(dec2)`
`//    && op == '+', '-', '*', or '/'`
`// POST: (op == '+') --> dec1+dec2 printed as an int value`
`//    && (op == '-') --> dec1-dec2 printed as an int value`
`//    && (op == '*') --> dec1*dec2 printed as an int value`
`//    && (op == '/') --> dec1/dec2 printed as a float value`

Chapter 2

2.1 a. Only `myprog.cpp` must be recompiled.
  b. All of the object (`.obj`) files must be relinked.

2.2 Only (a) and (d) are general enough to be useful to many programmers.

2.3 a. Declarations i, iv, v, and vi.

2.4 b. `int( NextRand()*99.0 ) + 2`

2.6 a. The functions `EnterData, Min, Max,` and `Mean`.

2.7 a.

  c. Any order will do.
  e. `rectang.cpp` and `polygon.cpp` must be modified and recompiled. Any program that imports items from `Rectang` or `Polygon` must be relinked.

2.8 a. `if (isdigit(inputChar))`
      `DoSomething();`
  c. `if (isalnum(inputChar))`
      `DoSomething();`
  e. `inputChar = tolower(inputChar);`

2.9   a. `strcpy(str1, "Hi, there");`

e. `if (strcmp(str1, str3) == 0)`
   `cout << "Same";`
`else`
   `cout << "Different";`

2.10 a. The precondition for `strcpy` says that the first parameter must be large enough to hold the result. If the string in `str3` has more than 49 characters, the result may be disastrous.

2.12
```
void GetPassword()
{
    char inString[81];    // Room for one full line + '\0'

    cout << "Establish a password of up to " << MAXLEN
        << " characters.\n"
        << "Type password then <RETURN> --> ";

    cin >> inString;
    if (strlen(inString) > MAXLEN) {
        inString[MAXLEN] = '\0';
        cout << "*** Only first " << MAXLEN << " chars retained ***\n";
    }
    strcpy(passStr, inString);
}

Boolean ValidUser()
{
    char inString[81];    // Room for one full line + '\0'

    cout << "Type password then <RETURN> --> ";
    cin >> inString;
    return ( strcmp(inString, passStr) == 0 );
}
```

Chapter 3

3.1 a. Add new student to list,
Remove student from list,
Sort the list alphabetically, . . .

c. Look up a word's definition,
Look up a word for its spelling,
Browse, . . .

e. Plow it under,
Seed,
Irrigate,
Harvest, . . .

h. Pick up shopping cart,
Wander through aisles,
Pick up a bargain,
Check out, . . .

i. Check inventory,
Place new order,
Pay distributor,
Hire checkout clerk, . . .

3.3 a. SomeClass and int
   b. Func1, Func2, Func3, and someInt
   d. Func1, Func2, and Func3
   g. ii

3.4 a.
```
class SavAcct {
  public:
      void  Deposit( float amt );
      void  Withdraw( float amt, Boolean& refused );
      float CurrBalance() const;
      SavAcct( float initDeposit );
  private:
      float balance;
};
```

3.5 Only b and d.

3.6 3.5
98.6

3.8 No. This module does not encapsulate data. It merely groups two related functions together.

3.10 a. `RandGen gen[100];`
   b. Declaration of this array invokes the default constructor `RandGen()` for each array element. It is impossible to invoke the parameterized constructor for each array element. Thus all 100 class instances are initialized to the default seed.

3.11 b.
```
// CLASSINV: 0 <= count <= 100
//          && data[0..count-1] == the entered integers
//          && (statsValid) --> minVal, maxVal, and meanVal are the
//                              smallest, largest, and average of
//                              data[0..count-1]
```

3.12 a. <u>Specification:</u>
```
void AddOne();
    // POST: This fraction == this fraction<entry> + 1
```
<u>Implementation:</u>
```
void FracType::AddOne()
    //....................................................
    // POST: This fraction == this fraction<entry> + 1
    //....................................................
{
    numer += denom;
}
```

   d. <u>Specification:</u>
```
friend void operator++( /* inout */ FracType& frac );
    // POST: frac == frac<entry> + 1
```
<u>Implementation:</u>
```
void operator++( /* inout */ FracType& frac )
    //....................................................
    // POST: frac == frac<entry> + 1
    //....................................................
{
    frac.numer += frac.denom;
}
```

Chapter 4

4.1 a. Arrays must have homogeneous components, but records may have heterogeneous components. Array components are selected by indices or subscripts, which are values from a type that has a one-to-one correspondence with the integers. Record components are selected by identifiers representing field names.

c. Lists are linear data structures; sets are nonlinear.

4.2 a. (p, q, #, X, A, N)

d. (p, q, #, A, N, Y)

4.3 **stk1**   **stk2**

a. | B | | M |

d. | M   P   A | | |

4.4 **q1**   **q2**

a. (B)   (M)

b. (A, C)   (P, M, D)

4.5 **s1**   **s2**

a. {B, e, +, c, X}   Unchanged

Note: There is no error deleting 'Y' from s2. According to the rules of set difference,

$$\{B, e, +, c, X\} - \{Y\} = \{B, e, +, c, X\}.$$

b. Unchanged   {e}

4.6 The Enqueue algorithm is as follows:

```
mainStk.Push(newItem);
// ASSERT: newItem is at rear of queue (at top of mainStk)
```

The following function is used to simplify the Dequeue algorithm:

```
void Transfer( /* inout */ CharStack& stk1,
               /* out */   CharStack& stk2 )
    //...............................................
    // PRE:  stk2.IsEmpty()
    // POST: stk2 contains items of stk1 in reverse order
    //    && stk1.IsEmpty()
    //...............................................
{
    while ( !stk1.IsEmpty() ) {
        stk2.Push(stk1.Top());
        stk1.Pop();
    }
}
```

The Dequeue algorithm is as follows:

```
Transfer(mainStk, auxStk);
auxStk.Pop();
Transfer(auxStk, mainStk);
// ASSERT: Char at front of queue (at bottom of mainStk) removed
```

4.8
```
int Cardinality( /* in */ CharSet someSet )
{
    int ch;
    int numElts = 0;

    for (ch = 0; (unsigned int) ch < 128; ch++)
        if (someSet.IsElt(char(ch)))
            numElts++;
    return numElts;
}
```

Chapter 5

5.1 a. `visitingProf.age`

c. `visitingProf.name.last`

e. `visitingProf.currentCourseLoad.course[0].dept`

h. `scienceProf[2].currentCourseLoad.course[1].number`

j.
```
scienceProf[31].name.firstInit = 'A';
strcpy(scienceProf[31].name.last, "Becker");
scienceProf[31].age = 35;
scienceProf[31].homeDept = compSci;
scienceProf[31].annualSalary = 38000;
scienceProf[31].currentCourseLoad.count = 2;
scienceProf[31].currentCourseLoad.course[0].dept = compSci;
scienceProf[31].currentCourseLoad.course[0].number = 110;
scienceProf[31].currentCourseLoad.course[1].dept = compSci;
scienceProf[31].currentCourseLoad.course[1].number = 222;
```

5.2 a.
```
enum VegVariety {
    corn, bean, tomato, carrot
};
enum VegColor {
    red, green, orange, yellow, white, purple
};
struct VegType {
    VegVariety variety;
    int        growingPeriod;
    VegColor   fruitColor;
};
VegType oneVegetable;
```

c.
```
typedef char String15[16];
struct StockType {
    String15 name;
    float    high;
    float    low;
    float    current;
    float    change;
};
StockType stock[500];
```

e.
```
typedef char String20[21];
struct EntryType {
    String20 word;
    int      pageReferenceCount;
    int      pageNumber[15];
};
EntryType entry[1000];
```

5.3 a. `favoritePossession.purchaseDate`

c. `favoritePossession.house.sqFeet`

f. `majorPossession[0].article = furniture;`

i. `majorPossession[4].article = other;`
`strcpy(majorPossession[4].oth.descrip, "Stereo");`
`majorPossession[4].purchaseDate.mo = 11;`
`majorPossession[4].purchaseDate.day = 29;`
`majorPossession[4].purchaseDate.yr = 1989;`
`majorPossession[4].hundredsVal = 21;`

5.4 a. `drawing[2].whichType = point;`
`drawing[2].pt.location.row = 123;`
`drawing[2].pt.location.col = 321;`

c. `drawing[2].whichType = line;`
`drawing[2].ln.leftEnd.row = 5;`
`drawing[2].ln.leftEnd.col = 10;`
`drawing[2].ln.rightEnd.row = 20;`
`drawing[2].ln.rightEnd.col = 50;`

Chapter 6

6.1 a. Base:

$$\text{If } N = 0, \text{ then } I^N = 1.$$

Recursive:

$$\text{If } N > 0, \text{ then } I^N = I * I^{N-1}.$$

b. Base:

$$\text{If } M = N + 1, \text{ then } M > N.$$

Recursive:

$$\text{If } M = K + 1 \text{ and } K > N, \text{ then } M > N.$$

6.3 a. <number>   ::= <digitSeq> . <digitSeq>
          | . <digitSeq>
<digitSeq> ::= <digit> | <digit> <digitSeq>
<digit>   ::= 0 | 1 | 2 | 3 | 4 | 5 | 6 | 7 | 8 | 9

6.4 One Small Step: Multiply the current product by the number N.
Complete the Solution: Compute the product of all numbers less than N.

6.5 b. One Small Step: Add one number to the running sum.
Complete the Solution: Compute the sum of all remaining numbers.

```
int SumOfInts( /* in */ int m,
               /* in */ int n )
{
    if (m == n)
        return n;
    else
        return m + SumOfInts(m+1, n);
}
```

6.8   a.   `0123456789`

```
0
1    WWWW
2    WbcW
3    WadW
4    WfeW
5    WWWW
```

6.10 a. `DDCEBF`

b. Whenever `param1 > param2` or whenever (`param1-param2`) is an odd integer.

c. `DDDDDD`

6.11 a. 0

c. 502

Chapter 7

7.1

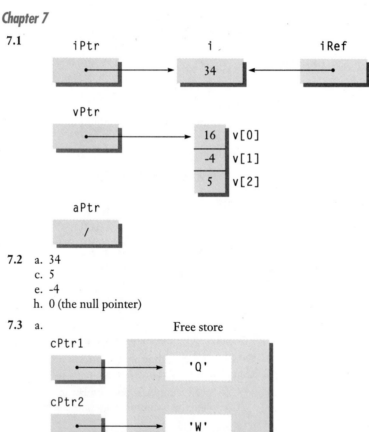

7.2   a. 34

c. 5

e. -4

h. 0 (the null pointer)

7.3   a.

7.5 a.

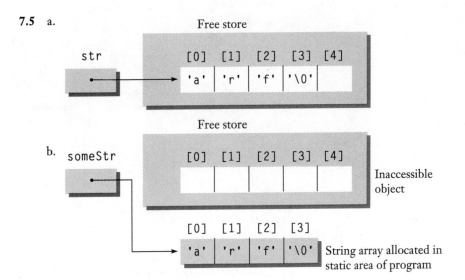

7.8 In vector.h, the only change is to add the word const and an ampersand (&) in the declaration of the formal parameter vec2:

```
void operator=( /* in */ const IntVec& vec2 );
```

Passing vec2 by reference prevents the copy-constructor from executing, and the word const prevents the operator= function from modifying vec2.

Likewise, in vector.cpp, the only change is to add the word const and an ampersand in the declaration of vec2:

```
void IntVec::operator=( /* in */ const IntVec& vec2 )
```

The function body remains the same.

7.10 The following function needs to modify its parameter, so the parameter is passed by reference. The data type of the parameter is int*, so the correct syntax for the formal parameter is int*& ptr.

```
void Deallocate( int*& ptr )
    //............................................................
    // PRE:  ptr is either NULL or was previously assigned from an
    //       execution of the "new" operator
    // POST: Dynamic data pointed to by ptr has been deallocated
    //    && ptr == NULL
    //............................................................
{
    delete ptr;
    ptr = NULL;
}
```

Chapter 8

8.1 a. StuPtr
b. StudentType

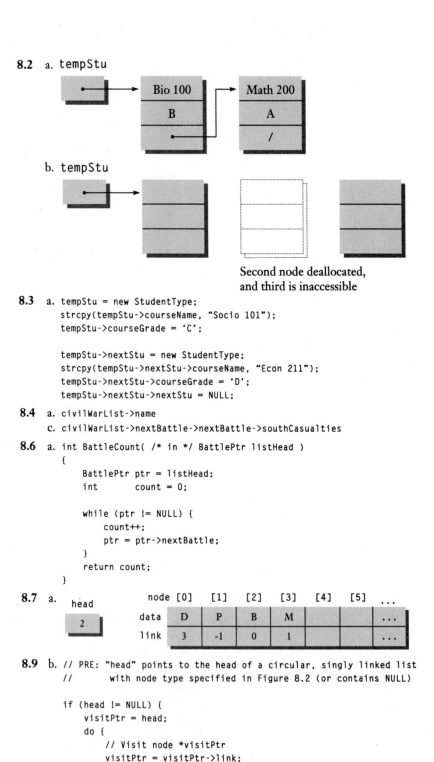

8.2 a. tempStu

Bio 100 / B

Math 200 / A / /

b. tempStu

Second node deallocated, and third is inaccessible

8.3 a.
```
tempStu = new StudentType;
strcpy(tempStu->courseName, "Socio 101");
tempStu->courseGrade = 'C';

tempStu->nextStu = new StudentType;
strcpy(tempStu->nextStu->courseName, "Econ 211");
tempStu->nextStu->courseGrade = 'D';
tempStu->nextStu->nextStu = NULL;
```

8.4 a. `civilWarList->name`

c. `civilWarList->nextBattle->nextBattle->southCasualties`

8.6 a.
```
int BattleCount( /* in */ BattlePtr listHead )
{
    BattlePtr ptr = listHead;
    int       count = 0;

    while (ptr != NULL) {
        count++;
        ptr = ptr->nextBattle;
    }
    return count;
}
```

8.7 a.

	node [0]	[1]	[2]	[3]	[4]	[5]	...
head: 2	data	D	P	B	M			...
	link	3	-1	0	1			...

8.9 b.
```
// PRE: "head" points to the head of a circular, singly linked list
//      with node type specified in Figure 8.2 (or contains NULL)

if (head != NULL) {
    visitPtr = head;
    do {
        // Visit node *visitPtr
        visitPtr = visitPtr->link;
    } while (visitPtr != head);
}
```

8.11 a.
```
Boolean EqualLists( /* in */ NodePtr ptr1,
                    /* in */ NodePtr ptr2 )
{
    if (ptr1==NULL || ptr2==NULL)
        return (ptr1==ptr2);
    if (ptr1->data != ptr2->data)
        return FALSE;
    return EqualLists(ptr1->link, ptr2->link);
}
```

Chapter 9

9.1 a. ii

b. iii

9.3 If a queue is implemented as an array without wrap-around subscripts, a Dequeue operation forces all remaining array elements to be shifted up by one position. The ring buffer eliminates such data movement.

With a stack, Pushes and Pops do not cause other array elements to be shifted anyway. There is no advantage to a ring buffer, and the disadvantage is the loss of one array element—the required "unused" element.

9.5 The reason is that there is already a precondition: the abstract class invariant. The user must guarantee this invariant before invoking any public function. The invariant that an integer be between 0 and 9 already implies that it is assigned.

9.6 This ADT is incomplete. Only positive fractions with a numerator of 1 can be constructed.

9.7 a. Any positive fraction m/n can be constructed by adding the m fractions $1/n + 1/n + \cdots + 1/n$. The zero fraction can be constructed by subtracting $1/n$ from $1/n$. Any negative fraction $-m/n$ can be constructed by subtracting m/n from the zero fraction.

9.8 One Small Step: Allocate a new node and copy the current node's data member into this new node.

Complete the Solution: Link this new node to a copy of the entire rest of the list.

9.13 a. 3

c. <7,3,2,1>

e. <2,1>

i. <2,3,2,1,1>

Chapter 10

10.2 a. False

c. True

10.4 a. At the end

10.5 a. An array of `PkgLotType` class instances:

```
PkgLotType lot[5];
```

b. Only one additional object is needed: a lotNumber object that specifies a particular parking lot. An operation ReadLotNumber is necessary to prompt for and input lotNumber from the user.

10.7 In our opinion, there are no has-a relationships in this problem. No objects are contained within other objects.

Object	Characteristics	Operations
currBalance	Money in dollars	AddCharge* MakePayment* AddInterest*† WriteBalance†
amtOfCharge	Money in cents	AddCharge ReadCharge*†
amtOfPayment	Money in cents	MakePayment ReadPayment*†
command	A single-letter user command	ReadCommand*†

* Denotes an operation that potentially changes the value of the object.
† Denotes an operation for which the object to the left has primary responsibility.

Chapter 11

11.1

	Abc	Def	Ghi
a.	alpha beta	alpha beta gamma	alpha beta gamma delta
c.	DoThis	DoThis DoThat	DoThis DoThat TryIt

11.2 a. Valid
  c. Valid
  e. Invalid. Converting from a pointer to a base class to a pointer to a derived class requires a type cast: ptr2 = (Pen*) sPtr.

11.3 a. 4
  d. 7
  e. 7

11.4 a. 4
  d. 4
  e. 7

11.5 a. Abc done
     Abc done
  b. Abc done
     Def done
     Abc done

11.6 **a.** A public base class is probably the better choice. The `Push` and `Pop` operations must be redefined to update the depth variable. If `NamedStack` is a private base class, `NamedStack2` must declare and implement *all* the operations. For example, `IsEmpty` must be declared and then implemented as

```
Boolean NamedStack2::IsEmpty() const
{
    return NamedStack::IsEmpty();
}
```

On the other hand, if `NamedStack` is a public base class, then only `Push` and `Pop` need overriding.

b.
```
//--------------------------------------------------------------------------
//  SPECIFICATION FILE (namedst2.h)
//  This module exports an ADT for a stack of integer values.
//  The maximum stack depth is MAX_DEPTH, an unspecified value.
//  NamedStack is a public base class of NamedStack2.
//--------------------------------------------------------------------------
#include "namedstk.h"

class NamedStack2 : public NamedStack {
public:
    int Depth() const;
        // POST: FCTVAL == Length(stack)

    void Push( /* in */ int newItem );
        // PRE:  Length(stack) < MAX_DEPTH  &&  Assigned(newItem)
        // POST: stack == AppendFront(stack<entry>,newItem)

    void Pop();
        // PRE:  Length(stack) >= 1
        // POST: stack == RemoveFront(stack<entry>)

    NamedStack2();
        // POST: Created(stack)  &&  stack == <>

    NamedStack2( const NamedStack2& otherStk );
        // POST: Created(stack)  &&  stack == otherStk

    ~NamedStack2();
        // POST: NOT Created(stack)
private:
    int depth;
};
```

11.8 Below is the specification file:

```
//--------------------------------------------------------------------------
//  SPECIFICATION FILE (pencil.h)
//  This module exports a Pencil class (derived from the Supply class).
//  Supply is a public base class of Pencil.
//--------------------------------------------------------------------------
#ifndef PENCIL_H
#define PENCIL_H

#include "supply.h"
```

```
class Pencil : public Supply {
public:
    void Personalize( const char* newName );
        // PRE:  Assigned(newName)
        // POST: Advertising name (if any) replaced by newName

    void Display() const;
        // POST: Item description, stock no., quantity, price, and
        //       advertising name have been written to standard output

    Pencil( /* in */ const char* description,
            /* in */ int         stockNumber,
            /* in */ int         initQuantity,
            /* in */ float       initPrice    );
        // PRE:  All parameters assigned
        // POST: New object created, with private data initialized
        //       by the input parameters
        //    && There is no advertising name

    Pencil( const Pencil& otherPencil );
        // POST: New object created, with private data initialized
        //       by otherPencil's private data

    ~Pencil();
        // POST: Object destroyed
private:
    char* advName;
};


#endif
```

11.9 a. The data type of the item vector is Supply*, but the Supply class has no member function named Personalize.

Chapter 12

12.1 a. T1   j. T2
     c. T2   l. T2
     e. T2   o. T1
     g. T2

12.2

	T1	**T2**		**T1**	**T2**
a.	$O(X^2)$	$O(X)$	j.	$O(1)$	$O(X)$
c.	$O(Y^{15})$	$O(Y^{16})$	l.	$O(W^9)$	$O(9^W)$
e.	$O(Z^2)$	$O(Z^3)$	o.	$O(X^3{*}Y)$	$O(X{*}Y)$
g.	$O(N^2)$	$O(N^2 \log N)$			

12.4 a. Linear (hence, polynomial)
     c. Exponential
     e. Logarithmic
     g. Constant
     i. Polynomial

12.5 a. $O(N^2)$ is quadratic.
     c. $O(2^N)$ is exponential.
     e. $O(N)$ is linear.
     g. $O(\log N)$ is logarithmic.

12.6 a. $O(X^3)$
    d. $O(X^2)$
    h. $O(X \log_2 X)$

12.7 a. $O(X)$
    c. $O(X \log_2 X)$

12.8 a.

[0]	5
[1]	54
[2]	24
[3]	
[4]	
[5]	358
[6]	457
[7]	162
[8]	187
[9]	80

b. k / 10 % 10

f.

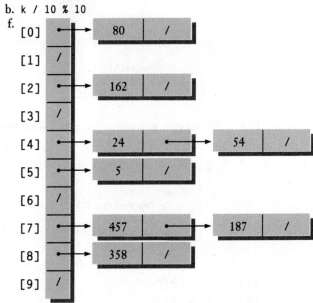

	Comparisons	**Data movements**
12.10 a.	$O(N)$	Zero = $O(1)$
c.	$O(N \log N)$	Zero = $O(1)$

12.12 a. $O(N^2)$ for an N^2 sort
        $O(N \log N)$ for an $N \log N$ sort

Chapter 13

13.1 a. i, ii, and vi are all trees.

b. iii and iv are not trees, because a node cannot have multiple parents. v is not a tree, because it has two roots.

13.2 a. 5

b. 0, 4, 6, 9

c. Level 2

e. 8

j. 3

l. This is a best case, because it is a full binary tree.

n. 5, 3, 0, 4, 8, 6, 9

13.4 a. 0

13.5 c.
```
int NodeCount( /* in */ NodePtr ptr )
{
    if (ptr == NULL)
        return 0;
    return 1 + NodeCount(LChild(ptr)) + NodeCount(RChild(ptr));
}
```

13.6 a. The key is to traverse the *right* subtree first, then visit the node, then traverse the left subtree:

```
void RevInorderTrav( /* in */ NodePtr ptr )
{
    if (ptr != NULL) {
        RevInorderTrav(RChild(ptr));
        Visit(ptr);
        RevInorderTrav(LChild(ptr));
    }
}
```

13.7 a. ((3 * 4) / (7 + 2))

13.8 a. 3 * 4 / 7 + 2

13.9 a. / * 3 4 + 7 2

13.10 a. 3 4 * 7 2 + /

13.11 a.

c.

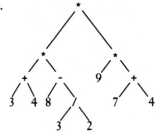

e.

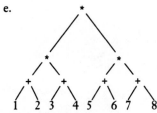

13.12 a. + 7 * 8 - 4 1
   c. * * + 3 4 - 8 / 3 2 * 9 + 7 4

13.13 a. 7 8 4 1 - * +
   c. 3 4 + 8 3 2 / - * 9 7 4 + * *

13.14 a. 47

INDEX